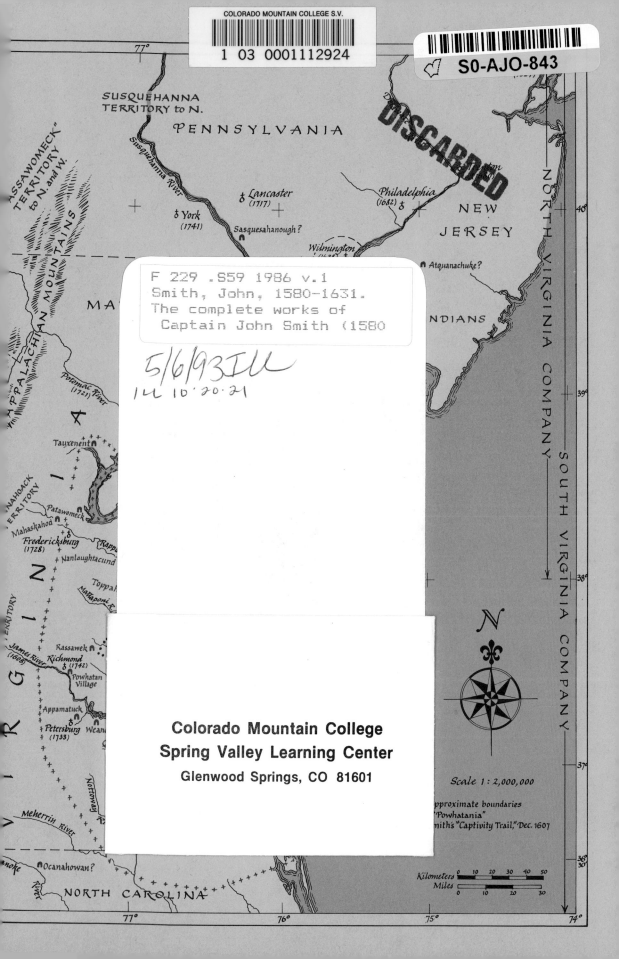

COLORADO MOUNTAIN COLLEGE S.V.

1 03 0001112924

S0-AJO-843

DISCARDED

SUSQUEHANNA
TERRITORY to N.

PENNSYLVANIA

NORTH VIRGINIA COMPANY

"ASSAWOMECK"
TERRITORY
to N. and W.

APPALACHIAN MOUNTAINS

Susquehanna River

♀ Lancaster
(1717)

♀ York
(1741)

Sasquesahanough?

Wilmington

Philadelphia
(1682) ♀

NEW
JERSEY

Atquanachuke?

MA

NDIANS

Potomac River
(1721)

40°

39°

SOUTH VIRGINIA COMPANY

F 229 .S59 1986 v.1
Smith, John, 1580-1631.
The complete works of
   Captain John Smith (1580

5/6/93 ILL
ILL 10·20·21

Tauxenent

NAHOACK
TERRITORY
Patawomeck
Mahaskahod
Fredericksburg
(1728)
Nanlaughtacund

Toppa

Mataponi R.

James River
(1608)
Rassawek
Richmond
♀ (1742)
Powhatan
Village

Appamattuck

Petersburg
(1733)
Wean

ERRITORY

V I R G I N I A

Colorado Mountain College
Spring Valley Learning Center
Glenwood Springs, CO 81601

N

38°

37°

Scale 1 : 2,000,000

pproximate boundaries
"Powhatania"
mith's "Captivity Trail," Dec. 1607

Meherrin River

NOTTOWAY

noke
Ocanahowan?

NORTH CAROLINA

Kilometers 0 10 20 30 40 50
Miles   0   10   20   30

36°
30'

77°   76°   75°   74°

THE COMPLETE WORKS OF

Captain John Smith

The Armorial Bearings of
CAPTAIN JOHN SMITH
of Virginia.
as Recorded at the College of Arms, London, by Sir William
Segar, Garter Principal King of Arms, 19 August, 1625.

Conrad Swan
Rouge Dragon

Rouge Dragon Pursuivant of Arms

THE COMPLETE WORKS OF

Captain John Smith

(1580–1631)

in Three Volumes

Edited by

Philip L. Barbour

VOLUME I

Published for
The Institute of Early American History and Culture
Williamsburg, Virginia
by The University of North Carolina Press
Chapel Hill and London

© 1986 The University of North Carolina Press
All rights reserved
Manufactured in the United States of America

Library of Congress Cataloging in Publication Data

Smith, John, 1580–1631.
   The complete works of Captain John Smith (1580–
1631)

      Bibliography: p.
      Includes index.
      1. Virginia—History—Colonial period, ca. 1600–
1775—Collected works.   2. New England—History—
Colonial period, ca. 1600–1775—Collected works.
3. America—Discovery and exploration—English—
Collected works.   I. Barbour, Philip L.
II. Institute of Early American History and Culture
(Williamsburg, Va.)   III. Title.
F229.S59   1986   975.5′02   81-10364

   ISBN 0-8078-1525-X   AACR2

[Official copy of John Smith's coat of arms made for the editor from the copy in the College of Arms, London (Dr. Conrad Swan, York Herald). The original document that Zsigmond Báthory gave Smith was evidently treasured by him until, at the suggestion of a friend, possibly Samuel Purchas or Sir Robert Cotton (*True Travels*, 15n), it reached the hands of Sir William Segar by 1625. Segar recorded "a true coppy of the same" in the register of the then "Heralds of Arms" (*ibid.*, 18). The original was returned to Smith, who bequeathed it to Thomas Packer (see Smith's will, Document iv, Volume III, below). Only the copy in the College of Arms is known to survive.]

SPONSORED BY
The Jamestown-Yorktown Foundation
The National Endowment for the Humanities
The Newberry Library
and
The Institute of Early American History and Culture

The Institute of Early American History and Culture
is sponsored jointly by The College of William and Mary
and The Colonial Williamsburg Foundation.

Preparation of these volumes was made possible in part
by a grant from the Research Materials Program
of the National Endowment for the Humanities,
an independent federal agency.

In addition to the major sponsorship of the agencies listed on p. v,
editorial work on these volumes was assisted also by grants from
the Jennings Charitable Trust,
the Jane and Dan Gray Charitable Foundation,
and the Sterling Morton Charitable Trust.

To the memory of all those
who purposefully or accidentally
have contributed to the preservation
of the manuscripts, books, drawings, and maps
that make it possible today
to edit, annotate, index, and value
the records of the past.

ADVISORY BOARD

Lewis A. McMurran, Jr.
David B. Quinn
Parke Rouse, Jr.
Lawrence W. Towner
Wilcomb E. Washburn
David Woodward

ASSISTANT EDITORS

J. Frederick Fausz
Lucy Trumbull Brown
Cynthia Carter Ayres

FOREWORD

On December 21, 1980, the editor of these volumes, Philip L. Barbour, died in Petersburg, Virginia. He had turned eighty-two that same day and was en route to Williamsburg from Louisville, Kentucky, his hometown.

At the time of Mr. Barbour's death, each of the three volumes in the set was in a different stage of editing. For reasons that need not be explained here, Volume II had been prepared for the compositor first. By fall 1980 this volume was in page proof, and Mr. Barbour had had a chance to make final corrections. Volume I and Volume III had not yet been typeset, but for both of these volumes Mr. Barbour's editorial work was basically complete. In the case of Volume I, the manuscript had already been perused by a recognized authority on John Smith's period, and Mr. Barbour had responded to detailed criticisms and had been able to make appropriate changes. He had also approved most of the copy editing that had been done on the volume. The manuscript of Volume I, then, was entirely ready for the compositor by the end of 1980.

Volume III had not yet been sent to an outside reader for criticism prior to Mr. Barbour's death, nor had the manuscript been finally copy edited. It should be emphasized, however, that in the course of preparation of the manuscript, Mr. Barbour had been in regular consultation with editors at the Institute of Early American History and Culture, and his work had been scrutinized piecemeal. In consequence, neither the outside critical reading nor the final copy editing resulted in any significant changes in the manuscript.

The Institute did not have for Volumes I and III the benefit of Mr. Barbour's close reading of the galley and page proof, which has been a considerable handicap, especially in the case of the substantive footnotes. On the other hand, the copy text of all three volumes had been prepared by Mr. Barbour long before his death, and the faithfulness of the text presented here to that copy text has been authenticated by multiple oral readings of the copy text against the proofs by members of the Institute staff.

Mr. Barbour had undertaken only preliminary planning of the index before he died. Knowing, however, that preparation of the index was a task too massive for him at his advanced age and that page proof of Volume III would not be available for another year, he requested, only months before he died, that the Institute arrange to have Mrs. Alison M. Quinn take over the job, which she was able to do.

It was Mr. Barbour's goal to have his editorial tasks completed by 1980, the quadricentennial anniversary of Smith's birth, and happily this goal was achieved. We are grateful, too, that Mr. Barbour thought to ensure the financial health of the project by a provision in his will—a complete surprise to the Institute staff—assigning a portion of his estate for Institute use. The Barbour fund was critically important at the last stages of editorial and production work.

Thad W. Tate, Director
Institute of Early American
History and Culture

PREFACE AND ACKNOWLEDGMENTS

The first attempt to present Capt. John Smith's works objectively and with sympathetic understanding of their character was made by Edward Arber in 1884. Before that, and since the days of their original printing, only scattered bits had been republished for one or another reason—on occasion even merely to disparage or glorify the man or what he wrote, depending on the publisher's bent. Arber, perhaps spurred by the specific doubts raised in the nineteenth century regarding Smith personally, collected and reprinted all but one of the major works, and added thereto a considerable section dedicated to contemporary writings relevant to Smith's career. This work, entitled *Captain John Smith ... Works, 1608–1631* (Birmingham, 1884), has now served for a century as the basic edition of Smith. Its excellence, rather than any want of assiduity on the part of more recent scholars, has certainly been responsible for the lack of a later edition. Yet modern research soon made a revision desirable, and that meant an edition that would supply such notes and comments as would make Smith more fully understandable.

The present edition includes a transcription of Smith's letter to Francis Bacon of 1618, which was omitted by Arber but constitutes the first draft of Smith's *New Englands Trials* (1620). This latter in turn was reprinted with additions in *New Englands Trials* (1622). Although the three versions are identical in part, each later one contains added material, thereby providing some insight into the development of Smith's plans for colonization.

Next, Arber omitted the *Sea Grammar* from his edition, presumably on the grounds that it is a mere expansion of Smith's *Accidence*. In this case, however, the omission is more serious than in that of the letter to Bacon. The material Smith added to the *Sea Grammar* was taken, generally verbatim, from one of the manuscript copies then circulating of Sir Henry Mainwaring's "Dictionary of Sea Terms" (the title is variously phrased), which was not printed until long after both Mainwaring and Smith were dead. Smith did not outrightly copy Mainwaring's book, but he used it as a source for good definitions of nautical terms that for the most part he had already published in his *Accidence*, much as the present editor has used the *Oxford English Dictionary* to explain obscure or obsolete words. The difference is that today we acknowledge our debts to our sources, while in 1627 few borrowing writers bothered to do so, and rarely indeed was the original writer, thus abused, known to complain.

A third kind of omission was Arber's failure to see the importance of passages in Samuel Purchas's *Hakluytus Posthumus, or Purchas His Pilgrimes* ... (London, 1625), that contain excerpts from Smith's notes or to recognize the importance of other documents in Purchas that add to our knowledge of Smith, or in the case of the *True Travels* provide an earlier version of a later work. Parenthetically, we may add that two poems by Smith have been discovered recently in the form of published commendatory verses for books by friends. These indirectly confirm Smith's authorship of the poem that introduces the *Advertisements*.

In the case of the present editor, a fading memory of a visit to Jamestown's 300th anniversary in 1907 persuaded him to return for the 350th anniversary in 1957. This brought about renewed interest in Smith and the acquisition of a copy of Arber. Finding that some details of southeastern European geography that had perplexed Arber were quite simple to verify through modern historical maps, the present editor undertook first an explanatory article or two, and then deliberately set out to try his luck with a biography of Smith based on known facts, illustrated with controlled flights of imagination but virtually devoid of bald legend. At that point, he became acquainted with Bradford Smith and his then recent *Captain John Smith: His Life and Legend* (Philadelphia, 1953). There, in an appendix by Dr. Laura Polanyi Striker, he found evidence of the first scholarly investigation into the Hungarian and provincial Austrian sources.

To pass over extraneous details, the editor's training in linguistics and experience as a newspaperman and intelligence officer had long since been that of an investigator. Impartial investigations in European archives steadily yielded circumstantial evidence in support of Smith's personal narratives, making the biography in progress a fait accompli. But, more important, these investigations aroused the interest of Dr. Lawrence W. Towner, then editor of the *William and Mary Quarterly*, to the extent that the desirability of a new edition of Smith's works was broached.

Arber's original edition had become scarce, as had even the reissue of 1895 and the reprint of 1910 with a new introduction by A. G. Bradley. Then, there were the works omitted by Arber (the letter to Bacon, the *Sea Grammar*, and the bits included as "Fragments" in Volume III of this edition), and there was the need for annotation, including the results of the latest research in many fields. Dr. Towner had already considered attacking the problem singlehandedly, but early in 1960 he got in touch with the present editor with the idea of joining forces. Due to other commitments on both parts, however, nothing concrete resulted from our discussions.

Finally, in 1969, five years after the publication of the present editor's life of Smith (*The Three Worlds of Captain John Smith*, Boston, 1964), the Jamestown Foundation celebrated the 350th anniversary of the first Virginia

Assembly. On this occasion, the chairman of the foundation, the Honorable Lewis A. McMurran, Jr., privately approached the editor with his own independent plan for publishing a complete and annotated edition of all Smith's works, including those omitted by Arber, and proposed entrusting this to the present editor. Agreement was soon reached. Dr. Towner (by then occupied with the Newberry Library, of which he is now president and librarian), willingly committed his dream to the present editor, and the Jamestown Foundation (now the Jamestown-Yorktown Foundation) contributed the funds necessary for further research, as well as partial support for publication. In this way, the editor was able to take charge by 1971. Although many problems remained to be solved, thanks to the efforts of Lewis McMurran and Lawrence Towner, the objective has become a reality. The many others who have helped make this edition possible, in addition to these "prime movers" (as Smith would have called them), are mentioned below.

A basic acknowledgment of debt to my forerunners in treating of John Smith's works is meet and proper, even though a wide and deep chasm often divides our aims and our conclusions. This chasm is the passage of time: the *chronos* of Homer, from which we have formed the word "chronology." With the passage of time, Smith's Elizabethan expansiveness became boasting within a generation, and by 1850 was labeled "lying." Yet those critics who began about 1850 to appraise Smith's work should be thanked, for ill informed though they were, they opened the door to just evaluation.

My most lasting debt in connection with this work, however, is to those who made its specific production possible. I therefore begin my acknowledgments with those who have granted me the most practical aid.

Foremost of these is the National Endowment for the Humanities, to which I express my hearty thanks for a grant in direct support of my research in 1972, and, four years later, for a Folger Library–NEH Senior Fellowship toward the same end, and in response to the need for study in greater depth of several problems raised particularly by Smith's *True Travels*. Another sponsor, already mentioned, is the Jamestown-Yorktown Foundation, heir to the Jamestown Foundation, whose generosity has been of help to me personally as well as to publication. And finally, two other sponsors have lent their support in more ways than one: the Newberry Library, Chicago; and the Institute of Early American History and Culture, Williamsburg, Virginia. They have been represented in part by an Advisory Board composed of the Honorable Lewis A. McMurran, Jr., Professor David Beers Quinn, Parke Rouse, Esq., Dr. Lawrence W. Towner, Dr. Wilcomb E. Washburn, and Dr. David Woodward. To all of these I extend my sincerest appreciation for advice and support. Dr. Thad W. Tate, director of the Institute of Early American History and Culture, has been the principal administrator of the project almost from its inception. His leadership has been essential to its success. In addition, I wish to recognize the efforts on my behalf of the editorial staff of the Institute at Williamsburg, Lucy Trumbull Brown, Dr. J. Frederick Fausz, and Dr. Norman S. Fiering. Without their keen attention to the minutiae that are encountered in such a work many flaws would not have been detected. For the oversights and errors that remain, I alone am responsible.

My debt is also great, however, to many other individuals and organizations. In addition to those listed in my *Three Worlds* (xi–xiii) who have since renewed their help, staff members in many previously unexplored libraries and archives have cooperated in great ways and small. Two or three sound scholars have remained skeptical (I would not want it otherwise), or disagreed with this or that analysis; but I believe I can truthfully state that the bulk of those whom I have consulted are in reasonable concord with the interpretations I have advanced here and there where highly moot historical questions are involved. Many of the results are to be found in the footnotes, above all in Volume III.

Here then, in order to avoid a list of acknowledgments reminiscent of a scholar's guide, I will single out a handful of scholars and archivists whose personal opinions have in some way influenced my work on Smith during the past five years. I am indebted particularly to Professor Quinn, already mentioned, who has freely given me the benefit of his unequaled familiarity with the entire period and area involved and thus has served as a welcome mentor for the edition as a whole. On specific matters and in specific fields, I am beholden to Dr. Franz Pichler, archivist in Graz, Austria; to the "Nicolae Iorga" Institute of History, Bucharest, and especially to Dr. Maria Holban, formerly of the staff of that institute; to the Topkapı Palace Archives and Library, Istanbul, and especially Sayın Ibrahim Baybura; to Francis W. Skeat, Esq., Fellow of the British Society of Master Glass Painters for advice on heraldic matters; to Dr. Karl Pišec, Maribor (Yugoslavia), for helping to identify Smith's "Olumpagh"; to Professor Gustav Bayerle, Department of Uralic and Altaic Languages, Indiana University, Bloomington, for clarification of certain aspects of the "Long War" (1593–1606); to Dr. Mehemet Kocakülah, graduate student at the University of Louisville (Kentucky), for help with Turkish titles; and to the staff of the Folger Shakespeare Library, Washington, D.C., and its director, Dr. O. B. Hardison. Many others are mentioned in the footnotes, in order to keep this section within bounds.

In conclusion, I wish to acknowledge also the help of my associate and assistant for thirty years, Wolfgang Rennert, whose work on the index was interrupted by his sudden untimely death on March 2, 1977.

Philip L. Barbour
Williamsburg, Virginia, 1980

CONTENTS

The True Travels, Adventures, and Observations
of Captaine John Smith (1630)
123

Advertisements for the Unexperienced Planters
of New England, or Any Where (1631)
253

Fragments
309

Auxiliary Documents
371

MAPS AND
ILLUSTRATIONS

EDITORIAL METHOD*

The editor's goal throughout has been to present the texts of Smith's works as faithfully as possible. The changes introduced are of two kinds, systematic and ad hoc. All ad hoc changes have been recorded meticulously by page and line number in the sections entitled "Textual Annotation" that follow each of Smith's works. More will be said below about the guiding principles behind these ad hoc changes. The systematic changes, most of which are merely typographical, have been introduced silently in accordance with the following rules.

1. Where necessary, "i" and "u" have been altered to represent vowel sounds exclusively; "j" and "v" have been altered to represent consonants exclusively. The makeshift "vv" has been changed to the modern "w," and the old forms of "s" have been changed to the modern "s."

2. Contractions have been expanded throughout: "Master" for "Mr.," "Captain" for "Cap[t].," "Sir" for "Sʳ," "lordship" for "Lᵖ," etc.; "the," "that," etc., have been substituted for "yᵉ," "yᵗ," etc. ("y" was a graphic variant of the runic letter *thorn*, still used in modern Icelandic, with the value of "th"); "and" replaces the ampersand; and "etc." replaces "&c." The tilde (a graphic variant "m" or "n" often reduced to a macron or short superior line) has been replaced by expanding the word, as in "them" or "then" for "thẽ," or "assistance" for "assistãce."

3. The numerous italicized words in the first editions (mostly proper names) have here been set in roman, except in the case of poetry, where we have followed the original mixture of italics and roman exactly. Otherwise, we have confined the use of italics to ships' names, Indian words (other than proper nouns) that do not appear in standard English dictionaries, and a few obscure foreign words and phrases. In one or two cases, such as the lists of immigrants and their occupations, italics have been retained or added for the sake of typographical clarity.

4. Almost all changes in punctuation are recorded in the Textual Annotation, except for a few additions or deletions of commas or full stops in the marginalia, which was often erratically typeset, and the silent addition of end-of-line hyphens that in certain obvious cases had been inadvertently dropped by the seventeenth-century compositor (e.g., a line ending after "pit" with the next line beginning "ched").

*This statement on editorial method has been prepared by the staff of the Institute of Early American History and Culture.

5. Speeches and other direct quotations, which normally were not set off by inverted commas in the seventeenth century, have been recognized in this edition by the introduction of a line space above and below the extract material.

6. The original running heads have been discarded along with the paging of the seventeenth-century editions. Page breaks are indicated by a double vertical rule (||), and the original folio is set in boldface in brackets in the margin. *All page references to Smith material in these volumes are to these boldface folios, not to the modern pagination.* The catchwords have also been dropped.

All other adjustments of the text, whether of punctuation, spelling, or word order, are listed in the Textual Annotation. It is perhaps necessary to comment a little on the editorial philosophy underlying these ad hoc alterations. First of all, obvious misprints have been corrected. Although in Smith's time the degree of standardization now prevailing in matters of orthography and punctuation did not exist, enough agreement existed to enable us to identify actual printer's errors as such. Correction of typographical mishaps such as inverted letters, triple consonants, and repeated words need no defense, but, in addition, we have made alterations in the copy text when it appeared logical to assume that if either Smith or his printers had noticed the "error," it would have been corrected. On the other hand, hundreds of "misspellings" in the modern sense have not been touched because they were common (or even uncommon) variants at the time. However, even though the editor has been extremely chary of making any changes at all in spelling, in a number of cases sound editorial considerations have justified some alterations. Since every one of these is listed in the Textual Annotation appended to each work of Smith's, the reader is free to check and, if so desired, reverse the editor's decision.

With regard to changes in punctuation, the same rules have been applied. When the text could easily be misunderstood by, or even be unintelligible to, the modern reader, we have altered the punctuation, based on our best judgment of how it would have been done if the compositor had minded his type. Here, too, the Textual Annotation will serve as a check and a resource for the specialist. Generally, no matter how peculiar the punctuation, if the text is comprehensible we have let it stand. The punctuation has been altered, then, only in cases of unusual ambiguity or obscurity. It has never been changed solely in the interest of modernizing or standardizing.

The Textual Annotation following each work of Smith's includes also two lists pertaining to the problems posed by words hyphenated at the end of the line. The first list records those words that in the copy text were hyphenated at the end of the line, thus raising for the editor the question of whether the hyphen should be retained when the same word fell in the middle of a line in the present edition. In deciding whether a word is normally hyphenated or whether it has been hyphenated only as part of an end-of-line word division, the editor has been guided by what he took to be Smith's typical usage. Since a decision on hyphenation is a form of emendation not unlike the correction of a supposed typographical error, the reader can use this first hyphenation list as a means of reconstructing the text as it was before editing. The second hyphenation list records those words hyphenated at the end of the line in the present edition for which the hyphen should be retained when transcribing from this edition. In other words, it corrects for the ambiguity that is often present when a word is divided at the end of the line. One does not know if it is word division brought about by the number of spaces left in the line or if the word is one that is to be hyphenated no matter where it falls in the line. The second list, then, does not reflect editorial discretion; it simply records that the word in question was hyphenated in the copy text and was found that way in the middle of a line.

Before concluding, a word must be said about the copy texts for this edition. The compositor was supplied with xerographic or printed facsimiles of Smith's works on which certain editorial changes had been made, as indicated above. The facsimiles were chosen for readability and availability, and in some cases two or three different copies of Smith's books were used. In consequence, in most instances no single library copy of a Smith work can be cited as the copy text. However, in all cases we have worked with the first editions of Smith's publications; there are no historical reasons for using any later editions under the assumption that Smith himself corrected or altered material for subsequent editions. The one partial exception to this rule is as follows: Since the *Generall Historie* is in some respects a compilation or reprint of some of Smith's earlier books, we have occasionally used that 1624 publication as a standard. All textual changes based on the *Generall Historie* are so indicated in the Textual Annotation, and many footnotes make comparisons between different versions of the same material in various of Smith's works. We have not found it necessary, on the other hand, to collate systematically the extant copies of Smith's works. There are variations from copy to copy, but these are invariably extremely minor, and after a century or so of Smith studies, no one has yet turned up a single important variation of this kind from copy to copy. Many years of research into John Smith's life and writings has brought to the editor's attention a number of these minor variations; these are noted in the Textual Annotation by the addition of the phrase "in some copies," without any further specificity.

ABBREVIATIONS
AND SHORT TITLES

ABBREVIATIONS

marg.
Marginalia, notes printed in margins of Smith's works.

repr.
Reprinted.

sig.
Signature, a letter or mark at the bottom of each gathering (folded sheet) in a book. In the absence of printed page numbers, reference is made instead to the signature, the order of the leaf in the gathering, and the side of the leaf. E.g., A1$^{r[ecto]}$ and A1$^{v[erso]}$ for the front and back of the first page in signature A; A2^r for the front of the second, etc.

SHORT TITLES

Arber, *Smith, Works*
Edward Arber, ed., *Captain John Smith ... Works, 1608–1631*, 2 vols., The English Scholar's Library Edition, No. 16 (Birmingham, 1884).

Barbour, "Earliest Reconnaissance," Pt. I or Pt. II
Philip L. Barbour, "The Earliest Reconnaissance of the Chesapeake Bay Area: Captain John Smith's Map and Indian Vocabulary," *Virginia Magazine of History and Biography*, Pt. I, LXXIX (1971), 280–302; Pt. II, LXXX (1972), 21–51.

Barbour, *Jamestown Voyages*
Philip L. Barbour, ed., *The Jamestown Voyages under the First Charter, 1606–1609*, 2 vols. (Hakluyt Society, 2d Ser., CXXXVI–CXXXVII [London, 1969]).

Barbour, *Pocahontas*
Philip L. Barbour, *Pocahontas and Her World* (Boston, 1970).

Barbour, *Three Worlds*

Philip L. Barbour, *The Three Worlds of Captain John Smith* (Boston, 1964).

Bradford, *Plymouth Plantation*

William Bradford, *Of Plymouth Plantation, 1620–1647*, ed. Samuel Eliot Morison (New York, 1952).

DAB

Dictionary of American Biography.

Deane, *Smith's Relation*

Charles Deane, ed., *A True Relation of Virginia, by Captain John Smith* (Boston, 1866).

DNB

Dictionary of National Biography.

Hakluyt, *Principal Navigations*

Richard Hakluyt, *The Principal Navigations, Voyages, Traffiques and Discoveries of the English Nation*, 3 vols. (London, 1598–1600).

Kingsbury, *Va. Co. Records*

Susan Myra Kingsbury, ed., *The Records of the Virginia Company of London*, 4 vols. (Washington, D.C., 1906–1935).

OED

Oxford English Dictionary, 13 vols. (Oxford, 1933).

Purchas, *Pilgrimage*

Samuel Purchas, *Purchas his Pilgrimage. Or Relations Of The World* ... (London, 1613).

Purchas, *Pilgrimes*

Samuel Purchas, *Hakluytus Posthumus, or Purchas His Pilgrimes* ..., 4 vols. (London, 1625).

Quinn, *Roanoke Voyages*

David Beers Quinn, ed., *The Roanoke Voyages, 1584–1590*, 2 vols. (Hakluyt Society, 2d Ser., CIV–CV [London, 1955]).

Sabin, *Dictionary*

Joseph Sabin *et al.*, eds., *A Dictionary of Books Relating to America*, 29 vols. (New York, 1868–1936). Vol. XX, containing the bibliography of Capt. John Smith, was prepared by Wilberforce Eames over a period of 25 years or more and was published in 1927–1928, with an independent reprint.

Siebert, "Virginia Algonquian"

Frank T. Siebert, Jr., "Resurrecting Virginian Algonquian from the Dead: The Reconstituted and Historical Phonology of Powhatan," in James M. Crawford, ed.,

	Studies in Southwestern Indian Languages (Athens, Ga., 1975), 285–453.
STC	A. W. Pollard and G. R. Redgrave, comps., *A Short-Title Catalogue of Books Printed in England, Scotland, and Ireland, 1475–1640,* 2 vols. (London, 1926; repr. 1969).
Strachey, *Historie*	William Strachey, *The Historie of Travell into Virginia Britania,* ed. Louis B. Wright and Virginia Freund (Hakluyt Society, 2d Ser., CIII [London, 1953]).
VMHB	*Virginia Magazine of History and Biography.*
WMQ	*William and Mary Quarterly.*

WORKS BY CAPT. JOHN SMITH

Accidence	*An Accidence or The Path-way to Experience. Necessary for all Young Sea-men* . . . (London, 1626).
Advertisements	*Advertisements For the unexperienced Planters of New England, or any where* . . . (London, 1631).
Broadside	Broadside prospectus of *The Generall Historie of Virginia* . . . (London, 1623).
Description of N.E.	*A Description of New England: or The Observations, and discoveries, of Captain John Smith* . . . *in the North of America* . . . (London, 1616).
Generall Historie	*The Generall Historie of Virginia, New-England, and the Summer Isles* . . . (London, 1624).
"Letter to Bacon"	Letter to Sir Francis Bacon (1618).
Map of Va.	*A Map of Virginia. With a Description of the Countrey, the Commodities, People, Government and Religion* (Oxford, 1612).
New Englands Trials (1620) and (1622)	*New Englands Trials* . . . (London, 1620, 1622).
Proceedings	*The Proceedings of the English Colonie in Virginia since their first beginning from England in* . . . *1606, till this present 1612* . . . (Oxford, 1612) [Pt. II of *Map of Va.*].

BIOGRAPHICAL
DIRECTORY

The Biographical Directory has been specifically designed to direct the reader through the more obscure byways of Elizabethan and Jacobean biography, with particular reference to the works of Capt. John Smith. No "famous" personage has been listed unless there is some direct connection with Smith, and the extent to which the biographies are detailed has been determined by either the amount of firm information available or the significance of the personage in Smith's career. The Directory thus falls short of adhering to a precise pattern, as it also falls short of providing sources in every case.

Practicality has been the editor's basic principle, and this has eliminated detailed references to (1) sources in little-known languages such as Rumanian, Turkish, and Hungarian, and (2) the very many notes made by the editor over nearly twenty years in nearly three dozen archives in the United States, England, France, Austria, Spain, Italy, and such cities as Munich, Istanbul, Copenhagen, and so on. To cite the former would be idle because of the languages and the scarcity of sources in other than major libraries; to cite the latter would take more space than is practical.

In short, this is a directory, not an encyclopedia. The short titles listed below have been used for the principle sources, in addition to those given in the Short Titles list for this volume. A few particularly pertinent, isolated works are named in the Biographical Directory with full bibliographical details.

SHORT TITLES FOR THE
BIOGRAPHICAL DIRECTORY

Bentley, *Stage*	Gerald Eades Bentley, *The Jacobean and Caroline Stage*, 7 vols. (Oxford, 1941–1968).
DCB	*Dictionary of Canadian Biography*, vol. I.
Enc. Br.	*The Encyclopedia Britannica*, 11th ed., 29 vols. (Cambridge, 1910–1911).
Enc. Isl.	*Encyclopaedia of Islam*, 1st ed., 5 vols. (Leiden, 1908–1938); new ed., vols. I–IV (Leiden, 1954–1978).

Enc. It.	*Enciclopedia Italiana di Scienze, Lettere ed Arti*, 36 vols. (Rome and Milan, 1929–1952).
Espasa Calpe	*Enciclopedia Universal Ilustrada Europeo-Americana, Espasa-Calpe*, 70 vols. in 72 (Barcelona, 1907–1930).
Gookin and Barbour, *Gosnold*	Warner F. Gookin and Philip L. Barbour, *Bartholomew Gosnold, Discoverer and Planter: New England—1602, Virginia—1607* (Hamden, Conn., 1963).
Grande Encyclopédie	*La Grande Encyclopédie*, 31 vols. (Paris, 1886–1902).
Greg, *Licensers*	W. W. Greg, *Licensers for the Press, Etc., to 1640* ... (Oxford, 1962).
Hamor, *True Discourse*	Ralphe Hamor, *A True Discourse Of The Present Estate Of Virginia* ... (London, 1615).
Hind, *Engraving*	Arthur M. Hind, *Engraving in England in the Sixteenth and Seventeenth Centuries*, 3 vols. (Cambridge, 1952–1964).
Jester, *Adventurers*	Annie Lash Jester, ed. and comp., in collaboration with Martha Woodroof Hiden, *Adventurers of Purse and Person: Virginia, 1607–1625* (Princeton, N.J., 1956).
Koeman, *Atlantes*	Cornelis Koeman, ed. and comp., *Atlantes Neerlandici. Bibliography of ... Atlases ...*, 5 vols. (Amsterdam, 1967–1971).
McKerrow, *Dictionary*	R. B. McKerrow, gen. ed., *A Dictionary of Printers and Booksellers in England, Scotland and Ireland ... 1557–1640* (London, 1910).
OCD	*Oxford Classical Dictionary.*
Plomer, *Dictionary*	Henry R. Plomer, *A Dictionary of the Booksellers and Printers Who Were at Work in England, Scotland and Ireland from 1641 to 1667* (London, 1907).
Plomer, *Short History*	Henry R. Plomer, *A Short History of English Printing, 1476–1898* (London, 1900).

Quinn, *New England*   David B. Quinn and Alison M. Quinn, eds.,
Voyages   *The English New England Voyages, 1602–1608*
                                  (Hakluyt Society, 2d Ser., CLXI [London,
                                  1983]).

Shaw, *History*   Stanford Shaw, *History of the Ottoman Empire*
                                  and Modern Turkey, vol. I, *Empire of the Gazis:*
                                  The Rise and Decline of the Ottoman Empire,
                                  1280–1808 (Cambridge, 1976).

Williams, *Index*   Franklin Burleigh Williams, Jr., *Index of*
                                  Dedications and Commendatory Verses in English
                                  Books before 1641 (London, 1962).

ABBAY, THOMAS (fl. 1608–1612), Jamestown colonist, 2d supply; author of
    dedications in the *Map of Va.* and the *Proceedings*; identity as yet
    unknown.
ABBOT, GEORGE (1562–1633), archbishop of Canterbury; one of the dedicatees
    of the *Advertisements*; see *DNB, Enc. Br.*, etc.
ABBOT, JEFFREY (fl. 1608–1612), Jamestown colonist, 1st supply, apparently
    not related to the archbishop; known to Smith as able and loyal, yet
    executed for unrecorded reasons; see *Generall Historie*, 110, and Hamor,
    True Discourse, 27.
ALEXANDER, SIR WILLIAM (c. 1577–1640), earl of Stirling, poet, statesman, and
    colonial promoter; see *DNB*, and Thomas H. McGrail, *Sir William*
    Alexander, First Earl of Stirling: A Biographical Study (Edinburgh, 1940).
ARCHER, CAPT. GABRIEL (c. 1575–1609/1610), original Jamestown colonist;
    educated at Cambridge and Gray's Inn (1593), but never called to the
    bar; associated with Bartholomew Gosnold (q.v.) in 1602 (wrote a report)
    and in 1606–1607 (report attributed to him); returned to England in
    1608, by then an avowed opponent of John Smith's; arrived back in
    Virginia in Aug. 1609 to lead an anti-Smith faction; died during the
    "starving time" in the winter of 1609/1610; see the account in Barbour,
    Pocahontas, 60–66.
ARGALL, SIR SAMUEL (1580–1626), navigator and administrator, knighted in
    1622; double cousin-by-marriage of Sir Thomas Smythe (q.v.) and
    brother-in-law of Lord De La Warr's wife's uncle; commissioned to test a
    shorter route to Virginia, he later succeeded Christopher Newport (q.v.)
    as pilot for Virginia, though briefly; abducted Pocahontas early in 1613

and a few months later wiped out a nascent French colony in Maine; acting Virginia governor from 1617 to 1619, he soon joined Sir Ferdinando Gorges (q.v.) in the renewed New England colonial effort; commanded a ship in an expedition to Spain (1625–1626), on the heels of which he suddenly died; see *DAB*; *DCB*; *DNB*; Seymour V. Connor, "Sir Samuel Argall: A Biographical Sketch," *VMHB*, LIX (1951), 162–175; Dorothy S. Eaton, "A Voyage of 'ffisshinge and Discovvery,'" Library of Congress, *Quarterly Journal of Current Acquisitions*, X (1953), 181–184; and Barbour, *Pocahontas*.

ASPLEY, JOHN (fl. 1624), "Student in Physicke, and Practitioner of the Mathematicks, in … London" (from title page of his *Speculum Nauticum* [1624]); see *Accidence*; *Sea Grammar*; and D. W. Waters, *The Art of Navigation in England in Elizabethan and Early Stuart Times* (New Haven, Conn., 1958).

AURELIUS ANTONINUS, MARCUS (A.D. 121–180), Roman emperor and Stoic philosopher; the "Marcus Aurelius" available to Smith was almost certainly not the "Meditations," but a didactic novel by Antonio de Guevara (q.v.) based on the emperor's life and character; see *True Travels*, 2n.

BARNES, JOSEPH (1546–1618), printer to the university and bookseller in Oxford; see Introduction to *Map of Va.*, and McKerrow, *Dictionary*, 22–23.

BARRA, JAN (JOHN) (fl. 1604–1634), Dutch engraver, came to England c. 1623; his title page for the *Generall Historie* was one of his first works; see Hind, *Engraving*, III, 95.

BASTA, GEN. GIORGIO (1540–c. 1607), count of Huszt, imperial commander in the "Long War," military writer; a ruthless tactician who brought "a peace of the grave" to Transylvania; see *Enc. It.*

BÁTHORY, ZSIGMOND (SIGISMUNDUS) (1572–1613), prince of Transylvania, nephew of István Báthory, king of Poland, married to a first cousin of Emperor Rudolph II and through her connected with Sigismund III of Sweden and Philip III of Spain; an unstable ruler in a time of unusual difficulty for his country; caught between the Ottoman and Holy Roman empires, Zsigmond abdicated at least three times; in the absence of any biography in English, see László Makkai, *Histoire de Transylvanie* (Paris, 1946).

BERTIE, ROBERT (1582–1642), Baron Willoughby of Eresby, 1st earl of Lindsey, later admiral of the ship-money fleet and general of the king's forces; son of the famous Elizabethan general Peregrine Bertie, Robert toured France (*True Travels*, 2), studied a wide range of subjects, and above all appears to have befriended John Smith, albeit inconspicuously. Robert's grandmother Catherine Willoughby, dowager duchess of Suffolk, had been an ardent Puritan. The count of Plouër, whose son (see Gouyon Family, below), befriended Smith, could hardly have failed to know her. His other grandmother, Margaret Golding, was related to the Gosnolds and the Wingfields, with whom Smith set out for Virginia. His wife, Elizabeth Montagu, could well have had a part in Smith's being appointed to the council in Virginia, and after the Virginia episode, Robert himself could have introduced Smith to the theatrical clique, including Richard Gunnell (q.v.). None of these helping hands can be identified in documents, yet it is surely worth mentioning that Robert Bertie or his shade seems to be standing by at nearly every event in John Smith's eventful life. Genealogical tables for the Bertie family are in Barbour, *Three Worlds*, 419–421.

BOCSKAI, ISTVÁN (1557–1606), chief councillor of Zsigmond Báthory (q.v.), his nephew; driven to take sides with the Turks by General Basta's outrages in Transylvania in 1602 and later, Bocskai in 1605 was elected prince by the diet in Medias, supported by the Ottoman sultan, and acknowledged by the Habsburg court, making possible the Zsitvatorok Treaty of 1606 ending the "Long War"; a few months later he died, apparently of poison; see *Enc. Br.*

BRATHWAIT, RICHARD (1588–1673), prolific poet, wrote verses for the *True Travels*; see *DNB*, and Matthew Wilson Black, *Richard Brathwait: An Account of His Life and Works* (Philadelphia, 1928).

BRENDAN, SAINT (fl. c. A.D. 484–c. 578), Irish monk, abbot, and missionary; legend says he sailed across the N Atlantic and discovered an island; see *DNB*.

BRERETON (BRIERTON), JOHN (1572–1619 or later), divine, Caius College, Cambridge, M.A. 1596; curate at Lawshall near Hessett, Suffolk, where he apparently got to know the Bacons, cousins of Bartholomew Gosnold (q.v.), with whom he sailed to New England in 1602; wrote an account (drawing also on Verrazzano's letter published by Hakluyt); rector near Gosnold's home in 1619, where he died; see *DNB*, and *DAB*.

BREREWOOD (BRYERWOOD), EDWARD (1565?–1613), antiquary and mathematician, author of *Enquiries touching the Diversity of Languages, and Religions* (1614); professor at Gresham College; see *Sea Grammar*, 51n, and *DNB*.

BRY, THEODORE DE (1527 or 1528–1598), engraver, of Liège, established at Strasbourg by 1560, visited England in 1586/1587, applied for citizenship in Frankfurt-am-Main in 1588, then returned to England to work on John White's drawings of "Virginia"; Johann Theodor (1561–1623) was his son; see Hind, *Engraving*, I, 124–126.

BUCK(E), GEORGE (fl. 1627), author of commendatory verses for the *Sea Grammar*; this Buck(e) seems to be the same as the "great-nephew" of Sir

George Buc (see Williams, *Index*, 26), and the "George Buck, Gent.," who published *An Eclog of Crownes* ... (1635); see *DNB*, s.v. "Buc, Sir George" (d. 1623).

BURLEY, NICOLAS (fl. 1627), author of commendatory verses for the *Sea Grammar*; otherwise unidentified.

BURTON, ROBERT (1577–1640), author of *The Anatomy of Melancholy* (1621), under the pen name of Democritus Junior; celebrated by Smith in the sixth state of the Smith/Hole map of Virginia with "Democrites Tree"; furthermore, Burton had a brother George who may have been the George Burton who arrived in Jamestown in 1608 and accompanied Smith to Werowocomoco on Dec. 29; "Burtons Mount" on the same map could have been named for either Burton; see Barbour, *Three Worlds*, 375.

BUTLER (BOTELER), CAPT. NATHANIEL (1577?–c. 1640), ship captain and governor of Bermuda, author of the *History of the Bermudaes*, which was the basis for Bk. V of Smith's *Generall Historie*, and of the *Dialogues*; sailed against Cádiz with Argall (q.v.) *et al.* in 1625, and sailed on the Île de Ré expedition in 1627. Butler's sister married John Cornelius (q.v.). See *DNB*.

CALVERT, GEORGE (c. 1580–1632), 1st Lord Baltimore; private secretary to Robert Cecil, earl of Salisbury, from 1606 to 1612; projector of the Maryland colony, member of the Virginia Co. from 1609 to 1620; see *DNB*; *DAB*; and Lawrence C. Wroth, *Tobacco or Codfish: Lord Baltimore Makes His Choice* (New York, 1954).

CARLTON, ENSIGN THOMAS (fl. 1602–1616), mercenary soldier with Smith in Transylvania, author of commendatory verses; otherwise unknown.

CARY (CAREY), HENRY (fl. 1617–1631), 4th Baron Hunsdon, Viscount Rochfort, 1st earl of Dover, grandson of Henry Carey (first cousin of Queen Elizabeth), and second cousin of Thomas West, Lord De La Warr (q.v.); dedicatee of the *True Travels*.

CAUSEY, NATHANIEL (fl.1608–1627), Jamestown colonist, 1st supply (in the *Phoenix*), 1608; wounded in 1622 massacre, he visited England, but was back in Virginia in 1627; see Jester, *Adventurers*, s.v. "Cawsey."

CECIL FAMILY: for Lord Burleigh and the earls of Salisbury and Exeter, see *DNB*.

CECILL, THOMAS (fl. 1630), engraver; contributed an unregistered coat of arms to the *True Travels*, based on Robert Vaughan's (q.v.) two devices in the map of Ould Virginia; see Hind, *Engraving*, III, 31, 45, and plate 20b.

CHAMBERLAIN, JOHN (1554–1628), news gatherer and letter writer; educated at Cambridge, but took up no profession; his letters are an invaluable source of historical information; see Norman Egbert McClure, ed., *The Letters of John Chamberlain*, 2 vols. (Philadelphia, 1939).

CLERKE, ROBERT (fl. 1616), an obscure bookseller who was licensed to print Smith's *Description of N.E.*; he appears also to have been the engraver of the portrait in the corner of Smith's map of New England (McKerrow, *Dictionary*, 70); his name was later erased (Hind, *Engraving*, II, 273).

CODRINGTON, JOHN (1580s?–1622?), author of commendatory verses for the *Description of N.E.*; Jamestown colonist with the 2d supply in 1608; despite the sketchiness of available data, he was certainly admitted to the Inner Temple, July 16, 1616, after his return to England; his will indicates that he was a man of some means; he was connected with the Fettiplaces (q.v.) by marriage; see R. H. Codrington, *Memoir of the Family of Codrington of Codrington* . . . (Letchworth, Herts., 1910).

COKE, SIR EDWARD (1552–1634), judge, writer on law, chief justice of the king's bench, but he finally lost favor with both James I and Charles I; Smith inserted a leaf of address to him in *New Englands Trials* (1620); see *DNB*, and Catherine Drinker Bowen, *The Lion and the Throne: The Life and Times of Sir Edward Coke, 1552–1634* (London, [1957]).

CORNELIUS, JOHN (fl. 1601–1609), goldsmith and merchant; member of the East India and Virginia companies, he sponsored Samuel Argall's (q.v.) exploratory 1609 voyage to Virginia; his wife was Elizabeth Butler, sister of Capt. Nathaniel Butler (q.v.).

COTTON, SIR ROBERT BRUCE (1571–1631), politician and antiquarian; educated at Cambridge, he began a collection of manuscripts, coins, etc., in 1588, part of which survives in the British Library today; see *DNB*, and Hope Mirrlees, *A Fly in Amber: . . . Sir Robert Bruce Cotton* (London, [1962]).

CRASHAW, RAWLEY (RALEIGH) (fl. 1608–1622), companion of Smith in Virginia and author of commendatory verses; a presumed but unverified relative of Rev. William Crashaw (q.v.).

CRASHAW, REV. WILLIAM (1572–1626), divine, poet, and bibliophile; supporter of the Virginia Co. and of John Smith, as well as of William Strachey (q.v.); responsible for interesting William Symonds (q.v.) in the publication of the *Map of Va.*; see *DNB*, and P. J. Wallis, *William Crashawe, the Sheffield Puritan* (privately printed by the Hunter Archaeological Society, 1963).

CRUSO, JOHN (fl. 1632–1681), civilian author of military works; despite his 1632 matriculation at Caius College, Cambridge, the publication of his *Militarie Instructions for the Cavallrie* at Cambridge that same year, with its broad and detailed basis in the classics, suggests that Cruso may have been the I. C. of the verses commending the *True Travels*; see *DNB*.

DALE, SIR THOMAS (fl. 1588–1619), deputy governor and marshal of Virginia; began as a mercenary in the Dutch forces; during a variegated career he rose to a captaincy and made many friends, including Sir Thomas Gates (q.v.) and Sir Robert Cecil, earl of Salisbury; in 1611 he volunteered for Virginia, where his success is well known; in England in 1616 Dale entered the service of the East India Co. and died in Java in 1619; see *DAB*, and especially Darrett B. Rutman, "The Historian and the Marshal: A Note on the Background of Sir Thomas Dale," *VMHB*, LXVIII (1960), 284–294.

DAVIES (DAVIS), JAMES, commander of Fort St. George at Sagadahoc in Maine (1606–1608). This was an attempt to plant a colony in "north Virginia," named "New England" a few years later by Smith; see Quinn, *New England Voyages*.

DAVIES, JOHN, of Hereford (1565?–1618), poet and writing master, author of commendatory verses for the *Description of N.E.*; see *DNB*, and Introduction to *Description of N.E.*

DAVIES (DAVIS), ROBERT, sergeant major at Fort St. George (1606–1608). As a skilled pilot he spent most of these two years commanding the *Mary and John* or the *Gifte of God* carrying colonists to and from Sagadahoc. The journal of the voyage of the *Mary and John* in 1607, used by William Strachey (q.v.), was probably written by Robert Davies; see Quinn, *New England Voyages*.

DAWSON, JOHN (fl. 1613–1634), printer in London who typeset Bks. I–III of the *Generall Historie* (see Haviland, John, below, and Introduction to the *Generall Historie*); admitted master printer in Jan. 1621 (McKerrow, *Dictionary*, 85).

DELARAM, FRANCIS (fl. 1615–1624), engraver, possibly of Netherlands origin; engraved portraits of Frances Howard, duchess of Richmond and Lennox, and Sir William Segar, among others; see Hind, *Engraving*, II, 215, 230, and plates 132b, 132c.

DE LA WARR, LORD: see West, Thomas.

DERMER (variously spelled), THOMAS (fl. 1614–1621), navigator and explorer; after his initial 1614 voyage with Smith, he spent part of 1616–1618 in Newfoundland with John Mason, later founder of New Hampshire, where he met Tisquantum (q.v.); in 1619 Sir Ferdinando Gorges (q.v.) commissioned him as commander of an expedition to New England, where he remained until exploring trips took him to Virginia, where he was killed by Indians in 1621; see *DCB*.

DONE, JOHN (fl. 1624–1633), author of commendatory verses for the *Generall Historie* and of *Polydoron: or a miscellania of morall, philosophicall and theologicall sentences* (1631); not to be confused with John Donne, dean of St. Paul's.

DROESHOUT, MARTIN (1601–c. 1652), English engraver, of Dutch extraction, famous for his portrait of Shakespeare (1623); he worked with John Payne on the illustrations for the *True Travels*, he doing the engraving; see Hind, *Engraving*, II, 341, 361.

EGERTON, SIR JOHN (1579–1649), 1st earl of Bridgwater, a title for which George Villiers (q.v.), then earl of Buckingham, is said to have extorted £20,000 from him (*DNB*); Smith inserted a leaf of address to him in *New Englands Trials* (1620).

ELSTRACK, RENOLD (1570–1625 or later), English engraver, of Dutch origin; did a portrait of Zsigmond Báthory; see Hind, *Engraving*, II, 163–214.

FEREBY, ANTHONY (fl. 1621–1640), author of commendatory verses for the *True Travels*, purveyor to the Ordnance Office; see *Calendar of State Papers, Domestic Series, 1629–ca. 1640*.

FETTIPLACE (PHETTIPLACE), MICHAEL and WILLIAM (fl. 1608–1616), brothers, gentlemen colonists of the 1st supply, and loyal supporters of John Smith during his Jamestown career; scions of an ancient Norman family, the Fettiplaces were well connected in England and well behaved in Virginia; together, they composed commendatory verses for the *Description of N.E.*, to which Richard Wiffin (q.v.) lent a hand as a token of his loyalty. Michael and William's great-aunt Dorothy Fettiplace married a great-uncle of Smith's friend John Codrington (q.v.).

FISHER, BENJAMIN (fl. 1621–1637), bookseller, licensed with Jonas Man (q.v.) to publish the *Accidence*, along with other notable works; see McKerrow, *Dictionary*, 104–105.

GATES, SIR THOMAS (fl. 1585–1621), governor of Virginia; sailed with Drake when Ralegh's Roanoke colony was rescued, fought in the Dutch wars, and sailed with the 1596 Cádiz expedition, etc.; patentee of the Virginia Co. in 1606; obtained leave from the Dutch States General to go to Virginia in 1608 and after serving the Jamestown cause well, returned to the Netherlands in 1621, where he died; see *DNB*, and *DAB*.

GENTLEMAN, TOBIAS (fl. 1612–1614), fisherman and writer on fishery; consulted by John Keymor (q.v.); author of *Englands way to win wealth . . .* (London, 1614), which strongly influenced *New Englands Trials*; see *DNB Supplement*.

GILBERT, CAPT. BARTHOLOMEW (fl. 1597–1603), naval captain, somehow involved in privateering and the fraudulent sale of a diamond to Queen Elizabeth, but cleared of any guilt; a cousin of Bartholomew Gosnold (q.v.) by marriage, he took part in Gosnold's 1602 voyage and was killed by Indians in 1603; see Gookin and Barbour, *Gosnold*, and Quinn, *New England Voyages*.

GIRAY, GAZI (GHAZI) (fl. 1588–1608), khan of Crimea, then tributary to the Ottoman Empire; younger brother of Mehmet Giray Khan, who had openly defied the sultan, Murat III, was deposed in 1584, and later killed; Mehmet was followed by Islam Giray Khan, who was succeeded in 1588 by Gazi Giray, another brother; in 1601 Gazi came to the aid of Mehmet III (q.v.) with a considerable Tatar force that swept into Transylvania on its way west, mostly skirmishing and raiding, until Gazi set up winter quarters in today's Yugoslavia, where he wrote a volume of verse, *Good and Evil*; see the *Enc. Isl.*; Shaw, *History*, 183; and W.E.D. Allen, *Problems of Turkish Power in the Sixteenth Century* (London, 1963).

GOAD(E), MASTER DOCTOR THOMAS (fl. 1615–1638), chaplain to Archbishop Abbot, precentor of St. Paul's; licensed *New Englands Trials* (1620) and the *Generall Historie*; see Greg, *Licensers*, 37–38.

GONZAGA, FERRANTE II (1563–1630), governor of High Hungary (*True Travels*, 8), cousin of Vincenzo, duke of Mantua (q.v.); his services in the "Long War" and elsewhere were so appreciated by Archbishop Ferdinand II of Styria that the latter, soon after his election as Holy Roman emperor, raised Ferrante's domain of Guastalla to a duchy, and created him duke thereof in 1621; see *Espasa Calpe*, and *Enc. It.*, s.v. "Gonzaga" and "Guastalla."

GONZAGA, VINCENZO (1562–1612), duke of Mantua, noted for his piety, his sense of justice, and his liberality, the last of which made his court one of the most brilliant in Europe; a cousin of the Holy Roman emperor through his mother, Vincenzo led an Italian army into Hungary to thwart the infidel Turk — with little success; for a vivid description of this late Renaissance Italian incursion into the Balkans, see Maria Bellonci, *A Prince of Mantua: The Life and Times of Vincenzo Gonzaga*, trans. Stuart Hood (New York, 1956).

GOOS, ABRAHAM (fl. 1614–1629), Dutch map engraver and printseller, who first printed Norwood's map of Bermuda; he was a cousin and pupil of Jodocus Hondius (q.v.); see Koeman, *Atlantes*.

GORGES, SIR FERDINANDO (1568–1647), naval and military commander, "father of English colonisation in America" (*DNB*), and onetime backer of Smith; see Richard Arthur Preston, *Gorges of Plymouth Fort: A Life of Sir Ferdinando Gorges, Captain of Plymouth Fort, Governor of New England, and Lord of the Province of Maine* (Toronto, 1953).

GOSNOLD, CAPT. BARTHOLOMEW (c. 1572–1607), explorer and planter in New England and Virginia, onetime privateer; in 1602, a pioneer explorer in New England; in 1606, undoubtedly a recruiter of colonists for Virginia, of whom one was probably Smith (through Robert Bertie [q.v.], whose aunt married Sir John Wingfield [q.v.], a first cousin of Gosnold's uncle's wife, as well as a second cousin of Edward Maria Wingfield [q.v.]); see Gookin and Barbour, *Gosnold*, and Quinn, *New England Voyages*. A genealogical table of the Gosnold family, as well as pertinent ties, is in Barbour, *Three Worlds*, 419–421.

GOUYON FAMILY, COUNTS OF PLOUËR. Charles Gouyon I, of Plouër, Brittany, had been a page of Charles IX of France (1550–1574), but had turned Protestant; he had fought against the duke of Mercoeur (q.v.), aided by English troops, and had fled to England with his family; his sons,

Amaury II, count of Plouër (born c. 1577), Charles II, viscount of Pommerit (born c. 1582), and Jacques, baron of Marcé (born c. 1584), were friends of Smith's c. 1600–1601; see Barbour, *Three Worlds*.

GRENT, WILLIAM (fl. 1617–1626), educated at Hart Hall, Cambridge, and Middle Temple c. 1626 (D.D., according to Hind, *Engraving*, III, 5, 174, 359); compiled a broadside "Map of the World 1625"; sailed for "the great river of Gambra" with Captain Jobson "to discover ... those rich mines of Gago or Tumbatu" (*True Travels*, 36n); wrote commendatory verses for the *Generall Historie*.

GRIFFIN, MISTRESS [ANNE] (fl. 1618–1621), widow of Edward, son of John Griffin of Llandunes, near Denbigh, who had bought out Eliot's Court Press in 1618; on Edward's death in 1621, his widow joined John Haviland (q.v.); see Plomer, *Dictionary*, 86–87.

GUEVARA, ANTONIO DE (1480?–1545), Spanish prelate and author, famous for his *Libro de Marco Aurelio* (1529), an adaptation of Marcus Aurelius's "Meditations"; Lyly's *Euphues* was modeled after his prose style; see *Espasa Calpe*.

GUILLIM, JOHN (1565–1621), herald; author of *A Display of Heraldrie ...* (1610), for which John Davies of Hereford (q.v.) and Sir William Segar wrote commendatory verses; he systematized the science of heraldry; see note to *True Travels* title page, and *DNB*.

GUNNELL, RICHARD (c. 1585?–1634), actor, theatre manager, and dramatist; author of commendatory verses for the *Description of N.E.*; see Bentley, *Stage*, II, 454–458, IV, 516–519, and Philip L. Barbour, "Captain John Smith and the London Theatre," *VMHB*, LXXXIII (1975), 277–279.

HAGTHORPE, JOHN (1585–after 1627), author of commendatory verses, poet, and perhaps the naval captain of that name; the poet had ties with the Saltonstalls (q.v.), through Wye Saltonstall's mother; see *DNB*.

HAKLUYT, REV. RICHARD (1552–1616), younger cousin of Richard Hakluyt, the lawyer; preacher, advocate of English expansion overseas, geographer, editor, translator, and broadly one of the "key figures in a group of intellectual clerics"; see D. B. Quinn, ed., *The Hakluyt Handbook*, 2 vols. (Hakluyt Society, 2d Ser., CXLIV–CXLV [London, 1974]).

HAMOR, RALPHE (fl. 1609–1626), Jamestown colonist, apparently with the 3d supply in 1609; became a councillor in 1611, visited England in 1614, and was a staunch supporter of the colony; despite the obscurity surrounding him, it is known that he had children by a first wife and married a second time before 1623 (Jester, *Adventurers*, 138); author of *A True Discourse Of The Present Estate of Virginia* (London, 1615).

HARSNETT, SAMUEL (1561–1631), archbishop of York; educated at Cambridge, collated to the archdeaconry of Essex in 1603, he promptly published a *Declaration of egregious popish impostures*, from which Shakespeare took the names of the spirits in *King Lear*; his High Church leanings kept him in trouble with the Puritans (*DNB*, and *Enc. Brit.*). He is one of the dedicatees of Smith's *Advertisements*.

HAVILAND, JOHN (fl. 1613–1638), printer in London who set Bks. IV–VI of Smith's *Generall Historie*; in 1621 Haviland joined with Edward Griffin's widow (q.v.) and founded an important printing business; in 1627 they printed Smith's *Sea Grammar*, but the following year he began entering books in his own name and soon became one of the three leading printers in London, along with Miles Fletcher and Robert Young; in 1630 Haviland printed Smith's *True Travels* for Thomas Slater, in quasi-modern spelling, and followed with the *Advertisements* in 1631, sold by Robert Milbourne (q.v.); see McKerrow, *Dictionary*, 131–132, and Plomer, *Short History*, 170.

HAWKINS, MA[STER], author of commendatory verses for Smith's *True Travels*, probably the William Hawkins (fl. 1622–1637) who was sizar at Christ's College, Cambridge (M.A., 1626), and then schoolmaster at Hadley, Suffolk; author of Latin verses between 1630 and 1634 and of a comedy published in 1627 by Robert Milbourne (q.v.); see Bentley, *Stage*, IV, 538–539.

HAWKINS, SIR RICHARD (1562?–1622), naval commander, only son of Sir John (1532–1595); sailed on a voyage round the world in 1593, but was caught and defeated in battle with Spanish ships off the Ecuadorian coast in 1594; a long term of imprisonment in Peru and Spain ended in 1602–1603; his most important work was his *Observations in his Voiage into the South Seas* (1622); see *DNB*.

HAY, JAMES (fl. 1603–1636), earl of Carlisle; highly esteemed by James I and served as a diplomat in Europe; see *DNB*, and *True Travels*, 52.

HEALEY, JOHN (fl. 1609–1610), translator, especially of Bishop Joseph Hall's *Mundus alter et idem*, a satire on the New World (*DNB*, and Barbour, *Jamestown Voyages*, I, 168, n. 1); tentatively identified as the "I. H." of the dedication "To the Courteous Reader" in the *True Relation*, though he remains an obscure personage.

HEATH, SIR ROBERT (1575–1649), judge, attorney general in 1625; Smith printed a special dedication to him in the *Accidence*.

HERBERT, WILLIAM (1580–1630), earl of Pembroke, famous for his ties with Shakespeare, but less well known as an investor in the Virginia, Northwest Passage, and Bermuda companies (*DNB*, etc.); dedicatee of Smith's *True Travels*.

HOLE, WILLIAM (fl. 1607–1620s), engraver, and sculptor of the king's seals, etc., as well as for the mint; a friend of many notables, his engraving of Smith's map seems to have been unique for him; see Hind, *Engraving*, II, 316–317, 339–340.

HONDIUS, JODOCUS (JOOS DE HONDT) (1563–1612), Flemish engraver, calligrapher, scientist, cartographer, and publisher; migrated to England c. 1584, where he worked with Emory Molyneux on the first English terrestrial globe of 1592 and became famous for his "wall-map of Europe" of 1595; continued Mercator's *Atlas Major*, purchased Mercator's plates after his return to Holland, and published his first edition in 1606; his sons Justus and Henrik continued his work; the smaller plates of his *Atlas Minor* (1607) appeared in England in Purchas's *Pilgrimes* (1625) and Wye Saltonstall's *Historia Mundi* (1635); see Hind, *Engraving*, I, 154–156, and Koeman, *Atlantes*.

HOWARD, CHARLES (1536–1624), earl of Nottingham, lord high admiral, etc. (see *DNB*); he was a first cousin in the male line of Thomas Howard, father of Smith's benefactress, Frances (q.v.), "the Double Duchess," and in the female line of Anne Boleyn, mother of Queen Elizabeth.

HOWARD, FRANCES (1579?–1639), daughter of Thomas, Viscount Howard of Bindon, and the patron of Smith's *Generall Historie*; upon the death of her second husband, Edward Seymour (q.v.), earl of Hertford, she married Ludovick Stuart, 2d earl of Lennox and later duke of Richmond, which alliance made her one of the richest women in England. It is notable that her father's brother Charles and his first cousins Queen Anne Boleyn and Queen Catherine Howard were all three executed, and Frances's own first cousin the premier duke of England, Thomas, duke of Norfolk, also died on the scaffold.

HUDSON, HENRY (fl. 1607–1611), navigator famed for his four voyages, from the last of which he never returned; friend of Smith's, he explored New York Bay and the Hudson River in 1609 in Dutch pay and was sent by English merchants to search for a northwest passage in 1610; see *DNB*; *DAB*; etc.; and Llewelyn Powys, *Henry Hudson* (London, 1927).

HUME, DAVID (1560?–1630?), controversialist, historian, and poet, of Wedderburn, Berwickshire; began travels c. 1580 in France, where he published tracts and books (*DNB*), but John Smith is the only witness to his presence there in 1599 or 1600 (*True Travels*, 2).

HUNT, REV. ROBERT (c. 1569–1608), M.A., first preacher in Jamestown with original colonists, formerly of Reculver, Kent; what little is known about him is summed up in Charles W. F. Smith, "Chaplain Robert Hunt and His Parish in Kent," *Historical Magazine of the Protestant Episcopal Church*, XXVI (1957), 15–33, while pertinent documents are in Barbour, *Jamestown Voyages*.

HUNT, MASTER THOMAS (fl. 1614), shipmaster for Smith in his 1614 voyage, during which he stole more than twenty Indians to sell into slavery in Spain, thereby damaging Anglo-Indian relations for many years.

IAPAZAWS (IAPAZOUS) (fl. 1610–1619), brother of the "King of Potomac," werowance of Paspatanzie; perhaps fretting under Powhatan's over-lordship, he helped Samuel Argall (q.v.) in engineering the kid-napping of Pocahontas; see Hamor, *True Discourse*, and *Generall Historie*, 112.

INGHAM, EDWARD (fl. 1627–1630), author of commendatory verses for Smith's *Sea Grammar* and *True Travels*; identity as yet unknown; see Williams, *Index*, 103.

JAMES, RICHARD (1582–1638), scholar, author of commendatory verses for Smith, nephew of Thomas James, Bodley's first librarian; after traveling extensively, as far as Muscovy, where he compiled an invaluable Russian-English vocabulary, Richard James became librarian for Sir Robert Bruce Cotton (q.v.); see *DNB*, and *Oxford Slavonic Papers*, X (1962), 46–59.

JEFFERAY(E), MASTER JOHN (fl. 1626–1630), D.D., chaplain to Archbishop Abbot (q.v.) and rector of Old Romney; licensed Smith's *True Travels*; see Greg, *Licensers*, 51–52.

JENKINSON, ANTHONY (fl. 1546–1611), merchant, sea captain, traveler; member of the Mercers' Company; received passport from Suleiman I in 1553 to travel in Ottoman Empire; captain-general of the Muscovy Co.'s fleet to Russia and their agent there for three years; authorized to travel in Persia and Central Asia in 1562, becoming the first Englishman to do so; he wrote a brief account of his travels 1546–1572; see *DNB*.

JONES, WILLIAM (fl. 1601–1626), printer, licensed for *New Englands Trials* (1620); a Puritan, imprisoned for some months, he sometimes printed for Michael Sparke, the bookseller; see McKerrow, *Dictionary*, 160–161.

JONSON, BEN (1572–1637), the dramatist (*DNB*, etc.); Smith's description of Pocahontas in his dedication to Frances Howard (q.v.) (*Generall Historie*, 2), was used verbatim in Jonson's *The Staple of News*, end of Act II.

JORDEN, EDWARD (1569–1632), physician and chemist, probably the author of commendatory verses for Smith's *Sea Grammar* and *True Travels*; his *Discourse of naturall bathes* was published for Michael Sparke, publisher of Smith's *Generall Historie*.

KENDALL, CAPT. GEORGE (fl. 1600–1607), original Jamestown colonist, executed "for a mutiny" in late 1607; apparently a former "servant" (employee) of Sir Robert Cecil, secretary of state and later earl of Salisbury; see Philip L. Barbour, "Captain George Kendall: Mutineer or Intelligencer?" *VMHB*, LXX (1962), 297–313, and John G. Hunt, "Captain George Kendall of Virginia, 1607," *National Genealogical Society Quarterly*, LIX (1971), 263–265.

KEYMOR (KEYMER), JOHN (fl. 1610–1620), economic writer; his *Observation made upon the Dutch fishing* may have been written c. 1601, but was first published in 1664; see *New Englands Trials* (1620 and 1622).

KHISSL, HANNS JACOB (fl. c. 1601), baron of Kaltenbrunn, court war counselor of Archduke Ferdinand (later Emperor Ferdinand II); appointed lieutenant colonel of the arsenal, Apr. 12, 1601; see *True Travels*, and J. Franz Pichler, "Captain John Smith in the Light of Styrian Sources," *VMHB*, LXV (1957), 335–336.

KINGSTON, FELIX (fl. 1597–1651), printer in London, originally a grocer, licenser with Clement Knight (q.v.) of Smith's *Accidence*; briefly one of the three king's printers in Ireland; see Plomer, *Dictionary*, 109–110.

KNIGHT, CLEMENT (fl. 1594–1629), draper and bookseller in London, joint licenser as warden of the Stationers' Company of Smith's *Accidence* with Felix Kingston (q.v.) and of the *Sea Grammar* with Edmund Weaver; see McKerrow, *Dictionary*, 166.

LEIGH, CAPT. CHARLES (1572–1605), merchant and voyager; early attracted by the separatist Puritanism of Robert Browne (1550–1633), Leigh attempted to plant a religious colony on the Magdalen Islands in the Gulf of St. Lawrence in 1597; failing in this, he traded in Algiers from 1600 to 1601, pursued pirates in the Mediterranean from 1601 to 1602, and later set out for Guiana, where he attempted in 1604 to settle a colony on the modern Oyapock River, only to die on board the ship sent to relieve him; this was the voyage in which Smith "should have beene a partie" (*True Travels*, 49); Leigh was a younger brother of Sir Oliph, "an encourager of maritime enterprise"; see *DNB*, and *DCB*.

LOW, GEORGE (fl. 1612–1614/1616), printer in London, known only for Smith's map of New England and an edition of William Byrd and Orlando Gibbons's *Parthenia* (1612?); see McKerrow, *Dictionary*, 178.

LOWNES, MASTER HUMPHREY (fl. 1587–1629), master of the Stationers' Company, licensed Smith's *True Relation, Description of N.E., New Englands Trials*, and *Generall Historie*; as a printer he was responsible for such famous works as Sidney's *Arcadia*, Spenser's *Faerie Queen*, and Bacon's *Apothegmes*; see McKerrow, *Dictionary*, 178–179.

M., S., author of commendatory verses for Smith; not satisfactorily identified as yet; see Williams, *Index*, 122.

MACARNESSE, THOMAS (fl. 1624), author of commendatory verses for the *Generall Historie*; "a Lincolnshire man" who has not been identified despite a thorough search in the Record Office, Lincoln.

MAINWARING, SIR HENRY (1587–1653), navigator, privateer, pirate, and nautical writer; Smith made full use of his manuscript "Dictionary" for the *Sea Grammar*; see *DNB*, and G. E. Manwaring and W. G. Perrin, eds., *The Life and Works of Sir Henry Mainwaring* (Navy Records Society, 2 vols., LIV, LVI [London, 1920, 1922]).

MAN, JONAS (fl. 1607–1626), bookseller in London, licensed with Benjamin Fisher (q.v.) to print Smith's *Accidence* (though neither name is shown); Man later transferred his copyrights to Fisher.

MARKHAM, GERVASE (c. 1568–1637), prolific writer, linguist, soldier under Essex, horse breeder, farmer, etc.; Smith's titles of *Accidence* and *Sea Grammar* were evidently inspired by Markham's works; see F. N. L. Poynter, *A Bibliography of Gervase Markham* (Oxford, 1962).

MARTIN, CAPT. JOHN (c. 1567–1632?), original Jamestown colonist, son of Sir Richard, the master of the mint and lord mayor of London (1534–1617), and brother-in-law of Sir Julius Caesar, the master of the rolls; always a contentious figure, about whom little is recorded beyond his quarrels; there is no full biography, but see Samuel M. Bemiss, "John Martin, Ancient Adventurer," *VMHB*, LXV (1957), 209–221, and James P. C. Southall, "Captain John Martin of Brandon on the James," *VMHB*, LIV (1946), 21–67.

MARTIN, RICHARD (1570–1618), member of the London Council for Virginia and friend of William Strachey, secretary of the Jamestown colony; though expelled from Middle Temple for his behavior in 1591, Martin became a barrister in 1602 and was "Prince of Revels" at Middle Temple c. 1605; later he was a member of the so-called "Mermaid Tavern Club," founded by Sir Walter Ralegh, which included Ben Jonson, John Donne, Thomas Coryate, possibly Shakespeare, and many other personalities.

MEADE, RICHARD (fl. 1629), author of commendatory verses for Smith's *True Travels*, his identity is uncertain.

MEHMET III (1566–1603), sultan of Turkey; inherited the "Long War" on his father's death in 1595, and left it for his son Ahmet I to conclude; after one decisive victory at Keresztes, Hungary, in 1595 and a defeat by Zsigmond Báthory (q.v.) and Mihai Viteazul (q.v.), Mehmet left military affairs to his viziers and led an indolent life in the Topkapı Saray, Istanbul; see Shaw, *History*, 184–186.

MELDRITCH, COL. (fl. 1601–1602), a military commander in the imperial army under whom Smith served during the "Long War"; despite efforts by Dr. Laura Polanyi Striker, Dr. J. Franz Pichler, and this editor to identify him, no firm case has yet been made; see Introduction to Fragment J, Vol. III.

MERCOEUR, PHILIPPE-EMMANUEL DE LORRAINE, DUKE OF (1558–1602); ardently Roman Catholic, he opposed Henry IV as king of France, but had to give way by 1598; a capable but hardly inspired leader, he entered the service of Rudolph II, a distant cousin, in the "Long War," but died on his way back to France to recruit more troops; see *Grande Encyclopédie*.

METHAM, GEORGE (fl. 1590s), son of George, son of Sir Thomas; caretaker of John Smith's small estate during his minority, he was related by marriage to Peregrine Bertie, Lord Willoughby, and to Sir John Wingfield (q.v.), who married Willoughby's sister, Susan; in addition, in

Smith's generation there were ties between a Metham and a son of Thomas Sendall (q.v.), the King's Lynn merchant to whom Smith was apprenticed; see *True Travels*, 2.

MIHAI VITEAZUL ("MICHAEL THE BRAVE") (1558?–1601), prince of Walachia, then an autonomous tributary state in the Ottoman Empire; at first *ban* (governor) of Craiova, in 1593 he was appointed voivode of all Walachia by the Turkish grand vizier, perhaps to assure his cooperation when the "Long War" broke out, but Mihai found the price too high and revolted in 1594; in 1595 the new sultan, Mehmet III (q.v.), retaliated, but his army was soundly defeated by Mihai in league with Zsigmond Báthory (q.v.) of Transylvania; this encouraged the neighboring Moldavian prince to rebel, thereby involving Mehmet's ally, the Tatar Khan of Crimea, and brought Sigismund III of Poland down to occupy Moldavia to keep the Tatars out; meanwhile Zsigmond Báthory abdicated, leaving Mihai virtually alone between the two empires; in a desperate effort to maintain independence, Mihai extended his league with the Habsburgs, but in the end he was treacherously murdered by order of Basta (q.v.), the imperial general, on Aug. 18, 1601, and by 1605 Walachia, Transylvania, and Moldavia were again ruled by native princes under the suzerainty of the Turkish sultan; see the brief biography by Nicolae Iorga in the *Grande Encyclopédie*; full biographies exist only in Rumanian, Hungarian, and German.

MILBOURNE, ROBERT (fl. 1623–1642/1643), bookseller in London who handled Smith's *Advertisements*; Milbourne also published Edward Waterhouse's *Relation of the Barbarous Massacre* (1622); see Kingsbury, *Va. Co. Records*, III, 541, and Plomer, *Dictionary*, 127–128.

MILDMAY (or MILEMER), THOMAS, unidentifiable due to his uncertain surname.

MOCKET, RICHARD (1577–1618), warden of All Souls, Oxford; actively employed licensing books at Stationers' Hall; author of two Latin religious treatises; see *DNB*.

MONTLUC (better, MONLUC), BLAISE DE (1502–1577), Gascon army captain, marshal of France in 1574; renowned for his *Commentaires* (1592); see *Grande Encyclopédie*.

MURAT III (1546–1595), sultan, grandson of Suleiman I; his wife Safiye Sultan strengthened the so-called "sultanate of the women"; Murat helped put István Báthory on the Polish throne, to counter Habsburg influence; admitted the first English ambassador and merchants; in the west, mutual frontier raids led to the "Long War"; see Shaw, *History*, 179–184.

NAMONTACK (fl. 1608), trusted servant of Powhatan, used to help, and spy on, the English on their first visit to Werowocomoco early in 1608; exchanged for Thomas Savage (q.v.) to learn the ways of the English and sent to England with Christopher Newport (q.v.); see Barbour, *Three Worlds*.

NEWPORT, CAPT. CHRISTOPHER (1560–1617), mariner; sailed for Brazil in 1581, but left ship because of a quarrel and somehow made his way back to England; after 1590 commanded privateers in the West Indies, soon taking out a share in the enterprise; chosen to command the Virginia Co.'s fleet in 1606 as "well practised" in those waters, he served the company for five years; employed by the East India Co. in 1612, he died at Bantam; see K. R. Andrews, "Christopher Newport of Limehouse, Mariner," *WMQ*, 3d Ser., XI (1954), 28–41.

NORTON, ROBERT (d. 1625, aged over 50), engineer and gunner, son of Thomas Norton, the lawyer and poet, coauthor with Sir Thomas Sackville of *The Tragedie of Gorboduc*; Robert was granted the post of engineer of the Tower of London for life in 1624; he and John Smith exchanged commendatory verses for one another; see *DNB*.

NORWOOD, RICHARD (1590?–1675), surveyor and mathematician; sent to survey Bermuda by the Bermuda Co. and produced a map in 1622, which exists only in manuscript copy; measured out one degree of latitude in England in terms of miles with astounding accuracy; returned to Bermuda and died there; see *DNB*; *Generall Historie*, 169n; and Wesley F. Craven and Walter B. Hayward, eds., *Journal of Richard Norwood Surveyor of Bermuda* (New York, 1945).

OPECHANCANOUGH (fl. 1607–1644), younger half-brother of Powhatan (q.v.), werowance of Pamunkey, later overlord of Powhatania; both wily and determined, he was the unwavering enemy of the English; he captured Smith in Dec. 1607, but bowed to Powhatan's conciliatory policy; keeping in the background while Powhatan lived, he came more to the fore when Opitchapam/Itoyatin (q.v.) briefly succeeded Powhatan, and commanded the massacre of 1622 as soon as his own authority was recognized; shaken but not broken when the colonists struggled to their feet again, Opechancanough made one last desperate effort to dislodge the English in 1644, when he was almost certainly over ninety; see Barbour, *Pocahontas*.

OPITCHAPAM (ITOYATIN) (fl. 1607–1618), next younger half-brother of Powhatan, werowance of Pamunkey; entertained Smith in 1608; succeeded Powhatan in 1618, but he kept behind the scenes; the date of his death is unknown.

OPOSSUNOQUONUSKE (fl. 1607–1610), weroansqua of a small Appamatuck village and the independent sister of the tribal werowance, she attended the ceremony when Smith was first brought before Powhatan and again when he returned early in 1608; nearly three years later she was killed by the English in retaliation for the massacre of fourteen colonists; see Strachey, *Historie*, 64.

O'ROURKE, BRIAN (fl. c. 1603–1629), an Irish gentleman, grandson of Brian Ballach and son of Brian-na-Mota, who inherited a strong aversion to

Englishmen, yet was taken to England for his education; beginning in
1619 he was almost constantly in and out of prison, but was finally freed
with the aid of a generous grant from King James; his commendatory
verses for the *Generall Historie* are the last recorded word from or about
him; see Barbour, *Three Worlds*, 486, n. 5.

PASSE, SIMON VAN DE (c. 1595–c. 1647), Dutch engraver, son of Crispin,
worked in England with his father, brothers, and sister; engraved
portraits of Pocahontas (q.v.), Ludovick Stuart, duke of Richmond and
Lennox, and Sir Thomas Smythe (q.v.), as well as the smaller engraving
of John Smith for the map of New England; see Hind, *Engraving*, II,
266–268, 273.

PASSE, WILLEM VAN DE (fl. 1600–1637), brother of Simon (q.v.); engraved a
portrait of Frances Howard (q.v.), duchess of Richmond and Lennox;
see Hind, *Engraving*, II, 293.

PERCY, GEORGE (1580–1632), younger brother of the 9th earl of North-
umberland, Henry Percy; educated at Gloucester Hall, Oxford, and
Middle Temple; traveled in the Netherlands and in Ireland and sailed
for Virginia with the first colonists; his manuscript account of the
"Starving Time" in Virginia (1609–1610) and its aftermath reflects
ennui coupled with sickness more than any other emotion; see Philip L.
Barbour, "The Honorable George Percy, Premier Chronicler of the First
Virginia Voyage," *Early American Literature*, VI (1971), 7–17.

PHETTIPLACE: see FETTIPLACE.

POCAHONTAS (1595?–1617), favorite daughter of Powhatan (q.v.); Pocahontas was the one potential peacemaker between the unwanted Englishmen and her own people; after the legendary meeting with Smith in
Powhatan's residence, she seems to have worked unremittingly in the
interests of the English; ultimately she was baptized and married John
Rolfe (q.v.); she died in Gravesend, apparently of some pulmonary
congestion brought on by the polluted air of London; see Barbour,
Pocahontas.

POOLE, JONAS (fl. 1607–1612), mariner, served under Captain Newport (q.v.)
on first exploration of James River in 1607; in 1610 sailed "for a northern
discovery" for the Muscovy Co. and a year later "to fish near Green-
land"; returning from Spitzbergen in 1612, he was "basely murdered
betwixt Ratcliffe and London"; see *DNB*.

POPHAM, SIR JOHN (1531–1607), chief justice of the king's bench, noted for his
severity; interested in colonization, he helped bring into being both the
London and Plymouth companies for "Virginia" colonization; primary
backer of Plymouth Co. until his death in June 1607; see *DNB*, and
Quinn, *New England Voyages*.

POTS (POTTS), RICHARD (fl. 1608–1612), clerk of the council in Virginia; the
compilation of Smith's *Proceedings* has been ascribed largely to him; he

arrived in Jamestown with the 1st supply, Jan. 2, 1608, and probably
returned to England in Sept. 1610; neither his identity nor his
contribution to Smith has been precisely determined.

POTTER, CHRISTOPHER (1591–1646), preacher, provost of Queens College,
Oxford; possibly the author of the commendatory verses ascribed to
"C.P." in the *True Travels*; see *DNB*.

POWELL, NATHANIEL (fl. 1607–1622), navigator and original Jamestown
colonist; accompanied Smith on the second Chesapeake Bay expedition
and wrote part of the account thereof in the *Proceedings* (pp. 36–41) in
collaboration with Anas Todkill (q.v.); credited by Alexander Brown
with being a surveyor, but this seems unlikely in view of the London
Council's appointment of William Claiborne as surveyor in 1621 when
Powell was still in Virginia; see Kingsbury, *Va. Co. Records*, III, 477.

POWHATAN (1540s?–1618), overlord of tidewater Virginia; named for his chief
fortified village, Powhatan near the James River falls, he inherited five
other villages, to which he added more than a score by conquest or
intimidation; despite legends to the contrary (see *DAB*), he appears to
have been an unusual Algonkian despot, similar to Bashabes in Maine.

PRING, CAPT. MARTIN (1580–1626?), sea captain; commanded a small
expedition to New England under license from Sir Walter Ralegh in
1603; in 1604 he was master of the *Olive Plant* under Capt. Charles Leigh
(q.v.), but revolted because of hard fare and the like; returned to London
aboard a chance Dutch ship; in 1606 he sailed to New England again, for
Sir John Popham (q.v.), and is said to have brought back an "exact
discovery of the North Virginia coast"; served the East India Co.,
probably from 1608; he is said to have made another voyage to Virginia
in 1626 and to have died on his return to England; see *DNB*.

PURCHAS, REV. SAMUEL (1577–1626), B.D., Cambridge, curate in 1601, vicar
of Eastwood, near Southend, where he began to assemble material for
what became his *Pilgrimage. Or Relations Of The World* . . . (1st ed., 1613);
this received such acclaim that he was inducted as rector of St. Martin's,
Ludgate, and appointed chaplain to the archbishop of Canterbury in
1614; Richard Hakluyt (q.v.), in whose footsteps Purchas evidently
wanted to follow, died in 1616, leaving a vast collection of documents
and books of travel that soon became Purchas's; this led to his embarking
on the huge work known to all historians of the period, the *Pilgrimes*; he
and Smith became friends about 1611, and much of Smith's work was
reprinted by Purchas; see Barbour, "Samuel Purchas," in J. A. Leo
Lemay, ed., *Essays in Early Virginia Literature Honoring Richard Beale Davis*
(New York, 1977), for further details and references to other sources.

RATCLIFFE: see SICKLEMORE, JOHN.

RAWDON (ROYDON), SIR MARMADUKE (1582–1646), London merchant who
married a wealthy heiress; traded, largely in wines, in France, Portugal,

the Netherlands, and elsewhere, and later invested capital in Barbados; see references in Robert Davies, ed., *The Life of Marmaduke Rawdon of York* (Camden Society, LXXXV [1863]), which treats Sir Marmaduke's nephew.

RICH, SIR NATHANIEL (1585?–1636), merchant adventurer, probably the eldest son of Richard Rich (author of *Newes from Virginia* [1610]), who was an illegitimate son of Richard, 1st Baron Rich; Sir Nathaniel was consequently a "cousin" of Robert Rich, earl of Warwick, of Bermuda and Virginia fame; see *DNB*.

ROBINSON, EDWARD (fl. 1601–1616), sergeant with Smith in Transylvania; author of commendatory verses for the *Description of N.E.*; otherwise unknown.

ROE, SIR THOMAS (1581?–1644), ambassador; Prince Henry sent him "upon a discovery to the West Indies" from 1609 to 1610; in 1614, at the suggestion of, and financed by, the East India Co., James I appointed him ambassador to the court of Jahangir, the "Great Mogul"; other embassies followed, all of them marked by good judgment and sagacity; see *DNB*.

ROLFE, JOHN (1585–1622), son of John and Dorothea Mason Rolfe, of Heacham, Norfolk, presumed husband of Pocahontas, and if so identical with the John Rolfe who sailed for Virginia in 1609 in the *Sea Adventure*, was wrecked off Bermuda, and finally reached Jamestown on June 23, 1610; he died apparently before the massacre in 1622; for doubts about Rolfe's identity, see Wilson Miles Cary, *VMHB*, XXI (1913), 208; for further details, see Barbour, *Pocahontas*.

ROSIER, JAMES (d. 1609), Cambridge graduate, became a Catholic, sent in 1605 by Sir Thomas Arundell, a Catholic, to collect information possibly leading to a Catholic colony in modern New England, and to write a report; published *A true relation* that same year, and in 1625 a version from manuscript was printed in Purchas's *Pilgrimes*, IV, 1659–1667, with the addition of a valuable Maine-Algonkian vocabulary; see Quinn, *New England Voyages*.

SALTONSTALL, SIR SAMUEL (1580s?–1641), draper, son of Sir Richard, the lord mayor of London, and first cousin of Sir Richard (1586–1658) of the Massachusetts Bay Co. (see *DNB*); Sir Samuel was imprisoned for thirteen years for unknown reasons, but released by the efforts of his sister's husband, Sir Thomas Myddelton, and perhaps for that reason kept in the background; he had interests in the West Indies and proved a friend and protector to John Smith; see *Sea Grammar*, and *True Travels*.

SALTONSTALL, WYE (fl. 1619–1640), son of Sir Samuel (q.v.), poet and translator; published some eight books, one of which was his translation into English of *Historia Mundi*, ... *written by Judocus* [*sic*] *Hondius*, which includes a copy of Smith's engraved portrait on the map of New England; see *Sea Grammar*, and *DNB*.

SANDYS, SIR EDWIN (1561–1629), statesman, parliamentarian; second son of Edwin Sandys, archbishop of York; M.P., 1604–1611 and 1621; quickly took a leading position in the House of Commons; basically opposed to extreme royal prerogatives, Sandys became and remained obnoxious to James; interested in colonization, he became a member of the London Council of the Virginia Co. (acting as assistant treasurer 1617–1619 and treasurer 1619–1620) as well as of the East India Co., and later, the Bermuda Co.; see *DNB*, and Wesley Frank Craven, *Dissolution of the Virginia Company: The Failure of a Colonial Experiment* (New York, 1932).

SANDYS, GEORGE (1578–1644), poet, traveler, translator, and treasurer of the council in Virginia, youngest brother of Sir Edwin (q.v.); author of *A relation of a journey* [to Turkey] (1615) and translator of Ovid's *Metamorphoses*; see *DNB*, and Richard Beale Davis, *George Sandys, Poet-Adventurer* (London, 1955).

SAVAGE, THOMAS (1594?–before 1633), "laborer, boy," later ensign, colonist of the 1st supply, apparently of the old Cheshire family of Savages of Rock Savage; given to Powhatan (q.v.) in exchange for Namontack (q.v.) in 1608; learned the Powhatan language and Indian customs and proved of great value as a reliable interpreter (see *Proceedings*); celebrated in an Indian song, Savage settled on the Eastern Shore, raised a family, and died there; see Martha Bennett Stiles, "Hostage to the Indians," *Virginia Cavalcade*, XII (Spring 1962), 5–11.

SCRIVENER, MATTHEW (1580–1609), son of Rauff Scrivener of Ipswich, colonist with 1st supply, and the first "new" member of the local council in 1608; at the start a loyal friend and aide to Smith, after Captain Newport's (q.v.) third departure in Dec. 1608 he suffered a "decline in his affection" and began to act arbitrarily; was drowned on a foolhardy canoe trip in Jan. 1609.

SENDALL, THOMAS (fl. 1577–1614), prominent merchant of King's Lynn, Norfolk, to whom Smith was apprenticed; see *True Travels*, and Bradford Smith, *Captain John Smith: His Life and Legend* (Philadelphia, 1953), 30–31.

SEYMOUR, EDWARD (1539?–1621), earl of Hertford, oldest surviving son of Edward "the Protector" (1506?–1552), brother of Queen Jane Seymour and thus uncle of King Edward VI; secretly married Catherine Grey, sister of Lady Jane Grey, who was, after Lady Jane's execution, the next in succession to the crown after Queen Mary and Queen Elizabeth; thus involved in court and legal intrigues, Hertford led a difficult life; his friendliness to John Smith may at first have been prompted by Robert Bertie (q.v.), whose grandmother Catherine, duchess of Suffolk, had ties with Hertford, and he in turn may have influenced his second wife, Frances Howard (q.v.) (later duchess of Richmond and Lennox), to be helpful to Smith; see *DNB*.

SICKLEMORE, JOHN (fl. 1607–1609), alias Capt. John Ratcliffe; master of the pinnace *Discovery* on the original Jamestown voyage (1606–1607) and member of the local council; at first friendly to, and later at odds with, John Smith, Sicklemore/Ratcliffe remains an enigma as to who he was and why he was appointed to the council; although several baptisms of boys named John Sicklemore are registered in Ipswich for the 1570s and early 1580s, it is impossible to identify any with "Captain John"; see Barbour, *Jamestown Voyages, passim*.

SICKLEMORE, MICHAEL (fl. 1608), colonist with the 1st supply; chiefly noted for his unsuccessful attempt to find traces of Ralegh's "Lost Colony" at Roanoke, etc., as noted in the *Proceedings*, 57, 90; little is known about him; an extended inspection of Suffolk County archives (which contain many references to the Sicklemores) has not brought to light anyone named Michael Sicklemore.

SMITH, N. (fl. 1616), author of commendatory verses for the *Description of N.E.* and the *Generall Historie*; identity uncertain, but see the Brief Biography of Captain John Smith, below.

SMYTH, JOHN, of Nibley (1567–1640), genealogical antiquary, steward for the Berkeley family and, later, of the hundred and liberty of Berkeley; adventurer in the Virginia Co., he later backed Berkeley Hundred, Virginia; a regular attendant at the company courts, he was the first to propose the writing of a history of the colony; see *DNB*, s.v. "Smith," and many references in Kingsbury, *Va. Co. Records*.

SMYTHE, SIR THOMAS (1558?–1625), outstanding merchant in London, governor of the East India Co., treasurer of the Virginia Co., and others; see *DNB* for details.

SOMERS, SIR GEORGE (1554–1610), mariner; after a life dedicated to the sea, he was one of the chief movers in the founding of the London Virginia Co., and one of its four patentees; named admiral of Virginia in 1609, he was wrecked off Bermuda, got ashore, and built two barks with which he transported 150 colonists to Jamestown in 1610; he returned to Bermuda for supplies and died there, it is said, of overeating; see *DNB*.

SPELMAN, HENRY (1595–1623), Jamestown colonist, 2d supply; son of Erasmus Spelman, the brother of Sir Henry, the well-known antiquarian; all doubt regarding the identity of young Henry was removed many years ago by the discovery of the will of his great-uncle, in which he was disinherited (*VMHB*, XV [1907–1908], 305); in trouble at home, he continued his independent way in Virginia, but was killed by treachery; see particularly the *Generall Historie*, 105, 108, 120, 151, 161.

STRACHEY, WILLIAM (1572–1621), member of the Essex minor gentry, educated at Emmanuel College, Cambridge, and Gray's Inn, London; moved in literary and dramatic circles, had a brief career as a diplomat in Istanbul, and in 1609 decided to try his fortune in Virginia; sailing with Gates (q.v.), Somers (q.v.), and Newport (q.v.), he was wrecked off Bermuda, landing at Jamestown only in 1610; meanwhile Matthew Scrivener (q.v.), briefly secretary of the colony, was drowned, and Strachey received the post; first writing an account of the shipwreck (which somehow reached Shakespeare's ears and provided fodder for *The Tempest*), Strachey put together *The Historie of Travell into Virginia Britania*, which was neither finished nor published in his lifetime, but which constitutes with John Smith's works our chief source of information about the Virginia Algonkians; returning to England in 1611, Strachey suffered continuous disappointments until his death; for details, see S. G. Culliford, *William Strachey, 1572–1621* (Charlottesville, Va., 1965), and Strachey's *Historie*.

STUKELY, SIR LEWIS (fl. 1603–1620), vice-admiral of Devon; was appointed guardian of Pocahontas's (q.v.) son, Thomas Rolfe, in 1617, and in the following year was involved in the arrest of Sir Walter Ralegh, a cousin; see *DNB*.

SUTCLIFFE, DR. MATTHEW (1550?–1629), dean of Exeter; founder of Chelsea College, where Samuel Purchas (q.v.) worked on his *Pilgrimes*; member of the Virginia Council, principal backer of the Plymouth Co., and later, member of the Council for New England, he was a prime backer of voyages to New England, including John Smith's projects; see *DNB*.

SYMONDS, REV. WILLIAM (1556–1616?), D.D., divine, schoolteacher, rector, and author; in 1599 he was presented by Robert Bertie (q.v.) to the rectory of Halton Holgate, Lincolnshire; later, preacher at St. Saviour's, Southwark, he undertook to help publish the *Proceedings* (as well as Smith's *Map of Va.*), at the suggestion of "Master Croshaw," probably Rev. William of Crashaw (q.v.); see *DNB*, and *Proceedings*.

TAHANEDO (fl. 1605–1607), an Algonkian Indian from Maine who had been kidnapped by George Waymouth (q.v.) in 1605; Thomas Hanham, a patentee of the Plymouth Co., brought him back in 1606, and he was of great help to the Sagadahoc colony; see Quinn, *New England Voyages*.

TANNER, SALO. (fl. 1629), author of commendatory verses for the *True Travels*; identity unknown.

THORPE, THOMAS (fl. 1584–1625), bookseller in London; published plays from 1604 and Shakespeare's *Sonnets* in 1609; his identification as the "T. T." of the commendatory verses for the *Generall Historie* seems logical in the light of other similar contributions by Thorpe.

TINDALL, ROBERT (fl. 1606–1610), sailor and gunner for Prince Henry; nothing seems to be known about him beyond his sketch map and odd references to him; see Barbour, *Jamestown Voyages*.

TISQUANTUM (SQUANTUM) (fl. 1605?–1622), Algonkian Indian from Massachusetts (possibly Maine); Gorges (q.v.), when old, said he was one of Waymouth's (q.v.) five Indians taken to England in 1605, but this is mistaken; probably brought to England in 1611 and put ashore at Cape Cod by Smith in 1614, Smith's captain, Thomas Hunt (q.v.), caught him and twenty other Indians and sold them as slaves in Spain; Tisquantum escaped to London, where he was befriended by the treasurer of the Newfoundland Co.; sent back to America, he met Thomas Dermer (q.v.), who brought him once more back to England in 1618; a year later, Dermer put him ashore again in New England, where he found all of his tribe dead (of smallpox?); in 1621 Tisquantum visited the Pilgrims at Plymouth and became their interpreter; see *DCB*.

TODKILL, ANAS (fl. 1607–1612?), at first servant of Capt. John Martin (q.v.), he was the only colonist to go on both of the Chesapeake Bay expeditions and to be present as well at the earlier visit to Powhatan (q.v.) and the later Pamunkey confrontation; credited as part author of four of the six sections of history in the *Proceedings* and *Generall Historie*; see Bradford Smith, *Captain John Smith: His Life and Legend* (Philadelphia, 1953), and Barbour, *Three Worlds*.

TRABIGZANDA, CHARATZA (from the Greek for "girl from Trebizond"), ladylove in 1602 of the Turk Captain Bogall, for whom he bought Smith in the Danube slave market at Axiopolis; she and her brother, the timariot, appear to have been Greeks assimilated to Turkish life.

TRADESCANT (TREDESKYN), JOHN, the younger (fl. 1607–1637), traveler, naturalist, and gardener, of English descent, married in Kent; interested himself in Virginia c. 1617; studied plants in arctic Muscovy in 1618 and sailed with Sir Robert Mansell and Capt. Samuel Argall (q.v.) against the Algiers pirates in 1620, bringing back "the Algiers apricot"; served Buckingham and later Charles I, establishing a "physic garden" and museum at South Lambeth; named a beneficiary in Smith's will; see *DNB*, and Mea Allen, *The Tradescants* (London, 1964).

UTTAMATOMAKKIN (fl. 1616), husband of Powhatan's (q.v.) daughter Matachanna, he accompanied Pocahontas (q.v.) to London; known there as Tomocomo, he was a frequent guest at the home of Dr. Theodore Gulston, a parishioner of Samuel Purchas's (q.v.) church and a scholar, where Purchas had an opportunity to hear him "discourse" on his country and religion, to see him dance, and so on; deeply disillusioned by his visit, Uttamatomakkin returned to Virginia anything but a friend of the English; see Barbour, *Pocahontas*.

VAUGHAN, ROBERT (c. 1600–1663 or before), English engraver of Welsh origin and ties; student of heraldry and antiquarian, he combined accuracy with romantic invention (Hind, *Engraving*, III, 48–49, 83–84); engraved title pages, book illustrations, and portraits, including the map of Ould Virginia for the *Generall Historie*, with its amusing Welsh joke.

VILLIERS, GEORGE (1592–1628), duke of Buckingham, royal favorite; see *DNB*.

WAYMOUTH, CAPT. GEORGE (fl. 1601–1612), mariner, forerunner in North American exploration, as well as a knowledgeable naval architect; sent to search for a northwest passage by the East India Co. in 1602 (despite his encouraging report there was no follow-up); in 1605, with the earl of Southampton and Sir Thomas Arundell as sponsors, Waymouth sailed to explore the modern New England coast with an eye toward English colonization, the most significant outcome of which was the kidnapping of five "Salvages" whose presence in England subsequently weighted the balance in favor of pursuing just such colonization; see *DNB*; *DCB*; and Quinn, *New England Voyages*.

WEST, FRANCIS (1586–1633?), younger brother of Thomas (West) (q.v.), Lord De La Warr, Jamestown colonist with the 3d supply in 1609, he shortly antagonized Smith; later the same year he seemingly deserted the colony, but rejoined his brother afterward; appointed admiral of New England in 1622, he divided his time between the two colonies; see *DNB*.

WEST, THOMAS (1577–1618), 3d or 12th Baron De La Warr, a grandson of a first cousin of Queen Elizabeth's and a second cousin of Henry (q.v.), earl of Dover, to whom Smith dedicated his *True Travels*; served under Essex in Ireland and in 1602 became a member of the Privy Council; in 1609 he became a member of the London Virginia Co.; in 1610 he was appointed first governor and captain-general of Virginia for life and promptly sailed for Jamestown; taken ill, he returned to London in 1611; sailing back to Virginia in 1618, he died en route; see *DNB*, and *DAB*.

WESTON, THOMAS (fl. 1619–1646), ironmonger; possessed of some means, he became an adventurer in New England, where he succeeded in irritating the Pilgrims despite their indebtedness to him, perhaps because of his "squeezing all he could out of them"; soon migrating to Virginia, he there engaged in fishing and trading voyages to Maine; in trouble with the law in Virginia, he retreated to Maryland and from there to England, where he died; see Bradford, *Plymouth Plantation*, 37n.

WHITAKER, REV. ALEXANDER (1585–1617), divine, son of Rev. William (1548–1595); appointed to a living in northern England in 1608, he soon volunteered to go to Virginia, where he arrived with Sir Thomas Dale (q.v.) in 1611; he instructed Pocahontas (q.v.) from 1613 to 1614 and baptized her; in Mar. 1617 he was accidentally drowned; see Harry

Culverwell Porter, "Alexander Whitaker: Cambridge Apostle to Virginia," *WMQ*, 3d Ser., XIV (1957), 317–343.

WHITE, JOHN (1540s?–1593), English artist, perhaps of Cornish stock; connected with Ralegh's Roanoke colony as artist and then as governor from 1584 to 1590; previously in 1577 he made on-the-spot drawings of Eskimos on Frobisher Bay; see Paul Hulton and David Beers Quinn, eds., *The American Drawings of John White, 1577–1590* (London, 1964).

WHITHORNE, PETER (fl. 1543–1565), military writer, noted among other things for his translation of Machiavelli's *Arte of Warre* (1560–1562); see *DNB*.

WIFFIN(G), DAVID and RICHARD (fl. 1608–1616), colonists in the 1st supply, apparently brothers; authors of commendatory verses for the *Description of N.E.*, and obviously loyal friends of Smith's, both still remain obscure; see Barbour, *Jamestown Voyages*.

WINGFIELD, EDWARD MARIA (fl. 1586–1613), patentee, adventurer, and first president of the council in Virginia; of a distinguished family, Wingfield had served in Ireland and the Netherlands and had been prisoner in Lille with Sir Ferdinando Gorges (q.v.) in 1588; having sailed with the original colonists, he was elected in Virginia to head the governing council, but proved himself rather a gentleman than a practical administrator; at odds with Smith and apparently disliked by most of the colonists, he returned to England in 1608, where he slowly lapsed back into obscurity; author of the valuable "Discourse of Virginia"; see *DAB*, and Barbour, *Jamestown Voyages*.

WINGFIELD, SIR JOHN (fl. 1585–1596), son of a second cousin of Edward Maria's (q.v.), he married Susan Bertie, aunt of Smith's friend Robert (q.v.), later Lord Willoughby; granted the close-knit Wingfield family, it may well be that Sir John was instrumental in helping Smith get his appointment as a member of the local council, before Edward Maria discovered that Smith had a mind of his own; see *DNB*, and genealogical tables in Barbour, *Three Worlds*, 420–421.

WITHER, GEORGE (1588–1667), poet and pamphleteer; author of commendatory verses for the *Description of N.E.*; see *DNB*.

YEARDLEY, SIR GEORGE (c. 1587–1627), son of a London merchant tailor, Yeardley served in the Netherlands, where he got to know Sir Thomas Gates (q.v.); in 1609 he sailed for Virginia with Gates, but was shipwrecked off Bermuda; in 1616 Sir Thomas Dale (q.v.) appointed him deputy governor; relieved by Samuel Argall (q.v.) in 1617, Yeardley returned to England, where he was knighted in 1618 and appointed governor to succeed Thomas West, Lord De La Warr (q.v.); returning to Virginia in 1619 with instructions to summon the first legislative assembly in America, Yeardley was soon disgusted by the negligence of the London Council and retired to develop his private investment in Southampton Hundred; he returned to England in 1625, was again commissioned governor in 1626, sailed back, and died in office; see *DNB*, and *DAB*.

BRIEF BIOGRAPHY
OF CAPTAIN JOHN SMITH

Prologue

Eight air miles (12.8 km.) east by north of Louth, where young John Smith attended grammar school, lies the village of Saltfleetby All Saints. Within a radius, say, of two miles (3.2 km.) from this center, clockwise, lie Saltfleet, due north, Saltfleetby St. Clement, Theddlethorpe St. Helen, Theddlethorpe All Saints, and, due west, Saltfleetby St. Peter. In this small area there once lived at least two families named Smith/Smyth (the spelling does not matter). Despite the ubiquity of so common a surname, this can only doubtfully be an accident in such small villages so close together. We may even soundly argue that these Smiths/Smyths were related.

The better known of the two families, established by a John Smyth of Epping, Essex, had attained some degree of respectability in the early sixteenth century. This John's eldest son, also John, died in Epping in 1570, while a younger son, Richard, established a family in far-off Bristol (see below). The heir of the younger John was born about 1552 and was named Nicholas. Nicholas migrated to Lincolnshire, and established small estates in Theddlethorpe and Cawkwell (the two Theddlethorpes are not a mile apart, and Cawkwell is but five miles [8 km.] the other side of Louth). Nicholas's wife was Alice Bonvile, of Spaunton, Yorkshire. Their firstborn son was another Nicholas, who married the daughter of a knight, while their daughter Susan married Francis Guevara, surely a close relative of Antonio de Guevara, secretary of Peregrine Bertie, Lord Willoughby, when he died in 1601. Here we must turn to the other Smith/Smyth family of the neighborhood.

When Capt. John Smith entered the Free Grammar School of King Edward VI in Louth, the headmaster was Robert Smith of Saltfleetby St. Clement. This Smith is known to have had a brother named Nicholas. With Theddlethorpe only two miles south of Saltfleetby St. Clement and the Nicholas Smyth who lived there having reached the age of twenty-eight when Captain John was born, it seems highly probable that Robert's brother Nicholas and Nicholas Smyth of Theddlethorpe were the same man. Add to this the fact that it has long been postulated that Captain John was sent to the Louth school because the headmaster was a relative, and it will become reasonably evident that the N. Smith who wrote commendatory verses for the *Description of New England* in 1616 and in them called Captain John "cousin" was the same Nicholas Smyth of Theddlethorpe. Chronologically, it all fits together: Nicholas Smyth signed his will January 18, 1623, and died before May 28.

To bear out the deduced relationships between various recorded facts, documents in manuscript as well as early compilations in print are readily available in the Lincolnshire Archives, Lincoln (e.g., the "Owte Rents Dewe to the Manner of Louth"). These show that a "Master" John Smith owned specific properties in Louth that were inherited by a George Smith who died before 1613. These same properties were later held by "Alice Johnson, widow, late wife of Martin Johnson of Boston" (thirty-two miles south of Louth). Alice, Capt. John Smith's mother, is known to have married Martin Johnson within a year of the death of John Smith's father, George Smith, in 1596. Thus, through inheritance of property we establish the grandfather-grandson relationship between Master John Smith of Louth and Capt. John Smith of Willoughby.

By way of further details, we may note here that in 1552 "John Smythe and George Somerscales" donated eighteen shillings to the Guild of Our Lady in Louth "for the Frame and organs in the Ladies quere [choir]"; and in later years that the captain had inherited property in Great Carlton, which is but five miles from both Theddlethorpes.

Not only has it in this way been demonstrated that Capt. John Smith's grandfather was established in Louth as early as 1552, but also the known migrations of other Smith/Smyth families point to a mobility among Captain John's relatives heretofore considered unlikely. Earlier ancestors could just as easily have come from Lancashire to Lincoln or Louth as the Smyths of Epping could have moved to Louth or Bristol.

More important than this is the conjecture made firmer by recent investigations that Master John Smith of Louth was in some way related to the John Smyth of Epping (d. 1570), and that the latter's son Nicholas (1552–1623) was the author of the commendatory verses mentioned above.[1] Despite the genuine humility that surrounded Captain John's father, much evidence has recently been brought out to show that the family was far from insignificant locally, and probably was related (at least by marriage) to personages of some distinction in the entourage of the Barons Willoughby of Eresby. Lincolnshire tradition would have it that George Smith, John's father, was a well-to-do man.

---

1. The clue to the conjectural tie between John Smith of Louth and Captain John was first supplied to the editor by R. N. Benton, King Edward VI Grammar School, Louth, Lincolnshire (retired), in the summer of 1967. Ten years later, working on the present edition of Smith, the editor spent some time in the Research Room, Office of the County Archivist, The Castle, Lincoln, where he found the material used here. The chief sources were the "Lough Old Corporation Records," the "Louth Grammar School Rentals," the "Booke of Owte Rents" already mentioned, and the *Notitiæ Ludæ, or Notices of Louth* (Louth, 1834), and other printed works in the library. The editor owes especial thanks to Mr. Benton, and to the county archivist, C. M. Lloyd, M.A.

In short, the doughty captain was evidently not a boasting braggart, but a man of parts in his own microcosm whose convictions carried him beyond the smug routine of the traditionalists who all but destroyed him. The three phases of Smith's career outlined below will bear this out.

Early Life[2]

John Smith, son of George and Alice (Rickard) Smith, was baptized in Willoughby by Alford, Lincolnshire, on January 9, 1580. Of his paternal grandfather, John Smith of nearby Louth, we have evidence only that he was a property owner, and from Captain John we know that the family originated in Cuerdley, near Liverpool, Lancashire. Young John's mother's family had apparently migrated to Lincolnshire from Yorkshire a generation or more before, and by 1580 or so had acquired a certain social status in both counties. Still, neither side of John Smith's family could have been "upper class" in any sense. Socially they were yeomen.

Smith had a customary schooling in Alford, part of it quite possibly under the noted preacher Francis Marbury, father of the even more famous Anne Hutchinson of New England, who was born in Alford in 1591. For unexplained reasons, young John attempted to run away from school in 1593, but his father "stayed" him, and in 1595, after some further schooling in Louth, he was apprenticed to a rich merchant in King's Lynn, some sixty miles (96 km.) away. But when Smith's father died early in 1596, and his mother remarried within a year (as was not uncommon in those days), Smith did not delay long in terminating his apprenticeship, amicably. The Dutch war of independence from Spain beckoned him, and in 1596 or 1597, after his father's estate had been settled, he joined a company of English volunteers. Although this much is clear in his *True Travels* (1630), it seems likely that at least part of Smith's military service was in France, where English contingents had been sent to aid Henry IV in establishing himself on the throne. In any event, peace being concluded in France in 1598, by 1599 Smith was back in England.

This date is established by two facts: Smith says that "he found meanes to attend Master Perigrine Barty into France";[3] and Peregrine Bertie, son of Lord Willoughby of Eresby, was granted a license "to travel for 3 years" on June 26, 1599. Bertie's father, be it noted, was John Smith's landlord. Despite this, and because of Lord Willoughby's expensive position under Queen Elizabeth, Smith had hardly reached Orléans with Peregrine when the

---

2. This biography is based on the editor's *The Three Worlds of Captain John Smith* (Boston, 1964), and partly follows his article on Smith in the 1975 edition of the *Encyclopedia Americana*, but it also takes into account the results of investigations up to Jan. 1, 1977.
3. *True Travels*, 2.

latter's older brother let it be known that Smith's upkeep could not be paid. He simply lacked the funds.

Back across the Channel Smith went, not without adventure (including shipwreck). In Willoughby, or Alford, however, he got to know a visiting Italian nobleman of Greek extraction, who taught him horsemanship while instilling in him a violent dislike of the Turks. After all, Mehmet the Conqueror had driven the Greeks out of Constantinople less than 150 years before. The nobleman seems to have left for Yorkshire to get married in mid-1600, and his absence plus news of renewed hostilities in the Netherlands may naturally have led Smith back to the Continent. Briefly put, Smith's wanderings soon ended with a tour of the Mediterranean in a merchant ship with a captain inclined toward piracy. In this way, he became involved in a fracas with a large Venetian trader and in the end landed in Italy with a share of prize money. Thus provided for financially, he decided, late in 1600, to join the Austrian forces then engaged in the "Long War" against the Turks (1593–1606).

Promoted to captain for his services in Hungary, in the spring of 1602 Smith was sent to Transylvania (now northwestern Rumania). There, during a siege, he accepted challenges to single combat in three duels that resulted in his beheading three Turkish officers. Later, wounded in a skirmish with Tatar allies of the Turks, he was captured and sold as a slave to a Turk who in turn gave him to his sweetheart in Istanbul, a girl of Greek descent. Before long, she apparently fell in love with Smith. As a result, she sent him to her brother, head of a *timar* (government fief), near the Black Sea, to "sojourne to learne the language, and what it was to be a Turke."[4] We may soundly infer that she intended to marry him and wanted him to get training for a career in the imperial service, which was open to Christian converts. Smith, however, unwilling to undergo the almost sadistic disciplining required for such aspirants, and surely not wanting to become a Turk in any case, eventually escaped by murdering the brother and fleeing back through Russia and Poland to Transylvania. Finding that country in different hands, he looked for and found the prince under whom he had served, Zsigmond Báthory, and was handsomely rewarded early in December 1603. Then, after traveling in Europe and looking for further soldiering in Morocco, Smith must have returned to England during the winter of 1604–1605. Let it be added here that, although this account is Smith's alone, circumstantial evidence supports his story broadly, and at times in detail.

Founding of Jamestown

Back in London, Smith got caught up in the plans to colonize Virginia. A royal charter licensing such activities was signed on April 10, 1606, and the

4. *Ibid.*, 24.

Virginia Company was formed. The first colonists sailed on December 19–20, 1606, with John Smith named as one of the members of the council in Virginia, and at last Jamestown was founded on May 13, 1607.

Possibly three hundred years before, however, Algonkian Indians had pushed down from the north into the area, and their hereditary chief, Powhatan, was just then expanding his realm into a tidewater Virginia "empire." The unwelcome English colony was resisted, ambushed, raided, and cajoled, alternatively, in the hope that it would go away. But John Smith, propelled into leadership largely by the colonists' prevailing sickly inertia, retaliated in kind. Though he had little backing, he would not yield.

In December 1607, Smith and a handful of companions out exploring ran across a large band of Indians hunting deer under the leadership of a werowance (tribal chief) who was one of Powhatan's half-brothers. Smith, captured, was taken for a white werowance whose fate had to be determined by Powhatan himself, since it was not customary to put werowances to death. Off the Indians marched him, by a circuitous route, to the Great Chief's residence. There, impressed by Smith's self-confidence and by such supernatural instruments as a pocket compass, Powhatan seems to have invoked an Indian custom and adopted Smith into his tribe as a subordinate werowance. A ceremony followed in which Powhatan's little daughter Pocahontas played an unclear role. After that, Smith was subjected to further inquiry and finally returned to Jamestown on January 2, 1608, escorted by a squad to guide, help, and protect him. This episode was the source of the Pocahontas legend.

Meanwhile, the policies formulated in London, along with dilatory and insufficient supplies, gradually led to alienation between Smith and some of the other leading colonists, especially Capt. Christopher Newport, who was in charge of the colony's lifeline to London. As a result, Smith pursued his own policy so far as he could, and during June, July, and August, left Jamestown to explore Chesapeake Bay and its tributary rivers. This provided not only the food the colony needed, but eventually also the material for his *Map of Virginia*, a descriptive book accompanied by a map of the whole region. At that time, however, bad government in Jamestown led to near anarchy, and to Smith's election as the president of the local council in September.

Under Smith's administration the settlement took better root. He strengthened defenses, enforced discipline as far as he could, and encouraged agriculture. Nevertheless, the London Council found need to reorganize the company on a broader basis. They patterned a local administration along the lines of British monarchical rule. Two knights, Sir Thomas Gates and Sir George Somers, were consequently dispatched with Captain Newport to lay the groundwork for the later arrival of a baron as lord governor and captain general. These two top men and Newport, sailing in one ship despite orders to the contrary, were wrecked off Bermuda, but the rest of the supply fleet in convoy arrived safely, bringing back to Jamestown several members of the anti-Smith faction who had returned to England. The remaining weeks of Smith's presidency were thus disrupted by what amounted to mutiny. A brother of the future lord governor felt at liberty to disobey Smith, general disorganization broke out, and Smith, on a voyage to quell an Anglo-Indian encounter near modern Richmond, was accidentally incapacitated by a gunpowder burn. The outcome was that he had to sail back to England early in October 1609.

Colonial Propagandist

In London Smith dedicated himself to promoting Virginia, but his intransigence on matters of policy stood in his way, and he got no further commission from the Virginia Company. In fact, his *Map of Virginia* had to be printed in Oxford, the London publishers apparently being unwilling to flout the mercantile "establishment." In April 1614, however, Smith obtained backing in the West Country for a voyage to modern Maine and Massachusetts Bay, which he named New England with Prince Charles's approval. In spite of the major cartographical and the minor financial success of this voyage, Smith's self-assertiveness once more blocked his proposals. Apart from an abortive return voyage to New England, Smith never went to sea again. Taking up his pen, he produced eight books in the next sixteen years. To some degree, both the Pilgrims and the Massachusetts Puritans accepted his advice, and the government of Virginia fell into a basic pattern not unlike that which he had proposed. Thus, supported and encouraged only by a small group of loyal friends, John Smith lived in or near London until he was taken ill and died, June 21, 1631.

Smith in History

Smith's adventures, none too remarkable for the times, aroused much skepticism in the nineteenth century, even as his self-centered style of writing had irritated some near-contemporaries in the seventeenth. The chief difficulty was, first, the diversity of accounts Smith published regarding Pocahontas. Since he hardly could have understood what was going on in December 1607, his inconsistency is not remarkable, yet legend made the Indian maiden his passion and in time even his wife, although everybody knows that she married John Rolfe. Then some scholars began to assail the historical side of his writings, creating a "gascon and braggart" having nothing in common with the factual Smith but the name. Only quite recent research has established him for what he was.

As a writer, John Smith apologized for his "owne rough pen," yet he left to posterity one of the basic ethnological studies of the tidewater Algonkians of the early seventeenth century; an invaluable, if one-sided, contemporary history of early Virginia; the earliest well-defined maps of Chesapeake Bay and the New England coast; and the first printed dictionary of English nautical terms. Briefly, his works can be divided into the following categories, according to their main theme and despite overlapping: Colonial Exploration and History (*True Relation, Map of Virginia, Proceedings, Description of New England, Generall Historie* [which includes or modifies all of these], and the last third of *True Travels*); Propaganda (*New Englands Trials* [both editions] and *Advertisements*); Nautical Affairs (*Accidence* and *Sea Grammar*); Memoirs (*True Travels* [first twenty chapters]). In addition there are the "Fragments," published in Volume III of this edition. Speculation about Smith's personality is well-nigh irresistible, but specialists in psychology should note that Smith himself was the independent author of only a relatively small part of all that was published in his name.

GENERAL INTRODUCTION

Sometime between fifteen and twenty years after John Smith's death, the Reverend Dr. Thomas Fuller included a brief biography of him in his *History of the Worthies of England*, a sort of encyclopedia describing each county of England and Wales, with short biographies of those whom he considered the most important natives. The *Worthies*, as the book is often called, is actually more attractive for its anecdotes and digressions than for its encyclopedic content, for Fuller was not noted for accuracy. In the case of Smith, mistakenly listed among the "Worthies of Cheshire," it is worth noting that he, Sir George Somers, and George Sandys were the only three signalized whose careers were directly connected with the colonization of America. Even then, Sir George was dismissed as "discoverer" of Bermuda and Sandys as a translator of Ovid, while Fuller's judgment of Smith was that "his perils, preservations, dangers, deliverances ... seem to most men above belief, to some beyond truth," and his "many strange performances ... are cheaper credited than confuted." Indeed, Fuller adds, "it soundeth much to the diminution of his deeds, that he alone is the herald to publish and proclaim them."[1] In mitigation of this, Fuller states that he got his information from "Master Arthur Smith, his kinsman and my school-master," a man under whom Fuller "had lost some time" when he was four to eight years of age, and in connection with whom he queries a relationship with the "worshipful family of the Smiths at Hatherton [Cheshire]."[2] Hatherton, incidentally, is about thirty-five miles (56 km.) from Cuerdley, Lancashire, where John Smith's family had lived.

After Dr. Fuller's mild expression of disbelief, Smith's name remained unsullied and partly forgotten for some two centuries.[3] Then Charles Deane, after a brief note in 1859, issued an edition of Smith's *True Relation* in 1866, in which a long footnote (pp. 38–40) called attention to the "marked discrepancies" between Smith's various accounts of the Pocahontas episode. Deane's fellow Bostonian Henry Adams (then a budding expatriate serving as secretary to his father, the United States minister to the Court of St. James), subsequently published a thirty-page review of Deane's book in the *North American Review*, CIV (1867), 1–30. In this, "Adams, seeking to attract

1. Thomas Fuller, *The History of the Worthies of England* (London, 1662), 1, 275–276.
2. *Ibid.*
3. A full list of works on Smith is printed in Philip L. Barbour, *The Three Worlds of Captain John Smith* (Boston, 1964), 521–527.

attention to himself, examined the Pocahontas story . . . and classified Smith as a liar."[4] Others followed suit[5] until by the end of the nineteenth century *lack of basic knowledge* fanned a flicker of curiosity and doubt into a fiery controversy that not even the appearance of Arber's 1884 edition of Smith's works brought completely under control.

It is not the aim or desire of the present editor to put an end to the argument. What he hopes to present is as much factual information as may make Smith's writings understandable, along with such circumstantial evidence as has direct bearing on them, and to supply "informed" conjecture or guesswork where needed to supply continuity or integration. All theoretical, presumptive, or hypothetical elements are clearly indicated, so far as the editor's attention has not flagged, and even facts are occasionally stressed as such for the sake of clarity. Indeed, without a judicious bit of explanatory supposition, the facts themselves can well be misleading.

One considerable element for which it is difficult to find a place in an edition such as this is the matter of differing interpretation or inferences, for John Smith has been the subject of manifold study. To simplify investigation, various aspects of his career are summarized below.

Smith as Autobiographer

In a broad sense, everything John Smith himself wrote was autobiographical. (The bulk of what was published under his name was collected from others.) His first work, the *True Relation*, bears evidence of being a letter designed to tell a friend or backer what happened to *him* from the time he sailed until the day he dispatched it to England. Damaged as it clearly was by injudicious editing, it still bears little trace of any interest in the colony as a whole;[6] thus matters alien to Smith may be assumed to have been lacking. The next seven works regard events and developments with Smith's eye even when they are almost purely descriptive, as in the *Map of Virginia* and the *Accidence/Sea Grammar*. Then the *True Travels* is for the greater part openly auto-biographical and is generally so classified, while the last, the *Advertisements*, is little more than a Smithian "voice of experience." It is true that Smith's contemporaries seem to have regarded the *True Travels* as res gestae patterned after Caesar's *Commentaries* (see Richard James's commendatory verses in the *Generall Historie*, sig. A5^r), and our own contemporary Paul Delany includes it

4. Everett H. Emerson, *Captain John Smith* (New York, 1971), 94.
5. They are listed in Edward Arber, ed., *Travels and Works of Captain John Smith . . .* , A New Edition, with a Biographical and Critical Introduction by A. G. Bradley (Edinburgh, 1910), xxviii–xxix.
6. Cf. George Percy's necrology in Philip L. Barbour, ed., *The Jamestown Voyages under the First Charter, 1606–1609*, 2 vols. (Hakluyt Society, 2d Ser., CXXXVI–CXXXVII [London, 1969]), I, 143–145.

in the category of "travel memoirs."[7] Yet all in all the editor feels that Smith was an autobiographer with other strong interests.

Smith as Compiler

Only on one occasion (*True Travels*, 51n), has the editor ventured to liken the Smith corpus to Richard Hakluyt's *Principal Navigations* or to the even more comprehensive *Pilgrimes* of his friend Samuel Purchas. Smith's objectives were far more circumscribed than those of either, and he had neither the available time nor the inclination for their breadth of scope — even if at the end of his life he contemplated a "history of the Sea" (*Advertisements*, 26). Nevertheless, for the restricted subject of "English colonization of North America, 1600–1630," the sum total of his work exceeds in detail that of Hakluyt and Purchas. In execution he is less accurate than Hakluyt in transcribing material and far less painstaking in acknowledging sources, and in personal interjections he resembles Purchas more. Yet he is always John Smith — actor, participant, propagandist, and often excessively apologist for himself.

From this point of view, it is unwise to regard Smith as an editor. In Hakluyt's case, despite some evidence of editing, the definitive bibliography of his works bears the subtitle "Works compiled, translated or published by Richard Hakluyt,"[8] with no mention of "editor." Even Purchas's merciless wielding of shears hardly constitutes "editing." With Smith, only when it came to reprinting his own works can he really be said to have edited them (cf. the *Map of Virginia* and the *Proceedings* vs. the *Generall Historie*, Books II and III respectively). Otherwise Smith sought rather to weave his source material into his own accounts, modifying it almost ad libitum, while still painstakingly preserving the original text where it served his purpose.

Smith as Geographer

The term "geographer" is perhaps more appropriate for Smith than "surveyor, cartographer, or mere map-maker." Regrettably, the bulk of critical articles on this subject is either absurdly partisan or an exercise in statistics. Among the more outrageous of the former was that by Alexander Brown. Brown produced a map that had been misfiled by the Public Record Office, London, as Smith's work,[9] and "was inclined to think" that the Virginia section of the so-called Velasco map "was compiled and drawn by Robert Tyndall or by Captain [Nathaniel] Powell,"[10] although the one

---

7. Paul Delany, *British Autobiography in the Seventeenth Century* (London, 1969), 110, 117.
8. D. B. Quinn, ed., *The Hakluyt Handbook*, 2 vols. (Hakluyt Soc., 2d Ser., CXLIV–CXLV [London, 1974]), II, 461.
9. Alexander Brown, ed., *The Genesis of the United States*, 2 vols. (Boston, 1890), II, 596–597.
10. *Ibid.*, I, 458.

surviving map by Tindall does not bear this out, and no map by or attributed to Powell is known to exist. This inconvenience, however, did not deter Worthington Chauncey Ford a generation later from stating: "I am inclined to advance the claim that Powell, a skilled surveyor, made the plat form, or basis, of the Smith map, and is entitled to the credit of it."[11] Apart from the gratuitous description of Powell's training, a more recent professional geographer has far more soundly observed that "the map [of Virginia], whether made by Smith or by Nathaniel Powell or by other members of his party *under Smith's direction* ... is a remarkable production considering the conditions under which it was made."[12] This is also the present editor's opinion on the subject.

Smith was a geographer in the sense that Sir Walter Ralegh was, and like Ralegh may have drawn some details himself.[13] Smith it was, not Powell or Tindall, who saw to it that William Hole produced the map that goes by Smith's name, just as Ralegh was to do with Hole two or three years later. How much or how little Smith contributed is irrelevant. That he had some basic knowledge of, or qualifications for, mapmaking is attested by the list of reference books on navigation in the *Accidence*, 36–37.

Smith as Ethnographer

A professional study of John Smith's contribution to the ethnology of the Indian tribes, particularly in tidewater Virginia, is still a desideratum. Although Smith is virtually the only source for ethnographic information about the Indians, supplemented by William Strachey's additions made between 1610 and 1611, modern studies such as John R. Swanton's *The Indians of the Southeastern United States*, Smithsonian Institution, Bureau of American Ethnology, Bulletin 137 (Washington, D.C., 1946), only sort out and summarize Smith's observations, but do not evaluate them. Nevertheless, a careful inspection of Regina Flannery's *An Analysis of Coastal Algonquian Culture* (Washington, D.C., 1939), will show how well the traits (attitudes, habits, practices), recorded by Smith correspond with those of related tribes, and help determine the overall picture, including local traits in some areas. As for a preliminary survey of Smith's transcriptions of Indian place-names and current words and phrases, see Philip L. Barbour, "The Earliest Reconnaissance of the Chesapeake Bay Area: Captain John Smith's Map and Indian Vocabulary," *Virginia Magazine of History and Biography*, LXXIX

11. Worthington Chauncey Ford, "Captain John Smith's Map of Virginia, 1612," *Geographical Review*, XIV (1924), 441.

12. George W. White, "Geological Observations of Captain John Smith in 1607–1614," *Illinois Academy of Science Transactions*, XLVI (1953), 125. Italics added.

13. See R. A. Skelton, "Ralegh as a Geographer," *Virginia Magazine of History and Biography*, LXXI (1963), 131–149.

(1971), 280–302, LXXX (1972), 21–51, and the notes on Smith's vocabulary in the *Map of Virginia*, below. Christian F. Feest, "Virginia Algonquians," in William C. Sturtevant, ed., *Handbook of North American Indians*, XV, *Northeast*, ed. Bruce G. Trigger (Washington, D.C., 1978), 253–270, is a summary of current research and knowledge.

Smith as Soldier and Governor

A preliminary word on Smith's rise to the presidency of the council in Virginia is here appropriate. He was appointed to the local council by His Majesty's Council for Virginia by virtue of orders dated December 10, 1606.[14] Although provision was made for thirteen councillors,[15] only seven sailed with the original fleet.[16] Of these, Edward Maria Wingfield was one of the patentees, Christopher Newport and Bartholomew Gosnold were admiral and vice-admiral of the fleet and had experience in American waters. John Martin was son of the master of the mint, George Kendall was related to the earl of Pembroke and to Sir Edwin Sandys, a parliamentary leader, and John Ratcliffe was ship captain of the third ship. Only Smith's presence remains to be explained. Somebody must have recommended him, and that somebody must have had a basis to go on, for Smith was a nobody while at least three original colonists who were not named to the council were of some standing: George Percy was brother of the earl of Northumberland; Anthony Gosnold was brother of Bartholomew Gosnold, the vice-admiral; and Gabriel Archer had sailed with Bartholomew Gosnold to Cape Cod in 1602.

While it may be idle to attempt to guess, it could be that Smith's accounts of military experience in the "Low Countries" (the Netherlands, Belgium, and northeastern France), and in eastern Europe, coupled with his escape from Tatary, qualified him as a Miles Standish for the Virginia venture. (Wingfield's military experience had been brief and inconsequential.) If this was the case, some of the critics of the *True Travels* should have second thoughts.

Whatever the position proposed for Smith in the colony may have been, it is obvious that his instincts were militaristic; discipline and training for self-defense were among his mottos. He bowed to superior authority, but expected that authority to be capable and effective. Incapability on Wingfield's part loosed Smith's wrath, and when Wingfield was legally deposed from the seat of authority in favor of the still more incompetent Ratcliffe, Smith's disgust was complete.

Smith sailed on two voyages of exploration in Chesapeake Bay. Soon

14. Barbour, *Jamestown Voyages*, I, 45–46, II, 382.
15. *Ibid.*, I, 36.
16. *Ibid.*, II, 382.

after his return, he was elected president of the council (September 10, 1608). Then about Michaelmas (September 29) Newport arrived at Jamestown with a letter for the president, which is now lost. The content of this was such that in short order Smith replied with a letter of protest against Newport. This letter Newport took with him when he sailed again (early December?), leaving Smith in virtually sole command. Under the pressure of events, a brief period of discipline was inaugurated in Jamestown, which seems to have worked for the colony's benefit.[17]

A new charter was put into effect in 1609, with Sir Thomas Gates as governor and Smith in charge of defense at Old Point Comfort, thus combining the authority vested in those days in social (or political) rank with the capability of experience on the spot. Had it not been for untoward accidents, the arrangement might well have put the colony on its feet. As it was, Smith's bright outlook for 1608–1609 was destroyed, Smith himself left for England with his term barely finished, and Jamestown came dangerously near to extinction.

Smith as Sailor and Admiral

Edward Arber has not been the only editor to show some surprise at the publication in 1626 of Smith's *Accidence . . . Necessary for all Young Sea-men.*[18] Yet anyone who has read the *True Travels* will know that Smith chanced to be involved in a trading voyage when he was twenty and sailed the Mediterranean from near Marseilles to the Levant, that he took ship with a French captain to Morocco in 1604, and that he was a prisoner on a French privateer in 1615 (*True Travels*, 4–5, 34; *Description of New England*, 50–57). His learning in his youth about seamanship as well as trading and fighting was only natural. Indeed, it seems likely that Smith's encounter with the authority of Wingfield (or Newport) off the Canaries early in 1607 may have been due to his knowing something about handling a ship or where to get water on Gran Canaria. His title of "admiral" must have been granted to him (officially or tacitly) because of his voyage to New England in 1614, when he had been captain in charge of the tiny fleet and when he had directed the coastal survey on which his map was based. In this way, his *Accidence* was born of his own experience. Then, taking advantage of a manuscript copy of Sir Henry Mainwaring's "Dictionary" (first published in 1644), he expanded the *Accidence* into the *Sea Grammar*, putting more than common effort into

17. Stephen Saunders Webb's "Army and Empire: English Garrison Government in Britain and America, 1569 to 1763," *William and Mary Quarterly*, 3d Ser., XXXIV (1977), 6–7, surely goes too far: Smith did not "militarize Virginia government," but years later the government fell into a basic pattern not unlike what Smith had proposed in 1623/1624—at all times, strong defense.
18. Arber, *Smith, Works*, 786.

"researching," and utilizing practically all works published by that date (*Accidence*, 33, 36–37; *Sea Grammar*, 69, 83 [73]).

Smith as Trader

This subject of course involves relations with the Indians. According to George Percy, the colony's "cape merchant" or commissary, Thomas Studley, died on August 28, 1607. On September 10, Wingfield was deposed as president (as has been mentioned), and shortly thereafter "the new President [Ratcliffe] ... committed the managing of all things abroad [at large] to captaine Smith."[19] This meant that Smith not only was able to (and did) stir the colony into productive activity, but also was responsible for trade with the Indians, especially gewgaws for food. Those who have considered Smith as primarily a militarist have overlooked the stress Smith continuously placed on trade, and on the need to keep the Indians at hand and also at peace. The Indians were not to be persecuted away, for they supplied food, but the English had to maintain their readiness for combat through strict discipline.

This basic philosophy of survival and growth forced Smith to travel in order to trade; travel and trade forced him to explore; and all put together forced him to learn the language and the ways of the Indians. Smith was a relatively ill-educated man, yet experience in Europe had taught him a modicum of French, Italian, and probably Spanish. In addition, it had trained him in seamanship (as we have seen), in combat, and in survival, while his modest social background in England had instilled in him an appreciation of what it is to be the underdog in a class-conscious society (Smith himself of course would not have thought of it in those terms). All of this served him admirably in his Indian "policy," if ad hoc solutions to unexpected problems can constitute a policy. Obviously, the Indians had to supply the colony with food, since the colonists were too lazy to supply themselves by working in the fields, but the colonists had to reimburse the Indians through barter. It was not right to browbeat the Indians, but neither should the Indians steal or take potshots at the colonists. And Smith's troubles with the silly, unrealistic orders from London, as well as the silly, unrealistic behavior of the colonists in Virginia, made all of this extremely real to him. He was not a trained administrator. He was a reasonably successful improviser.

By the same token, when Smith's career led him to lay down the musket and the compass, he had to improvise with the pen. As he had learned to use the first two, so he learned to use the last. In the meanwhile, his writings reflect weakness and uncertainty in style, conservative use of dialect words in English in company with occasional borrowings from foreign languages, and

19. Barbour, *Jamestown Voyages*, I, 144, 219, II, 385.

the particularity of putting down his thoughts at random, in his own way, with little regard to organization.

All of this makes Smith difficult to read at times: his antiquated syntax conflicts with the modernity of most of his language. Yet it all clarifies Smith's character and habits. To get along, he insists, one must do business in some fashion (such as trading in the Mediterranean or in America) while bowing to the demands of the circumstances, and one must know how to fight when necessary, and be ready at all times. Characteristically, at the end of his life, Smith was urging the development of the fishing industry in New England, while arguing for self-discipline and readiness for self-defense.

Smith and His Latter-Day Critics

Jarvis M. Morse has already recapitulated the bulk of critical comment on Smith and his writings, both pro and con, in an article published in 1935.[20] It seems proper here to run over Morse's conclusions in the light of recent research. Without going into detail, it is evident that most of the carping criticism revolves around two foci: Smith's rescue by Pocahontas and his soldiering in eastern Europe. But what Morse barely implies (if even that) is what is primary: the Indians and the Turkish war were two subjects about which the critics knew little or nothing. What really happened when Pocahontas "saved Smith's life" we can never know; but Indian customs provide an explanation, and the exercise of tact for the benefit of the Virginia Company in London could explain the seemingly contradictory accounts. By the same token, the matter of the Ferneza "book" on Smith in Transylvania is still unsolved (see the Purchas version in the Fragments), but local history and Turkish customs offer circumstantial evidence that the story is most likely true. All that was needed was for Morse, and the critics he criticized, to dig deeper.

When it came to Alexander Brown's *Genesis* and the obsessive dislike of Smith it exhibits, Morse was on surer ground. Morse contrasted Brown with Justin Winsor's *Narrative and Critical History*, which was already in print when Brown began work, but without indicating that Brown *could* have consulted Winsor. More to the point, however, Morse called attention to Smith's portrayal of "the spirit of his times" and stressed the value of Smith's description of the founding of Plymouth by the Pilgrims.

Some years after Morse, Bradford Smith, obviously with the aim of restoring Smith's reputation, called on a Hungarian scholar, Dr. Laura Polanyi Striker, and thus for the first time serious investigation of the problems created by the *True Travels* began.[21] Striker and Bradford Smith

20. Jarvis M. Morse, "John Smith and His Critics: A Chapter in Colonial Historiography,' *Journal of Southern History*, I (1935), 123–137.
21. Bradford Smith, *Captain John Smith: His Life and Legend* (Philadelphia, 1953).

went on to make fruitful contact with Austrian and Yugoslav scholars. The editor is happy to have known Bradford Smith and to have corresponded with Dr. Striker, both of whom are now deceased. In brief summation, appreciative mention must also be made of Professor Everett H. Emerson's *Captain John Smith* (New York, 1971).

The Legendary John Smith

So much has been written about the John Smith of legend (along with Pocahontas, usually), and so much that is pure legend has been written about John Smith that a summary of either would be beyond the purview of an edition that strives to be basically factual. Regarding the former, the editor can refer to a brief mention in his *Three Worlds*, 394, and to Jay B. Hubbell's "The Smith-Pocahontas Story in Literature."[22] For the legendary (non-factual) writings about Smith, these are perhaps even more extensive. For example, at least since Charles Deane wrote "Smith was a true knight errant,"[23] Smith has been so labeled.[24] Yet one wonders why the label should have persisted. In fact, to read Deane's note, Smith would appear to have been more of a Casanova than a hero of medieval romances. As a matter of fact, Smith was essentially practical, more like Sancho Panza than Don Quixote. Were not the "tufftaffaty humorists" whom Smith derided (*Proceedings*, 13), closer to the knights? If we look for knights errant in Virginia, even though loveless, they might be found in Edward Maria Wingfield, with his aloof gentility, and George Percy, who kept a "continual and dayly Table for Gentlemen of fashion" in Jamestown, in 1611. Smith paid ladies their proper compliments while seeing life as it was.[25]

Bibliographical Note on the Arber Text of Smith's Works

As is shown in the bibliographical note following each of Smith's works printed here, several titles were reissued or appeared in new editions between 1632 and 1699. Then, a few years later, translations of parts of the *Generall Historie* and the *True Travels* appeared, first in Dutch in 1706–1707, and then in German in 1782.

It was the next century, however, before new English editions began to come out, first in Virginia in 1819, and later in New England. Nevertheless, it was not until 1884 that an edition of Smith's collected works was published. In that year, Edward Arber (1836–1912), a distinguished English professor,

---

22. *VMHB*, LXV (1957), 275–300.
23. *A True Relation of Virginia, by Captain John Smith* (Boston, 1866), 40.
24. See Marshall W. Fishwick, "Virginians on Olympus: 1. The Last Great Knight Errant," *VMHB*, LVIII (1950), 40–57.
25. For Percy, see John W. Shirley, "George Percy at Jamestown, 1607–1612," *ibid.*, LVII (1949), 239.

editor, and bibliographer, put out a thick volume entitled *Capt. John Smith, President of Virginia, and Admiral of New England. Works. 1608–1631.*

Complete but for the *Sea Grammar*, the full text of the letter to Bacon, and a few odds and ends, Arber's edition included an introduction composed largely of reprints of other material that had bearing on Smith and early Virginia. Carefully edited, with relatively few errors of transcription or printing, the work is scholarly yet sympathetic. Writing not long after the initial efforts to "debunk" Smith in this country, Arber was perceptive enough to remark, "To deny the truth of the Pocahontas incident is to create more difficulties than are involved in its acceptance." The same applies to other "incidents" attacked by the critics, many if not all of which have since been confirmed or found to be supported by circumstantial evidence.

1884.   *Capt. John Smith, President of Virginia, and Admiral of New England. Works. 1608–1631.* The English Scholar's Library Edition, No. 16, ed. Edward Arber (Birmingham).

1895.   *Capt. John Smith of Willoughby by Alford, Lincolnshire; President of Virginia, and Admiral of New England. Works. 1608–1631.* The English Scholar's Library of Old and Modern Works, 2 Pts., ed. Edward Arber (repr. Westminster).

1910.   *Travels and Works of Captain John Smith, President of Virginia, and Admiral of New England, 1580–1631,* ed. Edward Arber. A New Edition, with a Biographical and Critical Introduction by A[rthur] G[ranville] Bradley, Parts I and II (Edinburgh).

1967.   A photo-offset reprint of the foregoing (New York).

Since Arber's death facsimiles of nearly all of Smith's works have become available. Since these are in process of printing by more than one publisher at the time of writing, it is impractical to attempt a complete list.

THE COMPLETE WORKS OF
Captain John Smith

VOLUME I

A TRUE RELATION

of Such Occurrences and
Accidents of Noate
as Hath Hapned
in Virginia . . .

1608

INTRODUCTION

While the story of John Smith's later life can be written with relatively few gaps, precisely what he did during his first twenty-six years is far from simple to determine. This period will be discussed in the Introduction to his *True Travels*, in Volume III. His activities from mid-December 1606 until June 2, 1608, however, are sketched by his own pen in the *True Relation*, and historians should be on firm ground already. Unfortunately, they are not.

The *True Relation*, originally a letter, was published without Smith's knowledge, permission, or supervision.[1] It was also ruthlessly edited and hastily and badly printed to an unusual degree. Both the editing and the rush to press fitted the Virginia Company's interests. The *True Relation* was the first account of the Jamestown colony's first year to reach London. There, rumors of disillusionment and dissatisfaction in Virginia were already rife. Word had got out that one member of the local council had been executed for treason; that factions were splitting the local government; that tons of "gold" brought back to London had proved to be "guilded durt" (as Smith put it); that the Indians were far less tractable than early reports had intimated and stragglers outside Jamestown's flimsy ramparts were not safe; that starvation threatened the colony while most of the colonists sat on their hands; and that John Smith had all but been clubbed to death by the Indian "emperor" Powhatan.

Thus when Smith's letter arrived in London, it was eagerly read. Much of its contents were optimistic, and the mere "rough" style of the young Lincolnshire soldier-turned-colonist was convincing. Yet it is evident that it contained episodes not suitable for wide reading and details that could disturb potential investors. So members of the company who read what Smith reported, indirectly and discreetly forwarded the letter to one "I. H.," who prepared it for publication. This writer has been identified as John Healey, a capable translator who had shown interest in Virginia and was not overburdened with work. In this way, Smith's *True Relation* was entered for publication less than six weeks after its arrival in London.

Such was the haste to publish the book that a title page was struck off with no mention of Smith, but with the name of Thomas Watson as author. Watson, who may well have been the person to whom Smith's letter was

---

1. Smith's original letter probably filled up to 40 sheets of paper, foolscap size, folded once to resemble an unbound booklet. It was most likely written with a goose quill pen in the so-called "English" or "secretary" hand.

addressed, quickly denied authorship, and the printer, still in haste, changed one line of type and inserted "by a Gentleman." By then someone had told Healey that Smith wrote the original letter, and after another gaffe, the thin volume at last appeared with an explanation in the foreword that Healey had "learned that the saide discourse was written by Captaine Smith, who is one of the Counsell there in Virginia."[2] All of this was so confusing that when the Reverend Samuel Purchas used the book in compiling his first work, *Purchas his Pilgrimage* . . . (London, 1613), he did not know that Smith was the author, and since he had met Smith in person by then, he acknowledged his source in a marginal note as "Newes from Virginia and a MS of Cap. Smith" ("Newes from Virginia" was the running head of the *True Relation*).[3] Only in modern times has the confusion been dissipated.

Nevertheless, the text of Smith's book remains in a sorry state. Between misprints and Healey's cuts, it is not an easy book to read or to clarify editorially. The present editor has therefore thought it wise to present a facsimile of the original, with an edited text on facing pages. There, errors of both "I. H." and the printer are pointed out, and indication is made of passages where cuts are evident or suspected. For the latter, reference is made wherever possible to parallel passages, often in Smith's other works, occasionally in "discourses" by his associates in the colony: Edward Maria Wingfield, George Percy, Gabriel Archer, Francis Perkins, and others.

In addition, the editor has provided a recension of the narrative of Smith's capture by the Indians, his restraint at their hands for several weeks, and his final liberation, in which Pocahontas clearly played a role. This seems to be doubly necessary because of superficially contradictory versions in Smith's other works, as well as what appears to be some manipulation of the text by John Healey. This recension follows the present Introduction.

A word is now needed to explain the facsimile text that has been used. While working on the *Jamestown Voyages* in 1965 and 1966, the editor noticed a British Museum (now British Library) copy of the *True Relation* cataloged as long ago as 1787 (present shelf mark C.33.c.5) that contains manuscript annotations in an early hand.[4] These notes were of such pertinence that the help of half a dozen specialists at the British Library, the Houghton Library, Harvard, and the Folger Shakespeare Library was solicited, and it has been established that in all probability the handwriting can be dated as of the last half of Smith's life. This copy was therefore chosen for facsimile reproduction here, and where the annotations were trimmed for binding, a reconstruction of the text is provided in footnotes in alphabetical series. While the annotator

2. See below, sig. ¶1ᵛ.
3. See the facsimile; and Samuel Purchas, *Purchas his Pilgrimage. Or Relations Of The World . . .* (London, 1613), 638n.
4. These annotations were not noted in Joseph Sabin *et al.*, eds., *A Dictionary of Books Relating to America*, XX (New York, 1927–1928), 256.

is still not certainly identified, there is a remote possibility, based on hand-writing, that it was Purchas annotating from hearsay (one expert noticed that Purchas's letter "k" was unusual, although the hand "is that of any educated person"). But in any event the comments are those of someone well informed about Virginia.

Summary

The original Virginia settlers appear to have boarded their three ships at Blackwall, just east of London, on December 19, 1606, and the fleet dropped down the Thames with the tide after midnight.[5] The commander was Capt. Christopher Newport, a veteran mariner in West Indian waters since 1590. Newport's lieutenant was Capt. Bartholomew Gosnold, a dozen years his junior, who had explored the coast of New England in 1602. The third in command, Capt. John Sicklemore, "commonly called Ratcliffe," remains an obscure personality. The three ships were the *Susan Constant* (120 tons), the *Godspeed* (40 tons), and the *Discovery* (20 tons).[6]

The fleet was much delayed, chiefly by storms, but the coast of Virginia was finally sighted at dawn on April 26, 1607.[7] After various adventures, the colonists chose a site some forty miles up the James River from Old Point Comfort, and on the following day, May 14, 1607, they disembarked and planted a colony called James Fort (later Jamestown), in honor of King James.

There was much dissension from the outset, and soon a combination of heat, unsuitable clothing, and bad water, along with improper diet, brought on physical disorders of epidemic proportions. Among the leaders, Gosnold succumbed to some intestinal ailment (hardly malaria or yellow fever as sometimes has been suggested), while Sicklemore (Ratcliffe) proved both ailing and self-seeking. Then, the first elected president of the council (i.e., the de facto governor), Edward Maria Wingfield, evinced eminent qualities as a gentleman, but none as chief executive, and before long John Smith, apparently one of the few colonists possessed of common sense, emerged as the leader of the colony. A year later he was elected president of the council.

Meanwhile, between a desperate attempt to supply Jamestown with food and to carry out the explorations desired by the adventurers who had financed the expedition, Smith not only bargained for provisions but also eventually exposed himself to capture by Indians on a hunting foray in the wilderness near the headwaters of the Chickahominy River, northeast of

---

5. George Percy wrote, "On Saturday, the twentieth of December . . . the fleet fell from London" (Percy's "Discourse," in Philip L. Barbour, ed., *The Jamestown Voyages under the First Charter, 1606–1609*, 2 vols. [Hakluyt Society, 2d Ser., CXXXVI–CXXXVII (Cambridge, 1969)], I, 129).

6. See Barbour, *Jamestown Voyages*, I, 55–57, II, 378.

7. *Ibid.*, I, 133.

modern Richmond. This resulted in his being led captive before the
"emperor" Powhatan, where he was questioned about the colonists' objectives and apparently subjected to some sort of ritual or trial that ended in
his being adopted into the Powhatan tribe—as was not uncommon among
the Algonkians when a valiant "werowance" (military or political commander) was captured. Powhatan's daughter Pocahontas, then a girl of
eleven or twelve, was somehow involved in the ceremony (Smith was con-
vinced that she saved his life), and this gave rise to the Smith-Pocahontas
legend two centuries after. Powhatan then named Smith werowance of
Capahowasic, an honor that Smith did not refuse, although he did not
occupy the post.

Smith, now unwittingly a subordinate chief, was aided in every way by
Powhatan until Newport returned to Virginia and upset the delicate balance.
Nevertheless, Smith managed to tide over the difficulties, and trading and
friendly—though mutually distrustful—relations resumed. Newport sailed
back to England on April 10, 1608. Ten days later a strayed companion ship
commanded by Capt. Francis Nelson arrived. Smith hurriedly finished the
account of the colony that he had been writing, and when Nelson sailed for
England on June 2, he entrusted it to him. Intended as a personal communication to a friend, it was mangled and hurried into print, as has been stated.

Note on Editorial Method

The presentation here of a facsimile of the original printing of the *True
Relation* on pages facing a specially edited transcription has a twofold purpose: that of preserving, on the one hand, the utmost accuracy and that of
offering, on the other hand, a text that is legible and intelligible. As has been
already stated, the 1608 text is clearly corrupt. Self-evident cutting and
broadly acknowledged textual modifications appear on almost every page,
frustrating all attempts to incorporate modern annotation in the book as it
was first printed. A more radical approach is necessary if we are to have a
text that at least attempts to recapture what John Smith wrote. Hence the
need to couple the text left us by "I. H." with a first step toward recon-
stituting Smith's original manuscript.

These complications made it impossible to handle the *True Relation* in
precisely the same fashion as the rest of Smith's works. The major difference
in editorial style introduced here is that the editor's substantive annotation
of the text is placed at the end of the book, rather than at the bottom of the
page. (Hereafter in these three volumes, the editor's substantive annotation
appears consistently at the foot of the page.) In this case only, the footnote
space has been reserved for transcription and discussion of the handwritten
marginal comments on the facsimile pages. In addition to this modification,
the edited text itself contains insertions in square brackets of editorial sug-

gestions, mostly bearing on paragraphing. Brackets also enclose indications of omissions, both self-evident [. . .] and presumptive [. . . ?]. More modern concepts of breaking up long unparagraphed passages have been introduced silently (the facsimile provides the original version), along with capital letters in conformity. Other changes in punctuation and so on have been made sparingly, only for the sake of intelligibility, and are indicated in the Textual Annotation that appears at the end of this book.

Recension of the Narratives of Smith's Captivity

In attempting to reconstruct one of the most important episodes in Smith's life, the editor could wish that both Smith and the deposed president, Wingfield, had had something of the orderly mind of George Percy (or, later, Samuel Argall), especially with regard to dates. We know from Francis Perkins, who arrived with Newport on his return voyage, that the first "supply" reached Jamestown on January 2, 1608 (a Saturday), and from both Smith and Wingfield that Smith had been escorted back from his month-long captivity early in the morning that same day.[1] Wingfield specifies, however, that Smith did not leave Jamestown until December 10, 1607, and at the same time states that Powhatan "sent him home" on January 8, and that Newport came "the same evening." Perkins's date is shown correct by the fact that he and Wingfield both state that Jamestown was nearly burned down on January 7, after Newport's (and Perkins's) arrival. Then, Wingfield implies, and Smith states, that Smith was away from Jamestown for one month. Since Wingfield has the date of his return six days too late, it is possible that the date he gives for Smith's departure is in fact the date when he heard that Smith was captured. This could easily have been six days after he left. Nevertheless, for the purpose of the recension that follows, the editor has accepted Wingfield's "Dec. 10," while warning the reader that an adjustment of about six days must be made somewhere in the chronology. However, the date of Smith's return is accurate.

The chronology for the following recension is:

December 3 or 10 (Thursday)	Smith's Departure
——— (Friday or Saturday)	Capture
December 26 (Saturday)	Arrival at Menapacute
December 30 (Wednesday)	Brought to Powhatan
January 2 (Saturday)	Return to Jamestown

The excerpts included in the recension have been left in the order

1. *Proceedings*, 14.

printed, with one exception: in the *True Relation* the description of the Indian religious ceremony is found after the narration of Smith's march as a captive through the Indian hunting towns; here this description is placed in the middle of the narration so that it may be more easily compared with the descriptions in the *Generall Historie* and Purchas's *Pilgrimage*.

The recension is based on Smith's *True Relation*, Smith's *Generall Historie*, and Samuel Purchas's *Purchas his Pilgrimage. Or Relations Of The World . . .* (1613).

True Relation	*Generall Historie*	*Pilgrimage*
[B4ᵛ] . . . a quarter of Venison and some ten pound of bread I had for supper, . . . my gowne, points and garters, my compas and a tablet they gave me again. . . .	[47] . . . and ere long more bread and venison was brought him then would have served twentie men, . . . Yet in this desperate estate to defend him from the cold, one Maocassater brought him his gowne, . . .	
The King [Opechanca-nough] tooke great delight in understanding the manner of our ships, . . . I desired he would send a messenger to Paspahegh [Jamestown], with a letter I would write, by which they shold under-stand, how kindly they used me, and that I was well, least they should revenge my death: this he granted and sent three men, in such weather, as in reason were unpossible by any naked to be indured: . . . The next day after my letter, came a salvage to my lodging, with his sword to have slaine me, but being by my guard inter-cepted, . . . this was the father of him I had slayne, . . .	Two dayes after a man would have slaine him (but that the guard prevented it) for the death of his sonne, . . . In part of a Table booke he writ his minde to them at the Fort, what was intended, how they should follow that direction to affright the messengers, . . . according to his request they went to James towne, in as bitter weather as could be of frost and snow, and within three dayes returned with an answer. . . .	
. . . the King presently con-ducted me to another King-dome, ‖ [C1ʳ] upon the top	[48] . . . then they led him to the Youghtanunds, the Mattapanients, the Payanka-	[638] Three or foure daies after his taking, seven of their Priestes in the house

True Relation

Generall Historie

Pilgrimage

of the next northerly river, called Youghtanan. Having feasted me, he further led me to another branch of the river, called Mattapanient; to two other hunting townes they led me, . . . After this foure or five dayes march, we returned to Rasaweack, the first towne they brought me too, where binding the Mats in bundels, they marched two dayes journey . . . to . . . Menapacute in Pamaunke, where the King inhabited: . . . [C3^r] . . . three or foure dayes after my taking seven of them in the house where I lay, each with a rattle began at ten a clocke in the morning to sing about the fire, which they invironed with a Circle of meale, and after, a foote or two from that, at the end of each song, layde downe two or three graines of wheate, continuing this order till they have included sixe or seven hundred in a halfe Circle, and after that two or three more Circles in like maner, a hand bredth from other: That done, at each song, they put betwixt everie three, two or five graines, a little sticke, so counting as an old woman her Pater noster. . . . One disguised with a great Skinne, his head hung round with little Skinnes of Weasels, and other vermine, with a Crownet of feathers on his head, painted as ugly as the divell, . . . Till sixe a clocke in the Evening, their howling would continue ere they would depart.

tanks, the Nantaughtacunds, and Onawmanients, . . . and backe againe by divers other severall Nations, to the Kings habitation at Pamaunkee, . . . Not long after, early in a morning a great fire was made in a long house, and a mat spread on the one side, as on the other, on the one they caused him to sit, . . . and presently came skipping in a great grim fellow, all painted over with coale, mingled with oyle; and many Snakes and Wesels skins stuffed with mosse, and all their tayles tyed together, so as they met on the crowne of his head in a tassell; and round about the tassell was as a Coronet of feathers, the skins hanging round about his head, backe, and shoulders, and in a manner covered his face; with a hellish voyce and a rattle in his hand. With most strange gestures and passions he began his invocation, and environed the fire with a circle of meale; which done, three more such like devils came rushing in . . . and then . . . three more as ugly as the rest; . . . at last they all sat downe right against him; three of them on the one hand of the chiefe Priest, and three on the other. Then all with their rattles began a song, which ended, the chiefe Priest layd downe five wheat cornes: then . . . he began a short Oration: . . . and then layd down three graines more. After that, . . . ever

where he lay, each with a Rattle, (setting him by them) began at ten of the clocke in the morning, to sing about a fire, which they invironed with a circle of Meale, at the end of every song, (which the chiefe Priest began, the rest following) laying downe two or three Graines of Wheate: and after they had thus laide downe six or seven hundred in one Circle, accounting their songes by Graines, as the Papists their Orisons by Beades, they made two or three other circles in like manner, and put at the end of every song, betwixt every two, or three, or five Graines, a litle sticke. The High Priest disguised with a greate skinne, his head hung round with little skinnes of Weasils, and other Vermine, with a crownet of Feathers, painted as ugly as the Divell, . . . thus till six of the clocke in the evening, they continued these howling devotions, and so held on three daies. . . . [639] . . . The high-Priests head-tire is thus made. They take a great many Snakes skinnes stuffed with mosse, as also of Weasils and other Vermines skinnes, which they tie by their tailes, so that all the tailes meete on the top of the head like a great Tassell. The faces of their Priests are painted as ugly as they can devise: in their hands they have rattells, . . .

True Relation	*Generall Historie*	*Pilgrimage*

laying downe so many cornes as before, till they had twice incirculed the fire; that done, they tooke a bunch of little stickes prepared for that purpose, continuing still their devotion, and at the end of every song and Oration, they layd downe a sticke betwixt the divisions of Corne. Till night, neither he nor they did either eate or drinke, and then they feasted merrily, with the best provisions they could make. Three dayes they used this Ceremony; . . .

[C1ʳ] . . . the next day another King . . . called Kekataugh, . . . invited me to feast at his house; the people from all places flocked to see me, each shewing to content me. . . . From hence this kind King [Opechanca-nough] conducted mee to a place called Topahanocke, a kingdome upon another River northward: the cause of this was, that the yeare before, a shippe had beene in the River of Pamaunke, who having beene kindly enter-tained by Powhatan their Emperour, . . . returned thence, and discovered the River of Topahanocke, where . . . he slue the King, and tooke of his people, and they supposed I were hee. But the people reported him a great man . . . and using mee kindly, the ‖ [C1ᵛ] next day we departed. . . . The next night I lodged at a hunting town of Powhatans, and the next day arrived at

Opitchapam the Kings brother invited him to his house, where, . . . he bid him wellcome; . . . At his returne to Opechancanoughs, all the Kings women, and their children, flocked about him for their parts [of leftover food], . . .

True Relation	*Generall Historie*	*Pilgrimage*

Werowocomoco . . . where
the great king is resident: by
the way we passed by the top
of another little river . . .
called Payankatank. . . .

Arriving at Werawocomoco,
their Emperour proudly lying
uppon a Bedstead a foote
high upon tenne or twelve
Mattes, richly hung with
manie Chaynes of great
Pearles about his necke, and
covered with a great Covering
of *Rahaughcums*: At his heade
sat a woman, at his feete
another, on each side sitting
uppon a Matte uppon the
ground were raunged his
chiefe men on each side the
fire, tenne in a ranke, and
behinde them as many yong
women, each a great Chaine
of white Beades over their
shoulders, their heades
painted in redde, and [he]
with such a grave and
Majesticall countenance, as
drave me into admiration to
see such state in a naked
Salvage, hee kindly wel-
comed me with good wordes,
and great Platters of sundrie
Victuals, assuring mee his
friendship, and my libertie
within foure dayes; hee much
delighted in Opechanca-
noughs relation . . . Hee
asked mee the cause of our
comming; . . . [C2r] . . .
demaunded why we went
further with our Boate; . . .
Many Kingdomes hee
described mee to the heade of
the Bay, which seemed to bee
a mightie River, issuing from
mightie Mountaines betwixt

At last they brought him to
Meronocomoco, where was
Powhatan their Emperor.
Here more then two hundred
. . . stood wondering at him,
. . . till Powhatan and his
trayne had put themselves in
their greatest braveries.
Before a fire upon a seat like
a bedsted, he sat covered
with a great robe, made of
Rarowcun skinnes, and all
the tayles hanging by. On
either hand did sit a young
wench of 16 or 18 yeares, and
along on each side the house,
two rowes ‖ [49] of men, and
behind them as many
women, with all their heads
and shoulders painted red;
many of their heads bedecked
with the white downe of
Birds; but every one with
something: and a great
chayne of white beads about
their necks. At his entrance
. . . all the people gave a
great shout. The Queene of
Appamatuck was appointed
to bring him water to wash
his hands, and . . . having
feasted him after their best
barbarous manner they
could, a long consultation
was held, but the conclusion
was, two great stones were
brought before Powhatan:
then as many as could layd
hands on him, dragged him
to them, and thereon laid his
head, and being ready with

the two Seas. . . . [C2ᵛ] In
describing to him the territories of Europe, which was
subject to our great King . . . ,
I gave him to understand the
. . . terrible manner of fighting were under captain
Newport . . . [Powhatan
then] desired mee to forsake
Paspahegh [Jamestown], and
to live with him upon his
River, . . . hee promised to
give me . . . what I wanted
to feede us, Hatchets and
Copper wee should make
him, and none should dis-
turbe us. This request I
promised to performe: and
thus having with all the
kindnes hee could devise,
sought to content me:

their clubs, to beate out his
braines, Pocahontas the
Kings dearest daughter,
when no intreaty could prevaile, got his head in her
armes, and laid her owne
upon his to save him from
death: whereat the Emperour
was contented he should live
to make him hatchets, and
her [Pocahontas] bells,
beads, and copper; . . .

Two dayes after, Powhatan
having disguised himselfe in
the most fearefullest manner
he could, caused Captaine
Smith to be brought forth to
a great house in the woods,
and there upon a mat by the
fire to be left alone. . . . then
Powhatan more like a devill
then a man . . . came unto
him and told him now they
were friends, and presently
he should goe to James
towne, to send him two great
gunnes, and a gryndstone,
for which he would give him
the Country of Capahowosick,
and for ever esteeme him as
his sonne Nantaquoud.

hee sent me home with 4.
men, . . . [C3ᵛ] . . . From
Weramocomoco is but 12.
miles, yet the Indians trifled
away that day, and would

So to James towne with 12
guides Powhatan sent him.
That night they quarterd in
the woods, he still expecting
. . . every houre to be put to

True Relation	*Generall Historie*	*Pilgrimage*

not goe to our Forte . . . but in certaine olde hunting houses of Paspahegh we lodged all night. The next morning ere Sunne rise, we set forward for our Fort, where we arrived within an houre, . . .

one death or other: for all their feasting. . . . The next morning betimes they came to the Fort, . . .

Chronology of Events in Jamestown, 1606–1608*

1606

(Fri.) *Dec. 19.*	The colonists set sail (*Proceedings*, 2).
(Sat.) *Dec. 20.*	Down river from London (Percy).

1607

(Mon.) *Jan. 5.*	Anchored in the Downs (Percy).
c. (Fri.) *Jan. 30.*	No longer in sight of England (*Proceedings*, 2).
c. (Tues.) *Feb. 17.*	Conjectured arrival at Gran Canaria.
c. (Sat.–Sun.) *Feb. 21–22.*	Departure from the Canaries; Smith "restrained as a prisoner" (*Proceedings*, 5).
(Mon.) *Mar. 23.*	Arrived at Martinique (Percy).
(Tues.) *Mar. 24.*	Anchored at Dominica (Percy).
(Thurs.) *Mar. 26.*	Had sight of Marie-Galante (Percy).
(Fri.) *Mar. 27.*	Sailed along Guadeloupe to Nevis (Percy); there "a paire of gallowes was made" for Smith, in an attempt to hang him (*True Travels*, 57).
(Fri.) *Apr. 3.*	Set sail from Nevis (Percy).
(Sat.) *Apr. 4.*	Sailed along St. Eustatius and Saba and anchored in the harbor of St. Thomas, Virgin Islands (Percy).
(Mon.) *Apr. 6.*	Passed by Vieques and San Juan, Puerto Rico (Percy).
(Tues.) *Apr. 7.*	Arrived at Mona and took on water (Percy).
(Thurs.) *Apr. 9.*	Visited the Isle of Moneta and laded two boats full of eggs and fowl (Percy).
(Fri.) *Apr. 10.*	Set sail from Mona (Percy).
(Tues.) *Apr. 14.*	Passed the Tropic of Cancer (Percy).
(Tues.) *Apr. 21.*	Forced to "lie at hull" because of a tempest (Percy).
(Wed.–Sat.) *Apr. 22–25.*	Sounded but found no ground (Percy).

*Sources: John Smith's works as presented in this edition, and the following accounts printed in Philip L. Barbour, ed., *The Jamestown Voyages under the First Charter, 1606–1609* (Hakluyt Society, 2d Ser., CXXXVI–CXXXVII [Cambridge, 1969]), I, indicated by surnames only: Gabriel Archer, 80–98; George Percy, 129–146; Francis Magnel, 151–157; Francis Perkins, 158–163; and Edward Maria Wingfield, 211–234.

The Julian calendar, ten days behind the Gregorian, is retained throughout.

(Sun.) *Apr. 26.*	"Descried the Land of Virginia" about four in the morning (Percy); at nightfall the colonists had their first skirmish with the Indians.
(Mon.) *Apr. 27.*	Began to assemble the shallop, which had been dismantled for the voyage over. Explored "eight miles up into the Land" (Percy).
(Tues.) *Apr. 28.*	Launched the shallop in which Newport took a party as far as the modern Elizabeth River (Percy).
(Wed.) *Apr. 29.*	Set up a cross by Chesapeake Bay, naming the point Cape Henry (Percy).
(Thurs.) *Apr. 30.*	The fleet crossed the bay to Old Point Comfort, near the village of Kecoughtan (Percy).
(Fri.–Sun.) *May 1–3.*	Entertained by Indians (Percy).
(Mon.) *May 4.*	The fleet came to a Paspahegh village where the colonists were entertained with "much welcome"; a werowance from across the river "seemed to take displeasure" from the colonists' being with the Paspahegh (Percy).
(Tues.) *May 5.*	Went to visit the werowance across the river (Percy).
(Fri.) *May 8.*	The colonists sailed up the James River to the "Countrey of Apamatica," where "there came many stout and able Savages to resist" them (Percy). Peace was made, however, and three days appear to have been spent exploring on foot.
(Tues.) *May 12.*	The colonists went back to their ships and discovered a point of land just below modern Jamestown Island they named "Archers Hope" (Percy).
(Wed.) *May 13.*	Came to their "seating place" (Percy), 8 mi. (13 km.) upstream; chosen by Wingfield, overruling Gosnold (*True Relation*, sig. A3ᵛ).
(Thurs.) *May 14.*	Landed all their men (Percy); about midnight some Indians sailed close by, causing an alarm; "not long after" two messengers came from the werowance of Paspahegh, saying he was coming "with a fat Deare" (Percy).
(Mon.) *May 18.*	The werowance arrived with 100 armed Indians, but after a fight, went away "in great anger" (Percy).

(Tues.) *May 19.*   Percy and others went for a stroll "some foure miles . . . to a Savage Towne" (Percy).

(Wed.) *May 20.*   The Paspahegh werowance sent 40 men "with a Deare, to our quarter" (Percy).

(Thurs.) *May 21.*   Captain Newport took a party on an exploring expedition in the shallop (Archer), spending the night with the Weanocks, enemies of Paspahegh.

(Fri.) *May 22.*   The party went "some 16 myle further," picking up some friendly Indians; they sailed in all 38 mi. (61 km.) that day (Archer).

(Sat.) *May 23.*   They continued on to the falls at modern Richmond, where they mistook the local werowance, Tanx ("Little") Powhatan, for his father, the "emperor" (Archer).

(Sun.) *May 24.*   Whitsunday. Newport angered Tanx Powhatan by setting up a cross and claiming the region for King James. That night Newport's party went back downstream to Arrohattoc (Archer and Percy).

(Mon.) *May 25.*   The party "satt banquetting all the forenoone" with the Arrohattoc werowance, then sailed down to "Kynd Womans Care" (Archer).

(Tues.) *May 26.*   The party went ashore to visit Queen Opossunoquonuske, then met Powhatan's brother Opechancanough a few miles below, and finally anchored for the night 21 mi. (34 km.) from Jamestown (Archer; but see Strachey, *Historie*, 64; and *Generall Historie*, 49). That same day, Paspahegh attacked Jamestown with 200 men, causing casualties, but was repulsed by the ships' ordnance (Archer; *True Relation*, sig. A4ʳ; and *Generall Historie*, 42).

(Wed.) *May 27.*   The party went ashore but grew suspicious and hurried home (Archer).

(Thurs.) *May 28.*   Labored at fortifying the fort (Archer; *True Relation*, sig. A4ᵛ; and *Generall Historie*, 42).

(Fri.) *May 29.*   The Indians attacked again, but did not hurt any of the English (Archer).

(Sun.) *May 31.*   The Indians "came lurking in the thickets," and Eustace Clovell was shot; he died June 8 (Archer).

(Mon.) *June 1.*   Some 20 Indians "appeared, shott dyvers arrowes, . . . and rann away" (Archer).

(Thurs.) *June 4.*	Three Indians shot at a colonist outside the palisade, but "missed the skynne" (Archer).
(Sat.) *June 6.*	A petition was drawn up for reformation of "certayne preposterous proceedinges" (Archer).
(Mon.) *June 8.*	Clovell died; two Indians presented themselves unarmed, "crying 'friends,'" but a guard shot at them, and they ran (Archer).
(Wed.) *June 10.*	"The Counsell scanned the . . . petition," Newport urged the colonists to work together, and Captain Smith was sworn in as councillor (Archer).
(Sat.) *June 13.*	Eight Indians lying "close among the weedes" shot Mathew Fitch in the breast and ran away (Archer).
(Sun.) *June 14.*	Two Indians presented themselves unarmed, naming the friends and foes of the colonists, and advising the English to cut down the tall weeds (Archer).
(Mon.) *June 15.*	The fort was finished, "triangle wise" (Percy).
(Tues.) *June 16.*	Two Indians appeared with a ruse to capture Newport, but failed (Archer).
(Sun.) *June 21.*	The colonists took communion and had a farewell dinner with Newport (Archer). Opechancanough sent a message of peace (*True Relation*, sig. A4^v).
(Mon.) *June 22.*	Captain Newport sailed for England (Percy; Wingfield; and *True Relation*, sig. A4^v; Archer omits the entry, and *Proceedings* and *Generall Historie* give June 15).
(Thurs.) *June 25.*	An Indian came from "the great Poughwaton with the words of peace" (Wingfield).
(Fri.) *July 3.*	Seven or eight Indians presented President Wingfield "a Dear from Pamaonke [Opechancanough]; they enquired after our shipping [Newport's ships]" (Wingfield).
	"About this tyme divers of our men fell sick" (Wingfield).
(Mon.) *July 27.*	The "King of Rapahanna [Quiyoughcohanock] demanded a canoa which was restored" (Percy).
(Thurs.) *Aug. 6.*	"John Asbie" died of the "bloudie Flixe" (Percy).
(Sun.) *Aug. 9.*	"George Flowre" died of the "swelling" (Percy).

(Mon.) *Aug. 10.*   "William Bruster" died of a wound given by the Indians (Percy).

(Fri.) *Aug. 14.*   "Jerome Alikock" died "of a wound"; the same day, "Francis Midwinter" and "Edward Moris" died "suddenly" (Percy).

(Sat.) *Aug. 15.*   "Edward Browne" and "Stephen Galthrope" died (Percy).

During these weeks, Wingfield told Smith to his face, in Gosnold's tent, that "it was proved . . . that he [Smith] begged in Ireland like a rogue, without lycence" (Wingfield), drawing a sharp retort from Smith.

(Sun.) *Aug. 16.*   "Thomas Gower" died (Percy).

(Mon.) *Aug. 17.*   "Thomas Mounslie" died (Percy).

(Tues.) *Aug. 18.*   "Robert Pennington" and "John Martin," son of Capt. John Martin, died (Percy).

(Wed.) *Aug. 19.*   "Drue Piggase" died (Percy).

(Sat.) *Aug. 22.*   Capt. Bartholomew Gosnold died; all the ordnance in the fort was shot off with many volleys (Percy; also Wingfield; *True Relation*, sig. A4^v; *Proceedings*, 10; and *Generall Historie*, 44). About this time the Indians began to bring fresh corn for barter (Wingfield).

(Mon.) *Aug. 24.*   "Edward Harington" and "George Walker" died (Percy).

(Wed.) *Aug. 26.*   "Kenelme Throgmortine" died (Percy).

(Thurs.) *Aug. 27.*   "William Roods" died (Percy).

(Fri.) *Aug. 28.*   "Thomas Stoodie [Studley], Cape Merchant" died (Percy).

About this time George Kendall was deposed from the council and confined in the pinnace (Percy; Wingfield; *True Relation*, sigs. A4^v–B1^r, etc.).

(Fri.) *Sept. 4.*   "Thomas Jacob" died (Percy).

(Sat.) *Sept. 5.*   "Benjamin Beast [Best]" died (Percy).

(Thurs.) *Sept. 10.* Ratcliffe, Smith, and Martin, constituting a majority of councillors present, signed a warrant to depose President Wingfield (Wingfield); Ratcliffe was elected in Wingfield's place (*True Relation*, sig. B1^r; Percy gives Sept. 11 as the date).

(Fri.) *Sept. 11.*	The new president made a speech telling the colony why Wingfield was deposed (Wingfield).
(Thurs.) *Sept. 17.*	After complaints by John Robbinson and John Smith, Wingfield was tried, and Robbinson got £100 and Smith £200 "damages for slaunder" (Wingfield).
(Fri.) *Sept. 18.*	"Ellis Kinistone" and "Richard Simmons" died (Percy).
(Sat.) *Sept. 19.*	"Thomas Mouton" died (Percy). By this time Smith had been made cape merchant (*True Relation*, sig. B1ʳ).
	[For the rest of 1607, dates can only be conjectured. In summary: a sharp decrease in food supplies from the Indians forced Smith to initiate trading voyages in the shallop (*Proceedings*, 11); unrest in Jamestown led to a mutiny, and Kendall was executed (Wingfield; Magnel; and *Proceedings*, 12); about Nov. 1, the council decided that the pinnace and barge should sail to the Falls (Powhatan village) for supplies (*True Relation*, sig. B1ᵛ).]
(Mon.) *Nov. 9* to c. (Sun.) *Nov. 15 (more likely, Nov. 19–25).*	Smith made three successful trading voyages up the Chickahominy River (*True Relation*, sig. B2ʳ–B3ʳ).
(Thurs.) *Dec. 10 (more likely, Dec. 3 or 4).*	Smith "went up" the Chickahominy (Wingfield; *True Relation*, sig. B3ʳ).
(Fri.) *Dec. 11 (Dec. 4 or 5?).*	Smith reached Apocant, 40 mi. (64 km.) up the river (*True Relation*, sig. B3ʳ).
(Sat.) *Dec. 12 (Dec. 5 or 6?).*	Smith went on by canoe, was captured by an Indian hunting party under Opechancanough, and taken to a temporary lodge (*ibid.*, sig. B3ᵛ).
	Three or four days later Smith witnessed certain Indian rites or conjurations (*ibid.*, sig. C3ʳ), after which he was marched around for four or five days and then led to Opechancanough's residence (*ibid.*, sig. C1ʳ).
c. (Fri.) *Dec. 25.*	Smith was entertained and then led to the Rappahannock River (*ibid.*, sig. C1ʳ⁻ᵛ).
(Tues.) *Dec. 29.*	Smith was lodged in a hunting town (*ibid.*, sig. C1ᵛ).
(Wed.) *Dec. 30.*	Smith taken before Powhatan.

1608

(Fri.) *Jan. 1.*   Powhatan sent Smith "home" (*True Relation*, sig. C3^v).

(Sat.) *Jan. 2.*   Smith reached Jamestown, where Newport arrived from England the same night (*ibid.*; Perkins).

(Thurs.) *Jan. 7.*   A fire destroyed "all the houses in the fort" at Jamestown (Perkins and Wingfield).

Newport having brought instructions from London to find "any of them sent by Sir Walter Raleigh" (*Generall Historie*, 71), the Paspahegh werowance was pressed into helping, but he went no farther than Warraskoyack (*True Relation*, sig. C4^r).

Feb. ?   Newport, Scrivener, Smith, and "30 or 40 chosen men" visited Powhatan at Werowocomoco (*True Relation*, sig. C4^r; *Proceedings*, 27–28).

(Wed.) *Mar. 9.*   Newport's party returned to Jamestown (Wingfield).

(Sun.) *Apr. 10.*   Newport sailed for England (Wingfield; *True Relation*, sig. D4^r).

(Wed.) *Apr. 20.*   Francis Nelson arrived (*True Relation*, sig. E1^r).

(Thurs.) *June 2.*   Smith left the fort to explore Chesapeake Bay and parted company with Nelson, who was sailing for England, at Cape Henry (*Generall Historie*, 55).

A TRVE RE-
lation of such occur-

rences and accidents of noate as
hath hapned in Virginia since the first
planting of that Collony, which is now
resident in the South part thereof, till
the last returne from
thence.

Written by Captaine Smith *one of the said Collony, to a*
worshipfull friend of his in England.

LONDON

Printed for *Iohn Tappe*, and are to bee solde at the Grey=
hound in Paules-Church-yard, by *W. W.*

1608

[The editor is grateful to the New York Public Library for permission to reproduce this title page.]

TO THE COURTEOUS READER.[1]

Courteous, Kind and indifferent[2] Readers, whose willingnesse to reade and heare this following discourse, doth explaine to the world your hearty affection, to the prosecuting and furtherance of so worthy an action: so it is, that like to an unskilfull actor, who having by misconstruction of his right Cue, over-slipt himselfe, in beginning of a contrary part,[3] and fearing the hatefull hisse of the captious multitude, with a modest blush retires himselfe in private; as doubting[4] the reprehension of his whole audience in publicke, and yet againe upon further deliberation, thinking it better to know their censures at the first, and upon submission to reape pardon, then by seeking to smother it, to incurre the danger of a secret scandall: Imboldening himselfe upon the curteous kindnesse of the best, and not greatly respecting the worst, comes fourth againe, makes an Apollogie for himselfe, shewes the cause of his error, craves pardon for his rashnes, and in fine, receives a generall applauditie of the whole assemblie: so I gentle Readers, happening upon this relation by chance (as I take it, at the second or third hand) induced thereunto by divers well willers of the action, and none wishing better towards it then my selfe, so farre foorth as my poore abilitie can or may stretch too, I thought good to publish it: but the Author being absent from the presse,[5] it cannot be doubted but that some faults have escaped

in the printing, especially in the names of Countries, ‖ Townes, and People, which are somewhat strange unto us: but most of all, and which is the chiefe error, (for want of knowledge of the Writer) some of the bookes were printed under the name of Thomas Watson, by whose occasion I know not, unlesse it were the over rashnesse, or mistaking of the workemen, but since having learned that the saide discourse was written by Captaine Smith, who is one of the Counsell there in Virginia: I thought good to make the like Apollogie, by shewing the true Author so farre as my selfe could learne, not doubting, but that the wise noting it as an error of ignorance, will passe it over with patience, and if worthy an applauditie, to reserve it to the Author, whose paines in my judgement deserveth commendations; somewhat more was by him written, which being as I thought (fit to be private) I would not adventure to make it publicke. What more may be expected concerning the scituation of the Country, the nature of the clime,[6] number of our people there resident, the manner of their government, and living, the commodities to be produced, and the end and effect it may come too, I can say nothing more then is here written, only what I have learned and gathered from the generall consent[7] of all (that I have conversed withall[8]) aswell marriners as others, which have had imployment that way; is that the Country is excellent and pleasant, the clime temperate and healthfull, the ground fertill and good, the commodities to be expected (if well followed) many, for our people, the worst being already past, these former having indured the heate of the day, whereby those that shall succeede, may at ease labour for their profit, in the most sweete, coole, and temperate shade: the action most honorable, and the end to the high glory of God, to the erecting of true religion among Infidells, to the overthrow of superstition and idolatrie, to the win-ning of ‖ many thousands of wandring sheepe, unto Christs fold, who **[¶2ʳ]** now, and till now, have strayed in the unknowne paths of Paganisme, Idolatrie, and superstition: yea, I say the Action being well followed, as by the grave Senators,[9] and worthy adventurors, it hath beene worthily begunne: will tend to the everlasting renowne of our Nation, and to the exceeding good and benefit of our Weale publicke in generall: whose Counsells,[10] labours, godly and industrious en-devours, I beseech the mightie Jehovah to blesse, prosper, and further, with his heavenly ayde, and holy assistance.

Farewell.
I.H.[11]

N.B. Page references to Smith works in the notes refer in all instances to the page numbers of the original editions, which are in boldface numerals in brackets in the margins.

A
True relation of such occurrences
and accidents of note, as hath hapned in *Vir-*
ginia, since the first planting of that Collony,
which is now resident in the South part
thereof, till the last returne.

a

Inde Sir , commendations remembred, &c. You shall vnderstand that after many crosses in the downes by tempests, wee arriued safely vppon the Southwest part of the great Canaries: within foure or fiue daies after we set saile for Dominica, the ~~26~~ of Aprill: the first land we made, wee fell with Cape Henry, the verie mouth of the Bay of Chissiapiacke, which at that present we little expected, hauing by a cruell storme bene put to the Northward: anchoring in this Bay twentie or thirtie went a shore with the Captain, and in comming aboard, they were assalted with certaine Indians, which charged them within Pistoll shot: in which conflict, Captaine Archer and Mathew Morton were shot: wherupon, Captaine Newport seconding them, made a shot at them, which the Indians little respected, but hauing spent their arrowes retyred without harme, and in that place was the Box opened, wherin the Counsell for Virginia was nominated: and arriuing at the place where wee are now seated, the Counsell was sworne, the President elected, which for that yeare was Maister Edm. Maria Wingfield, where was

16'

A 3   made

a. [l. 7]. "26" altered to "16" and entered in the margin; "26" is correct. The error was possibly due to calendar confusion or misunderstanding of the badly mutilated text.

A TRUE RELATION^[A3ʳ]

of such occurrences and accidents
of note, as hath hapned in Virginia,
since the first planting of that Collony,
which is now resident in the
South part[12] thereof, till the
last returne.

KINDE Sir, commendations remembred, etc.[13] You shall understand that after many crosses in the downes[14] by tempests, wee arrived safely uppon the Southwest part of the great Canaries: [. . .][15]

Within foure or five daies after, we set saile for Dominica, [. . .][16]

The 26. of Aprill: the first land we made, wee fell with Cape Henry,[17] the verie mouth of the Bay of Chissiapiacke,[18] which at that present we little expected, having by a cruell storme bene put to the Northward: anchoring in this Bay twentie or thirtie went a shore with the Captain,[19] and in comming aboard, they were assalted with certaine Indians,[20] which charged them within Pistoll shot: in which conflict, Captaine Archer and Mathew Morton were shot:[21] wherupon Captaine Newport seconding them, made a shot at them, which the Indians little respected, but having spent their arrowes retyred without harme. And in that place was the Box opened, wherin the Counsell for Virginia was nominated: [. . .][22]

And arriving at the place where wee are now seated, the Counsell was sworne, the President elected, which for that yeare was Maister Edward[23] Maria Wingfield, [. . .] where was

Newes from Virginia.

made choice for our scituation, a verie fit place for the erecting of a great cittie, about which some contention passed betwixt Captaine Wingfield and Captaine Gosnold, notwithstanding all our prouision was brought a shore, and with as much speede as might bee wee went about our fortification.

The two and twenty day of Aprill, Captain Newport and my selfe with diuers others, to the number of twenty two persons, set forward to discouer the Riuer, some fistic or sirtie miles, finding it in some places broader, & in some narrower, the Countrie (for the moste part) on each side plaine high ground, with many fresh Springes, the people in all places kindely intreating vs, daunsing and feasting vs with Strawberries, Mulberies, Bread, Fish, and other their Countrie prouisions whereof wee had plenty: for which Captaine Newport kindely requited their least fauours, with Bels, Pinnes, Needles, beades or Classes, which so contented them that his liberallitie made them follow vs from place to place, and euer kindely to respect vs. In the midway staying to refresh our selues in a little Ile foure or fiue sauages came vnto vs which described vnto vs the course of the Riuer, and after in our iourney, they often met vs, trading with vs for such prouision as wee had, and ariuing at Arsaticke, hee whom we supposed to bee the chiefe king of all the rest, moste kindely entertained vs, giuing vs in a guide to go with vs vp the Riuer to Powhatan, of which place their great Emperor taketh his name, where he that they honored for King vsed vs kindely. But to finish this discouerie, we passed on further, where within an ile we were intercepted with great craggy stones ẏ in midst of the riuer, where the water falleth so rudely, and with such a violence, as not any boat can possibly passe, and so broad disperseth the streame, as there is not past fiue or sixe foote at a low water, and to the shore scarce passage with a barge, the water floweth foure foote, and the freshes by reason of the Rockes haue left markes of the inundations 8. or 9. foote: The south side is plaine low ground, and the north side high mountaines,

b. [ll. 14–15]. A clover drawn in the margin calls attention to the "provisions" available.

c. [l. 23]. "Arsatecke," changed to read "Arsaticke"; a commoner spelling was "Arrohattoc" (see n. d, below; and n. 28 to edited text).

made choice for our scituation, a verie fit place for the erecting of a **[A3ᵛ]**
great cittie, about which some contention passed betwixt Captaine
Wingfield and Captaine Gosnold.[24] Notwithstanding all our provision was brought a shore, and with as much speede as might bee
wee went about our fortification.

The two and twenty day of Aprill,[25] Captain Newport and my
selfe with divers others, to the number of twenty two persons, set
forward to discover the River, some fiftie or sixtie miles, finding it in
some places broader, and in some narrower; the Countrie (for the
moste part) on each side plaine high ground, with many fresh
Springes, the people in all places kindely intreating[26] us, daunsing
and feasting us with strawberries, Mulberies, Bread, Fish, and other
their Countrie provisions wherof we had plenty: for which Captaine
Newport kindely requited their least favours with Bels, Pinnes,
Needles, beades or Glasses,[27] which so contented them that his
liberallitie made them follow us from place to place, and ever kindely
to respect us. In the midway staying to refresh our selves in a little
Ile foure or five savages came unto us which described unto us the
course of the River, and after in our journey, they often met us,
trading with us for such provision as wee had, and ariving at Arsatecke,[28] hee whom we supposed to bee the chiefe King of all the rest,
moste kindely entertained us, giving us a guide to go with us up the
River to Powhatan, of which place their great Emperor taketh his
name, where he that they honored for King used us kindely. But to
finish this discoverie, we passed on further, where within a mile[29] we
were intercepted with great craggy stones that in midst of the river,
where the water falleth so rudely, and with such a violence, as not
any boat can possibly passe, and so broad disperseth the streame, as
there is not past five or sixe Foote at a low water, and to the shore
scarce passage with a barge, the water floweth foure foote, and the
freshes[30] by reason of the Rockes have left markes of the inundations
8. or 9. foote: The south side is plaine low ground, and the north side
high

Newes from Virginia.

mountaines, the rockes being of a grauelly nature, interlaced with many vains of glistring spangles That night we returned to Powhatan: the next day (being Whitsunday after dinner) we returned to the fals, leauing a mariner in pawn with the Indians for a guide of theirs, hee that they honoured for King followed vs by the riuer. That afternoone we trifled in looking vpon the Rockes and riuer (furtherhe would not goe) so there we erected a crosse, and that night taking our man at Powhatans, Cap. Newport congratulated his kindenes with a Gown and a Hatchet: returning to Arsetecke, and stayed there the next day to obserue the height therof, & so with many signes of loue we departed. The next day the Queene of Agamatuck kindely intreated vs, her people being no lesse contented then the rest, and from thence we went to another place, (the name whereof I doe not remember) where the people shewed vs the manner of their diuing for Mussels, in which they finde Pearles.

That night passing by Weanock some twentie miles from our fort, they according to their former churlish condition, seemed little to affect vs, but as wee departed and lodged at the point of Weanock, I the people the next morning seemed kindely to content vs, yet we might perceiue many signes of a more Iealousie in them then before, and also the Hinde that the King of Arseteck had giuen vs, altered his resolution in going to our fort, and with many kinde circumstances left vs there. This gaue vs some occasion to doubt some mischiefe at the fort, yet Capt. Newport intended to haue visited Paspahegh and Tappahanocke, but the instant change of the winde being faire for our return we repaired to the fort withall speed, where the first we heard was that 400. Indians the day before had assalied the fort, & suppzised it, had not God (beyond al their expectations) by meanes of the shippes at whom they shot with their Ordinances & Muskets, caused them to retire, they had entred the fort without our own men, which were then busied in setting Corne, their armes beeing then in drie fats & few ready but certain Gentlemé of their own, in which conflict

---

d. [l. 10]. "Arsetecke," changed to "Arsaticke."

e. [ll. 12–13]. "Agamatock," corrected to read "Apametuck"; in the margin, "Apamettuc[k?]" (trimmed in binding).

f. [l. 18]. In margin, "Weeanocke," with the last letter struck through.

mountaines, the rockes being of a gravelly nature, interlaced with **[A4ʳ]**
many vains of glistring spangles.

That night we returned to Powhatan: the next day (being Whitsunday[31] after dinner) we returned to the fals, leaving a mariner in
pawn with the Indians for a guide of theirs. Hee that they honoured
for King followed us by the river. That afternoone we trifled in looking upon the Rockes and river (further he would not goe) so there
we erected a crosse,[32] and that night taking our man at Powhatans,
Captaine Newport congratulated[33] his kindenes with a Gown and a
Hatchet: returning to Arsetecke, and stayed there the next day to
observe the height[34] therof, and so with many signes of love we departed. The next day the Queene of Apamatuck kindely intreated
us, her people being no lesse contented then the rest, and from thence
we went to another place, (the name whereof I doe not remember)
where the people shewed us the manner of their diving for Mussels,
in which they finde Pearles.[35]

That night passing by Weanock[36] some twentie miles from our
Fort, they according to their former churlish condition, seemed
little to affect us, but as wee departed and lodged at the point of
Weanocke,[37] the people the next morning seemed kindely to content
us. Yet we might perceive many signes of a more Jealousie[38] in them
then before, and also the Hinde[39] that the King of Arseteck had given
us, altered his resolution in going to our Fort, and with many kinde
circumstances[40] left us there. This gave us some occasion to doubt
some mischiefe at the Fort, yet Captaine Newport intended to have
visited Paspahegh and Tappahanocke, but the instant change of the
winde being faire for our return we repaired to the fort with all speed,
where the first we heard was that 400. Indians the day before had
assalted the fort, and supprised it.[41] Had not God (beyond al their
expectations) by meanes of the shippes at whom they shot with their
Ordinances[42] and Muskets, caused them to retire, they had entred
the fort with our own men, which were then busied in setting Corne,
their armes beeing then in drie-fats[43] and few ready but certain
Gentlemen of their own, in which

g. [l. 21]. "Weanocke," with the last letter struck through.
h. [l. 24]. In margin, "Arsaticke" (see nn. c and d, above).
i. [l. 28]. "Tappahanocke," crossed out in text; in margin, "Quiocqahan[-]nock"
(damaged by trimming).

Newes from Virginia,

conflict, most of the Counsel was hurt, a boy slaine in the Pinnas, and thirteene or fourteene more hurt Withall speede we
pallisadoed our Fort: (each other day) for sixe or seauen daies
we had alarums by ambuscadoes, and foure or fiue cruelly
wounded by being abroad: the Indians losse wee know not,
but as they report three were slain and diuers hurt.

Captaine Newport hauing set things in order, set saile for
England the 22 of Iune, leauing prouision for 13. or 14
weeks. The day before the Ships departure, the King of Pamaunke sent the Indian that had met vs before in our discouerie, to assure vs peace, our fort being then pali'adoed round,
and all our men in good health and comfort, albeit, that throgh
some discontented humors, it did not so long continue, for the
President and Captaine Gosnold, with the rest of the Counsell, being for the moste part discontented with one another, in
so much, that things were neither carried with that discretion
nor any busines effected in such good sort as wisdome would,
nor our owne good and safetie required thereby, and throcugh
the hard dealing of our President, the rest of the counsell beeing diuerslie affected through his audacious commaund, and
for Captaine Martin, (albeit verie honest) and wishing the
best good, yet so sicke and weake , and my selfe so disgrac'd
through others mallice, through which disorder God (being
angrie with vs) plagued vs with such famin and sicknes, that
the liuing were scarce able to bury the dead: our want of sufficient and good victualls, with continuall watching, foure or
fiue each night at three Bullwarkes, being the chiefe
cause: onely of Sturgion wee had great store, whereon our men would so greedily surfet, as it cost manye
their liues: the Sack, Aquauitie, and other preseruatiues for
our health, being kept onely in the Presidents hands, for his
owne diet, and his few associates: shortly after Captaine Gosnold fell sicke, and within three weekes died , Captaine Ratcliffe being then also verie sicke and weake, and my selfe hauing also tasted of the extremitie therof, but by Gods assistãce
being well recouered. Kendall about this time, for diuers
                                                            reasons

---

conflict, most of the Counsel was hurt, a boy slaine in the Pinnas, and
thirteene or fourteene more hurt. With all speede we pallisadoed our
Fort:[44] (each other day) for sixe or seaven daies we had alarums by
ambuscadoes,[45] and foure or five cruelly wounded by being abroad:
the Indians losse wee know not, but as they report three were slain
and divers hurt. [. . .][46]

Captaine Newport having set things in order, set saile for
England the 22 of June, leaving provision for 13. or 14 weeks.[47] The
day before the Ships departure, the King of Pamaunke sent the
Indian that had met us before in our discoverie, to assure us peace,[48]
our fort being then palisadoed round, and all our men in good health
and comfort, albeit, that throgh some discontented humors, it did not
so long continue, for the President and Captaine Gosnold, with the
rest of the Counsell, being for the moste part discontented with one
another, in so much, that things were neither carried[49] with that discretion nor any busines effected in such good sort as wisdome would,
nor our owne good and safetie required thereby,[50] and through the
hard dealing of our President, the rest of the counsell beeing diverslie
affected through his audacious commaund, [. . .] and for Captaine
Martin, (albeit verie honest) and wishing the best good, yet so sicke
and weake, and my selfe so disgrac'd through others mallice, through
which disorder God (being angrie with us) plagued us with such
famin and sicknes, that the living were scarce able to bury the dead:
our want of sufficient and good victualls, with continuall watching,
foure or five each night at three Bulwarkes, being the chiefe cause:
onely of Sturgion wee had great store, whereon our men would so
greedily surfet, as it cost manye their lives; the Sack, Aquavitie, and
other preservatives for our health, being kept onely in the Presidents
hands, for his owne diet, and his few associates: [. . .][51] shortly after
Captaine Gosnold fell sicke, and within three weekes died,[52] Captaine Ratcliffe being then also verie sicke and weake, and my selfe
having also tasted of the extremitie therof, but by Gods assistance
being well recovered. Kendall about this time, for divers

Newes from Virginia.

reasons deposed from being of the Councell: and shortly after it pleased God (in our extremity) to moue the Indians to bring vs Corne, ere it was halfe ripe, to refresh vs, when we rather expected when they would destroy vs : about the tenth of September there was about 46. of our men dead, at which time Captaine Wingefield hauing ordred the affaires in such sort, that he was generally hated of all, in which respect with one consent he was deposed from his presidencie, and Captaine Ratcliffe according to his course was elected.

Our prouision being now within twentie dayes spent, the Indians brought vs great store both of Corne and bread ready made : and also there came such abundance of Fowles into the Riuers, as greatly refreshed our weake estates, whereuppon many of our weake men were presently able to goe abroad. As yet we had no houses to couer vs, our Tents were rotten, and our Cabbins worse then nought: our best commoditie was Yron which we made into little chissels, the president, and Captaine Martins sicknes, constrayned me to be Cape Marchant, and yet to spare no paines in making houses for the company, who notwithstanding our misery, little ceased their mallice, grudging and muttering. As at this time were most of our chiefest men either sicke or discontented, the rest being in such dispaire, as they would rather starue and rot with idlenes, then be perswaded to do any thing for their owne reliefe without constraint: our victualles being now within eighteene dayes spent, and the Indians trade decreasing, I was sent to the mouth of y' riuer, to Kegquouhtan an Indian Towne, to trade for Corne, and try the riuer for Fish, but our fishing we could not effect by reason of the stormy weather. The Indians thinking vs neare famished, with carelesse kindnes, offred vs little pieces of bread & small handfulls of beanes or wheat, for a hatchet or a piece of copper: In the like maner I entertained their kindnes, and in like scorne offered them like commodities, but the Children, or any that shewed extraordinary kindnes; I liberally contented with free giftes, such trifles as well contented them: finding this colde comfor-

13   comfor-

k. [margin, at top]. "Choapock: [Pipposco? *crossed out*] weeroance [of?] the Quiocqua[ha]nocks[?] did a[ll]wayes at o[ur] greatest nee[de] supply us w[ith] victualls of [all?] sortes which hee [did?] not withstanding the Continuall w[ant?] which wee had in [the?] rest of his Con[try?] and upon his death bed cha[rged?] his people that [they?] should for e[ver?] keepe good qu[iet?] with the English[.] Pippisco no[w]

reasons deposed from being of the Councell: and shortly after it **[B1ʳ]**
pleased God (in our extremity) to move the Indians to bring us
Corne, ere it was halfe ripe, to refresh us, when we rather expected
when[53] they would destroy us: about the tenth of September there
was about 46. of our men dead,[54] at which time Captaine Wingefield
having ordred the affaires in such sort that he was generally hated of
all, in which respect with one consent he was deposed from his presidencie, and Captaine Ratcliffe according to his course[55] was elected.

Our provision being now within twentie dayes spent, the Indians
brought us great store both of Corne and bread ready made:[56] and
also there came such aboundance of Fowles into the Rivers, as
greatly refreshed our weake estates, whereuppon many of our weake
men were presently able to goe abroad. As yet we had no houses to
cover us, our Tents were rotten, and our Cabbins worse than nought:
[. . .][57] Our best commoditie was Yron which we made into little
chissels, [. . .][58]

The president, and Captaine Martins sicknes, constrayned me
to be Cape Marchant,[59] and yet to spare no paines in making houses
for the company, who notwithstanding our misery, little ceased their
mallice, grudging and muttering. As at this time were most of our
chiefest men either sicke or discontented, the rest being in such dispaire, as they would rather starve and rot with idlenes, then be perswaded to do anything for their owne reliefe without constraint:
[. . .][60] our victualles being now within eighteene dayes spent, and
the Indians trade decreasing, I was sent to the mouth of the river, to
Kegquouhtan, an Indian Towne, to trade for Corne, and try the
river for Fish, but our fishing we could not effect by reason of the
stormy weather. The Indians thinking us neare famished, with carelesse kindnes offred us little pieces of bread and small handfulls of
beanes or wheat, for a hatchet or a piece of copper: In the like maner
I entertained their kindnes, and in like scorne offered them like commodities, but the Children, or any that shewed extraordinary
kindenes, I liberally contented with free gifte, such trifles as wel
contented them; finding this colde

---

weeroance doth not for[get] his predecess[ors?] Testament:" (see William Strachey, *The
Historie of Travell into Virginia Britania*, ed. Louis B. Wright and Virginia Freund [Hakluyt
Society, 2d Ser., CIII (London, 1953)], 64–65).
    l. [l. 4]. The second "when" is erroneously inked out (see n. 53 to the edited text).
    m. [ll. 27–30]. In margin, "Keequotancke" (Kecoughtan, modern Hampton, Vir-
ginia); "Musquasone" (unidentified, presumably in the same area); "Fort Henr[ie and]
Fort Charl[es]" (on either side of Southampton River [now the Hampton River], built
in mid-1610).

Newes from Virginia.

comfort, I anchored before the Towne, and the next day returned to trade, but God (the absolute disposer of all heartes)
altered their conceits, for now they were no lesse desirous of
our commodities then we of their Corne: vnder colour to
fetch fresh water, I sent a man to discouer the Towne,
their Corne, and force, to trie their intent, in that they desired me vpto their houses: which well vnderstanding, with
foure shot I visited them, with fish, oysters, bread and deere,
they kindly traded with me and my men, beeing no lesse in
doubt of my intent, then I of theirs, for well I might with
twentie men haue fraughted a Shippe with Corne: The
Towne conteineth eighteene houses, pleasantly seated vpon
three acres of ground, vppon a plaine, halfe inuironed with
a great Bay of the great Riuer, the other parte with a Baye
of the other Riuer falling into the great Baye, with a little Ile fit for a Castle in the mouth thereof, the Towne
adioyning to the maine by a necke of Land of sixtie pardes.
With sixteene bushells of Corne I returned towards our
Forte: by the way I encountred with two Canowes of Indians, who came aboord me, being the inhabitants of waroskoyack, a kingdome on the south side of the riuer, which is in
breadth 5. miles and 20 mile or neare from the mouth : with
these I traded, who hauing but their hunting prouision, requested me to returne to their Towne, where I should load
my boat with corne, & with near thirtie bushells I returned to
the fort, the very name whereof gaue great comfort to our des-
spairing company: time thus passing away, & hauing not aboue
14. daies victuals left, some motions were made about our presidents & Capt. Archers going for England, to procure a supply, in which meane time we had reasonablly fitted vs with
houses, and our President & Capt. Martin being able to walk
abroad, with much adoe it was concluded, that the pinnace and
barge should goe towards Powhatan, to trade for corne:Lotts
were cast who should go in her, the chance was mine, & while
she was arigging, I made a voiage to Topohanack, where a-
riuing, there was but certain women & children who fled from
their houses, yet at last I drew them to draw neare, truck they
durst

n. [ll. 20 21]. "Waroskoyack"; in margin, "[. . . sk?]ohiucke." "Warraskoyack"
enjoys an exceptional variety of spellings.

o. [l. 35]. "Topohanack," not altered here (see n. i, above). Perhaps the annotator
thought it was another name.

comfort, I anchored before the Towne, and the next day returned to **[B1ᵛ]**
trade, but God (the absolute disposer of all heartes) altered their
conceits, for now they were no lesse desirous of our commodities then
we of their Corne:[61] under colour to fetch fresh water, I sent a man
to discover the Towne, their Corne, and force, to trie their intent, in
that they desired me up to their houses: which well understanding
with foure shot I visited them. With fish, oysters, bread and deere,
they kindly traded with me and my men, beeing no lesse in doubt of
my intent, then I of theirs, for well I might with twentie men have
fraighted a Shippe with Corne: The Towne conteineth eighteene
houses, pleasantly seated upon three acres of ground, uppon a plaine,
halfe invironed with a great Bay of the great River, the other parte
with a Baye of the other River falling into the great Baye, with a little
Ile fit for a Castle in the mouth thereof, the Towne adjoyning to the
maine by a necke of Land of sixtie yardes. [. . .][62] With sixteene
bushells of Corne I returned towards our Forte: by the way I encountred with two Canowes of Indians, who came aboord me, being
the inhabitants of Waraskoyack, a kingdome on the south side of the
river, which is in breadth 5. miles and 20 mile or neare from the
mouth:[63] with these I traded, who having but their hunting provision requested me to returne to their Towne, where I should load
my boat with corne, and with near thirtie bushells I returned to the
fort, the very name wherof gave great comfort to our desparing
company:

Time thus passing away, and having not above 14. daies vituals
left, some motions were made about our presidents and Captaine
Archers going for England, to procure a supply,[64] in which meane
time we had reasonablly fitted us with houses, and our President and
Captaine Martin being able to walk abroad, with much ado it was
concluded that the pinnace and barge should goe towards Powhatan,[65] to trade for corne: Lotts were cast who should go in her. The
chance was mine, and while she was a rigging, I made a voiage to
Topohanack, where ariving, there was but certain women and children who fled from their houses, yet at last I drew them to draw
neere. Truck they

· Newes from Virginia.

durſt not, come they had plenty, & to ſpoile J had no cõmiſſion: In my returne to Paſpahegh, J traded with that churliſh & trecherous nation: hauing loaded 10 oz 12 buſhels of corne, they offred to take our pieces and ſwozds, yet by ſtelth, but ſeeming to diſlike if they were ready to aſſault vs, yet ſtäding vpon our guard in coaſting the ſhoze, diuers out of the woods would meet with vs with cozn & trade, but leaſt we ſhould be conſtraind, either to indure ouermuch wzong oz directly fal to reuenge, ſeing them dog vs, from place to place, it being night, & our neceſſitie not fit foz warres, we tooke occaſion to returne with 10 buſhells of cozne: Cap. Martin after made 2 iourneis to that nation of Paſpahegh but eache time returned with 8. oz 10. buſhells. All things being now ready foz my ieurney to Powhatan, foz the perfozmance thereof, J had 8. men and my ſelfe foz the barge, as well foz diſcouerie, as trading, the Pinnace, 5. Marriners: & 2. landmen to take in our ladings at conuenient places. The 9 of Nouember J ſet fozward foz the diſcouery of the country of Chikhamania, leauing the pinnace the next tide to followe and ſtay foz my comming at Point weanock, 20 miles from our fozt: the mouth of this riuer falleth into the great riuer at Paſpahegh, 8 miles aboue our fozt: that afternoone J ſtayed the eb, in the bay of Paſpahegh with the Indiãs: towards the euening certaine Indians haled me, one of them being of Chikahamania, offred to cõduci me to his country, the Paſpabegheans grudged therat: along we went by moonelight, at midnight he bzought vs befoze his Towne, deſiring one of our men to go vp with him, whom he kindely intertained, and returned back to the barge: the next mozning J went vp to the towne, and ſhewed them what copper and hatchets they ſhold haue foz cozne, each family ſeeking to giue me moſt content: ſo long they cauſed me to ſtay ẏ 100 at leaſt was expecting my comming by the riuer with cozne, what J liked J bought, and leaſt they ſhould perceiue my too great want J went higher vp the riuer: this place is called Manoſquoſick a quarter of a mile from the riuer, conteining thirtie oz foztie henſes, vppon an exceeding high land: at the foote of the hill towards the riuer, is a plaine wood, watered with many ſpzinges, which fall twentie yardes right downe

B 2   in o

p. [l. 18]. In margin, "Chickcahom[a?]niacke," now usually "Chickahominy."
q. [l. 25]. "Paspabegheans"; a misprint which the annotator has corrected.
r. [ll. 33–36]. In margin, "They moch[e?—uncertain; some sort of deceit] him for the na[me] of it is woo[??]niucke." Though the existence of Manosquosick may be

durst not, corne they had plenty, and to spoile I had no commission: **[B2ʳ]**
[. . .][66] In my returne to Paspahegh, I traded with that churlish and
trecherous nation:[67] having loaded 10 or 12 bushels of corne, they
offred[68] to take our pieces and swords, yet by stelth, but seeming to
dislike it, they were ready to assault us, yet standing upon our guard
in coasting the shore, divers out of the woods would meet with us
with corn and trade. But least we should be constrained, either to
indure overmuch wrong or directly fal to revenge, seeing them dog
us, from place to place, it being night, and our necessitie not fit for
warres, we tooke occasion to returne with 10 bushells of corne: Captaine Martin after made 2 journies to that nation of Paspahegh but
eache time returned with 8. or 10. bushells.[69]

All things being now ready for my journey to Powhatan, for the
performance thereof, I had 8. men and my selfe for the barge, as well
for discoverie, as trading; the Pinnace, 5. Marriners, and 2. landmen
to take in our ladings at convenient places. The 9 of November[70] I
set forward for the discovery of the country of Chikhamania, leaving
the pinnace the next tide to followe and stay for my comming at
Point Weanock, 20 miles from our fort: the mouth of this river falleth
into the great river at Paspahegh, 8 miles above our fort: that afternoone I stayed the eb, in the bay of Paspahegh with the Indians:
towards the evening certaine Indians haled me, one of them being of
Chikahamania, offred to conduct me to his country, the Paspa-
hegheans grudged[71] therat: [. . .] along we went by moonelight, at
midnight he brought us before his Towne, desiring one of our men
to go up with him, whom he kindely intertained, and [I] returned
back to the barge: the next morning I went up to the towne, and
shewed them what copper and hatchets they shold have for corne,
each family seeking to give me most content: so long they caused me
to stay that 100 at least was expecting my comming by the river with
corne. What I liked I bought, and least they should perceive my too
great want I went higher up the river:

This place is called Manosquosick[72] a quarter of a mile from the
river, conteining thirtie or fortie houses, uppon an exceeding high
land: at the foote of the hill towards the river, is a plaine wood,
watered with many springes, which fall twentie yardes right downe

---

doubted, the Smith/Hole map shows an "Ozenick" ("Ozaniocke" in the Smith/Zúñiga
map of 1608 [see Philip L. Barbour, ed., *The Jamestown Voyages under the First Charter,
1606–1609* (Hakluyt Society, 2d Ser., CXXXVI–CXXXVII [Cambridge, 1969]), I,
238–240]), and a few lines below (top of sig. B2ᵛ) Smith mentions an "Oraniocke."
Since the sound represented by *z* almost certainly did not exist in the local Algonkian
dialect and since a manuscript *r* could be mistaken for a *z* it is likely that this annotation
should read "Wooraniucke" (or "Wooreniucke"). See *ibid.*, 177; and Philip L. Barbour,
"The Earliest Reconnaissance of the Chesapeake Bay Area: Captain John Smith's Map
and Indian Vocabulary," *Virginia Magazine of History and Biography*, Pt. I, LXXIX
(1971), 295, s.v. "Oraniocke."

Newes from Virginia.

into the riuer: right against ý same is a great marish, of 4 or 5.
miles circuit, deuided in 2 Ilands, by the parting of the riuer,
abounding with ý foule of all forts: a little from thence is a
Towne called Oraniocke, I farther discouered the Townes
of Mangh, Apamock, Werawahone, & Mamanahūt: at eche
place kindely vsed, especially at the last, being the hart of the
Countrey, where were assembled 200. people with such abundance of corne, as hauing laded our barge, as also I might haue
laded a ship: I returned to Paspahiegh, & considering ý want
of corne at our fort, it being night, with ý eb, by midnight
I ariued at our fort, where I found our Pinnas run aground:
the next morning I vnladed seauē hogsheds into our store, the
next morning I returned againe: the second day I ariued at
Mamanahūt, wher ý people hauing heard of my cōming, were
ready with ; or 400. baskets litle & great, of which hauing laded my barge, with many signes of great kindnes I returned:
at my departure they requested me to heare our pieces, being in
the midst of the riuer, which in regard of ý eccho seemed a peale
of ordnance, many birds and fowles they see vs dayly kil that
much feared them, so desirous of trade wer they, ý they would
follow me with their canowes, & for any thing giue it me, rather then returne it back so I vnladed agoin 7 or 8. hogsheds
at our fort. Hauing thus by Gods assistance gotten good store
of corne, notwithstanding some bad spirits not content with
Gods prouidence, still grew mutinous, in so much, that our
president hauing occasion to chide the smith for his misbeha-
nor, he not only giue him bad langrage, but also offered to strike
him with some of his tooles, for which rebellious act the smith
was by a Iury condemned to be hanged, but being vppon the
ladder continuing very obstinate, as hoping vpon a rescue:
when he saw no other way but death with him, he became penitent, & declared a dangerous conspiracy, for which Captaine
Kendall as principal, was by a Iury condēned & shot to death.
This conspiracy appeased, I set forward for the discouery of
the Riuer of Chicka Hamania: this third time I discouered ý
Townes of Matapamient, Morinogh, Ascacap, moysenock
Righkahauck, Nechanichock, Mattalūt, Attamuspincke, &
diuers others, their plenty of corne I found decreased, yet la-
ding

for Matapament much abused . . . for there is not
such a name for any towne in all ý country . . .
. . . Matapament

into the river: right against the same is a great marsh, of 4. or 5. miles **[B2ᵛ]**
circuit, devided in 2 ilands, by the parting of the river, abounding
with fish and foule of all sorts; a mile from thence is a Towne called
Oraniocke; I further discovered the Townes of Mansa, Apanaock,
Werawahone, and Mamanahunt at eche place kindely used, especially at the last, being the hart of the Country, where were assembled
200. people with such aboundance of corne, as having laded our
barge, as also I might have laded a ship: I returned to Paspahhegh,
and considering the want of Corne at our Fort, it being night, with
the ebb, by midnight I arived at our fort, where I found our Pinnis
run aground: [. . .][73] the next morning I unladed seaven hogsheds
into our store.

The next morning I returned againe: the second day I arived
at Mamanahunt,[74] wher the people having heard of my comming,
were ready with 3 or 400. baskets litle and great, of which having
laded my barge, with many signes of great kindnes I returned: at my
departure they requested me to hear our pieces, being in the midst
of the river, which in regard of the eccho seemed a peale of ordnance.
Many birds and fowles they see us dayly kil that much feared them,
[. . .][75] so desirous of trade wer they, that they would follow me with
their canowes, and for any thing give it me, rather then returne it
back, so I unladed again 7 or 8. hogsheads at our fort. Having thus
by Gods assistance gotten good store of corne, notwithstanding some
bad spirrits not content with Gods providence still grew mutinous,
in so much, that our president having ocasion to chide the smith for
his misdeamenor,[76] he not only gave him bad language, but also
offred to strike him with some of his tooles, for which rebellious act
the smith was by a Jury condemned to be hanged. But being uppon
the ladder continuing verry obstinate, as hoping upon a rescue, when
he saw no other way but death with him, he became penitent, and
declared[77] a dangerous conspiracy, for which Captaine Kendall as
principal, was by a Jury condemned and shot to death.[78] This conspiracy appeased, I set forward for the discovery of the River of
Chickahominy: this third time I discovered the Townes of Matapamient, Morinogh, Ascacap, Moysenock, Righkahauck, Nechanichock, Mattalunt, Attamuspincke, and divers others.[79] Their plenty
of corne I found decreased, yet la-

s. [below bottom line]. At foot, "The Naturalls much abused him/for there is not
such a name for any towne in all the Country saving the first[:] Matapanient." These
"nonexistent" towns are not mentioned elsewhere in Smith's works (see Philip L. Barbour, "Chickahominy Place-Names in Captain John Smith's *True Relation*," *Names*, XV
[1967], 216–227; and Barbour, *Jamestown Voyages*, II, 477–480).

Newes from Virginia.

ding the barge, I returned to our fort: our ſtore being now indifferently wel prouided with corne, there was much adoe for to haue the pinace goe for England, againſt which Captain Martin & my ſelfe, ſtanding chiefly againſt it, and in fine after many debatings, pro & contra, it was reſolued to ſtay a further reſolutiõ: this matter alſo quieted, I ſet forward to finiſh this diſcouery, which as yet I had neglected in regard of ẙ neceſſitie we had to take in prouiſion whilſt it was to be had: 40. miles I paſſed vp ẙ riuer, which for the moſt part is a quarter of a mile broad, & 3. fatham & a half deep, exceeding oſey, many great low mariſhes, & many high lãds, especially about ẙ midſt at a place called Moyſonicke, a Peninſule of 4. miles cicuit, betwixt two riuers ioyned to the main, by a necke of 40. or 50. yards, and 40. or 50 yards from the high water marke: on both ſides in the very necke of the maine, are high hills and dales, yet much vnhabited, the Ile declining in a plaine fertile corne field, the lower end a low marſh, more pientic of ſwannes, cranes, geeſe, duckes, and mallards & diuers ſorts of fowles none would deſire: more plaine fertile planted ground, in ſuch great proportions as there I had not ſcene, of a light blacke ſandy mould, the cliffes commonly red, white and yellowe coloured ſand, & vnder red & white clay, fiſh great plentý, & people abou:ndance, the moſt of their inhabitants, in view of ẙ necke of Land, where a better ſeat for a towne canuot be deſired: at the end of forty miles this riuer ſurroneth many low Ilands, at each high water browned for a mile, where it baiteth it ſelfe, at a place called ꝫ pokant the higheſt Towne inhabited. 10. miles higher I diſcouered with the barge in the mid way, a great tree hindred my paſſage which I cut in twe: heere the riner became narrower, 8. 9 or 10. foote at a high water, and 6. or 7. at a lowe: the ſtreame exceeding ſwi t, & the bottom hard channell, the ground moſt part a low plaine, ſandy ſoyle, this occaſioned me to ſuppoſe it might iſſue from ſome lake or ſome broad ford, for it could not be far to the head, but rather then I would endanger the barge, yet to haue beene able to reſolue this doubt, & to diſcharge the imputation of malicious tungs, that halfe ſuſpected I durſt not for ſo long delaying, ſome of the company as deſirous as my ſeif, we reſolued te hier a Ca-

t. [l. 12]. "Moysonicke"; in margin, "no such tow[ne]."

ding the barge, I returned to our fort: our store being now indifferently wel provided with corne, there was much adoe for to have the
pinace goe for England, against which Captain Martin and my selfe,
standing chiefly against it, and in fine[80] after many debatings, pro et
contra, it was resolved to stay a further resolution:[81]

This matter also quieted, I set forward to finish this discovery,[82]
which as yet I had neglected in regard of the necessitie we had to take
in provision whilst it was to be had: 40. miles I passed up the river,
which for the most part is a quarter of a mile broad, and 3. fatham
and a half deep, exceeding osey,[83] many great low marshes, and
many high lands, especially about the midst at a place called Moysonicke,[84] a Peninsule of 4. miles circuit, betwixt two rivers joyned
to the main, by a neck of 40. or 50. yards, and 40. or 50 yards from
the high water marke: on both sides in the very necke of the maine,
are high hills and dales, yet much inhabited, the Ile declining in a
plaine fertile corne field, the lower end a low marsh. More plentie of
swannes, cranes, geese, duckes, and mallards and divers sorts of
fowles none would desire: more plaine fertile planted ground,[85] in
such great proportions as there, I had not seene, of a light blacke
sandy mould, the cliffes commonly red, white and yellowe coloured
sand, and under, red and white clay, fish great plenty, and people
aboundance, the most of their inhabitants, in view of the neck of
Land, where a better seat for a towne cannot be desired:[86]

At the end of forty miles this river invironeth many low ilands,
at each high water drowned for a mile,[87] where it uniteth it selfe at
a place called Apokant the highest Towne inhabited. 10. miles
higher I discovered with the barge in the mid way, a great tree
hindred my passage which I cut in two: heere the river became
narrower, 8. 9 or 10. foote at a high water, and 6. or 7. at a lowe: the
streame exceeding swift, and the bottom hard channell,[88] the ground
most part a low plaine, sandy soyle. This occasioned me to suppose
it might issue from some lake or some broad ford, for it could not be
far to the head, but rather then I would endanger the barge, yet to
have beene able to resolve this doubt, and to discharge the imputation of malicious tungs, that halfe suspected I durst not for so long
delaying, some of the company as desirous as my self, we resolved to
hier a Ca-

Newes from Virginia.

now, and returne with the barge to Pocant, there to leaue the barge secure, and put our selues vppon the aduenture: the country onely a bast and wilde wildernes, and but onely that Towne: within three or foure mile we hired a Canow, and 2. Indians to row vs ye next day a fowling: hauing made such prouision for the barge as was needfull, I left her there to ride, with expresse charge not any to go ashore til my returne. Though some wise men may condemne this too bould attempt of too much indiscretion, yet if they well consider the friendship of the Indians, in conducting me, the desolatenes of the country, the probabilitie of some lacke, & the malicious iudges of my actions at home, as also to haue some matters of worth to incourage our aduenturers in england, might well haue caused any honest minde to haue done the like, as well for his own discharge as for the publike good: hauing 2 Indians for my guide & 2 of our own company, I set forward, leauing 7 in the barge: hauing discouered 20 miles further in this desart, the riuer stil kept his depth and breoth, but much more combred with trees: here we went ashore (being some 12 miles higher then ye barge had bene) to refresh our selues, during the boyling of our vituals: one of the Indians I tooke with me, to see the nature of the soile, & to crosse the boughts of the riuer, the other Indian I left with M. Robbinson and Thomas Emry, with their matches light and order to discharge a peece, for my retreat at the first sight of any Indian, but within a quarter of an houre I heard a loud cry, and a hollowing of Indians, but no warning peece, supposing them surprized, and that the Indians had betraid vs, presently I seazed him & bound his arme fast to my hand in a garter, with my pistoll ready bent to be reuenged on him: he aduised me to fly, and seemed ignorant of what was done, but as we went discoursing, I was struck with an arrow on the right thigh, but without harme: vpon this occasion I espied 2 Indians drawing their bowes, which I preuented in discharging a french pistoll: by that I had charged againe 3 or 4 more did the like, for the first fell downe and fled: at my discharge they did the like, my hinde I made my barricado who offered not to striue, 20. or 30. arrowes were shot at me but short, 3 or 4 times I had discharged my pistoll ere the

king

now, and returne with the barge to Apocant, there to leave the barge
secure, and put our selves uppon the adventure:[89] the country onely
a vast and wilde wildernes, and but onely that Towne: within three
or foure mile we hired a Canow, and 2. Indians to row us the next
day a fowling:[90] having made such provision for the barge as was
needfull, I left her there to ride, with expresse charge not any to go
ashore til my returne. Though some wise men may condemn this too
bould attempt of too much indiscretion, yet if they well consider the
friendship of the Indians in conducting me, the desolatenes of the
country, the probabilitie of some lacke,[91] and the malicious judges of
my actions at home, as also to have some matters of worth to incourage our adventurers in England, might well have caused any
honest minde to have done the like, as wel for his own discharge[92] as
for the publike good:

Having 2 Indians for my guide and 2 of our own company, I set
forward, leaving 7 in the barge: having discovered 20 miles further
in this desart, the river stil kept his depth and bredth, but much more
combred[93] with trees: here we went ashore (being some 12 miles
higher then the barge had bene) to refresh our selves. During the
boyling of our vituals, one of the Indians I tooke with me, to see the
nature of the soile, and to crosse the boughts[94] of the river, the other
Indian I left with Master Robbinson and Thomas Emry, with their
matches light and order to discharge a peece, for my retreat at the
first sight of any Indian. But within a quarter of an houre I heard a
loud cry, and a hollowing of Indians, but no warning peece; supposing them surprised, and that the Indians had betraid us, [. . .][95]
presently I seazed him and bound his arme fast to my hand in a garter,
with my pistoll ready bent[96] to be revenged on him: he advised me
to fly, and seemed ignorant of what was done, but as we went discoursing, I was struck with an arrow on the right thigh, but without
harme: upon this occasion I espied 2 Indians drawing their bowes,
which I prevented in discharging a French pistoll:[97]

By [the time?] that I had charged againe 3 or 4 more did the
like, for the first fell downe and fled: at my discharge they did the
like; my hinde I made my barricado, who offered not to strive.[98] 20.
or 30. arrowes were shot at me, but short, 3 or 4 times I had discharged my pistoll ere the

u

Newes from Virginia.

king of Pamaůck called Opeckǎkenough with 200 men, in-
uironedme, eache drawing their bowe, which done they laid
them vpon the ground, yet without shot, my hinde treated betwixt them and me of conditions of peace, he discouered me to
be the Captaine, my request was to retire to ȳ boate, they demaunded my armes, the rest they saide were slaine, onely
me they would reserue : the Indian importuned me not to
shoot. In retiring being in the midst of a low quagmire, and
minding them more then my steps, I slept fast into the quagmire, and also the Indian in drawing me foorth : thus surprised, I resolued to trie their mercies, my armes I caste from
me, till which none durst approch me : being ceazed on me, they
drew me out and led me to the King, I presented him with
a compasse diall, describing by my best meanes the vse thereof,
whereat he so amazedly admires, as he suffered me to proceed
in a discourse of the roundnes of the earth, the course of the
sunne, moone, starres and plannets, with kinde speeches and
bread he requited me, conducting me where the Canow lay
and Iohn Robbinson slaine, with 20 or 30. arrowes in him.
Emry I saw not, I perceiued by the aboundance of fires
all ouer the woods, at each place I expected when they would
execute me, yet they vsed me with what kindnes they
could : approching their Towne, which was within 6 miles
where I was taken, onely made as arbors and couered with
mats, which they remoue as occasion requires : all the women and children, being aduertised of this accident, came
foorth to meet them, the King well guarded with 20 bowmen
5 flanck and reare, and each flanck before him a sword & a pece,
and after him the like, then a bowman, then I on each hand
a boweman : the rest in file in the reare, which reare led foorth
amongst the trees in a bushion, eache his bowe and a handfull
of arrowes, a quiuer at his back grimly painted : on eache
flanck a sargeant, the one running alwaies toward the front
the other towards the reare, each a true pace and in exceeding
good order, this being a good time continued, they cast themselues in a ring with a daunce, and so each man departed to
            his

u. [margin, at top]. "Apachancka[no?] was indeede [a?] weeraonce bu[t] not
K[inge]: of Pa[wma]unckett: for [his?] brother Powh[aton?] the Emporor wa[s] Kinge
of that p[lace?/people?]."

king of Pamaunck called Opeckankenough[99] with 200 men, invironed me, eache drawing their bowe, which done they laid them upon the ground, yet without shot; my hinde treated betwixt them and me of conditions of peace. He discovered me to be the Captaine.[100] My request was to retire to the boate; they demaunded my armes, the rest they saide were slaine, onely me they would reserve: the Indian importuned me not to shoot. In retiring being in the midst of a low quagmire, and minding them more then my steps, I stept fast into the quagmire, and also the Indian in drawing me forth: thus surprised, I resolved to trie their mercies, my armes I caste from me, till which none durst approch me: being ceazed on me, they drew me out and led me to the king. I presented him with a compasse diall, describing by my best meanes the use therof, whereat he so amazedly admired, as he suffered me to proceed in a discourse of the roundnes of the earth, the course of the sunne, moone, starres and plannets.[101] With kinde speeches and bread he requited me, conducting me where the Canow lay and John Robbinson slaine, with 20 or 30. arrowes in him. Emry I saw not, [. . .][102] I perceived by the aboundance of fires all over the woods, [. . .][103]

At each place I expected when they would execute me, yet they used me with what kindnes they could: approaching their Towne, which was within 6 miles where I was taken, onely made as arbors and covered with mats, which they remove as occasion requires:[104] all the women and children, being advertised of this accident, came foorth to meet them, the King well guarded with 20 bowmen 5 flanck and rear, and each flanck before him a sword and a peece, and after him the like, then a bowman, then I on each hand a boweman, the rest in file in the reare, which reare led foorth amongst the trees in a bishion,[105] eache his bowe and a handfull of arrowes, a quiver at his back grimly painted: on eache flanck a sargeant, the one running alwaies towards the front the other towards the reare, each a true pace and in exceeding good order. This being a good time continued, they caste themselves in a ring with a daunce, and so eache man departed to

Newes from Virginia.

his lodging, the Captain conducting me to his lodging, a quarter of Uenison and some ten pound of bread J had for supper, what J left was reserued for me, and sent with me to my lodging: each morning 3. women presented me three great platters of fine bread, more venison then ten men could deuour J had, my gowne, points and garters, my compas and a tablet they gaue me againe, though 8 ordinarily guarded me, J wanted not what they could deuise to content me: and still our longer acquaintance increased our better affection: much they threatned to assault our forte, as they were solicited by the king of

v ~uwinckapunck~ : ~Paspahey gh~

Paspahegh who shewed at our fort great signes of sorrow for this mischance: the king tooke great delight in vnderstanding the manner of our ships, and sayling the seas, the earth & skies and of our God: what he knew of the dominicns he spared not to acquaint me with, as of certaine men ~clothed~ at a place called

w ~onahawan:~

Ocanahonan, cleathed like me, the course of our riuer, and that within 4 or 5 daies iourney of the falles, was a great turning of salt water: J desired he would send a messenger to Paspahegh, with a letter J would write, by which they shold vnderstand, how kindly they vsed me, and that J was well, least they should reuenge my death: this he granted and sent three men, in such weather, as in reason were vnpossible, by any naked to be indured: their cruell mindes towards the fort J had deuerted, in describing the ordinance & the mines in the fields, as also the reuenge Captain Newport would take of them at his returne, their intent, J incerted the fort, the people of Ocanahonum and the back sea, this report they after found diuers Indians that confirmed: the next day after my letter, came a saluage to my lodging, with his sword to haue slaine me, but being by my guard intercepted, with a bowe andarrow he offred to haue effected his purpose: the cause J knew not, till the King vnderstanding thereof came and told me of a man a dying, wounded with my pistoll: he tould me also of another J had slayne, yet the most concealed they had any hurte: this was the father of him J had slayne, whose furye to preuent, the King presently conducted me to another kingdome,

vpon

v. [l. 11]. "Paspahegh"; in margin, "[W?]awinckapunck[,] [King?]e of Paspaheygh." Strachey has a paragraph on "*Wowinchopunck* Weroance of *Paspahegh*" (*Historie*, 66–67).

w. [ll. 15–16]. "Ocanahonan"; in margin, "[Oc]onahawan"; and in ll. 26–27, below, "Ocanahonum." The phrase "as of certaine men cloathed at a place called

his lodging, the Captain conducting me to his lodging; a quarter of **[B4ᵛ]**
Venison and some ten pound of bread I had for supper, what I left
was reserved for me, and sent with me to my lodging:[106] each morning 3. women presented me three great platters of fine bread, more
venison then ten men could devour I had; my gowne, points and
garters,[107] my compas and a tablet they gave me again. Though 8
ordinarily guarded me, I wanted not what they could devise to content me: and still our longer acquaintance increased our better
affection: much they threatned to assault our forte, as they were
solicited by the King of Paspahegh who shewed at our fort great
signes of sorrow for this mischance: [. . .][108]

The King[109] tooke great delight in understanding the manner
of our ships, and sayling the seas, the earth and skies and of our God:
what he knew of the dominions[110] he spared not to acquaint me with,
as of certaine men cloathed at a place called Ocanahonan,[111]
cloathed like me, the course of our river, and that within 4 or 5 daies
journey of the falles was a great turning of salt water:[112] I desired he
would send a messenger to Paspahegh,[113] with a letter I would write,
by which they shold understand, how kindly they used me, and that
I was well, least they should revenge my death: this he granted and
sent three men, in such weather, as in reason were unpossible by any
naked to be indured: their cruell mindes towards the fort I had
deverted, in describing the ordinance and the mines in the fields, as
also the revenge Captain Newport would take of them at his returne.
Their intent, I incerted[114] the fort, [. . .] the people of Ocanahonum
and the back sea, this report they after found divers Indians that
confirmed.

The next day after my letter, came a salvage to my lodging, with
his sword to have slaine me, but being by my guard intercepted,
with a bowe and arrow he offred to have effected his purpose: the
cause I knew not, till the King understanding thereof came and told
me of a man a dying, wounded with my pistoll: he tould me also of
another I had slayne, yet the most concealed they had any hurte:
this was the father of him I had slayne, whose fury to prevent,[115] the
King presently conducted me to another Kingdome,

Ocanahonan" has been corrected to read, "as of certaine men at a place 6 dayes jorny
beyond Ocanahonan." See the *Generall Historie*, 110: "five daies journey from us"; and
Philip L. Barbour, "Ocanahowan and Recently Discovered Linguistic Fragments from
Southern Virginia, *c*. 1650," in William Cowan, ed., *Papers of the Seventh Algonquian Conference, 1975* (Ottawa, 1976), 2–17.

Newes from Virginia.

upon the top of the next northerly riuer, called Youghtanan, hauing feasted me, he further led me to another branch of the riuer, called Mattapament, to two other hunting townes they led me, and to each of thefe Countries, a taufe of the great Emperour of Powhatan, whom as yet I fuppofed to bee at the Fals, to him I tolde him I muft goe, and fo returne to Pafpahegh, after this foure or fiue dayes march, we returned to Rafawrack, the firft towne they brought me to, where binding the Mats in bundels, they marched two dayes iourney, and croffed the Riuer of Youghtanan, where it was as broad as Thames: fo conducting me to a place called *Menapacute in Pamaunke, where ye King inhabited: the next day another King of that nation called Kekataugh, hauing receiued fome kindnes of me at the Fort, kindly inuited me to feaft at his houfe, the people from all places flocked to fee me, each fhewing to content me. By this the great King hath foure or fiue houfes, each containing fourefcore or an hundred foote in length, pleafantly feated vpon an high fandy hill, from whence you may fee wefterly a goodly low Country, the riuer before the which his crooked courfe caufeth many great Marfhes of exceeding good ground. An hundred houfes, and many large plaines are here togither inhabited, more abundance of fifh fowle, and a pleafanter feat cannot be imagined: the King with fortie Bowmen to guard me, intreated me to difcharge my Piftoll, which they there prefented me with a mark at fix fcore to ftrike therwith but to fpoil the practife I broke the cocke, whereat they were much difcontented though a chaunce fuppofed.

From hence this kind King conducted mee to a place called Rapahanocke, a kingdome vpon another Riuer northward: the caufe of this was, that the yeare before, a fhippe had béene in the Riuer of Pamaunke, who hauing béene kindly entertained by Powhatan their Emperour, they returned thence, and difcouered the Riuer of Rapahanocke, where being receiued with like kindneffe, yet he flue the King, and tooke of his people, and they fuppofed I were hee, but the people reported him a great man that was Captaine, and being mee kindly, the

C   next

---

x. [l. 1]. "Youghtanan"; with the *u* struck through and *t* added at the end. In margin, "Yoghtanun[t]."

y. [l. 3]. "Mattapament"; in margin, "Matappa[nient?]"; cf. n. s, above.

z. [l. 5]. In text, "of Pewhakan"; the "of" was deleted, and "Pewhakan" was changed to "Powhatan."

upon the top of the next northerly river, called Youghtanan. Having **[Cr^r]**
feasted me, he further led me to another branch of the river, called
Mattapanient; to two other hunting townes they led me, and to each
of these Countries, a house of the great Emperour of Powhatan,
whom as yet I supposed to bee at the Fals, to him I tolde him I must
goe, and so returne to Paspahegh.[116] After this foure or five dayes
march, we returned to Rasaweack,[117] the first towne they brought
me too, where binding the Mats in bundels, they marched two dayes
journey, and crossed the River of Youghtanan, where it was as
broad as Thames: so conducting me to a place called Menapacute
in Pamaunke, where the King inhabited: the next day another King
of that nation called Kekataugh, having received some kindnes of
me at the Fort, kindly invited me to feast at his house; the people
from all places flocked to see me, each shewing to content me.

By this the great King hath foure or five houses, each containing
fourescore or an hundred foote in length, pleasantly seated upon an
high sandy hill, from whence you may see westerly a goodly low
Country, the river before the which his crooked course causeth many
great Marshes of exceeding good ground. An hundred houses, and
many large plaines are here togither inhabited, more abundance of
fish and fowle, and a pleasanter seat cannot be imagined: the King
with fortie Bowmen to guard me, intreated me to discharge my
Pistoll, which they there presented me, with a mark at six score to
strike therwith[118] but to spoil the practice I broke the cocke, whereat
they were much discontented though a chaunce supposed.[119]

From hence this kind King conducted mee to a place called
Topahanocke, a kingdome upon another River northward: the
cause of this was, that the yeare before, a shippe had beene in the
River of Pamaunke, who having beene kindly entertained by Powhatan their Emperour, they returned thence, and discovered the
River of Topahanocke, where being received with like kindnesse, yet
he slue the King, and tooke of his people, and they supposed I were
hee. But the people reported him a great man that was Captaine, and
using mee kindly, the

aa. [ll. 7–8]. In text, "marsh, we returned to Rasawrack"; "marsh" being corrected
to "march." In margin, "no such towne." Rasaweack was a hunting camp only (see sig.
B4^r, above).

bb. [l. 10]. An asterisk before "River," and in margin, "or Creeke."

cc. [l. 11]. An asterisk after "Thames," and in margin, "at London."

dd. [l. 11]. "Menapacute"; in margin, "no [such?] pla[ce?]." But both the Smith/
Hole and the Smith/Zúñiga maps show its location.

ee. [l. 29]. "Topahanocke," changed to "Rapahanocke" (see Barbour, "Earliest
Reconnaissance," Pt. I, 298, s.v. "Rappahanock II").

ff. [l. 33]. "Topahanocke" again changed to "Rapahanocke"; in margin, "Rappahannock[e?]" (see ibid.).

Newes from Virginia.

next day we departed.

gg *Rappah mc*

hh *Nantaugs tacum*

This Riuer of Topahanock, seemeth in breadth not much lesse then that we dwell vpon. At the mouth of the Riuer is a Countrey called Cuttata women vpwards is Marraugh tacum Tapohanock, Appamatuck, and Nantaugs tacum , at Topmanahocks, the head issuing from many Mountaines, the next night I lodged at a hunting town of Powhatams, and the next day arriued at Waranacomoco vpon the riuer of Pamauncke, where the great king is resident: by the way we passed by the top of another little riuer , which is betwixt the two called Payankatank. The most of this Countrey though Desert, yet exceeding fertil, good timber, most hils and dales, in each valley a cristall spring.

ii

jj *made of A beast*
a Rarecowne
...

Arriuing at Weramocomoco, their Emperour proudly lying vppon a Bedstead a foote high vpon tenne or twelus Mattes, richly hung with manie Chaynes of great Pearles about his necke , and couered with a great Couering of Rahaughcums : At his heade sat a woman, at his feete another, on each side sitting vppon a Matte vppon the ground were raunged his chiefe men on each side the fire, tenne in a ranke, and behinde them as many yong women, each a great Chaine of white Beades ouer their shoulders : their heades painted in radde and with such a graue and Maiesticall countenance, as draue me into admiration to see such state in a naked Saluage, hee kindly welcomed me with good wordes, and great Platters of sundrie Victuals , assuring mee his friendship, and my libertie within foure dayes, hee much delighted in Opechan Comoughs relation of what I had described to him, and oft examined me vpon the same. Hee asked mee the cause of our comming, I tolde him being in fight with the Spaniards our enemie, being ouer powred, neare put to retreat, and by extreame weather put to this shore, where landing at Chesipiack, the people shot vs, but at Kequoughtan they kindly vsed vs, we by signes demaunded fresh water, they described vs by the Riuer was all fresh water, at Paspahegh, also they kindly vsed vs, our Pinasse being leake wee were infoxed to

Eer

gg. [ll. 2–3]. "Topahanock"; in margin, "Rappahannock ffl:" (for "Fl:" Latin *flumen*, "river").

hh. [l. 5]. "Nantaugs tacum," which should be one word, as should "Cuttata women" and "Marraugh tacum," above; in margin, "[Na?]ntsattaqunt" (cf. "Nonsowhaticond" in Ra[l]phe Hamor, *A True Discourse Of The Present Estate Of Virginia . . .* [London, 1615], 54).

next day we departed.[120] This River of Topahanock seemeth in   **[C1ᵛ]**
breadth not much lesse then that we dwell upon. At the mouth of
the River is a Countrey called Cuttatawomen; upwards is Mar-
raughtacum, Tapohanock, Appamatuck, and Nantaugstacum; at
Topmanahocks, the head issuing from many Mountaines.[121] The
next night I lodged at a hunting town of Powhatans, and the next
day arrived at Werowocomoco upon the river of Pamauncke, where
the great king is resident: by the way we passed by the top of another
little river, which is betwixt the two, called Payankatank. The most
of this Countrey though Desert, yet exceeding fertil, good timber,
most hils and dales, in each valley a cristall spring. [. . . ?][122]

Arriving at Werawocomoco,[123] their Emperour proudly lying
uppon a Bedstead a foote high upon tenne or twelve Mattes, richly
hung with manie Chaynes of great Pearles about his necke, and
covered with a great Covering of *Rahaughcums*:[124] At his heade sat a
woman, at his feete another, on each side sitting uppon a Matte
uppon the ground were raunged his chiefe men on each side the fire,
tenne in a ranke, and behinde them as many yong women, each a
great Chaine of white Beades over their shoulders, their heades
painted in redde, and [he] with such a grave and Majesticall countenance, as drave me into admiration to see such state in a naked
Salvage, [. . .][125] hee kindly welcomed me with good wordes, and
great Platters of sundrie Victuals, assuring mee his friendship, and
my libertie within foure dayes; hee much delighted in Opechancanoughs relation of what I had described to him, and oft examined
me upon the same.[126] Hee asked mee the cause of our comming; I
tolde him, being in fight with the Spaniards our enemie, beeing over
powred, neare put to retreat, and by extreame weather put to this
shore, where landing at Chesipiake, the people shot us, but at
Kequoughtan they kindly used us; we by signes demaunded fresh
water; they described us up the River was all fresh water; at Paspahegh, also they kindly used us; our Pinnasse being leake[127] wee were
enforced to

ii. [l. 14]. "Weramocomoco," with an ink blot over the first *m* in an obvious attempt
to correct it to *w*; however, "Waranacomoco" was allowed to stand in l. 8, above.

jj. [ll. 17–22]. In margin, "[M]ade of A beast [call?]ed a Raracoone [, the?] skinne
very well [dress?]ed and arty[fic]ially sowed to[get]hur" (see Barbour, "Earliest Reconnaissance," Pt. II, 32, s.v. "aroughcun").

Newes from Virginia.

ſtay to mend her, till Captaine Newport my father came to
conduct vs away. He demaunded why we went further with
our Boate, I tolde him, in that I would haue occaſion to
talke of the backe Sea, that on the other ſide the mainc, where
was ſalt water, my father had a childe ſlaine, whiche wee
ſuppoſed Menocan his enemie had done whoſe death we intended to reuenge.

After good deliberation, hee began to deſcribe mee the
Countreys beyonde the Falles, with many of the reſt, confirming what not onely Opechancanoyes, and an Indian
which had beene priſoner to Powhatan had before tolde mee,
but ſome called it fiue dayes, ſome ſixe, ſome eight, where the
ſayde water daſhed amongeſt many ſtones and rockes, each
Roane which cauſed oft tymes the heade of the Riuer to bee
brackiſh: Anchanachuck he deſcribes to bee the people that
had ſlaine my brother, whoſe death hee would reuenge. He
deſcribed alſo vpon the ſame Sea, a mighty Nation called
Pocoughtronack, a fierce Nation that did eate men, and
warred with the people of Moyaoncer, and Patoromerke,
Nations vpon the toppe of the heade of the Bay, vnder his
territories, where the yeare before they had ſlain an hundred,
he ſignified their crownes were ſhauen, long haire in the necke,
tied on a knot, Swords like Pollaxes.

Beyond them he deſcribed people with ſhort Coates, and
Sleeues to the Elbowes, that paſſed that way in Shippes
like ours. Many kingdomes hee deſcribed mee to the heads
of the Bay, which ſeemed to bee a mightie Riuer, iſſuing
from mightie Mountaines betwixt the two Seas, the people
cloathed at Ocamahowan. He alſo confirmed, and the Southerly Countries alſo, as the reſt, that reported vs to be within a
dz. e a halfe of Mangoge, two dayes of Chawwonock, 6. ſtō
Roonock, to the ſouth part of the backe ſea: he deſcribed a countrie called Anone, where they haue abundance of Braſſe,
and houſes walled as ours. I requited his diſcourſe, ſeeing what pride hee had in his great and ſpacious Dominions, ſeeing that all hee knewe were vnder his Territories.

stay to mend her, till Captaine Newport my father came to conduct us away. He demaunded why we went further with our Boate; I tolde him, in that I would have occasion to talke of the backe Sea, that on the other side the maine, where was salt water, my father had a childe slaine, whiche wee supposed Monocan his enemie had done[128] whose death we intended to revenge.

After good deliberation, hee began to describe mee the Countreys beyonde the Falles, with many of the rest, confirming what not onely Opechancanoyes, and an Indian which had beene prisoner to Powhatan had before tolde mee, but some called it five dayes, some sixe, some eight, where the sayde water dashed amongest many stones and rockes, each storme which caused oft tymes the heade of the River to bee brackish:[129] Anchanachuck[130] he described to bee the people that had slaine my brother, whose death hee would revenge. Hee described also upon the same Sea a mighty Nation called Pocoughtronack,[131] a fierce Nation that did eate men, and warred with the people of Moyaoncer, and Pataromerke,[132] Nations upon the toppe of the heade of the Bay, under his territories, where the yeare before they had slain an hundred; he signified their crownes were shaven, long haire in the necke, tied on a knot, Swords like Pollaxes.[133]

Beyond them he described people with short Coates, and Sleeves to the Elbowes, that passed that way in Shippes like ours. Many Kingdomes hee described mee to the heade of the Bay, which seemed to bee a mightie River, issuing from mightie Mountaines betwixt the two Seas. The people cloathed at Ocanahonan he also confirmed, and the Southerly Countries also, as the rest, that reported us to be within a day and a halfe of Mangoge, two dayes of Chawwonock, 6. from Roanoke, to the south part of the backe sea: he described a countrie called Anone, where they have abundance of Brasse, and houses walled as ours. I requited his discourse, seeing what pride hee had in his great and spacious Dominions, seeing that all hee knewe were under his Territories.[134]

Newes from Virginia.

In deſcribing to him the territozies of Europe, which was ſubiect to our great Ring whoſe ſubiect I was, the innumerable multitude of his ſhips, I gaue him to vnderſtand the noyſe of Trumpets, and terrible manner of fighting were vnder captain Newport my father, whom I intituled the Meworames which they call Ring of all the waters, at his greatneſſe hee admired, and not a little feared : hee deſired mee to forſake Paſpaliegh, and to liue with him vpon his Riuer, a Countrie called Capa Howaſicke : hee pzomiſed to giue me Cozne, Ueniſon, oz what I wanted to ſaue vs, Hatchets and Copper wee ſhould make him, and none ſhould diſturbe vs. This requeſt I pzomiſed to pzfozme : and thus hauing with all the kindnes hee could deuiſe, ſought to content me : hee ſent me home with 4. men, one that vſually carried my Gowne and Knapſacke after me, two other loded with bzead, and one to accompanie me.

This Riuer of Pamaunke is not paſt twelue mile from that we dwell on, his courſe nozthweſt, and weſterly, as the other. Weraocomoco, is vpon ſalt water, in bzedth two myles, and ſo keepeth his courſe without any tarrying ſome twenty miles, where at the parting of the freſh water and the ſalt, it diuideth it ſelfe into two partes, the one part to Goughland, as bzoad as Thames, and nauigable, with a Boate thzeeſcoze oz foureſcoze miles, and with a Shippe fiftie, exceeding crooked, and manie low grounds and mariſhes, but inhabited with aboundance of warlike and tall people. The Countrey of Youghtomam, of no leſſe wozth, onely it is lower, but all the ſoyle, a fatte, fertill, ſandie ground. Aboue Manapacumter, many high ſandie Mountaines. By the Riuer is many Rockes, ſeeming if not of ſeuerall Mines : The other bzanch a little leſſe in bzeadth, yet extendeth not neare ſo farre, noz ſo well inhabited, ſomewhat lower, and a white ſandie, and a white clay ſoyle : here is their beſt Terra Sigillata : The mouth of the Riuer, as I ſee in the diſcouerie therof with captain Newport, is halfe a mile bzoad, & within foure miles not aboue a Masket ſhot : the channell exceeding god and deepe, the Riuer ſtraight to the deuiſions. Kiskirk the neareſt Nation to the entrances.

Their

In describing to him the territories of Europe, which was sub- **[C2ᵛ]**
ject to our great King whose subject I was, [and] the innumerable
multitude of his ships, I gave him to understand the noyse of Trumpets, and terrible manner of fighting were under captain Newport
my father, whom I intituled the Meworames which they call King
of all the waters.[135] At his greatnesse hee admired, and not a little
feared: hee desired mee to forsake Paspahegh, and to live with him
upon his River, a Countrie called Capahowasicke: hee promised to
give me Corne, Venison, or what I wanted to feede us, Hatchets and
Copper wee should make him, and none should disturbe us. This
request I promised to performe: and thus having with all the kindnes
hee could devise, sought to content me: hee sent me home with 4.
men, one that usually carried my Gowne and Knapsacke after me,
two other loded with bread, and one to accompanie me.[136]

   This River of Pamaunke is not past twelve mile[137] from that we
dwell on, his course northwest and westerly, as the other. Weraocomoco is upon salt water, in bredth two myles, and so keepeth his
course without any tarrying some twenty miles, where at the parting
of the fresh water and the salt, it divideth it selfe into two partes, the
one part to Goughland, as broad as Thames, and navigable, with a
Boate threescore or fourescore miles, and with a Shippe fiftie, exceeding crooked, and manie low grounds and marishes, but inhabited
with aboundance of warlike and tall people. The Countrey of
Youghtanand, of no lesse worth, onely it is lower, but all the soyle,
a fatte, fertill, sandie ground. Above Menapacunt, many high sandie
Mountaines. By the River is many Rockes, seeming if not of severall
Mines: The other branch a little lesse in breadth, yet extendeth not
neare so farre, nor so well inhabited; somewhat lower, and a white
sandie, and a white clay soyle: here is their best Terra Sigillata:[138]
The mouth of the River, as I see in the discoverie therof with captain
Newport, is halfe a mile broad, and within foure miles not above a
Masket shot:[139] the channell exceeding good and deepe, the River
straight to the devisions. Kiskirk[140] the nearest Nation to the
entrances.

Newes from Virginia.

Their religion and Ceremonie I obſerued was thus: thre oꝛ foure dayes after my taking ſeuen of them in the houſe where I lay, each with a rattle began at ten a clocke in the moꝛning to ſing about the fire, which they inuironed with a Circle of meale, and after a foote oꝛ two from that, at the end of each ſong, layde downe two oꝛ thꝛee graines of wheate, continuing this oꝛder till they haue incloſed ſixe oꝛ ſeuen hundꝛed in a halfe Circle, and after that two oꝛ thꝛee moꝛe Circles in like maner, a hand bꝛedth from other: that done, at each ſong, they put betwixt euerie thꝛee, two oꝛ fiue graines, a little ſticke, ſo counting as an old woman her Pater noſter.

One diſguiſed with a great Skinne, his head hung round with little Skinnes of Weaſels, and other vermine, with a Crownet of feathers on his head, painted as vgly as the diuell, at the end of each ſong will make many ſignes and demonſtrations, with ſtrange and vehement actions, great cakes of Deare ſuet, Deare, and Tobacco he caſteth in the fire, till ſixe a clocke in the Euening, their howling would continue ere they would depart. Each moꝛning in the coldeſt froſt, the pꝛincipall to the number of twentie oꝛ thirtie, aſſembled themſelues in a rouud circle, a good diſtance from the towne, where they told me they there conſulted where to hunt the next day: ſo fat they fed mee, that I much doubted they intended to haue ſacrificed mee to the Quiyoughquoſicke, which is a ſuperiour power they woꝛſhip, a moꝛe vglier thing cannot be deſcribed: one they haue foꝛ chief ſacrifices, which alſo they call Quiyoughquoſick: to cure the ſick, a man with a Rattle, and extreame howling, ſhowting, ſinging, and ſuch biolent geſtures, and Anticke actions ouer the patient will ſucke out blood and flegme from the patient out of their vnable ſtomacke, oꝛ any diſeaſed place, as no labour will moꝛe tire them, Tobacco they offer the water in paſſing in fowle weather. The death of any they lament with great ſoꝛrow and weeping: their Kings they burie betwixt two mattes within their houſes, with all his beads, iewels, hatchets, and copper: the other in graues like ours. They acknowledge no reſurrection. Powhatan hath thꝛee bꝛethꝛen, and two ſiſters, each of his bꝛe-

C 2

Their religion and Ceremonie I observed was thus:[141] three or **[C3ʳ]**
foure dayes after my taking seven of them in the house where I lay,
each with a rattle began at ten a clocke in the morning to sing about
the fire, which they invironed with a Circle of meale, and after, a
foote or two from that, at the end of each song, layde downe two or
three graines of wheate, continuing this order till they have included
six or seven hundred in a halfe Circle, and after that two or three
more Circles in like maner, a hand bredth from other: That done,
at each song, they put betwixt everie three, two or five graines, a
little sticke, so counting as an old woman her Pater noster.

One disguised with a great Skinne, his head hung round with
little Skinnes of Weasels, and other vermine, with a Crownet of
feathers on his head, painted as ugly as the divell, at the end of each
song will make many signes and demonstrations, with strange and
vehement actions; great cakes of Deere suet, Deare, and Tobacco he
casteth in the fire. Till sixe a clocke in the Evening, their howling
would continue ere they would depart. Each morning in the coldest
frost, the principall to the number of twentie or thirtie, assembled
themselves in a round circle, a good distance from the towne, where
they told me they there consulted where to hunt the next day: so fat
they fed mee, that I much doubted they intended to have sacrificed
mee to the *Quiyoughquosicke*, which is a superiour power they worship; a more uglier thing cannot be described: one they have for
chief sacrifices, which also they call *Quiyoughquosick*:[142] to cure the
sick, a man with a Rattle and extreame howling, showting, singing,
and such violent gestures, and Anticke actions over the patient will
sucke out blood and flegme from the patient out of their unable[143]
stomacke, or any diseased place, as no labour will more tire them.
Tobacco they offer [to] the water in passing in fowle weather. The
death of any they lament with great sorrow and weeping: their Kings
they burie betwixt two mattes within their houses, with all his beads,
jewels, hatchets, and copper: the other in graves like ours. They
acknowledge no resurrection.[144]

Powhatan hath three brethren, and two sisters, each of his bre-

---

kk. [l. 35]. After "ours" an "x" calls attention to a marginal annotation (l. 27 to
bottom of page): "This Author I fy[nde] in many errors w[hich?] they doe impute to
h[is?] not well understa[n]dinge the language[,] for they doe Ackno[w]ledge both
God [&] the Devill and that af[ter] thei are out of this world they shall r[ise?] againe in
anothe[r] world where the[y?] shall live at ea[se] and have great[e] store of bread a[nd]
venison and other [???]." While Strachey supports the annotator (*Historie*, 100), it is
doubtful that the English were capable, linguistically or philosophically, of understanding the Indians' religion (see John Rolfe, in Samuel Purchas, *Purchas his Pilgrimage. Or
Relations Of The World . . .* , 3d ed. [London, 1617], 952).

Newes from Virginia.

therein succeeded other.

For the Crowne, their heyres inherite not, but the first heyres of the Sisters, and so successiuely the weomens heires: For the Kings haue as many weomen as they will, his Subiects two, and most but one.

From Weramocomoco is but 12. miles, yet the Indians trifled away that day, and would not goe to our Forte by any perswasions : but in certaine olde hunting houses of Paspahegh we lodged all night. The next morning ere Sunne rise, we set forward for our Fort, where we arriued within an houre, where each man with the truest signes of ioy they could expresse welcommed mee, except M. Archer, and some 2. or 3. of his, who was then in my absence, sworne Counsellour, though not with the consent of Captaine Martin: great blame and imputation was laide vpon mee by them, for the losse of our two men which the Indians slew: insomuch that they purposed to depose me, but in the midst of my miseries, it pleased God to send Captaine Nuport, who arriuing there the same night, so tripled our ioy, as for a while these plots against mee were deferred, though with much malice against me, which captain Newport in short time did plainly see. Now was maister Scriuener, captaine Martin, and my selfe, called Counsellers.

Within fiue or sire dayes after the arriuall of the Ship, by a mischaunce our Fort was burned, and the most of our apparell, lodging and priuate prouision, many of our old men diseased, and of our new for want of lodging perished. The Empereur Powhatan each weeke once or twice sent me many presents of Deare, bread Raugroughcuns, halfe alwayes for my father, whom he much desired to see, and halfe for me: and so continually importuned by messengers and presents, that I would come to fetch the corne, and take the Countrie their king had giuen me, as at last Captaine Newport resolued to go see him. Such acquaintance I had amongst the Indians, and such confidence they had in me, as neare the Fort they would not come till I came to them, euery of them calling mee by my name, would not sell any thing till I had first receiued their presents, and what

they

theren succeeded other. For the Crowne, their heyres inherite not, **[C3ᵛ]**
but the first heyres of the Sisters, and so successively the weomens
heires: For the Kings have as many weomen as they will, his Subjects
two, and most but one.

From Weramocomoco is but 12. miles, yet the Indians trifled
away that day, and would not goe to our Forte by any perswasions:
but in certaine olde hunting houses of Paspahegh we lodged all
night.[145] The next morning ere Sunne rise, we set forward for our
Fort, where we arrived within an houre, where each man with the
truest signes of joy they could expresse welcommed mee, except
Master Archer and some 2. or 3. of his, who was then, in my absence,
sworne Counsellour, though not with the consent of Captaine
Martin:[146] great blame and imputation was laide upon mee by them
for the losse of our two men which the Indians slew, insomuch that
they purposed to depose me;[147] but in the midst of my miseries, it
pleased God to send Captaine Nuport, who arriving there the same
night,[148] so tripled our joy, as for a while these plots against me were
deferred, though with much malice against me, which captain Newport in short time did plainly see. Now was maister Scrivener,[149]
captaine Martin, and my selfe, called Counsellers.

Within five or six dayes after the arrivall of the Ship, by a mischaunce our Fort was burned,[150] and the most of our apparell, lodging and private provision, many of our old men diseased,[151] and of
our new for want of lodging perished. The Emperour Powhatan
each weeke once or twice sent me many presents of Deare, bread,
Raugroughcuns,[152] halfe alwayes for my father, whom he much desired
to see, and halfe for me: and so continually importuned by messengers and presents, that I would come to fetch the corne, and take
the Countrie their King had given me, as at last Captaine Newport
resolved to go see him.[153] Such acquaintance I had amongst the
Indians, and such confidence they had in me, as neare the Fort they
would not come till I came to them, every of them calling me by my
name, would not sell any thing till I had first received their presents,
and what

Newes from Virginia.

they had that I liked, they deferred to my diseretion: but after
acquaintance, they vfually came into the Fort at their plea-
fure: The Prefident, and the reft of the Councell, they knewe
not, but Captaine Newports greatneffe I had fo deferibed, as
they conceyued him the chiefe, the reft his childzen, Officers, and
feruants. We had agreed with ye king of Paſpahegh, to conduct
two of our men to a place called Panawicke beyond Reonok,
where he repozted many men to be apparelled. We landed
him at Warraskoyack, where playing the villaine, and dela-
ting vs fo2 rewards, retorned within thze o2 loure dayes after
without going forther. Captaine Newport, maifter Scriuener, and my felfe, found the mouth of Pamaunck river, some
25 o2 30. miles nozthward from Cape Herrie, the chanell
good as befoze expzeffed.

Arriuing at Weramocomoca, being iealous of the intent of
this politick faluage, to difcouer his intent the better, I with 20.
fhot armed in Jacks went afhoze, the Bay where he dwelleth
hath in it 3 cricks, and a mile and a halfe from the chanel all of,
being conducted to the towne, I found my felfe mistaken in the
cracke, fo2 they al there were within leffe then a mile, the Empe-
ro2s fonne called Naukaquawis, the captaine that tooke me, and
diuerfe others of his chiefe men conducted me to their kings habitation: but in the mid way I was intercepted by a great creek
ouer which they had made a bzidge of grained ftakes & railes,
the king of Kiskieck, and Namontack, who all the iourney the
king had fent to guide vs, had conducted vs this paffage, which
caufed me to fufpect fome mifchiefe: the barge I had fent to meet
me at the right landing, when I found my felfe firft deceyued,
and knowing by experience the moft of their courages to p2o-
cæde from others feare, thcugh fewe lyked the paffage, I intermingled the kings fonne, our conductozs, and his chiefe men
amongft ours, and led fozward, leauing halfe at the one ende
to make a guard fo2 the paffage of the Front. The Indians
fæing the weakeneffe of the Bzidge, came with a Canow, and
tooke me in of the middeft with foure o2 fiue moze, being landed
wee made a guard fo2 the reft till all were paffed, two in
a ranke

they had that I liked, they deferred to my discretion: but after acquaintance, they usually came into the Fort at their pleasure: The
President, and the rest of the Councell, they knewe not, but Captaine
Newports greatnesse I had so described, as they conceyved him the
chiefe, the rest his children, Officers, and servants. We had agreed
with the king of Paspahegh to conduct two of our men to a place
called Panawicke,[154] beyond Roanoke, where he reported many men
to be apparelled. [. . .] Wee landed him at Warraskoyack, where
playing the villaine, and deluding us for rewards, [he] returned
within three or foure dayes after without going further.

Captaine Newport, maister Scrivener, and my selfe, found the
mouth of Pamuncks river, some 25. or 30. miles northward from
Cape Henrie,[155] the chanell good as before expressed.

Arriving at Weramocomoca, being jealous[156] of the intent of
this politick[157] salvage, to discover his intent the better, I with 20.
shot armed in Jacks[158] went a shore; the Bay where he dwelleth hath
in it 3. cricks, and a mile and a halfe from the chanel all os.[159] Being
conducted to the towne, I found my selfe mistaken in the creeke, for
they al there were within lesse then a mile; the Emperors sonne called
Naukaquawis,[160] the captaine that tooke me, and diverse others of
his chiefe men, conducted me to their kings habitation, but in the
mid way I was intercepted by a great creek over which they had
made a bridge of grained stakes[161] and railes. The king of Kiskieck,
and Namontack, who all the journey the king had sent to guide us,
had conducted us this passage, which caused me to suspect some mischiefe: the barge I had sent to meet me at the right landing, when I
found my selfe first deceyved, and knowing by experience the most
of their courages to proceede from others feare, though fewe lyked
the passage, I intermingled the Kings sonne, our conductors, and his
chiefe men amongst ours, and led forward, leaving halfe at the one
ende to make a guard for the passage of the Front.[162] The Indians,
seeing the weaknesse of the Bridge, came with a Canow, and tooke
me in of the middest with foure or five more, being landed wee made
a guard for the rest till all were passed. Two in

Newes from Virginia.

a ranke we marched to the Emperors house. Before his house stood fortie or fiftie great Platters of fine bread, being entred the house, with loude tunes they all made signes of great ioy. This proude saluage, hauing his finest women, and the principall of his chiefe men assembled, sate in rankes as before is expressed, himselfe as vpon a Throne at the vpper ende ot the house, with such a Maiestie as I cannot expresse, nor yet haue often seene, either in Pagan or Christian, with a kinde countenance hee bad mee welcome, and caused a place to bee made by himselfe to sit, I presented him a sute of red cloath, a white Greyhound, and a Hatte, as Iewels he esteemed them, and with a great Oration made by three of his Nobles) if there be any amongst Saluages) kindly accepted them, with a publike confirmation of a perpetuall league and friendship.

After that, he commaunded the Queene of Apamatuc, a comely yeng Saluage, to giue me water, a Turkie-cocke, and breade to eate : being thus feasted, hee began his discourse to this purpose. Your kinde visitation doth much content mee, but where is your father whom I much desire to see, is he not with you. I told him he remained aboord, but the next day he would come vnto him, with a merrie countenance he asked me for certaine peeces I which promised him, when I went to Paspahegh, I told according to my promise, that I proffered the man that went with me foure Demy Culuerings, in that he so desired a great Gunne, but they refused to take them, whereat with a lowde laughter, he desired to giue him some of lesse burthen, as for the other I gaue him them, being sure that none could carrie them : but where are these men you promised to come with you, I told him without, who therevpon gaue order to haue them brought in, two after two, euer maintaining the guard without. And as they presented themselues euer with thankes, he would salute me, and caused each of them to haue foure or fiue pound of bread giuen them. This done, I asked him for the corne and ground he promised me. He told me I should haue it, but he expected to haue all these men lay their armes at his feet, as did his subiects. I tolde him that was a ceremonie our enemies

ll

ll. [ll. 12–13]. "Nobles, if there be any amongst Salvages, kindly"; the commas are inked over by parentheses, perhaps for greater emphasis as was then a common practice.

a ranke we marched to the Emperors house. Before his house stood   **[C4ᵛ]**
fortie or fiftie great Platters of fine bread; being entred the house,
with loude tunes they all made signes of great joy. This proude
salvage, having his finest women, and the principall of his chiefe men
assembled, sate in rankes as before is expressed, himselfe as upon a
Throne at the upper ende of the house, with such a Majestie as I
cannot expresse, nor yet have often seene, either in Pagan or Christian; with a kinde countenance hee bad mee welcome, and caused a
place to bee made by himselfe to sit. I presented him a sute of red
cloath, a white Greyhound, and a Hatte; as Jewels he esteemed
them, and with a great Oration made by three of his Nobles, if there
be any amongst Salvages, kindly accepted them, with a publike confirmation of a perpetuall league and friendship.

    After that, he commaunded the Queene of Appomattoc, a
comely yong Salvage, to give me water, a Turkie-cocke, and breade
to eate: being thus feasted, hee began his discourse to this purpose.[163]

Your kinde visitation doth much content mee, but where is your
father whom I much desire to see, is he not with you.

I told him he remained aboord, but the next day he would come unto
him; with a merrie countenance he asked me for certaine peeces
which I promised him, when I went to Paspahegh. I told [him]
according to my promise, that I proffered the man that went with
me foure Demy Culverings,[164] in that he so desired a great Gunne,
but they refused to take them; whereat with a lowde laughter, he
desired [me] to give him some of lesse burthen, as for the other I gave
him them, being sure that none could carrie them: [. . .][165]

But where are these men you promised to come with you.

I told him without, who[166] therupon gave order to have them brought
in, two after two, ever maintaining the guard without. And as they
presented themselves ever with thankes, he would salute me, and
caused each of them to have foure or five pound of bread given them.
This done, I asked him for the corne and ground he promised me.
He told me I should have it, but he expected to have all these men
lay their armes at his feet, as did his subjects. I tolde him that was a
ceremonie our ene-

Newes from Virginia.

mies defired, but neuer our friends, as we prefented our felues vnto him, yet that he fhould not doubt of our friend-fhip: the next day my father would giue him a child of his, in full affurance of our loues, and not only that, but when he fhould thinke it conuenient, wée would deliuer vnder his fubiection the Country of Manacam and Pocoughtao-nack his enemies.

This fo contented him, as immediatly with attentiue filence, with a lewd oration he proclaimed me Awerowanes of Powhaton, and that all his fubiects fhould fo efféeme vs, and no man account vs ftrangers nor Paipaheghans, but Powhatans, and that the Cozas, weomen and Country, fhould be to vs as to his owne people: this proffered kindnes for many reafons we contemned not, but with the beft Languages and fignes of thankes I could expreffe, I tooke my leaue.

The King rifing from his feat, conducted me foorth, and caufed each of my men to haue as much mere bread as hée could beare: giuing me fome in a bafket, & as much he fent a board for a prefent to my Father: victuals you muft know is all there wealth, and the greateft kindnes they could fhew vs: arriuing at the Riuer, the Barge was fallen fo lowe with the ebbe, though I had giuen order and oft fent to preuent the fame, yet the meffengers deceiued me, the Skies being very thicke and rainie, the King vnderftanding this mif-chance, fent his Sonne and Mamontacke, to conduct mée to a great houfe fufficient to lodge mée, where entring I faw it hung round with bowes and arrowes.

The Indians vfed all diligence to make vs fires, & giue vs content: the kings Orators prefently entertained vs with a kinde oration, with expreffe charge that not any fhould fteale, or take out bowes or arrowes, or offer any iniury.

Prefently after he fent me a quarter of Venizon to ftay my ftomacke: in the euening hee fent for me to come onely

D.   with

mies desired, but never our friends, as we presented our selves unto **[Dı^r]**
him, yet that he should not doubt of our friendship: the next day my
Father would give him a child of his, in full assurance of our loves,
and not only that, but when he should thinke it convenient, wee
would deliver under his subjection the Country of Manacam and
Pocoughtaonack his enemies.[167]

This so contented him, as immediatly with attentive silence, with
a lowd oration he proclaimed me a werowanes of Powhatan, and that
all his subjects should so esteeme us, and no man account us strangers
nor Paspaheghans, but Powhatans, and that the Corne, weomen
and Country, should be to us as to his owne people: this proffered
kindnes for many reasons we contemned not, but with the best languages and signes of thankes I could expresse, I tooke my leave.

The King, rising from his seat, conducted me foorth, and caused
each of my men to have as much more bread as hee could beare,
giving me some in a basket, and as much he sent a board for a present
to my Father: victuals you must know is all there wealth, and the
greatest kindnes they could shew us: arriving at the River, the Barge
was fallen so low with the ebbe, [. . .]¹⁶⁸ though I had given order
and oft sent to prevent the same, yet the messengers deceived mee.
The Skies being very thicke and rainie, [. . .]¹⁶⁹ the King understanding this mischance, sent his Sonne and Namontack, to conduct mee
to a great house sufficient to lodge mee, where entring I saw it hung
round with bowes and arrowes.

The Indians used all diligence to make us fires, and give us content: the kings Orators presently entertained us with a kinde oration,
with expresse charge that not any should steale, or take out bowes
or arrowes, or offer any injury. [. . .]¹⁷⁰

Presently after he sent me a quarter of Venizon to stay my
stomacke: in the evening hee sent for mee to come onely

Newes from Virginia.

with two that with me : the company I gaue order to stand vpon their guard, & to maintaine two sentries at the ports all night. To my supper he set before me meate for twenty men, & seeing I could not eate, hee caused it to be giuen to my men : for this is a generall custome, that what they giue, not to take againe, but you must either eate it, giue it away, or carry it with you : two or three houres we spent in our auncient discourses, which done, I was with a fire stick lighted to my lodging.

The next day the King conducting mee to the Riuer, shewed me his Canowes , and described vnto me how hee sent them ouer the Baye, for tribute Beades: and also what Countries paide him Beads, Copper or Skins. But seeing Captaine Nuport , and Maister Scriuener , comming a shore, the King returned to his house, and I went to mete him, with a trumpet before him , wee marched to the King: who after his old manner kindly receiued him , especially a Boy of thirteen yeares old, called Thomas Saluage, whom he gaue him as his Sonne : he requited this kindnes with each of vs a great basket of Beanes, and entertaining him with the former discourse, we passed away that day, and a greed to bargaine the next day, and so returned to our Pinnis : the next day comming a shore in like order, the King hauing kindly entertained vs with a breakfast, questioned with vs in this manner.

Why we came armed in that sort, seeing hee was our friend, and had neither bowes nor arrowes, what did wee doubt : I told him it was the custome of our Country , not doubting of his kindnes any waies , wherewith though hee semed satisfied, yet Captaine Nuport caused all our men to retire to the water side, which was some thirtie score from thence: but to preuent the worst, Maister Scriuener or I were either the one or other by the Barge, experience had well taught me to beleeue his friendship, till conuenient opportunity suffered him to betray vs , but quickly this politi-
tian

with two shot with me: the company I gave order to stand upon their **[D1ᵛ]**
guard, and to maintaine two sentries at the ports[171] all night. To my
supper he set before me meate for twenty men, and seeing I could not
eate, hee caused it to be given to my men: for this is a generall
custome, that what they give, not to take againe, but you must either
eate it, give it away, or carry it with you: two or three houres we spent
in our aunciant[172] discourses, which done, I was with a fire stick
lighted to my lodging.

The next day the King, conducting mee to the River, shewed
me his Canowes, and described unto me how hee sent them over the
Baye, for tribute Beades, and also what Countries paide him Beads,
Copper or Skins. But seeing Captaine Nuport, and Maister Scrivener,
comming a shore, the King returned to his house, and I went to
meete him.[173] With a trumpet[174] before him, wee marched to the
King: who after his old manner kindly received him, especially a
Boy of thirteen yeares old, called Thomas Salvage, whom he gave
him as his Sonne: he requited this kindnes with each of us a great
basket of Beanes, and entertaining him with the former discourse,
we passed away that day, and agreed to bargaine the next day, and
so returned to our Pinnis: the next day comming a shore in like order,
the King having kindly entertained us with a breakfast, questioned
with us in this manner.

Why we came armed in that sort, seeing hee was our friend, and
had neither bowes nor arrowes, what did wee doubt? I told him it
was the custome of our Country, not doubting of his kindnes any
waies. Wherewith, though hee seemed satisfied, yet Captaine Nuport
caused all our men to retire to the water side, which was some thirtie
score[175] from thence: but to prevent the worst, Maister Scrivener or
I were either the one or other by the Barge. Experience had well
taught me to beleeve his friendship, till convenient opportunity
suffred him to betray us; but quickly this politi-

Newes from Virginia.

tian had perceiued my absence, and cunningly sent for ma;
I sent for Maister Scriuener to supply my place, the King
would demaund for him, I would againe releeue him, and
they sought to satisfie our suspition with kind Language, and
not being agreed to trade for corne, hee desired to see all our
Hatchets and Copper together, for which he would giue vs
corne, with that auncient tricke the Chickahominiens had
oft acquainted me: his offer I refused, offering first to see
what hee would giue for one piece, hee seeming to despise the
nature of a Merchant, did scorne to sell, but we freely should
giue him, and he liberally would requite vs.

Captaine Nuport would not with lesse then twelue great
Coppers try his kindnes, which he liberally requited with
as much corne as at Chickahmania, I had for one of lesse
proportion: our Hatchets hee would also haue at his owne
rate, for which kindnes hee much seemed to affect Captaine
Nuport, some few bunches of blew Beades I had, which he
much desired, and seeing so few, he offered me a basket of two
peckes, and that which I drew to bee it 2x peckes at the least,
and yet seemed contented and desired more: I agreed with
him the next day for two bushells, for ye ebbe now constrained vs to returne to our Boate, although he earnestly desired vs to stay dinner which was a prouiding, and being ready he sent aboard after vs, which was bread and ven zon,
sufficient for fiftie or sixtie persons.

The next day hee sent his Sonne in the morning not to
bring a shore with vs any pieces, least his wromen and children should feare. Captaine Nuports good beliefe would
haue satissfied that request, yet twentie or twentie fiue shot
we got a shore: the King importuning mee to leaue my
armes a board, much misliking my sword, pistol and target,
I told him the men that slew my Brother with the like
tearmes had perswaded me, and being vnarmed shot at vs,
and so betraide vs.

He oft entreated Captaine Nuport that his men might
D 2   leaue

mm   *Virginia Barmudas*

mm. [bottom of page]. The words "Virginia Barmudas" are inscribed below the signature in a bold secretary hand, without apparent pertinence.

tian[176] had perceived my absence, and cunningly sent for mee; I **[D2ʳ]**
sent for Maister Scrivener to supply my place, the King would demaund for him, I would againe releeve him, and they sought to
satisfie our suspition with kind Language, [. . .][177] and not being
agreed to trade for corne, hee desired to see all our Hatchets and
Copper together, for which he would give us corne; with that
auncient tricke the Chickahomaniens had oft acquainted me: his
offer I refused, offering first to see what hee would give for one piece.
Hee seeming to despise the nature of a Merchant, did scorne to sell,
but we freely should give him, and he liberally would requite us.

   Captaine Nuport would not with lesse then twelve great Coppers[178] try his kindnes, which he liberally requited with as much
corne as at Chickahamania, I had for one of lesse proportion: our
Hatchets hee would also have at his owne rate, for which kindnes hee
much seemed to affect Captaine Nuport. Some few bunches of blew
Beades I had, which he much desired, and seeing so few, he offred
me a basket of two pecks, and that which I drew to be three pecks at
the least,[179] and yet [he] seemed contented and desired more: I
agreed with him the next day for two bushells, for the ebbe now constrained us to returne to our Boate, although he earnestly desired us
to stay [for] dinner which was a providing, and being ready he sent
aboard after us, which was bread and venizon, sufficient for fiftie or
sixtie persons.[180]

   The next day hee sent his Sonne in the morning not to bring a
shore with us any pieces, least his weomen and children should feare.
Captaine Nuports good beliefe would have satisfied that request, yet
twentie or twentie five shot we got a shore: the King importuning
mee to leave my armes a board, much misliking my sword, pistol and
target, I told him the men that slew my Brother with the like tearmes
had perswaded me, and being unarmed shot at us, and so betraide
us.

   He oft entreated Captaine Nuport that his men might

Newes from Virginia.

leaue their armes, which still hee commanded to the water ſide, this day we ſpent in trading for blew Beads, and ha-uing neare ſtraigbted our Barge.

Captaine Nuport returned with them that came abord, leauing me and Maiſter Scriuener a ſhore, to follow in Ca-nowes; into one I got with fiue of our men, which being lanched a ſtones caſt from the ſhore ſtuck faſt in the Oſe: Maiſter Scriuener ſeeing this example, with ſeuen or eight more paſſed the dreadfull bridge, thinking to haue found deeper water on the other creeke, but they were infozced to ſtay with ſuch entertainment as a ſaluage, being forced a-ſhore with wind and raine, hauing in his Canow, as com-monly they haue, his houſe and houſhold, inſtantly ſet vp a houſe of mats which ſuccored them from the ſtorme.

The Indians ſeeing me peſtred in the Oſe, called to me, fiue or ſeuen of the Kings chiefe men threw off their ſkins, and to the middle in Oſe, came to bear me out on their heads, their impoztunacie cauſed me better to like the Canow then their curteſie, excuſing my deniall for feare to fall into the Oſe, deſiring them to bring me ſome wood, fire, and mats, to couer me, and I would content them: each preſently gaue his helpe to ſatiſfie my requeſt, which paines a hoꝛſe would ſcarce haue indured, yet a couple of bells richly contented them.

The Emperoꝛs ſent his Seaman Mantiuas in the eue-ning with bread and biſtnall for me and my men, he no moꝛe ſcripulous then the reſt ſeemed to take a pride in ſhewing how litle he regarded that miſerable cold and durty paſſage, though a dogge would ſcarce haue indured it. this kindnes I found, when I litle expected leſſe then a miſchiefe, but the blacke night parting our companies, ere midnight the flud ſerued to carry vs aboard: the next day we came a-ſhore, the King with a ſolemne diſcourſe cauſing all to de-part, but his principall men, and this was the effect when as hee perceiued that we had a deſire to inuade Monacum, a-gainſt

leave their armes, which still hee commanded to the water side, **[D2ᵛ]**
[. . .]¹⁸¹ this day we spent in trading for blew Beads, and having
neare fraighted our Barge. [. . .]¹⁸²

Captaine Nuport returned with them that came abord, leaving
me and Maister Scrivener a shore, to follow in Canowes; into one I
got with sixe of our men, which beeing lanched a stones cast from the
shore stuck fast in the Ose: Maister Scrivener seeing this example,
with seven or eight more passed the dreadfull bridge, thinking to
have found deeper water on the other creeke, but they were inforced
to stay with such entertainment¹⁸³ as a salvage, being forced ashore
with wind and raine, having in his Canow, as commonly they have,
his house and houshold, instantly set up a house of mats which suc-
coured them from the storme.

The Indians seeing me pestred in the Ose, called to me; sixe or
seven of the Kings chiefe men threw off their skins, and to the middle
in Ose, came to bear me out on their heads. Their importunacie
caused me better to like the Canow then their curtesie, excusing my
deniall for feare to fall into the Ose, desiring them to bring me some
wood, fire, and mats, to cover me, and I would content them: each
presently gave his helpe to satisfie my request, which paines a horse
would scarce have indured, yet a couple of bells richly contented
them.

The Emperor sent his Seaman Mantiuas¹⁸⁴ in the evening with
bread and victuall for me and my men; he no more scripulous¹⁸⁵
then the rest seemed to take a pride in shewing how litle he regarded
that miserable cold and durty passage, though a dogge would scarce
have indured it. This kindnes I found, when I litle expected lesse
then a mischiefe, but the blacke night parting our companies, ere
midnight the flood [tide] served to carry us aboard: the next day we
came ashore, the King with a solemne discourse, causing all to depart, but his principall men, [. . .] and this was the effect when as
hee perceived that we had a desire to invade Monacum, a-

Newes from Virginia.

gainſt whom he was no profeſſed enemy, yet thus farre he
would aſſiſt vs in this enterprise: Firſt hee would ſend his
ſpies, perfectly to vnderſtand their ſtrength and ability to
fight, with which he would acquaint vs himſelfe.

Captaine Nuport would not be ſeene in it himſelfe, being great Werowances, they were to ſtay at home, but I,
Maiſter Scriuener, and two of his Sonnes, and Opechan-
kaneugh. The King of Pamaunke ſhould haue 100 of
his men to goe before as though they were hunting, they
giuing vs notiſe where was the aduantage we ſhould kill
them, the weomen and young childzen he wiſhed we ſhould
ſpare, & bzing them to him only 100. oz 150. of cur men he
held ſufficient for this exploit: our boats ſhould ſtay at the
falls, where we might hew timber, which we might conuey
each man a piece till we were paſt the ſtones, and there
ioyne them, to paſſe our men by water, if any were ſhot, his
men ſhould bzing them backe to our boats, this faire tale
had almoſt made Captaine Nuport vndertake, by this
meanes to diſcouer the South ſea, which will not be without treeherie, if we ground our intent vpon his conſtan-
cie.

This day we ſpent in trading, dancing, and much mirth,
the King of Pamaunke ſent his meſſenger, as yet not knowing Captaine Nuport, to come vnto him: who had long
expected mee, deſiring alſo my Father to viſite him : the
meſſenger ſtayed to conduct vs, but Powhatan vnderſtanding that we had Hatchets lately come from Paſpahegh,
deſired the next day to trade with vs, and not to go further.

This new tricke he cunningly put vpon him, but onely
to haue what hee liſted, and to try whether we would go oz
ſtay. Opechankenoughs meſſenger returned that wee
would not come: the next day his Daughter came to entreat
me, ſhewing her Father had hurt his legge, and much ſoz-
rowed he could not ſee me.

gainst whom he was no professed enemy, [...] yet thus farre hee **[D3^r]** would assist us in this enterprise: First hee would send his spies, perfectly to understand their strength and ability to fight, with which he would acquaint us himselfe.[186]

Captaine Nuport would not be seene in it himselfe, being great Werowances, they would stay at home, but I, Maister Scrivener, and two of his Sonnes, and Opechankanough, the King of Pamaunke, should have 100. of his men to goe before as though they were hunting, they giving us notise where was the advantage we should kill them. The weomen and young children he wished we should spare, and bring them to him. Only 100. or 150. of our men he held sufficient for this exploit: our boats should stay at the falls, where we might hew timber, which we might convey each man a piece till we were past the stones, and there joyne them, to passe our men by water; if any were shot, his men should bring them backe to our boats. This faire tale had almost made Captaine Nuport undertake, by this meanes to discover the South sea, which will not be without trecherie, if wee ground our intent upon his constancie.

This day we spent in trading, dancing, and much mirth. The King of Pamaunke sent his messenger, as yet not knowing Captaine Nuport, to come unto him, who had long expected mee, desiring also my Father to visite him: the messenger stayed to conduct us, but Powhatan understanding that we had Hatchets lately come from Paspahegh, desired the next day to trade with us, and [for us] not to go further.[187]

This new tricke he cunningly put upon him, but onely to have what hee listed, and to try whether we would go or stay. Opechankenoughs messenger returned [saying] that wee would not come: the next day his Daughter came to entreate me, shewing her Father had hurt his legge, and much sorrowed he could not see me.

Newes from Virginia.

Captaine Nuport being not to bée perswaded to goe in, that Powhatan had desired vs to stay: sent her away with the like answer, yet the next day vpon better consideration intreatie preuailed, and wee anchored at Cinquoteck the first stwaine about the parting of the riuer, where dwelled two Kings of Pamaunke, Brothers to Powhatan: the one called Opitchapam, the other Kuatough, to these I went a shore, who kindly intreated mée and Maister Scriuener, sending some presents aboard to Captaine Nuport, whilst we were trucking with these Kings.

Opechankanough his wife, wcomen, and children came to méete me with a naturall kind affection, hée séemed to reioyce to sée me.

Captaine Nuport came a shore, with many kind discourses wée passed that forenoone: and after dinner, Captaine Nuport went about with the Pinnis to Menapacant which is twenty miles by water, and not one by land: Opechankanough, conducted me and Maister Scriuener by land, where hauing built a feasting house a purpose to entertaine vs with a kind Oration, after their manner and his best prouision, kindly welcomed vs, that day he would not trucke, but did his best to delight vs with content: Captaine Nuport arriued towards euening, whom the King presented with fiue great platters of fine bread, and Punsaroomanays the next day till noone wee traded: the King feasted all the company, and the afternoone was spent in playing, dauncing, and delight, by no meanes hée would haue vs depart till the next day, he had feasted vs with venison, for which he had sent, hauing spent his first and second prouision in expecting our comming: the next day he performed his promise, giuing more to vs three, then would haue sufficed 30. and in that we carried not away what we left, hée sent it after vs to the Pinnis, with what words or signes of loue hée could expresse, we departed.

Captaine Nuport in the Pinnis, leauing mée in the
                                                    Barge

nn. [l. 7]. "Opitchapam"; in margin, "[O]pochoppam," and just below, "[I?]toyatene." These were two names for the same brother (see the *Generall Historie*, 153 [on Opitchapam] and 125 [on Itopatin, or Itoyatin]).

oo. [l. 11]. "Opechankanough"; in margin, "[A]pachanckano" (see n. u, above).

Captaine Nuport being not to bee perswaded to goe, in that **[D3ᵛ]**
Powhatan had desired us to stay, sent her away with the like answer.
Yet the next day upon better consideration intreatie prevailed, and
wee anchored at Cinquoateck, the first towne above the parting of
the river, where dwelled two Kings of Pamaunke, Brothers to Powhatan: the one called Opitchapam, the other Katatough.[188] To these
I went a shore, who kindly intreated mee and Maister Scrivener,
sending some presents aboard to Captaine Nuport, whilst we were
trucking with these Kings.

Opechankanough his wife, weomen, and children[189] came to
meete me with a naturall kind affection, hee seemed to rejoyce to see
me.

Captaine Nuport came a shore. With many kind discourses wee
passed that forenoone: and after dinner, Captaine Nuport went
about with the Pinnis to Menapacant which is twenty miles by water,
and not one by land:[190] Opechankanough conducted me and Maister
Scrivener by land, where having built a feasting house a purpose to
entertaine us with a kind Oration, after their manner and his best
provision, kindly welcomed us. That day he would not trucke, but
did his best to delight us with content: Captaine Nuport arrived towards evening, whom the King presented with sixe great platters of
fine bread, and *Pansarowmana*.[191] The next day till noone wee traded:
the King feasted all the company, and the afternoone was spent in
playing, dauncing, and delight; by no meanes hee would have us
depart till the next day, he had feasted us with venizon, for which he
had sent, having spent his first and second provision in expecting our
comming: the next day he performed his promise, giving more to us
three, then would have sufficed 30. and in that we carried not away
what we left, hee sent it after us to the Pinnis. With what words or
signes of love he could expresse, we departed.

Captaine Nuport in the Pinnis, leaving mee in the

---

pp. [ll. 24–25]. "Pansarowmana," corrected to read, "Pansaromanans"; in margin,
"Pansaromanans [are?] accounted a very [da]ynty dish amongst [the]m, beeing made
of the [cor]ne when it is greene [boy?]led and so mingled [am]ongst beanes and so [kep]t
all the yeare, which is [wh]en it is boyled very [swe?]ete and wholesom [me?]ate."

Newes from Virginia.

large to digge a rocke, where wee supposd a Mine at
Cinquaoteck, which done,ere midnight I arriued at Weracomoco, where our Pinnis anchored, being 20.miles
from Cinquaorecke, the next day we tooke leaue of Powhatan, who in regard of his kindnes gaue him an Indian,
he well affected to goe with him for England in stead of his
Sonne, ȳ cause I assure me was to know our strength and
Countries condition: ȳ next day we arriued at Kiskiack,the
perple so scornefally entertained vs, as with what signes
of scorne and discontent we could.we departed and returned
to our Fort with 2,0. bushells of Corne, our president being not wholy recouered of his sicknes, in discharging, his
Piece brake and split his hand off, which he is not yet well
recouered.

At Captaine Nuports arriuall,wee were bictualled for
twelue weekes , and hauing furnished him of what hee
thought good, hee set saile for England the tenth of Aprill :
Maister Scriuener and my selfe with our shallop , accompanied him to Captaine Hendrek.

Powhatan hauing for a farewell, sent him fiue or sire
mens loadings, with Turkeyes for swords, which hee sent
him in our return to ȳ fort:we discouered the riuer of Nausamd, a proud warlike Nation, as well we may testified,at
our first arriuall at Chesiapiack: but that iniury Captaine Nuport well reuenged at his returne, where some
of them intising him to their Ambuscadoes by a daunce, hee
perceiuing their intent,with a vally of musket shot , slew
one, and shot one or two more, as themselues confesse, the
King at our ariuall sent for me to come vnto him:I sent him
word what commodities I had to exchange for wheat, and
if he would as had the rest of his Neighbours, conclude a
Peace,we were contented,at last he came downe before the
Boate which rid at anchor some fortie yards from ȳ shore,
he signified to me so come a shore, and sent a Canow with
foure or fiue of his men, two whereof I desired to come a-
board

Barge to digge a rocke,[192] where wee supposed a Mine at Cinquaoteck, [. . .] which done, ere midnight I arrived at Weracomoco,
where our Pinnis anchored, being 20. miles[193] from Cinquaotecke.
The next day we tooke leave of Powhatan, who in regard of his
kindnes gave him an Indian, he well affected[194] to goe with him for
England in steed of his Sonne, the cause I assure me was to know
our strength and countries condition: the next day we arrived at
Kiskiack, the people so scornefully entertained us, as with what
signes of scorne and discontent we could, we departed and returned
to our Fort with 250. bushells of Corne. Our president being not
wholy recovered of his sicknes, in discharging his Piece brake and
split his hand, of which he is not yet well recovered.[195]

At Captaine Nuports arrivall, wee were victualled for twelve
weekes, and having furnished him of what hee thought good, hee set
saile for England the tenth of Aprill:[196] Maister Scrivener and my
selfe with our shallop, accompanied him to Cape Henrie.

Powhatan having for a farrewell, sent him five or sixe mens
loadings, with Turkeyes for swords, which hee sent him in our return
to the fort:[197]

[. . .] we discovered the river of Nansemond,[198] a proud warlike
Nation, as well we may testified,[199] at our first arrivall at Chesiapiack:
but that injury Captaine Nuport well revenged at his returne,[200]
where some of them intising him to their Ambuscadoes by a daunce,
hee perceiving their intent, with a volley of musket shot, slew one,
and shot one or two more, as themselves confesse. The King at our
arivall sent for me to come unto him: I sent him word what commodities I had to exchange for wheat, and if he would, as had the
rest of his Neighbours, conclude a Peace, we were contented. At last
he came downe before the Boate which rid at anchor some fortie
yards from the shore; he signified to me to come a shore, and sent a
Canow with foure or five of his men, two whereof I desired to come a-

Newes from Virginia.

board & to stay, & I would send two to talke with their King
a shore, to this hee agreed: the King wee presented with a
piece of Copper, which he kindly excepted, and sent for victualls to entertaine the messengers.

Maister Scriuener and my selfe also, after that, went a
shore: the King kindly feasted vs, requesting vs to stay to
trade till the next day, which hauing done, wee returned to
the Fort, this riuer is a musket shot broad, each side being
should bares, a narrow channell, but three fadom, his course
for eighteene miles, almost direatly South, and by West,
where beginneth the first inhabitants, for a mile it turneth
direatly East, towards the West, a great bay and a white
chaukie Iland, conuenient for a Fort: his next course
South, where within a quarter of a mile, the riuer diuiceth
in two, the neck a plaine high Corne field, the wester bought
a high plaine likewise, the Northeast answerable in all respects: in these plaines are planted aboundance of houses
and people, they may containe 1000. Acres of most excellent fertill ground, so sweete, so pleasant, so beautifull, and
so strong a prospect, for an inuincible strong Citty, with so
many commodities, that I know as yet I haue not seene:
This is within one daies iourney of Chawwonocke, the
riuer falleth into the Kings riuer, within twelue miles of
Capé-hendicke.

At our Fort, the tooles we had were so ordinarily stolen
by the Indians, as necessity inforced vs to correct their bra-
uing theeuerie: for he that stole to day, durst come againe
the next day. One amongst the rest, hauing stolen two
swords, I got the Counsels consent to set in the bilboes:
the next day with three more, he came with their imbered
swords in the midst of our men to steale, their custome is to
take any thing they can ceaze off, onely the people of Pa-
mounke, wee haue not found stealing: but what others
can steale, their king receiueth.

I bad them depart, but flourishing their swords, they
seemed

board and to stay, and I would send two to talke with their King a
shore. To this hee agreed: the King wee presented with a piece of
Copper, which he kindly accepted, and sent for victualls to entertaine the messengers.

Maister Scrivener and my selfe also, after that, went a shore:
the King kindly feasted us, requesting us to stay to trade till the next
day, which having done, we returned to the Fort. This river is a
musket shot broad, each side being should bayes,[201] a narrow channell, but three fadom, his course for eighteene miles, almost directly
South, and by West, where beginneth the first inhabitants; for a mile
it turneth directly East, towards the West, a great bay and a white
chaukie Iland, convenient for a Fort: his next course South, where
within a quarter of a mile, the river divideth in two, the neck a plaine
high Corne field, the wester bought a high plaine likewise, the Northeast answerable in all respects: in these plaines are planted aboundance of houses and people. They may containe 1000. Acres of most
excellent fertill ground, so sweete, so pleasant, so beautifull, and so
strong a prospect, for an invincible strong Citty, with so many commodities, that I know as yet I have not seene: This is within one daies
journey of Chawwonocke.[202] The river falleth into the Kings river,
within twelve miles of Cape Henrie.

At our Fort, the tooles we had were so ordinarily stolen by the
Indians, as necessity inforced us to correct their braving theeverie:
for he that stole to day, durst come againe the next day. One amongst
the rest, having stolen two swords, I got the Counsels consent to set
in the bilboes:[203] the next day with three more, he came with their
woodden swords in the midst of our men to steale, their custome is to
take any thing they can ceaze off,[204] onely the people of Pamunke,
wee have not found stealing: but what others can steale, their King
receiveth.

I bad them depart, but flourishing their swords, they

Newes from Virginia.

seemed to defend what they could catch but out of our hands, his pride vrged me to turne him from amongst vs, whereof he offred to strike me with his sword, which I prevented, striking him first: the rest offring to reuenge the blow, receiued such an incounter, and fled; the better to affright them, I pursued them with fiue or sixe shot, and so chased them out of the Iland: the beginning of this broyle, litle expecting by his carriage, we durst haue refisted, hauing euen till that present, not bæne contradicted, especially them of Paspahegh: these Indians within one houre, hauing by other Saluages, then in the Fort, vnderstood that I threatned to be reuenged, came presently of themselues, and fell to working vpon our weares, which were then in hand by other Saluages, who seeing their pride so incountred, were so so submissiue, and willing to doe any thing as might be, and with trembling feare, desired to be friends within thræ daies after: From Nawsamond which is 30, miles from vs, the King sent vs a Hatchet, which they had stollen from vs at our being there: the messenger as is the custome, also wee well rewarded and contented.

The twenty of Aprill, being at worke, in hewing downe Trees, and setting Corne, an alarum caused vs with all spædo to take our armes, each expecting a new assault of the Saluages: but vnderstanding it a Boate vnder saile, our doubts were presently satisfied, with the happy sight of Maister Nelson, his many perrills of extreame stormes and tempests. His ship well, as his comp'ny could testifie his care in sparing our prouision, was well: but the prouidence thereof, as also of our stones, Hatchets, and other tooles, onely ours excepted, which of all the rest was most neceffary, which might inforce vs, to think either a seditious traitor to our action, or a most vnconscionable decciuer of our treasures. This happy arriuall of Maister Nelson in the Phenix, hauing bæne then about thræ monethes missing, after Captaine Nuports arriuall, being to all our expectations

E   pectations

seemed to defend what they could catch but out of our hands. His **[E1ʳ]**
pride urged me to turne him from amongst us, whereat he offred to
strike me with his sword, which I prevented, striking him first: the
rest offring to revenge the blow, received such an incounter, and
fled; the better to affright them, I pursued them with five or sixe
shot, and so chased them out of the Iland: the beginning of this
broyle, litle expecting by his carriage, we durst have resisted, having
even till that present not beene contradicted, especially them of
Paspahegh:²⁰⁵ these Indians within one houre, having by other
Salvages, then in the Fort, understood that I threatned to be revenged, came presently of themselves, and fell to working upon our
wears, which were then in hand by other Salvages, who seeing their
pride so incountred, were so submissive, and willing to doe any thing
as might be, and with trembling feare, desired to be friends within
three daies after: From Nansemond which is 30. miles from us, the
King sent us a Hatchet which they had stollen from us at our being
there:²⁰⁶ the messenger as is the custome, also wee well rewarded and
contented.

  The twenty of Aprill, being at worke, in hewing downe Trees,
and setting Corne, an alarum caused us with all speede to take our
armes, each expecting a new assault of the Salvages: but understanding it a Boate under saile, our doubts were presently satisfied, with
the happy sight of Maister Nelson, his many perrills of extreame
stormes and tempests [passed]. His ship well, as his company could
testifie, his care in sparing our provision, was well: but the providence thereof, as also of our stones, Hatchets, and other tooles, onely
ours excepted, which of all the rest was most necessary, which might
inforce us, to think either a seditious traitor to our action, or a most
unconscionable deceiver of our treasures. [. . .]²⁰⁷ This happy arrivall
of Maister Nelson in the *Phenix*, having beene then about three
monethes missing, after Captaine Nuports arrivall, being to all our
ex-

Newes from Virginia.

pectations lost: albeit, that now at the last, having bene long crossed with tempestuous weather, and contrary winds, his so vnexpected comming, did so ranish vs with exceeding ioy, that now we thought our selues as well stored, as our harts could with, both with a competent number of men, as also for all other needfull prouisions, till a farther supply should come vnto vs: whereupon the first thing that was concluded, was, that my selfe, and Maister Scriuener, should with 70. men goe with the best meanes we could prouide, to discouer beyond the Falls, as in our iudgements conueniently we might: sixe or seauen daies we spent only in learning, our men to march, fight, and scirmish in the woods, their willing minds to this action, so quickned their vnderstanding in this exercise, as in all iudgements we were better able to fight with Powhatans whole force: in our order battaile amongst the Trees, (for Thicks there is few) then the fort was to repasse 400. at the first assault, with some fortie or twenty shot, not knowing what to doe, nor how to vse a Piece: our warrant being sealed, Maister Nelson refused to assist vs with his voluntary Marriners, and himselfe as he promised, vnlesse we would stay home to pay the hire for shippe, and Marriners, for their stayed: and further there was some contrauersie, through the diuersitie of Contrary opinions, some alleadging, that how profitable, and to what good purpose soeuer our iourney should portend, yet our commission, commanding no certaine designe, we should be tared for the most indiscreete men in th' world, besides the wrong we should doe to Captaine Nuport, to whom only all discoueries did belong, and to no other: the meanes for guides, beside the vncertaine courses of the riuer, from which we could not erre much, each night would fortifie vs in two houres, better then that they first called the fort, their Townes vpon the riuer, each within one dayes iourney of other, besides our ordinary prouision, might well be supposed to adde reliefe: for truck and

pectations lost: albeit, that now at the last, having beene long crossed **[E1ᵛ]**
with tempestuous weather, and contrary winds, his so unexpected
comming, did so ravish us with exceeding joy, that now we thought
our selves as well fitted, as our harts could wish, both with a competent number of men, as also for all other needfull provisions, till a
further supply should come unto us: whereupon the first thing that
was concluded, was that my selfe and Maister Scrivener should with
70. men goe with the best meanes we could provide, to discover
beyond the Falls, as in our judgements conveniently we might: sixe
or seaven daies we spent only in trayning our men to march, fight,
and scirmish in the woods. These[208] willing minds to this action, so
quickned their understanding in this exercise, as in all judgements
wee were better able to fight with Powhatans whole force in our
order of battle amongst the Trees, (for Thicks[209] there is few) then
the Fort was to repulse 400. at the first assault, with some tenne or
twenty shot, not knowing what to doe, nor how to use a Piece: our
warrant being sealed, Maister Nelson refused to assiste us with the
voluntary Marriners, and himselfe, as he promised, unlesse we would
stand bound to pay the hire for shippe and Marriners for the time
they stayed: and further there was some contraversie, through the
diversitie of Contrary opinions, some alleadging that, how profitable and to what good purpose soever our journey should portend,
yet our commission, commanding no certaine designe, we should be
taxed for the most indiscreete men in the world, besides the wrong
we should doe to Captaine Nuport, to whom only all discoveries did
belong, and to no other:[210]

    The meanes for guides,[211] beside the uncertaine courses of the
river, from which we could not erre much, each night would fortifie
us in two houres, better then that they first called the Fort. Their
Townes upon the river, each within one dayes journey of other,
besides our ordinary provision, might well be supposed to adde
reliefe, for truck

Newes from Virginia.

¶ dealing only, but in loue & peace, as to the rest; if they assalted vs, their Townes they cannot defend, nor their luggage
so conuey, that we should not share, but abuse the worst, 16.
daies prouision we had of Cheese, Catmeale, and bisket besides our randeuous, we could and might haue had in the
ground. With fixe men, Captaine Martin, would haue vn-
dertaken it himselfe, leauing the rest to defend the Fort, and
plant our Corne: yet no reason could be reason, to procure
forward, though we were going aboard to set saile: These
discontents caused so many doubts to some, and discouragement to others, as our iourney ended: yet some of vs procured petitions to set vs toward, only with hope of our
owne confessons, our next course was to turne husbandmen, to fell Trees and set Corne. Fiftie of our men, we imployed in this seruice, the rest kept the Fort, to for the command of the president, and Captaine Martin, 30. daies the
ship perpetuan p'rall of certain matters which for some
cause I keepe priuate: the next exploit was an Indian hauing
stolen an axe, was so pursued by Maister Scriuener, & them
with him, as he threw it downe, and flying drew his bow
at any that durst incounter him: within foure or fiue dayes
after, Maister Scriuener and I, being a little from the Fort,
among the Corne, two Indians, each with a cudgell, and
all secretly painted with Terra sigillata, came circling about
mee, as though they would haue clubed me like a hare: I
knew their fainting loue is towards me, not without a deadly hatred, but to preuent the worst. I calling maister Scriuener retired to the Fort: the Indians seeing me suspect them,
with good tearmes, asked me for some of their men whom
they would beate, and went with me into our Fort, finding
one that lay ordinarily with vs, only for a spie: they offered
to beat him, I in perswading them to forbeare, they offered
to beginne with me, being new foure, for two other at each d
in like manner, came in on the other side the Fort: where-
vpon I caused to shut the Ports, and apprehend them. The

C 2   president

rr. [ll. 6–7]. In margin, "Hee that knowes n[othing?] feares nothing"; obviously
referring to Captain Martin.

and dealing only, but in love and peace, as with the rest. If they **[E2ʳ]**
assalted us, their Townes they cannot defend, nor their luggage so
convey that we should not share; but admit the worst, 16. daies
provision we had of Cheese, Oatmeale, and bisket besides, our
randevous,[212] we could and might have hid in the ground. With
sixe men, Captaine Martin, would have undertaken it himselfe,
leaving the rest to defend the Fort, and plant our Corne: yet no
reason could be reason to proceede forward, though we were going
aboard to set saile. These discontents caused so many doubts to some,
and discouragement to others, as our journey ended: yet some of us
procured petitions to set us forward, only with hope of our owne con-
fusions.[213] Our next course was to turne husbandmen, to fell Trees
and set Corne. Fiftie of our men, we imployed in this service, the rest
kept the Fort, to doe the command of the president, and Captaine
Martin, [while] 30. dayes the ship lay expecting the triall of certain
matters which for some cause I keepe private:[214] the next exploit
was an Indian, having stolen an Axe, was so pursued by Maister
Scrivener, and them next him, as he threw it downe, and flying drew
his bow at any that durst incounter him:[215] within foure or five dayes
after, Maister Scrivener and I, being a litle from the Fort among the
Corne, two Indians, each with a cudgell, and all newly painted with
Terrasigillata, came circling about mee, as though they would have
clubed me like a hare: I knew their faining love is towards me, not
without a deadly hatred, but to prevent the worst, I calling maister
Scrivener retired to the Fort: the Indians seeing me suspect them,
with good tearmes, asked me for some of their men whom they would
beate, and went with me into our Fort, finding one that lay ordinarily
with us, only for a spie: they offered to beat him.[216] I in perswading
them to forbeare, they offered to beginne with me, being now foure,
for two other arrayed in like manner, came in on the other side the
Fort: whereupon I caused to shut the Ports,[217] and apprehend them.
The

Newes from Virginia.

president and Counsell, being presently acquainted, remembring at the first assault, they came in like manner, and never else but against some villanie concluded to commit them to prison, and expect the euent, right more we ceazed at that present, an houre after came three or foure other strangers, extraordinarily fitted with arrowes, skinnes, and shooting gloues, their iealousie and feare, bewrayed their bad intent, as also their suspitions departure.

The next day came first an Indian, then another as Embassadors for their men, they desired to speake with me, our discourse was, that what Spades, Shouells, swords, or tooles they had stolne, to bring home (if not the next day, they should hang) the next newes was, they had taken two of our men, ranging in the woods, which mischiefe no punishment will prevent but hanging, and these they would should redeeme their owne 16. or 18. thus braving vs to our doores, we desired the president, and Captaine Martin, that afternoone to sally vpon them, that they might but know, what we durst to doe, and at night mand our Barge, and burnt their Townes, and spoiled, and destroyed, what we could, but they brought our men, and freely deliuered them : the president released one, the rest we brought well guarded, to Morning and Euening prayers. Our men all in armes, their trembling feare, then caused them to much sorrow, which till then scoffed, and scorned at what we durst doe, the Counsell concluded, that I should terrifie them with some torture, to know if I could know their intent, the next day I bound one in hold, to the maine Mast, and presenting sixe Muskets with match in the cockes, forcet him to desire life, to answere my demaunds he could not, but one of his Comouodos was of the counsell of Paspahegh, that could satisfie me : I releasing him out of sight, I affrighted the other, first with the rack, then with Muskets, which seeing, he desired me to stay, and hee wowld confesse to this execution : Master Scriuener came, his discourse was to
this

president and Counsell, being presently acquainted, remembring at **[E2ᵛ]**
the first assault, they came in like manner, and never else but against
some villanie, concluded to commit them to prison, and expect the
event;[218] eight more we ceazed at that present. An houre after, came
three or foure other strangers, extraordinarily fitted with arrowes,
skinnes, and shooting gloves; their jealousie and feare bewrayed their
bad intent, as also their suspitious departure.[219]

The next day came first an Indian, then another, as Embassadors for their men; they desired to speake with me. Our discourse
was, that what Spades, Shovells, swords, or tooles they had stolne,
to bring home (if not the next day, they should hang). The next
newes was, they had taken two of our men, ranging in the woods,
which mischiefe no punishment will prevent but hanging, and these
they would should redeeme their owne 16. or 18. thus braving us to
our doores. We desired the president, and Captaine Martin, that
afternoone to sally upon them, that they might but know, what we
durst to doe, and at night mand[220] our Barge, and burnt their
Townes, and spoiled, and destroyed, what we could, but they
brought our men, and freely delivered them: the president released
one, the rest we brought well guarded, to Morning and Evening
prayers. Our men all in armes, their trembling feare, then caused
them to much sorrow,[221] which till then scoffed and scorned at what
we durst doe. The Counsell concluded that I should terrifie them
with some torture, to know if I could know their intent. The next
day I bound one in hold[222] to the maine Mast, and presenting sixe
Muskets with match in the cockes,[223] forced him to desire life, to
answere my demaunds he could not, but one of his Comouodos[224]
was of the counsell of Paspahegh, that could satisfie me: I, releasing
him out of sight, I affrighted the other, first with the rack, then with
Muskets, which seeing, he desired me to stay, and hee would confesse to this execution:[225] Maister Scrivener come,[226] his discourse
was to

Newes from Virginia.

this eff:ct, that Paspehegh, the Chick..hamaniar, Yough:a-
num, Pamaunka, Mattapanien', & Kiskiack. Etcſe Nari;
ons were altogether a hunting that tooke me, Paſpahegh, &
Chicahamanya, had entrured to ſurpriſe vs at worke, to
haue had our tools: Powhatan, & al his would ſæ me frients,
till Captaine Nuports returne, that he had againe his man,
which he called Namontack, where with a great feaſt hæ
would ſo enamor Captain Nuport & his men, as they ſhould
ceaze on him, and the like traps would be laied for the reſt.

This trap for our tooles, we ſuſpected the chiefe occaſion
was foure daies before Powhatan had ſent the boy he had
to vs, with many Torkies to Maiſter Scriuener, and thee,
vnderſtanding I would go vp into his Countries to deſtroy
them, and he doubted it the more, in that I ſo oſt practiſed
my men, whoſe ſhooting he heard to his owne lodging, that
much feared his wiues, and childern; we ſent him word, we
entended no ſuch thing, but only to goe to Powhatan, to
ſeke ſtones to make Hatchets, except his men ſhoot at vs,
as Paſpahegh had told vs they would, which if they did
ſhoote but one arrowe, we would deſtroy them, and leaſt
this miſchiefe might happen, ſent the boy to acquaint him
thus much, and requeſt him to ſend vs Weanock, one of his
ſubiects for a guide, & boy he returned backe with his Cheſſ,
& apparell, which then we had giuen him, deſiring another
for him, & cauſe was, he was practiſing with the Chikahamanias, as the boy ſuſpected ſome villanie, by their extraordinary retoxt, & ſecret conference from whence they would ſend
him. The boy we kepe, now we would ſend him many meſ-
ſengers, & preſents, the guide we deſired he ſent vs, & withall requeſted vs to returne him, either the boy, or ſome other,
but none he could haue, & that day theſe Indians were apprehended, his ſonne with others & had loaded at our Fort,
returned, & being out of the Fort, rayled on vs, to diuers of
our men, to be enemies to him, & to & Chikamanias, not long
after Weanock & had bin with vs for our guide, whom we
kept to haue conducted vs in another iourny, to a miſe errute

C 3   returned,

this effect, that Paspahegh, the Chickahamanian, Youghtanum, **[E3ʳ]**
Pamunka, Mattapanient, and Kiskiack, these Nations were altogether a hunting that tooke me; Paspahegh, and Chicahamanya,
had entended to surprise us at worke, to have had our tools: Powhatan, and al his would seeme friends till Captaine Nuports returne,
that he had againe his man, which he called Namontack, where with
a great feast hee would so enamor[227] Captain Nuport and his men,
as they should ceaze on him, and the like traps would be laied for
the rest.

This trap for our tooles, we suspected[228] the chiefe occasion was
foure daies before Powhatan had sent the boy he had to us, with
many Turkies to Maister Scrivener, and mee, understanding I
would go up into his Countries to destroy them, and he doubted[229]
it the more, in that I so oft practised my men, whose shooting he
heard to his owne lodging, that much feared his wives, and children;
we sent him word, we entended no such thing, but only to goe to
Powhatan to seeke stones to make Hatchets, except his men shoot at
us, as Paspahegh had told us they would, which if they did shoote
but one arrowe, we would destroy them, and least this mischiefe
might happen, sent the boy to acquaint him thus much, and request
him to send us Weanock,[230] one of his subjects for a guide. The boy
he returned backe with his Chest, and apparell, which then we had
given him, desiring another for him, the cause was, he was practising
with the Chikahamanias, as the boy suspected some villanie, by their
extraordinary resort,[231] and secret conference from whence they
would send him. The boy we keepe, now we would send him many
messengers, and presents. The guide we desired he sent us, and
withall requested us to returne him either the boy, or some other, but
none he could have, and that day these Indians were apprehended,
his sonne with others that had loaded[232] at our Fort returned, and
being out of the Fort, rayled on[233] me, to divers of our men, to be
enemies to him, and to the Chikamanias. Not long after Weanock
that had bin with us for our guide, whom wee kept to have conducted
us in another journy, with a false excuse

Newes from Virginia.

returned, and secretly after him, Amocis the Paspaheyan, who alwaies they kept among us for a spie, whom the better to auoid suspicion, presently after they came to braue away: their presumptions induced me to take any occasion, not onely to try the honesty of Amocis, the spie, but also the meaning of these cunning tricks of their Emperour of Powhatan; whose true meaning Captaine Martin most confidently pleaded.

The confession of Macanoe, which was the counseller of Paspahegh: first I, then Master Scrue, upon their seuerall examinations, found by them all confirmed, that Paspahegh, and Chickahammenia did hate vs, and intended some mischiefe, and who they were that tooke me, the names of them that stole our tooles, and swords, and that Powhatan receiues them, they all agreed: certaine relics of shot we caused to be discharged, which caused each other to thinke that their fellowes had beene slaine.

Powhatan vnderstanding we detained certaine Saluages, sent his Daughter, a child of tenne yeares old, which not onely for feature, countenance, & proportion, much exceedeth any of the rest of his people, but for wit, and spirit, the onely Nonpariel of his Country: this hee sent by his most trustie messenger, called Rawhunt, as much exceeding in deformitie of person, but of a subtill wit, and craftie vnderstanding, he with a long circumstance, tolde me how well Powhatan, loued and respected mee, and in that I should not doubt any way of his kindnesse, he had sent his child, which he most esteemed, to see me, a Deere, and bread besides for a present: desiring me that the Boy might come againe which he loued exceedingly, his little Daughter hee had taught this lesson also: not taking notice at all of the Indeans that had beene prisoners three daies, till that morning that she saw their fathers, and friends come quietly, and in good tearmes to entreate their libertie.

Opechankanough, sent also vnto vs, that for his sake, we
                                                        would

(margin note in manuscript hand:) Pakahuntas / Matoa /

ss. [l. 19]. "Daughter"; in margin, "[Po]kahuntas," and just below, "Mator/." While the final r is clear, "Matoa" or "Matoaka" is found elsewhere (see Hamor's *True Discourse*, 59; Samuel Purchas, *Hakluytus Posthumus, or Purchas His Pilgrimes . . .* [London, 1625], IV, 1769, marg.).

returned, and secretly after him, Amocis the Paspaheyan, who **[E3ᵛ]** alwaies they kept amongst us for a spie, whom the better to avoide suspition presently after they came to beate[234] away: these presumptions induced me to take any occasion, not onely to try the honesty of Amocis, the spie, but also the meaning of these cunning trickes of their Emperour of Powhatan; whose true meaning Captaine Martin most confidently pleaded.[235]

The confession of Macanoe, which was the counseller of Paspahegh: [. . .][236] first I, then Maister Scrivener, upon their severall examinations, found by them all confirmed, that Paspahegh, and Chickahammania did hate us, and intended some mischiefe, and who they were that tooke me, the names of them that stole our tooles, and swords, and that Powhatan received them, they all agreed: certaine vollies of shot we caused to be discharged, which caused each other to thinke that their fellowes had beene slaine.

Powhatan, understanding we detained certaine Salvages, sent his Daughter, a child of tenne yeares old, which not only for feature, countenance, and proportion, much exceedeth any of the rest of his people, but for wit, and spirit, the only Nonpariel of his Country:[237] this hee sent by his most trustie messenger, called Rawhunt, as much exceeding in deformitie of person, but of a subtill wit and crafty understanding. He with a long circumstance told mee how well Powhatan loved and respected mee, and in that I should not doubt any way of his kindnesse, he had sent his child, which he most esteemed, to see me, a Deere and bread besides for a present: desiring me that the Boy might come againe, which he loved exceedingly, his litle Daughter hee had taught this lesson also: not taking notice at all of the Indeans that had beene prisoners thrce daies, till that morning that she saw their fathers and friends come quietly, and in good tearmes to entreate their libertie.

Opechaukanough sent also unto us, that for his sake, we

Newes from Virginia.

would release two that were his friends, and for a token
sent me his shooting Glove, and Bracer, which the day our
men was taken vpon, separating himselfe from the rest a
long time; intreated to speake with me, where in token of
peace, he had preferred me the same now all of them hauing
found their peremptorie conditions, but to increase our malice, which they seing vs begin to threaten to destroy them,
as familiarly as before, without suspition, or feare, came a-
mongst vs, to begge libertie for their men: In the afternoone
they being gone, we guarded them as before to the Church,
and after prayer, gaue them to Pocahuntas, the Kings
Daughter, in regard of her fathers kindnesse in sending
her: after hauing well fed them, as all the time of their imprisonment, we gaue them their bowes, arrowes, or
what else they had, and with much content, sent their
packing: Pocahuntas, also we requited, with such trifles
as contented her, to tel that we had vsed y Pasphey ans very
kindly in so releasing them The next day we had suspition
of some other practise for an Ambuscado, but perfectly wee
could not discouer it, two dayes after a Paspaheyan, came
to shew vs a glistering Minerall stone: and with signes demonstrating it to be in great abeundance, like vnto Rockes,
with some of it more, I was sent to seke to digge some
quantitie, and the Indean to conduct me: but suspecting
this some tricke to delude vs, for to get some Copper of vs,
or with some ambuscado to betray vs, seing him falter in his
tale, being two miles on our way, led him ashore, where
abusing vs from place to place, and seeking either to haue
drawne vs with him into the woods, or to haue stayed the
shippe: I shewed him Copper, which I promised to haue giuen him, if he had performed his promise, but for his scoffing
and abusing vs, I gaue him twentie lashes with a Rope,
and his bowes and arrowes, bidding him shoote if he durst,
and so let him goe.

    In all this time, our men being all or the most part well
recouered,

would release two that were his friends, and for a token sent me his **[E4ʳ]**
shooting Glove and Bracer,[238] which the day our men was taken
upon, separating himselfe from the rest a long time, intreated to
speake with me, where in token of peace, he had preferred[239] me the
same: now all of them having found their peremptorie conditions,
but to increase our malice, which they seeing us begin to threaten to
destroy them, as familiarly as before, without suspition or feare, came
amongst us to begge libertie for their men: In the afternoone, they
being gone, we guarded them as before to the Church, and after
prayer, gave them to Pocahuntas, the Kings Daughter, in regard of
her fathers kindnesse in sending her: after having well fed them, as
all the time of their imprisonment, we gave them their bowes,
arrowes, or what else they had, and with much content, sent them
packing: Pocahuntas also we requited, with such trifles as contented
her, to tel that we had used the Paspaheyans very kindly in so releasing them. The next day we had suspition of some other practise for
an Ambuscado, but perfectly wee could not discover it; two daies
after, a Paspaheyan came to shew us a glistering Minerall stone:[240]
and with signes demonstrating it to be in great aboundance, like unto
Rockes. With some dozen more, I was sent to seeke to digge some
quantitie, and the Indean to conduct me: but suspecting this some
tricke to delude us for to get some Copper of us, or with some ambuscado to betray us, seeing him falter in his tale, being two miles on
our way, led him ashore, where abusing us from place to place, and
so seeking either to have drawne us with him into the woods, or to
have given us the slippe: I shewed him Copper, which I promised to
have given him if he had performed his promise, but for his scoffing
and abusing us, I gave him twentie lashes with a Rope, and his bowes
and arrowes, bidding him shoote if he durst, and so let him goe.[241]

In all this time, our men being all or the most part well

Newes from Virginia.

recouered, and we not willing to trifle away moze time then
necessitie enfozced vs vnto, we thought good foz the better
content of the aduenturers, in some reasonable sozt to
fraight home Maister Nelson with Cedar wood, about
which, our men going with willing minds, was in very good
time effected, and the ship sent foz England; we now remaining being in good health, all our men well cõtented, frée
from mutinies, in loue one with another, ¢ as we hope in a
continuall peace with the Indians, where we doubt not but
by Gods gracious assistance, and the aduenturers willing
minds, and speedie furtherance to so honozable an action in
after times, to sée our Nation to enioy a Country, not onely
exceeding pleasant foz habitation, but also very pzofitable foz
comerce in generall, no doubt pleasing to almightie God,
honourable to our gracious Soueraigne, and commodious
generally to the whole Kingdome.

FINIS.

recovered, and we not willing to trifle away more time then neces- **[E4ᵛ]**
sitie enforced us unto, we thought good for the better content of the
adventurers in some reasonable sort to fraight home Maister Nelson
with Cedar wood, about which, our men going with willing minds,
was in very good time effected, and the ship sent for England; wee
now remaining being in good health, all our men wel contented, free
from mutinies, in love one with another, and as we hope in a continuall peace with the Indians, where we doubt not but by Gods
gracious assistance, and the adventurers willing minds and speedie
furtherance to so honorable an action in after times, to see our Nation
to enjoy a Country, not onely exceeding pleasant for habitation, but
also very profitable for comerce in generall, no doubt pleasing to
almightie God, honourable to our gracious Soveraigne, and commodious generally to the whole Kingdome.[242]

FINIS.

1. Inserted as sig. ¶ 1–2, a single leaf, between sig. A2ᵛ and A3ʳ, apparently after the book was in print. What follows bears out the haste and confusion attending the publication of Smith's account.

2. Fair, unbiased.

3. I.e., "having inadvertently spoken another player's lines"; a hint that "I. H." had connections in the theatre.

4. Dreading, fearing.

5. Authors not uncommonly went to the printing houses to read proof.

6. Region.

7. Consensus.

8. Often merely "with."

9. Councillors, counselors.

10. Opinions, private designs.

11. Very likely John Healey (see the Biographical Directory). Charles Deane dismissed the importance of "I. H." and his address somewhat briefly, without attempting to identify him (Charles Deane, ed., *A True Relation of Virginia, by Captain John Smith* [Boston, 1866]). Worthington Chauncey Ford, however, suggested Healey as the author (Massachusetts Historical Society, *Proceedings*, LVIII [1924–1925], 245–247). More recently Mr. Giles de la Mare, a London editor, independently reached the same conclusion (Barbour, *Jamestown Voyages*, I, 168n; and further personal communications, 1974–1975).

12. Modern Virginia.

13. Wording possibly supplied by "I. H."

14. The Downs was a protected rendezvous for ships off the east coast of Kent near Deal, where the fleet anchored Jan. 5, 1607, and suffered "great storms" (George Percy's "Discourse," in Barbour, *Jamestown Voyages*, I, 129).

15. Gran Canaria Island is probably meant. Capt. Christopher Newport, admiral in command, had watered there Apr. 6–9, 1590, on his first West Indian voyage (David Beers Quinn, ed., *The Roanoke Voyages, 1584–1590* [Hakluyt Society, 2d Ser., CIV–CV (London, 1955)], II, 600), and Smith himself had probably visited the island (see the *True Travels*, 39). A sentence or more has been cut here (see n. 16).

16. More cutting is obvious. Purchas states in a marginal note to his extract from Percy's "Discourse" that "the next day [after leaving the Canaries?] Capt. Smith was suspected for a supposed Mutinie, though never no such matter" (Barbour, *Jamestown Voyages*, I, 129).

17. See the *Proceedings*, 3; and the *Generall Historie*, 42. Percy supplies further detail (Barbour, *Jamestown Voyages*, I, 135).

18. Deane attempted to clarify the passage but misconstrued Percy's "Discourse" (*Smith's Relation*, 2n; see n. 16, above). For the name, see Quinn, *Roanoke Voyages*, I, 461n, II, 847–848; and Barbour, "Earliest Reconnaissance," Pt. I, 287.

19. I.e., Christopher Newport; see the Biographical Directory.

20. Cf. Percy's "Discourse" (Barbour, *Jamestown Voyages*, I, 133–134). Deane hazarded a guess as to the identity of the Indians (*Smith's Relation*, 3n). Arber mistakenly explained "aboard" (on board the ship) as "on land" (Edward Arber, ed., *Captain John Smith . . . Works, 1608–1631*, The English Scholar's Library Edition, No. 16 [Birmingham, 1884], 5).

21. For Gabriel Archer, see the Biographical Directory. According to Smith, Morton was an "expert Sea-man" with Sir Thomas Roe in South America (1610–1611) and later on "with command in the *East Indies*" (*True Travels*, 49). He is otherwise obscure.

22. A large cut, ignored by Deane, seems to have been made here, relating to Smith's exclusion from the council and the events between Sun. night, Apr. 26, and Wed., May 13, 1607. See Percy's "Discourse" for details (Barbour, *Jamestown Voyages*, I, 134–138).

23. "Edm." in the original.

24. See Percy's "Discourse" (Barbour, *Jamestown Voyages*, I, 138); and Charles E. Hatch, Jr., "Archer's Hope and the Glebe," *VMHB*, LXV (1957), 467–484. Deane summarizes Percy's "Discourse" in his notes (*Smith's Relation*, 4n).

25. "Thursday the xxith of May [1606]," according to Archer (Barbour, *Jamestown Voyages*, I, 81). Deane calls attention to Smith's slip (*Smith's Relation*, 5n). For the details of this exploration, see Barbour, *Jamestown Voyages*, I, 80–98.

26. I.e., "treating, dealing with"; common in Smith.

27. Gewgaws made of glass.

28. "Arsatecke" was a persistent alternative to "Arrohattoc." Smith's account here seems to be based on early, uncorrected notes; the "Relatyon" commonly attributed to Archer and sent to England in 1607 is better (Barbour, *Jamestown Voyages*, I, 84–89). The facts are that the werowance of Arrohattoc entertained Newport's party. Then the werowance of Powhatan village came downstream to see who they were. The latter werowance was the son of Great Powhatan, the "emperor," whom Smith first saw seven months later (see sig. C1ʳ, below).

29. Misread and printed as "within an ile"; not noted at the time. As in many cases, the misprint was ignored by Deane (*Smith's Relation*, 7). From the foot of the falls today it is 0.75 mi. to the mouth of Gillie Creek, just inside the southern city limits of Richmond. Powhatan village was probably on the high ground just N or S of this creek (see Barbour, "Earliest Reconnaissance," Pt. I, 297; and Barbour, *Jamestown Voyages*, II, 468, 474–475).

30. "Freshets."

31. May 24, 1607.

32. The "Relatyon" attributed to Archer specifies that Captain Newport "sett up a Crosse with this inscriptyon Jacobus Rex. 1607. and his owne name belowe" (Barbour, *Jamestown Voyages*, I, 88). Deane's notes are similar to these.

33. I.e., "acknowledged his pleasure or satisfaction (at)."

34. I.e., "latitude." Below, the colonists' visit to the queen of Appamatuck is described in Archer's "Relatyon" (Barbour, *Jamestown Voyages*, I, 91–92), also referred to by Deane. "Agamatock" was probably a misreading of the handwritten "Appamatuck"; the "p" could easily have been confused with a "g." "Appomattoc" is a post-17th-century spelling.

35. For further details, see *ibid.*, 92. This location was most likely a mile or so upstream from the E end of Eppes Island (*ibid.*, II, 466). Deane's note on the site was written a century before serious investigation began.

36. The Weanock tribe occupied both sides of the James River below modern Hopewell (see Ben C. McCary, *Indians in Seventeenth-Century Virginia*, Jamestown 350th Anniversary Historical Booklet No. 18 [Williamsburg, Va., 1957], 7; Barbour, "Earliest Reconnaissance," Pt. I, 301; and n. f to facsimile).

37. Perhaps modern Weyanoke Point (Barbour, *Jamestown Voyages*, II, 466), as intimated in Deane, *Smith's Relation*, 8n.

38. Animosity.

39. Servant, attendant; his name was Nauiraus, or Navirans (Barbour, *Jamestown Voyages*, I, 84–90).

40. I.e., "much ado, many formalities."

41. Archer's "Relatyon" says "above 200. of them" (Barbour, *Jamestown Voyages*, I, 95). However, neither he nor Smith was there. The Englishmen could not have numbered over 120, including the sailors. The werowance of Paspahegh, within whose hunting grounds the English had unknowingly settled, was always inimical to the colonists (cf. sig. E1ʳ, below; and n. qq to facsimile). He of Tappahanocke (later more correctly called Quiyoughcohanock), however, was always friendly (see sig. B1ʳ, below; and n. k to facsimile).

42. Large guns; cf. the *Accidence*, 24.

43. Casks or boxes for stacking guns.

44. "Palisadoed," Smith's characteristic use of a Spanish form in preference to French (cf. modern English "palisade"). Wingfield, and perhaps Newport, had been reluctant to fortify Jamestown on the basis of the "Instructions" they had (see the *Proceedings*, 4; and the *Generall Historie*, 42; the "Instructions" are in Barbour, *Jamestown Voyages*, I, 34–44).

45. Another Spanish form in place of French.

46. A considerable cut seems to have been made here (cf. the *Proceedings*, 5–6; and the *Generall Historie*, 42–43). "Abroad" means "outside the stockade, the house, the city."

47. Percy adds that Newport left 104 colonists "verie bare and scantie of victualls, furthermore in warres [among themselves] and in danger of the Savages," but with a promise of supplies within 20 weeks (Barbour, *Jamestown Voyages*, I, 143). Note the implied disparagement of Newport, carefully omitted in nearly two pages of notes by

Deane that seem intended to slight Smith (*Smith's Relations*, 10–11).

48. This passage was omitted in both the *Proceedings* and the *Generall Historie*. Wingfield independently testified that the Indian came from Opechancanough, not Powhatan, on June 25, not June 21, "with the worde of peace" (Barbour, *Jamestown Voyages*, I, 214–215). It is not known which date is correct.

49. Archaic for "conducted, managed"; today we might say "carried out."

50. The sentence seems truncated (cf. Wingfield's "Discourse," in Barbour, *Jamestown Voyages*, I, 213–218).

51. There may have been further meddling here.

52. Bartholomew Gosnold died on Aug. 22, 1607 (Percy's "Discourse," in Barbour, *Jamestown Voyages*, I, 144).

53. Green corn (maize), American "on the cob," was considered unripe by the English. In the concluding clause, the second "when" is correct if "expected" is taken in the archaic sense of "waited to see." Cf. n. l of facsimile.

54. Cf. the *Proceedings*, 10; the *Generall Historie*, 44; Percy's "Discourse" (in Barbour, *Jamestown Voyages*, I, 143–145); and Wingfield's "Discourse" (*ibid.*, 215). Deane suggests comparison with the condition of "the Pilgrims at Plymouth during the first winter and spring" (*Smith's Relation*, 13n). See William Bradford, *Of Plymouth Plantation, 1620–1647*, ed. Samuel Eliot Morison (New York, 1952), 77: "of 100 and odd persons, scarce fifty remained."

55. I.e., "in turn." He was the only ship captain present, with Gosnold dead and Newport away.

56. With their harvest ended, the Indians were probably eager to barter food for gewgaws. It should be noted, however, that Halley's comet was brilliant in the night sky from mid-Sept. to mid-Oct. Although no colonist seems to have noticed it, the Indians may well have, and they may have been influenced by the apparition.

57. Something seems to be missing; see n. 58, below.

58. The entire passage is amplified in the *Proceedings*, 11; and the *Generall Historie*, 45.

59. The officer in charge of purchase and sale or barter of goods (see the *Sea Grammar*, 34).

60. Although something seems to be missing here, the account that follows is somewhat more ample than that in the *Proceedings*, 11; and the *Generall Historie*, 45.

61. The *Generall Historie*, 44, also contains a detailed account of the manner in which "God . . . altered their conceits," which was credited and reprinted by Samuel Purchas without comment (*Pilgrimes*, IV, 1707). Deane found this "a very extravagant story . . . quite inconsistent with this account, and probably with the truth" (*Smith's Relation*, 16n). In view of Strachey's sidelights on Powhatan and the Kecoughtan Indians (*Historie*, 44, 68), the editor sees no basis for Deane's assertion. "Conceits" often meant "fanciful notions, whims." Below, "discover" usually meant "make a reconnaissance of."

62. The "little Ile" was surely Cape Comfort, mentioned in the "Relation" of Francis Magnel, one of Newport's sailors: "This Cape Comfort is an island which is at the entrance of a big river where the English live" (Barbour, *Jamestown Voyages*, I, 151–152, 157n). Percy described the naming of it in his "Discourse" (*ibid.*, 135), but Smith's first reference to the name is in the *Proceedings*, 40. Here the account appears to have been pruned again.

63. Warrascoyack was near the mouth of modern Pagan River, perhaps opposite Smithfield (Barbour, "Earliest Reconnaissance," Pt. I, 301). The James River is now 4.5 mi. wide here, and Old Point Comfort is about 18 mi. downstream by modern navigable channels.

64. Cf. the *Proceedings*, 12; and the *Generall Historie*, 46. It was probably less a matter of supplies than an urge to go home, but the sequence of events is less clear in this account than in the other two, most likely due to cutting.

65. I.e., Powhatan village.

66. "To spoil" here means "plunder, obtain by force." Something again seems to be missing, but in any case this marks the beginning of Smith's calculated policy of living by trade (forced if necessary) and not by combat.

67. Smith could not know that Jamestown was built on Paspahegh hunting grounds (cf. Frank G. Speck, *Chapters on the Ethnology of the Powhatan Tribes of Virginia*, Heye Foundation, *Indian Notes and Monographs*, I, No. 5 [New York, 1928], 320–321; and John L. Cotter, *Archeological Excavations at Jamestown, Virginia*, National Park Service,

Archeological Research Series, No. 4 [Washington, D.C., 1958], 6). The Paspaheghs resented the white squatters.

68. Tried, attempted.

69. "Only" should be added here (cf. Anas Todkill's remarks in the *Proceedings*, 25, and the *Generall Historie*, 54).

70. It was new moon on Nov. 8; since they went along "by moonlight," "9" may be a misprint for "19."

71. A passage seems to be missing.

72. See n. r to facsimile. For further discussion of the Chickahominy River excursions, see Barbour, "Chickahominy Place-Names," *Names*, XV (1967), 216–227; *Jamestown Voyages*, II, 477–482; "Earliest Reconnaissance," Pt. I, 285–302; and Ben C. McCary and Norman F. Barka, "The John Smith and Zuniga Maps in the Light of Recent Archaeological Investigations along the Chickahominy River," *Archaeology of Eastern North America*, V (1977), 73–86.

73. Again, something seems to be missing.

74. The site has been established beyond reasonable doubt by McCary and Barka, "Archaeological Investigations," *Archaeology of Eastern North America*, V (1977), 82. It must be one of four late sites within modern Wilcox Neck, across the Chickahominy from Lanexa.

75. Another cut was apparently made here.

76. Misconduct.

77. Announced, made known.

78. See Philip L. Barbour, "Captain George Kendall, Mutineer or Intelligencer?" *VMHB*, LXX (1962), 297–313.

79. See n. s to facsimile.

80. I.e., "in the end, finally."

81. Decision.

82. According to Wingfield, who was no more reliable about dates than Smith, this was on Thurs., Dec. 10, 1607 (Barbour, *Jamestown Voyages*, I, 226). It is curious that the following eight pages of text were condensed to one page in the *Proceedings*, 13–14, but reappear in large part in the *Generall Historie*, 46–49. Deane has a good many notes, without suggesting an explanation (*Smith's Relation*, 22–43). True, he points out difficulties with the punctuation and offers a lengthy digression on the "Pocahontas incident" without being constructive, but there is little if anything worth repeating here.

83. "Oozy."

84. See n. t to facsimile. McCary and Barka have found evidence of a site corresponding to the one named by Smith ("Archaeological Investigations," *Archaeology of Eastern North America*, V [1977], 82–83).

85. "Chickahominy" seems to mean "cleared place" (Barbour, *Jamestown Voyages*, I, 179n; and Barbour, "Earliest Reconnaissance," Pt. I, 287).

86. The apparent meaning is that the neighborhood of Moysonicke was well populated and that most of the inhabitants were within sight of the "towne" (or "place").

87. The modern dam at Matahunk Neck, c. 6 mi. downstream, has turned the area into swamp and marsh.

88. I.e., "riverbed." The significance of the next sentence, from Smith's point of view, lay in the London Council's instructions: "You must Observe . . . Whether the River on which you Plant Doth Spring . . . out of Lakes[;] if it be out of any Lake the passage to the Other Sea [the Pacific Ocean] will be the more Easy" (Barbour, *Jamestown Voyages*, I, 51).

89. Make the venture, at some hazard.

90. This was a plausible justification for the trip. Three of the colonists were killed. The remainder apparently took the barge back to Jamestown.

91. "Lacke" was a variant spelling of "lake"; common in the 16th and early 17th centuries.

92. Performance, execution of duty.

93. "Encumbered."

94. I.e., "bends, curves." Below, John Robbinson ("Jehu Robinson," in Barbour, *Jamestown Voyages*, I, 223) was a "gentleman"; Thomas Emry was a carpenter. The former had accused Wingfield of slander in Sept. and was awarded £100 damages by the same court that had given Smith £200 for a similar reason. This may have led Robbinson to volunteer to go with Smith.

95. Another passage was cut here with the antecedent of "him" omitted. The meaning is, "Supposing that the Indians we had hired had betrayed us, and that my companions had been surprised, I forthwith seized the one with me, and held him at gunpoint to prevent any further surprise" (see the *Generall Historie*, 46).

96. Aimed, leveled.

97. The French were leaders in pistol making (J. F. Hayward, *European Firearms* [London, 1955], 10).

98. I.e., "did not try to resist." "Barricado" is another one of Smith's Spanish preferences over French.

99. See n. u to facsimile. This is Smith's first mention of Opechancanough's name (the previous mention of "the King of Pamaunke" [sig. A4^v] seems rather to refer to Powhatan, despite Arber [*Smith, Works*, 8]). Opechancanough was the second in line for the overlordship after Powhatan and was about 60 years old at the time (see the Biographical Directory).

100. "He made known that I was a captain." A captain, tribal chief, or werowance was not put to death if captured (*Map of Va.*, 26; *Generall Historie*, 33). For "werowance," see n. 135, below.

101. For the compass, Smith seems to have taken a leaf from Thomas Harriot, *A briefe and true report of the new found land of Virginia* . . . (London, 1588), which relates how such things were used to mystify the Indians in North Carolina (see Richard Hakluyt, *The Principal Navigations, Voyages, Traffiques and Discoveries of the English Nation* [London, 1598–1600], III, 277). Later, Purchas summarized this passage without reference to the *True Relation* but referred to a MS "courteously communicated" to him by Smith (*Pilgrimage* [1613], 634). As for Smith's knowledge or understanding of astronomy, at best it was probably rudimentary Copernican.

102. Apparently another cut was made here.

103. The rest of the sentence is missing; the meaning is perhaps, "that Opechancanough and his men were on a deer hunt" (cf. top of sig. E3^r).

104. This was the hunting camp "Rasaweack" named below (sig. C1^r). Deane, lacking the Smith/Zúñiga map (see n. 122, below), mistakenly imagined that Smith was referring to Orapaks (later Powhatan's residence), regardless of Smith's clear statement that the town was "Rasawrack" (*Smith's Relation*, 27n, 30n).

105. Italian *biscione*, "great snake" (*Generall Historie*, 47: "Bissone"). While there is a reference to a display of this sort called a "bissa" in William Garrard's *The Art of Warre* . . . (London, 1591), 133–136, Smith must have picked up his form of the name during his European soldiering, 1597?–1602.

106. After dining with the Indian captain, Smith was apparently lodged elsewhere.

107. The gown was a cape-like upper garment; the points were strips of leather (or yarn or silk) used in place of buttons; garters kept the long stockings from falling down.

108. See n. v to facsimile; and n. 113, below. A passage about the king's activities may have been cut.

109. I.e., Opechancanough, not Wowinchopunck.

110. Powhatan's "empire."

111. Ocanahonan (Ocanahowan) seems to have been a Mangoak (non-Powhatan) town near the modern Virginia–North Carolina boundary, west of the Chowan River (see Barbour, "Ocanahowan and Recently Discovered Linguistic Fragments," in Cowan, ed., *Papers of the Seventh Algonquian Conference, 1975*, 3–17).

112. The "King's" phrase undoubtedly had reference to the salt springs in the mountains west of the falls, but was misunderstood.

113. Smith used the Indian name for the district where Jamestown was.

114. Apparently a misprint for "incensed," meaning "informed" (cf. Shakespeare's *Henry VIII*, V, i, 42–45: "I think I have Incensed the lords . . . that he is . . . a most arch heretic"). The punctuation here makes one suspect cutting (cf. Deane, *Smith's Relation*, 29n).

115. Hardly the true reason (cf. Barbour, *Jamestown Voyages*, II, 482).

116. Smith's confusion about the relative locations of Powhatan village, Powhatan's residence, and Paspahegh/Jamestown must have puzzled Opechancanough.

117. Printed "Rasawrack" (see n. aa to facsimile); perhaps better spelled "Rasawek"; the probable meaning is "in-between place" (see Barbour, "Earliest Reconnaissance," Pt. I, 298, where another place with the same name is mentioned, thereby invalidating Deane's surmise in *Smith's Relation*, 30n).

118. Presumably six score paces, or 600 feet; dueling pistols were only "reliable" at 100 feet, but so were Indian arrows: "Forty yards will they shoot levell [with direct aim]" (*Map of Va.*, 24). Smith did not want the Indians to realize the limitations of his weapons.

119. "Supposed" is used in the obsolete sense of "pretended": e.g., "though I pretended it was an accident."

120. "Discovered" here means "explored." This visit by some European ship about 1605–1606 has been the subject of study and speculation (Philip L. Barbour, *Pocahontas and Her World* [Boston, 1970], 6, and David Beers Quinn, *England and the Discovery of America, 1481–1620* [New York, 1974], 452–454). In any event, the local exoneration of Smith seems to have paved the way for the "Pocahontas episode" that followed in short order at Powhatan's residence (cf. n. 123, below).

121. For the first five names, see Barbour, "Earliest Reconnaissance," Pt. I, s.vv. "Cuttatawomen," "Moraughtacund," "Toppahanock," "Appomattoc," and "Nantaughtacund." "Topmanahocks" appears to be an error, perhaps due to cutting. The Smith/Hole map shows the country of the Mannahoacks at the top (head) of the Toppahanock River, in the midst of mountains. Deane remarks on the "sad work" of the printer here, as elsewhere, but nowhere does he stress the cutting admitted by "I. H." (*Smith's Relation*, 32n).

122. Smith's route is shown by a dotted line on the map of Virginia sent from London to Spain by Don Pedro de Zúñiga, Sept. 5/15, 1608, referred to as the Smith/Zúñiga map (see the *Generall Historie*, 48; and Barbour, *Jamestown Voyages*, I, 238–240). At this point, a passage that comprises all of sig. C3^r and the first several lines of sig. C3^v seems to have been shifted from here (see n. 141, below), as indicated by "[. . .]."

123. Here begins the now famous episode involving Pocahontas (who is not yet mentioned), which runs on to the middle of sig. C2^v and was greatly modified and augmented in the *Generall Historie*, 48–49, 121–122. Deane found the two accounts incompatible, and on the basis of this became "responsible for the attack on Smith's veracity" (Arber, *Smith, Works*, cxviii), which has since spread far and wide, despite rebuttals that began in 1882 (see Deane's notes in *Smith's Relation*, 33–40). See the recension in the introduction to this book.

124. "Raccoon skins"; see Barbour, "Earliest Reconnaissance," Pt. II, 32, s.v. "aroughcun." Below, Charles M. Andrews's note on two passages in Hakluyt and Purchas is pertinent: "It must be remembered that language of this sort was due in part to the inflated style of the day and in part to a desire to make an impression for propagandist purposes" (*The Colonial Period of American History* [New Haven, Conn., 1934], I, 58n). There is less inflated style in Smith than in most of his propagandist contemporaries.

125. This is the first appearance of the word "savage" for "Indian" in Smith's works. The epithet was common in England before the first Jamestown fleet sailed in 1606. The jerky style of writing here suggests cutting.

126. These statements read as if they were introduced by "I. H." to reassure potential backers of the Virginia venture. The promise of "libertie within foure dayes" more likely came at the end of Powhatan's cross-examination, while the reference to Smith's interview with Opechancanough seems out of place.

127. "Leaky"; a common variant spelling (see the *Accidence*, 13).

128. During the expedition of May 21–27, Smith had learned that the Monacans were enemies of Powhatan's (see n. 28, above; and Barbour, *Jamestown Voyages*, I, 87–88). On the Monacans, see, *inter alia*, David I. Bushnell, Jr., *The Five Monacan Towns in Virginia, 1607*, Smithsonian Institution, *Miscellaneous Collections*, LXXXII, No. 12 (Washington, D.C., 1930); and R. Westwood Winfree, "Monacan Farm, Powhatan County, Virginia," Archeological Society of Virginia, *Quarterly Bulletin*, XXVII (1972), 65–93. On the reference to the "backe Sea," see sig. B4^v, above. The "childe slaine" was obviously John Robbinson, gentleman (see sig. B4^r, above).

129. The phrase, "where the sayde water dashed amongst many stones and rockes," seems to be the basis for the annotation at the top of the Smith/Zúñiga map (see Barbour, *Jamestown Voyages*, I, 240).

130. The only instance of the name; probably an error for "Atquanachuke" (see the *Map of Va.*, 10; the *Proceedings*, 39, 45; and the *Generall Historie*, 25, 61, 68).

131. See the notation at the top right of the Smith/Zúñiga map (n. 129, above); and the references to the Bocootawwonaugh tribe in Strachey, *Historie*, 35–36, 57, 132.

132. "Moyaoncer" is clearly a mistake for "Moyaonce," while "Pataromerke" is a

garbled version of "Patawomecke," a common spelling of modern "Potomac." The only problem is with the former. There were two villages, on opposite sides of the Potomac, usually then spelled "Moyomps" and "Moyaones" (quite possibly the same name), the former of which was under Powhatan's control (at least allied to him), and the latter independent and even inimical (see Barbour, "Earliest Reconnaissance," Pt. I, 292). Smith appears to have meant "Moyomps" here, not "Moyaones."

133. Battle axes; i.e., tomahawks.

134. Although Smith can have understood little, his summary makes sense (see Strachey, *Historie*, 56–57, for a parallel, with "Anoeg" for Smith's "Anone").

135. See n. 100, above. A "werowance" (here misprinted "Meworames") was a chief, captain, or head of a village, often called a king by the colonists. The name was already familiar, in nine variegated spellings, from Hakluyt's *Principal Navigations*, III, 255. See Barbour, "Earliest Reconnaissance," Pt. II, 46–47.

136. The account is expanded in the *Generall Historie*, 49, and the squad enlarged to 12. ("Knapsack" was apparently soldier's slang then, imported from the Netherlands.)

137. According to Strachey, it was 15–16 mi. from Werowocomoco on the Pamunkey River to Jamestown (*Historie*, 57); the "other" river was the James. The sense of the passage that follows is that the Pamunkey (modern York) River extends 20 mi. above Werowocomoco, where it splits into two branches. One branch, the Youghtanund (modern Pamunkey) River, leads through "Goughland" (perhaps the same word, distorted), which is well populated, but above Menapacunt (above modern West Point) it flows between hills and riverine rocks that may contain minerals. The other branch, the Mattapanient (modern Mattaponi) River, is smaller and runs through less hilly, less populated terrain. Note that Smith had seen much of the Youghtanund but had barely glimpsed the Mattapanient.

138. An unctuous, astringent clay from the island of Lemnos, often mentioned by Smith, that was called "sigillata" because it was exported in tablets imprinted with the Ottoman sultan's seal. It was esteemed as a medicine and an antidote.

139. At modern Yorktown the mouth of the river is under 900 yards wide and, due to the terrain, must have been about the same in 1608. Smith's estimate of "halfe a mile" (880 yards) is very close. From that point for 4 mi. upstream, Smith estimated the breadth at "not above a musket shot," which has been sized up today as "the space ... at which a good [musket] marksman can hit a man, which is between 600 and 800 feet" (A. R. Hall, *Ballistics in the Seventeenth Century: A Study in the Relations of Science and War with Reference Principally to England* [Cambridge, 1952], 53). While it is true that the modern channel is only about 1,100 yards wide, and there are islands and marshes particularly along the left bank that may have been dry land then, Smith's "musket shot" still remains to be explained. Perhaps the range of some small ordnance (2,500 to 3,000 yards) was originally used, which would clarify the apparent discrepancy. Deane has possibly erred more than Smith in his note on the subject (*Smith's Relation*, 41n).

140. Kiskiack, here misprinted "Kiskirk," has been tentatively identified in an archaeological excavation near Yorktown (Barbour, "Earliest Reconnaissance," Pt. I, 288).

141. All of sig. C3^r and the first five lines of C3^v appear to belong after the paragraph ending "... in each valley a cristall spring" (sig. C1^v and n. 122, above). The passage was reprinted with minor alterations in Purchas, *Pilgrimage*, 638 (see Fragments, in Volume III of this edition).

142. *Quiyoughcosucks* (variously spelled) were petty gods and their priests. The name appears to mean "the just, or upright, ones," though it is impossible to know whether it was extended from the gods to include the priests, or vice versa (see Barbour, "Earliest Reconnaissance," Pt. II, 42; and Percy's "Discourse" in Barbour, *Jamestown Voyages*, I, 149–150).

143. Probably a misprint for "navle" (navel), as in the *Map of Va.*, 29, and the *Generall Historie*, 34, where there are further memoranda on curing the sick.

144. See n. kk to facsimile.

145. The apparently senseless delay is difficult to rationalize. One reason could be that Powhatan had "assured" Smith's liberty "within *foure* dayes" (editor's italics, see sig. C1^v, above). Another could be that Powhatan's spies on the Eastern Shore had already sighted Newport's ship (see below), and for some reason he did not want Smith to reach Jamestown until he was sure that Jamestown was the ship's destination (see Barbour, *Pocahontas*, 27, which should read "Paspahegh's houses," not "Powhatan's houses").

146. After the execution of Kendall and before Newport's return on Jan. 2, 1608, the local council was composed of President Ratcliffe (with two votes), Martin (with one), and Smith (also with one, but then "in durance vile"). Councillors could be appointed by a majority. With Wingfield deposed, Ratcliffe could appoint Archer by two votes over Martin's opposition.

147. *Sc.*, "from the council"; for fuller accounts, see the *Generall Historie*, 49, and Wingfield's "Discourse," in Barbour, *Jamestown Voyages*, I, 227.

148. Newport (here spelled "Nuport") arrived Jan. 2, 1608 (see Francis Perkins's letter in Barbour, *Jamestown Voyages*, I, 159; and Wingfield, *ibid.*, 227).

149. See the Biographical Directory.

150. Both Perkins and Wingfield give Thurs., Jan. 7, as the date of the fire (see Barbour, *Jamestown Voyages*, I, 160, 228).

151. The old planters had been deprived of what little ease they had.

152. See n. 124, above.

153. The disjointed sentence hints at a cut.

154. Panawick ("Panawaioc," etc.) appears on Theodore de Bry's map of North Carolina (based on John White's map), but its location is uncertain (Quinn, *Roanoke Voyages*, II, 849, 872). The incident is not mentioned in the *Proceedings* or the *Generall Historie*, though there is reference to it in the Smith/Zúñiga map (Barbour, *Jamestown Voyages*, I, 240). Strachey gives further information (*Historie*, 34). Note that some such phrase as "like me" is missing at the end of the sentence.

155. The mouth of the York ("Pamuncks") River is actually just under 30 mi. NW of Cape Henry; Smith's magnetic compass, however, would have shown a 4° variation west.

156. Suspicious.

157. Crafty.

158. Leather quilted jackets, often plated with iron.

159. As usual, "ooze" (here misprinted "os"). This spelling is the result of an obvious attempt, made in some copies only, to correct a mistaken "ost" for "ose" (see the latter on sig. D2ᵛ). Modern Purtan Bay has three creeks, or inlets: Bland, Leigh, and Purtan. Smith apparently mistook the first for the second and had to cross a "dreadful bridge" (sig. D2ᵛ, below). Despite the confused text, both the honesty of the guides and the cause of the colonists' anxiety are clear.

160. Transcribed as "Nantaquoud" and "Nantaquaus" in the *Generall Historie*, 49, 121.

161. I.e., "forked posts." Ottahotin was werowance of Kiskiack (Strachey, *Historie*, 69).

162. "The Rankes are called Frunts, because they stand foremost" (Gervase Markham, *The Soldiers Accidence* [London, 1625], 6). Below, "the bridge" was built for nimble-footed Indians, not for maladroit Englishmen in armor.

163. The exchanges of oratory between Powhatan and Smith are after the Classical pattern.

164. Cf. *Generall Historie*, 49, which mentions "two great gunnes, and a gryndstone." Demiculverins were cannons of about 4.5 in. bore, weighing 4,500 lbs. (*Accidence*, 34), or 3,400 lbs. (*Sea Grammar*, 70). This passage is not repeated in the *Generall Historie*, and the exact meaning of what follows is not clear.

165. A bridge is missing here; perhaps, "He then said (or asked): But where. . . ."

166. The sense requires "and I" instead of "who."

167. Despite the colonists' offers to conquer his enemies, Powhatan preferred first to conquer the colonists.

168. Some such phrase as "that it was aground" has been left out here.

169. Again, something seems to be missing.

170. Once more, something seems to be missing; perhaps also at the beginning of the paragraph. Note that Arber wrongly printed "our" for "out" in "take out bowes" (*Smith, Works*, 26; see also Barbour, *Jamestown Voyages*, I, 193n).

171. An absurd word for the doors to an Indian house, big as they may have been; literally, "gates."

172. "Auncient" means simply "former, earlier." Cf. the *Proceedings*, 18; and the *Generall Historie*, 51–52: "With many pretty Discourses to renew their old acquaintance."

173. Both the *Proceedings* and the *Generall Historie* dismiss the evening's events with a few words. The final "him" obviously refers to Newport, whose name is consistently

spelled "Nuport" from here to the end.

174. "Trumpeter." The military trumpet of Smith's day was a "natural" one, of limited range, but surely more strident than any sound the most stout-lunged Indian warrior could make. Below, the "basket of Beanes" is omitted in the *Proceedings*, 19, and the *Generall Historie*, 52, but Powhatan's return gift of Namontack is added (see the Biographical Directory).

175. Probably referring to paces: 3,000 ft., or more than half a mile.

176. Cf. "politic," sig. C4^r and n. 157, above.

177. Something about Powhatan seems to be missing here.

178. Large copper cooking pots used on shipboard; already in use as valuable trade goods in fur-trading coastal areas farther north.

179. Smith "drew him on" to give 3 pecks at least; cf. the *Proceedings*, 20; and the *Generall Historie*, 52.

180. There were 30 to 40 men in the party; see the *Proceedings*, 17–18; and the *Generall Historie*, 51. Despite some possible exaggeration, this account of the "blew Beades" is plausible.

181. Again, something seems to be missing. The sense is that Newport, seeking a compromise, allowed his men to carry arms, against Powhatan's wishes, but made them stay at the waterside, against Smith's better judgment.

182. The sentence has been truncated, but there is no parallel account elsewhere to hint at what is missing.

183. This mangled sentence merely means that Scrivener and his men made the best of it, "as a savage [would]."

184. Possibly "I. H.'"s misreading of "sonne Nantaquaus"; Powhatan had no "seamen," and "Mantiuas" does not occur elsewhere.

185. Variant of "scrupulous"; here "fastidious, finicky."

186. Something seems to be missing from the middle of this passage in two places; but it is evident that Powhatan was not eager to fight the Monacans, although he was willing to offer token aid to the English if they did.

187. Newport had apparently sent overland for more hatchets for trading. Since Powhatan did not want Opechancanough to get any, he resorted to trickery.

188. See n. nn to facsimile.

189. Although an emendation to read "Opechancanough, his wife, . . ." seems in order, it is possible that the meaning is "Opechancanough's wife . . . ," despite the later statement that "he seemed. . . ." The brevity and isolation of the paragraph lead the editor not to emend it, but to suggest that some pruning was done.

190. Judging by modern charts, the distance by water was probably half that.

191. See n. pp to facsimile; and Barbour, "Earliest Reconnaissance," Pt. II, 40. The dish was the Powhatan counterpart of New England "succotash."

192. This passage seems incomplete, and the incident is not mentioned in the *Proceedings*, 20, or in the *Generall Historie*, 52. The "Instructions" of the London Council, however, required that exploring parties should "try if they Can find any mineral" (Barbour, *Jamestown Voyages*, I, 51).

193. While the site of Werowocomoco (misspelled in text) has not yet been determined archaeologically, the editor subscribes to the suggested location at Purtan Bay, on the north (left) bank of modern York River, 11–12 mi. downstream from West Point (cf. McCary, *Indians in Seventeenth-Century Virginia*, 7). On that basis, it would have been about 15 mi. from Cinquaotecke, a distance roughly confirmed by the Smith/Hole map. Deane has disregarded other factors in arguing for 20-plus mi. (*Smith's Relation*, 59).

194. Namontack; see n. 174, above.

195. According to Wingfield, Newport and party returned to Jamestown Mar. 9 (Barbour, *Jamestown Voyages*, I, 228). This passage raises the question of how soon after their return Smith made the note on which this passage was based.

196. Wingfield and Archer went with him (*Proceedings*, 22; *Generall Historie*, 53). Deane suggests that the first sentence of the next paragraph should come here (*Smith's Relation*, 61) and the present editor concurs.

197. For the sequel, see the *Proceedings*, 23, and the *Generall Historie*, 54.

198. Something seems to have been cut at the beginning. "Nausamd" in the original is clearly an error for "Nawsamond" (sig. E1^r), itself a variant of the usual "Nansemond."

199. "We may testified" is most likely a misprint of "we many testified" (cf. "we two, we three, etc.").

200. There is no explanation of why this first revenge raid on the Indians took place (Smith disapproved of the idea; see the *Proceedings*, 95–96, and the *Generall Historie*, 91). The Nansemond River and the tribe of that name were 12 to 16 mi. (20 to 25 km.) W of the site of the encounter of nearly a year before (probably with the Chesapeake Indians; but see Quinn, *England and the Discovery of America*, 454–456). As a matter of fact, however, the whole area was virtually unknown. Robert Tindall had noted "Nattamonge" on his "Draughte" (Barbour, *Jamestown Voyages*, I, 105), but John Smith did not explore the region until after June 2, 1608. The present editor wonders if the editor of 1608 did not tamper with the account to vindicate Newport's actions (cf. Smith's letter to the Virginia Company, in the *Generall Historie*, 70–72).

201. Shallow bays.

202. Smith's guess at the location of Chawwonocke is reasonable (see the pocket map at the end of Quinn, *Roanoke Voyages*, II).

203. Long iron bars with sliding shackles to lock prisoners' ankles to the floor.

204. Now usually "seize on."

205. Garbled as this paragraph is, it is clear from it that the colonists generally were less determined than Smith. As to details, the end of the first sentence means, "they seemed to fight to keep anything they could snatch up, but for what we held in our hands." Then a cut was made, eliminating the antecedent of the masculine third-person pronoun, so that we do not know whose pride or who "offered" to strike Smith.

206. Cf. n. 198, above.

207. To understand this exceptionally bad passage, see the *Generall Historie*, 53. Briefly put, Nelson had wintered in the West Indies after being driven before a storm, and there had stocked up with food for himself and his men, and for Jamestown. Hatchets, tools, traitors, and deceivers are not mentioned. The trouble is much more than a mere matter of punctuation, as suggested in Deane, *Smith's Relation*, 64.

208. "These" has curiously been misread as "their" by both Deane (*Smith's Relation*, 65) and Arber (*Smith, Works*, 34).

209. "Thickets," dense undergrowth.

210. An overstated version of the London Council's "Instructions"; see Barbour, *Jamestown Voyages*, I, 50–51.

211. Smith's rebuttal, which follows and combines the opinions of others with his own, is badly worded (or edited).

212. "Rendezvous," here meaning "store of provisions"; an unusual use of the word.

213. I.e., "only with the prospect of our own discomfiture."

214. "I keepe private" sounds very much like "I. H." (see sig. ¶1ᵛ). Two of the "certain matters" may have been the gold fever (*Proceedings*, 25, 28; *Generall Historie*, 54) and Ratcliffe's "palace" (*Proceedings*, 28, 41; *Generall Historie*, 55, 66).

215. More time was needed to load and fire a gun than to nock and shoot an arrow.

216. The spy was Amocis (sig. E3ᵛ, below); no reason is given for the beating, and the passage has no exact parallel in the *Proceedings*, 24, or the *Generall Historie*, 54.

217. Here, "gates"; cf. sig. D1ᵛ and n. 171, above.

218. Await the outcome.

219. The meaning is, "Their mistrust and fear betrayed their evil designs, as did their apprehensive departure."

220. "Manned"; purely for the printer's convenience.

221. I.e., "made them grieve or mourn (loudly)." The daily prayers, with the minister in vestments and the colonists in armor, probably terrified the Indians.

222. I.e., "custody." The problems with the Indians were minimized in the *Proceedings*, 21–24, and the *Generall Historie*, 54.

223. I.e., the muskets were ready to fire.

224. Macanoe (see sig. E3ᵛ, below). "Comouodos" was likely a misreading of Smith's Spanish form "camaradas"—modern "comrade" had not yet taken definite shape in English.

225. "The action of carrying [a plan] into effect" (*OED*).

226. "Came" in some copies. The meaning is, "when Maister Scrivener had come, the Indian explained that. . . ."

227. Charm.

228. Arber suggests interpolating "[to be]" after "suspected" (*Smith, Works*, 37).

229. Suspected, feared.

230. Strachey confirms that "Weionock" was a "servant" of Powhatan's (*Historie*, 56).

231. Frequent or habitual meetings.

232. A misprint or misreading of "loged" or "lodged."

233. Now usually "railed against."

234. Deane reads "beare" (*Smith's Relation*, 71); the type is damaged, but an enlargement shows "beate."

235. Martin at that time apparently pleaded that Powhatan was "true"—not false or inimical.

236. Though the text is again mangled, it is clear that Smith and Scrivener repeated Macanoe's confession to other Indians and found that he told the truth.

237. See n. ss to facsimile. This is the first mention of Pocahontas in the *True Relation* as it was printed, but the casual way in which her name appears on the next page suggests that Smith's original letter had mentioned her before. On Pocahontas, see the Biographical Directory; Barbour, *Pocahontas*; and the editor's entry in Edward T. James *et al.*, eds., *Notable American Women: A Biographical Dictionary* (Cambridge, Mass., 1971), III, 78–81.

238. A guard for the wrist. The meaning of what follows seems to be that on the day of the affray (three days before), when some Englishmen were taken, Opechancanough had promised to send the articles to Smith as a gesture of peace.

239. Obsolete spelling of "proffered."

240. The English interest in such stones must have puzzled the Indians, whose sole "gems" were pearls and copper.

241. A passage seems to have been cut at the end of this paragraph. Despite preliminary pruning of one sort or another, the printer (and "I. H."?) found a single blank page remaining in the last gathering to accommodate both the end of the narrative and Smith's peroration. The former seems to have suffered.

242. This final paragraph seems to form a curious conclusion for a letter to a personal friend. Smith may well have written a few encouraging remarks as a close, but it seems entirely possible that "I. H." was primarily responsible for its propagandistic tone. In any event, Smith himself seldom if ever followed the text of the *True Relation* in his later works.

TEXTUAL ANNOTATION

AND BIBLIOGRAPHICAL NOTE TO

A True Relation

TEXTUAL ANNOTATION

The page numbers below refer to the boldface numerals in the margins of the present text, which record the pagination of the original edition used as copy text. The word or words before the bracket show the text as emended by the editor; the word or words after the bracket reproduce the copy text. The wavy dash symbol used after the bracket stands for a word that has not itself been changed but that adjoins a changed word or punctuation mark. The inferior caret, also used only after the bracket, signifies the location of missing punctuation in the copy text.

Page.Line

¶1ᵛ.13 somewhat] som:what
¶1ᵛ.14 publicke. What] ~ ∧ what
¶1ᵛ.15–16 nature of] ~ , ~
¶1ᵛ.22 excellent] execellent
¶1ᵛ.22–23 healthfull] health full
¶2ʳ.3 superstition] susperstition
A3ʳ.12 Canaries] Cauaries
A3ʳ.13 after, we] ~ ∧ ~
A3ʳ.25 harme. And] ~ , and
A3ᵛ.3 Gosnold. Notwithstanding] ~ , notwithstanding
A3ᵛ.9 narrower; the] ~ , ~
A3ᵛ.22 us a] ~ in ~
A3ᵛ.25 a mile] an ile
A3ᵛ.31 have] hane
A4ʳ.2 spangles.] ~ ∧
A4ʳ.5 theirs. Hee] ~ , hee
A4ʳ.7 further he] furtherhe
A4ʳ.12 Apamatuck] Agamatock
A4ʳ.21 us. Yet] ~ , yet
A4ʳ.27 with all] with-all (end-of-line hyphen)
A4ʳ.29 it. Had] ~ , had
A4ᵛ.2 hurt.] ~ ∧
A4ᵛ.17 thereby] whereby (in some copies)
A4ᵛ.22 plagued] inplagued (in some copies)
A4ᵛ.25–26 cause: onely] ~ , ~ (in some copies)
B1ʳ.17 The president] the ~

B1ʳ.26 Kegquouhtan, an] ~ ∧ ~
B1ʳ.33 kindenes, I] ~ : ~
B1ᵛ.7 them. With] ~ , with
B1ᵛ.18 Waraskoyack] waraskoyack
B1ᵛ.25 Time] time
B1ᵛ.31 her. The] ~ , the
B1ᵛ.35 neere. Truck] ~ , truck
B2ʳ.7 trade. But] ~ , but
B2ʳ.15 trading; the] ~ , ~
B2ʳ.19 Weanock] weanock
B2ʳ.31 corne. What] ~ , what
B2ʳ.33 This] this
B2ᵛ.3 sorts; a] ~ ∧ ~
B2ᵛ.13 The next] the ~
B2ᵛ.18–19 ordnance. Many] ~ , many
B2ᵛ.22 back, so] ~ ∧ ~
B2ᵛ.28 hanged. But] ~ , but
B2ᵛ.29 rescue, when] ~ : ~
B2ᵛ.34 Chickahominy] Checka Hamania
B2ᵛ.35 Moysenock, Righkahauck] moysenock ∧ ~
B2ᵛ.36 others. Their] ~ , their
B3ʳ.5 resolved] reolved
B3ʳ.6 This matter] this ~
B3ʳ.12 circuit] cicuit
B3ʳ.16 marsh. More] ~ , more
B3ʳ.19 there, I] ~ ∧ ~
B3ʳ.21 under, red] ~ ∧ ~
B3ʳ.24 At] at

Page.Line

C3ᵛ.13–14   them for]   ∼ , ∼

C3ᵛ.14   slew, insomuch]   ∼ : ∼

C3ᵛ.15   me; but]   ∼ , ∼

C3ᵛ.25–26   bread, Raugroughcuns] ∼ ‸ ∼

C4ʳ.7   Panawicke, beyond]   ∼ ‸ ∼

C4ʳ.7   Roanoke]   Roonok

C4ʳ.13   Cape Henrie]   Cape Henricke (in some copies). Cf. D4ʳ.16, below, where "Cape Henrie" was misprinted "Captaine Hendrick," and also D4ᵛ.21, below, where it is "Cape-hendicke." For a possible reason for the misprints, see Barbour, *Jamestown Voyages*, I, 190n.

C4ʳ.16   shore; the]   ∼ , ∼

C4ʳ.17   os. Being]   of, being (in some copies "oft, being")

C4ʳ.19   mile; the]   ∼ , ∼

C4ʳ.21   men, conducted]   ∼ ‸ ∼

C4ʳ.23   railes. The]   ∼ , the

C4ʳ.31–32   Indians, seeing]   ∼ ‸ ∼

C4ʳ.34   passed. Two]   ∼ , two

C4ᵛ.2   bread; being]   ∼ , ∼

C4ᵛ.7–8   Christian; with]   ∼ , ∼

C4ᵛ.9   sit. I]   ∼ , ∼

C4ᵛ.10   Hatte; as]   ∼ , ∼

C4ᵛ.14   Appomattoc]   Apamatuc

C4ᵛ.20   him; with]   ∼ , ∼

C4ᵛ.21   which I]   I which

C4ᵛ.21   Paspahegh. I]   ∼ , ∼

C4ᵛ.24   them; whereat]   ∼ , ∼

C4ᵛ.27   you.]   ∼ ,

D1ʳ.8   a werowanes]   A ∼

D1ʳ.14   King, rising]   ∼ ‸ ∼

D1ʳ.15–16   beare, giving]   ∼ : ∼

D1ʳ.20–21   mee. The]   ∼ , the

D1ʳ.22   Namontack]   Mamontacke

D1ᵛ.7   auncient]   aunent (end-of-line error)

D1ᵛ.11   Beades, and]   ∼ : ∼

D1ᵛ.14   him. With]   ∼ , with

D1ᵛ.26   waies. Wherewith,] ∼ , wherewith ‸

Page.Line

D1ᵛ.29   Barge. Experience]   ∼ , experience

D1ᵛ.31   us; but]   ∼ , ∼

D2ʳ.6   corne; with]   ∼ , ∼

D2ʳ.8–9   piece. Hee]   ∼ , hee

D2ʳ.15   Nuport. Some]   ∼ , some

D2ᵛ.14   me; sixe]   ∼ , ∼

D2ᵛ.16   heads. Their]   ∼ , their

D2ᵛ.23   Emperor]   Emperors

D2ᵛ.24   men; he]   ∼ , ∼

D2ᵛ.27   it. This]   ∼ , this

D2ᵛ.30   discourse, causing]   ∼ ‸ ∼

D3ʳ.7   Opechankanough, the]   ∼ . The

D3ʳ.7–8   Pamaunke, should]   ∼ ‸ ∼

D3ʳ.10   them. The]   ∼ , the

D3ʳ.11   him. Only]   ∼ , only

D3ʳ.15   water; if]   ∼ , ∼

D3ʳ.16   boats. This]   ∼ , this

D3ʳ.19   mirth. The]   ∼ , the

D3ʳ.21   him, who]   ∼ : ∼

D3ᵛ.1   goe, in that]   ∼ ‸ ∼ , ∼

D3ᵛ.2   stay, sent]   ∼ : ∼

D3ᵛ.2–3   answer. Yet]   ∼ , yet

D3ᵛ.4   Cinquoateck, the]   ∼ ‸ ∼

D3ᵛ.4   towne]   twaine

D3ᵛ.6   Katatough. To]   ∼ , to

D3ᵛ.13   shore. With]   ∼ , with

D3ᵛ.16   Opechankanough conducted]   ∼ , ∼

D3ᵛ.19   us. That]   ∼ , that

D3ᵛ.22   Pansarowmana. The]   ∼ ‸ the

D3ᵛ.24   delight; by]   ∼ , ∼

D3ᵛ.29   Pinnis. With]   ∼ , with

D4ʳ.3–4   Cinquaotecke. The]   ∼ , the

D4ʳ.10   Corne. Our]   ∼ , our

D4ʳ.12   hand, of which]   ∼ off, which

D4ʳ.16   Cape Henrie]   Captaine Hendrick (see C4ʳ.13, above)

D4ʳ.20   Nansemond]   Nausamd

D4ʳ.24   volley]   vally

D4ʳ.25   confesse. The]   ∼ , the

Page.Line			Page.Line	
D4^r.27	would, as] ~ ^ ~		E2^v.8	another, as] ~ ^ ~
D4^r.28	contented. At] ~ , at		E2^v.9	men; they] ~ , ~
D4^r.30	shore; he] ~ , ~		E2^v.9	me. Our] ~ , our
D4^v.2	shore. To] ~ , to		E2^v.11	hang). The] ~) ^ the
D4^v.3	accepted] excepted		E2^v.15	doores. We] ~ , we
D4^v.7	Fort. This] ~ , this		E2^v.23	doe. The] ~ , the
D4^v.10	inhabitants; for] ~ , ~		E2^v.23	concluded that] ~ , ~
D4^v.16	people. They] ~ , they		E2^v.24	intent. The] ~ , the
D4^v.20	Chawwonocke. The] ~ , the		E2^v.25	hold to] ~ , ~
			E2^v.28	I, releasing] ~ ^ ~
D4^v.21	Cape Henrie] Cape-hendicke (see C4^r.13, above)		E2^v.29	first with the rack] ~ ~ thereat (in some copies)
E1^r.1	hands. His] ~ , his		E2^v.31	come] came (in some copies)
E1^r.8	present not] ~ , ~		E3^r.2	Kiskiack, these] ~ . These
E1^r.13	so submissive] so ~ ~		E3^r.3	me; Paspahegh] ~ , ~
E1^r.15	Nansemond] Nawsemond		E3^r.5	friends till] ~ , ~
E1^r.25	testifie, his] ~ ^ ~		E3^r.10	occasion was] ~ , ~ (in some copies)
E1^v.7	was that] ~ , ~			
E1^v.7	selfe and] ~ , ~		E3^r.17	Powhatan to] ~ , ~
E1^v.10	trayning our] ~ , ~		E3^r.21	guide. The] ~ , the
E1^v.11	woods. These] ~ , these		E3^r.27	presents. The] ~ , the
E1^v.13	force in] ~ : ~		E3^r.28	him either] ~ , ~
E1^v.18	himselfe, as] ~ ^ ~		E3^r.30	Fort returned] ~ , ~
E1^v.19	shippe and] ~ , ~		E3^r.32	Chikamanias. Not] ~ , not
E1^v.21	alleadging that,] ~ , ~ ^		E3^v.3	suspition presently] ~ , ~
E1^v.21–22	profitable and] ~ , ~		E3^v.16	Powhatan, understanding] ~ ^ ~
E1^v.27	The meanes] the ~			
E1^v.29	Fort. Their] ~ , their		E3^v.16	Salvages, sent] ~ ^ ~
E1^v.32	reliefe, for] ~ : ~		E3^v.22	understanding. He] ~ , he
E2^r.1	rest. If] ~ ; if		E3^v.22	circumstance told] ~ , ~
E2^r.3	share; but] ~ , ~		E3^v.23	Powhatan loved] ~ , ~
E2^r.4	besides, our] ~ ^ ~		E3^v.25	Deere and] ~ , ~
E2^r.8	reason to] ~ , ~		E3^v.25	bread besides] ~ , ~
E2^r.11–12	confusions. Our] ~ , our		E3^v.31	Opechaukanough sent] ~ , ~
E2^r.17	Indian, having] ~ ^ ~			
E2^r.17	Axe, was] ~ ^ ~		E4^r.2	Glove and] ~ , ~
E2^r.20	Fort among] ~ , ~		E4^r.8	us to] ~ , ~
E2^r.21	Indians] Indiants		E4^r.8	afternoone, they] ~ ^ ~
E2^r.28	him. I] ~ , ~		E4^r.14	Pocahuntas also] ~ , ~
E2^v.3	villanie, concluded] ~ ^ ~		E4^r.16	suspition] snspition (inverted "u")
E2^v.4	event; eight] ~ , ~			
E2^v.4	present. An] ~ , an		E4^r.17	it; two] ~ , ~
E2^v.4	after, came] ~ ^ ~		E4^r.18	after, a] ~ ^ ~
E2^v.6	gloves; their] ~ , ~		E4^r.18	Paspaheyan came] ~ , ~

E4^r.20	Rockes. With]	~ , with
E4^r.22	us for]	~ , ~
E4^r.27	him if]	~ , ~

E4^v.3	adventurers in]	~ , ~
E4^v.9	minds and]	~ , ~

Hyphenation Record

The following list has been inserted at the request of the editorial staff of the Institute of Early American History and Culture. It records possible compound words that were hyphenated at the end of the line in the copy text. In each case the editor had to decide for the present edition whether to print the word as a single word or as a hyphenated compound. The material before the bracket indicates how the word is printed in the present edition; the material after the bracket indicates how the word was broken in the original. The wavy dash symbol indicates that the form of the word has been unchanged from the copy text. Numerals refer to the page number of the copy text (the boldface numerals in the margin in this edition) and to the line number (counting down from the boldface number) in the present edition.

¶1^r.6	himselfe]	him-selfe
¶1^v.20	aswell]	as-well
¶1^v.29	overthrow]	over-throw
A3^v.12	strawberries]	straw-berries
A4^r.33	drie-fats]	~
B1^r.13	abroad]	a-broad
B4^r.9	quagmire]	quag-mire
B4^r.34	themselves]	them-selves

D2^v.10	ashore]	a-shore
D2^v.30	ashore]	a-shore
D4^r.31– D4^v.1	aboard]	a-board
E2^r.12	husbandmen]	husband- men
E3^r.28	withall]	with-all

BIBLIOGRAPHICAL NOTE

Entry in the Stationers' Register

13 Augusti [1608]

William Welby.
John Tappe/
Entred for their copie under the handes
of. master. Wilson and Th[e]warden
Master Lownes/A booke called *A true
relation of suche occurrences and accidentes of
note as have happened in Virginia synce the
first plantinge of that Colonye which is nowe
resident in the south parte of Virginia till
master Nelsons comminge away from them
etc.* . . . . vi^d

(Edward Arber, ed., *A Transcript of
the Registers of the Company of
Stationers of London, 1554–1640
A.D.* . . . [London, 1875–1877],
III, 388).

Editions

Early:

1608. A || TRUE RE- || lation of such occur- || rences and accidents of noate as || hath hapned in Virginia since the first || planting of that Collony, which is now || resident in the South part thereof, till || the last returne from || thence. || *Written by Captaine* Smith *one of the said Collony, to a* || *worshipfull* friend of his in England. || [Woodcut of a ship.] || *LONDON* || Printed for *John Tappe*, and are to bee solde at the Grey- || hound in Paules-Church-yard, by. *W.W*. || 1608 ||

Quarto, pp. [44], unpaged. A–E in fours, the first blank; and ¶ in two, inserted after the title (*STC* 22795.7).

[Note: There was but one edition, with one setting of type, but there were three previous issues, affecting lines 10 and 11 of the title:

(a) *Written by a Gentleman of the said Collony to a worshipfull* || friend of his in England (*STC* 22795).

(b) *Written by* Th. Watson, *Gent. one of the said Collony, to a* || *worshipfull* friend of his in England (*STC* 22795.3).

(c) *Written by Captaine* Smith, *Coronell of the said Collony, to a* || *worshipfull* friend of his in England (*STC* 22795.5).

While it is uncertain whether (a) or (b) was the first issue (Worthington Chauncey Ford makes a good case for the latter in Massachusetts Historical Society, *Proceedings*, LVIII [1924–1925], 246), issue (c) was evidently someone's error. Most if not all surviving copies of this issue show attempts to blot out the first three and the last two letters of the word "Coronell," leaving the word "one." The reason for the several issues is clearly stated on sig. ¶1ᵛ. Note that the blank leaf before the title page bears sig. A, missing in B.M. copies.]

Modern:

1845. *Southern Literary Messenger*, XI, ed. Benjamin Blake Minor (Richmond, Va.).

1866. *A True Relation of Virginia, by Captain John Smith*, ed. Charles Deane, with introduction and notes (Boston).

1884, etc. *Smith . . . Works*, ed. Edward Arber (Birmingham). See the list of issues of the Arber text in the General Introduction at the beginning of this volume.

1896. *American History Leaflets: Colonial and Constitutional*, No. 27, ed. Albert Bushnell Hart and Edward Channing (New York), repr. 1912.

1907. *Narratives of Early Virginia, 1606–1625*, ed. Lyon Gardiner Tyler (New York), repr. 1930, 1959.

[1911]. *Readings in American History . . .* , ed. Edgar W. Ames, with biographies and notes (New York).

1969. *The Jamestown Voyages under the First Charter, 1606–1609*, ed. Philip L. Barbour (Cambridge).

A MAP OF VIRGINIA.

With a Description of the Countrey,
the Commodities, People,
Government and Religion

1612

INTRODUCTION*

Whereas the *True Relation* (1608) suffered from injudicious editing even before it was printed, Smith's 1612 publication has been subjected only to modern criticism, often in the form of myopic inspection. It is therefore wise that a fresh start be made here.

The original long title, pruned and modernized here for readier understanding, outlines the contents of both parts:

> [I] A Map of Virginia, With
> a Description of the Country, by
> Captain Smith: and
> [II] The Proceedings of Those Colonies,
> Taken Out of the Writings of Doctor
> Russell and others, by W[illiam]
> S[ymonds].
> Printed at Oxford by Joseph Barnes
> [manager of the press for the uni-
> versity, 1586–1617].

The first part, ordinarily though loosely referred to by the title *Map of Virginia*, consists of an engraved map and a descriptive text with information on the location of Virginia, and its geography, resources, and inhabitants. A quarto volume of only thirty-nine pages, it is virtually the fountainhead of what is known today of the Indians who inhabited the Chesapeake Bay area at the beginning of the seventeenth century.

Edward Arber was the first to point out that the printing of Smith's "book of travels" at the Oxford University Press was a "most singular fact," since that press usually "produced sermons, theological and learned Works, etc."[1] Eleven years later Falconer Madan added that Smith's book and Robert Burton's *Anatomy of Melancholy* (Oxford, 1621) were two of "the most important works produced at Oxford between 1585 and 1640."[2] Although in Burton's case the place of publication is not surprising since he lived and died in Oxford, Smith had no ties there and may never have visited the city (unless it was to revise proofs at Joseph Barnes's printing house). Yet when

---

*This work was printed in two parts, with twin title pages. The present Introduction deals with the first part only.

1. Edward Arber, ed., *Captain John Smith . . . Works, 1608–1631*, The English Scholar's Library Edition, No. 16 (Birmingham, 1884), I, 42.

2. Falconer Madan, *Oxford Books: A Bibliography* (Oxford, 1895), I, v, 83–85.

the course of events is taken into consideration, Arber's "singular fact" may not be so out of the way as it seemed to him. Although the evidence is purely circumstantial, it seems worth presenting.

Smith, disabled by a severe burn, returned to England late in 1609 without yet knowing that the Virginia Company had shown considerable appreciation of his work in Jamestown, and without having yet seen a copy of the new charter, signed only some six months before. He arrived in London, however, at a most inauspicious juncture. The reorganized company, now privately operated by royal license, had suffered a grave mishap at its very inception. For the same ships that took Smith home brought the news that the new governor, Sir Thomas Gates, the admiral, Sir George Somers, and the vice-admiral, Capt. Christopher Newport, were lost at sea on their way to take up their posts in Virginia, with all their letters of authority and other documents. Fortunately, the Council for Virginia had already planned to put a "lord governor and captain-general" over Gates, and thus a relief expedition could be organized with extraordinary speed. Sir Thomas West, third (or twelfth) Baron De La Warr, was appointed to take command, and on April 1, 1610, another fleet was on its way to Virginia.

Clearly, the councillors in London were too busy, and too troubled, to pay much attention to Capt. John Smith. He may have been put off politely, or he may have been merely brushed aside. The result was the same. The months dragged along, and by September 1610, London learned that the colony had been saved; Gates and De La Warr had joined forces in Jamestown, and Gates himself conveyed the tidings. An old friend or two of Smith's came back with Gates, and about the same time Smith found a new "best friend" in the elderly earl of Hertford, Sir Edward Seymour. Finding a "harbour" in his lordship's favor, and encouragement from his Virginia friends, Smith gathered together his notes, sketches, and keepsakes and set about writing a book.

A year passed. With a basic sketch map already in hand, Smith himself pulled together the text for the description of Virginia to go with the map, and with the aid of Richard Pots, clerk of the council in Virginia when Smith was president, he assembled various narratives from which the *Proceedings* was to be formed. Probably through Rawley Crashaw, a companion who had remained in Virginia, Smith got hold of the Reverend William Crashaw —for what immediate, specific purpose is not clear—and the Reverend William Whitaker. One or both of these put Smith in touch with a third preacher, William Symonds, an Oxford man then often to be found in the pulpit at St. Saviour's in Southwark, just across London Bridge from the Royal Exchange and other centers for news gathering. The rough copy for the *Proceedings* needed editorial advice, and Symonds gladly lent a hand. In this way, Smith's work came to be published in Oxford, and in two parts.

The map was engraved by William Hole, a well-known artist whom Smith apparently engaged sometime in 1611. Since Hole was not a cartographer, Smith supplied him with his own basic sketch map dating back to late 1608 and probably also with "regional" sketch maps of the rivers and other geographical details. In terms of the Latin then current, it can possibly best be said that Smith *collegit* (brought together, assembled) cards or sketches for Hole to use. To these he apparently added the Indians' verbal or manual descriptions (e.g., drawn with a stick in the sand) of unvisited or insufficiently explored regions. How much, or how little, of this Smith himself drafted is of small importance, especially since he seems never to have laid claim to any special ability in that field. What is significant is that he had the vision to get the map prepared and engraved.

Be that as it may, one chronological detail is important here. On March 12, 1611, Spain's ambassador to James I, Don Alonso de Velasco, sent a large manuscript map of northeast North America to Spain, which, as in the case of the Smith/Zúñiga map, no doubt is that stored in the Archivo General de Simancas, Valladolid, Spain, today. Careful inspection of the Velasco map points to a basic sketch of the Chesapeake Bay area, now lost, from which both the Velasco map and the more detailed one engraved by Hole were derived. Whether or not Smith did any or all of the drafting is not at issue here. Nor are the discrepant details an important matter, since there are valid explanations for these, such as the greatly reduced scale of the Velasco map as against Hole's. The important point is that the Velasco map establishes that the source of the Hole engraving was in existence early in 1611.

Smith's textual "Description of the Country," as distinct from the map, appears to have been inspired basically by Richard Hakluyt's *Principal Navigations, Voyages, Traffiques and Discoveries of the English Nation*, which had been completed in 1600 with the publication of Volume III, dealing with America. Hakluyt himself was one of the four patentees for the "Jamestown voyages," as the enterprise may succinctly be termed. His surrogate, the Reverend Robert Hunt, accompanied the original colonists as spiritual adviser. Most important of all, one or more copies of Hakluyt's book were taken along, too. Smith can hardly have failed to have had one handy.[3]

Thomas Harriot, however, who was "specially imploied" by Ralegh, was even more directly useful to Smith. His book *A briefe and true report of the new found land of Virginia* (London, 1588) had been available to Smith in

3. See the *Proceedings*, 28–36, with its reference to Ralph Lane's account of 1585–1586, from Richard Hakluyt's *The Principal Navigations, Voyages, Traffiques and Discoveries of the English Nation* (London, 1598–1600), III, 255–260. Smith appropriated two Indian words recorded by Lane: "werowances" ("kings," as defined by Lane); and "crenepos" ("their women," as explained by Hakluyt in a marginal note).

Virginia as reprinted by Hakluyt.[4] On his return, yet another reprint of the same work proved of great worth: that of the Flemish engraver and publisher Theodore de Bry, illustrated with de Bry's engravings based on John White's original drawings from life (Frankfurt am Main, 1590). Under Smith's guidance, both Hole and, later, Robert Vaughan[5] vicariously portrayed the Indians Smith saw around Chesapeake Bay in the likeness of the Indians White saw off Pamlico Sound. But it was Harriot's trained mind that accounted for de Bry, and de Bry inspired Smith's engravers.

As for the general organization of Smith's text, there is some slight reason to believe that he may have read José de Acosta's *Naturall and Morall Historie of the East and West Indies* (Seville, 1590), which had been translated by Edward Grimston (or Grimestone) and published in London in 1604. At least Smith's plan is broadly similar to Acosta's, even if there seems to be no evidence of direct borrowing, and it may be that the Reverend Samuel Purchas, when he got interested in Smith, made his copy available. Hakluyt's *Principal Navigations*, as we have noted, also gave Smith ideas. But for the rest, it was Smith's *Map of Virginia* that gave ideas to others.

William Strachey, the ex-secretary of the Jamestown colony, who returned to London late in 1611, was the first to follow in Smith's wake. Although it is remotely possible that Strachey had access to a manuscript copy of the *Map of Virginia* while in the colony early in that same year, it is certain that he had one soon after he got back home. Careful study of his *The Historie of Travell into Virginia Britania* shows that he incorporated about four-fifths of Smith's work bodily into his own. To this he added about twice as much more that he had collected himself during his fifteen to sixteen months' stay, beginning the year after Smith left Virginia. Strachey's complementary reinforcement of the *Map of Virginia* should be neither depreciated nor overlooked.[6]

Meanwhile, Samuel Purchas, B.D., vicar of Eastwood, near Southend-on-Sea at the mouth of the Thames, surrounded as he was by seafaring folk, had begun work on a large volume to be called *Purchas his Pilgrimage*, in which he planned to combine his religious calling with firsthand tales of foreign lands: "Relations," as he put it, "of the world and the religions observed in all ages and places discovered from the creation unto this present."[7] The Virginia colony, consequently, could not but interest Purchas, and through his colleagues in divinity in London, such as Crashaw and his associates, he must have heard about Smith and his book, full of the

4. Hakluyt, *Principal Navigations*, III, 266–280.

5. See caption to the "Map of Ould Virginia," following the first book of the *Generall Historie* in Vol. II.

6. For Strachey's debt to Smith, see S. G. Culliford, *William Strachey, 1572–1621* (Charlottesville, Va., 1965).

7. Purchas, *Purchas his Pilgrimage. Or Relations Of The World . . .* (London, 1613), title page.

"devilish" procedures of the American "savages" (from the French word *sauvages*, usually translated in those days as "wild-men"). If, then, Purchas had not already got in touch with Smith, he certainly did when Strachey came back with his harrowing tales.[8]

So it was that about the time Strachey returned, Purchas and Smith became or had become friends, and the former was able to publish a few extracts from the latter's manuscripts in the *Pilgrimage*, in 1613, including a fragment or two never printed by Smith himself.[9] The following year, Purchas noted in the second edition of the *Pilgrimage* (1614) that Smith's manuscript had been "since printed at Oxford" (p. 760), and this same notation was repeated in the third edition (1617), and in the 1626 reprint of the last mentioned.

Meanwhile, between 1617 and 1621, Purchas had started work on a new project, the enormous four-volume folio *Hakluytus Posthumus, or Purchas His Pilgrimes*, which appeared in 1625 (with an engraved title page dated 1624 in at least one copy). In this magnum opus Purchas found room to reprint the entire text of Smith's *Map of Virginia* as published in Oxford, with a few minor changes. But before the *Pilgrimes* appeared on the market, Smith himself had published the *Generall Historie of Virginia* (1624). In that work he included a reprint of the *Map of Virginia* as Book II, with minor changes of his own, but he almost rewrote the *Proceedings* for Book III. In short, inspired by Harriot but working according to his own understanding of what ought to be done, Smith produced a description of Virginia and its inhabitants that has been utilized ever since, with only the most trivial alterations, and to which Strachey's slightly later observations serve as a confirmation and handy complement.

In conclusion, it is worth noting here that the chance survival of a hand-written bill or invoice dated March 30, 1623, shows the importance that the Virginia Company then attached to Smith's work. Among the 115 titles of books sold to the company "at severall times" were:

> one copy of "Hackluites Voyadges,"
> three of "Smithes [Description of] New England [1616],"
> two of "Captaine Smithes book [Map of Virginia],"
> one "Heriotts booke of Virginia."[10]

The student of Smith's writings may find helpful the following table of broad correspondences between the *Map of Virginia*, Strachey's *Historie*, Smith's

8. Strachey's letter about the shipwreck on the reefs of Bermuda, "the Ile of Divels," was already known to Hakluyt, from whose estate Purchas finally retrieved it years later.

9. See the Fragments, in Vol. III.

10. Invoice, dated Mar. 30, 1623, found by the editor among the Ferrar Papers, Magdalene College, Cambridge. See David B. Quinn's published version, "A List of Books Purchased for the Virginia Company," *Virginia Magazine of History and Biography*, LXXVII (1969), 347–360.

Generall Historie, and Purchas's *Pilgrimes*, vol. IV; and between the *Map* and the various editions of Purchas's *Pilgrimage*.

Map of Va.	Strachey	Gen. Hist.	Pilgrimes
1–10	31–53	21–25	1691–1694
10–15		25–28	1694–1696
15–18 }	117–133	28–29	1696–1697
18–19		29	1697
19–29	70–87, 104–111	29–34	1697–1701
29–34	88–103	34–37	1701–1702
34–39		37–39	1703–1704

Map of Va.		Pilgrimage		
	(1613)	(1614)	(1617)	(1626)
1–2	634	760		834–835
9	640–641	767	953–954	842–844
2–19	635	761		836
29–34	639–640	768–769	950–956	839–841

Chronology of Events in Virginia, 1608–1612[*]

1608

June 2.   Smith sent his *True Relation* to England, and with it probably the Smith/Zúñiga map.

Sept. 10.   Smith elected president of the Virginia Council, after virtually completing his geographical and ethnological investigations. Shortly thereafter Captain Newport returned to Virginia with the second supply of colonists and brought a letter from the London Council that berated the colonists for their factiousness and "idle conceits."

c. Dec. 1.   Newport left on a return voyage to England, taking along Smith's "rude answer" to the London Council, as well as a "Mappe of the Bay and Rivers, with an annexed Relation of the Countries and Nations that inhabit them."

1609

Jan. 16.   Sometime before this date Newport reached England.

Feb. 18.   Robert Johnson's *Nova Britannia*, a promotional pamphlet inspired by King James's grant of a new charter, was entered for publication.

May 5.   Capt. Samuel Argall sent out to test a shorter route to Virginia, under a company commission.

May 23.   Second charter signed; Sir Thomas Smythe appointed treasurer. Also in May, the new council issued instructions to Sir Thomas Gates, as governor of Virginia, naming Sir George Somers admiral of Virginia, Capt. John Smith and others to the local council, and assigning Smith to the command of a fort to be built at Cape Comfort.

June 8.   Gates's fleet got out to sea from Falmouth.

July 13.   Argall arrived in Jamestown, after 69 days at sea (the 1606 voyage had taken 128 days).

July 24.   Gates and Somers's flagship caught by a hurricane and driven on the Bermuda reefs.

[*]The Julian calendar, ten days behind the Gregorian, is retained throughout.

Aug. 11–18. The surviving ships reached Jamestown. Archer, Ratcliffe, and other old enemies of Smith's stirred up trouble over the new charter (though nobody had a copy of it) but let Smith finish his term as president. Not long after, Smith was incapacitated by a severe burn, and the rebellious clique gained the upper hand. George Percy, youngest brother of the earl of Northumberland, reluctantly agreed to serve as president, apparently even before Sept. 10.

Aug. 18. Henry Hudson, a friend of Smith's, explored Delaware Bay, after picking up from where Smith's explorations had left off (approximately 37° 30′ N lat.). From there he sailed N to explore the river now named after him.

Oct. 4. Captain Ratcliffe wrote to Lord Salisbury that Smith "is sent home."

Nov. 9. Sometime before this date, Argall arrived back in England. Meanwhile, in Virginia the "starving time" had set in.

Nov. 27. In Bermuda, Gates and Somers determined to build boats to transport themselves to Virginia.

Nov. 30. Sometime before this date, Smith arrived in England.

Dec. 14. Lord De La Warr, Sir Thomas Smythe, and others entered for publication *A True and Sincere Declaration of the Purpose of the Plantation Begun in Virginia* to calm investors concerned over the loss of the flagship and to announce the immediate departure of a relief fleet commanded by De La Warr, now named lord governor and captain general for Virginia.

1610

Feb. 21. The Reverend William Crashaw, a Puritan, preached a farewell sermon before De La Warr, and on Apr. 1 the latter's fleet sailed from the Solent (Isle of Wight).

May 10. Gates set sail from Bermuda for Virginia in two pinnaces built on the island. At about the same time, George Percy undertook for the first time to sail from Jamestown down to Old Point Comfort to see if the colonists there were still alive.

May 21. Gates arrived with his men just in time to meet Percy, who was at Old Point Comfort, and two days later they were all reunited in Jamestown.

June 7. Finding "not past sixtie" colonists alive, out of 500, Gates abandoned Jamestown and put the survivors and his own men aboard three pinnaces. A few miles downstream, however, they met De La Warr, who had entered the bay the day before, and in short order all went back to Jamestown.

June 10. Sunday afternoon. De La Warr came ashore to take formal charge of the colony. Two days later he nominated his council, with William Strachey secretary and recorder.

c. *Sept. 1.* De La Warr's ships returned to England, bearing Gates, Newport, and others, along with Strachey's account of the Bermuda mis-adventure, "A True Reportory of the Wracke, and Redemption of Sir Thomas Gates." Important for John Smith was the highly probable return then of Richard Pots, an old Virginia colonist who had apparently acted as clerk of the council when Smith was president, and who was to take an important part in Smith's immediate plans, for the news of the colony's survival could not but give Smith a new purpose in life.

Nov. 8. Sir Thomas Smythe, Richard Martin, secretary of the Virginia Company, and others entered for publication *A True Declaration of the Estate of the Colony in Virginia*, a vindication based largely on Strachey's "Reportory." It is prob-able that the publication of this pamphlet was an immediate cause in Smith's completing plans for his own work, since Richard Pots, a knowledgeable acquaintance from Virginia now in England, and probably others, could help.

Nov. 9. Sir George Somers died in Bermuda.

Dec. 14. Richard Martin, secretary of the Virginia Company, apparently assailed by misgivings about Virginia, wrote privately to Strachey asking for an honest report of the colony.

1611

Mar. 12. Don Alonso de Velasco, Spanish ambassador to James I, sent to Philip III a manuscript map of NE North America (hereafter called the "Velasco map"), which was evidently based on various available maps, "plots," or sketches.

Mar. 26.   Smith appears to have employed the engraver William Hole shortly after this date.

Mar. 28.   De La Warr left Virginia, ill. Sir Thomas Dale had already sailed for Virginia with three ships bearing men, cattle, and supplies.

Nov. 1.   The earliest recorded performance of Shakespeare's *The Tempest*, in which he surely drew on William Strachey's "Reportory."

c. *Dec. 18.*   Shortly before this date Newport returned from Virginia with word of Gates's safe arrival there. Gates thereafter was employed by the East India Company. Argall seems to have replaced Newport in the Virginia service, and John Smith may have regarded this development as a favorable sign for himself. But by then William Hole presumably was at work on Smith's map, and William Crashaw and William Symonds may well have started to help Smith find a printer.

1612

Mar. 12.   The third charter, an amplification of the 1609 charter inspired by the knowledge that Bermuda was accessible and habitable and by the fear that Spain might now occupy it, was signed.

May 1.   Robert Johnson's *The New Life of Virginia* was entered for publication. Containing no map, no sound information about the Indians, and no historical details, this appears to have been the type of promotional literature considered most appropriate by Smythe's clique.

Aug. 7.   Purchas's *Pilgrimage* was entered for publication. In it he stated that the Smith/Hole map was in print, but implied that the accompanying text was not.

1613

Mar. 24.   Smith's *Map of Virginia* and *Proceedings* must have been in print by this date, since the legal year 1612 ended then. This is corroborated in the second edition of Purchas's *Pilgrimage*, which states in a marginal note that Smith's manuscript was "since printed at Oxford."

A MAP OF VIRGINIA.

VVITh A DESCRIPTI-
ON OF THE COVNTREY, THE
Commodities, People, Govern-
ment and Religion.

VVritten by Captaine SMITH, *sometimes Go-*
vernour of the Countrey.

WHEREVNTO IS ANNEXED THE
proceedings of those Colonies, since their first
departure from England, with the discourses,
Orations, and relations of the Salvages,
and the accidents that befell
them in all their Iournies
and discoveries.

TAKEN FAITHFVLLY AS THEY
were written out of the writings of

DOCTOR RVSSELL.	RICHARD WIEFIN.
THO. STVDLEY.	WILL. PHETTIPLACE.
ANAS TODKILL.	NATHANIEL POVVELL.
IEFFRA ABOT.	RICHARD POTS.

And the relations of divers other diligent observers there
present then, and now many of them in England.
By VV. S.

AT OXFORD,
Printed by Joseph Barnes. 1612.

[See the "Note on the Authors" following the Introduction to the *Proceedings* for comments on the "diligent observers."

"W. S." refers to William Symonds, D.D., who acted as editor for the *Proceedings* (see the Biographical Directory; and the *Proceedings*, 110).

The editor is grateful to the British Library for permission to reproduce this title page.]

TO THE RIGHT HONOURABLE
Sir Edward Semer Knight,
Baron Beauchamp, and Earle of Hartford,[1]
Lieutenant to his most excellent Majestie,
in the Countries of Somerset and
Wiltshire, my Honourable good
Lord and Maister.[2]

My Honourable Lord:

If Vertue be the soule of true Nobilitie[3] as wise men say, then blessed is your Lordship, that is every way noble, as well in vertue, as birth, and riches. Though riches now, be the chiefest greatnes of the great: when great and little are born, and dye, there is no difference: Vertue onely makes men more then men: Vice, worse then brutes. And those are distinguished by deedes, not words; though both be good, deedes are best, and of all evils, ingratitude the worst. Therfore I beseech you, that not to seeme ungratefull, I may present your Honour with this rude discourse, of a new old subject. It is the best gift I can give to the best friend I have. It is the best service I ever did to serve so good a worke: Wherin having beene discouraged for doing any more, I have writ this little: yet my hands hath been my lands this fifteene yeares in Europ, Asia, Afric,[4] or America.

In the harbour of your Lordships favour, I hope I ever shall rest secure, notwithstanding all weathers; lamenting others, that they fall into such miseries, as I foreseeing have foretold, but could not prevent. No more: but dedicating my best abilities to the honour and service of your renowned Vertues, I ever rest.

Your Lordships true and faithfull Servant,
John Smith

---

1. This printed dedication has been found in two surviving copies of the *Map of Va.*, one of them the earl's own copy, now in the New York Public Library (Joseph Sabin *et al.*, eds., *A Dictionary of Books Relating to America*, XX [New York, 1927–1928], 246–247). It is the only firm evidence we have that John Smith was befriended by the earl, whose wife Frances Howard upon the death of the earl married Ludovick Stuart, duke of Richmond and Lennox. John Smith listed the earl as an adventurer for Virginia in the 1620 roll, but this does not seem to be substantiated elsewhere (*Generall Historie*, 136; and see the Biographical Directory, s.v. "Seymour, Edward").

2. Dialectal form of "master," meaning "employer."

3. Cf. Juvenal, *Satire VIII*, line 20: "*nobilitas sola est atque unica virtus*"—virtue alone is true nobility. Smith's immediate source has not been spotted, but the moralizing that follows is better attributed to the spirit of the times than to any specific printed source.

4. This is the first mention of Smith's travels and adventures between c. 1597 and c. 1604, which are the subject of two-thirds of his *True Travels*.

TO THE RIGHT WORSHIPFULL
Thomas Watson, And John
Bingley, Esquiers:
P. F. Wisheth all Health
and Happinesse.[5]

As there is nothing more pretious in Man then vertue, so there is nothing worse then hatefull ingratitude. Though it be farre beyond my power, to requite, or deserve, the least of your favours, yet would I not neglect the opportunitie, to expresse my thankefulnesse. Being thus constrained both by dutie and affection, I hope you will pardon me for presenting your Worships with this little Booke; howbeit, it is not mine by Birth, yet it is by Gift, and purchase from the Presse. I esteeme of it as the best gift I can give, and I cannot give it to any, to mee more deare then your selves, and worthie Progenie, Friends, and Well-willers to this noble action, for whose recreation, and true satisfaction, I have occasioned the Impression, which if it give you content, my charge and paines is highly recompenced. So dedicating my best abilities to the exquisite judgement of your right worthie vertues;

I ever rest your Worships true and faithfull servant.
Philip Fote.

---

5. Thomas Watson was one of the tellers of the Exchequer and may be the same man as the Thomas Watson to whom the authorship of Smith's *True Relation* had been ascribed. John Bingley was also employed in the Exchequer. Both had been appointed members of the Council for Virginia under the third charter, Mar. 12, 1612. While the revised edition of Pollard and Redgrave's *Short-Title Catalogue* suggests that this dedication may possibly have been a joke ("as all copies have dedic[ation] To the Hand by T. A[bbay]"), a Philip Fote (or Foote) did get a license to sell clay for making tobacco pipes (see Philip L. Barbour, *The Three Worlds of Captain John Smith* [Boston, 1964], 291, 300, 468).

Least I should wrong any in dedicating this Booke to one: I have concluded it shal be particular to none. I found it only dedicated to a Hand, and to that hand I addresse it. Now for that this businesse is common to the world, this booke may best satisfie the world, because it was penned in the Land it treateth of. If it bee disliked of men, then I would recommend it to women, for being dearely bought, and farre sought, it should be good for Ladies. When all men rejected Christopher Collumbus: that ever renowned Queene Izabell of Spaine, could pawne her Jewels to supply his wants; whom all the wise men (as they thought themselves) of that age contemned. I need not say what was his worthinesse, her noblenesse, and their ignorance, that so scornefully did spit at his wants, seeing the whole world is enriched with his golden fortunes. Cannot this successfull example move the incredulous of this time, to consider, to conceave, and apprehend Virginia, which might be, or breed us a second India? hath not England an Izabell, as well as Spaine, nor yet a Collumbus as well as Genua?[6] yes surely it hath, whose desires are no lesse then was worthy Collumbus, their certainties more, their experiences no way wanting, only there wants but an Izabell, so it were not from Spaine.

T. A.[7]

---

6. Genua was the Latin name of Genoa (modern Italian, Genova).

7. Evidently the initials of Thomas Abbay, who is listed as a "diligent observer" on the title page of the *Proceedings*, appears as author of the address "To the Reader" (*Proceedings*, sig. A2ʳ⁻ᵛ), and is mentioned as a gentleman of the second supply that arrived late in Sept. 1608 (*ibid.*, 52). He is otherwise unidentified.

[*3ʳ]   Because many doe desire to knowe the maner of their
                     language, I have inserted these few words.⁸

*Ka ka torawincs*⁹ *yowo.* What call you this.

Nemarough. a man.¹

Crenepo. a woman.

Marowanchesso. a boy.

Yehawkans. Houses.

*Matchcores.*² Skins, or garments.

Mockasins. Shooes.

Tussan. Beds.

*Pokatawer.*³ Fire.

Attawp. A bowe.

Attonce. Arrowes.

Monacookes. Swords.

---

8. The most complete attempt at analysis of all Smith's Indian words and phrases
and the meanings he assigns to them is in Philip L. Barbour, "The Earliest Reconnais-
sance of the Chesapeake Bay Area: Captain John Smith's Map and Indian Vocabulary,"
Pt. II, *VMHB*, LXXX (1972), 21–51. More recently, however, Frank T. Siebert, Jr., has
published studies of nearly half of the total, correcting Barbour's work in a few instances
("Resurrecting Virginia Algonquian from the Dead: The Reconstituted and Historical
Phonology of Powhatan," in James M. Crawford, ed., *Studies in Southeastern Indian
Languages* [Athens, Ga., 1975], 285–453, hereafter cited as Siebert, "Virginia Algon-
quian"). Siebert's work, based on William Strachey's "Short Dictionary" (*The Historie
of Travell into Virginia Britania*, ed. Louis B. Wright and Virginia Freund [Hakluyt
Society, 2d Ser., CIII (London, 1953)], 174–207) rather than on Smith, has the advantage of supplying linguistic details known only to a specialist, but suffers from in-
adequacy with respect to early modern English handwriting, usage, and colonial history.
For this reason, it raises questions regarding the "phonemic representation of the Powhatan form" (Siebert, "Virginia Algonquian," 305–306) presented there.

Beyond Siebert and Barbour there are only scattered references to Smith's transcriptions, principally in two monographs by the late Reverend James A. Geary of
The Catholic University of America, "Strachey's Vocabulary of Indian Words Used
in Virginia, 1612" (Strachey, *Historie*, 209–214), and "The Language of the Carolina
Algonkian Tribes" (David Beers Quinn, ed., *The Roanoke Voyages, 1584–1590* [Hakluyt
Soc., 2d Ser., CIV–CV (London, 1955)], II, 873–900). For the problems involved, see
the facsimile of the Bodleian Library copy of Strachey's "Short Dictionary," in John P.
Harrington, "The Original Strachey Vocabulary of the Virginia Indian Language,"
Smithsonian Institution, Bureau of American Ethnology, *Anthropological Papers*, No. 46
(Washington, D.C., 1955), 189–202, with not a few slips; and Philip L. Barbour, "The
Function of Comparative Linguistics in the Study of Early Transcriptions of Indian
Words," *Studies in Linguistics*, XXIII (1973), 3–11.

9. More correctly, "ka katorawincs yowo" (see Siebert, "Virginia Algonquian,"
361); the "-cs" may represent the sound "sh" or "ch."

1. Siebert's suggestion of a misprint ("nemarough" for "nematough," *ibid.*, 355) is
apparently based solely on Strachey. Whether Strachey's copyist miscopied, or Smith's
printer misprinted, cannot be determined.

2. Siebert's analysis needs reworking (*ibid.*, 326); both Smith and Strachey clearly
have "r" in the second syllable. The Maryland form "matchcoat" cited by Siebert is
apparently not recorded before 1638.

3. Siebert has amplified and partly corrected Barbour here (*ibid.*, 340), adding
cognates from Micmac and from his own unpublished notes on Unami; Smith's final
"-r" is evidently redundant, though it may represent a breathing sound, or inaudible
whistle.

Aumoughhowgh. A Target.

Pawcussacks. Gunnes.

Tomahacks. Axes.

Tockahacks. Pickaxes.

Pamesacks. Knives.

Accowprets. Sheares.

Pawpecones.[4] Pipes.

Mattassin.[5] Copper.

Ussawassin.[6] Iron, Brasse, Silver, or any white mettal.

Musses.[7] Woods.

Attasskuss.[8] Leaves, weeds, or grasse.

Chepsin. Land.

Shacquohocan. A stone.

Wepenter,[9] a cookold.

Suckahanna. Water.

Noughmass. Fish.

|| *Copotone*.[1] Sturgion.   [*3ᵛ]

Weghshaughes. Flesh.

Sawwehone. Bloud.

Netoppew.[2] Friends.

Marrapough. Enimies.

Maskapow. The worst of the enimies.

Mawchick chammay. The best of friends.

Casacunnakack, peya quagh acquintan uttasantasough.[3] In how many
daies will there come hether any more English ships?

---

4. Musical pipes, cf. Natick, *pupehquon*, "an instrument of music." Here, Siebert
has apparently been led astray by Strachey's carelessness (*ibid.*, 367–368).

5. While the second element of this word, "-assin," clearly means "stone," Siebert's
conjecture that the first element, "matt-," represents a root meaning "uneven, jagged,"
seems farfetched. Geary's analysis, "mat- means 'red,'" corresponding with Barbour,
"Earliest Reconnaissance," Pt. II, 36, seems sounder semantically (see Quinn, *Roanoke
Voyages*, II, 897, s.v. "Tapisco").

6. Overlooked by Siebert, though he analyzes Strachey's "*osawas*, brass" in detail,
as a derivative from an element meaning "ore, mineral," plus a root meaning "yellow"
(Siebert, "Virginia Algonquian," 328–329, 409–410).

7. More accurately, "firewood, pieces of wood."

8. Siebert correctly emphasizes the meaning "reed, water weed" for this apparently
collective name, which may well have been primary in tidewater Virginia ("Virginia
Algonquian," 372).

9. The basic Algonkian element implies "sleeping together" (*ibid.*, 385).

1. A common Algonkian name for the sturgeon, appearing in various forms in
Abnaki, Narragansett, Delaware, etc. (Barbour, "Earliest Reconnaissance," Pt. II, 35).

2. More specifically, "my friend" (cf. Siebert, "Virginia Algonquian," 342).

3. The first word should probably be divided "casa cunnakack" (cf. "[nu]ssacon-
noke," the third day [singular], in Philip L. Barbour, "Ocanahowan and the Recently
Discovered Linguistic Fragments from Southern Virginia, *c.* 1650," in William Cowan,
ed., *Papers of the Seventh Algonquian Conference* [Ottawa, 1976], 2–17). The last word, an
unanalyzed designation, was still applied to the English in North Carolina in 1701, in
the form "Tosh shonte" (Barbour, "Earliest Reconnaissance," Pt. II, 46).

Their numbers.[4]

Necut. 1.
Ningh. 2
Nuss. 3.
Yowgh. 4.
Paranske. 5.
Comotinch. 6.
Toppawoss. 7.
Nusswash. 8.
Kekatawgh. 9.
Kaskeke.
They count no more but by tennes as followeth.
Case, how many.
Ninghsapooeksku. 20.
Nussapooeksku. 30.
Yowghapooeksku. 40.
Parankestassapooeksku. 50.[5]
Comatinchtassapooeksku. 60.
Nusswashtassapooeksku. 80.
Toppawousstassapooeksku. 70
Kekataughtassapooeksku. 90.
[*4ʳ*] || *Necuttoughtysinough.* 100.
Necuttweunquaough. 1000.
Rawcosowghs. Daies.
Keskowghes.[6] Sunnes.
Toppquough. Nights.
Nepawweshowghs.[7] Moones,
Pawpaxsoughes.[8] Yeares.
Pummahumps.[9] Starres.
Osies. Heavens.
Okes.[1] Gods.

---

4. There is a study in depth of the numbers from one to ten in Siebert, "Virginia Algonquian," 306–309, with extensive analyses.

5. Should read "Paransketassapooeksku." The typesetter misplaced the first "s."

6. Properly "Keshowghes." The word was undoubtedly intended to rhyme with "owes," the "-gh-" representing a breathing sound somewhat as in the German phrase "doch so"; the palatalization of the first sibilant ("sh" for "s"), however, may well have been accidental (indistinct speech or mishearing). Cf. *Rawcosowghs*, immediately preceding, and see Siebert's analysis ("Virginia Algonquian," 391).

7. Siebert has unfortunately omitted Smith's word, though he lists Strachey's "nepaus[c]he," meaning "sun" (*ibid.*, 392). Although this word seems to have meant "luminary" rather than either "sun" or "moon," a full inquiry into its semantics remains a desideratum.

8. Obviously a miscopy or a misprint of "popanow," meaning "winter" (see p. 16, below).

9. A problem word, not yet analyzed.

1. Perhaps the most puzzling word in Smith or Strachey (see p. 29, n. 4, below).

Quiyoughcosucks.[2] Pettie Gods, and their affinities.

Righcomoughes. Deaths.

Kekughes. Lives.

Mowchick woyawgh tawgh noeragh kaquere mecher.
    I am verie hungrie, what shall I eate?

Tawnor nehiegh Powhatan. where dwels Powwahtan.

Mache, nehiegh yowrowgh, orapaks. Now he dwels a great way hence
    at Orapaks.

Uttapitchewayne anpechitchs nehawper werowacomoco.
    You lie, he staide ever at Werowocomoco.

Kator nehiegh mattagh neer uttapitchewayne. Truely he is there I doe
    not lie.

*Spaughtynere keragh werowance mawmarinough kekaten wawgh
    peyaquaugh.* Run you then to the king mawmarynough and bid
    him come hither.

Utteke, e peya weyack wighwhip. Get you gone, and come againe
    quickly.

*Kekaten pokahontas patiaquagh ningh tanks manotyens neer mowchick
    rawrenock audowgh.* Bid Pokahontas[3] bring hither two little
    Baskets, and I wil give her white beads to make her a chaine.

FINIS.

2. Apparently an Algonkian parallel to the Greek Eumenides, "the Kindly Ones,"
a euphemism for the Furies. The *Quiyoughcosucks* were "the Upright Ones"—including
the priests ("affinities") who served them.

3. This reference to Pocahontas has been overlooked by some of Smith's critics. It
shows how he thought of her before her arrival in London in 1616.

Relevant to the foregoing word list and diminutive phrase book, it should be pointed
out here that the idea for such a list seems to have been a relatively novel one. Only three
or four such "curiosities" have been found by the editor in contemporary or earlier
works. It has been postulated, however, that Harriot, after studying the North Carolina
Indians at firsthand, "may have gone on to compile a short word-book" for just such
later expeditions as the one Smith joined (David B. Quinn, "Thomas Hariot and the
Virginia Voyages of 1602," *William and Mary Quarterly*, 3d Ser., XXVII [1970], 274). A
last-minute communication from Professor Quinn, however, states that "Harriot's manuscript on the Indian language was amongst the MSS deposited in Sion College, but was
destroyed with part of the library in the fire of London" of 1666 (personal communication to the editor, Jan. 1979). That Smith had such a book in Jamestown seems im-
probable, but Harriot could have shown it to him later, in London. William Strachey
could well have picked up the notion from Smith and expanded it into his "Short
Dictionary." The firm facts are that Smith recorded 137 Indian words, with a few errors
of transcription or translation, while Strachey's later vocabulary of 16 MS pages listed
nearly 600 more, including some duplication, as well as errors similar to Smith's.

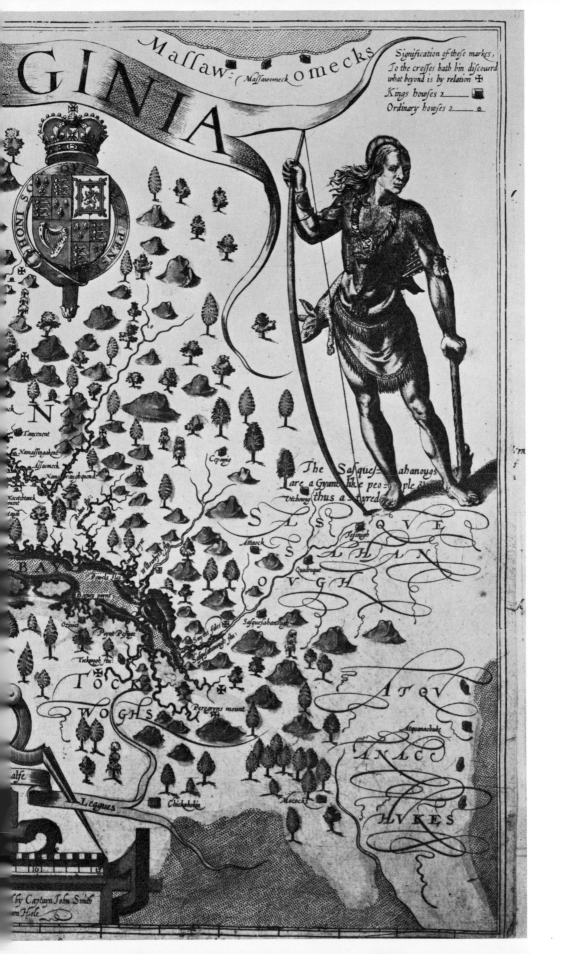

Maſſaw-·Maſſawomeck Omecks

Signification of theſe markes,
To the croſſes hath bin diſcouerd
what beyond is by relation ✠
Kings howſes 2 ▣
Ordinary howſes 2 ⊙

GINIA

HONI SOIT QVI MAL PENSE

N

Tauxenent

Namaſſingakent
Aſſaomeck
Nama Braughquund

Nacotchtanck
mount
Tagh

Cepowig

The Saſque-ſahanoygs
are a Gyant like peo=ple &
Vſchowig thus a tyred

S A S Q V E

Attaock   Jeſingh

S A H A N
Quadroque

O V G H

Powleys Ifland

BA

Kings fales

Poynt Pleyne

Sasquesahanough

Tockwogh flu:

A T O V
Sasquesahanoug flu:

Techkogh flu:

Ozinies

Aquanachuke

T O C K

W O G H S   Peregrews mount

A N A C C

alſe

Leagues   Chickahokin   Macocks

L V K E S

by Captayn John Smith
am Hole

[This is a slightly reduced reproduction of a print from the original plate, or first state, of William Hole's map of Virginia, based on sketches supplied by John Smith (the original dimensions were 32.2 × 40.6 cm.). Bibliographers have detected at least ten states of this map, three of which concern the *Map of Va.* as a book. For the tenth state, see the *Generall Historie*. The original plate lacks Smith's coat of arms and the dates 1607 (under Powhatan) and 1606 (under the scale). The second state had the two dates, and the third state, Smith's coat of arms.

For the Indian figures, Hole availed himself of the engravings made for Thomas Hariot's *A briefe and true report of the new found land of Virginia* . . . in Theodore de Bry's edition (Frankfurt am Main, 1590). The "Gyantlike" Sasquesahanough is all but a copy of de Bry's engraving No. III, "A weroan or great Lorde of Virginia," with changes in the coiffure, clothing, and armament, probably suggested by Smith. The inset of Powhatan in state, on the other hand, is a composite picture in which Hole mingled de Bry's No. XVII, "Their manner of pra[y]inge with Rattels abowt t[h]e fyer," with No. XXI, "The[i]r Idol Kiwasa," and No. XXII, "The Tombe of their Werowans or Cheiff Lordes" (see the reprint, with an introduction by Paul Hulton [New York, 1972]).

The compass card at the lower left shows that the map is oriented with N to the right—purely a matter of convenience. Note that the value of magnetic declination in lower Chesapeake Bay was approximately 4° 2′ W in 1608 (letter to the editor, Aug. 31, 1962, from the Chief of the Geophysics Division, Coast and Geodetic Survey, Washington, D.C.). In 1961 it was 6° 45′ W (see Coast and Geodetic Survey charts for that year).

In the scale of leagues, Hole used nautical leagues, at 20 to a degree of latitude (see the latitudinal markings just below). This gave 60 *nautical* miles to one degree of latitude, as opposed to the 69 *statute* miles (plus 14 rods) measured by Smith's friend Richard Norwood (see E. G. R. Taylor, *The Haven-finding Art: A History of Navigation from Odysseus to Captain Cook* [New York, 1956], 230; and the *Generall Historie*, 169n). Although this antique system still gives rise to occasional confusion involving knots and miles per hour, it need not concern readers unduly. Smith was too careless about figures for the difference between a statute mile of 5,280 feet and a nautical mile of c. 6,076 feet to matter.

Attention is called in the footnotes to significant variations between the Smith/Hole map and Smith's text, as well as the other sources that have survived. Additional information about the Indian names can be found in Philip L. Barbour, "The Earliest Reconnaissance of the Chesapeake Bay Area: Captain John Smith's Map and Indian Vocabulary," Pt. I, *VMHB*, LXXIX (1971), 280–302.

In the textual apparatus following this edition of the *Map of Va.*, the reader will find three schedules designed to help scholars and laymen alike. Schedule A lists the geographical limits of Smith's explorations, as indicated by the Maltese crosses, showing approximate modern locations. What lay beyond the crosses, as the legend to the map says, was "by relation" of the Indians. Schedule B lists the "Kings howses" (where the chiefs resided) and the "ordinary howses" (villages in all cases) as shown on the map. Schedule C gives the names and locations of peripheral nations or tribes conspicuously shown on the map, but barely known to Smith. In addition, following these three schedules, the editor has added a short specialized bibliography pertinent to the Smith/Hole map.

The editor is grateful to the British Library for permission to reproduce this map.]

THE DESCRIPTION [1]
OF VIRGINIA
By Captaine Smith.[1]

IRGINIA is a Country in America that lyeth betweene the degrees of 34 and 44 of the north latitude. The bounds thereof on the East side are the great Ocean. On the South lyeth Florida: on the North nova Francia. As for the West thereof, the limits are unknowne. Of all this country wee purpose not to speake, but only of that part which was planted by the English men in the yeare of our Lord, 1606. And this is under the degrees 37. 38. and 39. The temperature of this countrie doth agree well with English constitutions being once seasoned to the country. Which appeared by this, that though by many occasions our people fell sicke; yet did they recover by very small meanes and continued in health, though there were other great causes, not only to have made them sicke, but even to end their daies, etc.[2]

The latitude.

The sommer is hot as in Spaine; the winter colde as in Fraunce or England. The heat of sommer is in June, Julie, and August, but commonly the coole Breeses asswage the vehemencie of the heat. The chiefe of winter is halfe December, January, February, and halfe March. The colde is extreame sharpe, but here the proverbe is true that no extreame long continueth.[3]

The temperature.

In the yeare 1607 was an extraordinary frost in most of Europe, and this frost was founde as extreame in Virginia. But the next yeare

1. For a summary of the use made of this work in later books by Smith, Purchas, and Strachey, see the editor's Introduction, above. In l. 2, below, Smith has made the error of listing the N latitude of "Virginia" as 44° rather than 45°. See the *Generall Historie*, 21 and 203n.

2. A missing passage, indicated by "etc.," can be conjecturally restored from Strachey, *Historie*, 37–38: ". . . yet have they recovered againe by very smale meanes, without helpe of fresh dyett, or comfort of wholsome Phisique, there being at the first but fewe phisique Helpes, or skilfull surgeons, who knew how to applie the right Medecyne in a new Country or to search the quality and constitution of the Patient and his distemper, or that knew how to counsell, when to lett blood or not, or in necessity to use a Launce in that office at all." This lends support to the suggested possibility that Strachey had a manuscript copy of Smith's work before he left Virginia (see the Introduction, above).

3. This proverb appears as "No extreame will hold long," in Nicholas Breton, *Crossing of Proverbs: The Second Part* (London, 1616), repr. in Alexander B. Grosart, ed., *The Works in Verse and Prose of Nicholas Breton* (n.p., 1879), 6.

for 8. or 10. daies of ill weather, other 14 daies would be as Sommer.

The windes.   The windes here are variable, but the like thunder and lightning

[2] to purifie the aire, I have seldome either seene or ‖ heard in Europe. From the Southwest came the greatest gustes with thunder and heat. The Northwest winde is commonly coole and bringeth faire weather with it. From the North is the greatest cold, and from the East and South-East as from the Bermudas, fogs and raines.

Some times there are great droughts other times much raine, yet great necessity of neither, by reason we see not but that all the variety of needfull fruits in Europe may be there in great plenty by the industry of men, as appeareth by those we there planted.

The entrances.   There is but one entraunce by sea into this country and that is at the mouth of a very goodly Bay the widenesse whereof is neare 18.

Cape Henry.   or 20. miles. The cape on the Southside is called Cape Henry in honour of our most noble Prince. The shew of the land there is a white hilly sand like unto the Downes, and along the shores great plentie of Pines and Firres.

Cape Charles.   The north Cape is called Cape Charles in honour of the worthy Duke of Yorke. Within is a country that may have the prerogative[4] over the most pleasant places of Europe, Asia, Africa, or America, for large and pleasant navigable rivers, heaven and earth never agreed better to frame a place for mans habitation being of our con-

The country.   stitutions, were it fully manured and inhabited by industrious people. here are mountaines, hils, plaines, valleyes, rivers and brookes, all running most pleasantly into a faire Bay compassed but for the mouth with fruitfull and delightsome land. In the Bay and rivers are many Isles both great and small, some woody, some plaine,[5] most of them low and not inhabited. This Bay lieth North and South in which the water floweth neare 200 miles and hath a channell for 140 miles, of depth betwixt 7 and 15 fadome, holding in breadth for the most part 10 or 14 miles.[6] From the head of the Bay at the north, the land is mountanous, and so in a manner from thence by a South-west line; So that the more Southward, the farther off from the Bay

[3] are those mounetaines. From which fall ‖ certaine brookes which after come to five principall navigable rivers. These run from the Northwest into the Southeast, and so into the west side of the Bay, where the fall[7] of every River is within 20 or 15 miles one of an other.

The moun-   The mountaines are of diverse natures for at the head of the
taines.   Bay the rockes are of a composition like milnstones.[8] Some of marble, etc. And many peeces of christall we found as throwne downe by

4. Eminence, superiority.
5. Open, clear of woods.
6. The estimates are approximately accurate.
7. I.e., "outlet, mouth"; now obsolete. Smith obviously was not referring to the falls of the James River, or the rapids of the Appomattox River, and so on.
8. "Millstones"; this then archaic spelling was corrected in the *Generall Historie*, 22.

water from the mountaines. For in winter these mountaines are covered with much snow, and when it dissolveth the waters fall with such violence, that it causeth great inundations in the narrow valleyes which yet is scarce perceived being once in the rivers. These waters wash from the rocks such glistering tinctures that the ground in some places seemeth as guilded, where both the rocks and the earth are so splendent to behold, that better judgements then ours might have beene perswaded, they contained more then probabilities. The vesture of the earth in most places doeth manifestly prove the nature of the soile to be lusty and very rich. The colour of the earth we found in diverse places, resembleth *bole Armoniac, terra sigillata* and *lemnia,*[9] Fullers earth marle and divers other such appearances. But generally for the most part the earth is a black sandy mould, in some places a fat slimy clay, in other places a very barren gravell. But the best ground is knowne by the vesture it beareth, as by the greatnesse of trees or abundance of weedes, etc. `The soile.`

The country is not mountanous nor yet low but such pleasant plaine hils and fertle valleyes, one prettily crossing an other, and watered so conveniently with their sweete brookes and christall springs, as if art it selfe had devised them. By the rivers are many plaine marishes[1] containing some 20 some 100 some 200 Acres, some more, some lesse. Other plaines there are fewe, but only where the Savages inhabit: but all overgrowne with trees and weedes being a plaine wildernes as God first made it. `The vallyes.` `Plaines.`

On the west side of the Bay, wee said were 5. faire and ‖ delightfull navigable rivers, of which wee will nowe proceed to report. The first of those rivers and the next to the mouth of the Bay hath his course from the West and by North. The name of this river they call Powhatan according to the name of a principall country that lieth upon it. The mouth of this river is neere three miles in breadth, yet doe the shoules force the Channell so neere the land that a Sacre will overshoot it at point blancke. This river is navigable 100 miles, the shouldes and soundings are here needlesse to bee expressed.[2] It falleth from Rockes farre west in a country inhabited by a nation that they call Monacan. But where it commeth into our discoverie `[4]` `The river Powhatan.`

---

9. Properly *bole armeniac*, an astringent red clay brought from Armenia and used as an antidote and styptic, often along with *terra sigillata*. The latter, also an astringent (see the *True Relation*, sig. C2ᵛ and C2ᵛn), came from the island of Lemnos, and so was called also "terra lemnia"; thus, the passage should read "or lemnia." George Sandys, resident treasurer at Jamestown, 1621–1625, explained that when Jove threw Vulcan down from Olympus, he landed on Lemnos, "the earth in that place thereupon receiving those excellent vertues of curing of wounds, stopping of fluxes, expulsing poysons, etc., [is] now called Terra Sigillata," which is there gathered and sealed (*sigillata*) (*A Relation of a Journey Begun Anno Domini 1610* [London, 1673 (orig. publ. 1615)], 18).

1. In Smith's day, a variant of "marsh"; perhaps dialectal.

2. The mouth of the Powhatan (now James) River is about three mi. wide. A saker was a cannon smaller than a demiculverin with a range of half a mi. point-blank (cf. the *Accidence*, 34). From the mouth to the falls by the old channel is about 113 mi. (exaggerated to 150 mi. in the *Generall Historie*, 22).

it is Powhatan. In the farthest place that was diligently observed, are falles, rockes, showles, etc. which makes it past navigation any higher.[3] Thence in the running downeward, the river is enriched with many goodly brookes, which are maintained by an infinit number of smal rundles[4] and pleasant springs that disperse them-

The branches.   selves for best service, as doe the vaines of a mans body. From the South there fals into this river: First the pleasant river of Apama-tuck: next more to the East are the two rivers of Quiyoughcohanocke. A little farther is a Bay wherein falleth 3 or 4 prettie brookes and creekes that halfe intrench the Inhabitants of Warraskoyac then the river of Nandsamund, and lastly the brooke of Chisapeack. From the North side is the river of Chickahamania, the backe river of James Towne; another by the Cedar Isle, where we lived 10 weekes upon oisters, then a convenient harbour for fisher boats or smal boats at Kecoughtan, that so conveniently turneth it selfe into Bayes and Creeks that make that place very pleasant to inhabit, their corne-fields being girded therein in a manner as Peninsulaes. The most of these rivers are inhabited by severall nations, or rather families, of the name of the rivers. They have also in every of those places some Governour, as their king, which they call *Werowances*.[5] In a Peninsula

James Towne.   on the North side of this river are the English planted in a place by
[5]   them called James || Towne, in honour of the Kings most excellent Majestie, upon which side are also many places under the Wero-wances.

The severall   The first and next the rivers mouth are the Kecoughtans, who
inhabitants.   besides their women and children, have not past 20. fighting men. The Paspaheghes on whose land is seated the English Colony, some 40. miles from the Bay have not past 40. The river called Chicka-hamania neere 200. The Weanocks 100. The Arrowhatocks 30. The place called Powhatan, some 40. On the South side this river the Appamatucks have 60 fighting men. The Quiyougcohanocks, 25. The Warraskoyacks 40.[6] The Nandsamunds 200. The Chesapeacks are able to make 100. Of this last place the Bay beareth the name. In all these places is a severall commander, which they call Wero-wance, except the Chickhamanians, who are governed by the Priestes and their Assistants or their Elders called *Caw-cawwassoughes*.[7] In somer no place affordeth more plentie of Sturgeon, nor in winter

3. Cf. the fuller description in Hugh Jones, *The Present State of Virginia* (London, 1724), 133–134, modern edition by Richard L. Morton (Chapel Hill, N.C., 1956), 143. There seems to have been no awareness of the fall line in Smith's day.

4. Small streams, rivulets.

5. This word (variously spelled) for "king, chieftain, captain" was first recorded by Ralph Lane in 1585–1586 in the territory of the Chesepians, 15 mi. inland from the bottom of Chesapeake Bay and E of whatever tribe then occupied the Nansemond River region.

6. The Warraskoyacks were carelessly omitted in the *Generall Historie*, 23.

7. Later anglicized as "cockarouse"; cf. the *Generall Historie*, 38; and Robert Beverley, *The History and Present State of Virginia*, ed. Louis B. Wright (Chapel Hill, N.C. 1947), 226.

more abundance of fowle, especially in the time of frost. There was once taken 52 Sturgeons at a draught, at another draught 68. From the later end of May till the end of June are taken few, but yong Sturgeons of 2 foot or a yard long. From thence till the midst of September, them of 2 or three yards long and fewe others. And in 4 or 5 houres with one nette were ordinarily taken 7 or 8: often more, seldome lesse. In the small rivers all the yeare there is good plentie of small fish, so that with hookes those that would take paines had sufficient.

Foureteene miles Northward from the river Powhatan, is the river Pamaunke,[8] which is navigable 60 or 70 myles, but with Catches and small Barkes 30 or 40 myles farther. At the ordinary flowing of the salt water, it divideth it selfe into two gallant branches. On the South side inhabit the people of Youghtanund, who have about 60 men for warres. On the North branch Mattapament, who have 30 men. Where this river is divided the Country is called Pa-|| maunke, and nourisheth neere 300 able men. About 25 miles lower on the North side of this river is Werawocomoco, where their great King inhabited when Captain Smith was delivered him prisoner; yet there are not past 40 able men. But now he hath abandoned that, and liveth at Orapakes by Youghtanund in the wildernesse; 10 or 12 myles lower, on the South side of this river is Chiskiack, which hath some 40 or 50 men. These, as also Apamatuck, Arrohatock, and Powhatan, are their great kings chiefe alliance and inhabitance. The rest (as they report) his Conquests.

River Pamaunke.

The inhabitants.

[6]

Before we come to the third river that falleth from the mountaines, there is another river (some 30 myles navigable) that commeth from the Inland, the river is called Payankatanke, the Inhabitants are about some 40 serviceable men.

Payankatank River.

The third navigable river is called Toppahanock. (This is navigable some 130 myles).[1] At the top of it inhabit the people called Mannahoackes amongst the mountaines, but they are above the place we describe. Upon this river on the North side are seated a people called Cuttatawomen, with 30 fighting men. Higher on the river are the Moraughtacunds, with 80 able men. Beyond them Toppahanock with 100 men. Far above is another Cuttatawomen with 20 men. On the South, far within the river is Nantaughtacund having 150 men. This river also as the two former, is replenished with fish and foule.

Toppahanock River.

The inhabitants.

The fourth river is called Patawomeke and is 6 or 7 miles in

Patawomek River.

---

8. From Jamestown on the James to Kiskiack on the Pamaunk (Yorktown on the York) was close to 14 mi. by Indian trails. The York River is navigable today for a good 55 mi., with three-ft. depths for another 25 mi. It should be noted here that "Pamaunke" can easily be read as "Pamavuke" in the handwriting of the period: e.g., "Pamaunke" was printed "Pamavuke" at the end of this page and overleaf (corrected in this edition; see the Textual Annotation). The river is mentioned in the *True Relation*, sig. C2ᵛ.

1. The head of navigation at modern Fredericksburg is about 112 mi. from the mouth.

breadth. It is navigable 140 miles,[2] and fed as the rest with many sweet rivers and springs, which fall from the bordering hils. These hils many of them are planted, and yeelde no lesse plenty and variety of fruit then the river exceedeth with abundance of fish. This river is inhabited on both sides. First on the South side at the very entrance is Wighcocomoco and hath some 130 men, beyond them Sekacawone with 30. The Onawmanient with 100. Then Patawomeke with 160[3] able men. Here doth the river divide it selfe in- || to 3 or 4 convenient rivers; The greatest of the last is called Quiyough treadeth[4] north west, but the river it selfe turneth North east and is stil a navigable streame. On the westerne side of this bought[5] is Tauxenent with 40 men. On the north of this river is Secowocomoco with 40 men. Some what further Potapaco with 20. In the East part of the bought of the river, is Pamacacack with 60 men, After Moyowances[6] with 100. And lastly Nacotchtanke with 80 able men. The river 10 miles above this place maketh his passage downe a low pleasant vally over-shaddowed in manie places with high rocky mountaines; from whence distill innumerable sweet and pleasant springs.[7]

The inhabitants.

[7]

The fifth river is called Pawtuxunt, and is of a lesse proportion then the rest; but the channell is 16 or 18 fadome deepe in some places. Here are infinit skuls[8] of divers kinds of fish more then else-where. Upon this river dwell the people called Acquintanacksuak, Pawtuxunt and Mattapanient. 200 men was the greatest strength that could bee there perceived. But they inhabit togither, and not so dispersed as the rest. These of al other were found the most civill to give intertainement.

Pawtuxunt River.

Thirty leagues Northward is a river not inhabited, yet navigable; for the red earth or clay resembling bole Armoniack[9] the English called it Bolus. At the end of the Bay where it is 6 or 7 miles in breadth, there fall into it 4 small rivers, 3 of them issuing from diverse bogges invironed with high mountaines. There is one that commeth du north 3 or 4. daies journy from the head of the Bay and fals from rocks and mountaines, upon this river inhabit a people called Sasquesahanock. They are seated 2 daies higher then was passage for the discoverers Barge, which was hardly 2 toons, and

Bolus River.

The head of the Bay.

Sasquesa-hanock.

2. The distance from the Great Falls, just above Washington, D.C., to the mouth of the Potomac can be little more than 100 mi. For some reason, Samuel Purchas changed the figure to 120 mi. in *Purchas his Pilgrimage. Or Relations Of The World* . . . (London, 1613), 635. Possibly the 140 mi. is a misprint.

3. Increased to "more then 200" in the *Generall Historie*, 23.

4. Error for "trendeth"? "Trending" in the *Generall Historie*, 23.

5. Bend, curve; a parallel form to "bight."

6. For the confusion regarding this name, see Barbour, "Earliest Reconnaissance," Pt. I, 292. Nacotchtanke is modern Anacostia, Maryland.

7. For further description, see the *Generall Historie*, 58.

8. "Skuls" was a frequent spelling of "schools (shoals)" of fish.

9. See p. 3n, above. The following passage is somewhat altered in the *Generall Historie*, 24.

had in it but 12 men[10] to perform this discovery, wherein they lay above the space of 12 weekes upon those great waters in those unknowne Countries, having nothing but a little meale or oatmeale and water to feed them; and scarse halfe sufficient of that for halfe that time, but that by the ‖ Savages and by the plentie of fish they found in all places, they made themselves provision as opportunitie served; yet had they not a marriner or any that had skill to trim their sayles, use their oares, or any businesse belonging to the Barge, but 2 or 3, the rest being Gentlemen or as ignorant in such toyle and labour. Yet necessitie in a short time by their Captaines diligence and example, taught them to become so perfect, that what they did by such small meanes, I leave to the censure of the Reader to judge by this discourse and the annexed Map.[1] But to proceed, 60 of those Sasquesahanocks, came to the discoverers with skins, Bowes, Arrowes, Targets, Beads, Swords, and Tobacco pipes for presents. Such great and well proportioned men, are seldome seene, for they seemed like Giants to the English, yea and to the neighbours, yet seemed of an honest and simple disposition, with much adoe restrained from adoring the discoverers as Gods.[2] Those are the most strange people of all those Countries, both in language and attire; for their language it may well beseeme their proportions, sounding from them, as it were a great voice in a vault, or cave, as an Eccho. Their attire is the skinnes of Beares, and Woolves, some have Cassacks made of Beares heades and skinnes that a mans necke goes through the skinnes neck, and the eares of the beare fastned to his shoulders behind, the nose and teeth hanging downe his breast, and at the end of the nose hung a Beares Pawe, the halfe sleeves comming to the elbowes were the neckes of Beares and the armes through the mouth with pawes hanging at their noses. One had the head of a Woolfe hanging in a chaine for a Jewell, his Tobacco pipe 3 quarters of a yard long,[3] prettily carved with a Bird, a Beare, a Deare, or some such devise at the great end, sufficient to beat out the braines of a man, with bowes, and arrowes, and clubs, sutable to their greatnesse and conditions. These are scarse knowne to Powhatan. They can make neere 600 able and mighty men and are pallisadoed in their Townes to defend them

The description of a Sasquesahanough.

10. Smith refers here to his second voyage (*Proceedings*, 36); on the first he had 14 men (*ibid.*, 28–29). "Toons" is, of course, "tons."

1. The Smith/Hole map, already in print when these pages were in the press, appears at the beginning of this book.

2. The Sasquesahanocks spoke an Iroquoian language and lived on the Susquehanna River in what is now southeast Pennsylvania. Note that it was not uncommon for isolated peoples not in contact with the Old World to take Europeans for gods—e.g., in Mexico (cited in José de Acosta, *Naturall and Morall Historie*, ed. Clements R. Markham [Hakluyt Soc., 1st Ser., LX–LXI (London, 1880)], II, 514–516) and in the Pacific (mentioned in Olivier Leroy, *La Raison Primitive* [Paris, 1927], 221–224).

3. An 11-in. clay pipe has been unearthed at a Susquehannock site in Lancaster Co., Pennsylvania (Donald A. Cadzow, *Archaeological Studies of the Susquehannock Indians of Pennsylvania* [Harrisburg, Pa., 1936], 77–79). As for Smith's "3 quarters of a yard long," cf. n., following.

[9] from || the Massawomekes their mortall enimies. 5 of their chiefe Werowances came aboard the discoverers and crossed the Bay in their Barge. The picture of the greatest of them is signified in the Mappe. The calfe of whose leg was 3 quarters of a yard about, and all the rest of his limbes so answerable to that proportion, that he seemed the goodliest man that ever we beheld.[4] His haire, the one side was long, the other shore close with a ridge over his crown like a cocks combe. His arrowes were five quarters long, headed with flints or splinters of stones, in forme like a heart, an inch broad, and an inch and a halfe or more long. These hee wore in a woolves skinne at his backe for his quiver, his bow in the one hand and his clubbe in the other, as is described.

Tockwhogh River.

On the East side the Bay is the river of Tockwhogh, and upon it a people that can make 100 men, seated some 7 miles within the river: where they have a Fort very wel pallisadoed and mantelled with the barke of trees. Next to them is Ozinies with 60 men. More to the South of that East side of the Bay, the river of Rapahanock,

Rapahanock River.

Kuskarawaock River.

neere unto which is the river of Kuskarawaock. Upon which is seated a people with 200 men. After that is the river of Tants Wighcoco-moco, and on it a people with 100 men. The people of those rivers are of little stature, of another language from the rest, and very rude. But they on the river of Acohanock with 40 men, and they of Acco-mack 80 men doth equalize any of the Territories of Powhatan and speake his language, who over all those doth rule as king.

Wighcocomoco River.

Accomack River.

Chawoneck.

Southward they went to some parts of Chawonock and the Mangoags to search them there left by Sir Walter Raleigh; for those parts to the Towne of Chisapeack hath formerly been discovered by Master Heriots and Sir Raph Layne.[5] Amongst those people are thus

The several languages.

many severall nations of sundry languages, that environ Powhatans Territories. The Chawonokes, the Mangoags, the Monacans, the Mannahokes, the Masawomekes, the Powhatans, the Sasquesaha-

[10] || nocks, the Atquanachukes, the Tockwoghes, and the Kuscara-waokes.[6] Al those not any one understandeth another but by Inter-preters. Their severall habitations are more plainly described by this annexed Mappe, which will present to the eie, the way of the mountaines and current of the rivers, with their severall turnings, bayes, shoules, Isles, Inlets, and creekes, the breadth of the waters,

4. Despite conclusions reached by Francis Jennings in his "Glory, Death, and Transfiguration: The Susquehanna Indians in the Seventeenth Century," American Philosophical Society, *Proceedings*, CXII (1968), 15–53, the observations of many early explorers indicate that the North American Indians generally were substantially taller than Europeans. To men of the stature of Drake, John Smith, and even Jacques Le Moyne, a naked Indian over six ft. tall was a giant. There may be some exaggeration but after all, Smith is trying to show the Indian's unusually great size.

5. See the *Proceedings*, 57, for the details. Note that this passage in the *General Historie*, 25, substitutes Master John White for Ralegh and omits the rest of the sentence Ralegh had been beheaded virtually by command of King James in 1618.

6. See Schedules A–C, at the end of the Textual Annotation.

the distances of places and such like. In which Mappe observe this, that as far as you see the little Crosses on rivers, mountaines, or other places have beene discovered; the rest was had by information of the Savages, and are set downe, according to their instructions.

Of such things which are naturall in Virginia and how they use them.

Virginia doth afford many excellent vegitables and living Creatures, yet grasse there is little or none, but what groweth in lowe Marishes: for all the Countrey is overgrowne with trees, whose droppings continually turneth their grasse to weedes, by reason of the rancknesse of the ground which would soone be amended by good husbandry. The wood that is most common is Oke and Walnut, many of their Okes are so tall and straight, that they will beare two foote and a halfe square of good timber for 20 yards long; Of this wood there is 2 or 3 severall kinds. The Acornes of one kind, whose barke is more white, then the other, is somewhat sweetish, which being boyled halfe a day in severall waters, at last afford a sweete oyle, which they keep in goards to annoint their heads and joints. The fruit they eate made in bread or otherwise. There is also some Elme, some black walnut tree, and some Ash: of Ash and Elme they make sope Ashes. If the trees be very great, the ashes will be good, and melt to hard lumps, but if they be small, it will be but powder, and not so good as the other. Of walnuts there is 2 or 3 kindes; there is a kinde of wood we called Cypres, because both the wood, the fruit, and leafe did most resemble it, and of those trees there are || some neere 3 fadome about at the root very straight, and 50, 60, or 80 foot without a braunch.[7] By the dwelling of the Savages are some great Mulbery trees, and in some parts of the Countrey, they are found growing naturally in prettie groves.[8] There was an assay made to make silke, and surely the wormes prospered excellent well, till the master workeman fell sicke. During which time they were eaten with rats.

In some parts were found some Chesnuts[9] whose wild fruit equalize the best in France, Spaine, Germany, or Italy, to their tasts that had tasted them all. Plumbs there are of 3 sorts. The red and white are like our hedge plumbs, but the other which they call

Why there is little grasse.

Woods with their fruits.

Elme.

Walnuts.
Supposed Cypres.
[11]

Mulberies.

Chesnuts.

---

7. On the Virginia and Carolina trees, see Quinn, *Roanoke Voyages*, I, 351, 354, 365, and nn.

8. The red mulberry grows wild in this area, but it is said that the Chinese white mulberry is needed for silk culture.

9. Smith is probably referring to the dwarf chestnut, called the chinquapin (see Barbour, "Earliest Reconnaissance," Pt. II, 33, s.v. "chechinquamins"; and Oliver Perry Medsger, *Edible Wild Plants* [New York, 1967], 108–111).

Putchamins,[1] grow as high as a Palmeta: the fruit is like a medler; it is first greene then yellow, and red when it is ripe; if it be not ripe it will drawe a mans mouth awrie, with much torment, but when it is ripe, it is as delicious as an Apricock.

Cherries.

Vines.

They have Cherries and those are much like a Damsen,[2] but for their tastes and colour we called them Cherries. we see some few Crabs,[3] but very small and bitter. Of vines great abundance in many parts that climbe the toppes of the highest trees in some places, but these beare but fewe grapes. But by the rivers and Savage habitations where they are not overshadowed from the sunne, they are covered with fruit, though never pruined nor manured. Of those hedge grapes wee made neere 20 gallons of wine, which was neare as good as your French Brittish wine,[4] but certainely they would prove good were they well manured. There is another sort of grape neere as great as a Cherry, this they call *Messaminnes*,[5] they bee fatte, and the juyce thicke. Neither doth the tast so well please when they are made in wine. They have a small fruit growing on little trees, husked like a Chesnut, but the fruit most like a very small acorne. This they

Chechin-
quamens.

[12]

Rawcomens.
How they use
their fruits.

call *Chechinquamins*[6] which they esteeme a great daintie. They have a berry much like our gooseberry, in greatnesse, colour, and tast; those they call || *Rawcomenes*,[7] and doe eat them raw or boyled. Of these naturall fruits they live a great part of the yeare, which they use in this manner, The walnuts, Chesnuts, Acornes, and *Chechinquamens* are dryed to keepe. When they need them they breake them betweene two stones, yet some part of the walnut shels will cleave to the fruit. Then doe they dry them againe upon a mat over a hurdle. After they put it into a morter of wood, and beat it very small: that done they mix it with water, that the shels may sinke to the bottome.

Walnut milke.

This water will be coloured as milke, which they cal *Pawcohiscora*,[8] and keepe it for their use. The fruit like medlers they call *Putchamins*, they cast uppon hurdles on a mat and preserve them as Pruines. Of their Chesnuts and *Chechinquamens* boyled 4 houres, they make both

1. Now called persimmons (see Barbour, "Earliest Reconnaissance," Pt. II, 42; and Medsger, *Plants*, 77–79).
2. Probably the wild black cherry, smaller but more or less the color of the damson plum.
3. Crab apples.
4. "British" was occasionally used for "Breton, from Brittany." Smith had visited Brittany late in 1600 (*True Travels*, 4), and may have drunk a *vin du pays*, but the comparison is more likely with *muscadet* or *gros plant* brought in from Nantes (see Roger Dion, *Histoire de la vigne et du vin en France* . . . [Paris, 1959], 420, 429, 451).
5. Possibly the southern fox grape (see Barbour, "Earliest Reconnaissance," Pt. II, 37; and Medsger, *Plants*, 57–58).
6. See n. 9, above; and compare Harriot's "Sapúmmener" (Quinn, *Roanoke Voyages*, I, 354, II, 895).
7. Possibly the prickly wild gooseberry (see Barbour, "Earliest Reconnaissance," Pt. II, 42–43; and Medsger, *Plants*, 17–19).
8. Properly "pawcohiccora" (*Generall Historie*, 26; and Barbour, "Earliest Reconnaissance," Pt. II, 40). The hickory tree is named for this drink.

broath and bread for their chiefe men, or at their greatest feasts. Besides those fruit trees, there is a white populer, and another tree like unto it, that yeeldeth a very cleere and an odoriferous Gumme like Turpentine, which some called Balsom. There are also Cedars and Saxafras trees.[9] They also yeeld gummes in a small proportion of themselves. Wee tryed conclusions to extract it out of the wood, but nature afforded more then our arts.

Gummes.

Cedars.

Saxafras trees.

In the watry valleyes groweth a berry which they call *Ocought-anamins*[1] very much like unto Capers. These they dry in sommer. When they will eat them they boile them neare halfe a day; for otherwise they differ not much from poyson. *Mattoume* groweth as our bents do in meddows.[2] The seede is not much unlike to rie, though much smaller. this they use for a dainty bread buttered with deare suet.

Berries.

Matoume.

During Somer there are either strawberries which ripen in April; or mulberries which ripen in May and June. Raspises hurtes; or a fruit that the Inhabitants call *Maracocks*,[3] which is a pleasant wholsome fruit much like a lemond. Many hearbes in the spring time there are commonly dispersed throughout the woods, good for brothes and sallets, as Violets, Purslin,[4] Sorrell, etc. Besides many we used whose ‖ names we know not.

Strawberries.

Hearbs.

[13]

The chiefe roote they have for foode is called *Tockawhoughe*,[5] It groweth like a flagge in low muddy freshes. In one day a Savage will gather sufficient for a weeke. These rootes are much of the greatnes and taste of Potatoes. They use to cover a great many of them with oke leaves and ferne, and then cover all with earth in the manner of a colepit; over it, on each side, they continue a great fire 24 hours before they dare eat it. Raw it is no better then poison, and being

Rootes.

9. "Saxifrage" and "sassafras" were almost inextricably confused before Smith's day. The one was a European herb, known to Pliny, with leaves that were reputed to cure stones in the bladder. The other, discovered (and named) in Florida by the Spaniards, was a small tree, whose root had "power to comfort the liver," as the herbalist John Gerard (1545–1612) put it. The Carolina Algonkian name for sassafras was "winauk" (variously spelled), which may or may not be the same as the name of the Weanock tribe and village on the James River (see Quinn, *Roanoke Voyages*, I, 329n, which credits the French with the discovery of the plant and the Spaniards with the discovery of its reputed value in treating syphilis; Medsger, *Plants*, 205–207, for its true value; and Barbour, "Earliest Reconnaissance," Pt. I, 301, for the Indian tribe).

1. Possibly chokecherries (see Medsger, *Plants*, 49–51; and Barbour, "Earliest Reconnaissance," Pt. II, 39).

2. Possibly the large cane grass that forms the Virginia canebrakes (Medsger, *Plants*, 129). "Bent" is an English name for reedy or rush-like grass. On "mattoume," see Barbour, "Earliest Reconnaissance," Pt. II, 37.

3. "Raspises" was the common name for "raspberries" in Smith's day. Similarly, 'hurts' were "hurtleberries" (whortleberries), which became "huckleberries" in the American colonies. "Maracocks" were the lemonlike fruit of the passion vine, the name of which was corrupted into "maypop" about 1850, but its origin is uncertain (see Barbour, "Earliest Reconnaissance," Pt. II, 36).

4. "Purslane"; not to be confused with parsley.

5. "Tuckahoe," green arrow arum (Medsger, *Plants*, 196; and Barbour, "Earliest Reconnaissance," Pt. II, 44–45).

roasted, except it be tender and the heat abated, or sliced and dried in the sun, mixed with sorrell and meale or such like, it will prickle and torment the throat extreamely, and yet in sommer they use this ordinarily for bread.

Wighsacan a Root.

They have an other roote which they call *wighsacan*:[6] as th'other feedeth the body, so this cureth their hurts and diseases. It is a small root which they bruise and apply to the wound. *Pocones*,[7] is a small roote that groweth in the mountaines, which being dryed and beate in powder turneth red. And this they use for swellings, aches, annointing their joints, painting their heads and garments. They account it very pretious and of much worth. *Musquaspenne*[8] is a roote of the bignesse of a finger, and as red as bloud. In drying it will wither almost to nothing. This they use to paint their Mattes, Targets and such like.

Pocones a small Roote.

Musquaspenne, a Root.

Pellitory.
Sasafrage.

There is also Pellitory of Spaine, Sasafrage,[9] and divers other simples, which the Apothecaries gathered, and commended to be good, and medicinable.

Onyons.

In the low Marishes growe plots of Onyons containing an acre of ground or more in many places; but they are small not past the bignesse of the Toppe of ones Thumbe.

Their chiefe beasts are Deare.

Of beastes the chiefe are Deare, nothing differing from ours. In the deserts towards the heads of the rivers, ther are many, but amongst the rivers few. There is a beast they call *Aroughcun*,[1] much like a badger, but useth to live on trees as Squirrels doe. Their Squirrels some are neare as greate as ‖ our smallest sort of wilde rabbits, some blackish or blacke and white, but the most are gray.

Aroughcun.
Squirrels.

[14]

Assapanick a Squirrel flying.

A small beast they have, they call *Assapanick*[2] but we call them

6. This medicinal root has been identified as milkweed, *Asclepias syriaca* (Quinn, *Roanoke Voyages*, I, 444–446, II, 900). See Barbour, "Earliest Reconnaissance," Pt. II, 47. There is a drawing of the young shoots and buds in Lena C. Artz, "Native Plants Used by the North American Indians," Archeological Society of Virginia, *Quarterly Bulletin*, XXIX (1974–1975), 88.

7. Later spelled "puccoon"; see Barbour, "Earliest Reconnaissance," Pt. II, 41; and Frederick Webb Hodge, ed., *Handbook of American Indians North of Mexico*, Smithsonian Institution, Bureau of American Ethnology, Bulletin 30 (Washington, D.C., 1907, 1910), Pt. II, 315. These roots seem to have been used primarily as a balm and secondarily as a cosmetic. Purchas condensed the passage in a marginal note in his *Pilgrimage*, 640.

8. "Bloodroot," a dye; see Barbour, "Earliest Reconnaissance," Pt. II, 37.

9. See 12n, above, on "Sasafrage." Pellitory of Spain (pyrethrum), native to Barbary, was used as a medicine and toothache remedy. See Wyndham B. Blanton, *Medicine in Virginia in the Seventeenth Century* (Richmond, Va., 1930), 99–104. Samuel Purchas, in his reprint of this passage, supplies the Latin name of the plant (*Parietaria*), and adds a marginal note just below calling attention to "certain oxen [bison] found by Captaine Argall" early in 1613 (Purchas, *Hakluytus Posthumus, or Purchas His Pilgrimes . . .* [London, 1625], IV, 1695, 1765).

1. "Raccoon"; see the *True Relation*, sig. C1ᵛn; and Barbour, "Earliest Reconnaissance," Pt. II, 32, s.v. "aroughcun."

2. See Barbour, "Earliest Reconnaissance," Pt. II, 32. For King James's interest in flying squirrels, see Philip L. Barbour, ed., *The Jamestown Voyages under the First Charter 1606–1609* (Hakluyt Society, 2d Ser., CXXXVI–CXXXVII [Cambridge, 1969]), II 288.

flying squirrels, because spreading their legs, and so stretching the largenesse of their skins that they have bin seene to fly 30 or 40 yards. An Opassom[3] hath a head like a Swine, and a taile like a Rat, and is of the bignes of a Cat. Under her belly shee hath a bagge, wherein shee lodgeth, carrieth, and suckleth her young. *Mussascus*,[4] is a beast of the forme and nature of our water Rats, but many of them smell exceeding strongly of muske. Their Hares no bigger then our Conies, and few of them to be found. *(margin: Opassom. Mussascus.)*

Their Beares are very little in comparison of those of Muscovia and Tartaria. The Beaver is as bigge as an ordinary water dogge, but his legges exceeding short. His fore feete like a dogs, his hinder feet like a Swans. His taile somewhat like the forme of a Racket bare without haire, which to eate the Savages esteeme a great delicate. They have many Otters which as the Beavers they take with snares, and esteeme the skinnes great ornaments, and of all those beasts they use to feede when they catch them. *(margin: Beares. The Beaver. Otters.)*

There is also a beast they call *Vetchunquoyes*[5] in the forme of a wilde Cat. Their Foxes are like our silver haired Conies of a small proportion, and not smelling like those in England. Their Dogges of that country are like their Wolves, and cannot barke but howle, and their wolves not much bigger then our English Foxes. Martins, Powlecats, weessels and Minkes we know they have, because we have seen many of their skinnes, though very seldome any of them alive. But one thing is strange that we could never perceive their vermine[6] destroy our hennes, Egges nor Chickens nor do any hurt, nor their flyes nor serpents anie waie pernitious, where in the South parts of America they are alwaies dangerous and often deadly. *(margin: Vetchunquoyes. Foxes. Dogges. Martins. Polcats. Weesels and Minkes.)*

Of birds the Eagle is the greatest devourer. Hawkes there be of diverse sorts, as our Falconers called them, Spa- ‖ rowhawkes, Lanarets, Goshawkes, Falcons and Osperayes, but they all pray most upon fish. Partridges there are little bigger then our Quailes, wilde Turkies are as bigge as our tame.[7] There are wooosels or blackbirds with red shoulders, thrushes and diverse sorts of small birds, some red, some blew, scarce so bigge as a wrenne, but few in Sommer. In winter there are great plenty of Swans, Craynes, gray and white *(margin: Birds. **[15]**)*

3. See Barbour, "Earliest Reconnaissance," Pt. II, 39; and Carl G. Hartman, *Possums* (Austin, Tex., 1952). Georg Friederici has further references in his *Amerikanistisches Wörterbuch* . . . (Hamburg, 1960), 459–460.

4. "Muskrat" or "musquash" (see Barbour, "Earliest Reconnaissance," Pt. II, 38), possibly the same as Harriot's "maquówoc" (see Quinn, *Roanoke Voyages*, I, 355–356, II, 890; also cf. "sacquenúckot," *ibid*., II, 896).

5. Surely for "Uetchunquoyes," pronounced "wetch-" (see Barbour, "Earliest Reconnaissance," Pt. II, 45).

6. Vermin were objectionable or noxious animals in general.

7. Turkeys were domesticated in Mexico before the conquest, brought to Europe by 1530, and known in England by 1541. Thomas Tusser, agricultural writer, poet, and musician (who died in debtor's prison in 1580), testified that they played a part in "Christmas husbandlie fare" in his day (*Five Hundreth Pointes of Good Husbandrie* . . . London, 1573], sig. H3ᵛ). Below, "woosel" is a variant of "ouzel."

with blacke wings, Herons, Geese, Brants, Ducke, Wigeon, Dotterell, Oxeies, Parrats and Pigeons. Of all those sorts great abundance, and some other strange kinds to us unknowne by name. But in sommer not any or a very few to be seene.

Fish.

Of fish we were best acquainted with Sturgeon, Grampus, Porpus, Seales, Stingraies, whose tailes are very dangerous.[8] Brettes,[9] mullets, white Salmonds, Trowts, Soles, Plaice, Herrings, Conyfish, Rockfish, Eeles, Lampreyes, Catfish, Shades, Pearch of 3 sorts, Crabs, Shrimps, Crevises,[1] Oysters, Cocles and Muscles. But the most strange fish is a smal one so like the picture of St. George his Dragon,[2] as possible can be, except his legs and wings, and the Todefish[3] which will swell till it be like to brust, when it commeth into the aire.

The Rocks.

Concerning the entrailes of the earth little can be saide for certainty. There wanted good Refiners, for these that tooke upon them to have skill this way, tooke up the washings from the mounetaines and some moskered[4] shining stones and spangles which the waters brought down, flattering themselves in their own vaine conceits to have bin supposed what they were not, by the meanes of that ore, if it proved as their arts and judgements expected. Only this is certaine, that many regions lying in the same latitude, afford mines very rich of diverse natures. The crust also of these rockes would easily perswade a man to beleeve there are other mines then yron and steele, if there were but meanes and men of experience that knew the mine from spare.[5]

[16]   Of their Planted fruits in Virginia and how they use them.

How they divide the yeare.

They divide the yeare into 5. seasons. Their winter some call *Popanow*, the spring *Cattapeuk*, the sommer *Cohattayough*, the earing of their Corne *Nepinough*, the harvest and fall of leafe *Taquitock*.[6] From

8. For Smith's own encounter with a stingray, see the *Proceedings*, 34; and the *Generall Historie*, 27–28, 59.

9. "Bret[te]" was the Lincolnshire name for the turbot.

1. "Crayfish"; modern French *écrevisse*. "Shades" is possibly a unique variant of "shad" (plural).

2. Probably the sea robin; see John C. Pearson, "The Fish and Fisheries of Colonial Virginia," *WMQ*, 2d Ser., XXII (1942), 215, which contains an ichthyological discussion of Smith's entire list, including the scientific nomenclature for many of the species named.

3. "Toadfish," puffer; below, "brust" is an obsolete form of "burst."

4. I.e., "crumbling"; Lincolnshire and Yorkshire dialect.

5. "Spar"; the meaning of the phrase is, "that knew the ore from the rock in which it is found" (Barbour, *Jamestown Voyages*, II, 350n).

6. For the names of the seasons, see Barbour, "Earliest Reconnaissance," Pt. II,

September untill the midst of November are the chiefe Feasts and sacrifice. Then have they plenty of fruits as well planted as naturall, as corne, greene and ripe, fish, fowle, and wilde beastes exceeding fat.

The greatest labour they take, is in planting their corne,[7] for the country naturally is overgrowne with wood. To prepare the ground they bruise the barke of the trees neare the root, then do they scortch the roots with fire that they grow no more. The next yeare with a crooked peece of wood, they beat up the woodes by the rootes, and in that moulde they plant their corne. Their manner is this. They make a hole in the earth with a sticke, and into it they put 4 graines of wheate, and 2 of beanes. These holes they make 4 foote one from another; Their women and children do continually keepe it with weeding, and when it is growne midle high, they hill it about like a hop-yard.[8] *How they prepare the ground.*

In Aprill they begin to plant, but their chiefe plantation is in May, and so they continue till the midst of June. What they plant in Aprill they reape in August, for May in September, for June in October; Every stalke of their corne commonly beareth two eares, some 3, seldome any 4, many but one and some none. Every eare ordinarily hath betwixt 200 and 500 graines. The stalke being green hath a sweet juice in it, somewhat like a suger Cane, which is the cause that when they gather their corne greene, they sucke the stalkes: for as wee gather greene pease, so doe they their corne being greene, which excelleth their old. They plant also pease they cal *Assentamens,*[9] which are the same they cal in Italy, *Fagioli.* Their Beanes are the same the Turkes cal *Garnanses,*[1] but these they much esteeme for dainties. *How they plant.*

Their corne they rost in the eare greene, and bruising it in a morter of wood with a Polt,[2] lappe it in rowles in the leaves of their corne, and so boyle it for a daintie. They also reserve that corne late planted that will not ripe, by roasting it in hot ashes, the heat thereof drying it. In winter they esteeme it being boyled with beans for a **[17]** *How they use their corne.*

41-42, 34, 39, 44. Robert Beverley gave "cohonk" as the Indian name for "winter" (*ibid.,* 42), which may explain Smith's "some call" before "Popanow." On the Indian annual economic cycle in general, see John R. Swanton, *The Indians of the Southeastern United States,* Smithsonian Institution, Bureau of American Ethnology, Bulletin 137 (Washington, D.C., 1946), 255-265.

7. See pp. 18 and 22, below. Apparently the men helped prepare the ground, but the women did the actual planting (Swanton, *Indians of Southeastern United States,* 710).

8. Often "hop gardens."

9. See Barbour, "Earliest Reconnaissance," Pt. II, 32.

1. Chick-peas, called *garbanzos* in Spanish. This is a significant reference to Smith's experiences in Turkey, narrated in the *True Travels,* 24-32, and may be the first appearance of the word "garvances" in English print (not noted in the *OED,* under "calavance"). The unusual spelling "garnanses" must be a printer's error.

2. Pestle or club.

rare dish, they call *Pausarowmena*.[3] Their old wheat they first steep a night in hot water, in the morning pounding it in a morter. They use a small basket for their Temmes,[4] then pound againe the grout,[5] and so separating by dashing their hand in the basket, receave the flower[6] in a platter made of wood scraped to that forme with burning and shels. Tempering this flower with water, they make it either in cakes covering them with ashes till they bee baked, and then washing them in faire water they drie presently with their owne heat: or else boyle them in water eating the broth with the bread which they call *Ponap*.[7] The grouts and peeces of the cornes remaining, by fanning in a Platter or in the wind, away, the branne they boile 3 or 4 houres with water, which is an ordinary food they call *Ustatahamen*.[8] But some more thrifty then cleanly, doe burne the core of the eare to powder which they call *Pungnough*,[9] mingling that in

How they use their fish and flesh. their meale, but it never tasted well in bread, nor broth. Their fish and flesh they boyle either very tenderly, or broyle it so long on hurdles over the fire, or else after the Spanish fashion, putting it on a spit, they turne first the one side, then the other, til it be as drie as their jerkin beefe[1] in the west Indies, that they may keepe it a month or more without putrifying. The broth of fish or flesh they eate as commonly as the meat.

Planted fruits.   In May also amongst their corne they plant Pumpeons,[2] and a fruit like unto a muske millen, but lesse and worse, which they call *Macocks*.[3] These increase exceedingly, and ripen in the beginning of July, and continue until September. They plant also *Maracocks*[4] a wild fruit like a lemmon, which also increase infinitely. They begin

[18]   to ripe in Sep- ‖ tember and continue till the end of October. When all their fruits be gathered, little els they plant, and this is done by their women and children;[5] neither doth this long suffice them, for

3. The Virginia equivalent of "succotash," a Narragansett Indian word (see the *True Relation*, sig. D3ᵛn; and Barbour, "Earliest Reconnaissance," Pt. II, 40).

4. I.e., "sieve"; Lincolnshire and northern English dialect.

5. Coarse meal, peeled grain; what is meant is "hominy grits." Cf. "grouts and peeces," a few lines below.

6. "Flour," originally the "flower" or finest quality of meal. The modern distinction in spelling did not arise until later.

7. "Pone," or "corn pone"; perhaps a misprint of "apone" (see Barbour, "Earliest Reconnaissance," Pt. II, 32).

8. "Hominy" is a word derived from this (see the *True Travels*, 43; and Barbour, "Earliest Reconnaissance," Pt. II, 46).

9. Probably a misprint for "pungwough" (see Barbour, "Earliest Reconnaissance," Pt. II, 42).

1. "Jerked beef" was sliced and dried in the sun; from Spanish from Quechua *ccharqui*, "dried (flesh)." The Caribbean word for the process was *barbacóa*, whence "barbecue," which was not known in Virginia until later.

2. "Pumpkins."

3. "Gourds"; see Barbour, "Earliest Reconnaissance," Pt. II, 35.

4. See p. 12n, above.

5. See pp. 16 and 22, above.

neere 3 parts of the yeare, they only observe times and seasons, and live of what the Country naturally affordeth from hand to mouth, etc.

The commodities in Virginia or that may be had by industrie.

The mildnesse of the aire, the fertilitie of the soile, and the situation of the rivers are so propitious to the nature and use of man as no place is more convenient for pleasure, profit, and mans sustenance. Under that latitude or climat, here will live any beasts, as horses, goats, sheep, asses, hens, etc. as appeared by them that were carried thether. The waters, Isles, and shoales, are full of safe harbours for ships of warre or marchandize, for boats of all sortes, for transportation or fishing, etc. The Bay and rivers have much marchandable fish and places fit for Salt coats,[6] building of ships, making of iron, etc.[7]   *A proofe cattell will live well.*

Muscovia and Polonia doe yearely receave many thousands, for pitch, tarre, sope ashes, Rosen, Flax, Cordage, Sturgeon, masts, yards, wainscot, Firres, glasse, and such like, also Swethland[8] for iron and copper. France in like manner for Wine, Canvas, and Salt, Spaine asmuch for Iron, Steele, Figges, Reasons,[9] and Sackes. Italy with Silkes, and Velvets consumes our chiefe commodities. Holand maintaines it selfe by fishing and trading at our owne doores. All these temporize with other for necessities, but all as uncertaine as peace or warres. Besides the charge, travell, and danger in transporting them, by seas, lands, stormes, and Pyrats. Then how much hath Virginia the prerogative of all those florishing kingdomes for the benefit of our land, whenas within one hundred miles all those are to bee had, either ready provided by nature, or else to bee prepared, were there but industrious men to labour. Only of Copper wee may doubt is wanting, but there is good probabilitie that ‖ both copper and better minerals are there to be had for their labor. Other Countries have it. So then here is a place a nurse for souldiers, a practise for marriners, a trade for marchants, a reward for the good, and that which is most of all, a businesse (most acceptable to God) to bring such poore infidels to the true knowledge of God and his holy Gospell.   *The commodities.*   **[19]**

6. Variant spelling for "salt-cotes," salt houses.

7. Although there were two blacksmiths in Jamestown by 1608, the first machinery for "making" iron was not set up until 1619 (see Charles E. Hatch, Jr., and Thurlow Gates Gregory, "The First American Blast Furnace, 1619–1622," *VMHB*, LXX [1962], 259–296).

8. Sweden.

9. Obsolete spelling of "raisins." "Sacks" were white wines from Spain and the Canaries.

Of the naturall Inhabitants of Virginia.[1]

The land is not populous, for the men be fewe; their far greater number is of women and children. Within 60 miles of James Towne there are about some 5000 people, but of able men fit for their warres

The numbers.

scarse 1500.[2] To nourish so many together they have yet no means because they make so smal a benefit of their land, be it never so fertill.

700 men were the most were seene together when they thoght to have surprised Captaine Smith.

6 or 700 have beene the most hath beene seene together, when they gathered themselves to have surprised Captaine Smyth at Pamaunke, having but 15 to withstand the worst of their furie.[3] As small as the proportion of ground that hath yet beene discovered, is in comparison of that yet unknowne, the people differ very much in stature, especially in language, as before is expressed. Some being very great as the Sesquesahamocks; others very little, as the Wighcocomocoes:

A description of the people.

but generally tall and straight, of a comely proportion, and of a colour browne when they are of any age, but they are borne white.[4] Their haire is generally black, but few have any beards. The men

The barbers.

weare halfe their heads shaven, the other halfe long; for Barbers they use their women, who with 2 shels will grate away the haire, of any fashion they please. The women are cut in many fashions agreeable

The constitution.

to their yeares, but ever some part remaineth long. They are very strong, of an able body and full of agilitie, able to endure to lie in

The disposition.

the woods under a tree by the fire, in the worst of winter, or in the weedes and grasse, in Ambuscado in the Sommer. They are inconstant in everie thing, but what feare constraineth them to keepe.

[20] Craftie, || timerous, quicke of apprehension and very ingenuous. Some are of disposition fearefull, some bold, most cautelous,[5] all Savage. Generally covetous of copper, beads, and such like trash. They are soone moved to anger, and so malitious, that they seldome forget an injury: they seldome steale one from another, least their conjurers should reveale it, and so they be pursued and punished. That they are thus feared is certaine, but that any can reveale their offences by conjuration I am doubtfull. Their women are carefull not to bee suspected of dishonesty without the leave of their husbands. Each houshold knoweth their owne lands and gardens, and

The possessions.

most live of their owne labours. For their apparell, they are some time covered with the skinnes of wilde beasts, which in winter are dressed with the haire, but in sommer without. The better sort use

---

1. Purchas, *Pilgrimes*, IV, 1697, adds "and their customes" to the subhead.

2. As of this writing, the Indian population figures for Smith's day are under review, but no consensus seems to have been reached as yet.

3. This maximum show of fighting men (probably exaggerated by Smith) only confirms Smith's conviction that the land of Virginia was not populous. England's second city, Norwich, then had twice as many inhabitants as Powhatan's entire "empire."

4. Cf. the "Breif discription of the People" sent to London in 1607: "their skynn is tawny not so borne" (Barbour, *Jamestown Voyages*, I, 103).

5. Wary and wily; from Latin *cautela* (not *caution-em*).

large mantels of deare skins not much differing in fashion from the   Their attire.
Irish mantels.[6] Some imbrodered with white beads, some with
copper, other painted after their manner. But the common sort have
scarce to cover their nakednesse but with grasse, the leaves of trees,
or such like. We have seen some use mantels made of Turky feathers,
so prettily wrought and woven with threeds that nothing could bee
discerned but the feathers. That was exceeding warme and very
handsome. But the women are alwaies covered about their midles
with a skin and very shamefast[7] to be seene bare. They adorne themselves most with copper beads and paintings. Their women some   Their orna-
have their legs, hands, brests and face cunningly imbrodered[8] with   ments.
diverse workes, as beasts, serpentes, artificially wrought into their
flesh with blacke spots. In each eare commonly they have 3 great
holes, whereat they hange chaines bracelets or copper. Some of their
men weare in those holes, a smal greene and yellow coloured snake,
neare halfe a yard in length, which crawling and lapping her selfe
about his necke often times familiarly would kisse his lips. Others
wear a dead Rat[9] tied by the tail. Some on their heads weare the
wing of a bird, or some large feather with a Rat- || tell. Those Rattels   [21]
are somewhat like the chape[1] of a Rapier but lesse, which they take
from the taile of a snake. Many have the whole skinne of a hawke or
some strange fowle, stuffed with the wings abroad. Others a broad
peece of copper, and some the hand of their enemy dryed. Their
heads and shoulders are painted red with the roote *Pocone* braied to
powder mixed with oyle, this they hold in somer to preserve them
from the heate, and in winter from the cold. Many other formes of
paintings they use, but he is the most gallant that is the most mon-
strous to behold.

Their buildings and habitations are for the most part by the   Their build-
rivers or not farre distant from some fresh spring. Their houses are   ings.
built like our Arbors of small young springs[2] bowed and tyed, and
so close covered with mats, or the barkes of trees very handsomely,
that notwithstanding either winde, raine or weather, they are as
warme as stooves, but very smoaky, yet at the toppe of the house

6. Although Smith was said to have been in Ireland (see the Introduction to the
True Travels), and Strachey added the Irish word "falinges" in quoting this passage
(*Historie*, 71), there is no firm evidence that either of them ever visited the island. On
the Irish mantles, see the index to David Beers Quinn, *The Elizabethans and the Irish*
(Ithaca, N.Y., 1966).
    7. Modest; etymologically independent of "shamefaced."
    8. Tattooed.
    9. There were no rats before the arrival of the colonists. The reference is possibly
to "mussaneeks" (see Barbour, "Earliest Reconnaissance," Pt. II, 37–38), although
muskrats have also been suggested.
    1. The "chape" is the metal cap covering the tip of the scabbard of a rapier, dagger,
etc. This is most likely the earliest specific mention of the American rattlesnake, as suggested by Professor D. B. Quinn (cf. Mitford M. Mathews, ed., *A Dictionary of Americanisms
on Historical Principles* [Chicago, 1951], s.v. "rattlesnake").
    2. Saplings.

there is a hole made for the smoake to goe into right over the fire.

Their lodgings.   Against the fire they lie on little hurdles[3] of Reedes covered with a mat borne from the ground a foote and more by a hurdle of wood. On these round about the house they lie heads and points one by th'other against the fire, some covered with mats, some with skins, and some starke naked lie on the ground, from 6 to 20 in a house.

Their gardens.   Their houses are in the midst of their fields or gardens which are smal plots of ground. Some 20,[4] some 40. some 100. some 200. some more, some lesse, some times from 2 to 100 of those houses togither, or but a little separated by groves of trees. Neare their habitations is little small wood or old trees on the ground by reason of their burning of them for fire. So that a man may gallop a horse amongst these woods any waie, but where the creekes or Rivers shall hinder.

How they use their children.   Men women and children have their severall names according to the severall humor of their Parents. Their women (they say) are

[22]   easilie delivered of childe, yet doe they || love children verie dearly. To make them hardy, in the coldest mornings they wash them in the rivers and by painting and ointments so tanne their skins, that after a year or two, no weather will hurt them.

The industry of their women.   The men bestowe their times in fishing, hunting, wars and such manlike exercises, scorning to be seene in any woman-like exercise, which is the cause that the women be verie painefull and the men often idle. The women and children do the rest of the worke. They make mats, baskets, pots, morters, pound their corne, make their bread, prepare their victuals, plant their corne, gather their corne,[5] beare al kind of burdens and such like.

How they strike fire.   Their fire they kindle presently[6] by chafing a dry pointed sticke in a hole of a little square peece of wood, that firing it selfe, will so fire mosse, leaves, or anie such like drie thing, that will quickly burne.

Their order of diet.   In March and Aprill they live much upon their fishing weares, and feed on fish, Turkies and squirrels. In May and June they plant their fieldes and live most of Acornes, walnuts, and fish. But to mend their diet, some disperse themselves in small companies and live upon fish, beasts, crabs, oysters, land Torteyses, strawberries, mulberries, and such like. In June, Julie, and August they feed upon the rootes of *Tocknough* berries,[7] fish and greene wheat. It is strange to see how their bodies alter with their diet, even as the deare and wilde beastes

---

3. Smith refers to the rectangular frames lifting the Indian beds slightly from the ground; perhaps the "tussan" listed in the vocabulary at the beginning (sig. *3ʳ, above).

4. The *Generall Historie*, 31, has "Some 20 acres, some 40." and so on; and in the following line, a new sentence begins, "In some places from 2 to 50 of those houses. . . ."

5. Cf. pp. 16 and 18, above.

6. Quickly.

7. "Tocknough" is a misreading or misprint of "Tockuough" or "Tockwough" (see Barbour, "Earliest Reconnaissance," Pt. II, 44); probably the green arrow arum, the root of which is bulbous. Both the Indian name and the identity of the plant need further study.

they seeme fat and leane, strong and weak. Powhatan their great king and some others that are provident, rost their fish and flesh upon hurdles as before is expressed, and keepe it till scarce times.

For fishing and hunting and warres they use much their bow and arrowes. They bring their bowes to the forme of ours by the scraping of a shell. Their arrowes are made some of straight young sprigs which they head with bone, some 2 or 3 inches long. These they use to shoot at squirrels on trees. An other sort of arrowes they use made of reeds. These are peeced[8] with wood, headed with splinters ‖ of christall or some sharpe stone, the spurres of a Turkey, or the bill of some bird. For his knife he hath the splinter of a reed to cut his feathers in forme. With this knife also, he will joint a Deare or any beast, shape his shooes, buskins, mantels, etc. To make the noch of his arrow hee hath the tooth of a Bever, set in a sticke, wherewith he grateth it by degrees, His arrow head he quickly maketh with a little bone, which he ever weareth at his bracer,[9] of any splint of a stone, or glasse in the forme of a hart and these they glew to the end of their arrowes. With the sinewes of Deare, and the tops of Deares hornes boiled to a jelly, they make a glew that will not dissolve in cold water.

For their wars also they use Targets[10] that are round and made of the barkes of trees, and a sworde of wood at their backs, but oftentimes they use for swords the horne of a Deare put through a peece of wood in forme of a Pickaxe.[1] Some a long stone sharpned at both ends used in the same manner. This they were wont to use also for hatchets, but now by trucking they have plenty of the same forme of yron. And those are their chiefe instruments and armes.

Their fishing is much in Boats. These they make of one tree by bowing[2] and scratching away the coles with stons and shels till they have made it in forme of a Trough. Some of them are an elne[3] deepe, and 40 or 50 foot in length, and some will beare 40 men, but the most ordinary are smaller and will beare 10, 20, or 30. according to their bignes. Instead of oares, they use paddles and sticks with which they will row faster then our Barges. Betwixt their hands and thighes, their women use to spin, the barks of trees, deare sinews, or a kind of grasse they call *Pemmenaw*,[4] of these they make a thred very even and readily. This thred serveth for many uses: As about their housing,

How they make their bowes and arrowes.

[23]

Their knives.

Their Targets and Swords.

Their boats.

How they spin.

---

8. I.e., "put together to form one piece."

9. "Bracer" is still the name of the wrist guards used by fencers.

10. Light, round shields.

1. Cf. "tomahacks" and "tockahacks" in the vocabulary at the beginning (sig. *3^r).

2. Corrected to "burning" in the *Generall Historie*, 31. A handwritten "burn" could easily be mistaken for "bow."

3. "Ell"; the English ell was 45 in. long.

4. "Pemmenaw" means rather the thread than the grass (see Barbour, "Earliest Reconnaissance," Pt. II, 41).

Their fishookes. apparell, as also they make nets for fishing, for the quantity as for-mally braded as ours. They make also with it lines for angles. Their hookes are either a bone grated as they nock their arrows in the

[24] forme of a crooked pinne or fishook or of the splin- || ter of a bone tied to the clift of a litle stick, and with the ende of the line, they tie on the bate. They use also long arrowes tyed in a line wherewith they shoote at fish in the rivers. But they of Accawmack[5] use staves like unto Javelins headed with bone. With these they dart fish swimming in the water. They have also many artificiall weares in which they get abundance of fish.

In their hunting and fishing they take extreame paines; yet it being their ordinary exercise from their infancy, they esteeme it a pleasure and are very proud to be expert therein. And by their con-tinuall ranging, and travel, they know all the advantages and places most frequented with Deare, Beasts, Fish, Foule, Rootes, and Ber-ries. At their huntings they leave their habitations, and reduce them-

How they hunt. selves into companies, as the Tartars[6] doe, and goe to the most desert places with their families, where they spend their time in hunting and fowling up towards the mountaines, by the heads of their rivers, where there is plentie of game. For betwixt the rivers the grounds are so narrowe, that little commeth there which they devoure not. It is a marvel they can so directly passe these deserts, some 3 or 4 daies journey without habitation. Their hunting houses are like unto Arbours covered with mats. These their women beare after them, with Corne, Acornes, Morters, and all bag and baggage they use. When they come to the place of exercise, every man doth his best to shew his dexteritie, for by their excelling in those quallities, they get their wives. Forty yards will they shoot levell, or very neare the mark, and 120 is their best at Random.[7] At their huntings in the deserts they are commonly 2 or 300 together. Having found the Deare, they environ them with many fires, and betwixt the fires they place them-selves. And some take their stands in the midst. The Deare being thus feared by the fires and their voices, they chace them so long within that circle that many times they kill 6, 8, 10, or 15 at a hunt-ing. They use also to drive them into some narrowe point of land;

[25] || when they find that advantage and so force them into the river, where with their boats they have Ambuscadoes to kill them. When they have shot a Deare by land, they follow him like blood hounds

5. NE of Cape Charles City (see *ibid.*, Pt. I, 285).

6. See the *True Travels*, 26–31.

7. Shooting "at random" meant with speed, but without careful aim; shooting "level" meant carefully, with direct aim (see the *True Relation*, sig. C1ʳn). It is worth noting that the range of ancient composite bows (Roman Empire, c. A.D. 300–400) has been established: "bowmen were quite accurate up to 50 to 60 meters [55 to 66 yards]," with an effective range of "at least 160 to 175 meters [175–191 yards]" (Otto J. Maenchen-Helfen, *The World of the Huns: Studies in Their History and Culture* [Berkeley, Calif., 1973], 227). Obviously, with far less "sophisticated" weapons the Indians did very well indeed.

by the blood and straine and oftentimes so take them. Hares, Partridges, Turkies, or Egges,[8] fat or leane, young or old, they devoure all they can catch in their power. In one of these huntings they found Captaine Smith in the discoverie of the head of the river of Chickahamania, where they slew his men, and tooke him prisoner in a Bogmire, where he saw those exercises, and gathered these observations.

One Savage hunting alone, useth the skinne of a Deare slit on the one side, and so put on his arme, through the neck, so that his hand comes to the head which is stuffed, and the hornes, head, eies, eares, and every part as arteficially counterfeited[9] as they can devise. Thus shrowding his body in the skinne by stalking he approacheth the Deare, creeping on the ground from one tree to another. If the Deare chance to find fault, or stande at gaze, hee turneth the head with his hand to his best advantage to seeme like a Deare, also gazing and licking himselfe. So watching his best advantage to approach, having shot him, hee chaseth him by his blood and straine till he get him.   *One Savage hunting alone.*

When they intend any warres, the Werowances usually have the advice of their Priests and Conjurers, and their Allies and ancient friends, but chiefely the Priestes determine their resolution. Every Werowance, or some lustie fellow, they appoint Captaine over every nation. They seldome make warre for lands or goods, but for women and children, and principally for revenge. They have many enimies, namely all their westernely Countries beyond the mountaines, and the heads of the rivers. Upon the head of the Powhatans are the Monacans, whose chiefe habitation is at Russawmcake,[1] unto whome the Mouhemenchughes, the Massinnacacks, the Monahassanuggs, and other nations pay tributs.[2] Upon the head of the river of Toppahanock is a || people called Mannahoacks. To these are contributers the Tauxsnitanias, the Shackaconias, the Outponcas, the Tegoneaes, the Whonkentyaes, the Stegarakes, the Hassinnungas, and diverse others,[3] all confederats with the Monacans though many different in language, and be very barbarous living for most part of wild beasts and fruits: Beyond the mountaines from whence is the head of the river Patawomeke, the Savages report   *Their consultations.*   *Their enimies.*   **[26]**

8. "Egges" seems out of place; perhaps a garbled spelling of "geese."
9. Skillfully, ingeniously imitated.
1. Properly, "Rassaweake" (probably a misprint) (see Barbour, "Earliest Reconnaissance," Pt. I, 298, s.v. "Rassawek II"; and the *True Relation*, sig. C1ʳn). "Rassaweake" or "Rassawek" almost certainly means "in between, at the fork." It is the Algonkian name for (1) the King's house of the Monacans, and (2) the temporary hunting camp mentioned in the *True Relation*, sig. C1ʳ.
2. All three tribes are in Barbour, "Earliest Reconnaissance," Pt. I, 290, 292. The first two were visited by Newport late in 1608 (*Generall Historie*, 68; enthusiastically described in Strachey, *Historie*, 106, 131).
3. Also in Barbour, "Earliest Reconnaissance," Pt. I, 280, 300, 299, 294, 300, 302, 300, and 288, respectively. See the detailed account in the *Generall Historie*, 63–64, curiously omitted from the corresponding passages in the *Proceedings*, 40.

Massawo-
mekes.

inhabit their most mortall enimies, the Massawomekes[4] upon a great salt water, which by all likelyhood is either some part of Cannada some great lake, or some inlet of some sea that falleth into the South sea.[5] These Massawomekes are a great nation and very populous. For the heads of all those rivers, especially the Pattawomekes, the Pautuxuntes. The Sasquesahanocks, the Tockwoughes are continually tormented by them: of whose crueltie, they generally complained, and very importunate they were with Captaine Smith and his company to free them from these tormentors. To this purpose they offered food, conduct, assistance, and continuall subjection. To which he concluded[6] to effect, But the counsell then present emulating[7] his successe, would not thinke it fit to spare him 40 men to be hazarded in those unknowne regions, having passed (as before was spoken of) but with 12, and so was lost that opportunitie. Seaven boats full of these Massawomeks the discoverers encountred at the head of the Bay; whose Targets, Baskets, Swords, Tobacco pipes, Platters, Bowes and Arrowes, and every thing shewed, they much exceeded them of our parts, and their dexteritie in their small boats made of the barkes of trees sowed with barke and well luted with gumme,[8] argueth that they are seated upon some great water.

Their offer of
subjection.

Against all these enimies the Powhatans are constrained sometimes to fight. Their chiefe attempts are by Stratagems, trecheries, or surprisals. Yet the Werowances, women and children they put not to death but keepe them Captives.[9] They have a method in warre and for our plea- ‖ sures they shewd it us, and it was in this manner performed at Mattapanient.[1]

[27]

Their manner
of battell.

Having painted and disguised themselves in the fiercest manner they could devise. They divided themselves into two Companies, neare a 100 in a company. The one company Called Monacans, the other Powhatans. Either army had their Captaine. These as enimies

4. See the *Generall Historie*, 61–62; and the brief reference in the *Proceedings*, 39–40.
5. See the *True Relation*, sig. B4ᵛn.
6. Resolved.
7. Envying.
8. "Lute" was a sticky clay. Evidently these were the birchbark canoes of farther north, as opposed to the dugouts used in Virginia and North Carolina. The distribution of the two kinds of craft overlapped in southern New England, but there are few references to birchbark canoes south of the Massachusetts Bay area (Bert Salwen, "Indians of Southern New England and Long Island: Early Period," in William C. Sturtevant, ed., *Handbook of North American Indians*, XV, *Northeast*, ed. Bruce G. Trigger [Washington, D.C., 1978], 164). On possible connections between dugouts and Carib canoes, see William C. Sturtevant, "The Significance of Ethnological Similarities between Southeastern North America and the Antilles," *Yale University Publications in Anthropology*, No. 64 (New Haven, Conn., 1960), 26–27.
9. See the *True Relation*, B4ʳn.
1. Probably the chief tribal village on the river of that name, Mattapanient was not on the Smith/Hole map but did appear on the Smith/Zúñiga sketch (see Barbour, "Earliest Reconnaissance," Pt. I, 291, s.v. "Mattapanient III"). Henry Spelman's brief description of a battle between the Potomacs and the Massawomecks shows the same sort of fighting (Edward Arber, ed., *Captain John Smith . . . Works, 1608–1631*, The English Scholar's Library Edition, No. 16 [Birmingham, 1884], cxiv).

tooke their stands a musket shot one from another; ranked themselves 15 a breast and each ranke from another 4 or 5 yards, not in
fyle, but in the opening betwixt their fyles, So as the Reare could
shoot as conveniently as the Front. Having thus pitched the fields:
from either part went a Messenger with these conditions, that who-
soever were vanquished, such as escape upon their submission in 2
daies after should live, but their wives and children should be prize
for the Conquerers. The messengers were no sooner returned, but
they approached in their orders; On each flanke a Sarjeant, and in
the Reare an officer for leuitenant, all duly keeping their orders, yet
leaping and singing after their accustomed tune which they use only
in warres. Upon the first flight of arrowes they gave such horrible
shouts and screeches, as though so many infernall helhounds could
not have made them more terrible. When they had spent their
arrowes they joined together prettily, charging and retiring, every
ranke seconding other. As they got advantage they catched their
enimies by the haire of the head, and downe he came that was taken.
His enimie with his wooden sword seemed to beat out his braines,
and still they crept to the Reare, to maintaine the skirmish. The
Monacans decreasing, the Powhatans charged them in the forme of
a halfe moone; they unwilling to be inclosed, fled all in a troope to
their Ambuscadoes on whome they led them very cunningly. The
Monacans disperse themselves among the fresh men, whereupon the
Powhatans retired, with al speed to their seconds; which the Monacans seeing, took that advantage to retire againe to their owne battell,
and so each ‖ returned to their owne quarter. All their actions, voices   **[28]**
and gestures, both in charging and retiring were so strained to the
hight of their quallitie and nature, that the strangenes thereof made
it seem very delightfull.

    For their musicke they use a thicke cane, on which they pipe as   Their Musicke.
on a Recorder.[2] For their warres they have a great deepe platter of
wood. They cover the mouth thereof with a skin, at each corner they
tie a walnut, which meeting on the backside neere the bottome, with
a small rope they twitch them togither till it be so tought and stiffe,
that they may beat upon it as upon a drumme. But their chiefe instruments are Rattels made of small gourds or Pumpions shels. Of
these they have Base, Tenor, Countertenor, Meane and Trible.
These mingled with their voices sometimes 20 or 30 togither, make
such a terrible noise as would rather affright then delight any man.   Their enter-
If any great commander arrive at the habitation of a Werowance,   tainment.
they spread a mat as the Turkes[3] do a carpet for him to sit upon.
Upon an other right opposite they sit themselves. Then doe all with
a tunable[4] voice of showting bid him welcome. After this doe 2. or

    2. Called "pawpecone" by the Powhatans (see the vocabulary, sig. *3ʳ above; and
Barbour, "Earliest Reconnaissance," Pt. II, 41).
    3. Probably a recollection of Smith's captivity in Turkey (*True Travels*, 23–32).
    4. "Tuneful"; archaic.

more of their chiefest men make an oration, testifying their love. Which they do with such vehemency and so great passions, that they sweate till they drop, and are so out of breath they can scarce speake. So that a man would take them to be exceeding angry or starke mad. Such victuall as they have, they spend freely, and at night where his lodging is appointed, they set a woman fresh painted red with *Pacones* and oile, to be his bedfellow.

Their trade. Their manner of trading is for copper, beades, and such like, for which they give such commodities as they have, as skins, fowle, fish, flesh, and their country corne. But their victuall is their chiefest riches.

Their phisicke. Every spring they make themselves sicke with drinking the juice of a root they call *wighsacan*,[5] and water, whereof they powre[6] so great a quantity, that it purgeth them in a very violent maner; so

[29] that in 3 or 4 daies after they scarce || recover their former health. Sometimes they are troubled with dropsies, swellings, aches, and *Their chirurgery.* such like diseases; for cure wherof they build a stove in the form of a dovehouse[7] with mats, so close that a fewe coales therein covered with a pot, will make the pacient sweate extreamely.[8] For swellings also they use smal peeces of touchwood,[9] in the forme of cloves, which pricking on the griefe they burne close to the flesh, and from thence draw the corruption with their mouth. With this root *wighsacan* they ordinarily heal greene wounds. But to scarrifie a swelling or make incision their best instruments are some splinted[1] stone. Old ulcers or putrified hurtes are seldome seene cured amongst them. *Their charmes to cure.* They have many professed Phisitions, who with their charmes and Rattels with an infernall rowt[2] of words and actions will seeme to sucke their inwarde griefe from their navels[3] or their grieved places; but of our Chirurgians they were so conceipted, that they beleeved any Plaister would heale any hurt.

Of their Religion.

There is yet in Virginia no place discovered to bee so Savage in which the Savages have not a religion, Deare, and Bow, and Arrowes.

---

5. See p. 13, above. Swanton curiously states that the plant is "of European origin" (*Indians of Southeastern United States*, 247), but "wighsacan" has been identified with reasonable certainty as milkweed, a native Virginia plant (Barbour, "Earliest Reconnaissance," Pt. II, 47).
6. Variant of "pour."
7. Dovecote.
8. Cf. the Roman *calidarium* and the Finnish *sauna*.
9. Tinder; any easily ignited wood.
1. Split; an obsolete use of "splint."
2. "Rout," loud noise; Scottish and Lincolnshire word.
3. Cf. *True Relation*, sig. C3ʳ, where "navel [or navle]" has apparently been distorted into "unable."

All things that were able to do them hurt beyond their prevention, they adore with their kinde of divine worship; as the fire, water, lightning, thunder, our ordinance, peeces, horses, etc. But their chiefe God they worship is the Divell. Him they call *Oke*[4] and serve him more of feare then love. They say they have conference with him, and fashion themselves as neare to his shape as they can imagine. In their Temples they have his image evill favouredly carved, and then painted and adorned with chaines copper, and beades, and covered with a skin, in such manner as the deformity may well suit with such a God. By him is commonly the sepulcher of their kings. Their bodies are first bowelled, then dryed upon hurdles till they bee verie dry, and so about the most of their jointes and necke they hang bracelets or chaines of copper, pearle, and such like, || as they use to weare, their inwards they stuffe with copper beads and covered with a skin,[5] hatchets and such trash. Then lappe they them very carefully in white skins and so rowle them in mats for their winding sheetes. And in the Tombe which is an arch made of mats, they lay them orderly. What remaineth of this kinde of wealth their kings have, they set at their feet in baskets. These Temples and bodies are kept by their Priests.

Their God.

How they bury their kings.
[**30**]

For their ordinary burials they digge a deep hole in the earth with sharpe stakes and the corpes being lapped in skins and mats with their jewels, they lay them upon sticks in the ground, and so cover them with earth. The buriall ended, the women being painted all their faces with black cole[6] and oile, doe sit 24 howers in the houses mourning and lamenting by turnes, with such yelling and howling as may expresse their great passions.

Their ordinary burials.

In every Territory of a werowance is a Temple and a Priest 2 or 3 or more. Their principall Temple or place of superstition is at Uttamussack[7] at Pamaunke, neare unto which is a house Temple or place of Powhatans.

Their Temples.

Upon the top of certaine redde sandy hils in the woods, there are 3 great houses filled with images of their kings and Divels and Tombes of their Predecessors. Those houses are neare 60 foot in length built arbor wise after their building. This place they count so

4. Oke (Okee, Okeus) was the malevolent, vengeful god of the Powhatan tribe (see Purchas, *Pilgrimage* [1617 ed.], 954–955, which is summarized in Philip L. Barbour, *Pocahontas and Her World* [Boston, 1970], 168–173; and the brief note in Barbour, "Earliest Reconnaissance," Pt. II, 39, where it is suggested that the name and the deity may have been borrowed from the Iroquoian Hurons, despite many arguments to the contrary).

5. The phrase "and covered with a skin" appears to have been repeated here by printer's error (see p. 29); it was deleted in the *Generall Historie*, 35. Cf. similar accounts in Quinn, *Roanoke Voyages*, I, 425–427; and in Arber, *Smith, Works*, I, cix–cx. There is a summary in Swanton, *Indians of Southeastern United States*, 718–729.

6. Charcoal, soot, burnt wood.

7. The site of the principal Pamunkey temple (see Barbour, "Earliest Reconnaissance," Pt. I, 301).

holy as that but the Priestes and kings dare come into them; nor the Savages dare not go up the river in boats by it, but that they solemnly cast some peece of copper, white beads or *Pocones* into the river, for feare their *Oke* should be offended and revenged of them.

In this place commonly is[8] resident 7 Priests. The chiefe differed from the rest in his ornaments, but inferior Priests could hardly be knowne from the common people, but that they had not so many holes in their eares to hang their jewels at. The ornaments of the chiefe Priest was[9] certain attires for his head made thus. They tooke a dosen or 16 or ‖ more snake skins and stuffed them with mosse, and of weesels and other vermine skins a good many. All these they tie by their tailes, so as all their tailes meete in the toppe of their head, like a great Tassell. Round about this Tassell is as it were a crown of feathers, the skins hang round about his head necke and shoulders and in a manner cover his face. The faces of all their Priests are painted as ugly as they can devise, in their hands they had every one his Rattell, some base, some smaller.[1] Their devotion was most in songs which the chiefe Priest beginneth and the rest followed him, sometimes he maketh invocations with broken sentences by starts and strange passions, and at every pause, the rest give a short groane.

It could not bee perceived that they keepe any day as more holy then other; But only in some great distresse of want, feare of enimies, times of triumph and gathering togither their fruits, the whole country of men women and children come togither to solemnities. The manner of their devotion is, sometimes to make a great fire, in the house or fields, and all to sing and dance about it with rattles and shouts togither, 4 or 5 houres. Sometime they set a man in the midst, and about him they dance and sing, he all the while clapping his hands as if he would keepe time, and after their songs and dauncings ended they goe to their Feasts.

They have also divers conjurations, one they made when Captaine Smith was their prisoner[2] (as they reported) to know if any more of his countrymen would arive there, and what he there intended. The manner of it was thus. First they made a faire fire in a house; about this fire set 7 Priests setting him by them, and about the fire, they made a circle of meale. That done the chiefe Priest attired as is expressed began to shake his rattle, and the rest followed him in his song. At the end of the song, he laid downe 5 or 3 graines of wheat and so continued counting his songs by the graines, till 3 times they incirculed the fire, then they di- ‖ vided the graines by certaine

Marginal notes:
Their ornaments for their Priests.

[31]

Their times of solemnities.

Their conjurations.

[32]

8. Corrected to "are" in the *Generall Historie*, 35.
9. Corrected to "were" (*ibid.*).
1. "Some base, some treble" (Purchas, *Pilgrimage*, 639).
2. The rest of this paragraph is transferred in the *Generall Historie* from p. 36 to p. 48, with minor alterations.

numbers with little stickes, laying downe at the ende of every song a little sticke. In this manner they sat 8, 10, or 12 houres without cease, with such strange stretching of their armes, and violent passions and gestures as might well seeme strange to him they so conjured who but every houre expected his end: not any meat they did eat till late in the evening they had finished this worke, and then they feasted him and themselves with much mirth, but 3 or 4 daies they continued this ceremony.

They have also certaine Altar stones they call *Pawcorances*,[3] but these stand from their Temples, some by their houses, other in the woodes and wildernesses. Upon this they offer blood, deare suet, and Tobacco. These they doe when they returne from the warres, from hunting, and upon many other occasions. They have also another superstition that they use in stormes, when the waters are rough in the rivers and sea coasts. Their Conjurers runne to the water sides, or passing in their boats, after many hellish outcries and invocations, they cast Tobacco, Copper, *Pocones* or such trash into the water, to pacifie that God whome they thinke to be very angry in those stormes. Before their dinners and suppers the better sort will take the first bit, and cast it in the fire, which is all the grace they are known to use.

In some part of the Country they have yearely a sacrifice of children.[4] Such a one was at Quiyoughcohanock some 10 miles from James Towne and thus performed. Fifteene of the properest young boyes, betweene 10 and 15 yeares of age they painted white.[5] Having brought them forth the people spent the forenoone in dancing and singing about them with rattles. In the afternoone they put those children to the roote of a tree. By them all the men stood in a guard, every one having a Bastinado[6] in his hand, made of reeds bound together. This made a lane betweene them all along, through which there were appointed 5 young men ‖ to fetch these children: so every one of the five went through the guard to fetch a child each after other by turnes, the guard fearelesly[7] beating them with their Bastinadoes, and they patiently enduring and receaving all, defending the children with their naked bodies from the unmercifull blowes that pay them soundly though the children escape. All this while the

Their altars.

Sacrifices to the water.

Their solemne sacrifices of children.

[33]

---

3. Strachey's definition, *pokoranse*, "a mineral stone" (*Historie*, 196), helps little in the identification of Smith's word (see Barbour, "Earliest Reconnaissance," Pt. II, 40).

4. With regard to this paragraph, see Philip L. Barbour, "The Riddle of the Black Boyes," *VMHB*, LXXXVIII (1980), 148–154. Smith misinterpreted much of what he saw.

5. The marginal note in the *Generall Historie*, 36, adds: "which they call Black-boyes," an obvious error for "blake-boyes" ("blake" was a northern English dialect word meaning "pale, dead white"). See *ibid.*, 36n.

6. An erroneous English application of Spanish *bastonada*, "a blow with a cudgel," from *bastón*, "cudgel."

7. Boldly.

women weepe and crie out very passionately, providing mats, skinnes, mosse, and drie wood, as things fitting their childrens funerals. After the children were thus passed the guard, the guard tore down the trees, branches, and boughs, with such violence that they rent the body,[8] and made wreathes for their heads, or bedecked their haire with the leaves. What else was done with the children, was not seene, but they were all cast on a heape, in a valley as dead, where they made a great feast for al the company. The Werowance being demanded the meaning of this sacrifice,[9] answered that the children were not al dead, but that the *Oke* or Divell did sucke the blood from their left breast, who chanced to be his by lot, till they were dead, but the rest were kept in the wildernesse by the yong men till nine moneths were expired, during which time they must not converse with any, and of these were made their Priests and Conjurers. This sacrifice they held to bee so necessarie, that if they should omit it, their *Oke* or Divel and all their other *Quiyoughcosughes* which are their other Gods, would let them have no Deare, Turkies, Corne, nor fish, and yet besides, hee would make a great slaughter amongst them.

Their resur-   They thinke that their Werowances and Priestes which they
rection.   also esteeme *Quiyoughcosughes*, when they are dead, doe goe beyound the mountaines towardes the setting of the sun, and ever remaine there in forme of their *Oke*, with their heads painted with oile and *Pocones*, finely trimmed with feathers, and shal have beades, hatchets, copper, and tobacco, doing nothing but dance and sing, with all

[34] their Predecessors. But the common people they suppose ‖ shall not live after death.

To divert them from this blind idolatrie, many used their best indeavours, chiefly with the Werowances of Quiyoughcohanock, whose devotion, apprehension, and good disposition, much exceeded any in those Countries, who though we could not as yet prevaile withall to forsake his false Gods, yet this he did beleeve that our God as much exceeded theirs, as our Gunnes did their Bowes and Arrows and many times did send to the President, at James towne, men with presents, intreating them to pray to his God for raine, for his Gods would not send him any. And in this lamentable ignorance doe these poore soules sacrifice them selves to the Divell, not knowing their Creator.[1]

---

8. Trunk, main stem.

9. The single, though long, sentence—"The Werowance being demanded . . . and of these were made their Priests and Conjurers"—is expanded in Purchas, *Pilgrimes*, IV, 1702, with suppositions and elaborations that must have been born in Purchas's fertile brain, stimulated by a face-to-face meeting in London with Powhatan's son-in-law, Tomocomo (see Barbour, *Pocahontas*, 171–173).

1. The *Generall Historie*, 37, adds: "and we had not language sufficient, so plainly to expresse it as [to] make them understand it; which God grant they may."

Of the manner of the Virginians governement.

Although the countrie people be very barbarous, yet have they amongst them such governement, as that their Magistrats for good commanding, and their people for du subjection, and obeying, excell many places that would be counted very civill. The forme of their Common wealth is a monarchicall governement, one as Emperour ruleth over many kings or governours.[2] Their chiefe ruler is called Powhatan, and taketh his name of the principall place of dwelling called Powhatan. But his proper name is Wahunsonacock. Some countries he hath which have been his ancestors, and came unto him by inheritance, as the countrie called Powhatan, Arrohateck, Appamatuke, Pamaunke, Youghtanund, and Mattapanient. All the rest of his Territories expressed in the Map, they report have beene his severall conquests. In all his ancient inheritances, hee hath houses built after their manner like arbours, some 30 some 40 yardes long, and at every house provision for his entertainement according to the time. At Werowocomoco, he was seated upon the Northside of the river Pamaunke, some 14 miles from James Towne, where for the most part, hee was resident,[3] but he tooke so little pleasure in our neare neigh- ‖ bourhood, that were able to visit him against his will **[35]** in 6 or 7 houres, that he retired himself to a place in the deserts at the top of the river Chickahamania betweene Youghtanund and Powhatan. His habitation there is called Orapacks where he ordi- A description narily now resideth. He is of parsonage[4] a tall well proportioned of Powhatan. man, with a sower looke, his head somwhat gray, his beard so thinne that it seemeth none at al, his age neare 60; of a very able and hardy body to endure any labour. About his person ordinarily attendeth a guard of 40 or 50 of the tallest men his Country doth afford. Every His attendance night upon the 4 quarters of his house are 4 Sentinels each standing and watch. from other a flight shoot, and at every halfe houre one from the Corps du guard doth hollowe, unto whome every Sentinell doth answer round from his stand; if any faile, they presently send forth an officer that beateth him extreamely.

A mile from Orapakes in a thicket of wood hee hath a house in which he keepeth his kind of Treasure, as skinnes, copper, pearle, His treasurie. and beades, which he storeth up against the time of his death and buriall. Here also is his store of red paint for ointment, and bowes and arrowes. This house is 50 or 60 yards in length, frequented only by Priestes. At the 4 corners of this house stand 4 Images as Sentinels, one of a Dragon, another a Beare, the 3 like a Leopard[5] and the

2. In the face of this and other passages in the same spirit, it is interesting to remember that many authorities continue to refer to "the Powhatan Confederacy."
3. The *Generall Historie*, 37, adds: "when I was delivered him prisoner."
4. "Personage"; personal appearance.
5. The "Dragon" was surely a wolf, and the "Leopard" a lynx.

fourth like a giantlike man, all made evillfavordly,[6] according to their best workmanship.

His wives.

He hath as many women as he will, whereof when hee lieth on his bed, one sitteth at his head, and another at his feet, but when he sitteth, one sitteth on his right hand and another on his left. As he is wearie of his women, hee bestoweth them on those that best deserve them at his hands. When he dineth or suppeth, one of his women before and after meat, bringeth him water in a woden platter to wash his hands. Another waiteth with a bunch of feathers to wipe them insteed of a Towell, and the feathers when he hath wiped are dryed

[36] againe. His kingdome des- || cendeth not to his sonnes nor children, but first to his brethren, whereof he hath 3. namely Opitchapan,

His successors.

Opechancanough, and Catataugh, and after their decease to his sisters. First to the eldest sister then to the rest and after them to the heires male and female of the eldest sister, but never to the heires of the males.

He nor any of his people understand any letters wherby to write or read, only the lawes whereby he ruleth is custome. Yet when he

Their authority.

listeth his will is a law and must bee obeyed: not only as a king but as halfe a God they esteeme him. His inferiour kings whom they cal werowances are tyed to rule by customes, and have power of life and death at their command in that nature. But this word Werowance which we call and conster[7] for a king, is a common worde whereby they call all commanders: for they have but fewe words in their language, and but few occasions to use anie officers more then one commander, which commonly they call werowances. They all knowe

The tenor of their lands.

their severall landes,[8] and habitations, and limits, to fish, fowle, or hunt in, but they hold all of their great Werowance[9] Powhatan, unto whome they pay tribute of skinnes, beades, copper, pearle, deare, turkies, wild beasts, and corne. What he commandeth they dare not disobey in the least thing. It is strange to see with what great feare and adoration all these people doe obay this Powhatan. For at his feet they present whatsoever hee commandeth, and at the least frowne of his browe, their greatest spirits will tremble with feare: and no marvell, for he is very terrible and tyrannous in punishing

His maner of punishments.

such as offend him. For example hee caused certaine malefactors to be bound hand and foot, then having of many fires gathered great store of burning coles, they rake these coles round in the forme of a cockpit, and in the midst they cast the offenders to broyle to death. Somtimes he causeth the heads of them that offend him, to be laid

6. Often written as one word; "made to look ugly."

7. Variant of "construe," in the sense of "explain" here.

8. In the marginal note opposite, "tenor" was an archaic, if not obsolete, variant of "tenure."

9. The *Generall Historie*, 38, has: "Werowance, or *Caucorouse*, which is Captaine." The meaning is that the people have no rights or property other than from the great werowance, Powhatan.

upon the altar or sacrificing stone, and one with clubbes beates out
their braines. When he would punish any notorious enimie or
malefac- ‖ tor, he causeth him to be tied to a tree, and with muscle **[37]**
shels or reeds, the executioner cutteth of his joints one after another,
ever casting what they cut of into the fire; then doth he proceed with
shels and reeds to case the skinne from his head and face; then doe
they rip his belly and so burne him with the tree and all. Thus themselves reported they executed George Cassen.[10] Their ordinary correction is to beate them with cudgels. Wee have seene a man kneel-
ing on his knees, and at Powhatans command, two men have beat
him on the bare skin, till he hath fallen senselesse in a sound,[1] and
yet never cry nor complained.

In the yeare 1608, hee surprised the people of Payankatank his
neare neighbours and subjects.[2] The occasion was to us unknowne,
but the manner was this. First he sent diverse of his men as to lodge
amongst them that night, then the Ambuscadoes invironed al their
houses, and at the houre appointed, they all fell to the spoile, 24 men
they slewe, the long haire of the one side of their heades with the
skinne cased off with shels or reeds, they brought away.[3] They surprised also the women and the children and the Werowance. All
these they present[4] to Powhatan. The Werowance, women and children became his prisoners, and doe him service. The lockes of haire
with their skinnes he hanged on a line unto two trees. And thus he
made ostentation of as great a triumph at Werowocomoco, shewing
them to the English men that then came unto him at his appointment, they expecting provision, he to betray them, supposed to halfe
conquer them by this spectacle of his terrible crueltie.

And this is as much as my memory can call to mind worthie of
note; which I have purposely collected, to satisfie my friends of the
true worth and qualitie of Virginia. Yet some bad natures will not
sticke to slander the Countrey, that will slovenly spit at all things,[5]
especially in company where they can find none to contradict them.
Who though they were scarse ever 10 miles from James Town, or at
the most but at the falles; yet holding it a great disgrace that ‖ amongst **[38]**
so much action, their actions were nothing, exclaime of all things,

10. Purchas attributed the account of Cassen's "execution" to William White, a
laborer who had lived with the Indians apparently at that time: "William White reporteth . . . that . . . being stripped naked and bound to two stakes, with his backe against
a great fire: then did they rippe him and burne his bowels, and dried his flesh to the
bones, which they kept above ground in a by-roome" (*Pilgrimage* [1614 ed.], 767). Cassen
is briefly referred to in the *Proceedings*, 13, and the *Generall Historie*, 46.

1. "Swoon"; a variant spelling.

2. Strachey repeats the story of Payankatank (*Historie*, 44–45) and later adds an
account of a similar attack on the Chesapeake tribe (*ibid.*, 104–105).

3. The first report of "scalping" by the Virginia Indians; the verb seems to be first
recorded in 1676 (*OED*).

4. The *Generall Historie*, 38, uses the past tense, "presented."

5. Cf. *New Englands Trials* (1622), sig. D1ᵛ.

though they never adventured to knowe any thing; nor ever did any thing but devoure the fruits of other mens labours. Being for most part of such tender educations and small experience in martiall accidents, because they found not English cities, nor such faire houses, nor at their owne wishes any of their accustomed dainties, with feather beds and downe pillowes, Tavernes and alehouses in every breathing place, neither such plenty of gold and silver and dissolute liberty as they expected, had little or no care of any thing, but to pamper their bellies, to fly away with our Pinnaces, or procure their means to returne for England. For the Country was to them a miserie, a ruine, a death, a hell, and their reports here, and their owne actions there according.

Some other there were that had yearely stipends to pass to and againe for transportation:[6] who to keepe the mystery of the businesse in themselves, though they had neither time nor meanes to knowe much of themselves; yet al mens actions or relations they so formally tuned to the temporizing times simplicitie, as they could make their ignorances seeme much more, then al the true actors could by their experience. And those with their great words deluded the world with such strange promises as abused the businesse much worse then the rest. For the businesse being builded upon the foundation of their fained experience, the planters, the mony, time,[7] and meanes have still miscaried: yet they ever returning, and the Planters so farre absent, who could contradict their excuses? which stil to maintain their vaineglory and estimation, from time to time they have used such diligence as made them passe for truthes, though nothing more false. And that the adventurers might be thus abused, let no man wonder; for the wisest living is soonest abused by him that hath a faire tongue and a dissembling heart.

[39]   There were many in Virginia meerely projecting, verbal ‖ and idle contemplatours, and those so devoted to pure idlenesse, that though they had lived two or three yeares in Virginia, lordly, necessitie it selfe could not compell them to passe the Peninsula, or Pallisadoes of James Towne, and those wittie spirits, what would they not affirme in the behalfe of our transporters to get victuall from their ships, or obtaine their good words in England to get their passes. Thus from the clamors and the ignorance of false informers, are sprung those disasters that sprung in Virginia, and our ingenious verbalists[8] were no lesse plague to us in Virginia, then the Locusts to the Egyptians. For the labour of 30 of the best only preserved in Christianitie by their industrie the idle livers of neare 200 of the rest: who living neer 10 months of such naturall meanes, as the Country naturally of it

6. The reference is probably to Captain Newport.
7. The word is omitted from the *Generall Historie*, 39.
8. "One who deals in, or directs his attention to, words only, apart from reality or meaning" (*OED*); possibly the first appearance of the word in print.

selfe afforded, notwithstanding all this, and the worst furie of the Savages, the extremitie of sicknesse, mutinies, faction, ignorances, and want of victuall; in all that time I lost but 7 or 8 men, yet subjected the Savages to our desired obedience, and receaved contribution from 35 of their kings, to protect and assist them against any that should assalt them, in which order they continued true and faithful, and as subjects to his Majestie, so long after as I did govern there, untill I left the Country: since, how they have revolted, the Countrie lost, and againe replanted, and the businesses hath succeeded from time to time, I referre you to the relations of them returned from Virginia, that have bin more diligent in such observations.[9]

FINIS.

9. The *Generall Historie*, 39, adds: "John Smith writ this with his owne hand"; and omits "FINIS."

TEXTUAL ANNOTATION

AND BIBLIOGRAPHICAL NOTE TO

A Map of Virginia

TEXTUAL ANNOTATION

The page numbers below refer to the boldface numerals in the margins of the present text, which record the pagination of the original edition used as copy text. The word or words before the bracket show the text as emended by the editor; the word or words after the bracket reproduce the copy text. The wavy dash symbol used after the bracket stands for a word that has not itself been changed but that adjoins a changed word or punctuation mark. The inferior caret, also used only after the bracket, signifies the location of missing punctuation in the copy text.

Page.Line

[1ʳ].2	Semer] semer
[1ʳ].17	subject] subjest
[1ʳ].23	secure] sesure
*2ʳ.15	consider] cousider (inverted "n")
*3ᵛ.28	Nusswashtassapooeksku] Nussswashtassapooeksku
*4ʳ.15	hungrie, what] ~ ? ~
*4ʳ.18	Orapaks] orapaks
*4ʳ.20	Werowocomoco] werowocomoco
*4ʳ.28	ningh] niugh (inverted "n")
2.5	Bermudas] Barmadas
2.31	off from] offrom
3.3	Southeast] South east (end-of-line hyphen missing)
3.18	colour] coulor
3.20	and lemnia] ad ~ (from *Generall Historie*, 22)
4.5	according] accor- (end of line, the printer dropped the last syllable)
4.18	river: First] ~ . ~
4.29	families, of] ~ ‸ Of
5.15	or their] of ~
5.32–6.1	Pamaunke] Pamavuke
6.6	lower, on] ~ ; ~
6.7	Arrohatock] Irrohatock
6.15	myles). At] ~) ‸ ~
6.21	Nantaughtacund] Nautaughtacund

6.32–7.1	into] in to (end-of-line hyphen missing)
7.2	last] least
7.4	streame. On] ~ ‸ ~
7.11–12	springs. The] ~ , ~
8.4–5	3, the] ~ . The
8.5–6	labour. Yet] ~ , yet
11.5	silke, and] ~ , & and
12.3–4	Chechinquamens] Chechniquamens
12.17	and Saxafras] aud ~
12.20–21	Ocoughtanamins] Ocoughtanamnis
13.13	th'other] thother (from *Generall Historie*, 27)
13.20	and as red] aud ~ ~ (inverted "n")
14.8	suckleth] sucketh
14.21	Cat. Their] ~ , their
14.32	sorts, as] ~ ‸ ~
14.32	called them,] ~ ~ .
15.3	Partridges] Patrridges
15.22	Refiners, for] ~ . ~
15.26	what] that (from *Generall Historie*, 28)
16.13	more] mote
16.15	moulde] moulds
17.8	grout] great (see line 15, below)
19.2	minerals] munerals
19.15	Pamaunke] Pamavuke

Hyphenation Record

The following list has been inserted at the request of the editorial staff of the Institute of Early American History and Culture. It records possible compound words that were hyphenated at the end of the line in the copy text. In each case the editor had to decide for the present edition whether to print the word as a single word or as a hyphenated compound. The material before the bracket indicates how the word is printed in the present edition; the material after the bracket indicates how the word was broken in the original. The wavy dash symbol indicates that the form of the word has been unchanged from the copy text. Numerals refer to the page number of the copy text (the boldface numerals in the margin in this edition) and to the line number (counting down from the boldface number) in the present edition.

BIBLIOGRAPHICAL NOTE

Editions[*]

Early:

1612. *A MAP OF VIRGINIA.* || WITH A DESCRIPTI- || ON OF THE COUN-
TREY, THE || Commodities, People, Govern- || ment and Religion. || *Written by
Captaine* SMITH, *sometimes Go-* || *vernour of the Countrey.* || WHEREUNTO IS AN-
NEXED THE || proceedings of those Colonies, since their first || departure from
England, with the discourses, || Orations, and relations of the Salvages, || and the
accidents that befell || them in all their Journies || and discoveries. || *TAKEN FAITH-
FULLY AS THEY* || *were written out of the writings of* || DOCTOR RUSSELL. || THO.
STUDLEY. || ANAS TODKILL. || JEFFRA ABOT. || RICHARD WIEFIN. || WILL. PHETTI-
PLACE || NATHANIEL POWELL. || RICHARD POTS. || And the relations of divers other
diligent observers there || *present then, and now many of them in England,* || *By W. S.*
|| [Ornament] || *AT OXFORD,* || Printed by Joseph Barnes. 1612. ||
[Title of the second part:] THE || PROCEEDINGS OF || THE ENGLISH
COLONIE IN || Virginia since their first beginning from || England in the yeare
of our Lord 1606, || *till this present* 1612, *with all their* || *accidents that befell them in their*
|| *Journies and Discoveries.* || Also the Salvages discourses, orations and relations || of
the Bordering neighbours, and how they be- || came subject to the English. || *Un-
folding even the fundamentall causes from whence have sprang so many mise-* || *ries to the
undertakers, and scandals to the businesses taken faith-* || *fully as they were written out of the
writings of Thomas* || *Studley the first provant maister, Anas Todkill, Walter* || *Russell Doctor
of Phisicke, Nathaniell Powell,* || *William Phettyplace, Richard Wyffin, Tho-* || *mas Abbay,
Tho: Hope, Rich: Polts and* || *the labours of divers other dili-* || *gent observers, that were
* || *residents in Virginia. And perused and confirmed by diverse now resident in* || *England that
were actors in this busines.* || By W. S. || [Ornament] || *AT OXFORD,* || Printed by
Joseph Barnes. 1612. ||

Quarto: *Map of Va.*, pp. [8], 39; *Proceedings*, [4], 110. *Map of Va.*, in four, including title, "To the Hand" by "T. A.," and glossary of Indian words, A–E in fours;
Proceedings, A–O in fours, P in two, the second blank. (*STC* 22791).

[Copies in the New York Public Library and the Rosenbach Foundation
(Philadelphia) collections have inserted dedications to Sir Edward Seymour, earl
of Hertford, by John Smith; and the Kane copy, now at Princeton University, has
a dedication to Thomas Watson and John Bingley by Philip Fote, which the revised
STC suggests may be a joke, since all copies have the dedication "To the Hand,"
by T[homas] A[bbay]. But see Barbour, *Three Worlds*, 468, with a reference to
Philip Foote.]

[*] The *Map of Virginia* was not entered in the Stationers' Register.

1613. *Purchas his Pilgrimage. Or Relations Of The World* . . . (extracts from Smith's manuscripts), by Samuel Purchas (London).

1614. *Pilgrimage* (extracts from Smith's manuscripts), by Purchas (London).

1617. *Pilgrimage* (extracts), by Purchas (London).

1624. *The Generall Historie of Virginia, New-England, and the Summer Isles* . . . (virtual reprint of the *Map of Va.* and revised edition of the *Proceedings*) (London).

1625. *Hakluytus Posthumus, or Purchas His Pilgrimes* . . . (partly reprinted with omissions and additions), by Samuel Purchas (London).

Modern:

1884, etc. *Captain John Smith . . . Works, 1608–1631*, ed. Edward Arber (Birmingham). See the list of issues of the Arber text in the General Introduction at the beginning of this volume.

1907. *Narratives of Early Virginia, 1606–1625*, ed. Lyon Gardiner Tyler (New York) (repr. 1930, 1959).

1969. *The Jamestown Voyages under the First Charter, 1606–1609*, ed. Philip L. Barbour (Cambridge).

Schedule A.
Limits of Exploration 1607–1609 as Indicated
by Maltese Crosses on the Smith/Hole Map

The lists should be read clockwise, beginning with a point just south of Cape Henry in the Atlantic Ocean to a point north of Cape Charles. (Hole's scale is 20 leagues to 1° latitude, with 1 league equal to 3 nautical miles. To facilitate comparison with modern road and geographical maps, all leagues have been converted into statute miles.)

No.	Location on S/H Map	Approximate Modern Location
1.	5 leagues (17 mi.) S of Cape Henry	11 mi. S of Virginia Beach
2.	Chesapeack village	Near Lynnhaven
3.	Nandsamund village	Near Reids Ferry, Nansemond R.
4.	Chawons (vague)	Chowan R., N.C. (vague)
5.	6 leagues (21 mi.) SSW of Jamestown	Source of Grays Creek; distance exaggerated
6.	5.5 leagues (19 mi.) SSW of Paspahegh	Source of Chippokes Creek; distance exaggerated
7.	Mangoags (vague)	Between Meherrin and Roanoke rivers, N.C.
8.	2 leagues (7 mi.) S of Appamatuck village	At falls of Appomattox R., Petersburg
9.	4 leagues (14 mi.) WSW of Powhatan village	Westhampton (Richmond)
10.	6 leagues (21 mi.) NW of Powhatan village	North Anna R. (above Beaverdam?)
11.	2 leagues (7 mi.) NW of Cattachiptico	2–4 mi. above Manquin
12.	Source of Mattapanient R.	Mattaponi R., c. 5 mi. above Aylett
13, 14.	Two crosses, one opposite, one just below, Mahaskahod	At Rappahannock R. falls, Fredericksburg
15.	Source of Quiyough R.	Source of Aquia Creek (?)
16.	7.5 leagues (26 mi.) above Nacotchtank	Yellow Falls above Washington, D.C. (?)
17.	Source of Bolus R.	Patapsco R., 15 mi. W of Baltimore city hall, Md.
18.	2.5 leagues (8.6 mi.) from Willoughbyes R. mouth	Bush R., near Abingdon, Md. (?)
19.	Smyths fales, 7.5 leagues (26 mi.) from Sasqucsahanough R. mouth	Above Conowingo Dam, 10 mi. from Susquehanna R. mouth
20.	3.5 leagues (12 mi.) above head of Bay	A few miles above North East, Cecil Co., Md.
21.	Peregryns Mount	Possibly near Newark, Del.
22.	Source of Tockwogh R.	Source of Sassafras R., Del.
23.	2.5 leagues (8.6 mi.) ENE of Kuskarawaok	Nanticoke R., ENE of Seaford, Del.

No.	Location on S/H Map	Approximate Modern Location
24.	Source of Wighco[comoco] R.	Pocomoke R., near (above?) Snow Hill, Worcester Co., Md.
25.	6.5 leagues (22 mi.) NNE of Cape Charles	Near Nachipongo R., Hog Island Bay

Schedule B.
Indian Villages and River Names

The place and river names on the schedule below are listed in the same fashion as on the map, with the following exceptions: (1) English place and river names, along with the details of the changes made in the various states, are not listed below; and (2) peripheral nations or tribes, conspicuously shown on the map, but barely known to Smith, are not listed here, but rather on Schedule C. The spellings on this schedule follow those on the map. On this schedule the "Kings howses" are marked "KH."

Reading up, Powhatan [James] River, right bank.

1. KH Chesapeack
2. Mantoughquemend
3. Teracosick
4. KH Nandsamund
5. Mattanock
6. Mokete
7. KH Warraskoyack
8. Mathomauk
9. Nantapoyac
10. KH Quiyoughcohanock
11. Chawopo
12. KH Appamatuck
13. Mowhemcho
14. KH Massinacack
15. KH Monahassanugh
16. KH Rassawek

Reading down, Powhatan [James] River, left bank.

17. KH Monasukapanough
18. KH Powhatan [core of Powhatan's state]
19. KH Orapaks [Powhatan's residence, 1608]
20. KH Arrohateck
21. KH Weanock
22. KH Paspahegh

Reading up, Chickahamania [Chickahominy] River, right bank.
(The nation had no werowances, and no kings' houses.)

23. Menascosic
24. Mamanahunt
25. Paspanegh
26. Righkahauk
27. Nechanicok

Reading down, Chickahamania [Chickahominy] River, left bank.

28. Appocant
29. Moysonec
30. Askakep
31. Werawahon
32. Ozenick
33. Mattapanient

Reading down, Powhatan [James] River, left bank.

34. KH Kecoughtan

Reading up, Pamaunk [York] River, right bank.

35. KH Kiskiack

Reading up, Youghtanund [Pamunkey] River, right bank.

36. Matchut
37. Acconoc
38. Potauncac

39. Attamtuck
40. Pamuncoroy

Reading down, Youghtanund [Pamunkey] River, left bank.

41. Cattachiptico
42. Accossumwinck
43. KH Kupkipcock

44. KH Uttamussak
45. KH Menapucunt
46. Cinquoteck

Reading up, Mattapanient [Mattaponi] River, right bank.

47. Quackcohowaon
48. Myghtuckpassum

49. Passaunkack

Reading down, Mattapanient [Mattaponi] River, left bank.

50. Utcustank
51. Martoughquaunk
52. Muttamussinsack

53. Matchutt
54. Mamanassy

Reading down, Pamaunk [York] River, left bank.

55. Pasaughtacock
56. Poruptanck
57. Mattacock
58. KH Werowocomoco [Powhatan's
    residence, 1607]

59. Cantaunkack
60. Capahowasick [Powhatan's gift to
    John Smith]

Payankatank [Piankatank] River.

61. KH Payankatank

Reading up, Toppahanock [Rappahannock] River, right bank.

62. KH Opiscopank
63. Anrenapeugh
64. KH Nandtanghtacund
65. Checopissowo
66. Anaskenoans

67. Secobeck
68. Accoqueck
69. KH Shackaconia
70. KH Stegara
71. KH Hassniuga

Reading down, Toppahanock [Rappahannock] River, left bank.

72. KH Tanxsnitania
73. KH Mahaskahod
74. Massawoteck
75. Sockobeck
76. KH Cuttatawomen [II]
77. Waconiask

78. Monanask
79. Assuweska
80. Papiscone
81. Kerahocak
82. KH Pissaseck
83. Nawacaten

84. Mangoraca
85. Wecuppom
86. Matchopick
87. Pissacoack
88. Cawwontoll
89. Acquack
90. Winsack
91. Tantucquask
92. Poykemkack
93. Nawncutough (Nawnautough?)
94. KH Toppahanock
95. Poyektank

96. Menaskunt
97. Auhomesk
98. Powcomonet
99. Oquornock
100. KH Moraughtacund
101. Pawcocomocac
102. Nepawtacum
103. Kapawnich
104. Ottachugh
105. Chesakawon
106. KH Cuttatawomen [I]

Chesapeack Bay

107. Cinquack

Reading up, Patawomeck [Potomac] River, right bank.

108. KH Wighcocomoco
109. KH Cekakawwon
110. Uttamussamacoma
111. KH Onawmanient
112. Ozaiawomen
113. Mattacunt
114. KH Patawomeck

115. Quiyough
116. Pamacocack
117. KH Tauxenent
118. Namassingakent
119. Assaomeck
120. Namoraughquend
121. KH Massawomeck

Reading down, Patawomeck [Potomac] River, left bank.

122. KH Nacotchtanck
123. Tessamatuck
124. KH Moyaons
125. Cinquaoteck
126. KH Pamacocack
127. Nussamek

128. Mataughquamend
129. Nushemouck
130. Potapaco
131. KH Cecomocomoco
132. Monanauk

Reading up, Pawtuxunt [Patuxent] River, right bank.

133. KH Acquintanacsuck
134. Wasinacus
135. Acquaskack
136. Wasapokent
137. Macocanaco

138. Pocatamough
139. Quotough
140. Wosameus
141. Mattpanient

Reading down, Pawtuxunt [Patuxent] River, left bank.

142. Quactataugh
143. Wepanawomen
144. Tauskus
145. Wascocup

146. Onuatuck
147. KH Pawtuxunt
148. Quomo
149. Opanient

Northwest of Chesapeake Bay.

150. KH Cepowig

Reading up, Sasqusahanough [Susquehanna] River, right bank.

151. KH Attaock   152. KH Utchowig

Reading down, Sasqusahanough [Susquehanna] River, left bank.

153. KH Tesinigh   155. KH Sasquesahanough
154. KH Quadroque

North and Northeast of Chesapeake Bay.

156. KH Atquanachuke   158. KH Chickahokin
157. KH Macocks

The Eastern Shore, North to South.

159. KH [Tockwogh]   163. KH Kuskarawaok
160. KH Ozinies   164. KH Wighcocomoco
161. Nause   165. KH Accohanock
162. Nantaquack [origin of name   166. KH Accowmack
     Nanticoke]

If the 28 English place-names are added to the foregoing 166, the total is close to the estimate of "about two hundred place-names" in Joseph Sabin *et al.*, eds., *A Dictionary of Books Relating to America*, XX (New York, 1927–1928), 247.

Schedule C.
Nations or Tribes Peripheral to
Powhatan's Domain

1. The Chowans, first known to Ralegh's men, and not visited by Smith. They were of Algonkian speech.

2. The Mangoags, also first known to Ralegh's men, and not visited by Smith. They were Iroquoians (Tuscarora), though the name is Carolina Algonkian.

3. The Monacans seem to have been Siouans. Captain Newport penetrated their territory with a 120-man detachment in 1608, but what little Smith knew about them came from the Powhatans. The name is Algonkian, and possibly refers to their manner of digging the ground.

4. The Mannahoacks were probably of the same stock as the Monacans, but the name is possibly another version of "Mangoags," an abusive epithet meaning, roughly, "adders."

5. The Massawomecks, an Iroquoian people, were either the same as, or a people contiguous to, the Pocoughtaonacks mentioned in Smith's *True Relation* (sig. C2^r). For the possible identity of the two, see Bernard G. Hoffman, "Observations on Certain Ancient Tribes of the Northern Appalachian Province," Smithsonian Institution, Bureau of American Ethnology, *Anthropological Papers*, No. 70 (Washington, D.C., 1964).

6. The Sasquesahanoughs (later known as the Conestogas) were also Iroquoians, living to the east of the Massawomecks, above the falls in the Susquehanna River. The unusual size of the tribesmen Smith chanced to meet is attested by Thomas Campanius Holm, the Swede who published a small Susquehanna vocabulary in 1696.

7. The Atquanachukes appear in A. van der Donck's "Map of New Netherlands" (1656), about halfway between Philadelphia and Atlantic City. They were mentioned to Smith by the Tockwoghs, and their language may have been Algonkian, though not understood by the Powhatans.

8. The Tockwoghs were an Algonkian nation that later merged with the Kuskarawaoks to form the so-called Nanticokes of Pennsylvania.

9. The Kuskarawaoks, another Algonkian people, were famous for their manufacture of shell beads, locally called "roanoke," a southern counterpart of New England "wampum" or "peak."

Specialized Bibliography
Pertinent to the Smith/Hole Map

Alexander Brown, *The Genesis of the United States* (Boston, 1890), II, 596–597. Prejudiced.

Worthington Chauncey Ford, "Captain John Smith's Map of Virginia, 1612," *Geographical Review*, XIV (1924), 433–443. Mistaken hypothesis.

Coolie Verner, "The First Maps of Virginia, 1590–1673," *Virginia Magazine of History and Biography*, LVIII (1950), 3–15. Competent résumé.

Walter W. Ristow, "Captain John Smith's Map of Virginia," *Library of Congress Facsimile*, No. 1 (Washington, D.C., 1957). Excellent review, with a specialized bibliography.

Ben C. McCary, "John Smith's Map of Virginia," *Jamestown 350th Anniversary Booklet*, No. 3 (Williamsburg, Va., 1957). Sound and thorough.

Coolie Verner, "Smith's *Virginia* and Its Derivatives," *Map Collectors' Series*, No. 45 (London, 1968). Marred by typographical carelessness.

THE PROCEEDINGS

of the English Colonie

in Virginia,

[1606–1612] . . .

1612

INTRODUCTION

The *Proceedings* is an often uneven, unclear compilation of accounts of what happened to the settlers of the first permanent English colony on the western side of the Atlantic Ocean. Deficient in many respects though it be, it provides the only surviving comprehensive narrative of the undertaking during the period from late 1606 to mid-1610.

There are, however, several piecemeal accounts that are more detailed for this or that aspect of the story: the transatlantic voyage, the first explorations, the weeks immediately following the foundation of Jamestown, the period after the first deadly epidemic, and the "interregnum" from the close of Smith's administration to the rebirth of the colony under Lord De La Warr. These are the principal additional authorities:

1) George Percy, whose "Discourse" contains details of the sailing of the fleet and of the voyage after Martinique was sighted. He also chronicled the first landing in Virginia and the events from then until September 19, 1607, and included a partial necrology.[1]

2) The anonymous author of the "Relatyon" (probably Gabriel Archer, and so attributed in the present work), who recounted the river voyage up the James to modern Richmond and some subsequent developments in Jamestown from May 21 to June 21, 1607, when Captain Newport sailed back to England.[2]

3) Edward Maria Wingfield, whose "Discourse" is an apologia in which he stands up for his record as president of the council in Virginia and relates the events surrounding his deposition, with sidelights on the behavior of several colonists.[3]

4) William Strachey, whose "Reportory" narrates the shipwreck of Gates's flagship on July 23, 1609, the eventual landing in Jamestown, and the arrival of Lord De La Warr, c. July 15, 1610.[4]

5) George Percy, again, whose later "Relacyon" contains a detailed

1. See Samuel Purchas, *Hakluytus Posthumus, or Purchas His Pilgrimes* . . . (London, 1625), IV, 1685–1690 (repr. in Philip L. Barbour, ed., *The Jamestown Voyages under the First Charter, 1606–1609* [Hakluyt Society, 2d Ser., CXXXVI–CXXXVII (Cambridge, 1969)], I, 129–146).

2. MS in State Papers, Colonial, C.O. 1/1, fols. 46ʳ–52ʳ, Public Record Office, London (printed in Barbour, *Jamestown Voyages*, I, 80–98).

3. MS 250, Lambeth Palace Library (London), fols. 382–396 (printed in Barbour, *Jamestown Voyages*, I, 213–234).

4. Printed in Purchas, *Pilgrimes*, IV, 1734–1758 (repr. in Louis B. Wright, ed., *A Voyage to Virginia in 1609, Two Narratives: Strachey's "True Reportory" and Jourdain's Discovery of the Bermudas*, Jamestown Documents [Charlottesville, Va., 1964]).

account of the events in Jamestown from early August 1609 to April 22, 1612, though it was not written until after Smith's *Generall Historie* was published in 1624.[5]

There are of course other, less full, accounts scattered far and wide in England and the United States. From these, many details can be culled, especially for specific dates and personal names. But in none of these sources is anything to be found, so far as the editor's experience is concerned, which would negate or contradict any substantial statement in the *Proceedings*, such trivialities as dates or numbers excepted. Percy, for example, though he comes close to calling Smith a liar, goes Smith's *Generall Historie* one better by painting a more harrowing picture of the "starving time" in Jamestown than any passage there or in the *Proceedings*. Then, with magnificent artlessness, he states that while hundreds were dying of starvation in Jamestown, he, the acting governor, waited until mid-May 1610 to sail forty miles down the river to Old Point Comfort to find the colonists there "in good case [well off]" and "so well stored [supplied] thatt the Crabb fishes wherewith they had fedd their hogges would have bene a greate relefe unto us and saved many of our Lyves."[6]

Percy's pride was evidently hurt by Smith's greater interest in himself (naturally) than in Percy, whom Smith does slight. (The questions arise, how much did Percy do for the colony? and was Percy merely standing up for the blue bloods, one of whom was Wingfield?) But it is unfortunate for historians that Percy did not trouble to specify Smith's alleged "falseties and malicyous detractyons," which Percy mentioned to his brother, the earl of Northumberland, in a letter that served as a preface to his "Relacyon."[7]

In a sense, this is beside the point, because Percy's resentment was stirred by the *Generall Historie*, not by the *Proceedings*. But personal disparagement of this sort tends to spread into unexpected areas. While we can understand the social causes of the scorn a Percy or a Wingfield felt for a yeoman's son,[8] the animosity of Henry Adams, the Boston "Brahmin," and Alexander Brown of Nelson County, Virginia, toward John Smith of Lincolnshire is hardly defensible. Percy was petulant over lack of recognition of his importance. Brown merely despised Smith and all his works—including books in which Smith took little part.

To summarize the *Proceedings*, then, the participation of two or three (or more) writers can be established, at the risk of some error. We do not

5. MS 106, Elkins Collection, Free Library of Philadelphia (printed in *Tyler's Quarterly Historical and Genealogical Magazine*, III [1922], 259–282).

6. George Percy, "Trewe Relacyon," *Tyler's Qtly.*, III (1922), 268, with some errors in copying.

7. See Philip L. Barbour, "The Honorable George Percy, Premier Chronicler of the First Virginia Voyage," *Early American Literature*, VI (1971), 12–13.

8. See Robert Burton, *The Anatomy of Melancholy* . . . (Oxford, 1621; 2d ed., "By Democritus Junior," 1624), II, on "Baseness of Birth."

know, for example, if William Symonds saw to it that the proper names were inserted in the right places; indeed, the *Generall Historie* indicates that several were left out. Furthermore, the style of writing by and large is so loose that it is all but impossible to put a finger on any given passage and say, "this is so-and-so's work." Yet, if the names published in the *Proceedings* can be accepted as generally correct, the following observations may be sound.

The list of names of original settlers (pp. 6–8) was probably compiled by Thomas Studley, since he was responsible for the distribution of the colony's stores. But why the story of Smith's capture was reduced to less than a skeleton is a mystery that perhaps can be blamed on Symonds or one of his fellow divines. Other details, such as the attempts to abandon the colony, are attested in other records.

Chapters 1 and 2, which are credited in the *Proceedings* entirely to Studley, seem more likely to have been the work of John Smith, perhaps aided by others (see the *Generall Historie*, 50). Chapters 3 and 4 could well have been written primarily by Anas Todkill. Studley's name may persist as a coauthor only because the division into chapters was carelessly made.

That Walter Russell and Anas Todkill produced the material for Chapter 5 would not be surprising. Both of them went on the expedition therein described. By the same token, the combination of Nathaniel Powell and Anas Todkill is entirely logical for Chapter 6. It might even be suggested that Powell, not Studley, worked with Todkill on Chapters 3 and 4.

Chapters 7 to 9, including various lists of names, are ascribed to Richard Wiffin and William Phettiplace, as well as to Todkill. Here it is important to remember that both Wiffin and Phettiplace (along with the latter's brother Michael) collaborated in producing a lengthy bit of doggerel in commendation of Smith's *Description of New England*. That they were devoted followers of Smith is thus unquestioned, and this devotion is reflected in William Phettiplace's joining Richard Pots (the acknowledged compiler of the *Proceedings*) in preparing the rest of the book, barring a few paragraphs of unsigned post-Smithian narrative.

Such is the makeup of the *Proceedings*. Regardless of its many defects, it is an effective revelation of the tragicomic, melodramatic yet apathetic, and intensely human trials that beset the "invaders" of America.[9]

Printing History

In theory, this work was subjected to the editorial scrutiny of William Symonds (see the Biographical Directory). As has been pointed out in the Introduction to the *Map of Virginia*, the *Proceedings* forms the second part of

9. Cf. Francis Jennings, *The Invasion of America: Indians, Colonialism, and the Cant of Conquest* (Chapel Hill, N.C., 1975).

that work and was printed after the Smith/Hole map and that part of the accompanying text called "A Description of the Countrey." During the printing of the "Description," Symonds was presumably at work pulling together the at times incoherent narratives that Richard Pots had gathered, surely with the aid of Capt. John Smith. That the *Proceedings* was in fact regarded as a separate work is clearly indicated in Samuel Purchas's *Pilgrimage* (1614), in which he refers to Richard Pots, Thomas Studley, and the rest as the authors of the account of Bartholomew Gosnold's colonizing activities in the Chesapeake Bay area as distinguished from Smith's communications, which he notes have been "since printed at Oxford."[1] There is no hint that the Pots/Studley book was already in print at the time Purchas wrote, merely that Smith's book was.

By way of further differentiation between the two books, it may be pointed out that the type used in the *Proceedings* is "English" (14-point), while that of the *Map of Virginia* is "pica" (12-point),[2] requiring, of course, different cases of type, frames, and so on.

In any event, it is important that such readers as may study Smith's works from the historical, ethnographical, or other specialized point of view carefully consider the *Proceedings* before going on to read the *Generall Historie*, particularly Book III. This book is considerably expanded from the *Proceedings* and contains material not found there, but many footnotes that appear in this volume are not repeated in Volume II of this edition, to avoid excessive repetition. Indeed, such readers should exercise great care in comparing the two texts with an eye to building a complete text.

To the end of keeping Smith's period before the reader—the life-style and the philosophical yet narrow attitudes—the marginal notes of Purchas's reprinted version of the *Proceedings* have been quoted in full in their original places. Also, the editor has perhaps erred to the point of redundancy in "translating" common seventeenth-century words. The authors of the *Proceedings*, including Smith, lived in the age of Shakespeare, Bacon, and Ben Jonson, and they wrote in their language, though they did not have their command of that language. The editor's aim has been to dispel as many patches of Elizabethan and Jacobean fog (including wisps of dialect) as practicable.

With regard to the question of the extent to which Smith himself contributed to the accounts included in the *Proceedings*, there are details that he must have supplied here and there. There are other details that he could not have provided, though he may well have added personal touches. In fact, it seems especially probable that he had a considerable hand in the prepara-

1. Samuel Purchas, *Purchas his Pilgrimage. Or Relations Of The World . . .* (London, 1614), 756–757, 760.
2. At the editor's request, David Woodward of the Newberry Library, Chicago, confirmed this point.

tion of Chapters 1 and 2, as we have already observed. As noted on p. 15n, Studley is said to have died on August 28, 1607,[3] and a fortnight later Smith was appointed to take over some duties that must have been Studley's (p. 11). As a result, Smith could have acquired such papers and notes as Studley had, if any, and incorporated them with his own.

Note on the Authors Who Collaborated in the *Proceedings*

If Smith's *True Relation* suffered from poor editing and printers' carelessness, here the problem is a simple lack of elementary organization. On the title page of Part I (the *Map of Virginia* proper), the writings of eight authors are mentioned as sources for Part II (the *Proceedings*), but the title page of that part names nine. Then, the heading of Chapter 1 contains only six names, although Chapters 2, 4, 5, 6, 9, and 12 are signed by a total of seven. In addition, in the reprint of the *Proceedings* in the *Generall Historie*, Book III, the authorship varies from the original, with names of a few other contributors added. It therefore seems wise to summarize these details here. Since it is not the editor's intent to establish any of the putative authors as an author in fact, John Smith's contributions have been ignored in the following table.

Name	*Map of Va.*	*Proceedings*	*Gen. Hist.*
Abbay, Thomas	*2ʳ	A1ʳ, A2ᵛ	
Abbot, Jeffrey	title page		83
Bagnall, Anthony			66
Fenton, Robert			50
Harington, Edward[4]			50
Hope, Thomas		A1ʳ	
Momford, Thomas			59
Phettiplace, William[5]	title page	A1ʳ, 78, 104	83
Pots, Richard[6]	title page	A1ʳ, 104	94
Powell, Nathaniel	title page	A1ʳ, 41	66
Russell, Dr. Walter	title page	A1ʳ, 36	59
Studley, Thomas[7]	title page	A1ʳ, 15, 25	50
Tankard, William			94
Todkill, Anas	title page	A1ʳ, 25, 36, 41, 78	59, 66, 83
Wiffin, Richard	title page	A1ʳ, 78	83
Symonds, William, ed.	title page	A1ʳ, 110	41

3. See Purchas, *Pilgrimes*, IV, 1690; and Barbour, *Jamestown Voyages*, I, 144.
4. Died Aug. 24, 1607.
5. "G. P." in the *Generall Historie*, 94, is very likely an error for "W. P."
6. Pots probably assembled the material (see below, sig. A2ʳ).
7. Died Aug. 28, 1607.

THE
PROCEEDINGS OF
THE ENGLISH COLONIE IN
Virginia since their first beginning from
England in the yeare of our Lord 1606,
till this present 1612, with all their
accidents that befell them in their
Iournies and Discoveries.

Also the Salvages discourses, orations and relations
of the Bordering neighbours, and how they became subiect to the English.

Vnfolding even the fundamentall causes from whence haue sprang so many mise-
ries to the vndertakers, and scandals to the businesse: taken faith-
fully as they were written out of the writings of Thomas
Studley the first provant maister, Anas Todkill, Walter
Russell Doctor of Phisicke, Nathaniell Powell,
William Phettyplace, Richard Wyffin, Tho-
mas Abbay, Tho: Hope, Rich: Pots and
the labours of divers other dili-
gent observers, that were
residents in Virginia.

And perused and confirmed by diverse now resident in
England that were actors in this businesse.
By W. S.

AT OXFORD,
Printed by Joseph Barnes. 1612.

[Although the *Proceedings* constitutes the second part of the *Map of Virginia*, it was published as an independent volume, with its own title page (which makes no reference to the *Map of Virginia*) and its own address "To the Reader." Only at the very end does W[illiam] S[ymonds]'s *envoi* refer to Capt. John Smith's active intervention in its preparation. Expanded to form Bk. III of Smith's *Generall Historie* in 1624, the *Proceedings* was then reprinted, with many cuts, in Samuel Purchas's *Pilgrimes*, as chap. IV of bk. IX of pt. II, with an abridged version of the original title page and, after the list of authors, due credit to Smith: "and since enlarged out of the Writings of Captain John Smith, principall Agent and Patient in these Virginian Occurrents, from the beginning of the Plantation 1606. till Anno 1610. somewhat abridged." Purchas (*Hakluytus Posthumus, or Purchas His Pilgrimes* [London, 1625], IV, 1705) adds a marginal note pertinent to the name of Richard Pot[s]: "I have many written Treatises lying by me, written by Captaine Smith and others, some there, some here after [their] returne: but because these have alreadie seene the light, and containe a full relation of Virginian affaires, I was loth to wearie the Reader with others of this time."

For comments on the writers, see the editor's Introduction, above. "W. S." refers to the Reverend William Symonds, M.A., later created D.D.; see the Biographical Directory. "Rich: Polts" is Richard Pots.

The editor is grateful to The Newberry Library, Chicago, for permission to reproduce this title page.]

Long hath the world longed, but to be truely satisfied what Virginia is, with the truth of those proceedings, from whence hath flowne so manie reports of worth, and yet few good effects of the charge,[1] which hath caused suspition in many well willers that desire yet but to be truely satisfied therein. If any can resolve this doubt it is those that have lived residents in the land: not salers, or passengers, nor such mercinary contemplators, that only bedeck themselves with others plumes. This discourse is not from such, neither am I the author, for they are many, whose particular discourses are signed by their names. This solid treatise, first was compiled by Richard Pots,[2] since passing the hands of many to peruse, chancing into my hands, (for that I know them honest men, and can partly well witnesse their relations true) I could do no lesse in charity to the world then reveale; nor in conscience, but approve. By the advise of many grave and understanding gentlemen, that have pressed it, to the presse, it was thought fit to publish it, rather in its owne rude phrase then other waies. For that nothing can so purge that famous action from the infamous scandal some ignorantly have conceited, as the plaine simple and naked truth. For defect whereof the businesse is still suspected, the truth unknowne,[3] and the best deservers discouraged, and neglected, some by false reports, others by conjecture, and such power hath flattry to ingender of those, hatred and affection, that one is sufficient to beguile more, then 500 can ‖ keepe from being **[A2ᵛ]** deceived.

But this discourse is no Judge of mens manners, nor catalogue of their former courses; only a reporter of their actions in Virginia, not to disgrace any, accuse any, excuse any, nor flatter any; for which cause there is no wrong done but this, shortnesse in complaining, and so sparing in commending as only the reader may perceive the truth for his paines, and the action purged of foule slander; it can detract from none that intendeth there to adventure their fortunes; and to speake truly of the first planters, that brake the yce and beate the path, howsoever many difficulties obscured their indevours, he were worse then the worst of Ingrates, that would not spare them memory that have buried themselves in those forrain regions. From whose first adventures may spring more good blessings then are yet conceived. So I rest thine, that will read, peruse, and understand me. If

1. Returns on the investment.
2. Richard Pots had arrived on Jan. 2, 1608, and was apparently clerk of the council when Smith left in Oct. 1609 (*Generall Historie*, 94).
3. On Dec. 14, 1610, Richard Martin, secretary to the Virginia Company council in London, wrote to his friend William Strachey, secretary of the colony in Jamestown, asking for the truth (S. G. Culliford, *William Strachey, 1572–1621* [Charlottesville, Va., 1965], 123, 125).

you finde false orthography or broken English, they are small faultes in souldiers, that not being able to write learnedly, onlie strive to speake truely, and be understood without an Interpreter.

T. Abbay.[4]

4. Thomas Abbay arrived with the second supply, late in 1608; his family name was known in Hertfordshire.

THE PROCEEDINGS
of the English Colony in Virginia,
taken faithfully out of the writings of
Thomas Studly[1] Cape-marchant,
Anas Todkill, Doctor Russell,
Nathaniel Powell, William Phetiplace,
and Richard Pot, with the laboures
of other discreet observers, during
their residences.

Chapter 1.

IT might wel be thought, a countrie so faire (as Virginia is) and a people so tractable, would long ere this have beene quietly possessed, to the satisfaction of the adventurers, and the eternizing of the memorie of those that affected it. But because all the world doe see a defailement;[2] this following Treatise shall give satisfaction to all indifferent[3] readers, how the businesse hath beene carried, where no doubt they will easily understand and answer to their question, howe it came to passe there was no better speed and successe in those proceedings.

Captaine Bartholomew Gosnold,[4] the first mover of this plantation, having many yeares solicited many of his friends, but found small assistants; at last prevailed with some Gentlemen, as Master Edward Maria Wingfield, Captaine John Smith,[5] and diverse others who depended a yeare upon his projects, but nothing could be effected, till by their great charge and industrie it came to be appre-

The first mover of the action.

1. On Studley, see p. 15n, below.
2. Failure.
3. Unbiased, impartial.
4. Bartholomew Gosnold, seven or eight years Smith's senior, has been considered the prime mover of the Jamestown colony (see Philip L. Barbour, "Bartholomew Gosnold, Prime Mover of the Jamestown Colony," in Warner F. Gookin and Philip L. Barbour, *Bartholomew Gosnold, Discoverer and Planter, New England—1602, Virginia—1607* [Hamden, Conn., 1963], 191–218; and the Biographical Directory).
5. Smith placed his own name first in the *Generall Historie*, 41.

[2] hended by certaine of the Nobilitie, ‖ Gentrie, and Marchants, so that his Majestie by his letters patents, gave commission for establishing Councels, to direct here, and to governe, and to execute there; to effect this, was spent another yeare, and by that time, three ships were provided, one of 100 Tonns, another of 40. and a Pinnace of 20.[6] The transportation of the company was committed to Captaine Christopher Newport,[7] a Marriner well practised for the westerne parts of America. But their orders for governement were put in a box, not to be opened, nor the governours knowne untill they arived in Virginia.[8]

Orders for government.

On the 19 of December, 1606.[9] we set saile, but by unprosperous winds, were kept six weekes in the sight of England; all which time, Master Hunt[1] our Preacher, was so weake and sicke, that few expected his recoverie. Yet although he were but 10 or 12 miles from his habitation (the time we were in the downes) and notwithstanding the stormie weather, nor the scandalous imputations (of some few, little better then Atheists,[2] of the greatest ranke amongst us) suggested against him, all this could never force from him so much as a seeming desire to leave the busines, but preferred the service of God, in so good a voyage, before any affection to contest with his godlesse foes, whose disasterous designes (could they have prevailed) had even then overthrowne the businesse, so many discontents did then arise, had he not with the water of patience, and his godly exhortations (but chiefly by his true devoted examples) quenched those flames of envie, and dissention.

[3] Wee watred[3] at the Canaries,[4] wee traded with the Salvages at Dominica; three weekes we spent in refreshing our selvs amongst

6. According to Purchas, the ships were the *Susan Constant* (the flagship, with 71 men aboard), the *Godspeed* (commanded by Gosnold, with 52 men), and the *Discovery* (with 21), for a total of 144 men (Samuel Purchas, *Hakluytus Posthumus, or Purchas His Pilgrimes* . . . [London, 1625], IV, 1705). It has since been learned that the *Susan Constant* was rated at 120 tons (Philip L. Barbour, ed., *The Jamestown Voyages under the First Charter, 1606–1609* [Hakluyt Society, 2d Ser., CXXXVI–CXXXVII (Cambridge, 1969)], I, 55).

7. See the Biographical Directory.

8. This practice of secrecy, undoubtedly designed to protect the authority of the ship captain during the voyage, was to give rise to chaos in 1609 when the flagship, carrying the governor, his staff, and his orders, was wrecked on Bermuda, leaving Jamestown without any authorized leadership (see pp. 93–94, below).

9. George Percy wrote, "On Saturday[,] the twentieth of December . . . the fleet fell from London" (Purchas, *Pilgrimes*, IV, 1685; and Barbour, *Jamestown Voyages*, I, 129).

1. For Robert Hunt, M.A., see Barbour, *Jamestown Voyages*, I, 60–64; and the Biographical Directory.

2. "Atheist" seems to be merely a broad term of opprobrium here.

3. A not uncommon spelling of "watered."

4. In 1629 Smith wrote that he had been in the Canaries, apparently in 1604 (*True Travels*, 39). These ships watered there early in 1607. And on sailing from the Canaries, Smith was restrained as a prisoner (p. 5, below), perhaps for making some "impertinent" suggestion based on his previous experience. Anyone who disagreed with self-important

these west-India Iles;[5] in Gwardalupa[6] we found a bath so hot, as in
it we boiled porck as well as over the fire. And at a little Ile called
Monica,[7] we tooke from the bushes with our hands, neare 2 hogs-   *Monica an un-*
heads full of birds in 3 or 4 houres. In Mevis,[8] Mona, and the Virgin *frequented Ile*
Iles, we spent some time, where with a lothsome beast like a Crocadil, *full of birds.*
called a Gwayn,[9] Tortoses, Pellicans, Parrots, and fishes, we daily
feasted. Gone from thence in search of Virginia, the company was
not a little discomforted, seeing the Marriners had three daies passed
their reckoning and found no land, so that Captaine Ratcliffe (Captaine of the Pinnace) rather desired to beare up the helme to returne
for England, then make further search. But God the guider of all
good actions, forcing them by an extream storme to hul all night, did
drive them by his providence to their desired port, beyond all their
expectations, for never any of them had seene that coast. The first   *Their first*
land they made they called Cape Henry; where anchoring, Master   *landing.*
Wingfeild, Gosnoll, and Newport, with 30 others, recreating themselves on shore, were assalted by 5 Salvages, who hurt 2 of the English very dangerously.[1] That night was the box opened, and the
orders read, in which Bartholomew Gosnoll, Edward Wingfeild,
Christopher Newport, John Smith, John Ratliffe, John Martin, and
George Kendall, were named to bee the Councell, and to choose a   *Matters of*
President amongst them for a yeare, who with the Councell should   *government.*
governe. Matters of moment were to be examined by a Jurie, ‖ but   **[4]**
determined by the major part of the Councell in which the Prece-
dent[2] had 2 voices. Untill the 13 of May they sought a place to plant
in,[3] then the Councell was sworne, Master Wingfeild was chosen
Precident, and an oration made, whie Captaine Smith was not admitted of the Councell as the rest.
    Now falleth every man to worke, the Councell contrive the Fort,

---

gentlemen was "mutinous." See Philip L. Barbour, *The Three Worlds of Captain John
Smith* (Boston, 1964), 112–115, for suggestions as to what may have happened.
    5. According to Percy, the fleet reached the West Indies on Mar. 23 and "dis-
imboged" out of them on Apr. 10 (Purchas, *Pilgrimes*, IV, 1685–1686; and Barbour,
Jamestown Voyages, I, 129–133).
    6. Guadeloupe.
    7. Islote del Monito, Puerto Rico.
    8. Nevis; "Mevis" was a frequent misreading of the Spanish name, Nieves.
    9. Iguana.
    1. The two Englishmen were Capt. Gabriel Archer and Matthew Morton, a sailor
who later became a ship captain (see the *True Relation*, sig. A3ʳ; and the *True Travels*, 49).
    2. "Precedent" and "precident," below, were variant spellings of "president."
    3. A spot called Archer's Hope at the mouth of modern College Creek just below
Jamestown Island was considered a better site by Bartholomew Gosnold and others (see
Charles E. Hatch, Jr., "Archer's Hope and the Glebe," *Virginia Magazine of History and
Biography*, LXV [1957], 467–484; and Percy's "Observations," in Purchas, *Pilgrimes*, IV,
1688). Obviously, Gabriel Archer spotted the place; and the name "hope" was still
applied to a small bay or river mouth (Old English *hōp* related to modern Icelandic *hóp*,
"broad bay at the mouth of a river" [Jan de Vries, *Altnordisches Etymologisches Wörterbuch*
(Leiden, 1958), 248]).

the rest cut downe trees to make place to pitch their Tents; some provide clapbord[4] to relade the ships, some make gardens, some nets, etc. The Salvages often visited us kindly. The Precidents overweening jealousie would admit no exercise at armes, or fortification, but the boughs of trees cast together in the forme of a halfe moone by the extraordinary paines and diligence of Captaine Kendall. Newport, with Smith, and 20 others, were sent to discover the head of the river: by divers smal habitations they passed, in 6 daies they arrived at a towne called Powhatan, consisting of some 12 houses pleasantly seated on a hill; before it 3 fertil Iles, about it many of their cornefields. The place is very pleasant, and strong by nature. Of this place the Prince is called Powhatan, and his people Powhatans, to this place the river is navigable; but higher within a mile, by reason of the Rockes and Iles, there is not passage for a smal boate, this they call the Falles.[5] The people in al parts kindly intreated them, til being returned within 20 miles of James towne, they gave just cause of jealousie,[6] but had God not blessed the discoverers otherwise then those at the fort, there had then beene an end of that plantation; for **[5]** at the fort, where they arived the next day, ‖ they found 17 men hurt, and a boy slaine by the Salvages, and had it not chanced a crosse barre shot[7] from the ships strooke down a bough from a tree amongst them that caused them to retire, our men had all been slaine, being securely all at worke, and their armes in drie fats.[8]

Hereupon the President was contented the Fort should be pallisadoed, the ordinance mounted, his men armed and exercised, for many were the assaults, and Ambuscadoes of the Salvages, and our men by their disorderly stragling were often hurt, when the Salvages by the nimblenesse of their heeles well escaped. What toile wee had, with so smal a power to guard our workmen adaies, watch al night, resist our enimies and effect our businesse, to relade the ships, cut downe trees, and prepare the ground to plant our corne, etc. I referre to the readers consideration. Six weekes being spent in this manner, Captaine Newport (who was hired only for our transportation) was to return with the ships. Now Captaine Smith, who all this time from their departure from the Canaries was restrained as a prisoner upon

The discovery of the Falles and Powhatan.

The Fort assalted by the Salvages.

4. Clapboards were short, split oak staves used for cooperage and wainscoting. Virginia, it was hoped, would replace the Baltic as a major source.

5. A handy and well-illustrated article on the region is Robert L. Scribner, "Belle Isle," *Virginia Cavalcade*, V (Winter, 1955), 8–14.

6. Anxiety, apprehension.

7. A "crosse barre shot" was a round shot with "a long spike of Iron cast with it as if it did goe thorow the middest of it" (*Sea Grammar*, 67). Purchas states in a marginal note here, "I have also M[aster] Wingfields notes of these affaires: but would not trouble the Reader here with things more then troublesome there" (*Pilgrimes*, IV, 1706). These notes are presumably the same as or similar to the documents now in Lambeth Palace Library (London) and printed in Barbour, *Jamestown Voyages*, I, 213–234.

8. In this instance, "drie fats" refers to casks for stacking guns.

the scandalous suggestions of some of the chiefe[9] (envying his repute)
who fained he intended to usurpe the governement, murder the
Councell, and make himselfe king, that his confederats were dis-
pearsed in all the three ships, and that divers of his confederats that
revealed it, would affirme it, for this he was committed. 13 weekes
he remained thus suspected, and by that time the ships should returne
they pretended out of their commisserations,[1] to referre him to the
Councell in England to receave a ‖ check,[2] rather then by particulat- **[6]**
ing his designes make him so odious to the world, as to touch his life,
or utterly overthrowe his reputation; but he much scorned their
charitie, and publikely defied the uttermost of their crueltie. Hee
wisely prevented their pollicies, though he could not suppresse their
envies, yet so wel he demeaned himselfe in this busines, as all the
company did see his innocencie, and his adversaries malice, and
those suborned to accuse him, accused his accusers of subornation;
many untruthes were alleaged against him; but being so apparently
disproved begat a generall hatred in the harts of the company against
such unjust commanders; many were the mischiefes that daily
sprong from their ignorant (yet ambitious) spirits; but the good
doctrine and exhortation of our preacher Master Hunt reconciled
them, and caused Captaine Smith to be admitted of the Councell;[3]
the next day all receaved the Communion, the day following the   Captaine New-
Salvages voluntarily desired peace, and Captaine Newport returned   ports returne
for England with newes; leaving in Virginia 100. the 15 of June 1607. for England.

The names of them that were the first planters,
were these following.

Master Edward Maria Wingfield. ⎫
Captaine Bartholomew Gosnoll.   ⎪
Captaine John Smyth.   ⎬ *Councell.*
Captaine John Ratliffe.   ⎪
Captaine John Martin.   ⎪
Captaine George Kendall.   ⎭
‖ Master Robert Hunt *Preacher.*   **[7]**

9. "Chiefe" was used elliptically for "the chief people." See p. 3n, above.
1. I.e., they pretended their plan was in Smith's interest.
2. Reprimand.
3. While Master Hunt undoubtedly had something to do with Smith's admission to
the council, he is not specifically mentioned in the "Relatyon," attributed to Gabriel
Archer, which was sent to England with Newport on June 22; and Smith's chronology
is inaccurate. Smith was sworn one of the council on Wed., June 10, 1607; the following
Sun., June 14, two Indians came up, unarmed, and stated that four of the neighboring
chiefs would help promote peace with five unfriendly chiefs (naming them); the colonists
received the communion a week later, on Sun., June 21; and Newport sailed on Mon.,
June 22 (Barbour, *Jamestown Voyages*, I, 97–98; and Percy's "Discourse," *ibid.*, 143).

Master George Percie.
Anthony Gosnoll.[4]
Captaine Gabriell Archer.
Robert Ford.
William Bruster.
Dru Pickhouse.
John Brookes.
Thomas Sands.
John Robinson.
Ustis Clovill.
Kellam Throgmorton.
Nathaniell Powell.
Robert Behethland.
Jeremy Alicock.
Thomas Studley.
Richard Crofts.
Nicholas Houlgrave.
Thomas Webbe.
John Waler.
William Tankard.
Francis Snarsbrough.
Edward Brookes.
Richard Dixon.
John Martin.[5]
George Martin.
Anthony Gosnold.
Thomas Wotton, *Sierg.*[6]
Thomas Gore.
Francis Midwinter.

} *Gentlemen.*

[8]

|| William Laxon.
Edward Pising.
Thomas Emry.
Robert Small.

} *Carpenters.*

Anas Todkill.
John Capper.[7]

4. One Anthony Gosnold was Bartholomew's younger brother, not yet 30, who was drowned in the James River early in 1609; the other, listed 24 lines below, was the son of Bartholomew's first cousin Robert Gosnold IV and was about 19 in 1607. He remained in Virginia until 1621.

5. The identity of John and George Martin is uncertain, though one of them, if not both, must have been the son(s) of Capt. John Martin. Percy reports the death of John Martin on Aug. 18, 1607, and this may be the son who starved during Wingfield's presidency (see Barbour, *Jamestown Voyages*, I, 144, 220, 231). But John Martin was still a shareholder in the Virginia Company in 1620. A solution to the problem is still to be found.

6. "Surgeon."

7. In the original, "John Capper" was set on the same line with "Anas Todkill," for the convenience of the printer.

James Read, *Blacksmith*.
Jonas Profit, *Sailer*.
Thomas Couper, *Barber*.
John Herd, *Brick layer*.
William Garret, *Bricklayer*.
Edward Brinto, *Mason*.
William Love, *Taylor*.
Nicholas Skot, *Drum*.
John Laydon.
William Cassen.
George Cassen.
Thomas Cassen.
William Rods.
William White.
Ould Edward.   } *Labourers*.
Henry Tavin.
George Golding.
John Dods.
William Johnson.
William Unger.
William Wilkinson. *Surgeon*.
Samuell Collier.
Nathaniel Pecock.   } *Boyes*.
James Brumfield.
Richard Mutton.

with diverse others to the number of 105.

Chapter 2.
What happened till the first supply.

[9]

BEING thus left to our fortunes, it fortuned that within tenne daies scarse ten amongst us coulde either goe, or well stand, such extreme weaknes and sicknes oppressed us.[8] And thereat none need

The occasion of sicknesse.

8. The ascription of the autumn (1607) "sickness" to anopheles or aëdes mosquitoes has been invalidated by sounder medical diagnosis, but the precise cause remains uncertain. Unsanitary conditions and bad water unquestionably contributed to the virulence of the epidemic. Typhoid fever, dysentery, and beri-beri have been suggested as scientific causes; the inability of the colonists to dress suitably for the climate has been advanced as a contributory social source. In the absence of a definitive investigation, three studies can be mentioned: Wyndham B. Blanton, "Epidemics, Real and Imaginary, and Other Factors Influencing Seventeenth Century Virginia's Population," *Bulletin of the History of Medicine*, XXXI (1957), 454–462; Gordon W. Jones, "The First Epidemic in English America," *VMHB*, LXXI (1963), 3–10; and Darrett B. Rutman and Anita H. Rutman, "Of Agues and Fevers: Malaria in the Early Chesapeake," *William and Mary Quarterly*, 3d Ser., XXXIII (1976), 31–60 (the Rutmans note that "malaria was not notorious as a 'killer' disease" [p. 50]).

mervaile, if they consider the cause and reason, which was this;
whilest the ships staied, our allowance was somewhat bettered, by a
daily proportion of bisket which the sailers would pilfer to sell, give
or exchange with us, for mony, saxefras, furres, or love. But when
they departed, there remained neither taverne, beere-house nor
place of relief but the common kettell. Had we beene as free from all
sinnes as gluttony, and drunkennes, we might have bin canonized
for Saints; But our President would never have bin admitted, for
ingrossing to his privat, Otemeale, sacke, oile, aquavitæ,[9] beefe, egs,
or what not; but the kettel, that indeede he allowed equally to be
distributed, and that was halfe a pinte of wheat and as much barly
boyled with water for a man a day, and this having fryed some 26.
weeks in the ships hold, contained as many wormes as graines; so
that we might truely call it rather so much bran then corne, our
drinke was water, our lodgings castles in aire.[10] With this lodging and
diet, our extreame toile in bearing and planting pallisadoes,[11] so
strained and brui- ‖ sed us, and our continuall labour in the extremity of the heate had so weakned us, as were cause sufficient to
have made us as miserable in our native country, or any other place
in the world. From May, to September, those that escaped lived
upon Sturgion, and sea-Crabs, 50. in this time we buried. The rest
seeing the Presidents projects to escape these miseries in our Pinnas
by flight (who all this time had neither felt want nor sicknes) so
moved our dead spirits, as we deposed him; and established Ratcliffe in his place. Gosnoll being dead, Kendall deposed,[1] Smith
newly recovered, Martin and Ratliffe was by his care preserved and
relieved, but now was all our provision spent, the Sturgeon gone, all
helps abandoned, each houre expecting the fury of the Salvages;
when God the patron of all good indeavours in that desperate extreamity so changed the harts of the Salvages, that they brought such
plenty of their fruits, and provision as no man wanted.[2]

And now where some affirmed it was ill done of the Councel to

The sailers
abuses.

[10]

A bad Preci-
dent.

Plentie un-
expected.

9. A general name for spirits distilled from grapes or grain.
10. Daydreams, castles in Spain.
11. "Palisade"; fence made of stakes. The word was imported from Spanish long
before the French equivalent took over.
1. Percy informs us that Bartholomew Gosnold died on Aug. 22, 1607, after which
Kendall "was committed about hainous matters which was proved against him" (Barbour, *Jamestown Voyages*, I, 144). Late in Nov., Kendall was finally brought to trial, but
no English account states just when or just why. For a confused report, see that of the
Irish sailor Francis Magnel, which somehow reached Spain nearly three years later:
"they have executed in that James-fort of theirs a Catholic English Captain called Captain Tindol [Kendall], because they knew that he wanted to come to Spain to reveal to
His Majesty what goes on in that land" (*ibid.*, 156; see also the Biographical Directory,
s.v. "Kendall, Capt. George").
2. The fact of the matter was that the Indians had plenty of food to use for trade as
soon as their corn and beans ripened. The English, being unacquainted with corn "on
the cob" or "in the ear," attributed the Indians' haste to bring it "ere it was half ripe" to
the hand of God (see the *True Relation*, sig. B1ʳ).

send forth men so badly provided, this incontradictable reason will shew them plainely they are too ill advised to nourish such il conceipts; first the fault of our going was our owne, what coulde bee thought fitting or necessary wee had, but what wee should finde, what we should want, where we shoulde be, we were all ignorant, and supposing to make our passage in two monthes, with victuall to live, and the advantage of the spring to worke; we weare at sea 5. monthes[3] where we both spent our victuall and lost the opportunity of the time, and season to plant.

Such actions have ever since the worlds beginning beene subject to such accidents, and every thing of worth is found full of difficulties, but nothing so difficult as to establish a common wealth so farre remote from men and meanes, and where mens mindes are so untoward[4] as neither do well themselves nor suffer others; but to proceed. **[11]**

The new President, and Martin, being little beloved, of weake judgement in dangers, and lesse industry in peace, committed the managing of all things abroad to captaine Smith: who by his owne example, good words, and faire promises, set some to mow, others to binde thatch, some to build houses, others to thatch them, himselfe alwaies bearing the greatest taske for his own share, so that in short time, he provided most of them lodgings neglecting any for himselfe. This done, seeing the Salvages superfluity beginne to decrease (with some of his workemen) shipped himselfe in the shallop to search the country for trade. The want of the language,[5] knowledge to mannage his boat with out sailers, the want of a sufficient power, (knowing the multitude of the Salvages) apparell for his men, and other necessaries, were infinite impediments, yet no discouragement. Being but 6 or 7 in company he went down the river to Kecoughtan, where at first they scorned him, as a starved man, yet he so dealt with them, that the next day they loaded his boat with corne, and in his returne he discovered and kindly traded with the Weraskoyks. In the meane time those at the fort so glutted the Salvages with their commodities as they became not regarded. *The building of James Towne.* *The beginning of trade abroad.*

Smith perceiving (notwithstanding their late miserie) not any **[12]** regarded but from hand to mouth, (the company being well recovered) caused the Pinas to bee provided with things fitting to get provision for the yeare following; but in the interim he made 3. or 4. journies and discovered the people of Chickahamine. Yet what he carefully provided the rest carelesly spent. Wingfield and Kendall

3. Accurately, four months and a few days.
4. Shortsighted, contrary.
5. A "shallop" was a small boat that could be "cut down for stowage aboard ship" and "reassembled on the shore" (William A. Baker, "Notes on a Shallop," *American Neptune*, XVII [1957], 105–113). The period referred to was probably early Oct. Smith apparently had little command of the Powhatan language before mid-1608. The list of hindrances that follows is not really surprising.

living in disgrace, seeing al things at randome in the absence of
Smith, The companies dislike of their Presidents weaknes, and their
small love to Martins never-mending sicknes, strengthened themselves with the sailers, and other confederates to regaine their former
credit and authority, or at least such meanes abord the Pinas, (being
fitted to saile as Smith had appointed for trade) to alter her course
and to go for England. Smith unexpectedly returning had the plot
discovered to him, much trouble he had to prevent it till with store
of fauken and musket shot he forced them stay or sinke in the river,
which action cost the life of captaine Kendall.[6] These brawles are so
disgustfull, as some will say they were better forgotten, yet all men
of good judgement will conclude, it were better their basenes should
be manifest to the world, then the busines beare the scorne and shame
of their excused disorders. The President and captaine Archer not
long after intended also to have abandoned the country, which
project also was curbed, and suppressed by Smith.[7] The Spanyard
never more greedily desired gold then he victuall, which finding so
plentiful in the river of Chickahamine where hundreds of Salvages
in divers places stood with baskets expecting his com- || ming.[8] And
now the winter approaching, the rivers became so covered with
swans, geese, duckes, and cranes, that we daily feasted with good
bread, Virginia pease, pumpions, and putchamins, fish, fowle, and
diverse sorts of wild beasts as fat as we could eat them: so that none
of our Tuftaffaty humorists[9] desired to goe for England. But our
comædies never endured long without a Tragedie; some idle exceptions being muttered against Captaine Smith, for not discovering the
head of Chickahamine river, and taxed by the Councell, to bee too
slowe in so worthie an attempt. The next voyage hee proceeded so
farre that with much labour by cutting of trees in sunder[1] he made
his passage, but when his Barge could passe no farther, he left her in
a broad bay out of danger of shot,[2] commanding none should goe
ashore till his returne, himselfe with 2 English and two Salvages went
up higher in a Canowe, but hee was not long absent, but his men
went ashore, whose want of government, gave both occasion and
opportunity to the Salvages to surprise one George Casson, and much
failed not to have cut of the boat[3] and all the rest. Smith little dream-

6. "Fauken" was a variant spelling of "falcon," a kind of light cannon (see the *Sea
Grammar*, 70). For Kendall, see p. 10n.

7. The sentence "The President . . . by Smith" is out of sequence, and apparently
was inserted as an afterthought.

8. The end of this sentence is missing. Smith had treated his Chickahominy voyages
at much greater length in the *True Relation*, sig. B2ʳ–B3ᵛ, and the author of this passage
in the *Proceedings* (surely not Studley, since he was dead by then) seems to have relied on
some other version of the story.

9. Cranks in fancy clothes.

1. "Asunder."

2. This was at Apocant.

3. "Almost cut off the boat."

ing of that accident, being got to the marshes at the rivers head, 20 myles in the desert,[4] had his 2 men slaine (as is supposed) sleeping by the Canowe, whilst himselfe by fowling sought them victuall, who finding he was beset with 200 Salvages, 2 of them hee slew, stil defending himselfe with the aid of a Salvage his guid, (whome hee bound to his arme and used as his buckler,) till at last slipping into a bogmire they tooke him prisoner: when this newes came to the fort much was their sorrow for his losse, fewe expecting ‖ what ensued. **[14]** A month those Barbarians kept him prisoner,[5] many strange triumphes and conjurations they made of him, yet hee so demeaned himselfe amongst them, as he not only diverted them from surprising the Fort, but procured his owne liberty, and got himselfe and his company such estimation amongst them, that those Salvages admired him as a demi-God. So returning safe to the Fort, once more *The 3 projects* staied the Pinnas her flight for England, which til his returne, could *to abandon the* not set saile, so extreame was the weather, and so great the frost.[6] *fort.*

His relation of the plentie he had seene, especially at Werowocomoco, where inhabited Powhatan (that till that time was unknowne) so revived againe their dead spirits as all mens feare was abandoned. Powhatan having sent with this Captaine divers of his men loaded with provision, he had conditioned, and so appointed his trustie messengers to bring but 2 or 3 of our great ordenances, but the messengers being satisfied with the sight of one of them discharged, ran away amazed[7] with feare, till meanes was used with guifts to assure them our loves. Thus you may see what difficulties still crossed any good indeavour, and the good successe of the businesse, and being thus oft brought to the very period of destruction, yet you see by what strange meanes God hath still delivered it. As *A true proofe* for the insufficiencie of them admitted in commission, that errour *of Gods love to* could not be prevented by their electors, there being no other choice, *the action.* and all were strangers to each others education, quallities, or disposition;[8] and if any deeme it a shame to our nation, to have any **[15]** mention made of these e- ‖ normities, let them peruse the histories of the Spanish discoveries and plantations, where they may see how

4. A deserted, uninhabited place.
5. According to Wingfield, who is unreliable, Smith "went up the Ryver of the Chechohomynaies" on Dec. 10, and Powhatan "sent him home to owr Towne" on Jan. 8, 1608 (Barbour, *Jamestown Voyages*, I, 226–227), which would be 29 days. We know, however, that Captain Newport arrived on Jan. 2, when Smith had already returned (*ibid.*, 159). Smith's "a month" may therefore be approximately accurate, and Wingfield's first date as mistaken as the second.
6. See the *True Relation*, sigs. B3ʳ–C3ᵛ, for a fuller account; and the *Generall Historie*, 49, for the Pocahontas episode. The lack of sequential coherence between these concluding passages in chap. 2 (attributed to Studley) and the beginning of chap. 3 (seemingly derived from Studley and Todkill) points to different authorship, as well as inadequate editing by Symonds.
7. Terror stricken.
8. This is a keen summation of the basic trouble in the colony.

many mutinies, discords, and dissentions, have accompanied them and crossed their attempts, which being knowne to be particular mens offences, doth take away the generall scorne and contempt, mallice,[9] and ignorance might else produce, to the scandall and reproach of those, whose actions and valiant resolution deserve a worthie respect. Now whether it had beene better for Captaine Smith to have concluded with any of their severall projects to have abandoned the Countrie with some 10 or 12 of them we cal the better sort, to have left Master Hunt our preacher, Master Anthony Gosnoll, a most honest, worthie, and industrious gentleman, with some 30 or 40 others his countrie men, to the furie of the Salvages, famin, and all manner of mischiefes and inconveniences, or starved himselfe with them for company, for want of lodging, or but adventuring abroad to make them provision, or by his opposition, to preserve the action, and save all their lives, I leave to the censure of others to consider.

Of two evils the lesser was chosen.

Thomas Studley.[10]

Chapter 3.
The arrivall of the first supply[1] with their proceedings and returne.

[16] ALL this time our cares were not so much to abandon the Countrie, but the Treasurer and Councell in England were as diligent and carefull to supplie us. Two tall[2] ships they sent us, with neere 100 men, well furnished with all things could be imagined necessarie, both for them and us. The one commanded by Captaine Newport: the other by Captaine Nelson, an honest man and an expert marriner, but such was the leewardnesse[3] of his ship, that (though he were within sight of Cape Henry) by stormy contrarie windes, was forced so farre to sea, as the West Indies[4] was the next land for the repaire of his Masts, and reliefe of wood and water. But Captaine Newport got in, and arived at James towne, not long after the re-

The Phenix from Cape Henry forced to the west Indies.

9. Arber suggests this should read: "contempt, that mallice . . ." (Edward Arber, ed., *Captain John Smith . . . Works, 1608–1631*, The English Scholar's Library Edition, No. 16 [Birmingham, 1884], 99).

10. Studley could not have written all of this section, since he died on Aug. 28, 1607 (Barbour, *Jamestown Voyages*, I, 144). The *Generall Historie*, 50, significantly, adds the names of Robert Fenton, Edward Harrington (both of them otherwise unidentified), and especially Smith himself ("J. S.") for at least the last paragraph.

1. I.e., "additional body of persons (as well as supplies)."

2. "Tall" was frequently applied to ships that were high in proportion to their width.

3. "The ship's tendency to pull to the lee."

4. A good example of the difficulties of navigation in Smith's day. "The West Indies" possibly refers to the neighborhood of Spain's Hispaniola.

demption of Captaine Smith, to whome the Salvages every other day brought such plentie of bread, fish, turkies, squirrels, deare, and other wild beasts, part they gave him as presents from the king; the rest, hee as their market clarke set the price how they should sell.[5]

So he had inchanted those poore soules (being their prisoner) in demonstrating unto them the roundnesse of the world, the course of the moone and starres, the cause of the day and night the largenes of the seas the quallities of our ships, shot and powder, The devision of the world, with the diversity of people, their complexions, customes and conditions. All which hee fained to be under the command of Captaine Newport, whom he tearmed to them his father; of whose arri-‖val, it chanced he so directly prophecied,[6] as they esteemed him an oracle; by these fictions he not only saved his owne life, and obtained his liberty, but had them at that command, he might command them what he listed. That God that created al these things; they knew he adored for his God, whom they would also tearme in their discourses, the God of captaine Smith. The President and Councel so much envied his estimation amongst the Salvages (though wee all in generall equally participated with him of the good therof) that they wrought it into their understandings, by their great bounty in giving 4. times more for their commodities then he appointed, that their greatnesse and authority, as much exceeded his, as their bounty, and liberality; Now the arrivall of this first supply, so overjoyed us, that we could not devise too much to please the mariners. We gave them liberty to truck or trade at their pleasures. But in a short time, it followed, that could not be had for a pound of copper, which before was sold for an ounce. Thus ambition, and sufferance, cut the throat of our trade, but confirmed their opinion of Newports greatnes, (wherewith Smith had possessed[7] Powhatan) especially by the great presents Newport often sent him, before he could prepare the Pinas to go and visit him; so that this Salvage also desired to see him. A great bruit there was to set him forwarde: when he went he was accompanied, with captaine Smith, and Master Scrivener a very wise understanding gentleman newly arrived, and admitted of the Councell, and 30. or 40. chosen men for their guarde. Arriving at Werowocomo Newports conceipt of this great Salvage,

How Captaine
Smith got his
liberty.

[17]

Their opinion
of our God.

---

5. Cf. the *Generall Historie*, 50–51.

6. According to the *True Relation*, sig. C1ᵛ–C2ʳ, when Smith was first brought before Powhatan he had elaborated on the importance of Captain Newport, his "father," and Powhatan had promised his release within four days. Two days after this Powhatan had appeared before him, apparently garbed as high priest, and announced that "presently he should goe to James towne" (*Generall Historie*, 49). But because of delaying tactics by the Indians, Smith did not reach Jamestown for another two days. Newport arrived the evening of the day of Smith's return (Wingfield, "Discourse," in Barbour, *Jamestown Voyages*, I, 227). Hence, in a roundabout way, Smith had prophesied Newport's appearance. Ergo, he was an "oracle."

7. I.e., "instilled in." Smith's plan to impress Powhatan with Newport's importance was surely sound, but Newport abused it.

[**18**]
Smiths revisit-
ing Powhatan.

bred ‖ many doubts, and suspitions of treacheries; which Smith, to make appeare was needlesse, with 20. men well appointed, undertooke to encounter (with that number) the worst that could happen there names were.

Nathaniell Powell.	John Taverner.
Robert Beheathland.	William Dier.[8]
William Phettiplace.	Thomas Coe.
Richard Wyffin.	Thomas Hope.
Anthony Gosnoll.	Anas Todkell.

Powhatans first
entertainement
of our men.

with 10. others whose names I have forgotten. These being kindly received a shore, with 2. or 300. Salvages were conducted to their towne; Powhatan strained himselfe to the uttermost of his greatnes to entertain us, with great shouts of Joy, orations of protestations, and the most plenty of victuall hee could provide to feast us. Sitting upon his bed of mats, his pillow of leather imbroydred (after their rude manner) with pearle and white beades, his attire a faire Robe of skins as large as an Irish mantle,[9] at his head and feet a handsome young woman; on each side his house sate 20. of his concubines, their heads and shoulders painted red, with a great chaine of white beads about their necks.[10] Before those sate his chiefest men in like order in his arbor-like house. With many pretty discourses to renue their olde acquaintaunce; the great kinge and our captaine spent the time

[**19**]

The exchange
of a Christian
for a Salvage.

till the ebbe left our Barge a- ‖ ground, then renuing their feasts and mirth we quartred that night with Powhatan: the next day Newport came a shore, and received as much content as those people could give him, a boy named Thomas Savage[1] was then given unto Powhatan who Newport called his son, for whom Powhatan gave him Namontacke[2] his trusty servant, and one of a shrewd subtill capacity. 3. or 4. daies were spent in feasting dancing and trading, wherin Powhatan carried himselfe so prowdly, yet discreetly (in his Salvage manner) as made us all admire his natural gifts considering

8. For the subsequent behavior of this colonist, see pp. 87, 99, 102, below; and the *Generall Historie*, 86.

9. Cf. the *True Relation*, sig. C1ᵛ, which omits the reference to Irish mantles; and the *Map of Va.*, 20n, which does not mention Powhatan. The added reference here brings up the question of an alleged visit by Smith to Ireland that is discussed in the Introduction to the *True Travels*.

10. Regarding the chains of white beads, the specific idea of "wampum" as a medium of exchange in New England (cf. Roger Williams, *A Key Into the Language of America*, ed. John J. Teunissen and Evelyn J. Hinz [Detroit, Mich., 1973], 210) seems not to have been harbored in the minds of the Powhatan Indians (see Frank G. Speck, "The Functions of Wampum among the Eastern Algonkian," American Anthropological Association, *Memoirs*, VI, No. 1 [Lancaster, Pa., 1919]).

1. On Thomas Savage, see Martha Bennett Stiles, "Hostage to the Indians," *Virginia Cavalcade*, XII (Summer, 1962), 5–11; and the Biographical Directory.

2. See the Biographical Directory, s.v. "Namontack."

his education;[3] as scorning to trade as his subjects did, he bespake Newport in this manner.[4]

Captain Newport it is not agreeable with my greatnes in this pedling manner to trade for trifles, and I esteeme you a great werowans. Therefore lay me down all your commodities togither, what I like I will take, and in recompence give you that I thinke fitting their value.

Powhatans speech.

Captaine Smith being our interpreter, regarding Newport as his father, knowing best the disposition of Powhatan, told us his intent was but to cheat us; yet captaine Newport thinking to out brave this Salvage in ostentation of greatnes, and so to bewitch him with his bounty, as to have what he listed, but so it chanced Powhatan having his desire, valued his corne at such a rate, as I thinke it better cheape in Spaine, for we had not 4. bushels for that we expected 20. hogsheads. This bred some unkindnes betweene our two captaines,[5] Newport seeking to please the humor of the unsatiable Salvage; Smith to cause the Salvage to please him, but smothering his distast (to avoide the || Salvages suspition) glaunced[6] in the eies of Powhatan many Trifles who fixed his humour upon a few blew beads; A long time he importunatly desired them, but Smith seemed so much the more to affect them, so that ere we departed, for a pound or two of blew beads he brought over[7] my king for 2 or 300 bushels of corne, yet parted good friends. The like entertainement we found of Opechanchynough king of Pamaunke whom also he in like manner fitted, (at the like rates) with blew beads: and so we returned to the fort. Where this new supply being lodged with the rest, accidently fired the quarters, and so the Towne, which being but thatched with reeds the fire was so fierce as it burnt their pallizadoes (though 10. or 12 yardes distant) with their armes, bedding, apparell, and much private provision. Good Master Hunt our preacher lost all his library, and al that he had (but the cloathes on his backe,) yet none

Difference of opinions.

[20]

James towne burnt.

3. Rearing; the word "education" began to be used in the present-day sense some years after Smith died.

4. The speeches presented by Smith, be they Indian or English, should be taken as faithful only in spirit—and within the bounds of Anglo-Indian mutual comprehension. The handwritten notations found in one copy of Smith's *True Relation* maintain: "This Author I fy[nde] in many errors . . . [due] to h[is?] not well understa[n]dinge the language" (sig. C3ʳn), an assertion that is corroborated in a minor way by his apparent misunderstanding of several Indian words in his word list (e.g., see Philip L. Barbour, 'The Earliest Reconnaissance of the Chesapeake Bay Area: Captain John Smith's Map and Indian Vocabulary," Pt. II, *VMHB*, LXXX [1972], 42–43). The significant factor is the obvious oratorical gift of Powhatan and his subordinates (cf. Edna C. Sorber, "The Noble Eloquent Savage," *Ethnohistory*, XIX [1972], 227–236), to which Smith attempted to respond in the language of Shakespeare in his prime.

5. This occasion signaled the beginning of the tension between Smith and Newport.

6. In present-day English, "flashed."

7. Prevailed upon.

ever see him repine at his losse.[8] This hapned in the winter, in that extreame frost, 1607. Now though we had victuall sufficient, I meane only of Oatemeale, meale, and corne, yet the ship staying there 14. weeks[9] when shee might as well have been gone in 14. daies, spent the beefe, porke, oile, aquavitæ, fish, butter, and cheese, beere and such like; as was provided to be landed us. When they departed, what their discretion could spare us, to make a feast or two with bisket, pork, beefe, fish, and oile, to relish our mouths, of each somwhat they left us, yet I must confess those that had either mony, spare clothes, credit to give bils of payment, gold rings, furres, or any such commodities were ever welcome to this removing taverne, such ‖ was our patience to obay such vile commanders, and buy our owne provision at 15 times the valew, suffering them feast (we bearing the charge) yet must not repine,[10] but fast; and then leakage, ship-rats, and other casualties occasioned the losse, but the vessell and remnants (for totals) we were glad to receive with all our hearts to make up the account, highly commending their providence for preserving that. For all this plentie our ordinarie was but meale and water, so that this great charge little relieved our wants, whereby with the extreamity of the bitter cold aire more then halfe of us died, and tooke our deathes, in that piercing winter I cannot deny, but both Skrivener and Smith did their best to amend what was amisse, but with the President went the major part, that their hornes were too short. But the worst mischiefe was, our gilded refiners with their golden promises,[1] made all men their slaves in hope of recompence; there was no talke, no hope, no worke, but dig gold, wash gold, refine gold, load gold, such a brute[2] of gold, as one mad fellow desired to bee buried in the sandes, least they should by their art make gold of his bones. Little need there was and lesse reason, the ship should stay, their wages run on, our victuall consume, 14 weekes, that the Marriners might say, they built such a golden Church, that we can say, the raine washed neare to nothing in 14 daies. Were it that Captaine Smith would not applaud all those golden inventions, because

A ship idly loitring 14 weeks.

[21]

The effect of meere verbalists.

A needles charge.

8. The passage "Where this new supply . . . repine at his losse" is out of sequence chronologically. The fire had occurred on Jan. 7, 1608 (see the *True Relation*, sig. C3 and n. 150). Newport, Smith, *et al.* did not return from Werowocomoco until Mar. (Barbour, *Jamestown Voyages*, I, 228).

9. Smith's chronology is accurate. Newport stayed 14 weeks and one day.

10. Arber, *Smith, Works*, 104, suggests: "yet must we not repine. . . ."

1. Some of the colonists had thought they had found gold in the mud and sand of the north shore of the James River. While some historians, including the editor, have thought of pyrite or marcasite for this "fool's gold," it would seem more likely to have been flakes of mica, which "may be quite persistent in sediments and may develop a yellow to silver-colored sheen that is sometimes mistaken for gold" (D. C. Le Van, Geologist, Division of Mineral Resources of the Department of Conservation and Economic Development, Commonwealth of Virginia, Charlottesville, in a letter to the editor dated Sept. 16, 1975).

2. "Bruit," clamor.

they admitted him not to the sight of their trials, nor golden consultations I knowe not; but I heard him question with Captaine Martin[3] and tell him, except he would shew ‖ him a more substantiall triall, hee was not inamored with their durtie skill, breathing out these and many other passions, never any thing did more torment him, then to see all necessarie businesse neglected, to fraught such a drunken ship with so much gilded durt; till then wee never accounted Captaine Newport a refiner; who being fit to set saile for England, and wee not having any use of Parliaments, plaies,[4] petitions, admirals, recorders, interpreters, chronologers, courts of plea, nor Justices of peace,[5] sent Master Wingfield and Captaine Archer with him for England to seeke some place of better imploiment.

[22]

A returne to England.

Chapter 4.
The arivall of the Phœnix, her returne, and other accidents.

THE authoritie nowe consisting in refining,[6] Captaine Martin and the still sickly President, the sale of the stores commodities maintained their estates as inheritable revenews. The spring approching, and the ship departed, Master Skrivener and Captaine Smith divided betwixt them, the rebuilding our towne, the repairing our pallisadoes, the cutting downe trees, preparing our fields, planting our corne, and to rebuild our Church, and recover[7] our store-house; al men thus busie at their severall labours, Master Nelson arived with his lost *Phœnix* (lost I say, for that al men deemed him lost) landing safely his men; so well hee had mannaged his ill hap, causing the Indian[8] Iles to feed his company ‖ that his victuall (to that was left as before[9]) was sufficient for halfe a yeare. He had nothing but he freely imparted it, which honest dealing (being a marriner) caused us admire him, wee would not have wished so much as he did for us. Nowe to relade this ship with some good tidings, the President (yet notwithstanding[1] with his dignitie to leave the fort) gave order to Captaine Smith and Master Skrivener to discover and search the

The repairing of James towne.

[23]

---

3. This points to Todkill as the author. Todkill had been in Martin's employ (see p. 25, below).
4. Tricks, underhand proceedings.
5. With this list of legal offices and institutions Smith apparently intended to disparage Archer's inappropriate activities.
6. Omitted in the *Generall Historie* version (p. 53), this may have reference to Martin's "gold fever."
7. Put a new roof on.
8. West Indian.
9. "Added to what we had left over."
1. A printer's error lurks somewhere in "notwithstanding"; perhaps read, "it not standing with his dignitie."

60 appointed
to discover
Monacan.
commodities of Monacans countrie beyound the Falles, 60 able men was allotted their number, the which within 6 daies exercise, Smith had so well trained to their armes and orders, that they little feared with whome they should encounter. Yet so unseasonable was the time, and so opposite was Captaine Martin[2] to every thing, but only to fraught this ship also with his phantasticall gold, as Captaine Smith rather desired to relade her with Cedar, which was a present dispatch; then either with durt, or the reports of an uncertaine discoverie. Whilst their conclusion was resolving, this hapned.

An ill example
to sell swords
to Salvages.

Powhatans
trecherie.

[24]

The governours
weaknesse.

Smiths attempt
to suppresse
the Salvages
insolencies.

Powhatans
excuses.

Powhatan to expresse his love to Newport, when he departed, presented him with 20 Turkies, conditionally to returne him 20 Swords, which immediatly were sent him.[3] Now after his departure hee presented Captaine Smith with the like luggage, but not finding his humor obaied in sending him weapons, he caused his people with 20. devises to obtain them, at last by ambuscadoes at our very ports they would take them per force, surprise us at work, or any way, which was so long permitted that they became so insolent, there was no rule, the command from England was so straight not || to offend them as our authority bearers (keeping their houses) would rather be any thing then peace breakers: this charitable humor prevailed, till well it chaunced they medled with captaine Smith, who without farther deliberation gave them such an incounter, as some he so hunted up and downe the Ile, some he so terrified with whipping, beating and imprisonment, as for revenge they surprised two of his forraging disorderly souldiers, and having assembled their forces, boldly threatned at our ports to force Smith to redeliver 7. Salvages which for their villanies he detained prisoners, but to try their furies, in lesse then halfe an houre he so hampered their insolencies, that they brought the 2. prisoners desiring peace without any farther composition[4] for their prisoners, who being threatned and examined their intents and plotters of their villanies confessed they were directed only by Powhatan, to obtaine him our owne weapons to cut our own throats, with the manner how, where, and when, which wee plainely found most true and apparant, yet he sent his messengers and his dearest Daughter Pocahuntas[5] to excuse him, of the injuries done by his subjects, desiring their liberties, with the assuraunce of his love. After Smith had given the prisoners what correction hee

2. The *True Relation*, sig. E2[r], tells a different story: Captain Martin was willing to go himself, "yet no reason could be reason to proceede forward"—whatever specifically was meant by that. (A few lines below, in the same passage, Smith mentions "certain matters which for some cause I keepe private.")

3. The account that follows differs somewhat in detail from that in the *True Relation* sig. E2[r]–E3[r].

4. Terms.

5. This happened sometime between Apr. 20 and June 2, 1608. Pocahontas would hardly have been 13 yet, perhaps not even 12.

thought fit, used them well a day or two after, and then delivered them Pocahuntas, for whose sake only he fained to save their lives and graunt them liberty. The patient councel, that nothing would move to warre with the Salvages, would gladly have wrangled with captaine Smith for his cruelty, yet none was slaine to any mans knowledge, but it brought them in such feare and ‖ obedience, as his very name wold sufficiently affright them. The fraught of this ship being concluded to be Cedar, by the diligence of the Master, and captaine Smith shee was quickly reladed; Master Scrivener was neither Idle nor slow to follow all things at the fort; the ship falling to[6] the Cedar Ile, captaine Martin having made shift to be sicke neare a yeare, and now, neither pepper, suger, cloves, mace, nor nutmegs, ginger nor sweet meates in the country (to injoy the credit of his supposed art) at his earnest request, was most willingly admitted to returne for England, yet having beene there but a yeare, and not past halfe a year since the ague left him (that he might say somewhat he had seene) hee went twice by water to Paspahegh a place neere 7. miles from James towne, but lest the dew should distemper him, was ever forced to returne before night,[7] Thus much I thought fit to expresse, he expresly commanding me to record his journies, I being his man, and he sometimes my master.

Thomas Studly. Anas Todkill.[8]

[25]
A ship fraught
with Cedar.

The adventures
of Captaine
Martin.

6. Usually a ship "falls down to" in the sense of "falls downstream to [with the tide]."
7. Part of the passage on Martin was omitted in the *Generall Historie*, 54.
8. Todkill was evidently the author of the foregoing; see the Biographical Directory.

Their names that were landed in this supply:

Matthew Scriviner, *appointed to be of the Councell.*

Michaell Phetyplace.
William Phetyplace.
Ralfe Morton.
William Cantrill.
Richard Wyffin.
Robert Barnes.
George Hill.
|| George Pretty.
John Taverner.
Robert Cutler.
Michaell Sickelmore.
Thomas Coo.
Peter Pory.
Richard Killingbeck.
William Causey.[9]
Doctor Russell.
Richard Worley.
Richard Prodger.
William Bayley.
Richard Molynex.
Richard Pots.
Jefrey Abots.
John Harper.
Timothy Leds.
Edward Gurganay.
George Forest.
John Nickoles.
William Gryvill.

} *Gentlemen.*

Daniell Stalling *Jueller.*[10]
William Dawson *Refiner.*
Abraham Ransacke *Refiner.*
William Johnson *Goldsmith.*
Peter Keffer *a Gunner.*
Robert Alberton *a Perfumer.*
Richard Belfield *Goldsmith.*

9. Causey's first name was Nathaniel; cf. the *Generall Historie*, 55, and elsewhere.
10. Variant spelling of "jeweller."

‖ Raymond Goodyson.   [27]
John Speareman.
William Spence.[1]
Richard Brislow.
William Simons.
John Bouth.
William Burket.
Nicholas Ven.
William Perce.
Francis Perkins.[2]
Francis Perkins.   } *Labourers.*
William Bentley.[3]
Richard Gradon.
Rowland Nelstrop.
Richard Salvage.
Thomas Salvage.
Richard Miler.[4]
William May.
Vere.
Michaell.
Bishop Wyles.
John Powell.
Thomas Hope.
William Beckwith.
William Yonge.   } *Tailers.*
Laurence Towtales.
William Ward.

Christopher Rodes.
James Watkings.
Richard Fetherstone.[5]
James Burne.
‖ Thomas Feld.   } *Apothecaries.*   [28]
John Harford.
Post Gittnat *a Surgion.*
John Lewes *a Couper.*
Robert Cotten *a Tobaco-pipe-maker.*
Richard Dole *a blacke Smith.*

And divers others to the number of 120.[6]

1. William Spence is listed as a gentleman in the *Generall Historie*, 55.
2. Francis Perkins was a gentleman (see *ibid.*); the second Francis was his son (Barbour, *Jamestown Voyages*, I, 160).
3. Bentley is listed as a gentleman in the *Generall Historie*, 55, perhaps mistakenly.
4. Probably the same person as the Richard Milmer in the *Generall Historie*, 55.
5. Of these four "unclassified" colonists, only Richard Fetherstone appears to have been a gentleman; the other three were laborers.
6. The names of only 60% of the colonists are listed here.

Chapter 5.
The accidents that happened in the
Discoverie of the bay.

THE prodigality of the Presidents state went so deepe in the store
that Smith and Scrivener had a while tyed both Martin[7] and
him to the rules of proportion, but now Smith being to depart, the
Presidents authoritie so overswayed Master Scriveners discretion as
our store, our time, our strength and labours was idlely consumed to
fulfill his phantasies. The second of June 1608. Smith left the fort to
performe his discoverie; with this company.

Walter Russell *Doctour of Physicke.*[8]

Ralph Morton.
Thomas Momford.
William Cantrill.
Richard Fetherstone.[9]   } *Gentlemen.*
James Bourne.
Michael Sicklemore.

[29]

|| Anas Todkill.
Robert Small.
James Watkins.   } *Souldiers.*
John Powell.

James Read *blackesmith.*
Richard Keale *fishmonger.*
Jonas Profit *fisher.*

These being in an open barge of two tunnes burthen leaving the
Phenix at Cape-Henry[1] we crossed the bay to the Easterne shore and
fell with the Iles called Smiths Iles. The first people we saw were

Cape Charles.   2 grimme and stout Salvages upon Cape-Charles with long poles like
Javelings, headed with bone, they boldly demanded what we were,
and what we would, but after many circumstances,[2] they in time

Acawmacke.   seemed very kinde, and directed us to Acawmacke the habitation of
the Werowans where we were kindly intreated;[3] this king was the

7. The mention of Martin here seems to have been in error; see the *Generall Historie,*
55.

8. Doctors of "physicke," or physicians, "were men who had some university training, at least a B.A. degree, had read the classic authors in medicine, such as Hippocrates,
Aristotle, and Galen, and were trained to treat disease empirically" (John H. Raach,
A Directory of English Country Physicians, 1603–1643 [London, 1962], 11). Since surviving
records are far from complete, the editor has been unable to identify Walter Russell,
despite the help of the Royal College of Physicians. A *William* Russell was practicing
c. 1624 (*ibid.,* 79).

9. Fetherstone died within a few months; see p. 40, below.

1. On this occasion Smith delivered to Capt. Francis Nelson his famous letter, which
was soon to be published as the *True Relation.*

2. Much ado.

3. Treated.

comliest proper civill Salvage wee incountred: his country is a
pleasant fertill clay-soile. Hee tolde us of a straunge accident lately
happened him, and it was. Two dead children by the extreame
passions of their parents, or some dreaming visions, phantasie, or
affection moved them againe to revisit their dead carkases, whose
benummed bodies reflected to the eies of the beholders such pleasant
delightfull countenances, as though they had regained their vital
spirits.[4] This as a miracle drew many to behold them, all which,
(being a great part of his people) not long after died, and not any one
escaped.[5] They spake the language of Powhatan wherein they made
such descriptions of the bay, Iles, and rivers that often did us exceeding pleasure. Passing ‖ along the coast, searching every inlet, and
bay fit for harbours and habitations seeing many Iles in the midst of
the bay, we bore up for them, but ere wee could attaine them, such
an extreame gust of wind, raine, thunder, and lightning happened,
that with great daunger we escaped the unmercifull raging of that
ocean-like water. The next day searching those inhabitable[6] Iles
(which we called Russels Iles) to provide fresh water, the defect
whereof forced us to follow the next Easterne channell, which brought
us to the river Wighcocomoco. The people at first with great furie,
seemed to assault us, yet at last with songs, daunces, and much mirth,
became very tractable, but searching their habitations for water,
wee could fill but 3,[7] and that such puddle[8] that never til then, wee
ever knew the want of good water. We digged and searched many
places but ere the end of two daies wee would have refused two
barricoes of gold for one of that puddle water of Wighcocomoco.
Being past these Iles, falling with a high land upon the maine wcc
found a great pond of fresh water, but so exceeding hot, that we supposed it some bath: that place we called Point Ployer.[9] Being thus
refreshed in crossing over from the maine to other Iles, the wind and
waters so much increased with thunder, lightning, and raine, that
our fore-mast blew overbord and such mightie waves overwrought
us in that smal barge, that with great labour wee kept her from sink-
ing by freeing out the water, 2 daies we were inforced to inhabit these
uninhabited Iles, which (for the extremitie of gusts, thunder, raine,
stormes, and il weather) we called Limbo.[10] Repairing our fore saile

A strange
mortalitie of
Salvages.

[30]

An extreame
gust.

Russels Iles.

Wighco-
comoco.

An extreame
want of fresh
water.

The barge
neere sunk in
a gust.

4. The curious phrasing seems to have been William Symonds's. Smith tried to
improve on it in the *Generall Historie*, 56, without much success. See the Textual Annotation.

5. The editor has not chanced on any sound explanation of this phenomenon. Note
that it occurred before the first known landing of the Jamestown settlers on Cape Charles.

6. "Inhabitable" means "not habitable," hence "uninhabited" (*OED*).

7. Sc., "barricoes" or "kegs" (see the *Generall Historie*, 56).

8. Foul or dirty water such as is found in puddles.

9. The *Generall Historie*, 56, gives an incomplete explanation of the name; Amaury
II Goyon (or Gouyon), comte de Plouër, had befriended Smith during the winter of
1600/1601 in Brittany (see Barbour, *Three Worlds*, 21, 202).

10. Here probably "Hell," "Hades." Note in the Smith/Hole map of Virginia the
angry fish in the bay, off Limbo.

[31] with ‖ our shirts, we set saile for the maine[1] and fel with a faire river on the East called Kuskarawaocke, by it inhabit the people of Soraphanigh, Nause, Arsek, and Nautaquake that much extolled a great nation called Massawomekes,[2] in search of whome wee returned by Limbo, but finding this easterne shore shallow broken Iles, and the maine for most part without fresh water, we passed by the straights of Limbo for the weasterne shore. So broad is the bay here, that we could scarse perceive the great high Cliffes on the other side;[3] by them wee ancored that night, and called them Richards Cliffes. 30 leagues we sailed more Northwards, not finding any inhabitants, yet the coast well watred, the mountaines very barren, the vallies very fertil, but the woods extreame thicke, full of Woolves, Beares, Deare, and other wild beasts. The first inlet we found, wee called Bolus, for that the clay (in many places) was like (if not) Bole-Armoniacke:[4] when we first set saile, some of our gallants doubted nothing, but that our Captaine would make too much hast home; but having lien not above 12 daies in this smal Barge, oft tired at their oares, their bread spoiled with wet, so much that it was rotten (yet so good were their stomacks that they could digest it) did with continuall complaints so importune him now to returne, as caused him bespeake them in this manner.

The first notice of the Massawomecks.

Bolus river.

Smiths speech to his souldiers.

[32] Gentlemen if you would remember the memorable historie of Sir Ralfe Lane,[5] how his company importuned him to proceed in the discoverie of Morattico, alleaging, they had yet a dog, that being boyled with Saxafras leaves, would richly feed them in their returnes; what a shame would it be for you ‖ (that have beene so suspitious of my tendernesse) to force me returne with a months provision scarce able to say where we have bin, nor yet heard of that wee were sent to seeke; you cannot say but I have shared with you of the worst is past;[6] and for what is to come of lodging, diet, or whatsoever, I am contented you allot the worst part to my selfe; as for your feares, that I will lose my selfe in these unknowne large waters, or be swal-

1. The mainland, the Eastern Shore.
2. Smith seems to have been inspired to seek out the Massawomekes by Ralph Lane's account of his encounters with hostile tribes in North Carolina (*Generall Historie*, 6–9).
3. If the identification of the Kuskarawaocke with the modern Nanticoke River is correct, Chesapeake Bay would be about 25 km. (or better than 15 mi.) wide at its mouth. The cliffs are a bit farther to the N. They were named for Smith's mother (see the *True Travels*, 1). As for the 30 leagues (90 mi., or 145 km.), from Cove Point, just to the S of the cliffs in question, to the mouth of the Patapsco River (see n. 4, below) is about 20 leagues (60 mi., or 96 km.) by modern channels and direct sailing, and only 16 leagues according to the Smith/Hole map.
4. See the *Map of Va.*, 3n and 7. The Bolus must have been the Patapsco River, since the alternatives suggested by some writers do not allow for the 25 mi. (40 km.) or so of waterway shown on the Smith/Hole map.
5. See n. 2, above.
6. The *Generall Historie*, 57, has "in the worst which is past."

lowed up in some stormie gust, abandon those childish feares, for worse then is past cannot happen, and there is as much danger to returne, as to proceed forward. Regaine therefore your old spirits; for return I wil not, (if God assist me) til I have seene the Massa-womekes, found Patawomeck, or the head of this great water you conceit to be endlesse.

3 or 4 daies wee expected[7] wind and weather, whose adverse ex-treamities added such discouragements to our discontents as 3 or 4 fel extreame sicke, whose pittiful complaints caused us to returne, leaving the bay some 10 miles broad at 9 or 10 fadome water.

The 16 of June we fel with the river of Patawomeck: feare being gon, and our men recovered, wee were all contented to take some paines to knowe the name of this 9 mile broad river,[8] we could see no inhabitants for 30 myles saile; then we were conducted by 2 Salvages up a little bayed creeke toward Onawmament where all the woods were laid with Ambuscadoes to the number of 3 or 400 Salvages, but so strangely painted, grimed, and disguised, showting, yelling, and crying, as we rather supposed them so many divels. They made many bravadoes, but to appease ‖ their furie, our Captaine prepared with a seeming willingnesse (as they) to encounter them, the grazing of the bullets upon the river, with the ecco of the woods so amazed them, as down went their bowes and arrowes; (and exchanging hos-tage) James Watkins was sent 6 myles up the woods to their kings habitation: wee were kindly used by these Salvages, of whome wee understood, they were commaunded to betray us, by Powhatans direction, and hee so directed from the discontents of James towne. The like incounters we found at Patawomeck, Cecocawone and divers other places, but at Moyaones, Nacothtant and Taux,[1] the people did their best to content us. The cause of this discovery, was to search a glistering mettal, the Salvages told us they had from Patawomeck, (the which Newport assured that he had tryed to hold halfe silver) also to search what furres, metals, rivers, Rockes, nations,

The discovery of Patawomeck.

Ambuscados of Salvages.

[33]

A treacherous project.

---

7. Waited for a change in.
8. From Smith Point, NW across the mouth of the Potomac, to Point Lookout is over 10 mi., and from Smith Point to Nomini Bay (Onawmanient was somewhere there) is nearly 30 mi. Smith's rough estimates, however, were probably made at some point a few miles upstream; hence they are somewhat exaggerated, as probably also is the number of Indians waiting in ambush.
1. The Moyaones and Nacotchtank tribes are shown on the Smith/Hole map, the former at Anacostia, Maryland, the latter a few miles below, at the mouth of Piscataway Creek, Maryland. They were not subject to Powhatan. The Taux clearly lived in the same neighborhood, and their name seems to survive in Doag's Neck, on or near Piscata-way Creek (see Hamill Thomas Kenny, *The Origin and Meaning of the Indian Place Names of Maryland* [Baltimore, 1961], 150). All three were evidently subdivisions of the Conoy tribe, and this was "probably intermediate between the Nanticoke and the Powhatan Indians" (John R. Swanton, *The Indian Tribes of North America*, Smithsonian Institution, Bureau of American Ethnology, Bulletin 145 [Washington, D.C., 1952], 57).

Antimony

woods, fishings, fruits, victuals and other commodities the land afforded, and whether the bay were endlesse, or how farre it extended.
The mine we found 9 or 10 myles up in the country from the river,
but it proved of no value: Some Otters, Beavers, Martins, Luswarts,[2]
and sables we found, and in diverse places that abundance of fish
lying so thicke with their heads above the water, as for want of nets
(our barge driving amongst them) we attempted to catch them with
a frying pan, but we found it a bad instrument to catch fish with.

An abundant
plentie of fish.

Neither better fish more plenty or variety had any of us ever seene,
in any place swimming in the water, then in the bay of Chesapeack,
but they are not to be caught with frying-pans.[3] To expresse al our

[34]

|| quarrels, treacheries and incounters amongst those Salvages, I
should be too tedious; but in briefe at al times we so incountred them

How to deale
with the
Salvages.

and curbed their insolencies, as they concluded with presents to purchase peace, yet wee lost not a man, at our first meeting our captaine
ever observed this order to demaunde their bowes and arrowes
swords mantles or furres, with some childe for hostage, wherby he
could quickly perceive when they intended any villany. Having
finished this discovery (though our victuall was neare spent) he intended to have seene his imprisonment-acquaintances upon the river
of Toppahannock.[4] But our boate (by reason of the ebbe) chansing
to ground upon a many shoules lying in the entrance, we spied many
fishes lurking amongst the weedes on the sands, our captaine sport-
ing himselfe to catch them by nailing them to the ground with his
sword, set us all a fishing in that manner, by this devise, we tooke

A Stingray
very hurtfull.

more in an houre then we all could eat; but it chanced, the captaine
taking a fish from his sword (not knowing her condition) being much
of the fashion of a Thornebacke with a longer taile, whereon is a
most poysoned sting of 2. or 3. inches long, which shee strooke an
inch and halfe into the wrist of his arme the which in 4. houres had
so extreamly swolne his hand, arme, shoulder, and part of his body,
as we al with much sorrow concluded his funerall, and prepared his
grave in an Ile hard by (as himselfe appointed) which then wee
called Stingeray Ile after the name of the fish.[5] Yet by the helpe of a
precious oile Doctour Russell applyed, ere night his tormenting
paine was so wel asswaged that he eate the fish to his supper, which

---

2. Lynx.

3. Note that Jonas Profit, fisher, and Richard Keale, fishmonger, formed part of
Smith's company (p. 29, above).

4. See the *True Relation*, sig. C1r.

5. Cf. the *Map of Va.*, 15, with the spelling "stingraies." Here the word should
probably read "Stingray." Samuel Purchas has a pertinent marginal note on the subject:
"A Stingray very hurtfull, one in Foulenes [presumably Foulness Island, E of Southend]
was so swolne with the sting of a Ray thorow his thicke fishermans-boots, that he therof
died. An. 1613. and was so swolne that they could not bring his coffin out of the dore
but brake the wall (as they told me) for that purpose" (*Pilgrimes*, IV, 1714). For an
expanded version of Smith's accident, see the *Generall Historie*, 59, 63, where Bagnall is
erroneously credited with the cure.

|| gave no lesse joy and content to us, then ease to himselfe. Having **[35]**
neither Surgeon nor surgerie but that preservative oile, we presently
set saile for James Towne; passing the mouth of Pyankatanck, and
Pamaunke rivers, the next day we safely arrived at Kecoughtan. The
simple Salvages, seeing our captaine hurt, and another bloudy   The Salvages
(which came by breaking his shin) our number of bowes, arrowes,   affrighted with
swords, targets, mantles and furs; would needs imagine we had bin   their owne
at warres, (the truth of these accidents would not satisfie them) but suspition.
impaciently they importuned us to know with whom wee fought.
Finding their aptnes to beleeve, we failed not (as a great secret) to
tel them any thing that might affright them, what spoile wee had got
and made of the Masawomeckes. This rumor went faster up the river
then our barge; that arrived at Weraskoyack the 20. of Julie, where
trimming her with painted streamers, and such devises we made the
fort jealous of a Spanish frigot; where we all safely arrived the 21. of
July. There wee found the last supply, al sicke, the rest, some lame,
some bruised, al unable to do any thing, but complain of the pride   A needlesse
and unreasonable needlesse cruelty of their sillie President,[6] that had miserie.
riotously consumed the store, and to fulfill his follies about building
him an unnecessarie pallace in the woods had brought them all to
that miserie; That had not we arrived, they had as strangely tormented him with revenge. But the good newes of our discovery, and
the good hope we had (by the Salvages relation) our Bay had
stretched to the South-sea, appeased their fury; but conditionally
that Ratliffe should be deposed, and that captaine Smith would take
|| upon him the government; their request being effected, hee Sub- **[36]**
stituted Master Scrivener his deare friend in the Presidencie, equally
distributing those private provisions the other had ingrossed; ap-
pointing more honest officers to assist Scrivener, (who then lay
extreamelie tormented with a callenture) and in regard of the   The company
weaknes of the company, and heat of the yeare they being unable to left to live at
worke; he left them to live at ease, but imbarked himselfe to finish ease.
his discovery.

Written by Walter Russell and Anas Todkill.

6. Ratcliffe.

Chapter 6.
What happened the second voyage
to discover the Bay.

THE 20.[7] of July Captaine Smith set forward to finish the discovery with 12. men their names were

Nathaniell Powell.
Thomas Momford.
Richard Fetherstone. } *Gentlemen.*
Michaell Sicklemore.
James Bourne.
Anas Todkill.
Edward Pysing.
Richard Keale. } *Souldiers.*
Anthony Bagnall.[8]
James Watkins.
William Ward.
Jonas Profit.

[37]

The Salvages
admire fire-
workes.

The head of
the Bay.

An incounter
with the Mas-
sawomecks.

The winde beeing contrary caused our stay 2. or 3. ‖ daies at Kecoughtan the werowans feasting us with much mirth, his people were perswaded we went purposely to be revenged of the Massawomeckes. In the evening we firing 2. or 3. rackets, so terrified the poore Salvages, they supposed nothing impossible wee attempted, and desired to assist us. The first night we ancored at Stingeray Ile, the nexte day crossed Patawomecks river, and hasted for the river Bolus, wee went not much farther before wee might perceive the Bay to devide in 2. heads, and arriving there we founde it devided in 4, all which we searched so far as we could saile them; 2. of them wee found uninhabited, but in crossing the bay to the other, wee incountered 7. or 8. Canowes-full of Massawomecks.[9] We seeing them prepare to assault us, left our oares and made way with our saile to incounter them, yet were we but five (with our captaine) could stand; for within 2. daies after wee left Kecoughtan, the rest (being all of the last supply) were sicke almost to death, (untill they were seasoned to the country) having shut them under our tarpawling, we put their hats upon stickes by the barge side to make us seeme many, and so we thinke the Indians supposed those hats to be men, for they fled

7. Read: "The 24 of July" (*Generall Historie*, 59). They did not return to Jamestown until July 21, as stated on p. 35, above.

8. Bagnall was a chirurgeon, or surgeon (*Generall Historie*, 60). "The chirurgeons did strictly 'cutting' and as a result learned their trade by an apprenticeship to an older chirurgeon" (Raach, *Directory of Physicians*, 10–11; and p. 28n, above).

9. Apparently the English learned that the Indians were Massawomekes after they crossed the bay to the Tockwough River (see p. 38, below). This tribe spoke an Iroquoian language.

with all possible speed to the shoare, and there stayed, staring at the sailing of our barge, till we anchored right against them. Long it was ere we could drawe them to come unto us, at last they sent 2 of their company unarmed in a Canowe, the rest all followed to second them if need required; These 2. being but each presented with a bell, brought aborde all their fellowes, presenting the captain with veni-son, beares flesh, fish, bowes, arrows, ‖ clubs, targets, and beare- **[38]** skins; wee understood them nothing at all but by signes, whereby they signified unto us they had been at warres with the Tockwoghs the which they confirmed by shewing their green wounds; but the night parting us, we imagined they appointed the next morning to meete, but after that we never saw them.

Entring the River of Tockwogh the Salvages all armed in a   An incounter fleete of Boates round invironed us; it chanced one of them could   with the Tock-speake the language of Powhatan who perswaded the rest to a   woghs. friendly parly: but when they see us furnished with the Massawo-meckes weapons, and we faining the invention of Kecoughtan to have taken them perforce; they conducted us to their pallizadoed towne, mantelled with the barkes of trees, with Scaffolds like mounts, brested about with Barks very formally,[1] their men, women, and children, with dances, songs, fruits, fish, furres, and what they had kindly entertained us, spreading mats for us to sit on, stretching their best abilities to expresse their loves.

Many hatchets, knives, and peeces of yron, and brasse, we see,   Hatchets from which they reported to have from the Sasquesahanockes[2] a mighty   Sasquesa-people, and mortall enimies with the Massawomeckes; the Sasquesa-   hanock. hanocks, inhabit upon the chiefe spring of these 4.[3] two daies journey higher then our Barge could passe for rocks. Yet we prevailed with the interpreter to take with him an other interpreter to perswade the Sasquesahanocks to come to visit us, for their language are different: 3. or 4. daies we expected their returne then 60. of these giantlike-people came downe with presents of venison, Tobacco ‖ pipes,   **[39]** Baskets, Targets, Bowes and Arrows. 5 of their Werowances came boldly abord us, to crosse the bay for Tockwogh, leaving their men and Canowes, the winde being so violent that they durst not passe.

Our order was, dayly to have prayer, with a psalm, at which

---

1. This early 17th-century military jargon means, "they conducted us to their town, which had a palisade around it covered with barks of trees, with wooden scaffolds like defensive earthworks, those also protected by barks, according to the principles of military science."

2. The "Sasquesahanocks" were also an Iroquoian-speaking people, whose nearest important post was in Lancaster Co., Pennsylvania. Communication must have been uncertain, since Smith needed a Tockwough interpreter who spoke Powhatan and another interpreter to make sense in Tockwough of what the Susquehannas said. On the other hand, Smith had faced a similar problem in the Ottoman Empire (see the *True Travels*, 24n; and Introduction to Fragment J, in Vol. III).

3. They were situated at the head of the chief spring of the four leading into the bay.

solemnitie the poore Salvages much wondered: our prayers being done, they were long busied with consultation till they had contrived their businesse; then they began in most passionate manner to hold up their hands to the sunne[4] with a most fearefull song, then imbrac-

The Sasquesa-hanocks offer to the English.

ing the Captaine, they began to adore him in like manner, though he rebuked them, yet they proceeded til their song was finished, which don with a most strange furious action, and a hellish voice began an oration of their loves; that ended, with a great painted beares skin they covered our Captaine, then one ready with a chaine of white beads (waighing at least 6 or 7 pound) hung it about his necke, the others had 18 mantles made of divers sorts of skinnes sowed together, all these with many other toyes, they laid at his feet, strok-ing their ceremonious handes about his necke for his creation to be their governour, promising their aids, victuals, or what they had to bee his, if he would stay with them to defend and revenge them of the Massawomecks; But wee left them at Tockwogh, they much sorrow-ing for our departure, yet wee promised the next yeare againe to visit them; many descriptions and discourses they made us of At-quanahucke,[5] Massawomecke, and other people, signifying they

Cannida.

[40]

inhabit the river of Cannida, and from the French to have their hatchets, and such like tooles by trade, ‖ these knowe no more of the territories of Powhatan then his name, and he as little of them.

Pawtuxunt River.

Thus having sought all the inlets and rivers worth noting, we returned to discover the river of Pawtuxunt, these people we found very tractable, and more civill then any. Wee promised them, as also the Patawomecks, the next yeare to revenge them of the Massa-womecks. Our purposes were crossed in the discoverie of the river of

Toppahanock River.

Toppahannock, for wee had much wrangling with that peevish nation; but at last they became as tractable as the rest. It is an excel-lent, pleasant, well inhabited, fertill, and a goodly navigable river, toward the head thereof; it pleased God to take one of our sicke

Fetherstone buried.

(called Master Fetherstone) where in Fetherstons bay we buried him in the night with a volly of shot; the rest (notwithstanding their ill diet, and bad lodging, crowded in so small a barge in so many dangers, never resting, but alwaies tossed to and againe) al well

Payankatanke discovered.

recovered their healthes; then we discovered the river of Payanka-tank, and set saile for James Towne; but in crossing the bay in a faire calme, such a suddaine gust surprised us in the night with thunder and raine, as wee were halfe imployed in freeing out water, never

---

4. There are hints of sun worship among the Iroquois, and possibly also the Tock-wough (see the brief mention in John R. Swanton, "Sun Worship in the Southeast," *American Anthropologist*, N.S., XXX [1928], 212–213).

5. According to the Smith/Hole map, the Atquanachukes lived to the NE of the head of Chesapeake Bay. They were shown as living in central to central-eastern New Jersey on Dutch maps, beginning with Adriaen Block's manuscript map of 1614 (see W. P. Cumming, R. A. Skelton, and D. B. Quinn, *The Discovery of North America* [New York, 1972], 264–265).

thinking to escape drowning. Yet running before the winde, at last we made land by the flashes of fire from heaven, by which light only we kept from the splitting shore, until it pleased God in that black darknes to preserve us by that light to find Point Comfort, and arived safe at James Towne, the 7 of September, 1608.[6] where wee found Master Skrivener and diverse others well recovered, many dead, some sicke. The late President prisoner for || muteny, by the honest diligence of Master Skrivener the harvest gathered, but the stores, provision, much spoiled with raine. Thus was that yeare (when nothing wanted) consumed and spent and nothing done; (such was the government of Captain Ratliffe) but only this discoverie, wherein to expresse all the dangers, accidents, and incounters this small number passed in that small barge, with such watrie diet in these great waters and barbarous Countries (til then to any Christian utterly unknowne) I rather referre their merit to the censure[7] of the courteous and experienced reader, then I would be tedious, or partiall, being a partie;

Their proceed-ings at James Towne.

[41]

By Nathaniell Powell, and Anas Todkill.

Chapter 7.
The Presidencie surrendred to Captaine Smith, the arrivall and returne of the second supply: and what happened.

THE 10. of September 1608. by the election of the Councel, and request of the company Captaine Smith received the letters patents, and tooke upon him the place of President, which till then by no meanes he would accept though hee were often importuned thereunto. Now the building of Ratcliffes pallas staide as a thing needlesse; The church was repaired, the storehouse recovered;[8] buildings prepared for the supply we expected. The fort reduced to the forme of this figure,[9] the order of watch renued, the squadrons

QUERE, 8.

6. This is the first mention of (Old) Point Comfort in Smith's works, although it had been named (probably by Gabriel Archer, who had a penchant for such names) on Apr. 28, 1607 (Barbour, *Jamestown Voyages*, I, 135; modern New Point Comfort is about 25 km. [over 15 mi.] to the N, at the mouth of Mobjack Bay). Although there is an interesting study in "Tales of Old Fort Monroe," No. 10 (Fort Monroe Casemate Museum, Fort Monroe, Va., 1962), the fact that Point Comfort was an island in 1607 seems to have been stated only by the Irish sailor Francis Magnel (Barbour, *Jamestown Voyages*, I, 151). It is perhaps worth noting here that in his reprint of the *Proceedings*, Samuel Purchas omitted all the material added to this passage in the *Generall Historie*, 64–65, explaining, "For feare of tediousnesse I have left out the most" (*Pilgrimes*, IV, 1716).

7. Judgment, expressed opinion, estimation.

8. This work had been begun before Nelson arrived, in Apr., but apparently little was done during Smith's 14 weeks of exploration.

9. As mentioned in Barbour, *Jamestown Voyages*, II, 410n, "QUERE, 8" is evidently one of several printer's queries, here not deleted: "Where is the figure?" Purchas noted

[42] (each setting of the watch) trained. The ‖ whole company every Satturday exercised in a fielde prepared for that purpose; the boates trimmed for trade which in their Journey encountred the second supply,[10] that brought them back to discover the country of Monacan. How, or why, Captaine Newport obtained such a private commission as not to returne without a lumpe of gold, a certainty of the south sea or one of the lost company of Sir Walter Rawley I know not,[1] nor why he brought such a 5 pieced barge, not to beare us to that south sea, till we had borne her over the mountaines: which how farre they extend is yet unknowne. As for the coronation of Powhatan[2] and his presents of Bason, Ewer, Bed, Clothes, and such costly

Powhatans scorne when his curtesie was most deserved.

novelties, they had bin much better well spared, then so ill spent. For we had his favour much better, onlie for a poore peece of Copper, till this stately kinde of soliciting made him so much overvalue himselfe, that he respected us as much as nothing at all; as for the hiring of the Poles and Dutch to make pitch and tarre, glasse milles,[3] and sope-ashes, was most necessarie and well. But to send them and seaventy more without victuall to worke, was not so well considered; yet this could not have hurt us, had they bin 200. (though then we were 130 that wanted for our selves.) For we had the Salvages in that Decorum, (their harvest beeing newly gathered) that we feared not

No way but one to over-throwe the busines.

to get victuall sufficient had we bin 500. Now was there no way to make us miserable but to neglect that time to make our provision, whilst it was to be had; the which was done to perfourme this strange discovery, but more strange coronation; to loose that time, spend

[43] that vi-‖ctuall we had, tire and starve our men, having no means to carry victuall, munition, the hurt or sicke, but their owne backs. How or by whom they were invented I know not; But Captaine

---

that "The figure is left out" (*Pilgrimes*, IV, 1717), and the *Generall Historie* makes amends by stating that it was in "a five-square forme" (p. 66). Archaeological evidence can prove nothing, for the undoubted site has been washed into the James River, but it seems to be generally agreed that the fort was triangular, and not pentagonal (see John L. Cotter, *Archeological Excavations at Jamestown*, Virginia National Park Service, Archeological Research Series, No. 4 [Washington, D.C., 1958], 11–17).

10. Alexander Brown estimated that Smith was president for 19 days before Newport arrived with the second supply (*The First Republic in America: An Account of the Origin of This Nation* [Boston, 1898], 69).

1. Here Smith's protests against company policy begin in earnest.

2. Purchas's marginal comments here bear quoting: "Civility is not the way to win Savages, nor magnificence and bounty to reclaime Barbarians. Children are pleased with toyes and awed with rods; and this course of toies and feares hath always best prospered with wilde Indians either to doe them, or to make them good to us or themselves. This vanity of ours made Powhatan overvalue himselfe, his Corne, etc." (*Pilgrimes*, IV, 1717).

3. See J. C. Harrington's illuminating monograph, *Glassmaking at Jamestown: America's First Industry* (Richmond, Va., 1952), and J. Paul Hudson's well-illustrated *Glassmaking at Jamestown: One of the First Industries in America*, Jamestown Foundation (Jamestown, Va., n.d.). See also Barbour, *Jamestown Voyages*, II, 411n, which mentions the production of pitch, tar, and soap ashes as a colonial objective since 1584; only the glassmills were a new idea. For the Poles and Dutch, see p. 53, below.

Newport we only accounted the author, who to effect these projects had so gilded all our hopes, with great promises, that both company and Councel concluded[4] his resolution. I confesse we little understood then our estates, to conclude his conclusion, against al the inconveniences the foreseeing President alleadged. There was added to the councell one Captaine Waldo, and Captaine Winne two ancient souldiers and valiant gentlemen, but ignorant of the busines (being newly arrived). Ratcliffe was also permitted to have his voice, and Master Scrivener desirous to see strange countries, so that although Smith was President, yet the Councell had the authoritie, and ruled it as they listed; as for cleering Smiths objections, how pitch, and tarre, wanscot, clapbord, glasse, and sope ashes, could be provided to relade the ship; or provision got to live withal, when none was in the Country and that which we had, spent before the ships departed; The answer was, Captaine Newport undertook to fraught the Pinnace with corne, in going and returning in his discoverie, and to refraught her againe from Werawocomoco; also promising a great proportion of victuall from his ship, inferring that Smiths propositions were only devises to hinder his journey, to effect it himselfe; and that the crueltie Smith had used to the Salvages, in his absence, might occasion them to hinder his designes;[5] For which, al workes were left; and 120 chosen men were appointed for his guard, ‖ and Smith, to make cleere these seeming suspicions, that the Salvages were not so desperat, as was pretended by Captaine Newport, and how willing he was to further them to effect their projects, (because the coronation would consume much time) undertooke their message to Powhatan, to intreat him to come to James Towne to receive his presents. Accompanied only with Captaine Waldo, Master Andrew Buckler, Edward Brinton, and Samuell Collier; with these 4 hee went over land, against Werawocomoco, there passed the river of Pamaunke in the Salvages Canowes, Powhatan being 30 myles of, who, presently was sent for, in the meane time his women entertained Smith in this manner.

[44]
Captaine Smith with 4 goeth to Powhatan.

    In a faire plaine field they made a fire, before which he sitting uppon a mat; suddainly amongst the woods was heard such a hideous noise and shriking, that they betooke them to their armes, supposing Powhatan with all his power came to surprise them;[6] but the beholders which were many, men, women, and children, satisfied the Captaine there was no such matter, being presently presented with this anticke, 30 young women came naked out of the woods (only

The womens entertainement at Werawocomoco.

4. A rare use of "conclude" in the sense of "decided (in favor of)."
5. Newport was not the type not to retaliate.
6. The *Generall Historie*, 67, inserts here: "But presently [quickly, immediately] Pocahontas came, willing him to kill her if any hurt were intended. . . ." The entertainment, which is described below, was not without parallel in North Carolina years later, when 30-odd women and girls danced for John Lawson (John Lawson, *A New Voyage to Carolina*, ed. Hugh Talmage Lefler [Chapel Hill, N.C., 1967], 44–45).

covered behind and before with a few greene leaves) their bodies al painted, some white, some red, some black, some partie colour, but every one different; their leader had a faire paire of stagges hornes on her head, and an otter skinne at her girdle, another at her arme, a quiver of arrowes at her backe, and bow and arrowes in her hand, the next in her hand a sword, another a club, another a pot-stick, all hornd alike, the rest every one with their severall devises. These **[45]** feindes with most hellish ‖ cries, and shouts rushing from amongst the trees, cast themselves in a ring about the fire, singing, and dauncing with excellent ill varietie, oft falling into their infernall passions, and then solemnely againe to sing, and daunce. Having spent neere an houre, in this maskarado; as they entered; in like manner departed; having reaccommodated themselves, they solemnely invited Smith to their lodging, but no sooner was hee within the house, but all these Nimphes more tormented him then ever, with crowding, and pressing, and hanging upon him, most tediously crying, love you not mee? This salutation ended, the feast was set, consisting of fruit in baskets, fish, and flesh in wooden platters, beans and pease there wanted not (for 20 hogges) nor any Salvage daintie their invention could devise; some attending, others singing and dancing about them; this mirth and banquet being ended, with firebrands (instead of torches) they conducted him to his lodging.

Captain Smiths message.

The next day came Powhatan; Smith delivered his message of the presents sent him, and redelivered him Namontack,[7] desiring him come to his Father Newport to accept those presents, and conclude their revenge against the Monacans, whereunto the subtile Salvage thus replied.

Powhatans answer.

If your king have sent me presents, I also am a king, and this my land, 8 daies I will stay to receave them. Your father is to come to me, not I to him, nor yet to your fort, neither will I bite at such a baite: as for the Monacans, I can revenge my owne injuries, and as for Atquanuchuck, where you say your brother was slain, it is a con- **[46]** trary way from those parts you suppose it.[8] ‖ But for any salt water beyond the mountaines, the relations you have had from my people are false.

Wherupon he began to draw plots upon the ground (according to his discourse) of all those regions; many other discourses they had (yet both desirous to give each other content in Complementall courtesies) and so Captaine Smith returned with this answer.

7. Newport had taken Namontack to England in Apr. (see p. 19, above) and had just brought him back.
8. Smith, misunderstanding what he heard, had thought it was near the head of the Chickahominy River, where he was captured (see p. 39n, above; and the *True Relation*, sig. C2^r).

Upon this Captaine Newport sent his presents by water, which is neare 100 miles;[9] with 50 of the best shot, himselfe went by land which is but 12 miles, where he met with our 3 barges to transport him over. All things being fit for the day of his coronation, the presents were brought, his bason, ewer, bed and furniture set up, his scarlet cloake and apparel (with much adoe) put on him (being perswaded by Namontacke they would doe him no hurt.) But a fowle trouble there was to make him kneele to receave his crowne, he neither knowing the majestie, nor meaning of a Crowne, nor bending of the knee, indured so many perswasions, examples, and instructions, as tired them all. At last by leaning hard on his shoulders, he a little stooped, and Newport put the Crowne on his head. When by the warning of a pistoll, the boates were prepared with such a volly of shot, that the king start[1] up in a horrible feare, till he see all was well, then remembring himselfe, to congratulate[2] their kindnesse, he gave his old shoes and his mantle to Captain Newport. But perceiving his purpose was to discover the Monacans, hee laboured to divert his resolution, refusing to lend him either men, or guids, more then Namontack, and so (after some complementall[3] kindnesse || on both sides) in requitall of his presents, he presented Newport with a heape of wheat eares, that might contain some 7 or 8 bushels, and as much more we bought ready dressed in the towne, wherewith we returned to the fort.

[47]

The ship having disburdened her selfe of 70 persons, with the

Powhatans Coronation.

9. Purchas begins a long marginal notation at this point (*Pilgrimes*, IV, 1718). It is worth reproducing as illustrative of pious thinking in England in 1625:

"So much was done to buy repentance with more cost then worship. If we seeke Savages we loose them, if wee force them to seeke us, wee shal finde these shadowes of men close at our feet. I have read more stories of them then perhaps any man, and finde that a cruell mercy in awing Savages to feare us is better then that mercifull cruelty, which by too much kindenes hath made us feare them, or else by too much confidence to loose our selves. [This was written after the massacre. *Ed.*] Smith and Newport may by their examples teach the just course to be taken with such: the one breeding awe and dread, without Spanish or Panike terror, the other disgraced in seeking to grace with offices of humanity, those which are gracelesse. Neither doth it become us to use Savages with savagenesse, nor yet with too humaine usage, but in a middle path (medio tutissimus ibis) to goe and doe so that they may admire and feare us, as those whom God, Religion, Civility, and Art, have made so farre superior; yet to abuse them (unprovoked) as hostile slaves, or as meere beasts, with cruell and beastly severity, whom nature hath equally made men. This breedes desperate depopulations, as in the Spanish Indies hath been seene; that gentlenesse and unequall equity makes them proud and treacherous, as wofull experience hath taught in the late massacre. Our temperance and justice should be qualified with prudence and fortitude. Neither must wee make them beasts, nor yet value them as Christians, till we have made them such; and the way to make them Christian men, is first to make them civill men, to file off the rust of their humanity, which as children (the like in taming wilde Beasts) must be done with severe gentlenesse, and gentle severity, which may breede in them a loving awe, or awfull love, at least a just dread toward us, that feare may make them know us, and then the fault is ours if they see no cause to love us."

1. "Start" is a strong past tense that survived in English well into the 1600s.
2. "To express his pleasure at. . . ."
3. Additional and ceremonial.

first gentlewoman, and woman servant that arrived in our Colony; Captaine Newport with al the Councell, and 120 chosen men, set forward for the discovery of Monacan, leaving the President at the fort with 80. (such as they were) to relade the shippe. Arriving at the falles, we⁴ marched by land some forty myles in 2 daies and a halfe, and so returned downe the same path we went. Two townes wee discovered of the Monacans, the people neither using us well nor ill, yet for our securitie wee tooke one of their pettie Werowances, and lead him bound, to conduct us the way. And in our returne searched many places wee supposed mynes, about which we spent some time in refining, having one William Callicut a refiner, fitted for that purpose. From that crust of earth wee digged hee perswaded us to beleeve he extracted some smal quantitie of silver (and not unlikely better stuffe might bee had for the digging) with this poore trial being contented to leave this faire, fertill, well watred countrie. Comming to the Falles, the Salvages fained there were diverse ships come into the Bay to kill them at James Towne. Trade they would not, and find their corn we could not, for they had hid it in the woods, and being thus deluded we arrived at James Towne, halfe sicke, all complaining, and tired with toile, famine, and dis- ‖ content, to have only but discovered our gilded hopes, and such fruitlesse certaineties, as the President foretold us.

[48]

No sooner were we landed, but the President dispersed many as were able, some for glasse, others for pitch, tarre and sope ashes, leaving them, (with the fort) to the Councels oversight. But 30 of us he conducted 5. myles from the fort to learn to make clapbord, cut downe trees, and ly in woods; amongst the rest he had chosen Gabriell Beadell, and John Russell the only two gallants of this last supply, and both proper gentlemen: strange were these pleasures to their conditions, yet lodging eating, drinking, working, or playing they doing but as the President, all these things were carried so pleasantly, as within a weeke they became Masters, making it their delight to heare the trees thunder as they fell, but the axes so oft blistered there tender fingers, that commonly every third blow had a lowd oath to drowne the eccho; for remedy of which sin the President devised howe to have everie mans oathes numbred, and at night, for every oath to have a can of water powred downe his sleeve, with which every offender was so washed (himselfe and all) that a man should scarse heare an oath in a weeke.

By this, let no man think that the President, or these gentlemen spent their times as common wood-hackers at felling of trees, or such like other labours, or that they were pressed to any thing as hirelings or common slaves, for what they did (being but once a little inured)

---

4. Obviously not written by Smith. Chaps. 7–9 are signed by Richard Wiffin, William Phettiplace, and Anas Todkill, so that it is impossible to know which of the three (if any) wrote this account.

it seemed, and they conceited it only as a pleasure and a recreation.[5]
Yet 30 or 40 of such voluntary || Gentlemen would doe more in a day
then 100 of the rest that must bee prest to it by compulsion. Master
Scrivener, Captaine Waldo, and Captaine Winne at the fort, every
one in like manner carefully regarded their charge. The President
returning from amongst the woodes, seeing the time consumed, and
no provision gotten, (and the ship lay Idle, and would do nothing)
presently imbarked himselfe in the discovery barge, giving order to
the Councell, to send Master Persey after him with the next barge
that arrived at the fort; 2. barges, he had himselfe, and 20. men, but
arriving at Chickahamina, that dogged nation was too wel acquainted with our wants, refusing to trade, with as much scorne and
insolencie as they could expresse. The President perceiving it was
Powhatans policy to starve us, told them he came not so much for
their corne, as to revenge his imprisonment,[6] and the death of his
men murdered by them, and so landing his men, and ready to charge
them, they immediatly fled; but then they sent their imbassadours,
with corne, fish, fowl, or what they had to make their peace, (their
corne being that year bad) they complained extreamly of their owne
wants, yet fraughted our boats with 100 bushels of corne, and in like
manner Master Persies, that not long after us arrived; they having
done the best they could to content us, within 4. or 5. daies we
returned to James Towne.

Though this much contented the company (that then feared
nothing but starving) yet some so envied his good successe, that they
rather desired to starve, then his paines should prove so much more
effectuall then || theirs; some projects there was, not only to have
deposed him but to have kept him out of the fort, for that being
President, he would leave his place, and the fort without their con-
sents; but their hornes were so much too short to effect it,[7] as they
themselves more narrowly escaped a greater mischiefe.

All this time our old taverne made as much of all them that had
either mony or ware as could bee desired; and by this time they were
become so perfect on all sides (I meane Souldiers, Sailers, and Salvages,) as there was ten-times more care to maintaine their damnable
and private trade, then to provide for the Colony things that were
necessary. Neither was it a small pollicy in the mariners, to report in
England wee had such plenty and bring us so many men without
victuall, when they had so many private factors in the fort, that

Margin notes:

[49]
One gentle-
man better
then 20
lubbers.

The Chickaha-
mines forced to
contribution.

A bad reward
for well doing.
[50]

A good taverne
in Virginia.

---

5. An interesting sidelight on the English gentleman of the day. Smith could only
succeed in getting the gentlemen to work by diversionary tactics of this sort.

6. Smith seems to have understood that Powhatan was at the root of the Chickahominy embargo on trade with the English. For the Indians, as well as for the English,
revenge was "a sort of wild justice" (Francis Bacon, "Of Revenge," in *The Essays, or
Counsels, civil and moral* . . .). They would understand it.

7. Read: "their horns were much too short to effect it"; that is, the grumbling
minority was too weak. See p. 21, above, for a similar reference.

within 6. or 7. weekes after the ships returne,[8] of 2. or 300. hatchets, chissels, mattocks, and pickaxes scarce 20 could be found, and for

A bad trade of
masters and
sailers.

pike-heads, knives, shot, powder, or any thing (they could steale from their fellowes) was vendible; They knew as well (and as secretly) how to convay them to trade with the Salvages, for furres, baskets, mussaneekes,[9] young beastes or such like commodities, as exchange them with the sailers, for butter, cheese, biefe, porke, aquavitæ, beere, bisket, and oatmeale; and then faine, all was sent them from their friends. And though Virginia afford[10] no furs for the store, yet one mariner in one voyage hath got so many, as hee hath confessed to have solde in England for 30l.

[51]   Those are the Saint-seeming worthies of Virginia, ‖ that have notwithstanding all this, meate, drinke, and pay, but now they begin to grow weary, their trade being both perceived and prevented; none hath bin in Virginia (that hath observed any thing) which knowes not this to be true, and yet the scorne, and shame was the poore souldiers, gentlemen and carelesse governours, who were all thus bought and solde, the adventurers cousened, and the action overthrowne by their false excuses, informations, and directions, by this let all the world Judge, how this businesse coulde prosper, being thus abused by such pilfering occasions.

The proceedings and accidents,
with the second supply.

Skriveners
voiage to
Werawoco-
moco.

Master Scrivener was sent with the barges and Pinas to Werawocomoco, where he found the Salvages more ready to fight then trade, but his vigilancy was such, as prevented their projectes, and by the meanes of Namontack got 3. or 4. hogshead of corne, and as much Red paint which (then) was esteemed an excellent die.

Captaine Newport being dispatched with the tryals of pitch, tarre, glasse, frankincense, and sope ashes, with that clapbord and wainscot could bee provided met with Master Scrivener at point Comfort, and so returned for England, leaving us in all 200. with those hee brought us.[1]

The names of those in this supply are these.

Captaine Peter Winne.   } *were appointed to bee*
Captaine Richard Waldo. } *of the Councell.*

8. I.e., return to Virginia.
9. Possibly gray squirrels, which looked very different from the English red variety (see Barbour, "Earliest Reconnaissance," Pt. II, 38).
10. The *Generall Historie*, 70, has "afforded."
1. Smith's letter to the treasurer, sent to London with Newport but omitted here, appears in the *Generall Historie*, 70–72. Both the letter and the list of names that follows were omitted by Purchas (*Pilgrimes*, IV, 1719–1720).

|| Master Francis West.   **[52]**
Thomas Graves.
Rawley Chroshaw.
Gabriell Bedle.
John Russell.
John Bedle.
William Russell.
John Gudderington.
William Sambage.
Henry Collings.
Henry Ley.
Harmon Haryson.
Daniell Tucker.
Hugh Wollystone.   } *Gentlemen.*
John Hoult.
Thomas Norton.
George Yarington.
George Burton.
Henry Philpot.
Thomas Maxes.
Michaell Lowicke.
Master Hunt.[2]
Thomas Forest.
William Dowman.
John Dauxe.
Thomas Abbay.

Thomas Phelps.
John Prat.
John Clarke.
Jefry Shortridge.
|| Dionis Oconor.   **[53]**
Hugh Wynne.
David ap Hugh.
Thomas Bradley.   } *Tradesmen.*
John Burras.
Thomas Lavander.
Henry Bell.
Master Powell.[3]
David Ellys.
Thomas Gipson.

2. The identity of Master Hunt is uncertain. He may have been the Thomas Hunt who was listed as an adventurer in the 1609 charter.
3. This appears to have been the artisan Henry Powell, listed on p. 56, below.

Thomas Dowse.	
Thomas Mallard.	
William Taler.	
Thomas Fox.	
Nicholas Hancock.	
Walker.	*Laborers.*
Williams.	
Morrell.	
Rose.	
Scot.	
Hardwin.	
Milman.	
Hellyard.	*Boyes.*

Mistresse Forest and Anne Buras her maide, 8. Dutchmen, and Poles[4] with divers to the number of 70. persons.

<table>
<tr><td>Nansamund
forced to con-
tribution.</td><td>Those poore conclusions so affrighted us all with famine; that the President provided for Nansamund, tooke with him Captaine Winne and Master Scrivener (then returning from Captaine New-</td></tr>
</table>

[54] port). These people also ‖ long denied him trade, (excusing themselves to bee so commanded by Powhatan) til we were constrained to begin with them perforce, and then they would rather sell us some, then wee should take all; so loading our boats, with 100. bushels we parted friends, and came to James Towne, at which time, there was a marriage betweene John Laydon and Anna Burrowes, being the first marriage we had in Virginia.

Long he staied not, but fitting himselfe and captaine Waldo with 2. barges, from Chawopo, Weanocke and all parts there, was found neither corne nor Salvage, but all fled (being Jealous of our

Appamatucke
discovered.

intents) till we discovered the river and people of Appametuck, where we founde little that they had, we equally devided, betwixt the Salvages and us (but gave them copper in consideration). Master Persie and Master Scrivener went also abroad but could finde nothing.

The President seeing this procrastinating of time, was no course to live, resolved with Captaine Waldo, (whom he knew to be sure in time of need) to surprise Powhatan, and al his provision, but the unwillingnes of Captaine Winne, and Master Scrivener (for some private respects) did their best to hinder their project: But the President whom no perswasions could perswade to starve, being invited by Powhatan to come unto him, and if he would send him but men to build him a house, bring him a grinstone, 50. swords, some peeces, a cock and a hen, with copper and beads, he would loade his shippe with corne. The President not ignoraunt of his devises, yet unwilling

4. Regarding the Poles, see p. 81, below.

to neglect any opportunity, presently sent 3. Dutch-men and 2. English (having no vi- ‖ ctuals to imploy them, all for want therof **[55]** being idle) knowing there needed no better castel,[5] then that house to surprize Powhatan, to effect this project he took order with Captaine Waldo to second him if need required; Scrivener he left his substitute; and set forth with the Pinnas 2. barges and six and forty men which only were such as voluntarily offered themselves for his journy, the which (by reason of Master Scriveners ill successe) was censured very desperate, they all knowing Smith would not returne empty howsoever, caused many of those that he had appointed, to finde excuses to stay behinde.

Chapter 8.
Captaine Smiths journey to Pamaunke.

THE 29 of December hee set forward for Werawocomoco, his company were these.

In the Discovery barge, himselfe.

Robert Behethland.
Nathaniell Powell.[6]
John Russell.
Rawly Crashaw. } *Gentlemen.*
Michaell Sicklemore.
Richard Worlie.
Anas Todkill.
William Love.
William Bentley. } *Souldiers.*
Geoffery Shortridge.
Edward Pising.
William Warde.

In the Pinnace. **[56]**

Master George Persie, *brother to the Earle of Northumberland,*
Master Frauncis West, *brother to the Lord De-la-Ware.*
William Phetiplace *Captaine of the Pinnas.*
Jonas Profit *Master.*
Robert Ford *clarcke of the councell.*

---

5. Here in the sense of "visionary project or scheme."
6. The *Generall Historie*, 74, curiously, has "Nathanael Graves" by mistake; Powell is confirmed below (p. 66).

Michaell Phetiplace.
Geoffery Abbot *Sergeant.*
William Tankard.
George Yarington.   } *Gentlemen.*
James Bourne.[7]
George Burton.
Thomas Coe.
John Dods.
Edward Brinton.
Nathaniel Peacocke.
Henry Powell.
David Ellis.
Thomas Gipson.
John Prat.
George Acrigge.   } *Souldiers.*
James Reade.
Nicholas Hancocke.
James Watkins.
Anthony Baggly *Serg.*[8]
Thomas Lambert.
Edward Pising *Sergeant.*[9]

4. Dutchmen and Richard Salvage were sent by land, to build the house for Powhatan against our arrivall.

[57]   This company being victualled but for 3. or 4. daies || lodged the first night at Weraskoyack, where the President tooke sufficient provision. This kind Salvage did his best to divert him from seeing Powhatan, but perceiving he could not prevaile, he advised in this maner.

The good
counsell of
Weraskoyack.

Captaine Smith, you shall finde Powhatan to use you kindly, but trust him not, and bee sure hee hath no opportunitie to seaze on your armes, for hee hath sent for you only to cut your throats.

The Captaine thanked him for his good counsell, yet the better to try his love, desired guides to Chowanoke, for he would send a present to that king to bind him his friend. To performe this journey, was sent Michael Sicklemore, a very honest, valiant, and painefull souldier, with him two guids, and directions howe to search for the lost company of Sir Walter Rawley, and silke grasse:[1] then wee de-

7. Bourne is erroneously listed as Browne in the *Generall Historie*, 74.
8. Anthony Baggly, Serg[eant], is an error for Anthony Bagnall, Surgeon, as shown in various references.
9. Edward Pising was in the barge (see p. 55, above).
1. Thomas Harriot and others had discovered fibrous plants on the small islands around Roanoke Island, North Carolina, before or about Sept. 1585. These were said to yield "silk grass"—a potentially valuable commodity. See David Beers Quinn, ed.,

parted thence, the President assuring the king his perpetuall love, and left with him Samuell Collier his page to learne the language.

The next night being lodged at Kecoughtan 6 or 7 daies, the extreame wind, raine, frost, and snowe, caused us to keepe Christmas[2] amongst the Salvages, where wee were never more merrie, nor fedde on more plentie of good oysters, fish, flesh, wild foule, and good bread, nor never had better fires in England then in the drie warme smokie houses of Kecoughtan. But departing thence, when we found no houses, we were not curious[3] in any weather, to lie 3 or 4 nights together upon any shore under the trees by a good fire. 148 fowles the President, Anthony Bagly,[4] and Edward Pising, did kill at 3 shoots. At Kiskiack the frost forced us 3 or 4 daies also to suppresse the insolencie of those || proud Salvages; to quarter in their houses, and guard our barge, and cause them give us what wee wanted, yet were we but 12 with the President, and yet we never wanted harbour where we found any houses. The 12 of Januarie[5] we arrived at Werawocomoco, where the river was frozen neare halfe a mile from the shore; but to neglect no time, the President with his barge, so farre had approached by breaking the Ice as the eb left him amongst those oozie shoules, yet rather then to lie there frozen to death, by his owne example hee taught them to march middle deepe, more then a flight shot through this muddie frore[6] ooze; when the barge floted he appointed 2 or 3 to returne her abord the Pinnace, where for want of water in melting the salt Ice[7] they made fresh water, but in this march Master Russell (whome none could perswade to stay behind) being somewhat ill, and exceeding heavie, so overtoiled him selfe, as the rest had much adoe (ere he got a shore) to regaine life, into his dead benummed spirits. Quartering in the next[8] houses we found, we sent to Powhatan for provision, who sent us plentie of bread, Turkies, and Venison. The next day[9] having feasted us after his ordinarie manner, he began to aske, when we would bee gon, faining hee sent not for us, neither had hee any corne, and his people much lesse, yet for 40 swords he would procure us 40 bushels. The

Plentie of victuall.

148 Fowles killed at 3 shoots.

[58]

An ill march.

The Roanoke Voyages, 1584–1590 (Hakluyt Society, 2d Ser., CIV–CV [London, 1955]), I, 325n, for suggestions as to the plants concerned. The Indians are known to have used ramie fiber from stingless nettles and fibers from milkweed and yucca for making textiles (see A. C. Whitford, "Textile Fibers Used in Eastern Aboriginal North America," *Anthropological Papers of the American Museum of Natural History*, XXXVIII, Pt. I [New York, 1941], 9–13).

2. The Christmas season lasted until Twelfth Night. Six or seven days beginning Dec. 30 would include most of the period.

3. Eager.

4. Again an error for Bagnall; see p. 56n, above.

5. 1609.

6. Intensely cold, frozen.

7. The *Generall Historie*, 75, clarifies this: "in melting the ice, they made fresh water, for the river there was salt."

8. Nearest.

9. Jan. 13, 1609; Smith seldom supplies dates.

President shewing him the men there present, that brought him the message and conditions, asked him how it chaunced he became so forgetful, thereat the king concluded the matter with a merry laughter, asking for our commodities, but none he liked without gunnes and swords, || valuing a basket of corne more pretious then a basket of copper, saying he could eate his corne, but not his copper.

Powhatans subteltie.

[59]

Captaine Smithes discourse to Powhatan.

Captaine Smith seeing the intent of this subtil Salvage began to deale with him after this manner,

Powhatan, though I had many courses to have made my provision, yet beleeving your promises to supply my wants, I neglected all, to satisfie your desire, and to testifie my love, I sent you my men for your building, neglecting my owne: what your people had you have engrossed, forbidding them our trade, and nowe you thinke by consuming the time, wee shall consume for want, not having to fulfill your strange demandes. As for swords, and gunnes, I told you long agoe, I had none to spare. And you shall knowe, those I have, can keepe me from want, yet steale, or wrong you I will not, nor dissolve that friendship, wee have mutually promised, except you constraine mee by your bad usage.

Powhatans reply and flattery.

The king having attentively listned to this discourse; promised, that both hee and his Country would spare him what they could, the which within 2 daies, they should receave.

Yet Captaine Smith, (saith the king) some doubt I have of your comming hither, that makes me not so kindly seeke to relieve you as I would; for many do informe me, your comming is not for trade, but to invade my people and possesse my Country, who dare not come to bring you corne, seeing you thus armed with your men. To cleere us of this feare, leave abord your weapons, for here they are needlesse we being all friends and for ever Powhatans.

[60]

With many such discourses they spent the day, quartring that night in the kings houses. The next day he reviewed[1] his building, which hee little intended should proceed; for the Dutchmen finding his plenty, and knowing our want, and perceived[2] his preparation to surprise us, little thinking wee could escape both him and famine, (to obtaine his favour) revealed to him as much as they knew of our estates and projects, and how to prevent them; one of them being of so good a judgement, spirit, and resolution, and a hireling that was certaine of wages for his labour, and ever well used, both he and his countrimen, that the President knewe not whome better to trust, and

1. The *Generall Historie*, 75, has "renewed."
2. *Ibid.*, "perceiving."

not knowing any fitter for that imploiment, had sent him as a spie to discover Powhatans intent, then little doubting his honestie, nor could ever be certaine of his villany, till neare halfe a yeare after.

Whilst we expected the comming in of the countrie, we wrangled out of the king 10 quarters of corne for a copper kettle, the which the President perceived him much to affect, valued it at a much greater rate, but (in regard of his scarcety) hee would accept of[3] as much more the next yeare, or else the country of Monacan, the king exceeding liberall of that hee had not yeelded him Monacan. Wherewith each seeming well contented; Powhatan began to expostulate the difference betwixt peace and war, after this manner.

Captaine Smith you may understand, that I, having seene the death of all my people thrice,[4] and not one living of those 3 generations, but my selfe, I knowe the difference of peace and warre, better then any in my || Countrie. But now I am old, and ere long must die, my brethren, namely Opichapam, Opechankanough, and Kekataugh, my two sisters, and their two daughters, are distinctly each others successours, I wish their experiences no lesse then mine, and your love to them, no lesse then mine to you; but this brute from Nansamund[5] that you are come to destroy my Countrie, so much affrighteth all my people, as they dare not visit you; what will it availe you, to take that perforce, you may quietly have with love, or to destroy them that provide you food? what can you get by war, when we can hide our provision and flie to the woodes, whereby you must famish by wronging us your friends; and whie are you thus jealous of our loves, seeing us unarmed, and both doe, and are willing still to feed you with that you cannot get but by our labours? think you I am so simple not to knowe, it is better to eate good meate, lie well, and sleepe quietly with my women and children, laugh and be merrie with you, have copper, hatchets, or what I want, being your friend; then bee forced to flie from al, to lie cold in the woods, feed upon acorns, roots, and such trash, and be so hunted by you, that I can neither rest, eat, nor sleepe; but my tired men must watch, and if a twig but breake, everie one crie there comes Captaine Smith, then must I flie I knowe not whether, and thus with miserable feare end my miserable life; leaving my pleasures to such youths as you, which through your rash unadvisednesse, may quickly as miserably

Powhatans discourse of peace and warre.

[61]

---

3. *Ibid.*, "he would accept it, provided we should have as much more the next yeare. . . ."

4. Powhatan is apparently referring to drastic reverses or epidemics in his lifetime of which we have now little or no record.

5. The bruit, or rumor, from Nansemond "that from the *Chesapeack* Bay a Nation should arise, which should dissolve and give end to his Empier" was confirmed by William Strachey (*The Historie of Travell into Virginia Britania*, ed. Louis B. Wright and Virginia Freund [Hakluyt Soc., 2d Ser., CIII (London, 1953)], 104).

[62]

ende, for want of that you never knowe how to find? Let this therefore assure you of our loves and everie yeare our friendly trade shall furnish you ‖ with corne, and now also if you would come in friendly manner to see us, and not thus with your gunnes and swords, as to invade your foes.

To this subtil discourse the President thus replied.

Captaine
Smiths reply.

Seeing you will not rightly conceave of our words, wee strive to make you knowe our thoughts by our deeds. The vow I made you of my love, both my selfe and my men have kept. As for your promise I finde it everie daie violated, by some of your subjects, yet wee finding your love and kindnesse (our custome is so far from being ungratefull) that for your sake only, wee have curbed our thirsting desire of revenge, else had they knowne as wel the crueltie we use to our enimies as our true love and curtesie to our friendes. And I thinke your judgement sufficient to conceive as well by the adventures we have undertaken, as by the advantage we have by our armes of yours: that had wee intended you anie hurt, long ere this wee coulde have effected it; your people comming to me at James towne, are entertained with their bowes and arrowes without exception; we esteeming it with you, as it is with us, to weare our armes as our apparell. As for the dangers of our enimies, in such warres consist our chiefest pleasure, for your riches we have no use, as for the hiding your provision, or by your flying to the woods, we shall so unadvisedly starve as you conclude,[6] your friendly care in that behalfe is needlesse; for we have a rule to finde beyond your knowledge.

[63]

Manie other discourses they had, til at last they began to trade, but the king seing his will would not bee admitted as a lawe, our gard dispersed, nor our men ‖ disarmed, he (sighing) breathed his mind, once more in this manner.

Powhatans
importunitie
for to have
them unarmed,
to betray them.

Captaine Smith, I never used anie of[7] Werowances, so kindlie as your selfe; yet from you I receave the least kindnesse of anie. Captaine Newport gave me swords, copper, cloths, a bed, tooles, or what I desired, ever taking what I offered him, and would send awaie his gunnes when I intreated him: none doth denie to laie at my feet (or do) what I desire, but onelie you, of whom I can have nothing, but what you regard not, and yet you wil have whatsoever you demand. Captain Newport you call father, and so you call me, but I see for all

6. Read: "we shall *not* so unadvisedly starve. . . ." Smith was retorting to Powhatan's insinuation that the English "never knowe how to find" sustenance (p. 61), with his own insinuation that he had some tricks up his sleeve, too.
7. Both the *Generall Historie* and Purchas's *Pilgrimes* omit "of"; perhaps the original had "of my" or "of the."

us both, you will doe what you list, and wee must both seeke to content you: but if you intend so friendlie as you saie, sende hence your armes that I may beleeve you, for you see the love I beare you, doth cause mee thus nakedlie forget my selfe.

Smith seeing this Salvage but trifled the time to cut his throat: procured the Salvages to breake the ice, (that his boat might come to fetch both him and his corne) and gave order for his men to come ashore, to have surprised[8] the king, with whom also he but trifled the time till his men landed, and to keepe him from suspition, entertained the time with this reply.

Powhatan, you must knowe as I have but one God, I honour but one king; and I live not here as your subject, but as your friend, to pleasure you with what I can: by the gifts you bestowe on me, you gaine more then by trade; yet would you visite mee as I doe you, you should knowe it is not our customes to sell our curtesie as a vendible commoditie. Bring all your Country ‖ with you for your gard, I will not dislike of it as being over jealous. But to content you, to morrow I will leave my armes, and trust to your promise. I call you father indeed, and as a father you shall see I will love you, but the smal care you had of such a child, caused my men perswade me to shift for my selfe.

By this time Powhatan having knowledge, his men were readie: whilst the ice was breaking, his luggage[9] women, and children fledde, and to avoid suspition, left 2 or 3 of his women talking with the Captaine, whilst he secretly fled, and his men as secretlie beset the house, which being at the instant discovered to Captaine Smith, with his Pistol, Sword and Target, he made such a passage amongst those naked divels, that they fled before him some one waie some another, so that without hurt he obtained the Corps du-guard; when they perceived him so well escaped, and with his 8 men (for he had no more with him), to the uttermost of their skill, they sought by excuses to dissemble the matter, and Powhatan to excuse his flight, and the suddaine comming of this multitude, sent our Captaine a greate bracelet, and a chaine of pearle, by an ancient Orator that bespoke us to this purpose, (perceiving them from our Pinnace, a barge and men departing and comming unto us.)

Captaine Smith, our Werowans is fled, fearing your guns, and knowing when the ice was broken there would come more men, sent those of his to guard his corne from the pilfric,[1] that might happen without

Captaine Smiths discourse to delay time, that hee might surprise Powhatan.

[64]

Powhatans plot to have murdered Smith.

A chain of perle for a present.

His excuse.

8. The *Generall Historie*, 76, has "to surprise."
9. *Ibid.*, 77, "with his luggage."
1. "Pilfering"; obsolete. Above, read: "knowing *that* when the ice was broken. . . ."

your knowledge: now though some bee hurt by your misprision, yet
he is your friend, and so wil continue: and since the ice is open hee
[65] would have you send a- ‖ waie your corne; and if you would have his
companie send also your armes, which so affrighteth his people, that
they dare not come to you, as he hath promised they should.

Nowe having provided baskets for our men to carrie the corne, they
kindlie offered their service to gard our armes, that none should

Pretending to kill our men loded with baskets we forced the Salvages carrie them.

steale them. A great manie they were, of goodlie well appointed fellowes as grim as divels; yet the verie sight of cocking our matches
against them, and a few words, caused them to leave their bowes and
arrowes to our gard, and beare downe our corne on their own backes;
wee needed not importune them to make quick dispatch. But our
own barge being left by the ebb, caused us to staie, till the midnight
tide carried us safe abord, having spent that halfe night with such
mirth, as though we never had suspected or intended any thing, we
left the Dutchmen to build, Brinton to kil fowle for Powhatan (as by
his messengers he importunately desired) and left directions with our
men to give Powhatan all the content they could, that we might
injoy his company at our returne from Pamaunke.

Chapter 9.
How we escaped surprising at Pamaunke.

The dutchmen deceave Cap- taine Smith.

[66]

WEE had no sooner set saile, but Powhatan returned, and sent
Adam and Francis (2. stout Dutch men) to the fort, who faining to Captaine Winne that al things were well, and that Captaine
Smith had use for their armes, wherefore they requested newe ‖ (the
which were given them) they told him their comming was for some
extraordinary tooles and shift of apparell; by this colourable excuse,
they obtained 6. or 7. more to their confederacie, such expert theefes,
that presently furnished them with a great many swords, pike-heads,
peeces, shot, powder and such like. They had Salvages at hand ready
to carry it away, the next[2] day they returned unsuspected, leaving
their confederates to follow, and in the interim, to convay them a
competencie of all things they could, for which service they should
live with Powhatan as his chiefe affected: free from those miseries
that would happen the Colony. Samuell their other consort, Powhatan kept for their pledge, whose diligence had provided them, 300.
of their kinde of hatchets, the rest, 50. swords, 8. peeces, and 8. pikes
Brinton, and Richard Salvage seeing the Dutch-men so strangly diligent to accommodate the Salvages these weapons[3] attempted to have

2. The *Generall Historie*, 78, has "and the next. . . ."
3. *Ibid.*, "with weapons. . . ." Below, the "king" at "Pamaunke" was Opechanca
nough.

got to James Towne, but they were apprehended; within 2. or 3. daies we arrived at Pamaunke: the king as many daies, entertained us with feasting and much mirth: and the day he appointed to begin our trade, the President, with Master Persie, Master West, Master Russell, Master Beheathland, Master Powell, Master Crashaw, Master Ford, and some others to the number of 15. went up to Opechancanougs house (near a quarter of a mile from the river,) where we founde nothing, but a lame fellow and a boy, and all the houses about, of all things abandoned; not long we staide ere the king arrived, and after him came divers of his people loaded with bowes and arrowes, but such pinching commodities, and those esteemed at such a va- ‖ lue, as our Captaine beganne with him in this manner.

Opechanca-
noughs
abandoned.

[67]

Opechancanough the great love you professe with your tongue, seemes meere deceipt by your actions; last yeare you kindly fraughted our ship, but now you have invited me to starve with hunger. You know my want, and I your plenty, of which by some meanes I must have part, remember it is fit for kings to keepe their promise. Here are my commodities, wherof take your choice; the rest I will pro-portion, fit bargaines for your people.

Smiths speech
to Opechanca-
nough.

The king seemed kindly to accept his offer; and the better to colour his project, sold us what they had to our own content; promising the next day, more company, better provided; (the barges, and Pinnas being committed to the charge of Master Phetiplace) the President with his old 15 marched up to the kings house, where we found 4 or 5 men newly come with great baskets, not long after came the king, who with a strained cheerefulnes held us with discourse, what paines he had taken to keepe his promise; til Master Russell brought us in news that we were all betraied: for at least 6. or 700. of well appointed Indians had invironed the house and beset the fields. The king conjecturing what Russell related, we could wel perceive how the extremity of his feare bewrayed his intent: whereat some of our companie seeming dismaide with the thought of such a multitude; the Captaine incouraged us after this manner.

700 Salvages
beset the
English being
but 16.

Worthy countrymen were the mischiefes of my seeming friends, no more then the danger of these enemies, I little cared, were they as many more, if you ‖ dare do, but as I. But this is my torment, that if I escape them, our malicious councell with their open mouthed minions, will make mee such a peace-breaker (in their opinions) in England, as wil break my neck; I could wish those here, that make these seeme Saints, and me an oppressor. But this is the worst of all, wherin I pray aide me with your opinions; should wee begin with them and surprize this king, we cannot keep him and defend well our selves. If we should each kill our man and so proceede with al in this

Smiths speech
to his company.

[68]

nouse; the rest will all fly, then shall we get no more, then the bodies
that are slaine, and then starve for victuall: as for their fury it is the
least danger; for well you know, (being alone assaulted with 2 or 300
of them) I made them compound to save my life, and we are now
16 and they but 700. at the most, and assure your selves God wil so
assist us, that if you dare but to stande to discharge your peeces, the
very smoake will bee sufficient to affright them; yet howsoever (if
there be occasion) let us fight like men, and not die like sheep; but
first I will deale with them, to bring it to passe, we may fight for some
thing and draw them to it by conditions. If you like this motion,
promise me youle[4] be valiant.

The time not permitting any argument, all vowed to execute whatsoever he attempted, or die; whereupon the captaine, approaching
the king bespoke him in this manner.

Smiths offer
to Opechanca-
nough.

[69]

    I see Opechancanough your plot to murder me, but I feare it
not, as yet your men and mine, have done no harme, but by our
directions. Take therefore your arms; you see mine; my body shalbe
as naked as yours; ‖ the Ile in your river is a fit place, if you be contented: and the conqueror (of us two) shalbe Lord and Master over
all our men; otherwaies drawe all your men into the field; if you
have not enough take time to fetch more, and bring what number
you will, so everie one bring a basket of corne, against all which I
will stake the value in copper; you see I have but 15 men, and our
game shalbe the conquerer take all.

Opechanca-
noughs devise
to betray
Smith.

    The king, being guarded with 50 or 60 of his chiefe men, seemed
kindly to appease Smiths suspition of unkindnesse, by a great present
at the dore, they intreated him to receive. This was to draw him
without the dore where the present was garded with at the least 200
men and 30 lying under a greate tree (that lay thwart as a Barricado)
each his arrow nocked ready to shoot; some the President commanded to go and see what kinde of deceit this was, and to receive
the present, but they refused to do it, yet divers offered whom he
would not permit; but commanding Master Persie and Master West
to make good the house, tooke Master Powell and Master Beheathland to guard the dore, and in such a rage snatched the king by his
vambrace[5] in the midst of his men, with his pistoll ready bent against
his brest: thus he led the trembling king, (neare dead with feare)
amongst all his people,[6] who delivering the Captaine his bow and

    4. An obsolete form of "you'll."
    5. Forearm armor; see the *Generall Historie*, 79.
    6. Here again Purchas unburdens himself in an interesting marginal note (*Pil-
grimes*, IV, 1724): "Opechancanough taken prisoner amids his men. If this course had bin
taken by others Virginia by this had bin out of her cradle, and able to goe alone, yea to

arrowes, all his men were easily intreated to cast downe their armes, little dreaming anie durst in that manner have used their king; who then to escape himselfe, bestowed his presents in goodsadnesse.[7] And having caused all his multitude to approach disarmed; the President argued with them to this effect.

> I see you Pamaunkies the great desire you have to cut my throat; and my long suffering your injuries, have inboldened you to this presumption. The cause I have forborne your insolencies, is the promise I made you (before the God I serve) to be your friend, till you give me just cause to bee your enimie. If I keepe this vow, my God will keepe me, you cannot hurt me; if I breake it he will destroie me. But if you shoot but one arrow, to shed one drop of blood of any of my men, or steale the least of these beades, or copper, (I spurne before me with my foot) you shall see, I wil not cease revenge, (if once I begin) so long as I can heare where to find one of your nation that will not deny the name of Pamaunke; I am not now at Rasseweac[8] (halfe drownd with mire) where you tooke me prisoner, yet then for keeping your promise, and your good usage, and saving my life, I so affect you, that your denials of your treacherie, doth half perswade me to mistake my selfe. But if I be the marke you aime at, here I stand, shoote hee that dare. You promised to fraught my ship ere I departed, and so you shall, or I meane to load her with your dead carkases; yet if as friends you wil come and trade, I once more promise not to trouble you, except you give me the first occasion.

[70] Smiths discourse to the Pamaunkies.

Upon this awaie went their bowes and arrowes, and men, women, and children brought in their commodities, but 2 or three houres they so thronged about the President, and so overwearied him, as he retired himself to rest, leaving Master Beheathland and Master Powel to accept their presents; but some Salvage perceiving him fast asleepe, and the guard carelesly dispersed, 40 or 50 of their choice men ‖ each with an English sword in his hand, began to enter the house, with 2 or 300 others that pressed to second them. The noise and hast they made in, did so shake the house, as they awoke him from his sleep, and being halfe amazed[9] with this suddaine sight, betooke him straight to his sword and target,[10] Master Crashaw and some other charging in like manner, they thronged faster backe, then before forward. The house thus clensed, the king and his ancients,

The Salvages dissemble their intent.

[71]

Their excuse and reconcilement.

trade or fight. But names of peace have bred worse then wars, and our confidence hatched the miserable massacre by this perfidious Savage. And would God a Dale or Smith, or some such spirit were yet there [in 1625] to take this, that is the onely right course with those which know not to doe right, further for feare of suffering it enforceth. . . ."

7. Soberly or with dignity, and evidently sadly (usually written as two words).
8. See the *True Relation*, sigs. B4ʳ, C1ʳ.
9. Stupefied.
10. Buckler.

with a long oration came to excuse this intrusion. The rest of the day was spent with much kindnesse, the company againe renuing their presents of their best provision. And what soever we gave them, they seemed well contented with it.

Now in the meane while since our departure, this hapned at the fort, Master Scrivener willing to crosse[1] the surprizing of Powhatan; 9 daies after the Presidents departure, would needs visit the Ile of hogges, and took with him Captaine Waldo (though the President had appointed him to bee readie to second his occasions)[2] with Master Anthony Gosnoll[3] and eight others; but so violent was the wind (that extreame frozen time) that the boat sunke, but where or how, none doth knowe, for they were all drowned; onlie this was

The losse of Master Skrivener and others with a Skiffe.

knowne, that the Skiffe was much overloaded, and would scarse have lived in that extreame tempest, had she beene emptie; but by no perswasion hee could bee diverted, though both Waldo and 100 others doubted as it hapned.[4] The Salvages were the first that found their bodies, which so much the more encouraged them to effect

[72] their projects. To advertise the President of this heavie ‖ newes, none could bee found would undertake it, but the journey was often refused of all in the fort, untill Master Wiffin undertooke alone the

Master Wiffin his journey to the President.

performance thereof; wherein he was encountred with many dangers and difficulties, and in all parts as hee passed (as also that night he lodged with Powhatan) perceived such preparation for warre, that assured him, some mischiefe was intended, but with extraordinarie bribes, and much trouble, in three daies travell[5] at length hee found us in the midst of these turmoiles. This unhappie newes, the President swore him to conceale from the rest, and so dissembling his sorrow, with the best countenance he could, when the night approached, went safely abord with all his companie.

Powhatan constraineth his men to be trecherous.

Now so extreamely Powhatan had threatned the death of his men, if they did not by some meanes kill Captaine Smith, that the next day they appointed the Countrie should come to trade unarmed: yet unwilling to be treacherous, but that they were constrained, hating fighting almost as ill as hanging, such feare they had of bad successe. The next morning the sunne had not long appeared, but the fieldes appeared covered with people, and baskets to tempt

Their third attempt to betray us.

us ashore. The President determined to keepe abord, but nothing was to bee had without his presence, nor they would not indure[6] the sight of a gun; then the President seeing many depart, and being un-

---

1. Probably "to thwart"; certainly somehow to get in Smith's way.
2. "To second his needs; to back him up."
3. Bartholomew's brother.
4. "Feared that was what would happen."
5. Three days may be considered remarkably little; under the best of circumstances it would have taken him a day and a half.
6. Here, though the usage seems odd, the "not" is far from pleonastic; this is a case of outright double negative for emphasis.

willing to lose such a booty, so well contrived the Pinnace, and his barges with Ambuscadoes, as only with Master Persie, Master West, and Master Russell armed, he went ashore, others unarmed he appointed to receive what was brought; the Salvages floc- || ked before **[73]** him in heapes, and (the bancke serving as a trench for retreat) hee drewe them faire open to his ambuscadoes, for he not being to be perswaded to go to visit their king, the King came to visit him with 2 or 300 men, in the forme of two halfe moons, with some 20 men, and many women loaded with great painted baskets; but when they approached somewhat neare us, their women and children fled; for when they had environed and beset the fieldes in this manner, they thought their purpose sure; yet so trembled with fear as they were scarse able to nock their arrowes; Smith standing with his 3 men readie bent beholding them, till they were within danger of our ambuscado, who, upon the word discovered themselves, and he retiring to the banke;[7] which the Salvages no sooner perceived but away they fled, esteeming their heeles for their best advantage.

That night we sent to the fort Master Crashaw and Master Foard, who (in the mid-way betweene Werawocomoco and the fort) met 4 or 5. of the Dutch mens confederates going to Powhatan, the which (to excuse[8] those gentlemens Suspition of their running to the Salvages) returned to the fort and there continued.

The Salvages hearing our barge depart in the night were so terriblie affraide, that we sent for more men,[9] (we having so much threatned their ruine, and the rasing of their houses, boats, and canowes) that the next day the king sent our Captaine a chaine of pearle to alter his purpose; and stay his men, promising (though they wanted themselves) to fraught our ship, and bring it abord to avoid suspition, so that 5 or 6 daies after, || from al parts of the countrie within 10 or 12 miles, in the extreame cold frost, and snow, they brought us provision on their naked backes.

A chaine of pearle sent to obtaine peace.

[74]

Yet notwithstanding this kindnesse and trade; had their art and poison bin sufficient, the President with Master West and some others had been poysoned;[1] it made them sicke, but expelled it selfe; Wecuttanow a stout yong fellow, knowing hee was suspected for bringing this present of poison, with 40 or 50. of his choice companions (seeing the President but with a few men at Potauncac) so

The President Poysoned.

The offender punished.

7. The *Generall Historie*, 81, has "Barge."

8. "To seek to remove. . . ."

9. Read: "that we had sent for more men." Below, the *Generall Historie*, 81, has "wires," i.e., "weirs," instead of "canowes"; the "king" is Opechancanough.

1. Archer's "Relatyon" mentions a "Roote wherewith they [the Powhatan Indians] poisen their Arrowes" (Barbour, *Jamestown Voyages*, I, 90), but this seems not to have been identified; neither does the "poisonous substance" said to have been invented by the Nanticoke Indians on the Eastern Shore, Smith's Nantaquacks (see Frederick Webb Hodge, ed., *Handbook of American Indians North of Mexico*, Smithsonian Institution, Bureau of American Ethnology, Bulletin 30, II [Washington, D.C., 1910], 125).

prowdlie braved it, as though he expected to incounter a revenge; which the President perceiving in the midst of his companie did not onlie beat, but spurned him like a dogge, as scorning to doe him anie worse mischiefe; whereupon all of them fled into the woods, thinking they had done a great matter, to have so well escaped; and the townsmen remaining, presentlie fraughted our barge, to bee rid of our companies, framing manie excuses to excuse Wecuttanow (being son to their chiefe king but Powhatan[2]) and told us if we would shew them him that brought the poyson, they would deliver him to us to punish as wee pleased.

Men maie thinke it strange there should be this stir for a little corne, but had it been gold with more ease we might have got it; and had it wanted, the whole collonie had starved. We maie be thought verie patient, to indure all those injuries; yet onlie with fearing them, we got what they had. Whereas if we had taken revenge, then by their losse we should have lost our selvs.[3] We searched also the countries of Youghtanund and ‖ Mattapamient, where the people imparted that little they had, with such complaints and tears from women and children; as he had bin too cruell to be a Christian that would not have bin satisfied, and moved with compassion. But had this happened in October, November, and December, when that unhappie discoverie of Monacan was made,[4] we might have fraughted a ship of 40 tuns, and twice as much might have bin had from the rivers of Toppahannock, Patawomeck, and Pawtuxunt. The maine occasion of our temporizing with the Salvages was to part friends, (as we did) to give the lesse cause of suspition to Powhatan to fly; by whom we now returned, with a purpose, to have surprised him and his provision. For effecting whereof, (when we came against the towne) the President sent Master Wiffin and Master Coe ashore to discover and make waie for his intended project. But they found that those damned Dutch-men had caused Powhatan to abandon his new house, and Werawocomoco, and to carrie awaie all his corne and provision; and the people, they found (by their means so ill affected), that had they not stood well upon their guard, they had hardlie escaped with their lives. So the President finding his intention thus frustrated, and that there was nothing now to be had, and therefore an unfit time to revenge their abuses,[5] helde on his course for James

[75]
The Salvage want and poverty.

The Dutchmen did much hurt.

2. Powhatan's successor (presumably a "brother") was Opichapam (p. 61, above), also known as Itoyatin, Taughaiten, etc. (see Strachey, *Historie*, 69; and John Pory in Smith's *Generall Historie*, 143). Otherwise, the "chiefe king but Powhatan" might have been Opechancanough or Katataugh, Powhatan's other "brothers."

3. "Fearing" was often used in the causative sense of "frightening, causing to fear." As to revenge, again, see Barbour, *Jamestown Voyages*, II, 437n: "Smith was one of the few colonists who realized that trade or barter with the Indians was a *sine qua non* of survival. Therefore, they must neither be exterminated nor driven away."

4. The "unhappie discoverie" was the disastrous expedition to explore the Monacan territory.

5. Smith's forays were designed to benefit the colony, not merely to vent his rage on the Indians.

Towne; we having in this Jornie (for 25^l of copper 50^l of Iron and beads) kept 40 men 6. weekes,[6] and dailie feasted with bread, corne, flesh, fish, and fowle, everie man having for his reward (and in consideration of his commodities) a months provision; (no trade being allowed but for the store,) and we ‖ delivered at James Towne to the **[76]** Cape-Marchant 279 bushels of corne.

Those temporall proceedings to some maie seeme too charitable; to such a dailie daring trecherous people: to others unpleasant that we washed not the ground with their blouds, nor shewed such strange inventions, in mangling, murdering, ransaking, and destroying, (as did the Spaniards) the simple bodies of those ignorant soules; nor delightful because not stuffed with relations of heaps, and mines of gold and silver, nor such rare commodities as the Portugals and Spaniards found in the East and West Indies. The want wherof hath begot us (that were the first undertakers) no lesse scorne and contempt, then their noble conquests and valiant adventures (beautified with it) praise and honor. Too much I confesse the world cannot attribute to their ever memorable merit. And to cleare us from the worlds blind ignorant censure, these fewe words may suffise to any reasonable understanding.

It was the Spaniards good hap to happen in those parts, where were infinite numbers of people, whoe had manured the ground with that providence, that it afforded victuall at all times: and time had brought them to that perfection, they had the use of gold and silver, and the most of such commodities, as their countries afforded, so that what the Spaniard got, was only the spoile and pillage of those countrie people, and not the labours of their owne hands. But had those fruitfull Countries, beene as Salvage, as barbarous, as ill peopled, as little planted, laboured and manured as Virginia, their proper labours (it is likely) would have ‖ produced as small profit as **[77]** ours. But had Virginia bin peopled, planted, manured, and adorned, with such store of pretious Jewels, and rich commodities, as was the Indies: then, had we not gotten, and done as much as by their examples might bee expected from us, the world might then have traduced us and our merits, and have made shame and infamy our recompence and reward.

But we chanced in a lande, even as God made it. Where we found only an idle, improvident, scattered people; ignorant of the knowledge of gold, or silver, or any commodities; and carelesse of any thing but from hand to mouth, but for bables of no worth; nothing to encourage us, but what accidentally wee found nature afforded. Which ere wee could bring to recompence our paines, defray our charges, and satisfie our adventurers, we were to discover the country, subdue the people, bring them to be tractable, civil, and

6. Six weeks from Dec. 29, 1608 (p. 55, above), would have been Feb. 9, 1609. Above, read: "copper *and* 50^l of Iron and beads."

industrious, and teach them trades, that the fruits of their labours might make us recompence, or plant such colonies of our owne that must first make provision how to live of themselves, ere they can bring to perfection the commodities of the countrie, which doubtles will be as commodious for England, as the west Indies for Spaine, if it be rightly managed; notwithstanding all our home-bred opinions, that will argue the contrarie, as formerly such like have done against the Spaniards and Portugals. But to conclude, against all rumor of opinion, I only say this, for those that the three first yeares began this plantation, notwithstanding al their factions, mutenies, and miseries, **[78]** so gently corrected, ‖ and well prevented: peruse the Spanish Decades, the relations of Master Hacklut,[7] and tell mee how many ever with such smal meanes, as a barge of 2 Tunnes; sometimes with 7. 8. 9, or but at most 15 men did ever discover so many faire and navigable rivers; subject so many severall kings, people, and nations, to obedience, and contribution with so little bloud shed.

And if in the search of those Countries, wee had hapned where wealth had beene, we had as surely had it, as obedience and contribution, but if wee have overskipped it, we will not envy them that shall chance to finde it. Yet can wee not but lament, it was our ill fortunes to end, when wee had but only learned how to begin, and found the right course how to proceed.

By Richard Wiffin, William Phettiplace, and
Anas Todkill.[8]

Chapter 10.
How the Salvages became subject to the English.

W HEN the shippes departed,[9] al the provision of the store (but that the President had gotten) was so rotten with the last somers rain, and eaten with rats, and wormes, as the hogs would scarsely eat it, yet it was the souldiers diet, till our returnes: so that wee found **[79]** ‖ nothing done, but victuall spent, and the most part of our tooles, and a good part of our armes convayed to the Salvages. But now, casting up the store, and finding sufficient till the next harvest, the feare of starving was abandoned; and the company divided into tennes, fifteenes, or as the businesse required, 4 houres each day was

---

7. The "Spanish Decades" probably refers to Peter Martyr d'Anghiera's *Decades*, trans. Richard Eden (1555) and augmented by Richard Willes (1577); the "relations of Master Hacklut" were of course the *Principal Navigations*.
    8. The *Generall Historie*, 83, adds the name of Jeffrey Abbot.
    9. The date is not known; the editor has suggested the week of Nov. 27 to Dec. 3, 1608 (Barbour, *Jamestown Voyages*, II, 440n).

spent in worke, the rest in pastimes and merry exercise; but the untowardnesse of the greatest number, caused the President to make a
generall assembly, and then he advised them as followeth.

Countrimen, the long experience of our late miseries, I hope is
sufficient to perswade every one to a present correction of himselfe;
and thinke not that either my pains, or the adventurers purses, will
ever maintaine you in idlenesse and sloth; I speake not this to you
all, for diverse of you I know deserve both honor and reward, better
then is yet here to bee had: but the greater part must be more industrious, or starve, howsoever you have bin heretofore tolerated by the
authoritie of the Councell from that I have often commanded you,
yet seeing nowe the authoritie resteth wholly in my selfe,[10] you must
obay this for a law, that he that will not worke shall not eate[1] (except
by sicknesse he be disabled) for the labours of 30 or 40 honest and
industrious men shall not bee consumed to maintaine 150 idle
varlets. Now though you presume the authoritie here is but a shad-
dow, and that I dare not touch the lives of any, but my own must
answer it; the letters patents each week shall be read you, whose
contents will tell you the contrary. I would wish you therefore with-
out contempt seeke to observe these orders || set downe: for there are
nowe no more Councells[2] to protect you, nor curbe my indeavors.
Therefore hee that offendeth let him assuredly expect his due punishment.

The Presidents
advise to the
company.

[80]

Hee made also a table as a publike memoriall of every mans deserts,
to encourage the good, and with shame to spurre on the rest to
amendment. By this many became very industrious, yet more by
severe punishment performed their businesse; for all were so tasked,
that there was no excuse could prevaile to deceive him, yet the Dutch-
mens consorts so closely still convaid[3] powder, shot, swords, and
tooles, that though we could find the defect, we could not find by
whom it was occasioned, till it was too late.

All this time the Dutchmen remaining with Powhatan, received
them, instructing the Salvages their use. But their consorts not following them as they expected, to knowe the cause, they sent Francis
their companion (a stout young fellow) disguised Salvage like to the
glasse-house, (a place in the woods neere a myle from James Towne)[4]
where was the randavus for all their unsuspected villany. 40 men
they procured of Powhatan to lie in Ambuscadoe for Captaine

The Dutch-
mens plot to
murder Cap-
taine Smith.

10. Of the original councillors, Smith was the only one still surviving in Virginia.
1. The source of this is 2 Thess. 3:10.
2. The *Generall Historie*, 83, has "Counsellers."
3. Variant spelling of "conveyed."
4. Archaeological excavations started by the National Park Service in the fall of
1948 located the site just off the Old Road (and modern Colonial Parkway) about a mile
from Jamestown.

Smith, who no sooner heard of this Dutchman, but hee sent to apprehend him, who found he was gon, yet to crosse his returne to Powhatan, Captaine Smith presently dispatched 20 shot after him, and
then returning but from the glasse-house alone, hee incountred the
king of Paspaheigh, a most strong stout Salvage, whose perswasions
not being able to perswade him to his ambush, seeing him only armed
but with a fauchion, attempted to have shot him; but the President

[81] prevented his shot ‖ by grapling with him, and the Salvage as well
prevented him for drawing his fauchion, and perforce bore him into
the river to have drowned him; long they struggled in the water,
from whence the king perceiving two of the Poles[5] upon the sandes

Smith taketh
the king of
Paspaheigh
prisoner.

would have fled; but the President held him by the haire and throat
til the Poles came in; then seeing howe pittifully the poore Salvage
begged his life, they conducted him prisoner to the fort. The Dutchman ere long was also brought in, whose villany, though all this time
it was suspected, yet he fained such a formall excuse, that for want
of language, Win[6] had not rightly understood them, and for their
dealings with Powhatan, that to save their lives they were constrained to accommodate[7] his armes, of whome he extreamely complained to have detained them perforce; and that hee made this
escape with the hazard of his life, and meant not to have returned,
but only walked in the woods to gather walnuts: yet for all this faire
tale (there was so smal appearance of truth) hee went by the heeles;[8]
the king also he put in fetters, purposing to regaine the Dutch-men,
by the saving his life; the poore Salvage did his best, by his daily
messengers to Powhatan, but all returned that the Dutchmen would
not returne, neither did Powhatan stay them, and bring them fiftie
myles on their backes they were not able; daily this kings wives
children, and people, came to visit him with presents, which hee
liberally bestowed to make his peace, much trust they had in the
Presidents promise, but the king finding his gard negligent (though

[82] fettered) yet escaped. Captaine Win thinking to pur- ‖ sue him,
found such troopes of Salvages to hinder his passages, as they exchanged many volies of shot for flights of arrowes. Captaine Smith
hearing of this, in returning to the fort tooke two Salvages prisoners,

5. Although there may have been as many as four Poles in Jamestown at the time,
only these two have been mentioned in Smith's works. Ever since about 1927 Polish
Americans have been attempting to identify these first Polish immigrants, culminating
about the time of the 350th anniversary celebrations in Jamestown. A few years later,
and after thorough investigation on both sides of the Atlantic, the editor presented the
known facts of the case in "The Identity of the First Poles in America," *WMQ*, 3d Ser.,
XXI (1964), 77–92. It needs to be stated here only that their identity is still unknown;
not even their names have survived.

6. Capt. Peter Winne; see p. 89n, below.

7. Read: "to supply him with"; a rare and obsolete use of "accommodate."

8. I.e., was put in irons.

the one called Kemps, the other Kinsock,[9] the two most exact villaines in the countrie; with those, Captaine Win, and 50 chosen men
attempted that night to have regained the king, and revenged his
injurie and so had done if he had followed his directions, or bin
advised by those two villaines, that would have betraied both their
king and kindred for a peece of copper, but hee trifling away the
night, the Salvages the next morning by the rising of the sunne,
braved him come a shore to fight, a good time both sides let flie at
other, but wee heard of no hurt, only they tooke two Canows, burnt
the kings house and so returned.

The President fearing those bravadoes would but incourage the   The Salvages
Salvages, begun himselfe to trie his conclusions; whereby 6 or 7   desire peace.
Salvages were slaine, as many made prisoners; burnt their houses,
tooke their boats with all their fishing weares, and planted them at
James Towne for his owne use; and nowe resolved not to cease till he
had revenged himselfe upon al that had injured him. But in his
journey passing by Paspaheigh towards Chickahamina, the Salvages
did their best to draw him to their ambuscadoes; but seeing him
regardlesly passe their Countrey, all shewed themselves in their
bravest manner, to trie their valours; he could not but let flie, and
ere he could land, the Salvages no sooner knewe him, but they threw
downe their armes and desired peace; their Orator was a stout young
man ‖ called Ocanindge, whose worthie discourse deserveth to be   **[83]**
remembred; and this it was.

Captaine Smith, my master is here present in this company   Ocanindge his
thinking it Captaine Win, and not you; and of him hee intended to Oration.
have beene revenged, having never offended him: if hee have
offended you in escaping your imprisonment; the fishes swim, the
fowles flie, and the very beastes strive to escape the snare and live;
then blame not him being a man, hee would entreat you remember,
your being a prisoner, what paines he tooke to save your life;[10] if
since he hath injured you he was compelled to it, but howsoever, you
have revenged it with our too great losse. We perceive and well
knowe you intend to destroy us, that are here to intreat and desire
your friendship, and to enjoy our houses and plant our fields, of
whose fruit you shall participate, otherwise you will have the worst
by our absence, for we can plant any where, though with more
labour, and we know you cannot live if you want our harvest, and
that reliefe wee bring you; if you promise us peace we will beleeve

---

9. A mistake of some sort for "Tassore" (see p. 86, below; and various references in
the *Generall Historie*).

10. This is hardly substantiated in the *True Relation*, though there is a reference to
"the King of Paspahegh" (sig. B4ᵛ).

you, if you proceed in reveng, we will abandon the Countrie.

Upon these tearmes the President promised them peace, till they did us injurie, upon condition they should bring in provision, so all departed good friends, and so continued till Smith left the Countrie.

A Salvage
smothered at
James Towne,
and was
recovered.

Ariving at James Towne, complaint was made to the President that the Chickahaminos, who al this while continued trade, and seemed our friendes, by colour thereof were the only theeves, and amongst other things, a pistol being stolne, and the theefe fled, there

[84] || were apprehended 2 proper young fellows that were brothers, knowne to be his confederats. Now to regain this pistoll, the one we imprisoned, the other was sent to returne againe within 12 hours, or his brother to be hanged, yet the President pittying the poore naked Salvage in the dungeon, sent him victuall and some charcole for fire;[1] ere midnight his brother returned with the pistoll, but the poore Salvage in the dungeon was so smothered with the smoke he had made, and so pittiously burnt, that wee found him dead, the other most lamentably bewailed his death, and broke forth in such bitter agonies, that the President (to quiet him) told him that if herafter they would not steal, he wold make him alive againe, but little thought hee could be recovered, yet (we doing our best with aquavitæ and vineger) it pleased God to restore him againe to life,[2] but so drunke and affrighted that he seemed lunaticke, not understanding any thing hee spoke or heard, the which as much grieved and tormented the other, as before to see him dead; of which maladie (upon promise of their good behaviour afterward) the President promised to recover him and so caused him to be laid by a fire to sleepe, who in the morning (having well slept) had recovered his perfect senses; and then being dressed of his burning, and each a peece of copper given them, they went away so well contented, that this was spread amongst all the Salvages for a miracle, that Captaine Smith could make a man alive that is dead; these and many other such pretty accidents, so amazed and affrighted both Powhatan and all his people that from all parts with presents they desired peace,

[85] || returning many stolne things which wee neither demaunded nor thought of. And after that, those that were taken stealing (both Powhatan and his people) have sent them backe to James Towne to receive their punishment, and all the countrie became absolutely as free for us, as for themselves.

1. Purchas, *Pilgrimes*, IV, 1727, has a marginal note: "Charcole-smoke [is] an unusual murtherer by oversight, where no vent is left to it." He may have meant "usual," rather than "unusual."

2. A second Purchas comment appears a few lines below: "Perhaps the Jesuites wits have (besides meere lies) hatched many of their Indian Miracles from as unlikely egs as this by conjoyning industrie and opportunitie" (*ibid.*).

Chapter 11.

What was done in three monthes having victuall.
The store devoured by rats, how we lived 3 monthes
of such naturall fruits as the countrie afforded.

Now wee so quietly followed our businesse, that in 3 monthes we
made 3 or 4 last[3] of pitch and tarre, and sope ashes, produced a
triall of glasse, made a well in the forte of excellent sweete water
(which till then was wanting) built some 20 houses, recovered our
Church, provided nets and weares for fishing (and to stop the dis- *More done in*
orders of our disorderly theeves and the Salvages) built a blocke *3 monthes then*
house in the necke of our Ile, kept by a garrison, to entertaine the *3 yeares.*
Salvages trade, and none to passe nor repasse, Salvage, nor Christian,
without the Presidents order. 30 or 40 acres of ground we digged,
and planted; of 3 sowes in one yeare increased 60 and od pigges, and
neere 500 chickens brought up themselves (without having any
meate given them) but the hogges were transported to Hog Ile,[4]
where al- ‖ so we built a blocke house with a garrison, to give us **[86]**
notice of any shipping, and for their exercise they made clapbord,
wainscot, and cut downe trees against the ships comming. We built
also a fort for a retreat, neare a convenient river upon a high commanding hill,[5] very hard to be assaulted, and easie to be defended;
but ere it was halfe finished this defect caused a stay; in searching
our casked corne, wee found it halfe rotten, the rest so consumed with
the many thousand rats (increased first from the ships) that we knewe
not how to keepe that little wee had. This did drive us all to our wits
ende, for there was nothing in the countrie but what nature afforded.
Untill this time Kemps and Tassore, were fettered prisoners, and
daily wrought, and taught us how to order and plant our fields.
Whome now (for want of victuall) we set at libertie, but so wel were
they used, that they little desired it; and to express their loves, for 16
daies continuance, the Countrie[6] brought us (when least) 100 a daie
of squirrils, Turkies, Deare, and other wild beastes; but this want of
corne occasioned the end of all our workes, it being worke sufficient
to provide victuall. 60 or 80 with Ensigne Laxon were sent downe
the river to live upon oysters, and 20 with leiftenant Percie to trie for
fishing at Point-Comfort, but in 6 weekes, they would not agree once
to cast out their net.[7] Master West with as many went up to the falles,

3. A last of pitch was 12 or sometimes 14 barrels (*OED*).
4. Across the river and slightly downstream from Jamestown.
5. The reference is apparently to Smith's "New Fort," across the James River and
just E of Gray's Creek.
6. The *Generall Historie*, 86, has "Countrie people."
7. The *Generall Historie*, 86, adds "he being sicke and burnt sore with Gunpouder."

but nothing could bee found but a fewe berries and acornes; of that

The pains of
40 fed 150.

in the store every one had their equall proportion. Till this present

[87]

(by the hazard and endeavour of some 30 or 40) this whole number had ever been fed. Wee had more Sturgeon then ‖ could be devoured by dogge and man; of which the industrious, by drying and pownding, mingled with caviare, sorrel, and other wholsome hearbs, would make bread and good meate;[8] others would gather as much *Tockwough* roots in a day, as would make them bread a weeke, so that of those wilde fruites, fish and berries, these lived very well, (in regard of such a diet). But such was the most strange condition of some 150, that had they not beene forced nolens volens perforce to gather and prepare their victuall they would all have starved, and have eaten one another. Of those wild fruites the Salvages often brought us: and for that the President would not fulfill the unreasonable desire of those distracted lubberly gluttons, to sell, not only our kettles, howes, tooles, and Iron, nay swords, peeces, and the very ordenance, and houses, might they have prevailed but to have beene but idle, for those salvage fruits they would have imparted all to the Salvages; especially for one basket of corne they heard of, to bee at Powhatans, 50 myles from our fort, though he bought neere halfe of it to satisfie their humours, yet to have had the other halfe, they would have sold

Their desire to
destroy them-
selves.

their soules, (though not sufficient to have kept them a weeke). Thousands were their exclamations, suggestions, and devises, to force him to those base inventions, to have made it an occasion to abandon the Countrie. Want perforce constrained him to indure their exclaiming follies till he found out the author, one Dyer, a most craftie knave, and his ancient maligner, whom he worthely punished, and with the rest he argued the case in this manner.

[88]

The Presidents
speech to the
drones.

Fellow souldiers, I did little thinke any so false to report, or so many so simple to be perswaded, that I either intend to starve you, or that Powhatan (at this present) hath corne for himselfe, much lesse for you; or that I would not have it, if I knewe where it were to be had. Neither did I thinke any so malitious as nowe I see a great many, yet it shall not so much passionate me, but I will doe my best for my worst maligner. But dreame no longer of this vaine hope from Powhatan; nor that I wil longer forbeare to force you from your Idlenesse, and punish you if you raile. You cannot deny but that by the hazard of my life, many a time I have saved yours, when, might your owne wils have prevailed, you would have starved, and will doe still whether I will or no. But I protest by that God that made me, since necessitie hath not power to force you to gather for your selvs those fruits the earth doth yeeld, you shall not only gather for your

8. "Meat," as here, in Smith's day usually referred to solid food in general, not just animal flesh. On *Tockwough* roots, see the *Map of Va.*, 13n.

selves, but for those that are sicke: as yet I never had more from the
store then the worst of you; and all my English extraordinarie provision that I have, you shall see mee devide among the sick. And this
Salvage trash, you so scornfully repine at, being put in your mouthes
your stomacks can digest it, and therefore I will take a course you
shall provide it. The sicke shal not starve, but equally share of all
our labours, and every one that gathereth not every day as much as
I doe, the next daie shall be set beyond the river, and for ever bee
banished from the fort, and live there or starve.

This order many murmured, was very cruell, but it caused the
most part so well bestir themselves, that || of 200 men (except they **[89]**
were drowned) there died not past 7 or 8. As for Captaine Win, and But 7 of 200
Master Ley, they died ere this want happened,[9] and the rest died not died in 9
for want of such as preserved the rest. Many were billitted among months.
the Salvages, whereby we knewe all their passages, fieldes, and habitations, howe to gather and use their fruits, as well as themselves.

So well those poore Salvages used us, (that were thus Billited)
as divers of the souldiers ran away, to search Kemps our old prisoner. The Salvages
Glad was this Salvage to have such an occasion to testifie his love. returne our
For insteed of entertaining them, and such things as they had stolne, fugitives.
with all the great offers and promises they made them, to revenge
their injuries upon Captaine Smith, First he made himselfe sport, in
shewing his countrymen (by them) how he was used; feeding them
with this law who would not worke must not eat, till they were neere
starved, continuallie threatning to beate them to death, neither
could they get[1] from him, til perforce he brought them to our Captaine, that so well contented him, and punished them: as manie
others that intended also to have followed them, were rather contented to labour at home, then adventure to live Idle among the
Salvages, (of whom there was more hope to make better christians
and good subjects, then the one halfe of those that counterfeited
themselves both.) For so afeard were all those kings and the better
sorte of their people, to displease us, that some of the baser sort that
we have extreamelie hurt and punished for their villanies, would
hire us, we should not tell it to their kings or countrymen, who would
also repunish || them, and yet returne them to James Towne to con- **[90]**
tent the President, by that testimonie of their loves.

Master Sicklemore well returned from Chawonock, but found Search for
little hope and lesse certainetie of them were left by Sir Walter them sent by
Rawley.[2] So that Nathaniell Powell and Anas Todkill, were also, by Sir Walter
                                                                       Rawley.

9. What appears to be Peter Winne's last letter to London was dated Nov. 26, 1608
(see Barbour, *Jamestown Voyages*, I, 245–246); he died early in 1609.
    1. I.e., "get away from. . . ."
    2. Purchas adds a comment of his own to Smith's account: "Powhatan confessed
that hee had bin at the murther of that Colonie: and shewed to Captain Smith a Musket

the Quiyoughquohanocks, conducted to the Mangoages to search
them there. But nothing could we learne but they were all dead. This
honest, proper, good promis-keeping king,[3] of all the rest did ever
best affect us, and though to his false Gods he was yet very zealous,
yet he would confesse, our God as much exceeded his, as our guns
did his bowe and arrowes, often sending our President manie presents
to praie to his God for raine, or his corne would perish, for his Gods
were angrie. All this time to reclaime the Dutchmen, and one
Bentley an other fugitive, we imploied one William Volda (a Switzer
by birth) with pardons and promises to regaine them. Litle we then
suspected this double villaine, of anie villanie, who plainlie taught
us, in the most trust was the greatest treason. For this wicked hypo-

**The Dutch-
mens projects.**

crit, by the seeming hate he bore to the lewd condition of his cursed
countrimen, having this opportunitie by his imploiment to regaine
them, conveighed them everie thing they desired to effect their
project to destroie the colonie. With much devotion they expected
the Spanyard, to whom they intended to have done good service.
But to begin with the first oportunitie, they seeing necessitie thus inforced us to disperse our selves; importuned Powhatan to lend them
but his forces, and they would not onlie destroie our hogs, fire our

[91] towne, and be- ‖ traie our Pinnas; but bring to his service and subjection the most part of our companies.[4] With this plot they had
acquainted manie discontents and manie were agreed to their
divelish practise. But on Thomas Dowse and Thomas Mallard,
whose christian harts much relenting at such an unchristian act,
voluntarily revealed it to Captaine Smith: who did his best it might
be concealed, perswading Dowse and Malard to proceed in the confederacie: onlie to bring the irreclamable Dutch men, and inconstant Salvages in such a maner amongst his ambuscadoes as he had
prepared, as not manie of them shoulde ever have returned from out
our peninsula. But this brute comming to the ears of the impatient

---

barrell and a brasse Morter, and certaine peeces of Iron which had bin theirs" (*Pilgrimes*, IV, 1728). Long before Smith could have passed this information on to Purchas,
however, Newport had brought word to London not only about Powhatan and the
Roanoke colony, but also about survivors. In the instructions given to Sir Thomas Gates
by the Virginia Council in May 1609, there is a long paragraph about a desirable seat at
Oconahöen, in the neighborhood of which is Peccarecamicke, "where you shall finde
foure of the englishe alive, left by Sir Walter Rawely which escaped from the slaughter
of Powhaton of Roanocke" (Susan Myra Kingsbury, ed., *The Records of the Virginia
Company of London* [Washington, D.C., 1906–1935], III, 17). A summary of the whole
subject is available in Philip L. Barbour, "Ocanahowan and Recently Discovered Linguistic Fragments from Southern Virginia, *c.* 1650," in William Cowan, ed., *Papers of the
Seventh Algonquian Conference* (Ottawa, 1976), 2–17.

3. Possibly the same "Choapock" who is mentioned in a marginal manuscript note
to the *True Relation*, sig. B1ʳ.

4. The *Generall Historie*, 88, has "company." The sense of the preceding passage is
that the conspirators were hoping for help from Spanish ships, but seeing the company
temporarily vulnerable, they hoped to get Powhatan's assistance for an immediate
attack.

multitude, they so importuned the President to cut of those Dutch-men, as amongst manie that offered to cut their throates before the face of Powhatan.[5] Master Wiffin and Jefra Abot were sent to stab or shoot them; but these Dutch men made such excuses accusing Volday whom they supposed had revealed their project, as Abbot would not, yet Wiffin would, perceiving it but deceipt. The king understanding of this their imploiment, sent presentlie his messengers to Captaine Smith to signifie it was not his fault to detaine them, nor hinder his men from executing his command, nor did he nor would he maintaine them, or anie to occasion his displeasure. But ere this busines was brought to a point, God having seene our misery sufficient, sent in Captaine Argall[6] to fish for Sturgion with a ship well furnished with wine and bisket, which though it was not sent us, such were our occasions we tooke it at a price, but left him sufficient to ‖ returne for England, still dissembling Valdo his villany,[7] but certainlie hee had not escaped had the President continued.

Two gentlemen sent to kill them.

[92]

By this you may see, for all those crosses, treacheries, and dissentions, howe he wrastled and overcame (without bloud shed) all that hapned. Also what good was done, how few died, what food the country naturally affordeth, what small cause there is men shoulde starve, or be murdered by the Salvages, that have discretion to manage this[8] courage and industry. The 2. first years though by his adventures he had oft brought the Salvages to a tractable trade, yet you see how the envious authority ever crossed him, and frustrated his best endeavours. Yet this wrought in him that experience and estimation among the Salvages, as otherwaies it had bin impossible he had ever effected that he did; though the many miserable yet generous[9] and worthy adventures he had long and oft indured as wel in some parts of Africa, and America, as in the most partes of Europe and Asia[10] by land or sea had taught him much, yet in this case he

Note these inconveniences.

5. The sentence is completed in the *Generall Historie*, 88: "the first was Lieutenant Percy, and Master John Cuderington, two Gentlemen of as bold resolute spirits as could possibly be found."

6. There is a fairly comprehensive account of Samuel Argall in Philip L. Barbour, *Pocahontas and Her World* (Boston, 1970), especially pp. 66–76, 215–224, but consult the index. Argall was commissioned on Apr. 2, 1609, by the London Council for Virginia "to sett forward," as captain of the *Mary and John*, on "a fishing voiage to Virginia," on which he was "to shape his Course Sowthewest or neere thereunto and therby to beat it up the straytest way he can, accordinge to his offer made unto us, unto James Towne in Virgynya . . ." (see Dorothy S. Eaton, "A Voyage of 'ffishinge and Discovery,'" The Library of Congress, *Quarterly Journal of Current Acquisitions*, X [1953], 181–184). For further details, see the *Generall Historie*, 88n.

7. The *Generall Historie*, 88, clarifies the text somewhat: "The villany of Volday we still dissembled." Yet the true cause of so much infighting, as it is called today, still obscures what really happened—or was on the verge of happening. Smith's, or his associates', next paragraph reflects contemporary bewilderment.

8. The *Generall Historie*, 89, has "mannage them with courage and industrie."

9. Here, "gallant, courageous."

10. See the *True Travels*, chaps. 1–20.

was againe to learne his Lecture by experience. Which with thus much a doe having obtained, it was his ill chance to end, when hee had but onlie learned how to begin. And though hee left these un-knowne difficulties, (made easie and familiar) to his unlawfull suc-cessors, whoe onlie by living in James Towne, presumed to know more then al the world could direct them; though they had all his souldiers with their triple power, and twise triple better meanes, by what they have done in his absence, the world doth see: and what

[93] they would have done in his ‖ presence, had he not prevented their indiscretions:[11] it doth justlie approve what cause he had to send them for England. But they have made it more plaine since their returne, having his absolute authoritie freely in their power, with all the advantages, and opportunity that his labours had effected. As I am sorry their actions have made it so manifest, so I am unwilling to say what reason doth compell me to make apparant the truth, least I should seeme partial, reasonlesse, or malitious.

Chapter 12.
The Arivall of the third supply.

The alteration of the governe-ment.

To redresse those jarres and ill proceedings, the Councell in En-gland altered the governement and devolved the authoritie to the Lord De-la-ware.[12] Who for his deputie, sent Sir Thomas Gates, and Sir George Somers, with 9 ships and 500 persons, they set saile from England in May 1609. A smal catch perished at sea in a Herycano. The Admirall,[13] with 150 men, with the two knights, and their new commission, their bils of loading with al manner of direc-tions, and the most part of their provision arived not. With the other

The losse of Virginia.

7 (as Captaines) arived Ratliffe, whose right name was Sickelmore, Martin, and Archer. Who as they had been troublesome at sea, be-ganne againe to marre all ashore. For though, as is said, they were

[94] formerly deposed and sent for England: yet now ‖ returning againe, graced by the title of Captaines of the passengers, seeing the admirall wanting, and great probabilitie of her losse, strengthned themselves with those newe companies, so railing and exclaiming against Cap-

11. In other words, "though his successors have better means for achieving success, by what they have done in his absence the world doth see what they would have done in his presence, had he not prevented their indiscretions."

12. For a succinct account of what happened, see Barbour, *Jamestown Voyages*, II, 249–250. It only needs to be stated here that of the fleet of nine ships, the flagship with Gates, Somers, and Newport aboard was wrecked on a Bermuda reef, and a small ketch was lost at sea. The remaining seven ships straggled up the James River with three of Smith's ancient antagonists among the personnel and without any authorized person in command, or even a copy of any authoritative document.

13. I.e., the flagship.

taine Smith, that they mortally hated him, ere ever they see him.
Who understanding by his scouts the arivall of such a fleet (little
dreaming of any such supply) supposing them Spaniards, hee so
determined and ordered his affaires, as wee little feared their arivall,
nor the successe of our incounter, nor were the Salvages any way
negligent or unwilling, to aide and assist us with their best power. The Salvages
Had it so beene, wee had beene happy. For we would not have offer to fight
trusted them but as our foes, whereas receiving those as our countrie- under our
men and friends, they did their best to murder our President, to colours.
surprise the store, the fort, and our lodgings, to usurp the governement, and make us all their servants, and slaves to our owne merit. Mutinie.
To 1000 mischiefes those lewd[1] Captaines led this lewd company,
wherein were many unruly gallants packed thether by their friends
to escape il destinies, and those would dispose and determine of the
governement, sometimes one,[2] the next day another, to day the old
commission, to morrow the new, the next day by neither. In fine,
they would rule all or ruine all; yet in charitie we must endure them
thus to destroy us, or by correcting their follies, have brought the
worlds censure upon us to have beene guiltie of their bloods. Happy
had we bin had they never arrived; and we for ever abandoned, and
(as we were) left to our fortunes, for on earth was never more confusion, or miserie, then their factions occasioned.

The President seeing the desire those braves had to rule, seeing **[95]**
how his authoritie was so unexpectedly changed, would willingly have The planting
left all and have returned for England, but seeing there was smal Nansamund.
hope this newe commission would arive, longer hee would not suffer
those factious spirits to proceed. It would bee too tedious, too strange,
and almost incredible, should I particularly relate the infinite
dangers, plots, and practises, hee daily escaped amongst this factious
crue, the chiefe whereof he quickly laid by the heeles, til his leasure
better served to doe them justice; and to take away al occasions of
further mischiefe, Master Persie had his request granted to returne
for England, and Master West with 120 went to plant at the falles. A plantation of
Martin with neare as many to Nansamund, with their due pro- the falles.
portions, of all provisions, according to their numbers.

Now the Presidents yeare being neere expired,[3] he made Martin
President, who knowing his own insufficiencie, and the companies
scorne, and conceit of his unworthinesse, within 3 hours resigned it
againe to Captaine Smith, and at Nansamund thus proceeded. The
people being contributers[4] used him kindly: yet such was his jealous

1. Unprincipled, good-for-nothing.
2. Read: "sometimes one way. . . ."
3. The president of the council took office annually on Sept. 10. Smith was evidently trying to preserve some semblance of law and order.
4. Tribute payers.

The breach of
peace with the
Salvages.

feare, and cowardize, in the midst of his mirth, hee did surprize this poore naked king, with his monuments,[5] houses, and the Ile he inhabited; and there fortified himselfe, but so apparantly distracted with fear, as imboldned the Salvages to assalt him, kill his men, redeeme their king, gather and carrie away more then 1000 bushels of corne, hee not once daring to intercept them. But sent to the Presi-

[96] dent then at the Falles for 30 good shotte, which from James || towne immediatly were sent him, but hee so well imploid them, as they did just nothing, but returned, complaining of his childishnesse, that with them fled from his company, and so left them to their fortunes.

Master West having seated his men at the Falles, presently returned to revisit James Towne, the President met him by the way as he followed him to the falles: where he found this company so inconsiderately seated, in a place not only subject to the rivers inundation, but round invironed with many intollerable inconve-

Powhatan sold
for copper.

niences. For remedy whereof, he sent presently to Powhatan to sell him the place called Powhatan, promising to defend him against the Monacans, and these should be his conditions (with his people) to resigne him the fort and houses and all that countrie for a proportion of copper: that all stealing offenders should bee sent him, there to receive their punishment: that every house as a custome should pay him a bushell of corne for an inch square of copper, and a proportion of *Pocones* as a yearely tribute to King James, for their protection as a dutie: what else they could spare to barter at their best discreation.

Mutinies.

But both this excellent place and those good conditions did those furies refuse, contemning both him, his kind care and authoritie. The worst they could to shew their spite, they did. I doe more

5 suppresse
120.

then wonder to thinke how only with 5 men, he either durst, or would adventure as he did, (knowing how greedy they were of his blood) to land amongst them and commit to imprisonment the greatest spirits amongst them, till by their multitudes being 120. they forced him to

[97] retire; || yet in that retreate hee surprised one of the boates, wherewith hee returned to their shippe, wherein was their provisions, which also hee tooke. And well it chaunced hee found the marriners so tractable and constant, or there had beene small possibility he had ever escaped. Notwithstanding there were many of the best, I meane of the most worthy in Judgement, reason or experience, that from their first landing hearing the generall good report of his old souldiers, and seeing with their eies his actions so wel managed with discretion, as Captaine Wood, Captaine Web, Captaine Mone, Captaine Phitz-James, Master Partridge, Master White, Master Powell and divers others.[6] When they perceived the malice and con-

5. Temples or ossuaries where the dried bodies of chiefs and other eminences were preserved on raised platforms (see Henry Spelman's "Relation of Virginea," in Arber, *Smith, Works*, cx).

6. Other than the notice in Kingsbury, *Va. Co. Records*, III, 13, of the appointment of "Captaine Woode" to the council in Virginia, nothing is known about these mariners.

dition of Ratliffe, Martin, and Archer, left their factions; and ever
rested his faithfull friends: But the worst was, the poore Salvages that
dailie brought in their contribution to the President. That dis-
orderlie company so tormented those poore naked soules, by stealing their corne, robbing their gardens, beating them, breaking their
houses, and keeping some prisoners; that they dailie complained to
Captaine Smith he had brought them for protectors worse enimies
then the Monocans themselves; which though till then, (for his love)
they had indured: they desired pardon, if hereafter they defended
themselves, since he would not correct them, as they had long expected he would: so much they importuned him to punish their mis-
demeanores, as they offered (if hee would conduct them) to fight for
him against them. But having spent 9. daies in seeking to reclaime
them, shewing them how much they did abuse themselves ‖ with **[98]**
their great guilded hopes of seas, mines, commodities, or victories
they so madly conceived. Then (seeing nothing would prevaile with
them) he set saile for James Towne: now no sooner was the ship under
saile but the Salvages assaulted those 120 in their fort, finding some
stragling abroad in the woods they slew manie, and so affrighted the
rest, as their prisoners escaped, and they scarse retired, with the
swords and cloaks of these they had slaine. But ere we had sailed a
league our shippe grounding, gave us once more libertie to summon
them to a parlie. Where we found them all so stranglie amazed with
this poore simple assault, as they submitted themselves upon anie
tearmes to the Presidents mercie. Who presentlie put by the heeles
6 or 7 of the chiefe offenders, the rest he seated gallantlie at Powhatan, in their Salvage fort they built[7] and pretilie fortified with
poles and barkes of trees sufficient to have defended them from all
the Salvages in Virginia, drie houses for lodgings 300 acres of grounde
readie to plant, and no place so strong, so pleasant and delightful in
Virginia, for which we called it Nonsuch.[8] The Salvages also he
presentlie appeased; redelivering to every one their former losses.
Thus al were friends, new officers appointed to command, and the
President againe readie to depart. But at that Instant arrived Master
West, whose good nature with the perswasions and compassion of
those mutinous prisoners was so much abused, that to regaine their
old hopes new turboiles[9] arose. For the rest being possessed of al their
victuall munition and everie thing, they grew to that height in their
former factions, as there the President ‖ left them to their fortunes, **[99]**
they returning againe to the open aire at West Fort, abandoning

The breach of peace with the Salvages at the Falles.

An assault by the Salvages.

The planting of Nonsuch.

New peace concluded.

7. The *Generall Historie*, 92, has "in that Salvage Fort, readie built, and prettily
fortified. . . ."

8. Henry Spelman left a badly written and distorted account of this in his "Relation"
(see Arber, *Smith, Works*, cii).

9. Possibly a misprint of "garboils" (brawls); if not, it could be a distortion of
"troubles" or "turmoils" (unrecorded in *OED*). The meaning at the beginning of the
sentence is that West's compassion and good nature led him to be persuaded by the
mutinous prisoners.

Nonsuch, and he to James Towne with his best expedition, but this hapned him in that Journie.

Sleeping in his boat, (for the ship was returned 2 daies before,) accidentallie, one fired his powder bag, which tore his flesh from his bodie and thighes, 9. or 10. inches square in a most pittifull manner; but to quench the tormenting fire, frying him in his cloaths he leaped over bord into the deepe river, where ere they could recover him he was neere drownd. In this estat, without either Chirurgion, or chirurgery he was to go neare 100. miles.[10] Ariving at James Towne causing all things to bee prepared for peace or warres to obtain provision, whilest those things were providing, Martin, Ratliffe, and Archer, being to have their trials, their guiltie consciences fearing a just reward for their deserts, seeing the President unable to stand, and neare bereft of his senses by reason of his torment, they had plotted to have murdered him in his bed. But his hart did faile him

A bloody intent.

that should have given fire to that mercilesse pistol. So, not finding that course to be the best they joined togither to usurp the government, thereby to escape their punishment, and excuse themselves by accusing him. The President, had notice of their projects: the which to withstand, though his old souldiers importuned him but permit them to take of their heads that would resist his commaund, yet he

The governement usurped.

would not permit them, But sent for the masters of the ships and tooke order with them for his returne for England. Seeing there was

[100] neither chirurgion, nor chirur- || gery in the fort to cure his hurt, and the ships to depart the next daie, his commission to be suppressed[1] he knew not why, himselfe and souldiers to be rewarded he knew not how, and a new commission graunted they knew not to whom, the which so disabled that authority he had, as made them presume so oft to those mutinies and factions as they did. Besides so grievous were his wounds, and so cruell his torment, few expected he could live, nor was hee able to follow his businesse to regaine what they had lost, suppresse those factions and range the countries for provision as he intended, and well he knew in those affaires his owne actions and presence was as requisit as his experience, and directions, which now could not be; he went presently abord, resolving there to appoint them governours, and to take order[2] for the mutiners and their confederates. Who seeing him gone, perswaded Master Persie (to stay) and be their President, and within lesse then an howre was this mutation begun and concluded. For when the company understood Smith would leave them, and see the rest in Armes called Presidents and councellors, divers began to fawne on those new commanders,

10. From Jamestown to Powhatan village is about 74 mi. (120 km.) by modern charts (see Barbour, *Jamestown Voyages*, II, 465).

1. This would imply that it was not yet Sept. 10; but in so much confusion that date may have been overlooked.

2. Take measures, make arrangements.

that now bent all their wits to get him resigne them his commission, who after many salt and bitter repulses, that their confusion should not be attributed to him for leaving the country without government and authority; having taken order to bee free from danger of their malice; he was not unwilling they should steale it from him, but never consented to deliver it to any. But had that unhappy blast not hapned, he would quickly have quallified the heate of ‖ those humors and factions, had the ships but once left them and us to our fortunes, and have made that provision from among the Salvages, as we neither feared Spanyard, Salvage, nor famine: nor would have left Virginia, nor our lawfull authoritie, but at as deare a price as we had bought it, and paid for it. What shall I say? but thus we lost him, that in all his proceedings, made Justice his first guid, and experience his second; ever hating basenesse, sloth, pride, and indignitie, more then any dangers; that never allowed more for himselfe, then his souldiers with him; that upon no danger would send them where he would not lead them himselfe; that would never see us want what he either had, or could by any meanes get us; that would rather want then borrow, or starve then not pay; that loved actions more then wordes, and hated falshood and cousnage[3] worse then death: whose adventures were our lives, and whose losse our deathes. Leaving us thus with 3 ships, 7 boates, commodities ready to trade, the harvest newly gathered, 10 weekes provision in the store, 490 and odde persons, 24 peeces of ordinances, 300 muskets, snaphances and fire lockes, shot, powder, and match sufficient, curats,[4] pikes, swords, and moryons[5] more then men: the Salvages their language and habitations wcl knowne to 100 well trained and expert souldiers; nets for fishing, tooles of all sortes to worke, apparell to supply our wants, 6 mares and a horse, 5 or 600 swine, as many hens and chickens; some goates, some sheep; what was brought or bread there remained, but they regarded nothing but from hand to mouth, to consume that we had, tooke care for no- ‖ thing but to perfit[6] some colourable complaints against Captaine Smith, for effecting whereof, 3 weekes longer they stayed the 6 ships[7] til they could produce them. That time and charge might much better have beene spent, but it suted well with the rest of their discreations.

Now all those Smith had either whipped, punished, or any way disgraced, had free power and liberty to say or sweare any thing, and from a whole armefull of their examinations this was concluded.

The causes why Smith left the countrie and his commission.

[101]

[102]

Their complaints and proofe against him.

3. Variant spelling of "cozenage."
4. "Cuirasses."
5. "Morions" were a kind of helmet without beaver or visor.
6. Obsolete spelling of "perfect." The meaning is: "they did nothing but to develop their complaints against Smith and held up the departure of the ships an extra three weeks for that purpose."
7. Three weeks from Sept. 10 would have been Oct. 1.

The mutiners at the Falles, complained hee caused the Salvages assalt them, for that hee would not revenge their losse, they being but 120, and he 5 men and himselfe, and this they proved by the oath of one hee had oft whipped for perjurie and pilfering. The dutch-men that he had appointed to bee stabd for their treacheries, swore he sent to poison them with rats baine. The prudent Councel, that he would not submit himselfe to their stolne authoritie. Coe and Dyer, that should have murdered him, were highly preferred[8] for swearing, they heard one say, he heard Powhatan say, that he heard a man say: if the king would not send that corne he had, he should not long enjoy his copper crowne, nor those robes he had sent him: yet those also swore hee might have had corne for tooles but would not. The truth was, Smith had no such ingins as the king demanded, nor Powhatan any corne. Yet this argued he would starve them. Others complained hee would not let them rest in the fort (to starve) but forced them to the oyster bankes, to live or starve, as he lived himselfe. For

[103] though hee had of his owne private provisi- ‖ ons sent from England, sufficient; yet hee gave it all away to the weake and sicke, causing the most untoward (by doing as he did) to gather their food from the unknowne parts of the rivers and woods, that they lived (though hardly) that otherwaies would have starved, ere they would have left their beds, or at most the sight of James Towne to have got their own victuall. Some propheticall spirit calculated hee had the Salvages in such subjection, hee would have made himselfe a king, by

Pocahontas
Powhatans
daughter.

marrying Pocahontas, Powhatans daughter. It is true she was the very nomparell of his kingdome, and at most not past 13 or 14 yeares of age.[9] Very oft shee came to our fort, with what shee could get for Captaine Smith, that ever loved and used all the Countrie well, but her especially he ever much respected: and she so well requited it, that when her father intended to have surprized him, shee by stealth in the darke night came through the wild woods and told him of it. But her marriage could no way have intitled him by any right to the kingdome, nor was it ever suspected hee had ever such a thought, or more regarded her, or any of them, then in honest reason, and discreation he might. If he would he might have married her, or have done what him listed. For there was none that could have hindred his determination. Some that knewe not any thing to say, the Councel instructed, and advised what to sweare. So diligent they were in this businesse, that what any could remember, hee had ever done, or said in mirth, or passion, by some circumstantiall oath, it was applied to their fittest use, yet not past 8 or 9 could say much and that nothing

8. Probably "recommended" here.
9. I.e., in 1609; Pocahontas was probably born in 1595 or 1596 (see Barbour, *Pocahontas*, xix).

but circumstances,[10] which ‖ all men did knowe was most false and
untrue. Many got their passes by promising in England to say much
against him. I have presumed to say this much in his behalfe for that
I never heard such foule slaunders, so certainely beleeved, and urged
for truthes by many a hundred, that doe still not spare to spread
them, say them and sweare them, that I thinke doe scarse know him
though they meet him, nor have they ether cause or reason, but their
wills, or zeale to rumor or opinion. For the honorable and better sort
of our Virginian adventurers I think they understand it as I have
writ it. For instead of accusing him, I have never heard any give him
a better report, then many of those witnesses themselves that were
sent only home to testifie against him.

Richard Pots, W. P.[1]

When the ships departed Captaine Davis[2] arived in a smal Pin-   The planting
nace with some 16 proper men more, to those were added a company   at Point Com-
from James Towne under the command of Captaine Ratliffe to   fort.
inhabit Point-Comfort. Martin and Master West having lost their
boates, and neere halfe their men amongst the Salvages, were returned to James Towne, for the Salvages no sooner understood of
Captaine Smiths losse, but they all revolted, and did murder and
spoile all they could incounter. Now were we all constrained to live
only of that which Smith had only for his owne company, for the rest
had consumed their proportions. And now have we 20 Presidents
with all their appurtenances, for Master Persie was so sicke he could
not goe nor stand. But ere all was consumed, Master West and Ratliffe each with a pinnace, and 30 or 40 men wel appointed, sought
abroad ‖ to trade, how they carried the businesse I knowe not, but
Ratliffe and his men were most slaine by Powhatan, those that   Ratliffe slain
escaped returned neare starved in the Pinnace. And Master West   by Powhatan.
finding little better successe, set saile for England. Now wee all found
the want of Captaine Smith, yea his greatest maligners could then
curse his losse. Now for corne, provision, and contribution from the
Salvages; wee had nothing but mortall wounds with clubs and
arrowes. As for our hogs, hens, goats, sheep, horse, or what lived, our
commanders and officers did daily consume them, some small proportions (sometimes) we tasted till all was devoured, then swords,
arrowes, peeces, or any thing we traded to the Salvages, whose
bloody fingers were so imbrued in our bloods, that what by their
crueltie, our Governours indiscreation, and the losse of our ships; Of

10. Circumstantial evidence.
1. This is surely for William Phettiplace.
2. This seems to have been Capt. James Davies of the Sagadahoc colony in Maine,
later a resident of Virginia (see the Biographical Directory). The pinnace *Virginia* had
been built in Maine and was the first ship built by Englishmen on this side of the Atlantic
(see Barbour, *Jamestown Voyages*, II, 280).

500, within 6 monthes after there remained not many more then 60. most miserable and poore creatures.[3] It were to vild[4] to say what we endured; but the occasion[5] was only our owne, for want of providence, industrie, and governement, and not the barrennesse and defect of the countrie, as is generally supposed, for till then in 3 yeares (for the numbers were landed us) we had never landed sufficient provision for 6 months; such a glutton is the sea, and such good fellowes the marriners, wee as little tasted of those great proportions for their provisions, as they of our miseries, that notwithstanding ever swaid and overruled the businesse: though we did live as is said, 3 yeares chiefly of what this good countrie naturally affordeth: yet now had we beene in Paradice it selfe (with those gover- ‖ nours) it would not have beene much better with us, yet was there some amongst us, who had they had the governement, would surely have kept us from those extremities of miseries, that in 10 daies more would have supplanted us all by death.

The fruits of improvidences.

[106]

But God that would not it should bee unplanted, sent Sir Thomas Gates, and Sir George Sommers, with a 150 men, most happily preserved by the Berondoes[6] to preserve us. Strange it is to say how miraculously they were preserved, in a leaking ship, in those extreame stormes and tempests in such overgrowne seas 3 daies and 3 nights by bayling out water. And having given themselvs to death, how happily when least expected that worthy Captaine Sir George Somers, having line all that time cuning[7] the ship before those swalowing waves, discovered those broken Iles, where how plentifully they lived with fish and flesh, what a paradice this is to inhabit, what industrie they used to build their 2 ships, how happily they did transport them to James Towne in Virginia, I refer you to their owne printed relations.

The arivall of Sir Thomas Gates with 150.

But when those noble knights did see our miseries (being strangers in the country) and could understand no more of the cause but by their conjecture, of our clamors and complaints, of accusing or excusing one an other, they imbarked us with themselves, with the best means they could, and abandoning James Towne set saile for England.[8]

James Towne abandoned.

But yet God would not so have it, for ere wee left the river we met the Lord de-la-ware, then governour for the countrie, with 3

The arival of the Lord Laware.

---

3. This entire story is confirmed and embellished independently by George Percy ("Relacyon," MS copy in The Free Library of Philadelphia, printed with some slips in *Tyler's Quarterly Historical and Genealogical Magazine*, III [1922], 259–282).

4. Base, disgusting; obsolete variant of "vile."

5. Cause; i.e., fault.

6. The Bermudas.

7. Also spelled "con"; "to direct the steering of a ship." Above, "line" should be "lain."

8. Only Sir Thomas Gates had prevented the colonists from burning Jamestown to the ground (Percy, "Relacyon," MS copy, p. 18, and *Tyler's Qtly.*, III [1922], 269).

ships exceeding well furnished ‖ with al necessaries fitting, who [107]
againe returned them to the abandoned James Towne, the 9. of
June, 1610. accompanied with Sir Ferdinando Wainman, and divers
other gentlemen of sort. Sir George Somers, and Captaine Argall he
presentlie dispatcheth to require the Bermondas to furnish them with
provision: Sir Thomas Gates for England to helpe forward their supplies: himselfe neglected not the best was in his power for the furtherance of the busines and regaining what was lost. But even in the
beginning of his proceedings, his Lordship had such an incounter
with a scurvy sickenesse, that made him unable to weld[9] the state of
his body, much lesse the affaires of the colonie, so that after 8.
monthes sicknesse, he was forced to save his life by his returne for
England.

In this time Argall not finding the Bermondas, having lost Sir   2 Ships sent to
George Somers at sea, fell on the coast of Sagadahock,[10] where re-   the Bermundas.
freshing himselfe, found a convenient fishing for Cod. With a tast
whereof hee returned to James towne, from whence the Lord De-la-
ware sent him to trade in the river of Patawomecke, where finding an
English boy those people had preserved from the furie of Powhatan,
by his acquaintance had such good usage of those kind Salvages, that
they fraughted his ship with corne, wherewith he returned to James
Towne, and so for England with the Lord governour; yet before his
returne, the adventurers had sent Sir Thomas Dale with 3 ships,   The arival of
men and cattell, and all other provisions necessarie for a yeare, all   Sir Thomas
which arived the 10 of May, 1611.   Dale.

Againe, to second him with all possible expedition ‖ there was   [108]
prepared for Sir Thomas Gates, 6 tall ships with 300 men, and 100
kyne, with other cattel, with munition and all manner of provision
could bee thought needfull, and they arived about the 1 of August
next after safely at James towne.

Sir George Somers all this time was supposed lost: but thus it   Sir George
hapned, missing the Bermondas, hee fell also as did Argall with   Somers arivall
Sagadahock, where being refreshed, would not content himselfe with   at the Ber-
that repulse, but returned againe in the search; and there safely   mondas and
arived. But overtoiling himselfe on a surfeit died.[1] And in this Cedar   dieth.
ship built by his owne directions, and partly with his owne hands,
that had not in her any iron but only one bolt in her keele, yet well
endured thus tossed to and againe in this mightie Ocean, til with his
dead body she arived in England at fine, and at Whitchurch in
Dorsetshire, his body by his friends was honourably buried, with

9. Control, manage; obsolete variant of "wield."
10. See "A briefe Relation of the Discovery and Plantation of New England," in
James Phinney Baxter, ed., *Sir Ferdinando Gorges and His Province of Maine* (Boston, 1890),
207–208. The "English boy" mentioned below was Henry Spelman.
1. Apparently of overwork and overeating; cf. the *Generall Historie*, 176.

many volies of shot, and the rights of a souldier. And upon his Tombe was bestowed this Epitaph

His Epitaph.

Hei mihi Virginia, quod tam cito præterit æftas,
    Autumnus sequitur, sæviet inde & hyems.
At ver perpetuum nascetur, & Anglia læta,
    Decerpit flores, Floryda terra tuos.

Alas *Virginia* Somer so soone past
Autume succeeds and stormy winters blast,
Yet Englands joyfull spring with Aprill shewres,[2]
O *Floryda*, shall bring thy sweetest flowers.

[109]   Since there was a ship fraughted with provision, and 40 men, and another since then with the like number and provision to stay in the Countrie 12 months with Captaine Argall.[3]

The Lord governour himselfe doth confidently determine to goe with the next, or as presently as hee may in his owne person, with sundry other knights and gentlemen, with ships and men so farre as their meanes will extend to furnish: as for all their particular actions since the returne of Captaine Smith, for that they have beene printed from time to time, and published to the world, I cease farther to trouble you with any repetition of things so well knowne, more then are necessarie. To conclude the historie, leaving this assurance to all posteritie, howe unprosperously things may succeed, by what changes or chances soever. The action is honorable and worthie to bee approved, the defect whereof hath only beene in the managing the businesse; which I hope now experience hath taught them to amend, or those examples may make others to beware, for the land is as good as this booke doth report it.

FINIS.

[110] Captaine Smith I returne you the fruit of my labours, as Master Croshaw[4] requested me, which I bestowed in reading the discourses, and hearing the relations of such which have walked, and observed the land of Virginia with you. The pains I took was great: yet did

---

2. "Showers."

3. The opening of this paragraph should read: "Since the supply of August 1611, another ship came freighted with provision and 40 men, and then still another. . . ." This paragraph and the peroration that follows seem to be by another hand or hands, the peroration perhaps by William Symonds.

4. Despite Arber, *Smith, Works,* 174, the editor believes this refers to the Rev. William Crashaw, who has very kind words for John Smith and the entire 1612 book in his "Epistle Dedicatorie" addressed to Ralph, Lord Eure, lord president of Wales, in Alexander Whitaker's *Good Newes from Virginia* (London, 1613), sig. C4ᵛ.

the nature of the argument, and hopes I conceaved of the expedition, give me exceeding content. I cannot finde there is any thing, but what they all affirme, or cannot contradict: the land is good: as there is no citties, so no sonnes of Anak:[5] al is open for labor of a good and wise inhabitant: and my prayer shall ever be, that so faire a land, may bee inhabited by those that professe and love the Gospell.

Your friend
W. S.[6]

5. The sons of Anak were giants (Numbers 13: 27–28, 33).
6. William Symonds.

TEXTUAL ANNOTATION TO

The Proceedings
of the English Colonie
in Virginia

TEXTUAL ANNOTATION

The page numbers below refer to the boldface numerals in the margins of the present text, which record the pagination of the original edition used as copy text. The word or words before the bracket show the text as emended by the editor; the word or words after the bracket reproduce the copy text. The wavy dash symbol used after the bracket stands for a word that has not itself been changed but that adjoins a changed word or punctuation mark. The inferior caret, also used only after the bracket, signifies the location of missing punctuation in the copy text.

Page.Line

19.7   capacity. 3.]   ~ , ~ (from
            Generall Historie, 52)

19.10   education; as]   ~ , ~

19.14   werowans. Therefore]
            ~ , ~

19.18   Powhatan, told]   ~ ^ ~

19.23–24   hogsheads. This]   ~ , ~

20.6–7   Opechanchynough]
            Spechanchynough

20.22   pork, beefe]   ~ ^ ~

20.23   confess]   confest

21.4   fast; and]   ~ , ~ (based on
            Generall Historie, 52)

21.13   President]   Presidents (from
            Generall Historie, 53)

21.15–16   recompence; there]   ~ , ~
            (from *Generall Historie*, 53)

21.19   bones. Little]   ~ , little

21.marg.   A needles]   a ~

23.2   yeare. He]   ~ , he (from
            Generall Historie, 53)

23.5   tidings, the]   ~ . The (from
            Generall Historie, 53)

23.13   this]   his

23.19   him. Now]   ~ ; ~

23.21   humor obaied]   ~ , ~

24.20   love. After]   ~ , after
            (based on *Generall Historie*,
            54)

24.26   knowledge, but]   ~ ^ ~
            (from *Generall Historie*, 54)

25.5   fort; the]   ~ , ~ (from
            Generall Historie, 54)

25.7   nutmegs]   nugmets

27.1   Raymond]   Ramon

28.3   Surgion]   Curgion (*Generall
            Historie*, 55, has "Chir-
            urgion," but *Proceedings*, 8,
            has "Surgeon," with same
            change in *Generall Historie*,
            44)

29.10   Smiths Iles. The]   ~ , ~ ^
            the (based on *Generall
            Historie*, 55)

29.18   was. Two]   ~ ? ~ (in some
            copies; see Purchas,
            Pilgrimes, IV, 1712)

30.9   Wighcocomoco. The]   ~ ,
            the (from *Generall Historie*,
            56)

Page.Line

30.13   water. We]   ~ , we (from
            Generall Historie, 56)

30.18   Ployer. Being]   ployer,
            being (based on *Generall
            Historie*, 56)

31.2   Kuskarawaocke]   Kuskar-
            anaocke (based on *Generall
            Historie*, 56)

31.7   shore. So]   ~ ^ ~

32.18   Patawomeck: feare]   ~ ^ ~
            (in some copies)

32.25   divels. They]   ~ , they
            (based on *Generall Historie*,
            58)

33.9   Patawomeck, Cecocawone]
            ~ ^ ~

33.10   Moyaones, Nacothtant]
            ~ ^ ~ (from *Generall
            Historie*, 58)

33.25   they are]   there (from
            Generall Historie, 58)

34.9   imprisonment-acquaint-
            ances]   imprisonments,
            acquaintance (from
            Generall Historie, 58)

34.23   Stingeray]   stingeray

34.24   Russell]   Russels

35.3   Pyankatanck]   pyankatanck

35.8   warres, (the]   ~ , ^ ~ (from
            Generall Historie, 59)

35.9–10   fought. Finding]   ~ , find-
            ing (based on *Generall
            Historie*, 59)

35.11   them, what]   ~ ^ ~

35.12   Masawomeckes. This]   ~ ,
            this (from *Generall Historie*,
            59)

35.13   Weraskoyack]   weraskoyack

35.16   July. There]   ~ , there
            (from *Generall Historie*, 59)

37.3–4   Massawomeckes. In]   ~ , in
            (from *Generall Historie*, 60)

37.12   Massawomecks. We]   ~ ,
            we

37.15   for]   or (from *Generall
            Historie*, 60)

37.20   with all]   withall (from
            Generall Historie, 60)

37.24   a bell]   all ~ (from *Generall
            Historie*, 60)

Page.Line

39.2 Arrows. 5]　∼ , ∼ (from *Generall Historie*, 60)

40.5 any. Wee]　∼ , wee

40.13 notwithstanding]　notwith-anding

40.20 drowning. Yet]　∼ , yet (based on *Generall Historie*, 64)

40.23 Comfort]　comfort

41.12 Powell]　Poell

41.23 buildings]　building (from *Generall Historie*, 66)

42.4–5 Monacan. How]　∼ , how (from *Generall Historie*, 66)

42.10 unknowne. As]　∼) as (from *Generall Historie*, 66)

42.16 glasse milles]　∼ , ∼ (see Barbour, *Jamestown Voyages*, II, 411, 411n)

43.2–3 backs. How]　∼ , how (from *Generall Historie*, 66)

43.11 arrived). Ratcliffe]　∼) ∧ ∼

44.6 presents. Accompanied]　∼ , accompanied

44.21 different; their]　∼ , ∼

45.6 reaccommodated]　re accommodated (end-of-line hyphen missing)

45.10 mee? This]　∼ . ∼ (from *Generall Historie*, 67)

45.22 them. Your]　∼ ∧ your (from *Generall Historie*, 68)

46.3–4 false. Wherupon]　∼ , wherupon (from *Generall Historie*, 68)

46.9 miles; with]　∼ , ∼ (based on *Generall Historie*, 68)

47.12 downe the]　∼ to ∼ (from *Generall Historie*, 68)

47.13 neither]　neithet (in some copies)

47.18 purpose. From]　∼ , from (from *Generall Historie*, 68)

48.25–26 recreation. Yet]　∼ , ∼

49.10 Chickahamina, that]　∼ ∧ ∼ (from *Generall Historie*, 69)

49.10 nation was]　∼ , ∼ (from *Generall Historie*, 69)

Page.Line

50.6 taverne made]　∼ , ∼ (from *Generall Historie*, 69)

50.9 care to]　∼ , ∼ (from *Generall Historie*, 69)

50.11 necessary. Neither]　∼ , neither (from *Generall Historie*, 70)

52.28 Prat]　Part (from *Generall Historie*, 72)

52.30 Jefry]　(original has an in-verted "a" for the "y")

53.1 Dionis]　Dius (from *Generall Historie*, 72)

53.3 David ap Hugh]　Davi Uphu (from *Generall Historie*, 72)

53.9 David]　Davi (from *Generall Historie*, 73)

53.28–29 Newport). These]　∼) , these (based on *Generall Historie*, 73)

54.4 bushels]　bussels (in some copies)

54.6 Burrowes, being]　∼ ∧ ∼ (in some copies)

54.9 Weanocke]　weanocke

54.13–14 consideration). Master Persie and]　∼ ∧ ∧ ∼) ∼ , ∼ (based on *Generall Historie*, 73)

54.16 procrastinating]　procasti-nating

54.25 corne. The]　∼ , the (from *Generall Historie*, 73)

55.6 voluntarily]　volentarily

57.3 provision. This]　∼ ; ∼ (from *Generall Historie*, 74)

57.5–6 maner. Captaine]　∼ , ∼ (from *Generall Historie*, 74)

57.8–9 throats. The]　∼ ; the (from *Generall Historie*, 74)

57.22 Kecoughtan. But]　∼ , ∼ (based on *Generall Historie*, 74)

58.10 frore]　froye

58.16 spirits. Quartering]　∼ , quartering (from *Generall Historie*, 75)

59.3 Salvage began]　∼ ; ∼ (based on *Generall Historie*, 75)

Page.Line

59.11 demandes. As] ~ , as (from *Generall Historie*, 75)

59.12 spare. And] ~ ₍ ~

59.14 promised, except] ~ , (~ (from *Generall Historie*, 75)

59.18–19 receave. Yet] ~ , yet (from *Generall Historie*, 75)

59.21 I would] J ~

60.2 houses. The] ~ , the (from *Generall Historie*, 75)

60.5 escape both] ~ , ~ (from *Generall Historie*, 75)

60.5 him and] ~ , ~ (from *Generall Historie*, 75)

60.16 affect] effect (from *Generall Historie*, 75)

61.18 acorns, roots] ~ ₍ ~ (from *Generall Historie*, 76)

61.21 I flie] J ~

62.7 kept. As] ~ , as (from *Generall Historie*, 76)

62.12 I thinke] J ~

63.4 I receave] J ~

63.6 I offered] J ~

63.10 I see] J ~

63.13 I may] J ~

63.13 I beare] J ~

63.21 I have] J ~

63.21 I honour] J ~

63.22 I live] J ~

63.23 I can] J ~

64.2 I will] J ~

64.4 I will] J ~

64.16 him), to] ~) ₍ To (based on *Generall Historie*, 77)

65.2 his people] this ~

65.3 promised] promiseed

65.3–4 should. Nowe] ~ : nowe (based on *Generall Historie*, 77)

66.2 was for] ~ , ~

66.3 apparell; by] ~ , ~ (from *Generall Historie*, 78)

66.6 like. They] ~ , they (based on *Generall Historie*, 78)

66.13 rest, 50.] ~ . ~

67.7 promise. Here] ~ , here (from *Generall Historie*, 78)

Page.Line

68.8 selves. If] ~ , if (from *Generall Historie*, 79)

68.20 vowed to] ~ , ~ (from *Generall Historie*, 79)

69.11 with at] ~ (~ (from *Generall Historie*, 79)

69.17 Powell] Poell

70.5 If I keepe] Jf J ~

70.6 I breake] J ~

70.9–10 I begin] J ~

70.10 I can] J ~

70.11 I am] J ~

70.11 Rasseweac] Rasseneac (based on *Generall Historie*, 80)

70.18 I once] J ~

71.14 Ile] Jle

72.3 alone the] ~ , ~ (from *Generall Historie*, 80)

72.16–17 constrained, hating] ~ ₍ ~

72.17 fighting almost] ~ , ~ (based on *Generall Historie*, 80)

73.19 Salvages) returned] ~ ₍ ~

73.23 king sent] ~ , ~ (from *Generall Historie*, 81)

74.9 Potauncac)] Potauncat—)

75.7 had from] ~ ; ~ (from *Generall Historie*, 81)

75.12 provision. For] ~ , for (from *Generall Historie*, 82)

75.13 Coe ashore] ~ , ~ (from *Generall Historie*, 82)

75.16 Werawocomoco] werawocomoco

75.17–18 affected), that] ~ ₍ , ~

75.24 flesh, fish] ~ ₍ ~

76.16 reasonable] reasonably (from *Generall Historie*, 82)

76.24 Salvage, as] ~ ₍ ~ (from *Generall Historie*, 82)

77.4 then, had] ~ ₍ ~

77.22 done against] ~ , ~ (from *Generall Historie*, 82)

78.1 prevented: peruse] ~) ~ (from *Generall Historie*, 82)

79.17 selfe, you] ~ ; ~

79.20 men shall] ~ , ~ (from *Generall Historie*, 83)

Page.Line

80.2	nowe no] ∼ , ∼ (from *Generall Historie*, 83)
80.6	spurre] spurne
80.15	to knowe] (∼ ∼
80.16	like] ∼)
80.18	villany. 40] ∼ , ∼ (based on *Generall Historie*, 83)
81.15	walnuts] walenuts (based on *Generall Historie*, 84)
81.17	fetters, purposing] ∼ ; ∼
81.25	escaped. Captaine] ∼ ; ∼ (from *Generall Historie*, 84)
82.8	injurie and] ∼ (∼
82.15	bravadoes would] ∼ , ∼
82.17	burnt] burut
82.20	him. But] ∼ , but (from *Generall Historie*, 84)
82.24	valours; he] ∼ , ∼
83.marg.	Ocanindge] Gcanindge
83.8	then] them
83.11	losse. We] ∼ , we
83.23	that] ihat
85.16	garrison, to] ∼ ∧ ∼
85.18	without] with out (end-of-line hyphen missing)
85.18	order. 30] ∼ , ∼
85.21	Hog] hog (from *Generall Historie*, 86)
86.11	Untill] untill
86.11	Kemps] Keinps
86.20	Point-Comfort] point-comfort (based on *Generall Historie*, 86)
87.7	diet). But] ∼) ∧ but (based on *Generall Historie*, 86)
87.10	another. Of] ∼ : of
87.15–16	Salvages; especially] ∼ , ∼
87.19–20	weeke). Thousands] ∼) ∧ thousands (based on *Generall Historie*, 86)
87.22	Countrie] Counrrie
88.9	raile. You] ∼ , you (based on *Generall Historie*, 86)
88.25–89.1	that of 200] that 200 (the catchword "of" omitted at the top of p. 89)
89.4	Many] many

89.10	For] for
89.10–11	stolne, with] ∼ ∧ ∼ (from *Generall Historie*, 87)
89.17	well] we (from *Generall Historie*, 87)
90.3	Chawonock] chawonock
90.marg.	for] fo
90.7	dead. This] ∼ , this (from *Generall Historie*, 87)
90.13	angrie. All] ∼ ∧ all (based on *Generall Historie*, 87–88)
90.16	double villaine] ∼ villanie (from *Generall Historie*, 88)
90.19	imploiment] imploimenr
91.4	Dowse] Douese
91.7	Dowse] Douese
91.9	ambuscadoes as] ∼ , ∼ (from *Generall Historie*, 88)
91.11	peninsula] penisula
92.14	did; though] ∼ , ∼
92.15	adventures he] ∼ , ∼ (from *Generall Historie*, 89)
92.15	long and] ∼ , ∼ (from *Generall Historie*, 89)
92.23	them; though] ∼ ∧ ∼
93.7	me to] ∼ , ∼
93.12	governement and] ∼ : ∼
93.13	Gates] Gales
93.14	persons, they] ∼ . ∼
93.15	1609. A] ∼ ∧ a
94.6	scouts the] ∼ , ∼ (from *Generall Historie*, 90)
94.10–11	power. Had] ∼ , had (from *Generall Historie*, 90)
94.12	trusted] trused
94.marg.	colours] coulors
94.15–16	merit. To] ∼ , to (based on *Generall Historie*, 90)
96.10	Powhatan to] ∼ , ∼ (from *Generall Historie*, 91)
96.21	The worst] the ∼
96.26–97.1	retire; yet] ∼ , ∼
97.14	President. That] ∼ , that
97.25	themselves] ∼ , (from *Generall Historie*, 92)
98.2	hopes of] ∼ , ∼
98.16	the Salvages] their ∼ (from *Generall Historie*, 92)

Page.Line		Page.Line	
98.18	Nonsuch] ɴonsuch	104.17	Point-Comfort] ~-comfort
98.18	The Salvages] the ~	105.8	arrowes. As] ~ , ~
98.25	grew] grow (from *Generall*	105.20	months; such] ~ ˌ ~
	Historie, 92)	105.marg.	improvidences] imp
99.2	West Fort] west fort (based		ovidences
	on *Generall Historie*, 92)	106.8	Strange] strange
99.14	trials, their] ~ ˌ ~ (based	106.11	bayling] bapling
	on *Generall Historie*, 92)	106.14	swalowing] sawlowing
100.12	be; he] ~ , ~	106.25	river we] ~ ; ~
101.18	muskets, snaphances and]	107.22	governour; yet] ~ , ~
	~ ˌ snaphanches, ~	108.2	tall] tale
101.23	chickens] chicken	108.14	body] bo- (end of line,
101.24	sheep; what] ~ , ~		printer dropped the second
102.3	That] that		syllable)
102.6	those Smith] ~ , ~	108.14	fine] line
104.marg.	Point Comfort] point com-	108.marg.	His] his
	fort	109.13	soever. The] ~ , ~

Hyphenation Record

The following lists have been inserted at the request of the editorial staff of the Institute of Early American History and Culture. The list immediately below records possible compound words that were hyphenated at the end of the line in the copy text. In each case the editor had to decide for the present edition whether to print the word as a single word or as a hyphenated compound. The material before the bracket indicates how the word is printed in the present edition; the material after the bracket indicates how the word was broken in the original. The wavy dash symbol indicates that the form of the word has been unchanged from the copy text. Numerals refer to the page number of the copy text (the boldface numerals in the margin in this edition) and to the line number (counting down from the boldface number) in the present edition.

Page.Line		Page.Line	
10.5	sea-Crabs] ~	75.15	Dutch-men] ~
17.13	overjoyed] over-joyed	86.20	Point-Comfort] ~
19.23–24	hogsheads] hogs-heads	92.13	otherwaies] other-waies
28.14	overswayed] over-swayed	102.12	dutch-men] ~
35.24	South-sea] ~	106.marg.	La-ware] ~
37.marg.	fire-workes] ~	107.17–18	De-la-ware] ~
72.12	abord] a-bord		

The list below contains words found as hyphenated compounds in the copy text that unavoidably had to be broken at the end of the line at the hyphen in the present text. In quoting or transcribing from the present text, the hyphen should be retained for these words. Numerals refer to the page number of the copy text (the boldface numerals in the margin in this edition) and line number (counting down from the boldface number).

Page.Line		*Page.Line*	
31.14–15	Bole-Armoniacke	38.25–26	giantlike-people
37.marg.	fire-workes	106.marg.	La-ware
38.1–2	beare-skins	107.17–18	De-la-ware

A DESCRIPTION
of New England . . .

1616

INTRODUCTION

While Smith's *Map of Virginia* was in press, meddlesome rumors were again sweeping over London about the disastrous conditions in the Jamestown colony. On July 9, 1612, for example, that diligent letter writer John Chamberlain, in the course of informing his friend Sir Dudley Carleton about a return visit of Don Pedro de Zúñiga as special ambassador to England, surmised that the latter would "expostulate" to King James "about our planting in Virginia." Chamberlain added tartly, "Wherin there will need no great contestation, seeing it is to be feared that that action will fall to the ground of it self, by the extreem beastly idleness of our nation, which . . . will rather die and starve then be brought to any labor or industrie to maintain themselves."[1] At the same time, the eagerness of some investors to back a colony in Bermuda indicated that quicker and surer profit was to be had there than in the slothful atmosphere of tidewater Virginia.

When the opportunity to invest in a Bermuda independent of the Virginia Company came in November, however, Smith had no funds available for that sort of "adventure."[2] But he was more than willing to hazard his skin again in the American wilderness, and after deciding that appeals to the Virginia Company were an exercise in futility, he set about looking elsewhere.

At about this time, 1611, Sir Ferdinando Gorges's interest in colonization was reawakened. He had originally become interested in the English colonization of America in 1605, when five Abenaki Indians accidentally arrived in Plymouth, England, where Gorges was governor of the fort.[3] Six years later he received another Indian, Epenow (this time from Martha's Vineyard), from Capt. Edward Harlow, a veteran of the Sagadahoc colony, who had just returned from the New England region. Gorges still had with him an Indian from the 1605 "accident," one Sassacomoit, who acted as a

1. Norman Egbert McClure, ed., *The Letters of John Chamberlain* (Philadelphia, 1939), I, 367.

2. See Smith's appeal for some sort of "reward" for his services in Virginia as late as May 2, 1621, in Susan Myra Kingsbury, ed., *The Records of the Virginia Company of London* (Washington, D.C., 1906–1935), I, 474.

3. Three of these Indians were given to Gorges by Capt. George Waymouth, who was returning to Dartmouth in July 1605 from an expedition to Monhegan Island. (Though Plymouth is only 30-odd mi. from Dartmouth, the reason for the gift is not known.) "This accident," Gorges later wrote, "must be acknowledged the means under God of putting on foot and giving life to all our plantations" (Sir Ferdinando Gorges, *A Briefe Narration of the Originall Undertakings of the Advancement of Plantations into the Parts of America . . .* [London, 1658] [Massachusetts Historical Society, *Collections*, 3d Ser., VI (Boston, 1837)], 51). See also David B. Quinn and Alison M. Quinn, eds., *The English New England Voyages, 1602–1608* (Hakluyt Society, 2d Ser., CLXI (London, 1983)).

rough interpreter after some of the linguistic difficulties between the Indians themselves had been solved.

Even before that, however, in March 1611, one Marmaduke Rawdon (or Roydon), a rich young merchant, married a still wealthier heiress and, with even more cash in his coffers, began looking for means to increase his income further through worldwide trade. Sir Ferdinando's new Indian, Epenow, by then had begun to talk about gold mines on Cape Cod—on the logical assumption that he would be sent home to help the English find them. That there were none was beside the point. Word of this golden disclosure naturally reached the ears of shipmaster Thomas Hunt, who seems to have been as unscrupulous as John Smith was guileless. Hunt somehow painted himself into a picture that made his participation in the venture plausible to Rawdon and Smith.

Whatever the details, Rawdon and his associates fitted out a small fleet for Smith (and Hunt), which sailed in March 1614, just about the time that Gorges started once more to plan in earnest. Gorges's aim was specifically Epenow's gold mine on Cape Cod, though to his associate backers he suggested a sounder source of revenue from fishing. But to the dismay of the good Plymouth merchants, Epenow managed to escape to Cape Cod without providing any clue to the whereabouts of the nonexistent mines, and the captain and crew were so discomfited that they turned tail and fled back to England without stopping even to fish. At that, Gorges lost heart, as well as money.

Smith, returning from his Rawdon-sponsored voyage, arrived in Plymouth soon after this debacle, bringing such evidence of success, albeit modest, that Gorges's enthusiasm was revivified. Nevertheless, between private conflicts of interest in London, as well as Plymouth, and even more serious conflicts of purpose, nothing more significant came out of Smith's design than a "fleet" of two ships that would fish for a cargo while Smith with sixteen companions found a place somewhere in New England to settle in for the winter.

On the heels of this attenuation of much grander plans, bad luck so plagued Smith's venture that he barely escaped with his life (and his notes for the *Description of New England*), while his other ship sailed on, under the command of Capt. Thomas Dermer, to return eventually to England without anything further being recorded or known today. In the face of Smith's failure, the editor cannot but join in the philosophical reflection that "it may be that his contribution to the future of the country which stirred him so greatly was thus as important as it would have been had he succeeded in his original plan to test the New England winter. The *Description of New England* did much to focus attention on that part of the New World."[4]

4. Richard Arthur Preston, *Gorges of Plymouth Fort: A Life of Sir Ferdinando Gorges, Captain of Plymouth Fort, Governor of New England, and Lord of the Province of Maine* (Toronto, 1953), 159.

The significance of the commendatory verses written for the *Description of New England* should not be overlooked. Verses, good, bad, and indifferent, were often prefixed to published works in Smith's day. For the historian they can be useful for the light they may throw on the subject in hand. In the case of Smith's *Description of New England*, passing over the friendly testimonials of no consequence, the following can be noted about the versifiers: John Davies was a poet of some small distinction, a writing master at Oxford, and one of the first authors to refer to Shakespeare (1603); Richard Gunnell was an actor, a dramatist, and a theatre manager, to whom Smith had certainly recounted tales of adventure in eastern Europe; George Wither was a voluminous champion of liberty and toleration; and the two ex-soldiers who close the book were companions of Smith's in Transylvania.[5]

Admittedly, there are few facts to go on for all periods of Smith's life, but this early book contains many hints that the years from the successful publication of his 1612 book until he all but spent himself on the *Generall Historie* saw many unrecorded or little-known experiences and personal contacts that attest to a more significant career than has generally been credited to him. Such inconspicuous witnesses as these versifiers form some of the "other men" who vouched for Smith and whom Thomas Fuller had not troubled to notice.[6]

It is proper to point out here that this work is in a sense Smith's first solid opus—the first book in which we see his character as explorer, narrator, and ethnographer merged with his vision, his propagandist bent, and his retrospective self-discovery. Here for the first time he lets drop, or indirectly introduces, a word or two of his experiential schooling in seamanship, soldiering, and surviving. These matters would form the core of his *True Travels* in 1629.

In conclusion, while it would be to little purpose to attempt to locate all the sources Smith used for side information after 1612, it is worth pointing out here that he did base his plans on knowledge available in printed books, as well as some in manuscript. His first recognizable reference to contemporary sources is found here,[7] and for the first time he draws on unacknowledged material for statistics or other pertinent data.[8] In addition, less specifically, sidelights on social conditions in England found in Smith are substantiated in such works as Robert Burton's *Anatomy of Melancholy* (first published in 1612) and the poems of John Taylor and Richard Brathwaite (1580–1653 and 1588?–1673, respectively)—all three of these writers being personally known to Smith. Finally, the *Description of New England* tells

---

5. For these and other versifiers, see the Biographical Directory.
6. Thomas Fuller, *The History of the Worthies of England*, new ed. (London, 1840 [orig. publ. 1744]), I, 276.
7. See the two "relations" mentioned on p. 4, below.
8. E.g., see p. 12n, below, and the highly probable debt to Tobias Gentleman's study of the fishing industry mentioned on p. 20n, below.

us that Smith "could speak French,"[9] while elsewhere direct borrowings from Spanish and Italian bear witness to some knowledge of those languages.[10] Smith, with little formal schooling, had at last found his métier.

Summary

Despite its rambling structure the *Description of New England* shows at least some conception of organization (for a man of action the handling of a quill pen must have been an ordeal). It broaches a more complicated subject than the straight narration of the *True Relation* or the description of the land and people in the *Map of Virginia*, in that it combines some of both, while tossing in an element of propaganda that is new for Smith. While he had pleaded for colonial Virginia on earlier occasions, in this work he began to "sell" colonization with arguments he had not used before. He now took it for granted that colonization was justifiable and necessary, and on that basis went on to show that a colony—especially one in New England—could be self-sustaining and even profitable from the outset, the harsh climate of New England notwithstanding.

The subsequent record of New England fully justifies Smith's confidence. Nevertheless, it took the determination of two disparate groups to bring the idea to fruition, groups that had the financial backing, the determination, and the willingness to work that were essential: the Pilgrims in 1620 and the Puritans in 1630. Smith could only urge, preach, back, and advise, while others slowly established what he so firmly believed in. His last work, the *Advertisements*, reflects his disappointment over not taking part.

The *Description of New England* is therefore to be regarded as much for what it preaches as for what it tells. Beginning with some fifteen pages of physical description, Smith digressed on colonization for half that space before returning to his subject. Then he indulged in another digression of a similar nature (pp. 30–45), with Classical references on great states as well as the very recent exploits of Spain and Portugal. A detailed narrative of his unsuccessful attempt to return to New England in 1615 follows, including details of his capture by French "pirates." Finally, the closing summation treats Adam and Eve, the Pharisees and publicans, and the importance of "planting of countries, and civilizing barbarous and inhumane Nations."

The whole work was reprinted in the *Generall Historie*, 203–227, somewhat amplified so that the entire reprinted text is about one-sixth longer than the original. Briefly put, the first four pages of the *Generall Historie* reprint contain some material not in the first two pages of the *Description of New*

---

9. See p. 52, below.
10. See the *True Travels*, 23, for borrowings from Italian; Smith's preference for Spanish forms rather than French (e.g., "ambuscado," *ibid.*, 12) seems significant.

England, but pages 206–221 follow pages 3–45 of the latter almost verbatim. Then there is some rearrangement and a few details added for the French episode, until the last two pages of the reprint follow the last three of the *Description of New England* closely.

Chronology of Early New England, 1602–1620[*]

1602

Capts. Bartholomew Gosnold and Bartholomew Gilbert (cousins by marriage, and unrelated to Sir Humphrey) set out to establish a small colony, explored part of the coast of Maine and Massachusetts, named Cape Cod, and built a small redoubt on Cuttyhunk Island near Martha's Vineyard, Massachusetts. Lack of provisions forced them to return to England on June 18/28, after a short stay.

1603

Capt. Martin Pring, on a trading voyage backed by Richard Hakluyt and others, explored Cape Cod Bay and settled briefly near the mouth of the Pamet River on Cape Cod. There were also French explorations around Nova Scotia in this year.

1604

Samuel de Champlain, in the pay of Pierre Du Gua de Monts, explored Nova Scotia and established a post on modern St. Croix Island, near the mouth of the St. Croix River, New Brunswick. From there he surveyed the coast as far as Pemaquid Point, Maine.

1605

May   Sir Thomas Arundell's expedition under Capt. George Waymouth arrived at Monhegan Island to explore the coast and to look for a site for a Catholic colony.

July 18/28   Arundell's expeditions returned to England, with five Abenaki Indians, three of whom Waymouth soon gave to Sir Ferdinando Gorges, then captain of Plymouth Fort.

Aug.   De Monts founded the first permanent settlement in Canada at Port Royal, near Annapolis, Nova Scotia.

---

[*] In this chronology both Old Style and New Style dates are given, since the English were using the Julian (O.S.) calendar and the French the Gregorian (N.S.).

1606

Apr. 10/20	Letters patent (the first charter) issued to two groups to "deduce" colonies in North America: the first, sponsored by London, for what is today Virginia; the second, by the West Country (Bristol, Exeter, Plymouth, etc.), for New England. Sir John Popham, lord chief justice of the king's bench, and Gorges were the paramount backers of the latter.
Aug. 12/22	The first of two ships sent by Popham and Gorges to establish a colony in "North Virginia" sailed, with two of Waymouth's five Indians on board, but was captured by Spaniards in the Straits of Florida and eventually sank in the Guadalquivir River in Spain. The second, which sailed shortly after the first, reached New England safely, with Popham's son-in-law Thomas Hanham as captain, and Martin Pring as pilot. One more Indian was on this ship.
Dec. 15/25?	When the first ship failed to arrive, Hanham left the Indian behind to help the next body of settlers and set sail for England.

1607

May 13/23	Jamestown founded in Virginia.
May 31/June 10	Two vessels were sent by Popham and Gorges to settle on the Maine coast. This time the leaders were Raleigh Gilbert, son of Sir Humphrey, and George Popham, a kinsman of the lord chief justice; the fourth of the Indians was with them.
June 10/20	Sir John Popham died. His son Sir Francis took over the management of the colonial enterprise.
Aug. 20/30	Capt. George Popham began the building of St. George's Fort at Sagadahoc. The next day the carpenters began work on the pinnace that was later named *Virginia*.

1608

June 23/July 3	Champlain founded Quebec, on his third voyage to "New France" (Canada).
spring–winter	The Sagadahoc colony had suffered from bitter cold weather, George Popham had died, and Gilbert had to return to England. Thus it was

decided to abandon the settlement, although it is not known just when. Certainly the colonists were back in England before George Popham's will was probated on Dec. 2/12.

1609

May 23/June 2   By this date, when the Virginia Company was reorganized under a second charter to provide broader financial backing, the Sagadahoc experiment had lapsed into inactivity.

c. Oct. 4/14   Smith left Jamestown forever.

1611

May 11/21   Champlain returned to Quebec for a stay of three months.

1612

Nov.   Champlain was appointed lieutenant to the first viceroy of Canada, the prince de Condé.

1613

Mar. 19/29   Champlain arrived at Tadoussac, and from there went W and up the Ottawa River to the Huron country, thereby opening the French route W. He soon returned to France, however, and did not continue his Canadian explorations until the spring of 1615, after Smith had come and gone from New England.

May 6/16   René Le Coq de la Saussaye landed in Nova Scotia on behalf of a wealthy French noblewoman, Madame Antoinette de Pons, marquise de Guercheville, wife of Charles du Plessis, duc de Liancourt and governor of Paris. La Saussaye was to establish a new French colony in "Acadia." Having done this, in name, in Nova Scotia, he promptly sailed to Mount Desert Island, Maine, where he went to work on an agricultural project.

June 22/July 2   Samuel Argall, who was fishing in the neighborhood of Mount Desert Island, having heard of the Frenchmen from local Indians, arrived to investigate. While the Frenchmen were ashore, Argall seized their ship. La Saussaye fled into the forest and Argall in the meantime pilfered all his papers. When the two finally confronted one another, La Saussaye was forced to sail off with half of his men, while the other half were taken aboard Argall's ship to go to Jamestown for questioning. The upshot was that the acting governor of Virginia, Sir Thomas Dale, commanded Argall to return to Nova Scotia or Maine and wipe out the French colony (or colonies). This Argall did, quickly and efficiently, having caught the French commander in Port Royal completely unawares.

Oct. 30/Nov. 9   Argall sailed back to Jamestown, having purged America S of 45° N latitude of all French intruders.

1614

Mar. 3/13   Smith sailed for New England.

June   Gorges sent Capt. Nicholas Hobson on a bootless voyage to New England.

late Aug.   Smith returned to England, having made at least a small profit, through furs and fishing.

1615

Mar.   Smith started for New England again, but had to turn back for repairs; his second ship went on and came home "well fraught" in Aug.

May 15/25   Champlain landed at Tadoussac once more, only to set out for the Indian village at modern Lachine Rapids.

June 24/July 4   Smith sailed from Plymouth heading to New England again, but ran afoul of pirates and a French privateer.

July–Oct.   Champlain undertook his great voyage up the Ottawa River and by portages reached Lake Huron.

1616

June 18/28   Printing of the *Description of N.E.* finished.

July–Dec.   Gorges sent Richard Vines to New England for trade and discovery; he wintered at or near Smith's Sowocatuck ("Ipswich," now Biddeford, Maine), living with the Indians. It is probable that such contacts with Europeans fresh from abroad produced the epidemic that decimated the Indian population in 1617.

Aug. 31–Sept. 10   Champlain returned to France, to learn that the viceroy of Canada, the prince de Condé, had been arrested.

Dec.   A letter from the Spanish ambassador to London stated that Smith had offered to accompany a whaling expedition "in the region of the North" and had given him a book, probably the *Description of N.E.*

1617

Jan.   Smith was promised a large fleet for New England, which turned out to be three ships.

Mar.   Smith's ships were pinned in Plymouth harbor by a southwester that blew for three months. (That same spring Sir Walter Ralegh entered Plymouth harbor early in Apr. and could not get away until June 12.) Smith abandoned his plans and returned to London.

Nov.–Dec.   The Pilgrims, in the Netherlands, began to interest themselves seriously in migrating to America and conferred with Sir Edwin Sandys of the Council for Virginia.

1618

Jan. 4/14   Sir Francis Bacon was named lord chancellor.

Apr.   Powhatan died in Virginia.

May 14/24   Champlain sailed back to Canada with plans for colonization on a large scale.

July 12/22   Bacon was raised to the peerage as Baron Verulam. Not long thereafter, both Smith and William Strachey addressed manuscripts to him: Smith with his first draft of what was to be *New Englands Trials*; Strachey with the third copy of his *Historie*. Both men hoped to get some sort of reward, and both failed.

Aug. 18/28   By this date Champlain was again in France, where he soon ran into political and legal trouble. Obliged to remain there until May 1620, he could then sail only as the administrator of an established colony. It was the end of his career as an explorer.

Oct. 29/Nov. 8   Sir Walter Ralegh, perhaps England's greatest colonial promoter, was beheaded.

1619

Apr. 28/May 8   Sir Edwin Sandys was made treasurer of the Virginia Company, replacing Sir Thomas Smythe.

May Argall returned to England, after two years as acting governor of Virginia.

June 9/19 A patent for the Pilgrims to settle in Virginia was granted by the Virginia Company.

Aug. First Africans brought to Virginia. About this time Capt. Thomas Dermer was exploring the NE coast of America for Gorges. He wintered in Virginia.

1620

Mar. 3/13 Gorges and his associates applied to the Privy Council for renewal of the rights of the "northern colony."

July 21/31 A reorganization of the "northern colony" was approved.

July 22/Aug. 1 The Pilgrims sailed from the Netherlands.

Nov. 3/13 A charter for the "Council for New England" was signed in England, giving Gorges and his associates jurisdiction over all of America between 40° and 48° N latitude.

Nov. 9/19 The Pilgrims accidentally ended up on Cape Cod.

Nov. 11/21 The Mayflower Compact was signed.

Dec. 11/21 Smith's *New Englands Trials* was entered for publication.

A DESCRIPTION

of *New England:*

OR

THE OBSERVATIONS, AND

difcoueries, of Captain *Iohn Smith* (Admirall
of that Country) in the North of *America*, in the year
of our Lord 1614: *with the fucceffe of fixe Ships,
that went the next yeare* 1615; *and the
accidents befell him among the
French men of warre:*

With the proofe of the prefent benefit this
Countrey affoords: whither this prefent yeare,
1616, *eight voluntary Ships are gone
to make further tryall.*

At LONDON
Printed by *Humfrey Lownes*, for *Robert Clerke*; and
are to be fould at his houfe called the Lodge,
in Chancery lane, ouer againft Lin-
colnes Inne. 1616.

A. p. 420.

[Smith's title of "Admiral of New England" seems to stem from 1617, when he was "contracted . . . to be Admirall" after he was unable to get away from Plymouth in that year (*New Englands Trials* [1622], sig. B3ʳ; and *Advertisements*, 16). There is obviously a chronological anomaly in his use of the title in the summer of 1616, unless it was, perhaps jokingly, conferred on him on his return from defeat at the hands of French privateers late in 1615. In the absence of substantiating evidence of any kind, the editor is inclined to go along with the suggestion of Richard Arthur Preston that the title was more of a promise than a gift, and that "if it was more than a figment of Smith's fervent imagination, [the promise] was never fulfilled" (*Gorges of Plymouth Fort: A Life of Sir Ferdinando Gorges, Captain of Plymouth Fort, Governor of New England, and Lord of the Province of Maine* [Toronto, 1953], 160).

It should be noted that Robert Clerke, mentioned at the bottom of the page, also engraved the accompanying map of New England (see the caption to the map).

Two title pages with specially printed presentation inscriptions have come to light relatively recently. One of these reads: "For the Right Honourable the/Lord Elesmore Lord High/Chancelor of England" (Joseph Sabin *et al.*, eds., *A Dictionary of Books Relating to America*, XX [New York, 1927–1928], 223); now in the Huntington Library, San Marino, Calif. The other has a similar inscription, "For the Right Honourable, Sir/Edward Coke, Lord Chiefe/Justice of England" and is now in the Folger Shakespeare Library, Washington, D.C. (see the following page). To provide for the inscriptions the decoration and one of the line dashes were omitted and the title lowered. The purpose of these inscriptions was obviously to obtain support for Smith's plans to colonize New England, though neither worthy appears to have paid any heed. In fact, "Lord Elesmore" (Sir Thomas Egerton, Baron Ellesmere) resigned from his office within a year due to ill health and was succeeded early in 1618 by Sir Francis Bacon (see the "Letter to Bacon," immediately following in this volume). Meanwhile, Smith proposed some sort of fishing-exploring expedition under the aegis of King Christian IV of Denmark, King James's brother-in-law (see the Fragments, in Vol. III). Verily, in those years Smith was "a voice crying in the wilderness."

The editor is grateful to the New York Public Library, Astor, Lenox and Tilden Foundations for permission to reproduce this title page.]

For the Right Honourable, Sir
Edward Coke, Lord Chiefe
Iustice of *England*.

A
DESCRIPTION
of *New England*:

OR

THE OBSERVATIONS, AND
discoueries, of Captain *Iohn Smith* (Admirall
of that Country) in the North of *America*, in the year
of our Lord 1614: *with the successe of sixe Ships,
that went the next yeare* 1615; *and the*
accidents befell him among the
French men of warre:

With the proofe of the present benefit this
Countrey affoords: whither this present yeare,
1616, *eight voluntary Ships are gone
to make further tryall.*

At LONDON
Printed by *Humfrey Lownes*, for *Robert Clerke*; and
are to be sould at his house called the Lodge,
in Chancery lane, ouer against Lin-
colnes Inne. 1616.

[The editor is grateful to the Folger Shakespeare Library for permission to reproduce this title page.]

TO THE HIGH
Hopeful Charles,
Prince of Great Britaine.

Sir:

So favourable was your most renowned and memorable Brother, Prince Henry, to all generous designes; that in my discovery of Virginia, I presumed to call two namelesse Headlands after my Soveraignes heires, Cape Henry, and Cape Charles.[1] Since then, it beeing my chance to range some other parts of America, whereof I heere present your Highness the description in a Map; my humble sute is, you would please to change their Barbarous names, for such English, as Posterity may say, Prince Charles was their Godfather. What here in this relation I promise my Countrey, let mee ‖ live or die the slave of scorne and infamy, if (having meanes) I make it not apparent; please God to blesse me but from such accidents as are beyond my power and reason to prevent. For my labours, I desire but such conditions as were promised me out of the gaines; and that your Highnesse would daigne to grace this Work, by your Princely and favourable respect[2] unto it, and know mee to be

Your Highnesse true and faithfull servant,
John Smith.

1. According to George Percy, "The nine and twentieth day [of April 1607] we set up a Crosse at Chesupioc Bay, and named that place Cape Henry" (Samuel Purchas, *Hakluytus Posthumus, or Purchas His Pilgrimes* . . . [London, 1625], IV, 1687; Philip L. Barbour, ed., *The Jamestown Voyages under the First Charter, 1606–1609* [Hakluyt Society, 2d Ser., CXXXVI–CXXXVII (Cambridge, 1969)], I, 135). Since Smith was then "under restraint," it is doubtful that he had anything to do with the naming of that promontory. He may well have named Cape Charles, however, since he was the first to explore that region (see the *Proceedings*, 29; and cf. the *Map of Va.*, 2).
2. Regard or consideration (of).

TO THE RIGHT HONOURABLE
and worthy Lords, Knights, and
Gentlemen, of his Majesties Councell,
for all Plantations and discoveries;
especially, of New England.

Seeing the deedes of the most just, and the writings of the most wise, not onely of men, but of God himselfe, have beene diversly traduced by variable judgements of the Times opinionists;[3] what shall such an ignorant as I expect? Yet reposing my selfe on your favours, I present this rude[4] discourse, to the worldes construction;[5] though I am perswaded, that few do think there may be had from New England Staple commodities, well worth 3 or 400000 pound a yeare, with so small charge, and such facilitie, as this discourse will acquaint you. But, lest your Honours, that know mee not, should thinke I goe by hearesay or affection; I intreat your pardons to say thus much of my selfe: Neere twice nine yeares,[6] I have beene taught by lamentable experience, aswell in Europe and Asia, as Affrick, and America, such honest adventures as the chance of warre doth cast

upon poore Souldiers. So that, if ‖ I bee not able to judge of what I have seene, contrived,[7] and done; it is not the fault either of my eyes, or foure quarters.[1] And these nine yeares, I have bent my endeavours to finde a sure foundation to begin these ensuing projects: which though I never so plainely and seriously propound; yet it resteth in God, and you, still to dispose of. Not doubting but your goodnesse will pardon my rudenesse, and ponder errours in the balance of good will; No more: but sacring[2] all my best abilities to the good of my Prince, and Countrey, and submitting my selfe to the exquisit judgements of your renowned vertue, I ever rest

Your Honours, in all honest service,

J. S.

---

3. Holders of variant opinions (derogatory).
4. Rough, unpolished.
5. Interpretation, views, opinion.
6. I.e., since 1598, give or take a year.
7. Helped to bring about.
1. Limbs.
2. Dedicating.

TO THE RIGHT WORSHIPFULL
Adventurers for the Countrey of
New England, in the Cities of
London, Bristow, Exceter, Plimouth,
Dartmouth, Bastable, Totneys, etc.
and in all other Cities and Ports,
in the Kingdome of England.

If the little Ant, and the sillie[3] Bee seek by their diligence the good of their Commonwealth; much more ought Man. If they punish the drones and sting them steales their labour;[4] then blame not Man. Little hony hath that hive, where there are more Drones then Bees: and miserable is that Land, where more are idle then well imployed. If the indeavours of those vermin be acceptable, I hope mine may be excuseable; Though I confesse it were more proper for mee, To be doing what I say, then writing what I knowe. Had I returned rich, I could not have erred: Now having onely such fish as came to my net, I must be taxed.[5] But, I would my taxers were as ready to adventure their purses, as I, purse, life, and all I have: or as diligent to furnish the charge, as I know they are vigilant to crop the fruits of my labours. Then would I not doubt (did God please I might safely arrive in New England, and safely returne) but to ‖ performe [¶4ᵛ] somewhat more then I have promised, and approve[6] my words by deeds, according to proportion.

I am not the first hath beene betrayed by Pirats: And foure men of warre, provided as they were, had beene sufficient to have taken Sampson, Hercules, and Alexander the great, no other way furnisht[7] then I was. I knowe not what assurance any have do passe the Seas, Not to bee subject to casualty as well as my selfe: but least this disaster may hinder my proceedings, or ill will (by rumour) the behoofefull worke I pretend;[8] I have writ this little: which I did thinke to have concealed from any publike use, till I had made my returnes speake as much, as my pen now doth.

But because I speake so much of fishing, if any take mee for such a devote[1] fisher, as I dreame of nought else, they mistake mee. I know

---

3. Insignificant.
4. Here, as often in Smith, the relative "that" has been dropped (see the beginning of the next paragraph).
5. Censured, blamed.
6. "Prove," as often in Smith.
7. No better furnished.
8. "The useful work I plan."
1. "Devoted."

a ring of golde from a graine of barley, aswell as a goldesmith: and
nothing is there to bee had which fishing doth hinder, but furder[2] us
to obtaine. Now for that I have made knowne unto you a fit place
for plantation, limited within the bounds of your Patent and Commission; having also received meanes, power, and authority by your
directions, to plant there a Colony, and make further search, and
discovery in those parts there yet unknowne: Considering, withall,
first those of his Majesties Councell, then those Cities above named,

[A1ʳ] and diverse others that have beene moved to lend ‖ their assistance
to so great a worke, doe expect (especially the adventurers) the true
relation or event[3] of my proceedings which I heare are so abused; I
am inforced for all these respects, rather to expose my imbecillitie to
contempt, by the testimonie of these rude lines, then all should condemne me for so bad a Factor,[4] as could neither give reason nor
account of my actions and designes.

Yours to command,
John Smith.

2. "Further," assist.
3. True story or factual outcome.
4. Agent.

IN THE DESERVED
Honour of the Author,
Captaine John Smith,
and his Worke.⁵

DAmn'd Envie is a sp'rite, that ever haunts
Beasts, mis-nam'd Men; Cowards, or Ignorants.
But, onely such shee followes, whose deere WORTH
(Maugre⁶ her malice) sets their glorie forth.
    If this faire Overture, then, take not; It
    Is Envie's spight (dear friend) in men-of-wit;
Or Feare, lest morsels, which our mouthes possesse,
Might fall from thence; or else, tis Sottishnesse.
    If either; (I hope neither) thee they raise;
    Thy *Letters⁷ are as Letters in thy praise;   *Hinderers.
Who, by their vice, improve (when they reproove)
Thy vertue; so, in hate, procure thee Love.
    Then, On firme Worth: this Monument I frame;
    Scorning for any Smith to forge such fame.

                Jo: Davies, Heref:

TO HIS WORTHY
Captaine the Author.

THat which wee call the subject of all Storie,
Is Truth: which in this Worke of thine gives glorie
To all that thou hast done. Then, scorne the spight
Of Envie; which doth no mans merits right.
    My sword may helpe the rest: my Pen no more
    Can doe, but this; I'ave⁸ said enough before.

        Your sometime souldier,
        J. Codrinton,⁹ now Templer.

---

5. This sonnet was reprinted in the *Generall Historie*, 95. John Davies also contributed the verses under the engraving of Smith in the corner of the map of New England (see the Biographical Directory).
    6. I.e., "in spite of"—common in English between 1300 and 1700.
    7. "Let" in the sense of "hinder" survives almost solely in the phrase "without let or hindrance."
    8. "I'ave" was a frequent spelling of modern "I've."
    9. John Codrinton (better, Codrington; also Cudderington) arrived in Jamestown with the second supply in 1608 (see the *Proceedings*, 52; and the Biographical Directory, s.v. "Codrington, John"). The verse was reprinted in the *Generall Historie*, 95.

TO MY WORTHY
friend and Cosen,[1]
Captaine John Smith.

*I*T *over-joyes my heart, when as thy Words*
Of these designes, with deeds I doe compare.
Heere is a Booke, such worthy truth affords,
None should the due desert thereof impare;
Sith thou, the man, deserving of these Ages,
Much paine hast ta'en for this our Kingdoms good,
In Climes unknowne, Mongst Turks *and Salvages,*[2]
T'inlarge our bounds; though with thy losse of blood.
  Hence damn'd Detraction: stand not in our way.
  Envie, it selfe, will not the Truth gainesay.

        N. Smith.

[A2ᵛ]

TO THAT WORTHY
and generous[3] Gentleman,
my verie good friend,
Captaine Smith.

*M*Ay Fate thy Project prosper, that thy name
May be eternised with living fame:
 Though foule Detraction Honour would pervert,
 And Envie ever waits upon desert:
In spight of Pelias,[4] *when his hate lies colde,*
Returne as Jason *with a fleece of Golde.*
  Then after-ages shall record thy praise,
  That a New England *to this Ile didst raise:*
And when thou dy'st (as all that live must die)
Thy fame live heere; thou, with Eternitie.

        R: Gunnell.[5]

1. Despite the stated relationship, the identity of "N. Smith" is far from certain (see the Biographical Directory). Again, the acrostic was reprinted in the *Generall Historie*, 95.

2. The rhyme here is purely visual.

3. Gallant, noble-minded.

4. Pelias was the half-brother of Jason's father. He sent Jason to Colchis, at the eastern end of the Black Sea, in quest of the Golden Fleece. The reference seems to be to John Smith's slavery in "Colchis"—i.e., Tatary.

5. Undoubtedly Richard Gunnell, manager of the new Fortune Theatre in London, and an actor and dramatist as well. For his friendship with Smith, see Philip L. Barbour, "Captain John Smith and the London Theatre," *Virginia Magazine of History and Biography*, LXXXIII (1975), 277–279; and the Biographical Directory. The verse is reprinted in the *Generall Historie*, 201–202.

TO HIS FRIEND
Captaine Smith, upon his
description of New England.

S*Ir; your Relations I have read: which shewe,*
Ther's reason I should honour them and you:[6]
And if their meaning I have understood,
I dare to censure, thus: Your Project's *good;*
And may (if follow'd) doubtlesse quit the paine,
With honour, pleasure and a trebble gaine;
Beside the benefit that shall arise
To make more happie our Posterities.
        For would we daigne to spare, though 'twere no more
Then what o're-filles, and surfets us in store,
To order Nature's *fruitfulnesse a while*
In that rude Garden, *you* New England *stile;*
With present good, ther's hope in after-daies
Thence to repaire what Time *and* Pride *decaies*
In this rich kingdome. And the spatious West
Beeing still more with English *blood possest,*
The Proud Iberians *shall not rule those Seas,*
To checke our ships from sayling where they please;
Nor future times make any forraine power
Become so great to force a bound to Our.
        Much good my minde fore tels would follow hence
With little labour, and with lesse expence.
Thrive therefore thy Designe, *who ere envie:*
England *may joy in* England's *Colony,*
Virginia seeke *her Virgine sisters good,*
Be blessed in such happie neighbourhood:
        Or, what-soere Fate pleaseth to permit,
        Be thou still honor'd for first mooving it.

                              George Wither,[7] *è societate Lincol.*

---

6. The rhyme points to the pronunciation "yo" rather than "yew," which is borne out by the spelling "yow" in many contemporary manuscripts as well as printed books.

7. Wither was a prominent poet and pamphleteer of Smith's day (see the Biographical Directory).

[A3ᵛ]

IN THE DESERVED HONOUR
of my honest and worthie Captaine,
John Smith, and his Worke.

C*Aptaine and friend; when I peruse thy booke*
(With Judgements *eyes) into thy* heart *I looke:*
*And there I finde (what sometimes-*Albyon *knew)*[8]
A Souldier, *to his* Countries-honour, *true.*
    Some fight for wealth; *and some for* emptie praise;
    But thou alone thy Countries Fame *to raise.*
With due discretion, *and* undanted heart,
I (oft) so well have seene thee act thy Part
    In deepest plunge of hard extreamitie,
    As forc't the troups of proudest foes to flie.
Though men of greater Ranke *and lesse* desert
Would Pish-*away thy* Praise, *it can not start*
    From the true Owner: *for, all good-mens tongues*
    Shall keepe the same. To them that Part belongs.
If, then, Wit, Courage, *and* Success *should get*
Thee Fame; *the Muse for* that *is in thy* debt:
    A part whereof (least able though I bee)
    Thus heere I doe disburse, to honor Thee.

Rawly Croshaw.[1]

---

8. Perhaps read: "(what sometimes 'Albyon' knew)." Parentheses were "the general way of indicating a *short* quotation" during the late 16th century and on into the early 17th century (Ronald B. McKerrow, *An Introduction to Bibliography for Literary Students* [Oxford, 1965 (orig. publ. 1927)], 317). Here, the reason for the punctuation is not clear.

1. See the Biographical Directory, s.v. "Crashaw, Rawley." The verse was reprinted in the *Generall Historie*, 95–96.

MICHAEL PHETTIPLACE, [A4ʳ]
William Phettiplace, and Richard Wiffing,
Gentlemen, and Souldiers under
Captaine Smiths Command:²
In his deserved honor for
his Worke, and worth.

W*Hy may not we in this Worke have our Mite,*
That had our share in each black day and night,
When thou Virginia *foild'st,*³ *yet kept'st unstaind;*
And held'st the King of Paspeheh *enchaind.*
Thou all alone this Salvage *sterne didst take.*
 Pamunkes king wee saw thee captive make.
Among seaven hundred of his stoutest men,
To murther thee and us resolved; when
Fast by the hand thou ledst this Salvage grim,
Thy Pistoll at his breast to governe him:
Which did infuse such awe in all the rest
*(Sith their drad*⁴ *Soveraigne thou had'st so distrest)*
That thou and wee (poore sixteene) safe retir'd
Unto our helplesse ships. *Thou (thus admir'd)*
Didst make proud Powhatan, *his subjects send*
To James *his Towne, thy censure to attend:*
And all Virginia's *Lords, and pettie Kings,*
*Aw'd by thy vertue, crouch,*⁵ *and Presents brings*
To gaine thy grace; so dreaded thou hast beene:
And yet a heart more milde is seldome seene;
So, making Valour Vertue, really;
Who hast nought in thee counterfet, or slie;
‖ *If in the sleight*⁶ *bee not the truest art,*   [A4ᵛ]
That makes men famoused for faire desert.
 Who saith of thee, this savors of vaine-glorie,
Mistakes both thee and us, and this true storie.
If it bee ill in Thee, *so well to doe;*
Then, is it ill in Us, *to praise thee too.*

2. See the Biographical Directory (for Michael and William Phettiplace, s.v. "Fetti-place"). The verse was reprinted in the *Generall Historie,* 96.
3. Here "foil" is used in the sense of "defeat"—Smith defeated the Indians, but kept the land "unstained."
4. Cf. Smith's "dread Soveraigne Queene Elizabeth" (*True Travels,* 4).
5. Cower; the "-s" in "brings" is for rhyme only.
6. Skill.

But, if the first bee well done; it is well,
To say it doth (if so it doth) excell!
Praise is the guerdon of each deere desert,
Making the praised act the praised part
With more alacritie: Honours *Spurre is* Praise;
Without which, it (regardlesse) soone decaies.
*   And for this paines of thine wee praise thee rather,*
That future Times may know who was the father
Of this rare Worke (New England) *which may bring*
Praise to thy God, and profit to thy King.

BECAUSE THE BOOKE WAS PRINTED ERE

the Prince his Highnesse had altered
the names, I intreate the Reader, peruse
this schedule; which will plainely shew him the
correspondence of the old names to the new.[7]

The old names.	The new.	The old names.	The new.
Cape Cod	Cape James[8]	Sowocatuck	Ipswitch
	Milford haven	Bahana	Dartmouth
Chawum	Barwick		Sandwich[4]
Accomack	Plimouth	Aucociscos Mount	Shooters hill
Sagoquas	Oxford	Aucocisco	The Base
Massachusets Mount	Chevit hill	Aumoughcawgen	Cambridge
Massachusets River	Charles River[1]	Kinebeck	Edenborough
Totant	Fawmouth	Sagadahock	Leeth
A Country not discovered	Bristow	Pemmaquid	S. Johns towne
Naemkeck	Bastable	Monahigan	Barties Iles
Cape Trabigzanda[2]	Cape Anne	Segocket	Norwich
Aggawom	Southhampton	Matinnack	Willowby's Iles
Smiths Iles	Smiths Iles	Metinnicut	Hoghton's Iles
Passataquack	Hull	Mecadacut	Dunbarton
Accominticus	Boston[3]	Pennobscot	Aborden
Sassanowes Mount	Snodon hill	Nusket[5]	Lowmonds

7. This inserted leaf is found only in some copies. The copy of the *Description of N.E.* carried by the Pilgrims in 1620 seems to have contained one (see n., following).

8. Of this, William Bradford wrote: "A word or two by the way of this cape. It was thus first named [Cape Cod] by Captain Gosnold and his company, Anno 1602, and after by Captain Smith was called Cape James; but it retains the former name amongst seamen" (William Bradford, *Of Plymouth Plantation, 1620–1647*, ed. Samuel Eliot Morison [New York, 1952], 60–61). Compare this insert with the reprint in the *Generall Historie*, 205, where "The Harbor at Cape Cod" is inserted one line below, opposite "Milforth haven."

1. In *Plymouth Plantation*, Book II, chap. 11 (written after 1630), Bradford quotes Smith's friend Thomas Dermer as writing that "Charlton" would be a better location than Plymouth, "because there the savages are less to be feared" (*Plymouth Plantation*, 82). This is the present site of Boston, just S of the Charles River, but it is interesting to note that "Charlton" had not been added to Smith's map before the eighth state, which seems to be found first in a copy of the *Advertisements* (1631). The implications are that the Pilgrims as late as c. 1631 were still interested enough in Smith's writings to have noticed such late changes made in the map.

2. The first, and best-spelled, mention of Smith's mistress in Istanbul, Charatza Trabigzanda (see the *True Travels*, 23).

3. This has nothing to do with modern Boston. Smith's Boston (Accominticus) seems to have been at the foot of modern Mount Agamenticus, between York Beach and Ogunquit, perhaps 40 mi. (65 km.) SW of Portland.

4. The *Generall Historie* adds a description but no "old name"—"A good Harbor within that Bay" (p. 205). The location was probably Back Cove, Portland.

5. Nusket (renamed for the Lomond Hills, which lie between the Firth of Forth and the Firth of Tay, Scotland) would seem, in the editor's opinion, to be the Naskeag Point at the E extremity of Penobscot Bay on modern maps. The *Generall Historie*, 205, lists separately the three places that Smith named himself.

ND

44½

Gunnels Ils   *Aberden*

The River Forth   *borough*

St Iohn Towne   *Norwich*

Lowmonds

Pines Ils

44

Pembrocks Bay

Heghton Ils

Barty Ils   *Willowby Ils*

ELIZABETH

43½

43

42½

A Scale of Leagues

2   6   8   10

Observed and described by Captayn John Smith

42

London
Printed by Geor: Low

[Simon van de Passe, the second son of the Dutch engraver Crispin van de Passe, seems to have drawn the map and the portrait of John Smith, even though the word "sculpsit" (engraved) is used at the bottom of the map. His work was probably accomplished between early Jan. and Mar. 24, 1617—witness the details on the portrait, "*Aetatis* 37, *Anno* 1616" (Smith was baptized Jan. 9, 1580; and the legal year 1616 ended Mar. 24, 1617). About the same time van de Passe did a drawing of Pocahontas, which must have been printed and in circulation before Feb. 22 (see Barbour, *Pocahontas and Her World* [Boston, 1970], 179). In both instances van de Passe's drawings were engraved by another artist: Compton Holland in the latter case, Robert Clerke in the former. Curiously, Clerke is little known either as an engraver or as a publisher (see the title page). Even more curiously, when the map was again used as an illustration for the *Generall Historie* in 1624, Clerke's name was erased. At the same time the name of the printer of the map was changed from George Low (who may have died) to James Reeve. Note that Humphrey Lownes printed the book but not the map.

The compass card shows orientation to the N. The scale of leagues, as in the map of Virginia, shows 20 leagues (60 mi.) to the degree of latitude (see the markings on the right and left margins). The latitudes of the various geographical features themselves are notably accurate, generally; e.g., modern charts show such sample readings as these: Aborden (upper right), identified with Penobscot village, modern Castine, 44° 25′ N lat.; Smiths Iles, modern Isles of Shoals, just below 43°; the mouth of the River Charles is at 42° 22′; and the top, or N, edge of Cape Cod is almost exactly right, at 42° 5′.

As a product of Smith's own surveying, the map of New England offers an interesting contrast with the Smith/Hole map of Virginia, in which a certain amount of hearsay evidence (from Indians, especially) was incorporated. For this map Smith struck out from the "Barty Iles" (Monahiggan, modern Monhegan Island) and headed to Lowmonds (Nusket, probably modern Naskeag Point), his farthest point to the NE. From there he followed the coast SW and S to the bottom of Massachusetts Bay, back up to Cape Cod, and then around and along the ocean side of the cape as far S as the rips and shoals, whence he scurried back to his ship, at or near Monhegan Island. If we may assume that Smith's exploring, surveying, and trading began about the middle of June (see the top of p. 2) and ended July 18 (see *New Englands Trials* [1620], sig. B3ʳ), in less than five weeks he had sailed roughly as far as he did on his Chesapeake Bay voyages from June 2 to Sept. 7, 1608.

The map was by no means the first to be made, and some previous sketches were consulted by Smith himself (apparently not Samuel de Champlain's *Carte géographique de la Nouvelle France* [Paris, 1612–1613]). But Smith's map is the most detailed of the early ones that survive, for the area covered in it: the coast of Maine W of Mount Desert Island, the narrow bit of New Hampshire, and E Massachusetts to the underside of Cape Cod (see p. 5n, below). Champlain's map had included the vast region to the N and E, and part of the area was covered in Sir William Alexander's map of 1624, which included the coast from Nantucket Island to the Straits of Belle Isle (in *An Encouragement to Colonies* . . . [London, 1625]). This was followed by a sketch map of the S part of New England appended to William Wood's *New Englands Prospect* . . . (London, 1634). Neither of these latter two maps rivaled the work of Champlain and Smith, and Wood went so far as to refer his readers "to the thrice memorable discoverer of those parts [N of the Bay] Captaine Smith, who hath likewise fully described the Southerne and North-east part of New England" (*ibid.*, 2).

It is unfortunate from the ethnological point of view that Smith listed only the English names that he and Prince Charles gave to the Indian localities on the map itself. To offset this, the endpaper maps in this edition show the locations of about two dozen Indian place-names mentioned in the text or listed in the inserted sheet at the beginning.

The editor is grateful to the William L. Clements Library, Ann Arbor, Michigan, for permission to reproduce the first state of this map, which appears here slightly reduced.]

A DESCRIPTION OF [1]
New-England, by Captaine John Smith.

N the moneth of Aprill, 1614. with two Ships from London, of a few Marchants,[1] I chanced to arrive in New-England, a parte of Ameryca, at the Ile of Monahiggan,[2] in 43½ of Northerly latitude: our plot was there to take Whales and make tryalls of a Myne of Gold and Copper. If those failed, Fish and Furres was then our refuge,[3] to make our selves savers howsoever: we found this Whale-fishing a costly conclusion: we saw many, and spent much time in chasing them; but could not kill any: They beeing a kinde of Jubartes,[4] and not the Whale that yeeldes Finnes and Oyle as wee expected. For our Golde, it was rather the Masters[1] device to get a voyage that projected it, then any knowledge hee had at all of any such matter. Fish and Furres was now our guard: and by our late arrival, and long lingring about the Whale, the prime of both those seasons were past ere wee perceived it; we thinking that their seasons served at all times: ‖ but wee found it otherwise; for, by the midst of June, the fishing failed. Yet in July and August some was taken, but not sufficient to defray so great a charge as our stay required. Of dry fish we made about

My first voyage to new-England.

[2]

1. *New Englands Trials* (1622), sig. B2^r, supplies the names: Capt. Marmaduke Roydon (see the Biographical Directory, s.v. "Rawdon"), Capt. George Langam, Master John Buley, and William Skelton. A relevant passage in a document presented to James I during the week following Easter Sunday, Apr. 13, 1623, on behalf of part of the Virginia Company is worth quoting here: "The grownd" of the employment of 42 sail of ships to Virginia "was in great parte holpen by the Discoveriye of the fishinge in newe England found out dureinge Sir Thomas Smiths government at the Charge of the Company by Sir Samuell Argall, Capteyne John Smith and others" (Susan Myra Kingsbury, ed., *The Records of the Virginia Company of London* [Washington, D.C., 1906–1935], IV, 150). While Argall may have reported on New England fishing anytime between autumn 1609 and spring 1615 (or later), there seems to be no record of it. Smith certainly was not financed by the Virginia Company. Robert Johnson, deputy treasurer and member of the council of the Virginia Company, is said to have drawn up the draft of this "Declaration," and Sir Nathaniel Rich perhaps revised it, but much is still unexplained.
  2. Modern Monhegan Island, 43° 46′ N lat. (69° 19′ W long.); 20 mi. (32 km.) SW of the entrance to Penobscot Bay.
  3. Protection against loss; called "guard" several lines below.
  4. Apparently the first appearance of the name in print in English. It was applied to a species of rorqual.
  1. "Master's"—referring to Thomas Hunt (see p. 47, below).

40000. of Cor fish[2] about 7000. Whilest the sailers fished, my selfe with eight or nine others of them might best bee spared; Ranging the coast in a small boat, wee got for trifles neer 1100 Bever skinnes, 100 Martins, and neer as many Otters; and the most of them within the distance of twenty leagues.[3] We ranged the Coast both East and West much furder; but Eastwards our commodities were not esteemed, they were so neare the French who affords them better: and right against us in the Main was a Ship of Sir Frances Popphames, that had there such acquaintance, having many yeares used onely that porte, that the most parte there was had by him.[4] And 40 leagues westwards were two French Ships, that had made there a great voyage by trade, during the time wee tryed those conclusions, not knowing the Coast, nor Salvages habitation. With these Furres, the Traine,[5] and Cor-fish I returned for England in the Bark: where within six monthes after our departure from the Downes, we safe arrived back.[6] The best of this fish was solde for five pound the hundreth, the rest by ill usage betwixt three pound and fifty shillings. The other Ship staied to fit herselfe for Spaine with the dry fish which was sould, by the Sailers reporte that returned, at forty ryalls the quintall, each hundred weighing two quintalls and a halfe.

[3]
The situation of
New England.

New England is that part of America in the Ocean Sea opposite to Nova Albyon[7] in the South Sea; discovered by the most memorable Sir Francis Drake in his voyage about the worlde. In regarde whereto this is stiled New England, beeing in the same latitude. New France,[8] off it, is Northward: Southwardes is Virginia, and all the adjoyning Continent, with New Granado, New Spain, New Andolosia[9] and the West Indies. Now because I have beene so oft asked

2. Salt fish, as opposed to dry fish or stockfish—literally "basket-fish," from corf, a kind of basket.

3. A radius of 20 leagues (60 mi.) would include Nusket, modern Naskeag, on the E, and Sowocatuck, near Portland, on the W.

4. Sir Francis was the only son of Lord Chief Justice Popham, promoter of the Sagadahoc colony, who died June 10, 1607. Sir Francis was treasurer of the "Plymouth Company," and when the colony was abandoned the following spring, he and his mother tried to keep the project alive by sending ships to the site and along the nearby coast (cf. the *Generall Historie*, 204). The colony's St. George's Fort was on the right bank of the Kennebec River, at the SE extremity of the town of Phipsburg, on the S shore of Atkins Bay (see Henry O. Thayer, ed., *The Sagadahoc Colony: Comprising the Relation of a Voyage into New England* [Gorges Society (Portland, Me., 1892)], 167–187). Curiously, most of this passage is missing from the reprint in the *Generall Historie*, 204.

5. "Train" probably refers to the oil from cod livers in this case.

6. "I . . . arived safe with my company the latter end of August" (*New Englands Trials* [1622], sig. B2ʳ). In the last sentence of this paragraph, note the absence of reference to Hunt, master of the "other ship," whose activities are mentioned on p. 47, below.

7. Roughly, California.

8. Canada.

9. Nueva Granada was the name given to modern Colombia in the 1530s; Nueva España was Mexico, somewhat enlarged; and Nueva Andalucía was northern Chile, expanded eastwards, by virtue of a *capitulación* dated May 21, 1534, but previously part of Colombia. What Smith meant by the names is uncertain, except for what is now Mexico.

such strange questions, of the goodnesse and greatnesse of those spatious Tracts of land, how they can bee thus long unknown, or not possessed by the Spaniard, and many such like demands; I intreat your pardons, if I chance to be too plaine, or tedious in relating my knowledge for plaine mens satisfaction.

Florida is the next adjoyning to the Indes, which unprosper-ously was attempted to bee planted by the French. A Country farre bigger then England, Scotland, France and Ireland,[10] yet little knowne to any Christian, but by the wonderful endevours of Ferdi-nando de Soto a valiant Spaniard: whose writings in this age is the best guide knowne to search those parts. Notes of Florida.

Virginia is no Ile (as many doe imagine)[11] but part of the Con-tinent adjoyning to Florida; whose bounds may be stretched to the magnitude thereof without offence to any Christian inhabitant. For from the degrees of 30. to 45.[1] his Majestie hath granted his Letters patents, the Coast extending South-west and North-east aboute 1500[2] ‖ miles; but to follow it aboard, the shore may well be 2000. at the least: of which, 20. miles is the most gives entrance into the Bay of Chisapeak, where is the London plantation: within which is a Country (as you may perceive by the description in a Booke and Map printed in my name of that little I there discovered) may well suffice 300000 people to inhabit. And Southward adjoyneth that part dis-covered at the charge of Sir Walter Rawley, by Sir Ralph Lane, and that learned Mathematician Master Thomas Heryot. Northward six or seaven degrees[3] is the River Sagadahock, where was planted the Westerne Colony, by that Honourable Patrone of vertue Sir John Poppham, Lord chief Justice of England. Ther is also a relation printed by Captaine Bartholomew Gosnould, of Elizabeths Iles: and an other by Captaine Waymoth, of Pemmaquid.[4] From all these diligent observers, posterity may be bettered by the fruits of their labours. But for divers others that long before and since have ranged Notes of Virginia. [4]

10. King James's Great Britain plus France was twice the size of modern Florida, Georgia, and South Carolina combined. But of course nobody knew how big King Philip's "Florida" was.

11. In Smith's day there was still a persistent tradition that NE North America was an island. Indeed, this had been confirmed as recently as 1599 in the "Edward Wright world map" (see reproduction in David Beers Quinn, ed., *The Hakluyt Handbook* [Hakluyt Society, 2d Ser., CXLIV (London, 1974)], 62–63), and in the Velasco map of 1611 (colored reproduction in W. P. Cumming, R. A. Skelton, and D. B. Quinn, eds., *The Discovery of North America* [New York, 1972], 264, 326). Despite Smith and Champlain, the "tradition" flourished as late as 1672 (Douglas R. McManis, *European Impressions of the New England Coast, 1497–1620* [Chicago, 1972], 37–40; see also p. 5n, below).

1. The correct limits stated in the "letters patents" were from 34° to 45° N latitude. Smith (or his printer) was persistently careless about these details.

2. By modern measure, about 1,360 mi.

3. More accurately, a little more than 6° 32'.

4. John Brereton, *A Briefe and true Relation of the Discoverie of the North part of Virginia* . . . (London, 1602); and James Rosier, *A True Relation of the most prosperous voyage made this present yeere 1605, by Captaine George Waymouth* . . . (London, 1605), respectively.

those parts, within a kenning[5] sometimes of the shore, some touching
in one place some in another, I must entreat them pardon me for
omitting them; or if I offend in saying that their true descriptions are
concealed, or never well observed, or died with the Authors: so that
the Coast is yet still but even as a Coast unknowne and undiscovered.
I have had six or seaven severall plots of those Northren parts, so unlike each to other, and most so differing from any true proportion, or
[5] resemblance of the Countrey, as they did ‖ mee no more good, then
so much waste paper, though they cost me more. It may be it was not
my chance to see the best; but least others may be deceived as I was,
or throgh dangerous ignorance hazard themselves as I did, I have
drawen a Map from Point to Point, Ile to Ile, and Harbour to Harbour, with the Soundings, Sands, Rocks, and Land-marks as I passed
close aboard the Shore in a little Boat;[6] although there be many
things to bee observed which the haste of other affaires did cause me
omit: for, being sent more to get present commodities, then knowledge by discoveries for any future good, I had not power to search as
I would: yet it will serve to direct any shall goe that waies, to safe
Harbours and the Salvages habitations: What marchandize and
commodities for their labour they may finde, this following discourse
shall plainely demonstrate.

Thus you may see, of this 2000. miles more then halfe is yet unknowne to any purpose: no not so much as the borders of the Sea are
yet certainly discovered.[7] As for the goodnes and true substances of
the Land, wee are for most part yet altogether ignorant of them, unlesse it bee those parts about the Bay of Chisapeack and Sagadahock:
but onely here and there wee touched or have seene a little the edges
of those large dominions, which doe stretch themselves into the
Maine, God doth know how many thousand miles; whereof we can
yet no more judge, then a stranger that saileth betwixt England and
[6] France can describe the Harbors ‖ and dangers by landing here or
there in some River or Bay, tell thereby the goodnesse and substances

5. Sight or view.
6. According to Samuel Eliot Morison, Smith's map "was not the best map of New
England that had been made, but by far the most accurate that had yet been published,
and made available" (*The Builders of the Bay Colony* [Boston and New York, 1930], 11).
This assertion seems unsupported by any evidence at hand, although there are less
detailed maps that cover greater areas—by Champlain (1612), Adriaen Block (MS of
1614), and the unidentified cartographer of the so-called Velasco map (early 1611). For
a sound assessment of Smith's map by a historical geographer, see McManis, *European
Impressions of the New England Coast*, 110–115. The editor is grateful to Dr. David Woodward, The Newberry Library, Chicago, for calling this monograph to his attention
(personal communications of Aug. 2 and Sept. 5, 1975).
7. Before 1609 almost nothing was known about the coast from Chesapeake Bay to
Cape Cod, despite such a well-known voyager as Giovanni da Verrazzano. Henry
Hudson started the new trend and was followed by Samuel Argall in 1610 and by the
Dutchmen Hendrick Christiaensen and Adriaen Block in 1610 or 1611 (Simon Hart,
Prehistory of the New Netherland Company [Amsterdam, 1959], 18–21). But 1614 seems to
mark the beginning of effectual exploration.

of Spaine, Italy, Germany, Bohemia, Hungaria and the rest. By this
you may perceive how much they erre, that think every one which
hath bin at Virginia understandeth or knowes what Virginia is: Or
that the Spaniards know one halfe quarter[8] of those Territories they
possesse; no, not so much as the true circumference of Terra Incognita, whose large dominions may equalize the greatnesse and goodnes
of America, for any thing yet known. It is strange with what small
power hee[9] hath raigned in the East Indes; and few will understand
the truth of his strength in America: where he having so much to
keepe with such a pampered[1] force, they neede not greatly feare his
furie, in the Bermudas, Virginia, New France, or New England;
beyond whose bounds America doth stretch many thousand miles:
into the frozen partes whereof one Master Hutson an English Mariner
did make the greatest discoverie of any Christian I knowe of, where
he unfortunately died.[2] For Affrica, had not the industrious Portugales ranged her unknowne parts, who would have sought for wealth
among those fryed Regions of blacke brutish Negers,[3] where notwithstanding all the wealth and admirable adventures and endeavours more then 140 yeares, they knowe not one third of those
blacke habitations. But it is not a worke for every one, to manage
such an affaire as makes a discoverie, and plants a Colony: It requires all the best parts of ‖ Art, Judgement, Courage, Honesty,   **[7]**
Constancy, Diligence and Industrie, to doe but neere well. Some are
more proper for one thing then another; and therein are to be imployed: and nothing breedes more confusion then misplacing and
misimploying men in their undertakings. Columbus, Cortez, Pitzara,
Soto, Magellanes, and the rest served more then a prentiship[4] to
learne how to begin their most memorable attempts in the West
Indes: which to the wonder of all ages succesfully they effected, when
many hundreds of others farre above them in the worlds opinion,
beeing instructed but by relation, came to shame and confusion in
actions of small moment, who doubtlesse in other matters, were both
wise, discreet, generous, and couragious. I say not this to detract any
thing from their incomparable merits, but to answer those question-

8. Perhaps a reminiscence of an ancient biblical phrase, such as the "ruler of the
halfe quarter of Bethzur" (Miles Coverdale's version of Nehemiah 3:16), now translated
in the New English Bible as "half the district." The meaning is "very little."

9. The reference is to "the Spaniard."

1. Spoiled by luxury.

2. For Henry Hudson, see the *Generall Historie*, 207; and the Biographical Directory.

3. On the English (and perhaps general European) conception of, and attitude
toward, black Africans, see P.E.H. Hair, "Guinea," in Quinn, ed., *Hakluyt Handbook*,
197–207. Among recent and more extensive studies, see Gary B. Nash, *Red, White, and
Black: The Peoples of Early America* (Englewood Cliffs, N.J., 1974), 156–182, for a general
study; and Edmund S. Morgan, *American Slavery, American Freedom: The Ordeal of Colonial
Virginia* (New York, 1975), for Virginia only. Smith, who had not been in black Africa
at all, here obviously uses the descriptive epithets he heard all around him.

4. "Apprenticeship"—a popular variant spelling.

lesse questions[5] that keep us back from imitating the worthinesse of their brave spirits that advanced themselves from poore Souldiers to great Captaines, their posterity to great Lords, their King to be one of the greatest Potentates on earth, and the fruites of their labours, his greatest glory, power and renowne.

The description of New England.

That part wee call New England is betwixt the degrees of 41. and 45: but that parte this discourse speaketh of, stretcheth but from Pennobscot to Cape Cod, some 75 leagues by a right line distant each from other:[6] within which bounds I have seene at least 40. severall habitations upon the Sea Coast, and sounded about 25 excellent **[8]** good Harbours;[7] || In many whereof there is ancorage for 500. sayle of ships of any burthen; in some of them for 5000:[8] And more then 200 Iles overgrowne with good timber, of divers sorts of wood, which doe make so many harbours as requireth a longer time then I had, to be well discovered.[9]

The particular Countries or Governments.

The principall habitation Northward we were at, was Pennobscot:[1] Southward along the Coast and up the Rivers we found Mecadacut, Segocket, Pemmaquid, Nusconcus,[2] Kenebeck, Sagadahock, and Aumoughcawgen; And to those Countries belong the people of Segotago, Paghhuntanuck, Pocopassum, Taughtanakagnet, Warbigganus, Nassaque, Masherosqueck, Wawrigweck, Moshoquen, Wakcogo, Passharanack,[3] etc. To these are allied the Countries of Aucocisco, Accominticus, Passataquack, Aggawom, and Naemkeck:[4] all these, I could perceive, differ little in language, fashion, or government: though most be Lords of themselves, yet

5. I.e., "to answer those questions—and there is no doubt that they are questions—that keep us back. . . ."
6. By modern measurement, the distance by air is about 180 mi. (288 km.). Smith's 75 leagues (225 mi.) seems strangely excessive, especially considering the 65 leagues (195 mi.) shown on his map.
7. The map is evidently intended to show the harbors only.
8. The *Generall Historie*, 208, has "one thousand." The "5000" may have been a misprint.
9. Explored and sounded.
1. This spot has been identified, with minimal likelihood of error, as the Castine peninsula (Fannie Hardy Eckstorm, *Indian Place-Names of the Penobscot Valley and the Maine Coast* [Orono, Me., 1941], 198–199). William Bradford supplies the detail that one Edward Ashley, a "profane young man," landed at Penobscot, "some fourscore leagues" from Plymouth (Bradford, *Plymouth Plantation*, 219, 219n). This was in 1631, and it is surprising that the Pilgrims would not have measured the distance better.
2. More correctly, "Musconcus"; probably the crossroads today called Muscongus, 2 mi. (3 km.) N of Round Pond on Muscongus Sound, but not shown on Smith's map.
3. These 11 tribes are listed (with minor changes in spelling) in the *Generall Historie*, 208, and the *Advertisements*, 14. Little or nothing is known about them, but see Dean R. Snow, *The Archaeology of New England* (New York, 1980).
4. These five "countries" can be identified with greater or less probability as follows: Aucocisco, "muddy bay" (Eckstorm, *Indian Place-Names*, 169), more likely in the neighborhood of Freeport than at Portland; Accominticus, near Ogunquit (see n. to inserted leaf following sig. A4ᵛ); Passataquack, probably a misprint for Pascataquack, near the mouth of the modern Piscataqua River, the southern boundary between Maine and New Hampshire; Aggawom, at or near Ipswich, Massachusetts; and Naemkeck, at or near Salem, Massachusetts.

they hold the Bashabes[5] of Pennobscot, the chiefe and greatest amongst them.

The next I can remember by name are Mattahunts; two pleasant Iles of groves, gardens and corne fields a league in the Sea from the Mayne. Then Totant, Massachuset, Pocapawmet, Quonahassit, Sagoquas, Nahapassumkeck, Topeent, Seccasaw, Totheet, Nasnocomacack, Accomack, Chawum;[6] Then Cape Cod by which is Pawmet and the Ile Nawset, of the language, and alliance of them of Chawum: The others are called Massachusets;[7] of another language, humor and condition: For their trade and marchandize; to each of their habitations they have || diverse Townes and people belonging; and by their relations and descriptions, more then 20 severall Habitations and Rivers that stretch themselves farre up into the Countrey, even to the borders of diverse great Lakes,[8] where they kill and take most of their Bevers and Otters. From Pennobscot to Sagadahock this Coast is all Mountainous and Iles of huge Rocks, but overgrowen with all sorts of excellent good woodes for building houses, boats, barks or shippes; with an incredible abundance of most sorts of fish, much fowle, and sundry sorts of good fruites for mans use. **[9]**

Betwixt Sagadahock and Sowocatuck there is but two or three sandy Bayes, but betwixt that and Cape Cod very many: especialy the Coast of the Massachusets is so indifferently mixed with high clayie or sandy cliffes in one place, and then tracts of large long ledges of divers sorts, and quarries of stones in other places so strangely divided with tinctured veines of divers colours: as, Free stone for building, Slate for tiling, smooth stone to make Fornaces and Forges for glasse or iron, and iron ore sufficient,[9] conveniently to melt in them: but the most part so resembleth the Coast of Devonshire, I thinke most of the cliffes would make such lime-stone: If they be not of these qualities, they are so like, they may deceive a better judgement then mine; all which are so neere adjoyning to those other advantages I observed in these parts, that if the Ore prove as good iron and steele in those parts, as I know it is within the bounds of || the **[10]** Countrey, I dare engage my head (having but men skilfull to worke

The mixture of an excellent soyle.

5. Bashabes (Bessabés, in French) was the most renowned sachem (or sagamore) in Maine. The name was not a title.

6. These villages or tribes were all located in Massachusetts.

7. The Massachuset tribe lived along the coast of Massachusetts Bay, at least as far N as Salem. The name means "at the great little hill" and refers to the Blue Hills S of Boston.

8. These were the lakes of modern Maine. The Great Lakes, in the modern sense of the name, were first explored by a European in 1615 (a year after Smith's trip), when Champlain reached the shores of Lake Huron by way of the Ottawa River.

9. This is surely based on a mixture of hope and hearsay, although Pierre Erondelle's translation of Marc Lescarbot's *Nova Francia* (London, 1609) states that the French "found quantitie of Steele among the Rockes" on the coast of New Brunswick (repr. in Purchas, *Pilgrimes*, IV, 1639). Smith's confidence grows as he continues.

the simples[10] there growing) to have all things belonging to the building and the rigging of shippes of any proportion, and good marchandize for the fraught, within a square of 10 or 14 leagues: and were it for a good rewarde, I would not feare to proove it in a lesse limitation.

A proofe of
an excellent
temper.

And surely by reason of those sandy cliffes and cliffes of rocks, both which we saw so planted with Gardens and Corne fields, and so well inhabited with a goodly, strong and well proportioned people, besides the greatnesse of the Timber growing on them, the greatnesse of the fish and the moderate temper[11] of the ayre (for of twentie

A proofe of
health.

five, not any was sicke, but two that were many yeares diseased before they went, notwithstanding our bad lodging and accidentall diet) who can but approove this a most excellent place, both for health and fertility? And of all the foure parts of the world that I have yet seene not inhabited, could I have but meanes to transport a Colonie, I would rather live here then any where: and if it did not maintaine it selfe, were wee but once indifferently well fitted, let us starve.

Staple com-
modities
present.

The maine Staple, from hence to bee extracted for the present to produce the rest, is fish; which however it may seeme a mean and a base commoditie: yet who will but truely take the pains and consider the sequell, I thinke will allow it well worth the labour. It is

[11]

strange to see what great ‖ adventures the hopes of setting forth men of war to rob the industrious innocent, would procure; or such massie promises in grosse: though more are choked then well fedde with

The Hol-
landers fishing.

such hastie hopes. But who doth not know that the poore Hollanders, chiefly by fishing, at a great charge and labour in all weathers in the open Sea, are made a people so hardy, and industrious? and by the venting this poore commodity to the Easterlings[1] for as meane, which is Wood, Flax, Pitch, Tarre, Rosin, Cordage, and such like (which they exchange againe, to the French, Spaniards, Portugales, and English, etc. for what they want) are made so mighty, strong and rich, as no State but Venice, of twice their magnitude,[2] is so well furnished with so many faire Cities, goodly Townes, strong Fortresses, and that aboundance of shipping and all sorts of marchandize, as well of Golde, Silver, Pearles, Diamonds, Pretious stones, Silkes, Velvets, and Cloth of golde; as Fish, Pitch, Wood, or such grosse commodities? What Voyages and Discoveries, East and West, North and South, yea about the world, make they? What an Army by Sea and Land, have they long maintained in despite of one of the

10. Medicinal herbs.

11. I.e., "the prevailing atmospheric conditions." A few lines below, "accidentall diet" means "living off the land."

1. Eastern or Baltic coast Germans, especially those living in the towns of the Hanseatic League.

2. The Republic of Venice had an area of over 50,000 sq. km. (19,300 sq. mi.); the Low Countries had considerably less than 33,000 sq. km. (13,000 sq. mi.) at the time of the 1609 truce with Spain.

greatest Princes of the world? And never could the Spaniard with all his Mynes of golde and Silver, pay his debts, his friends, and army, halfe so truly, as the Hollanders stil have done by this contemptible trade of fish. Divers (I know) may alledge many other assistances: But this is their Myne; and the Sea the || source of those silvered streames of all their vertue; which hath made them now the very miracle of industrie, the pattern of perfection for these affaires: and the benefit of fishing is that Primum mobile that turnes all their Spheres to this height of plentie, strength, honour and admiration. [12]

Herring, Cod, and Ling, is that triplicitie that makes their wealth and shippings multiplicities, such as it is, and from which (few would thinke it) they yearly draw at least one million and a halfe of pounds starling; yet it is most certaine (if records be true): and in this faculty they are so naturalized, and of their vents so certainely acquainted, as there is no likelihood they will ever bee paralleld, having 2 or 3000 Busses, Flat bottomes, Sword pinks, Todes,[3] and such like, that breedes them Saylers, Mariners, Souldiers and Marchants, never to be wrought out of that trade, and fit for any other. I will not deny but others may gaine as well as they, that will use it, though not so certainely, nor so much in quantity; for want of experience. And this Herring they take upon the Coast of Scotland and England; their Cod and Ling, upon the Coast of Izeland[4] and in the North Seas. *Which is fifteen hundred thousand pound.*

Hamborough, and the East Countries, for Sturgion and Caviare, gets many thousands of pounds from England, and the Straites:[5] Portugale, the Biskaines,[6] and the Spaniards, make 40 or 50 Saile yearely to Cape-blank,[7] to hooke for Porgos,[8] Mullet, and make Puttargo:[9] and New found Land, doth yearely fraught neere 800 sayle of Ships with a sillie leane || skinny Poore-John,[10] and Corfish, which at least yearely amounts to 3 or 400000 pound. If from all those parts such paines is taken for this poore gaines of fish, and by [13]

---

3. Smith seems to have drawn here on some such source as John Keymor's *Observation made upon the Dutch fishing, about the year 1601* (then in MS, published in London, 1664). Busses were two- or three-masted herring boats; flat-bottoms were a kind of barge; sword-pinks were pinks provided with leeboards (Dutch *zwaard*); and tode-boats were small fishing vessels (origin unknown).

4. Frequent variant of "Iceland."

5. The "Straits" of Gibraltar or, loosely, the Mediterranean.

6. Biscayners, people of Biscay, in N Spain—Basques.

7. Cape Blanco is on the W coast of Africa, in 20° N lat. (The statement in Frank T. Siebert, Jr., "The Identity of the Tarrantines, with an Etymology," *Studies in Linguistics*, XXIII [1973], 73, 73n, that "the Portuguese, Basques, and Spaniards fished off Cape Cod that year [1614]," is untenable.)

8. A very non-specific name for spiny fishes; here most likely to be the eastern Atlantic sea bream.

9. Properly "botargo," a relish made from the roe of mullet or tuna (tunny).

10. A name for hake or cod salted and dried for food (*OED*), "poor fare." A term of opprobrium suggesting "desiccated" when applied to a man (Shakespeare, *Romeo and Juliet*, I, i, 37, "thou hadst been poor John").

them hath neither meate, drinke, nor clothes, wood, iron, nor steele, pitch, tarre, nets, leades, salt, hookes, nor lines, for shipping, fishing, nor provision, but at the second, third, fourth, or fift hand, drawne from so many severall parts of the world ere they come together to be used in this voyage: If these I say can gaine, and the Saylers live going for shares, lesse then the third part of their labours, and yet spend as much time in going and comming, as in staying there, so short is the season of fishing; why should wee more doubt, then Holland, Portugale, Spaniard, French, or other, but to doe much better then they, where there is victuall to feede us, wood of all sorts, to build Boats, Ships, or Barks; the fish at our doores, pitch, tarre, masts, yards, and most of other necessaries onely for making? And here are no hard Landlords to racke us with high rents, or extorted fines to consume us, no tedious pleas in law to consume us with their many years disputations for Justice: no multitudes to occasion such impediments to good orders, as in popular States. So freely hath God and his Majesty bestowed those blessings on them that will attempt to obtaine them, as here every man may be master and owner of his owne labour and land; or the greatest part in a small time. If hee have nothing but his hands, he may set up this trade; and by in-

[14] || dustrie quickly grow rich; spending but halfe that time wel, which in England we abuse in idlenes, worse or as ill. Here is ground also as good as any lyeth in the height of forty one, forty two, forty three, etc. which is as temperate and as fruitfull as any other paralell in the world. As for example, on this side the line West of it in the South

Examples of the altitude comparatively.

Sea, is Nova Albion, discovered as is said, by Sir Francis Drake.[1] East from it, is the most temperate part of Portugale, the ancient kingdomes of Galazia,[2] Biskey, Navarre, Arragon, Catalonia, Castilia the olde, and the most moderatest of Castilia the new, and Valentia, which is the greatest part of Spain: which if the Spanish Histories bee true, in the Romanes time abounded no lesse with golde and silver Mines, then now the West Indies; the Romanes then using the Spaniards to work in those Mines, as now the Spaniard doth the Indians.

In France, the Provinces of Gasconie, Langadock, Avignon, Province, Dolphine, Pyamont, and Turyne,[3] are in the same paralel: which are the best and richest parts of France. In Italy, the provinces of Genua, Lumbardy, and Verona, with a great part of the most

1. Sir Francis Drake's Nova Albion was "within thirtie eight degrees towardes the [equatorial] line" (Richard Hakluyt, *The Principal Voyages, Traffiques and Discoveries of the English Nation* [London, 1598–1600], III, 440); apparently the vicinity of San Francisco Bay in modern California, which is roughly the latitude of Córdoba in southern Spain, and therefore considerably farther S than most of the cities and provinces named below.

2. Galicia; perhaps a misprint.

3. Note that Provence was the prototype of French provinces, and that Piedmont and Turin were dominions of the house of Savoy, which became Italian rather than French during the 50-year reign of Charles Emmanuel I (d. 1630).

famous State of Venice, the Dukedoms of Bononia,[4] Mantua, Ferrara, Ravenna, Bolognia, Florence, Pisa, Sienna, Urbine, Ancona, and the ancient Citie and Countrey of Rome, with a great part of the great Kingdome of Naples. In Slavonia, Istrya, and Dalmatia, with the Kingdomes of Albania.[5] In Grecia, that famous Kingdome of Macedonia, Bulgaria, Thessalia, Thracia, or Romania, where is seated ‖ the most pleasant and plentifull Citie in Europe, Constantinople. In Asia also, in the same latitude, are the temperatest parts of Natolia, Armenia, Persia, and China, besides divers other large Countries and Kingdomes in these most milde and temperate Regions of Asia. Southward, in the same height, is the richest of golde Mynes, Chily and Baldivia,[6] and the mouth of the great River of Plate, etc : for all the rest of the world in that height is yet unknown. Besides these reasons, mine owne eyes that have seene a great part of those Cities and their Kingdomes, as well as it,[7] can finde no advantage they have in nature, but this, They are beautified by the long labour and diligence of industrious people and Art. This is onely as God made it, when he created the worlde. Therefore I conclude, if the heart and intralls[8] of those Regions were sought : if their Land were cultured, planted and manured by men of industrie, judgement, and experience; what hope is there, or what neede they doubt, having those advantages of the Sea, but it might equalize any of those famous Kingdomes, in all commodities, pleasures, and conditions? seeing even the very edges doe naturally afford us such plenty, as no ship need returne away empty : and onely use but the season of the Sea, fish will returne an honest gaine, beside all other advantages; her treasures having yet never beene opened, nor her originalls wasted, consumed, nor abused.

The particular staple commodities that may be had. [16]

And whereas it is said, the Hollanders serve the Easterlings themselves, and other parts that want, ‖ with Herring, Ling, and wet Cod; the Easterlings, a great part of Europe, with Sturgion and Caviare; Cape-blanke, Spaine, Portugale, and the Levant, with Mullet, and Puttargo; New found Land, all Europe, with a thin Poore John : yet all is so overlaide with fishers, as the fishing decayeth, and many are constrained to returne with a small fraught. Norway, and Polonia, Pitch, Tar, Masts, and Yardes; Sweathland, and

[15]

---

4. Smith is confused here; Bononia was merely the Latin name of Bologna (see the next line).

5. This would seem to refer to the Albania of Skanderbeg, who died in 1467, after which the region joined the "Kingdome" of Macedonia, etc., under Turkish suzerainty. To supplement Smith's comment, it can be pointed out that the Black Sea lies roughly between the same parallels of latitude (41°–45°) as Smith's New England.

6. Smith has confused the land of Chile with the name of its conquistador, Pedro de Valdivia, who founded Santiago (33° 24′ S lat.). He may have obtained his information from the account by Lopez Vaz (of Elvas, Portugal) in Hakluyt, *Principal Navigations*, III, 778–802.

7. New England.

8. Variant spelling of "entrails."

Russia, Iron, and Ropes; France, and Spaine, Canvas, Wine, Steele, Iron, and Oyle; Italy and Greece, Silks, and Fruites. I dare boldly say, because I have seen naturally growing, or breeding in those parts the same materialls that all those are made of, they may as well be had here, or the most part of them, within the distance of 70 leagues for some few ages,[9] as from all those parts; using but the same meanes to have them that they doe, and with all those advantages.

The nature of ground approoved. First, the ground is so fertill, that questionless it is capable of producing any Grain, Fruits, or Seeds you will sow or plant, growing in the Regions afore named: But it may be, not every kinde to that perfection of delicacy; or some tender plants may miscarie, because the Summer is not so hot, and the winter is more colde in those parts wee have yet tryed neere the Sea side, then we finde in the same height in Europe or Asia; Yet I made a Garden upon the top of a Rockie Ile in 43. ½, 4 leagues[10] from the Main, in May, that grew so **[17]** well, as it served us for sallets in June and July. All sorts ‖ of cattell may here be bred and fed in the Iles, or Peninsulaes, securely for nothing. In the Interim till they encrease if need be (observing the seasons) I durst undertake to have corne enough from the Salvages for 300 men, for a few trifles; and if they should bee untoward[1] (as it is most certaine they are) thirty or forty good men will be sufficient to bring them all in subjection, and make this provision; if they understand what they doe:[2] 200 whereof may nine monethes in the yeare be imployed in making marchandable fish, till the rest provide other necessaries, fit to furnish us with other commodities.

The seasons for fishing approoved. In March, Aprill, May, and halfe June, here is Cod in abundance; in May, June, July, and August Mullet and Sturgion; whose roes doe make Caviare and Puttargo. Herring, if any desire them, I have taken many out of the bellies of Cods, some in nets; but the Salvages compare their store in the Sea, to the haires of their heads: and surely there are an incredible abundance upon this Coast. In the end of August, September, October, and November, you have Cod againe, to make Cor fish, or Poore John: and each hundred is as good as two or three hundred in the New-found Land. So that halfe the labour in hooking, splitting, and turning,[3] is saved: and you may have your fish at what Market you will, before they can have any in New-found Land; where their fishing is chiefly but in June and July: whereas it is heere in March, Aprill, May, September, October, and **[18]** ‖ November, as is said. So that by reason of this plantation, the Mar-

9. The sense seems to require the addition of the phrase "of time or effort" after "ages."

10. Monhegan Island is in that latitude (see p. 1, above), and is very nearly 4 leagues (12 mi.) S from modern Port Clyde.

1. Disinclined, intractable.

2. The *Generall Historie*, 211, clarifies: "if they [the English] understand what to doe."

3. Fishermen's jargon for the steps to be taken in drying cod for the market.

chants may have fraught both out and home: which yeelds an advantage worth consideration.

Your Cor-fish you may in like manner transport as you see cause, to serve the Ports in Portugale (as Lisbon, Avera, Porta port,[4] and divers others, or what market you please) before your Ilanders returne: They being tyed to the season in the open Sea; you having a double season, and fishing before your doors, may every night sleep quietly a shore with good cheare and what fires you will, or when you please with your wives and familie: they onely, their ships in the maine Ocean.

The Mullets heere are in that abundance, you may take them with nets, sometimes by hundreds, where at Cape blank they hooke them; yet those but one foot and a halfe in length; these two, three, or foure, as oft I have measured: much Salmon some have found up the Rivers, as they have passed: and heer the ayre is so temperate, as all these at any time may well be preserved.

Now, young boyes and girles Salvages, or any other, be they never such idlers, may turne, carry, and return fish, without either shame, or any great paine: hee is very idle that is past twelve yeares of age and cannot doe so much: and she is very olde, that cannot spin a thred to make engines to catch them.

For their transportation, the ships that go there to fish may transport the first: who for their pas- || sage will spare the charge of double manning their ships, which they must doe in the New-found Land, to get their fraught; but one third part of that companie are onely but proper to serve a stage,[5] carry a barrow, and turne Poor John: notwithstanding, they must have meate, drinke, clothes, and passage, as well as the rest. Now all I desire, is but this; That those that voluntarily will send shipping, should make here the best choise they can, or accept such as are presented them, to serve them at that rate: and their ships returning leave such with me, with the value of that they should receive comming home, in such provisions and necessarie tooles, armes, bedding and apparell, salt, hookes, nets, lines, and such like as they spare of the remainings; who till the next returne may keepe their boates and doe them many other profitable offices: provided I have men of ability to teach them their functions, and a company fit for Souldiers to be ready upon an occasion;[6] because of the abuses which have beene offered the poore Salvages, and the liberty both French, or any that will, hath to deale with them as

Imployment for poore people and fatherlesse children.

The facility of the plantation.
[19]

---

4. Aveiro is a seaport 88 km. (55 mi.) S of Oporto, birthplace of João Affonso, one of the earliest mariners to use the fishing grounds off Newfoundland; "Porta port" was a popular form of Port Oporto, itself a magnificent example of tautology. Below, "Ilanders" are Newfoundlanders.

5. A docking stage along the side of which boats drew up and unloaded their catch. It contained the cutting table. The cookhouse (for rendering train) and the flake (for drying cod) were separate structures.

6. I.e., "when needed"—in case of hostile attacks.

they please: whose disorders will be hard to reforme; and the longer the worse. Now such order with facilitie might be taken, with every port Towne or Citie, to observe but this order, With free power to convert the benefits of their fraughts to what advantage they please, and increase their numbers as they see occasion; who ever as they are **[20]** able to subsist of themselves, may beginne the new Townes in ‖ New England in memory of their olde: which freedome being confined but to the necessity of the generall good, the event (with Gods helpe) might produce an honest, a noble, and a profitable emulation.

Present com-
modities.

Salt upon salt[7] may assuredly be made; if not at the first in ponds, yet till they bee provided this may be used: then the Ships may transport Kine, Horse, Goates, course Cloath, and such commodities as we want; by whose arrivall[8] may be made that provision of fish to fraught the Ships that they stay not: and then if the sailers goe for wages, it matters not. It is hard if this returne defray not the charge: but care must be had, they arrive in the Spring, or else provision be made for them against the Winter.

Of certaine red berries called Alkermes[9] which is worth ten shillings a pound, but of these hath been sould for thirty or forty shillings the pound, may yearely be gathered a good quantitie.

Of the Musk Rat may bee well raised gaines, well worth their labour, that will endevor to make tryall of their goodnesse.

Of Bevers, Otters, Martins, Blacke Foxes, and Furres of price, may yearely be had 6 or 7000: and if the trade of the French were prevented, many more: 25000 this yeare were brought from those Northren parts into France; of which trade we may have as good part as the French, if we take good courses.

[21] Of Mynes of Golde and Silver, Copper, and ‖ probabilities of Lead, Christall and Allum, I could say much if relations were good assurances. It is true indeed, I made many trials according to those instructions I had, which doe perswade mee I need not despaire, but there are metalls in the Countrey: but I am no Alchymist, nor will promise more then I know: which is, Who will undertake the rectifying[10] of an Iron forge, if those that buy meate, drinke, coals, ore, and all necessaries at a deer rate gaine; where all these things are to be

---

7. Ipswich, Tobias Gentleman wrote in 1614, is "most convenient for the erecting of Salt-pans, for the making of Salt upon Salt, for that the Harbour is so good that at all times Ships may come unto them with Salt for Mayo [Maio I., Cape Verdes], or Spanish salt to make the brine" (*Englands way to win wealth* . . . [London, 1614], 24). Smith meant that salt brought over could be mixed with seawater to produce more salt.

8. At first the ships will come out with a salt lading. Later, when salt is made in New England, they will come out not in ballast but laden with colonists or goods for them and "by whose arrivall" (by means of whose arrival thus freighted) a lading of fish can be provided without them having to fish for it.

9. Kermes are the dried bodies of crimson insects (female only) found mainly on oaks and thought to be berries until the 18th century. A famous cordial was made from them. But Smith may have had in mind the bloodroot or partridgeberry, *Mitchella repens*.

10. Probably an error for "erectifying," a rare verb for "set up" or "build."

had for the taking up, in my opinion cannot lose.

Of woods seeing there is such plenty of all sorts, if those that build ships and boates, buy wood at so great a price, as it is in England, Spaine, France, Italy, and Holland, and all other provisions for the nourishing of mans life; live well by their trade: when labour is all required[1] to take those necessaries without any other tax; what hazard will be here, but doe much better? And what commoditie in Europe doth more decay[2] then wood? For the goodnesse of the ground, let us take it fertill, or barren, or as it is: seeing it is certaine it beares fruites, to nourish and feed man and beast, as well as England, and the Sea those severall sorts of fish I have related. Thus seeing all good provisions for mans sustenance, may with this facility be had, by a little extraordinarie labour, till that transported be increased; and all necessaries for shipping, onely for labour: to which may bee added the assistance of the Salvages, which may easily be had, if they be discreetly handled in their ‖ kindes;[3] towards fishing, **[22]** planting, and destroying woods. What gaines might be raised if this were followed (when there is but once men to fill your store houses, dwelling there, you may serve all Europe better and farre cheaper, then can the Izeland fishers, or the Hollanders, Cape blank, or New found Land: who must be at as much more charge, then you) may easily be conjectured by this example.

2000. pound will fit out a ship of 200. and 1 of a 100[4] tuns: If the dry fish they both make, fraught that of 200. and goe for Spaine, sell it but at ten shillings a quintall; but commonly it giveth fifteen, or twentie: especially when it commeth first, which amounts to 3 or 4000 pound: but say but tenne, which is the lowest, allowing the rest for waste, it amounts at that rate, to 2000 pound, which is the whole charge of your two ships, and their equipage: Then the returne of the money, and the fraught of the ship for the vintage,[5] or any other voyage, is cleere gaine, with your shippe of a 100 tuns of Train oyle,[6] besides the bevers, and other commodities; and that you may have at home within six monethes, if God please but to send an ordinarie passage. Then saving halfe this charge by the not staying of your ships, your victual, overplus of men and wages; with her fraught thither of things necessarie for the planters, the salt being there made: as also may the nets and lines, within a short time: if nothing were to bee expected but this, it might in time equalize your Hollanders gaines, if not exceed them: they returning but ‖ wood, pitch, tarre, **[23]**

An example of the gains upon every yeare or six monethes returne.

1. Read: "all that is required. . . ."
2. Fall off, dwindle away.
3. In their way, after their fashion.
4. Read: "1 [ship] of 100 tuns."
5. Probably new wine for England.
6. "Train" in Smith's time referred to fish oil generally, but here cod-liver oil was intended. The "oyle" could be from seals, walruses, or even whales. In later usage, "train" referred specifically to oil extracted from whale blubber by boiling.

and such grosse commodities; you wines, oyles, fruits, silkes, and such Straits commodities,[7] as you please to provide by your Factors, against such times as your shippes arrive with them. This would so increase our shipping and sailers, and so employ and encourage a great part of our idlers and others that want imployments fitting their qualities at home, where they shame to doe that they would doe abroad; that could they but once taste the sweet fruites of their owne labours, doubtlesse many thousands would be advised by good discipline, to take more pleasure in honest industrie, then in their humours of dissolute idlenesse.[8]

A description of the Countries in particular, and their situations.

But, to returne a little more to the particulars of this Countrey, which I intermingle thus with my projects and reasons, not being so sufficiently yet acquainted in those parts, to write fully the estate of the Sea, the Ayre, the Land, the Fruites, the Rocks, the People, the Government, Religion, Territories, and Limitations, Friends, and Foes: but, as I gathered from the niggardly[9] relations in a broken language to my understanding, during the time I ranged those Countries etc. The most Northren[1] part I was at, was the Bay of Pennobscot, which is East and West, North and South, more then ten leagues:[2] but such were my occasions,[3] I was constrained to be satisfied of them I found in the Bay, that the River ranne farre up into the Land, and was well inhabited with many people, but they

[24] were from their habitations, either fish- || ing among the Iles, or hunting the Lakes and Woods, for Deer and Bevers. The Bay is full of great Ilands, of one, two, six, eight, or ten miles in length, which divides it into many faire and excellent good harbours. On the East of it, are the Tarrantines, their mortall enemies, where inhabit the French, as they report that live with those people, as one nation or family.[4] And Northwest of Pennobscot[5] is Mecaddacut, at the foot of

---

7. Commodities from the Mediterranean, by way of the Strait of Gibraltar.

8. The disinclination of English gentlemen "of quality" to do any sort of work is stressed time and again in the literature of the period.

9. I.e., "given in a grudging way"; the language was "broken" in that the Indian languages of New England differed somewhat from those of Virginia, so that Smith cannot have understood all he heard.

1. "Northren" was no less popular a variant than "Southren."

2. Penobscot Bay measures more than 30 mi. (c. 50 km.) from Naskeag W to Rockland, and about the same from the mouth of the Penobscot River S to the open sea off Vinalhaven Island.

3. Business in hand.

4. The sense is that the Tarrantines are the mortal enemies of the Penobscot, and the French live in the Tarrantine territory. There were no Frenchmen left in the neighborhood after Samuel Argall's raid on Port Royal and Sainte-Croix, July to Nov. 1613 (see the *Generall Historie*, 115; and Philip L. Barbour, *Pocahontas and Her World* [Boston, 1970], 119-124, 146-147). But Charles de Biencourt struggled through the winter in Port Royal (modern Annapolis, Nova Scotia), over 150 mi. (c. 250 km.) up the Bay of Fundy from Naskeag (see the *Dictionary of Canadian Biography*, s.v. "Biencourt de Saint-Just, Charles de"). In the spring, Biencourt's father brought supplies and reinforcements, but Port Royal was too far away to concern John Smith.

5. Smith's description of the coast from here to the bottom of the page follows the map but gives the Indian names, not the English.

a high mountaine, a kinde of fortresse against the Tarrantines, ad-joyning to the high mountaines of Pennobscot, against whose feet doth beat the Sea :[6] But over all the Land, Iles, or other impediments, you may well see them sixteene or eighteene leagues from their situation. Segocket is the next; then Nusconcus, Pemmaquid, and Sagadahock. Up this River where was the Westerne plantation[7] are Aumuckcawgen, Kinnebeck, and divers others, where there is planted some corne fields. Along this River 40 or 50 miles, I saw nothing but great high cliffes of barren Rocks, overgrowne with wood: but where the Salvages dwelt there the ground is exceeding fat and fertill. Westward of this River, is the Countrey of Aucocisco, in the bottome of a large deepe Bay, full of many great Iles, which divides it into many good harbours. Sowocotuck is the next, in the edge of a large sandy Bay, which hath many Rocks and Iles, but few good harbours, but for Barks, I yet know. But all this Coast to Pennobscot, and as farre I could see Eastward of it is nothing but such high craggy Cliffy Rocks and stony ‖ Iles that I wondered such great **[25]** trees could growe upon so hard foundations. It is a Countrie rather to affright, then delight one. And how to describe a more plaine spectacle of desolation or more barren I knowe not. Yet the Sea there is the strangest fishpond I ever saw; and those barren Iles so furnished with good woods, springs, fruits, fish, and foule, that it makes mee thinke though the Coast be rockie, and thus affrightable; the Vallies, Plaines, and interior parts, may well (notwithstanding) be verie fertile. But there is no kingdome so fertile hath not some part barren: and New England is great enough, to make many Kingdomes and Countries, were it all inhabited. As you passe the Coast still Westward, Accominticus and Passataquack are two convenient harbors for small barks; and a good Countrie, within their craggie cliffs. Angoam is the next; This place might content a right curious judgement: but there are many sands at the entrance of the harbor: and the worst is, it is inbayed too farre from the deepe Sea. Heere are many rising hilles, and on their tops and descents many corne fields, and delightfull groves. On the East, is an Ile of two or three leagues in length; the one halfe, plaine morish grasse fit for pasture, with many faire high groves of mulberrie trees and gardens: and there is also Okes, Pines, and other woods to make this place an excellent habitation, beeing a good and safe harbor.

Naimkeck though it be more rockie ground (for Angoam is sandie) not much inferior; neither for the ‖ harbor, nor any thing I **[26]** could perceive, but the multitude of people. From hence doth stretch into the Sea the faire headland Tragabigzanda, fronted with three Iles called the three Turks heads:[8] to the North of this, doth enter a

---

6. The Longfellow Mountains do parallel the coast at about 50 mi. (80 km.) inland.
7. At Sagadahoc.
8. This is the first unmistakable evidence of the connection of Smith's coat of arms,

great Bay, where wee founde some habitations and corne fields: they report a great River, and at least thirtie habitations, doo possesse this Countrie. But because the French had got their Trade, I had no leasure to discover it. The Iles of Mattahunts are on the West side of this Bay, where are many Iles, and questionlesse good harbors: and then the Countrie of the Massachusets, which is the Paradise of all those parts: for, heere are many Iles all planted with corne; groves, mulberries, salvage gardens, and good harbors: the Coast is for the most part, high clayie sandie cliffs. The Sea Coast as you passe, shewes you all along large corne fields, and great troupes of well proportioned people: but the French having remained heere neere sixe weekes, left nothing, for us to take occasion[9] to examine the inhabitants relations, viz. if there be neer three thousand people upon these Iles; and that the River doth pearce many daies journeies the intralles of that Countrey. We found the people in those parts verie kinde; but in their furie no lesse valiant. For, upon a quarrell wee had with one of them, hee onely with three others crossed the harbor of Quonahassit[10] to certaine rocks whereby wee must passe; and there let flie their arrowes for our shot, till we were out of danger.

[27]   Then come you to Accomack,[1] an excellent good || harbor, good land; and no want of any thing, but industrious people. After much kindnesse, upon a small occasion, wee fought also with fortie or fiftie of those: though some were hurt, and some slaine; yet within an houre after they became friendes. Cape Cod is the next presents it selfe: which is onely a headland of high hils of sand, overgrowne with shrubbie[2] pines, hurts,[3] and such trash; but an excellent harbor for all weathers. This Cape is made by the maine Sea on the one side, and a great Bay on the other in forme of a sickle: on it doth inhabit the people of Pawmet: and in the bottome of the Bay, the people of Chawum. Towards the South and Southwest of this Cape, is found a long and dangerous shoale of sands and rocks. But so farre as I incircled it, I found thirtie fadom water aboard[4] the shore, and a strong

---

or device, with his first protectress, his Turkish mistress, Charatza Trabigzanda (see the *True Travels*, 12–18, 23).

9. Read: "the French . . . left nothing for us but to take occasion" to inform ourselves about the country and the people. The identity of the French is uncertain.

10. Modern Cohasset, on Massachusetts Bay, 25 mi. (40 km.) N of Plymouth.

1. Since the name Accomack seems to mean "land or place on the other side," since Patuxet is the name given by Bradford to the Indian town at Plymouth, and since Champlain's 1605 map of Plymouth Bay shows Indian houses and fields on both sides of the little river at Plymouth, it may be suggested that there were two (if not more) villages on the bay at or near Plymouth. It must be remembered that when the Pilgrims arrived the site was deserted, due to a disastrous epidemic among the Indians.

2. Now usually "scrubby" or "stunted," variant developments from the same Middle English verb.

3. "Hurtleberries"; huckleberries, or, more formally, the whortleberry, here referring to several species of *Vaccinium*.

4. I.e., "along." There would most likely have been soundings of 30 fathoms (150 to 180 ft., depending on which fathom Smith used) within 3 statute mi. of the shore at

current: which makes mee thinke there is a Channell about this shoale; where is the best and greatest fish to be had, Winter and Summer, in all that Countrie. But, the Salvages say there is no Channell, but that the shoales beginne from the maine at Pawmet, to the Ile of Nausit; and so extends beyond their knowledge into the Sea. The next to this is Capawack,[5] and those abounding Countries of copper, corne, people, and mineralls; which I went to discover this last yeare: but because I miscarried by the way, I will leave them, till God please I have better acquaintance with them. A good

The Massachusets, they report, sometimes have warres with the Bashabes of Pennobskot;[6] and are not ‖ alwaies friends with them of Chawun and their alliants: but now they are all friends, and have each trade with other, so farre as they have societie, on each others frontiers. For they make no such voiages as from Pennobskot to Cape Cod; seldom to Massachewset.[7] In the North (as I have said) they begunne to plant corne, whereof the South part hath such plentie, as they have what they will from them of the North; and in the Winter much more plenty of fish and foule: but both Winter and Summer hath it in the one part or other all the yeare; being the meane and most indifferent temper, betwixt heat and colde, of all the regions betwixt the Lyne and the Pole: but the furs Northward are much better, and in much more plentie, then Southward.

The remarkeablest Iles and mountains for Landmarkes are these; The highest Ile is Sorico,[8] in the Bay of Pennobskot: but the three Iles and a rock of Matinnack are much furder in the Sea; Metinicus is also three plaine Iles and a rock, betwixt it and Monahigan: Monahigan is a rounde high Ile; and close by it Monanis, betwixt which is a small harbor where we ride. In Damerils Iles is such another: Sagadahock is knowne by Satquin, and foure or five Iles in the mouth. Smyths Iles are a heape together, none neere them, against Accominticus. The three Turks heads are three Iles seen far to Sea-ward in regard of the headland.

The cheefe headlands are onely Cape Tragabigzanda and Cape Cod.

The cheefe mountaines, them of Pennobscot; the twinkling[1]

A good
Countrie.
[28]

The land-
markes.

[29]

Smith's Pawmet, the unnamed house on the map in the neighborhood of modern Nauset Beach Light. Some 20 statute mi. S of there Smith would have encountered the maze of currents and shoals between Monomy Point and Nantucket.

5. Capawack was the Indian name for Martha's Vineyard. There is nothing to indicate that he dared try to navigate through or around Nantucket Shoals.

6. See p. 8, above.

7. Despite Smith's assertion, which was based on brief experience, it would appear that the Indians did not entirely shun the open sea. See Horace P. Beck, *The American Indian as a Sea-Fighter in Colonial Times* (Mystic, Conn., 1959), 5–20.

8. Sorico has been identified as Isle au Haut, to the E of Vinalhaven (Eckstorm, *Indian Place-Names*, 99–100; Eckstorm is puzzled by the name).

1. I.e., "appearing and disappearing in rapid succession." There is a high hill NW of Casco Bay and some 10 mi. (16 km.) inland, and beyond are the White Mountains, but the editor is not in a position to suggest that they "twinkle."

mountaine of Aucocisco; the greate mountaine of Sasanou; and the high mountaine of Massachusit:[2] each of which you shall finde in the Mappe; their places, formes, and altitude. The waters are most pure, proceeding from the intrals of rockie mountaines; the hearbes and fruits are of many sorts and kindes: as alkermes, currans, or a fruit like currans, mulberries, vines, respices,[3] goos-berries, plummes, walnuts, chesnuts, small nuts, etc. pumpions,[4] gourds, strawberries, beans, pease, and mayze; a kinde or two of flax, wherewith they make nets, lines and ropes both small and great, verie strong for their quantities.[5]

Hearbs.

Woods.

Oke, is the chiefe wood; of which there is great difference in regard of the soyle where it groweth. firre, pyne, walnut, chesnut, birch, ash, elme, cypresse, ceder, mulberrie, plumtree, hazell, saxefrage,[6] and many other sorts.

Birds.

Eagles, Gripes,[7] diverse sorts of Haukes, Cranes, Geese, Brants, Cormorants, Ducks, Sheldrakes, Teale, Meawes, Guls, Turkies, Dive-doppers,[8] and many other sorts, whose names I knowe not.

Fishes.

Whales, Grampus, Porkpisces,[9] Turbut, Sturgion, Cod, Hake, Haddock, Cole,[1] Cusk, or small Ling, Shark, Mackerell, Herring, Mullet, Base, Pinacks,[2] Cunners,[3] Pearch, Eels, Crabs, Lobsters, Muskles, Wilkes,[4] Oysters, and diverse others etc.

Beasts.

Moos, a beast bigger then a Stagge; deere, red, and Fallow; Bevers, Wolves, Foxes, both blacke and other; Aroughconds,[5] Wild-

[30] cats, Beares, Otters, ‖ Martins, Fitches, Musquassus,[6] and diverse sorts of vermine, whose names I know not. All these and diverse other good things do heere, for want of use, still increase, and decrease with little diminution, whereby they growe to that abundance. You shall scarce finde any Baye, shallow shore, or Cove of sand, where you may not take many Clampes,[7] or Lobsters, or both at your pleasure, and in many places lode your boat if you please; Nor Iles where you finde not fruits, birds, crabs, and muskles, or all of them, for taking, at a lowe water.[8] And in the harbors we frequented, a

---

2. The highest of these "mountaines" is Massachusit, where today the Blue Hills Observatory rises to 849 ft. above sea level. "Sasanou" is Agamenticus.
   3. "Raspberries."
   4. "Pumpkins."
   5. Size, dimensions.
   6. "Sassafras"; see the *Map of Va.*, 12n.
   7. Vultures.
   8. Variant of "didapper," the dabchick or little grebe.
   9. Variant of "porpoises."
   1. Coalfish; also "pollock" or "podlock."
   2. Perhaps an error for "pinna," a shellfish.
   3. Blue perch (of the NE North American coast).
   4. Variant of "whelks."
   5. Raccoons.
   6. "Musquash," muskrat.
   7. An occasional variant of "clam," probably by association with a "clamp."
   8. The passage "And in . . . any place, but" was omitted in the *Generall Historie*, 216, apparently inadvertently.

little boye might take of Cunners, and Pinacks, and such delicate fish, at the ships sterne, more then sixe or tenne can eate in a daie; but with a casting-net, thousands when wee pleased: and scarce any place, but Cod, Cuske, Holybut, Mackerell, Scate, or such like, a man may take with a hooke or line what he will. And, in diverse sandy Baies, a man may draw with a net great store of Mullets, Bases, and diverse other sorts of such excellent fish, as many as his Net can drawe on shore: no River where there is not plentie of Sturgion, or Salmon, or both; all which are to be had in abundance observing but their seasons. But if a man will goe at Christmasse to gather Cherries in Kent, he may be deceived; though there be plentie in Summer: so, heere these plenties have each their seasons, as I have expressed. We for the most part had little but bread and vineger: and though the most part of July when the fishing decaied they wrought all day, laie abroade in the Iles ‖ all night, and lived on what they found, yet **[31]** were not sicke: But I would wish none put himself long to such plunges;[9] except necessitie constraine it: yet worthy is that person to starve that heere cannot live; if he have sense, strength and health: for, there is no such penury of these blessings in any place, but that a hundred men may, in one houre or two, make their provisions for a day: and hee that hath experience to mannage well these affaires, with fortie or thirtie honest industrious men, might well undertake (if they dwell in these parts) to subject the Salvages, and feed daily two or three hundred men, with as good corne, fish, and flesh, as the earth hath of those kindes, and yet make that labor but their pleasure: provided that they have engins,[10] that be proper for their purposes.

Who can desire more content, that hath small meanes; or but only his merit to advance his fortune, then to tread, and plant that ground hee hath purchased by the hazard of his life? If he have but the taste of virtue, and magnanimitie,[1] what to such a minde can bee more pleasant, then planting and building a foundation for his Posteritie, gotte from the rude earth, by Gods blessing and his owne industrie, without prejudice to any? If hee have any graine of faith or zeale in Religion, what can hee doe lesse hurtfull to any; or more agreeable to God, then to seeke to convert those poore Salvages to know Christ, and humanitie, whose labors with discretion will triple requite thy charge and paines? What so truely sutes with honour and ho- ‖ nestie, as the discovering things unknowne? erecting Townes, **[32]** peopling Countries, informing the ignorant, reforming things unjust, teaching virtue; and gaine to our Native mother-countrie a kingdom to attend her; finde imployment for those that are idle, because they know not what to doe: so farre from wronging any, as to cause Posteritie to remember thee; and remembring thee, ever

A note for men that have great spirits, and smal meanes.

9. Stresses.
10. Contrivances, implements.
1. Nobly ambitious spirit.

honour that remembrance with praise? Consider: What were the
beginnings and endings of the Monarkies of the Chaldeans, the
Syrians, the Grecians, and Romanes, but this one rule; What was it
they would not doe, for the good of the commonwealth, or their
Mother-citie? For example: Rome, What made her such a Mon-
archesse, but onely the adventures of her youth, not in riots at home;
but in dangers abroade? and the justice and judgement out of their
experience, when they grewe aged. What was their ruine and hurt,
but this; The excesse of idlenesse, the fondnesse of Parents, the want
of experience in Magistrates, the admiration of their undeserved
honours, the contempt of true merit, their unjust jealosies, their poli-
ticke incredulities, their hypocriticall seeming goodnesse, and their
deeds of secret lewdnesse? finally, in fine, growing onely formall
temporists, all that their predecessors got in many years, they lost in
few daies. Those by their pains and vertues became Lords of the
world; they by their ease and vices became slaves to their servants.
This is the difference betwixt the use of Armes in the field, and on the
[33] monuments of stones; ‖ the golden age and the leaden age, prosperity
and miserie, justice and corruption, substance and shadowes, words
and deeds, experience and imagination, making Commonwealths
and marring Commonwealths, the fruits of vertue and the conclusions of vice.

Then, who would live at home idly (or thinke in himselfe any
worth to live) onely to eate, drink, and sleepe, and so die? Or by consuming that carelesly, his friends got worthily? Or by using that
miserably, that maintained vertue honestly? Or, for being descended
nobly, pine with the vaine vaunt of great kindred, in penurie? Or
(to maintaine a silly shewe of bravery) toyle out thy heart, soule, and
time, basely, by shifts,[2] tricks, cards, and dice? Or by relating newes
of others actions, sharke[3] here or there for a dinner, or supper; deceive thy friends, by faire promises, and dissimulation, in borrowing
where thou never intendest to pay; offend the lawes, surfeit with
excesse, burden thy Country, abuse thy selfe, despaire in want, and
then couzen thy kindred, yea even thine owne brother, and wish thy
parents death (I will not say damnation) to have their estates?
though thou seest what honours, and rewards, the world yet hath for
them will seeke them and worthily deserve them.

I would be sory to offend, or that any should mistake my honest
meaning: for I wish good to all, hurt to none. But rich men for the
[34] most part are growne to that dotage, through their pride in ‖ their
wealth, as though there were no accident could end it, or their life.
And what hellish care do such take to make it their owne miserie,
and their Countries spoile, especially when there is most neede of

2. Expedients.
3. Sponge.

their imployment? drawing by all manner of inventions, from the Prince and his honest subjects, even the vitall spirits of their powers and estates: as if their Bagges,[4] or Bragges, were so powerfull a defence, the malicious could not assault them; when they are the onely baite, to cause us not to be onely assaulted; but betrayed and murdered in our owne security, ere we well perceive it.

May not the miserable ruine of Constantinople, their impregnable walles, riches, and pleasures last taken by the Turke (which are but a bit, in comparison of their now mightines) remember[5] us, of the effects of private covetousness? at which time the good Emperour held himselfe rich enough, to have such rich subjects, so formall in all excesse of vanity, all kinde of delicacie, and prodigalitie. His povertie when the Turke besieged, the citizens (whose marchandizing thoughts were onely to get wealth, little conceiving the desperate resolution of a valiant expert enemy) left the Emperour so long to his conclusions,[6] having spent all he had to pay his young, raw, discontented Souldiers; that sodainly he, they, and their citie were all a prey to the devouring Turke. And what they would not spare for the maintenance of them who adventured their lives to defend them, did serve onely their ‖ enemies to torment them, their friends, and countrey, and all Christendome to this present day. Let this lamentable example remember you that are rich (seeing there are such great theeves in the world to robbe you) not grudge to lend some proportion, to breed them that have little, yet willing to learne how to defend you: for, it is too late when the deede is a-doing. The Romanes estate hath beene worse then this: for, the meere covetousnesse and extortion of a few of them, so mooved the rest, that not having any imployment, but contemplation; their great judgements grew to so great malice, as themselves were sufficient to destroy themselves by faction: Let this moove you to embrace imployment, for those whose educations, spirits, and judgements, want but your purses; not onely to prevent such accustomed dangers, but also to gaine more thereby then you have. And you fathers that are either so foolishly fond, or so miserably covetous, or so willfully ignorant, or so negligently carelesse, as that you will rather maintaine your children in idle wantonness, till they growe your masters; or become so basely unkinde, as they wish nothing but your deaths; so that both sorts growe dissolute: and although you would wish them any where to escape the gallowes, and ease your cares; though they spend you here one, two, or three hundred pound a yeer; you would grudge to give halfe so much in adventure with them, to obtaine an estate, which in a small time but with a little assistance of your ‖ providence, might bee better then your owne. But if an Angell should tell you,

An example of secure covetousness.

[35]

[36]

4. "Bagges" of money.
5. Remind.
6. Fate.

that any place yet unknowne can afford such fortunes; you would not beleeve him, no more then Columbus was beleeved there was any such Land as is now the well knowne abounding America; much lesse such large Regions as are yet unknowne, as well in America, as in Affrica, and Asia, and Terra incognita; where were courses for gentlemen (and them that would be so reputed) more suiting their qualities, then begging from their Princes generous disposition, the labours of his subjects, and the very marrow of his maintenance.

The Authors conditions.

I have not beene so ill bred, but I have tasted of Plenty and Pleasure, as well as Want and Miserie: nor doth necessity yet, or occasion of discontent, force me to these endeavors: nor am I ignorant what small thanke I shall have for my paines; or that many would have the Worlde imagine them to be of great judgement, that can but blemish these my designes, by their witty objections and detractions: yet (I hope) my reasons with my deeds, will so prevaile with some, that I shall not want imployment in these affaires, to make the most blinde see his owne senselesnesse, and incredulity; Hoping that gaine will make them affect that, which Religion, Charity, and the Common good cannot. It were but a poore device in me, To deceive my selfe; much more the King, and State, my Friends, and Countrey, with these inducements: which, seeing his

[37] Majestie hath given ‖ permission, I wish all sorts of worthie, honest, industrious spirits, would understand: and if they desire any further satisfaction, I will doe my best to give it: Not to perswade them to goe onely; but goe with them: Not leave them there; but live with them there. I will not say, but by ill providing and undue managing, such courses may be taken, may make us miserable enough: But if I may have the execution of what I have projected; if they want to eate, let them eate or never digest Me.[7] If I performe what I say, I desire but that reward out of the gaines may sute my paines, quality, and condition. And if I abuse you with my tongue, take my head for satisfaction. If any dislike at the yeares end, defraying their charge, by my consent they should freely returne. I feare not want of companie sufficient, were it but knowne what I know of those Countries; and by the proofe of that wealth I hope yearely to returne, if God please to blesse me from such accidents, as are beyond my power in reason to prevent: For, I am not so simple, to thinke, that ever any other motive then wealth, will ever erect there a Commonweale; or draw companie from their ease and humours at home, to stay in

The planters pleasures, and profits.

New England to effect my purposes. And lest any should thinke the toile might be insupportable, though these things may be had by labour, and diligence: I assure my selfe there are who delight extreamly in vaine pleasure, that take much more paines in England,

7. I.e., ". . . or never consider what I have written." The capital "M" was possibly intentional, though it is printed "mee" in the *Generall Historie*, 219. In the next sentence, read: "reward . . . that may sute."

to enjoy it, then I should doe heere to gaine wealth suffici- ‖ ent: and
yet I thinke they should not have halfe such sweet content: for, our
pleasure here is still gaines; in England charges and losse. Heer
nature and liberty affords us that freely, which in England we want,
or it costeth us dearely. What pleasure can be more, then (being
tired with any occasion a-shore)[8] in planting Vines, Fruits, or Hearbs,
in contriving their owne Grounds, to the pleasure of their owne
mindes, their Fields, Gardens, Orchards, Buildings, Ships, and other
works, etc. to recreate themselves before their owne doores, in their
owne boates upon the Sea, where man woman and childe, with a
small hooke and line, by angling, may take diverse sorts of excellent
fish, at their pleasures? And is it not pretty sport, to pull up two
pence, six pence, and twelve pence, as fast as you can hale and veare
a line?[9] He is a very bad fisher, cannot kill in one day with his hooke
and line, one, two, or three hundred Cods: which dressed and dryed,
if they be sould there for ten shillings the hundred, though in England
they will give more then twentie; may not both the servant, the
master, and marchant, be well content with this gaine? If a man
worke but three dayes in seaven, he may get more then hee can spend,
unlesse he will be excessive. Now that Carpenter, Mason, Gardiner,
Taylor, Smith, Sailer, Forgers, or what other, may they not make
this a pretty recreation though they fish but an houre in a day, to take
more then they eate in a weeke: or if they will not eate it, because
there is so much better ‖ choise; yet sell it, or change it, with the fisher   [39]
men, or marchants, for any thing they want. And what sport doth
yeeld a more pleasing content, and lesse hurt or charge then angling
with a hooke, and crossing the sweete ayre from Ile to Ile, over the
silent streames of a calme Sea? wherein the most curious may finde
pleasure, profit, and content. Thus, though all men be not fishers:
yet all men, whatsoever, may in other matters doe as well. For necessity doth in these cases so rule a Commonwealth, and each in their
severall functions, as their labours in their qualities may be as profitable, because there is a necessary mutuall use of all.

    For Gentlemen, what exercise should more delight them, then   Imployments
ranging dayly those unknowne parts, using fowling and fishing, for   for gentlemen.
hunting and hauking? and yet you shall see the wilde haukes give
you some pleasure, in seeing them stoope[1] (six or seaven after one
another) an houre or two together, at the skuls[2] of fish in the faire
harbours, as those a-shore at a foule; and never trouble nor torment
your selves, with watching, mewing, feeding, and attending them:
nor kill horse and man with running and crying, See you not a hauk?

---

8. I.e., "any casual happening"; the parentheses are omitted in the *Generall Historie*,
219.
9. To "haul and veer" a line, in cod fishing.
1. Swoop; hawking jargon.
2. "Schools"; frequent spelling in this context.

For hunting also: the woods, lakes, and rivers, affoord not onely chase sufficient, for any that delights in that kinde of toyle, or pleasure; but such beasts to hunt, that besides the delicacy of their bodies for food, their skins are so rich, as may well recompence thy dayly labour, with a Captains pay.

[40]
**Imployments
for labourers.**

For labourers, if those that sowe hemp, rape, turnups, parsnips, carrats, cabidge, and such like; give 20, 30, 40, 50 shillings yearely for an acre of ground, and meat drinke and wages to use it, and yet grow rich: when better, or at least as good ground, may be had and cost nothing but labour; it seemes strange to me, any such should there grow poore.

My purpose is not to perswade children from their parents; men from their wives; nor servants from their masters: onely, such as with free consent may be spared: But that each parish, or village, in Citie, or Countrey, that will but apparell their fatherlesse children, of thirteene or fourteene years of age, or young maried people, that have small wealth to live on; heere by their labour may live exceeding well: provided alwaies that first there bee a sufficient power to command them, houses to receive them, meanes to defend them, and meet provisions for them; for, any place may bee overlain:[3] and it is most necessarie to have a fortresse (ere this grow to practice) and sufficient masters (as, Carpenters, Masons, Fishers, Fowlers, Gardiners, Husbandmen, Sawyers, Smiths, Spinsters,[4] Taylors, Weavers, and such like) to take ten, twelve, or twentie, or as ther is occasion, for Apprentises. The Masters by this may quicklie growe rich; these may learne their trades themselves, to doe the like; to a generall and an incredible benefit, for King, and Countrey, Master, and Servant.

[41]
**Examples of
the Spanyard.**

It would bee an historie of a large volume,[5] to recite the adventures of the Spanyards, and Portugals, their affronts, and defeats, their dangers and miseries; which with such incomparable honour and constant resolution, so farre beyond beleefe, they have attempted and indured in their discoveries and plantations, as may well condemne us, of too much imbecillitie, sloth, and negligence: yet the Authors of those new inventions, were held as ridiculous, for a long time, as now are others, that doe but seek to imitate their unparalleled vertues. And though we see daily their mountaines of wealth (sprong from the plants of their generous indevours) yet is our sensualitie and untowardnesse such, and so great, that wee either ignorantly beleeve nothing; or so curiously contest, to prevent wee knowe not what future events; that wee either so neglect, or oppresse and discourage the present, as wee spoile all in the making, crop all in the blooming; and building upon faire sand, rather then rough rockes, judge that

3. Overpowered.
4. "Spinners."
5. The lengthy digression from here to the top of p. 45 was slightly reworked for the *Generall Historie*, 220–221, but remains somewhat obscure in detail.

wee knowe not, governe that wee have not, feare that which is not; and for feare some should doe too well, force such against their willes to be idle or as ill. And who is he hath judgement, courage, and any industrie or qualitie with understanding, will leave his Countrie, his hopes at home, his certaine estate, his friends, pleasures, libertie, and the preferment sweete England doth afford to all degrees, were it not to advance his fortunes by injoying his deserts? whose prosperitie once appearing, will incourage others: but it must be cherish- || ed **[42]** as a childe, till it be able to goe, and understand it selfe; and not corrected, nor oppressed above its strength, ere it knowe wherefore. A child can neither performe the office, nor deedes of a man of strength, nor indure that affliction He is able; nor can an Apprentice at the first performe the part of a Maister. And if twentie yeeres bee required to make a child a man, seven yeares limited an apprentice for his trade: if scarce an age be sufficient to make a wise man a States man; and commonly, a man dies ere he hath learned to be discreet: If perfection be so hard to be obtained, as of necessitie there must bee practice, as well as theorick: Let no man much condemne this paradox opinion, to say, that halfe seaven yeeres is scarce sufficient, for a good capacitie, to learne in these affaires, how to carrie himselfe: and who ever shall trie in these remote places the erecting of a Colony, shall finde at the ende of seaven yeares occasion enough to use all his discretion: and, in the Interim all the content, rewards, gaines, and hopes will be necessarily required, to be given to the beginning, till it bee able to creepe, to stand, and goe, yet time enough to keepe it from running, for there is no feare it wil grow too fast, or ever to any thing; except libertie, profit, honor, and prosperitie there found, more binde the planters of those affaires, in devotion to effect it; then bondage, violence, tyranny, ingratitude, and such double dealing, as bindes free men to become slaves, and honest men turne knaves: which hath ever bin the ruine of the most popular || common- **[43]** weales; and is verie unlikelie ever well to begin in a new.[6]

Who seeth not what is the greatest good of the Spanyard, but these new conclusions, in searching those unknowne parts of this unknowne world? By which meanes hee dives even into the verie secrets of all his Neighbours, and the most part of the world: and when the Portugale and Spanyard had found the East and West Indies; how many did condemn themselves, that did not accept of that honest offer of Noble Columbus? who, upon our neglect, brought them to it, perswading our selves the world had no such places as they had found: and yet ever since wee finde, they still (from time to time) have found new Lands, new Nations, and trades, and still daily dooe finde both in Asia, Africa, Terra incognita, and America; so that there is neither Soldier nor Mechanick, from the Lord to the begger,

The blisse of Spaine.

6. Cf. the *Generall Historie*, 221, "to begin anew."

but those parts afforde them all imploiment; and discharge their Native soile, of so many thousands of all sorts, that else, by their sloth, pride, and imperfections, would long ere this have troubled their neighbours, or have eaten the pride of Spaine it selfe.

Now he knowes little, that knowes not England may well spare many more people then Spaine, and is as well able to furnish them with all manner of necessaries. And seeing, for all they have, they cease not still to search for that they have not, and know not; It is strange we should be so dull, as not maintaine that which wee have, **[44]** and pursue that wee ‖ knowe. Surely I am sure many would taste[7] it ill, to bee abridged of the titles and honours of their predecessors: when if but truely they would judge themselves; looke how inferior they are to their noble vertues, so much they are unworthy of their honours and livings: which never were ordained for showes and shadowes, to maintaine idlenesse and vice; but to make them more able to abound in honor, by heroycall deeds of action, judgement, pietie, and vertue. What was it, They would not doe both in purse and person, for the good of the Commonwealth? which might move them presently to set out their spare kindred in these generous designes. Religion, above all things, should move us (especially the Clergie) if wee were religious, to shewe our faith by our workes; in converting those poore salvages, to the knowledge of God, seeing what paines the Spanyards take to bring them to their adulterated faith. Honor might move the Gentrie, the valiant, and industrious; and the hope and assurance of wealth, all; if wee were that we would seeme, and be accounted. Or be we so far inferior to other nations, or our spirits so far dejected, from our auncient predecessors, or our mindes so upon spoile, piracie, and such villany, as to serve the Portugall, Spanyard, Dutch, French, or Turke (as to the cost of Europe, too many dooe) rather then our God, our King, our Country, and our selves? excusing our idlenesse, and our base complaints, by want of imploiment; when heere is such choise of all sorts, and for all **[45]** degrees, in the plan- ‖ ting and discovering these North parts of America.

My second voyage to New England.

Now to make my words more apparent by my deeds; I was, the last yeare, 1615. to have staied in the Countrie, to make a more ample triall of those conclusions with sixteene men; whose names were[8]

---

7. The *Generall Historie*, 221, has "take it ill."

8. There are a few differences between this list and the reprint in the *Generall Historie*, 222. "Robert Miter" and "Walter Chissick" are misprints for "Robert Miller" and "Walter Chissel" (or "Chisell"). The names appear properly in the *Generall Historie* and on p. 53, below. John Gosling is here a gentleman and in the *Generall Historie* is a soldier. The "two boies" and Robert Miller are here soldiers and in the *Generall Historie* "were to learne to be Sailers." And John Hall is omitted altogether from the reprint.

Thomas Dirmir.
Edward Stalings.
Daniel Cage.   } *Gentlemen.*
Francis Abbot.
John Gosling.

William Ingram.
Robert Miter.
David Cooper.   } *Souldiers.*
John Partridge,
and two boies.

Thomas Digbie.
Daniel Baker.
Adam Smith.   } *Sailers.*
Thomas Watson
Walter Chissick.
John Hall.

I confesse, I could have wished them as many thousands, had all other provisions bin in like proportion: nor would I have had so fewe, could I have had meanes for more: yet (would God have pleased wee had safely arrived) I never had the like authoritie, freedom, and provision, to doe so well. The maine assistance next God, I had to this small number, was my acquaintance among the Salvages; especially, with Dohannida,[9] one of their greatest Lords; who had lived long in England. By the meanes of this proud Salvage, I did not doubt but quickly to have gotte that credit with the rest of his friends, and alliants,[10] to have had as many of them, as I desired in any designe I intended, and that trade also they had, by such a kind of exchange || of their Countrie commodities; which both with ease **[46]** and securitie in their seasons may be used. With him and diverse others, I had concluded to inhabit, and defend them against the Terentynes;[1] with a better power then the French did them; whose tyranny did inforce them to imbrace my offer, with no small devotion. And though many may thinke me more bolde then wise, in regard of their power, dexteritie, treacherie, and inconstancie, having so desperately assaulted and betraied many others: I say but this (because with so many, I have many times done much more in Virginia, then I intended heere, when I wanted that experience Virginia taught me) that to mee it seemes no daunger more then ordinarie. And though I know my selfe the meanest of many thousands, whose apprehensive inspection can pearce beyond the boundes of my habilities, into the hidden things of Nature, Art, and Reason: yet I intreate such give me leave to excuse my selfe of so much imbecillitie, as to say, that in these eight yeares which I have been conversant with these affairs, I have not learned there is a great

9. See the Biographical Directory, s.v. "Tahanedo." The name is also transcribed as "Nahanada" (William Strachey, *The Historie of Travell into Virginia Britania*, ed. Louis B. Wright and Virginia Freund [Hakluyt Soc., 2d Ser., CIII (London, 1953)], 164–172).
    10. Variant of "allies."
    1. Seven years later, in 1621, William Bradford reported that the Massachusetts Bay Indians "were much afraid of the Tarentines, a people to the eastward which used to come in harvest time and take away their corn, and many times kill their persons" (Bradford, *Plymouth Plantation*, 89; cf. p. 24, above).

difference, betwixt the directions and judgement of experimentall knowledge, and the superficiall conjecture of variable relation: wherein rumor, humor, or misprision have such power, that oft times one is enough to beguile twentie, but twentie not sufficient to keep one from being deceived. Therefore I know no reason but to beleeve my own eies, before any mans imagination, that is but wrested from **[47]** the conceits of my owne projects, and indea- || vours. But I honor, with all affection, the counsell and instructions of judiciall directions, or any other honest advertisement; so farre to observe, as they tie mee not to the crueltie of unknowne events.

These are the inducements that thus drew me to neglect all other imployments, and spend my time and best abilities in these adventures. Wherein, though I have had many discouragements by the ingratitude of some, the malicious slanders of others, the false-nesse of friendes, the trechery of cowards, and slownesse of adven-turers; but chiefly by one Hunt,[2] who was Master of the ship, with whom oft arguing these projects, for a plantation, however hee seemed well in words to like it, yet he practiced to have robbed mee of my plots, and observations,[3] and so to leave me alone in a desolate Ile, to the fury of famine, and all other extreamities (lest I should have acquainted Sir Thomas Smith, my Honourable good friend, and the Councell of Virginia) to the end, he and his associates, might secretly ingrosse it, ere it were knowne to the State: Yet that God that alway hath kept me from the worst of such practices, delivered me from the worst of his dissimulations. Notwithstanding after my departure, hee abused the Salvages where hee came, and betrayed twenty seaven of these poore innocent soules, which he sould in Spaine for slaves, to moove their hate against our Nation, as well as to cause my proceed-ings to be so much the more difficult.

[48] Now, returning in the Bark, in the fift[4] of Au- || gust, I arrived at Plimouth: where imparting those my purposes to my honourable friende Sir Ferdinando Gorge,[5] and some others; I was so incouraged, and assured to have the managing their authoritie in those parts, during my life, that I ingaged my selfe to undertake it for them. Arriving at London, I found also many promise me such assistance, that I entertained Michaell Cooper the Master,[6] who returned with mee, and others of the company. How hee dealt with others, or others with him I know not: But my publike proceeding gave such

2. Master Thomas Hunt, mentioned on p. 1, above; see the Biographical Directory.

3. "He tried to rob me of my charts (plats) and notes."

4. "The latter end of August" (*New Englands Trials* [1620], sig. B3^r).

5. The spelling "Gorge," the name "Gorgeana" for a settlement on the Agamenti-cus River, and the Norman-French origin of the name (with silent "-s") seem to hint strongly that the family name Gorges was then pronounced "gorge," not "gorges." See p. 49n, below.

6. Cooper was master of the bark, the second ship mentioned on p. 1, above.

incouragement, that it became so well apprehended by some fewe of the Southren Company, as these projects were liked,[7] and he furnished from London with foure ships at Sea, before they at Plimouth had made any provision at all, but onely a ship cheefely set out by sir Ferdinando Gorge; which upon Hunts late trecherie among the Salvages, returned as shee went, and did little or nothing, but lost her time. I must confesse I was beholden to the setters forth of the foure ships that went with Cooper; in that they offered mee that imploiment if I would accept it: and I finde, my refusall hath incurred some of their displeasures, whose favor and love I exceedingly desire, if I may honestly injoy it. And though they doe censure me as opposite to their proceedings; they shall yet still in all my words and deedes finde, it is their error, not my fault, that occasions their dislike: for having ingaged my selfe in this businesse to the West Countrie; I had beene verie dishonest to have ‖ broke my promise; nor will I spend **[49]** more time in discoverie, or fishing, till I may goe with a companie for plantation: for, I know my grounds. Yet every one that reades this booke can not put it in practice; though it may helpe any that have seene those parts. And though they endeavour to worke me even out of my owne designes, I will not much envy their fortunes: but, I would bee sory, their intruding ignorance should, by their defailements,[8] bring those certainties to doubtfulnesse: So that the businesse prosper, I have my desire; be it by Londoner, Scot, Welch, or English, that are true subjects to our King and Countrey: the good of my Countrey is that I seeke; and there is more then enough for all, if they could bee content but to proceed.

At last it pleased Sir Ferdinando Gorge, and Master Doctor Sutliffe,[9] Deane of Exceter, to conceive so well of these projects, and my former imployments, as induced them to make a new adventure with me in those parts, whither they have so often sent to their continuall losse. By whose example, many inhabitants of the west Country, made promises of much more then was looked for, but their private emulations[10] quickly qualified that heat in the greater number; so that the burden lay principally on them, and some few Gentlemen my friends, in London. In the end I was furnished with

The occasion of my returne.

7. Cooper's expedition remains obscure, as does Smith's "promise" (mentioned at the top of the next page). Basically, Smith's interest lay in establishing a fishing colony; the backers he had so far found wanted little or nothing more than exploration and profitable summer fishing voyages (see Preston, *Gorges of Plymouth Fort*, 157, though some of his evidence seems shaky). See p. 49, below.

8. Failures.

9. Sir Ferdinando was a leading backer of the colonization of New England from the outset. Matthew Sutcliffe, the well-to-do dean of Exeter Cathedral, was promoter and benefactor of Chelsea College, where Samuel Purchas retired on occasion to work on his *Pilgrimes*, and backer of the colonial projects for Virginia and, more particularly, for New England. See the Biographical Directory for both Gorges and Sutcliffe.

10. Jealousies.

a Ship of 200. and another of 50. But ere I had sayled 120 leagues, shee broke all her masts; pumping each watch 5 or 6000 strokes:

[50]

My reimbark-
ment, incoun-
ters with pyrats
and imprison-
ment by the
French.

onely her spret saile ‖ remayned to spoon before the wind, till we had re-accommodated a Jury mast, and the rest, to returne for Plimouth. My Vice-admirall beeing lost, not knowing of this, proceeded her voyage:[1] Now with the remainder of those provisions, I got out again in a small Barke of 60 tuns with 30 men (for this of 200 and provision for 70) which were the 16 before named, and 14 other saylors for the ship. With those I set saile againe the 24 of June: where what befell me (because my actions and writings are so publicke to the world, envy still seeking to scandalize my indeavours, and seeing no power but death, can stop the chat[2] of ill tongues, nor imagination of mens mindes) lest my owne relations of those hard events, might by some constructors, be made doubtfull, I have thought it best to insert the examinations of those proceedings, taken by Sir Lewis Stukley a worthie Knight, and Viceadmirall of Devonshire;[3] which were as followeth.

Captaine Fry
his ship 140
tuns, 36 cast
peeces and
murderers, 80
men; of which
40, or 50.
were master
gunners.

[51]

The examination of Daniel Baker,[4] late Steward
to Captaine John Smith in the returne of Plimouth;
taken before Sir Lewis Stukley, Knight,
the eight of December 1615.

Who saith, being chased two dayes by one Fry, an English Pirate,[5] that could not board us, by reason of foule weather, Edmund Chambers, the Master, John Minter, his mate, Thomas Digby[6] the Pilot, and others importuned his saide Captaine to yeeld; houlding it unpossible hee should defend ‖ himselfe: and that the saide Captaine should send them his boate, in that they had none: which at last he concluded upon these conditions, That Fry the Pyrate should vow not to take any thing from Captaine Smith, that might over-throwe his voyage, nor send more Pirats into his ship then hee liked off; otherwaies, he would make sure of them he had, and defend himselfe against the rest as hee could.

More: he confesseth that the quarter-masters and Chambers received golde of those Pirats; but how much, he knoweth not: Nor would his Captain come out of his Caben to entertaine them; al-

---

1. The ship under the command of the vice-admiral was lost from view and pro-ceeded on its way, not knowing of the problems on Smith's ship.
2. "Chatter"; gossip.
3. On Sir Lewis Stukely, see the Biographical Directory. No trace of the examina-tion related below has been found in the archives of Devonshire, but the records for 1616 are incomplete (personal letter to the editor from Mrs. Miriam Wood, Assistant Archi-vist, Devon County Record Office, Exeter, dated Mar. 7, 1963).
4. See p. 45, above.
5. The English pirates were notorious in Smith's day.
6. See p. 45, above.

though a great many of them had beene his saylers, and for his love would have wafted us to the Iles of Flowers.[7]

At Fyall,[8] wee were chased by two French Pyrats, who commanded us Amaine. Chambers, Minter, Digby, and others, importuned againe the Captaine to yeeld; alledging they were Turks, and would make them all slaves: or Frenchmen, and would throw them all over board if they shot but a peece; and that they were entertained to fish, and not to fight: untill the Captaine vowed to fire the powder and split the ship, if they would not stand to their defence; whereby at last wee went cleere of them, for all their shot.

The one of 200, the other 20.

At Flowers, wee were chased by foure French men of warre;[1] all with their close fights[2] afore and after. And this examinants Captaine having provided for our defence, Chambers, Minter, Dig- ‖ by, and some others, againe importuned him to yeeld to the favour of those, against whom there was nothing but ruine by fighting: But if he would goe aboard them, in that hee could speake French, by curtesie hee might goe cleere; seeing they offered him such faire quarter, and vowed they were Protestants, and all of Rochell, and had the Kings commission onely to take Spaniards, Portugales, and Pyrats; which at last hee did: but they kept this examinates Captaine and some other of his company with him. The next day the French men of warre went aboard us, and tooke what they listed, and divided the company into their severall ships, and manned this examinates ship with the Frenchmen; and chased with her all the shippes they saw: untill about five or six dayes after upon better consideration, they surrendered the ship, and victualls, with the most part of our provision, but not our weapons.[3]

The Admirall 140 tuns, 12 peeces, 12 murderers, 90 men, with long pistols, pocket **[52]** pistols, musket, sword and poniard, the Vice-admirall 100 tuns, the Rere-admiral 60, the other 80: all had 250 men most armed as is said.

More: he confesseth that his Captain exhorted them to performe their voyage, or goe for New found Land to returne fraughted with fish, where hee would finde meanes to proceed in his plantation: but Chambers and Minter grew upon tearms they would not;[4] untill those that were Souldiers concluded with their Captaines resolution, they would; seeing they had clothes, victualls, salt, nets, and lines

The gentlemen and souldiers were ever willing to fight.

7. "Convoyed us to the island of Flores (Azores)"—a frequent rendezvous in those days.

8. Fayal is 150 mi. (240 km.) ESE of Flores.

1. For surviving French records of what follows, see Philip L. Barbour, "A French Account of Captain John Smith's Adventures in the Azores, 1615," *VMHB*, LXXII (1964), 293–303.

2. "Smal ledges of wood laid crosse one another like the grates of iron in a prisons window, betwixt the maine mast, and the fore mast" (*Sea Grammar*, 58). More broadly, Sir Henry Mainwaring explains, "generally any place wherein men may cover themselves and yet use their arms" ("The Seaman's Dictionary," in G. E. Manwaring and W. G. Perrin, eds., *The Life and Works of Sir Henry Mainwaring* [Navy Records Society (London, 1922)], II, 147).

3. This is borne out by the French account (see Barbour, "French Account," *VMHB*, LXXII [1964], 296).

4. The details about Chambers and Minter are omitted in the *Generall Historie*, 223.

sufficient, and expected their armes: and such other things as they wanted, the French men promised to restore, which the Captaine the

[53] next day went to seeke, and sent them about loading of ‖ commodities, as powder, match, hookes, instruments, his sword and dagger, bedding, aqua vitæ, his commission, apparell, and many other things; the particulars he remembreth not: But, as for the cloath, canvas, and the Captaines cloathes, Chambers, and his associats divided it amongst themselves, and to whom they best liked; his Captaine not having any thing, to his knowledge, but his wastecoat and breeches.[5] And in this manner going from ship to ship, to regaine our armes, and the rest; they seeing a sayle, gave chase untill night. The next day being very foule weather, this examinate came so neere with the ship unto the French men of warre, that they split the maine sayle on the others spret sayle yard. Chambers willed the Captaine come aboard, or hee would leave him: whereupon the Captaine commanded Chambers to send his boate for him. Chambers replyed shee was split (which was false) telling him hee might come if he would in the Admiralls boat. The Captaines answer was, he could not command her, nor come when hee would: so this examinate fell on sterne; and that night left his said Captaine alone amongst the French men, in this manner, by the command of Chambers, Minter, and others.

> *Daniel Cage, Edward Stalings, Gentlemen; Walter Chissell,*
> *David Cooper, Robert Miller, and John Partridge,*
> *beeing examined, doe acknowledge and confesse,*
> *that Daniel Baker his examination above*
> *writen is true.*[6]

[54] Now the cause why the French detayned me againe, was the
A double
treachery. suspicion this Chambers and Minter gave them, that I would revenge my selfe, upon the Bank,[7] or in New found Land, of all the French I could there incounter; and how I would have fired the ship, had they not overperswaded mee: and many other such like tricks to catch but opportunitie in this maner to leave me. And thus they returned to Plimouth; and perforce with the French I thus proceeded.

Being a Fleet of eight or nine sayle,[8] we watched for the West Indies fleet, till ill weather separated us from the other 8. Still we

5. From this passage to the end of the paragraph, the text is altered and largely cut in the *Generall Historie*, 223–224.

6. The mention of Baker is omitted and the conclusion changed in the *Generall Historie*, 224.

7. The Newfoundland Banks, which stretch some 300 mi. (nearly 500 km.) SE into the Atlantic and have depths of between 15 and 90 fathoms. Since about A.D. 1500 the Banks have been famous for the multitude of fish to be obtained there.

8. The next two pages are substantiated in the French records (see Barbour, "French Account," *VMHB*, LXXII [1964], 293–303).

spent our time about the Iles neere Fyall: where to keepe my per- A fleet of nine
plexed thoughts from too much meditation of my miserable estate, French men of
I writ this discourse;[9] thinking to have sent it you of his Majesties war, and fights
Councell, by some ship or other: for I saw their purpose was to take with the
all they could. At last we were chased by one Captain Barra,[1] an Spaniards.
English Pyrat, in a small ship, with some twelve peeces of ordinance,
about thirty men, and neer all starved. They sought by curtesie re-
leefe of us; who gave them such faire promises, as at last wee betrayed
Captaine Wolliston[2] (his Lieftenant) and foure or five of their men
aboard us, and then provided to take the rest perforce. Now my part
was to be prisoner in the gun-roum, and not to speake to any of them
upon my life: yet had Barra knowledge what I was. Then Barra perceiving wel these French intents, made ready to fight, and Wolliston
as resolutely regarded not their threats, ‖ which caused us demurre **[55]**
upon the matter longer, som sixteene houres; and then returned their
prisoners, and some victualls also, upon a small composition.[3] The
next wee tooke was a small English man of Poole[4] from New found
Land. The great caben at this present, was my prison; from whence
I could see them pillage those poore men of all that they had, and
halfe their fish. When hee was gone, they sould his poore cloathes at
the maine mast, by an outcry, which scarce gave each man seaven
pence a peece. Not long after, wee tooke a Scot fraught from Saint
Michaels[5] to Bristow: hee had better fortune then the other. For,
having but taken a boats loading of suger, marmelade, suckets,[6] and
such like, we discried foure sayle, after whom we stood; who forling
their maine sayles attended us to fight. But our French spirits were
content onely to perceive they were English rcd crosses.[7] Within a
very small time after, wee chased foure Spanish shippes came from
the Indies: wee fought with them foure or five houres, tore their
sayles and sides; yet not daring to board them, lost them. A poore
Carvell[8] of Brasile, was the next we chased: and after a small fight,
thirteene or fourteen of her men being wounded, which was the better A prize worth
halfe, we tooke her, with 370 chests of sugar. The next was a West 16000 crowns.
Indies man, of 160 tuns, with 1200 hides, 50 chests of cutchanell,[9] 14 A prize worth
200000
crownes.

9. Apparently only the part from Aug. 5, 1614, on (see p. 47, above).
1. Perhaps the same Captain Barrow mentioned in the *True Travels*, 59, who was
pardoned by James I.
2. Also pardoned by James I (see *ibid.*).
3. Settlement.
4. Five mi. W of modern Bournemouth, Dorset.
5. Saint Michaels (São Miguel) is the largest of the Azores; "Bristow" was a frequent
spelling of "Bristol."
6. Variant spelling of "succade"; candied fruit.
7. St. George's cross, emblem of England.
8. Variant of "caravel," a small, light sailing ship.
9. "Cochineal," a brilliant red dyestuff prepared from the dried body of the female
cochinilla, a Mexican insect.

coffers of wedges[1] of silver, 8000 ryalls of 8,[2] and six coffers of the King of Spaines treasure, besides the pillage and rich coffers of many rich

[56] passengers. Two || monethes they kept me in this manner to manage their fights against the Spaniards, and be a prisoner when they tooke any English. Now though the Captaine had oft broke his promise, which was to put me a-shore on the Iles,[3] or the next ship he tooke; yet at last, he was intreated I should goe for France in the Carvell of sugar: himself resolved still to keepe the Seas. Within two dayes after, we were haled by two West Indy men: but when they saw us wave them for the King of France,[4] they gave us their broad sides, shot through our mayne mast and so left us. Having lived thus, neer three moneths among those French men of warre; with much adoe, we arrived at the Gulion,[5] not far from Rochel; where in stead of the great promises they alwaies fed me with, of double satisfaction, and full content, they kept me five or six daies prisoner in the Carvell, accusing me to bee him that burnt their Colony in New France;[6] to force mee give them a discharge before the Judge of the Admiralty, and so stand to their curtesie for satisfaction, or lie in prison, or a worse mischiefe. To prevent this choise, in the end of such a storme

My escape   that beat them all under Hatches, I watched my opportunity to get
from the   a-shore in their boat; where-into, in the darke night, I secretly got:
French men.   and with a halfe pike that lay by me, put a drift for Rat Ile:[7] but the Current was so strong and the Sea so great, I went a drift to Sea; till it pleased God the winde so turned with the tide, that although I was all this fearefull night of gusts and raine, in the Sea, the space of 12

[57] || houres, when many ships were driven a shore, and diverse split (and being with sculling and bayling the water tired, I expected each minute would sinke mee) at last I arrived in an oazie Ile by Char-owne;[8] where certaine fowlers found mee neere drowned, and halfe dead, with water, colde, and hunger. By those, I found meanes to gette to Rochell; where I understood the man of warre which we left at Sea, and the rich prize was split, the Captaine drowned and halfe his companie the same night, within seven leagues of that place,

---

1. Ingots; so called because of their shape.
2. There were eight reales in a peso, or "piece of eight" as it was often called. A piece of eight was worth roughly 5 shillings when Smith was writing.
3. The Azores.
4. "Signaling with the fleur-de-lis."
5. L'Aiguillon, c. 16 mi. (25 km.) N of La Rochelle.
6. Capt. Samuel Argall (knighted, 1622) was the one commanded to wipe out the French colony (see p. 24n, above).
7. Île de Ré (Latin, *Ratis Insula*). This English version of the name gave rise to Robert Vaughan's little joke in the map of Ould Virginia (see the notes to this map in the *Generall Historie*; and cf. Sir Henry Mainwaring, "Discourse on Pirates," in Manwaring and Perrin, eds., *Life and Works of Mainwaring*, II, 40). The Latin *ratis* has nothing to do with a rat or, in this case, with a raft, as some have suggested; it was derived from a Celtic word meaning "fern," hence "Isle of Ferns" (René James and Louis Suire, *L'Île de Ré d'autrefois et d'aujourd'hui* [La Rochelle, 1959 (orig. publ. 1952)], 26).
8. The Charente River.

from whence I escaped alone, in the little boate, by the mercy of God; far beyond all mens reason, or my expectation. Arriving at Rochell, upon my complaint to the Judge of the Admiraltie, I founde many good words, and faire promises; and ere long many of them that escaped drowning, tolde mee the newes they heard of my owne death: these I arresting, their severall examinations did so confirme my complaint, it was held proofe sufficient. All which being performed according to the order of justice, from under the judges hand; I presented it to the English Ambassador then at Burdeaux,[9] where it was my chance to see the arrivall of the Kings great mariage brought from Spaine. Of the wrack of the rich prize some 36000.[1] crownes worth of goods came a shore and was saved with the Carvell, which I did my best to arrest: the Judge did promise me I shold have justice; what will bee the conclusion as yet, I know not. But under the colour[2] to take Pirats and West-Indie men (because the Spanyards will not || suffer the French trade in the West-Indies) any goods from thence, thogh they take them upon the Coast of Spaine, are lawfull prize; or from any of his territories out of the limits of Europe.

Leaving thus my businesse in France, I returned to Plimouth, to find them that had thus buried me amongst the French: and not onely buried mee, but with so much infamy, as such trecherous cowards could suggest to excuse their villanies: But my clothes, bookes, instruments, Armes, and what I had, they shared amongst them, and what they liked; fayning, the French had all was wanting; and had throwne them into the Sea, taken their ship, and all, had they not runne away and left me as they did. The cheeftaines of this mutinie that I could finde, I laied by the heeles; the rest, like themselves, confessed the truth as you have heard. Now how I have or could prevent these accidents, I rest at your censures.[3] But to the matter.

Newfound-land at the first, I have heard, was held as desperate[4] a fishing, as this I project in New England. Placentia,[5] and the Banke, were also as doubtfull to the French: But, for all the disasters happened mee, the businesse is the same it was: and the five ships (whereof one was reported more then three hundred tunnes) went forward; and found fish so much, that neither Izeland-man, nor

[margin:] Sir Thomas Edmunds.

They betraied mee having the broad seale of

[58]

England: and neere twentie sayle of English more, besides them concealed, in like maner were betrayed that year. My returne for England, 1615.

9. The ambassador, Sir Thomas Edmondes, attended the young king, Louis XIII, to Bordeaux early in Oct. 1615 and apparently remained there at least until Nov. 21, when Louis drove out to meet the Infanta Ana de Austria on her way to their royal wedding ceremony.

1. The *Generall Historie*, 226, has "some three thousand six hundred crownes worth." The smaller sum may be correct, considering the loss of the bulk of the "prize."

2. Pretext or pretense.

3. I.e., "expressed opinions," as often.

4. Dangerous, reckless.

5. Placentia is on the protected bay of that name, in the W part of the Avalon peninsula, which is to the SE of the main island.

The successe
of my vice
Admirall and

[59]

the foure ships
of London,
from New
England.

Newfound-land-man, I could heare of hath beene there, will goe any more to either place, if they may goe thither. So, that upon the returne of my Viceadmirall that proceeded on her voyage when I spent my ‖ masts, from Plimouth this yeare are gone foure or five saile: and from London as many; onely to make voyages of profit: where the Englishmen have yet beene, all their returnes together (except Sir Francis Popphames) would scarce make one a saver of neere a douzen I could nominate; though there be fish sufficient, as I perswade my selfe, to fraught yearely foure or five hundred sayle, or as many as will goe. For, this fishing stretcheth along the Coast from Cape Cod to Newfound-land, which is seaven or eight hundered miles at the least; and hath his course in the deepes, and by the shore, all the yeare long; keeping their hants and feedings as the beasts of the field, and the birds of the aire. But, all men are not such as they should bee, that have undertaken those voiages: and a man that hath but heard of an instrument, can hardly use it so well, as hee that by use hath contrived to make it. All the Romanes were not Scipioes: nor all the Geneweses, Columbuses: nor all Spanyards, Corteses: had they dived no deeper in the secrets of their discoveries, then wee, or stopped at such doubts and poore accidentall chances; they had never beene remembred as they are: yet had they no such certainties to begin as wee. But, to conclude, Adam and Eve did first beginne this innocent worke, To plant the earth to remaine to posteritie; but not without labour, trouble and industrie. Noe, and his family, beganne againe the second plantation; and their seede as it still increased, hath still planted new Countries, and one countrie

[60]   another: and so the world to that estate it is. But ‖ not without much hazard, travell,[6] discontents, and many disasters. Had those worthie Fathers and their memorable off-spring not beene more diligent for us now in these Ages, then wee are to plant that yet unplanted, for the after livers: Had the seede of Abraham, our Saviour Christ, and his Apostles, exposed themselves to no more daungers to teach the Gospell, and the will of God then wee; Even wee our selves, had at this present been as Salvage, and as miserable as the most barbarous Salvage yet uncivilized. The Hebrewes, and Lacedæmonians, the Goths, the Grecians, the Romanes, and the rest, what was it they would not undertake to inlarge their Territories, enrich their subjects, resist their enemies? Those that were the founders of those great Monarchies and their vertues, were no silvered idle golden Pharises, but industrious iron-steeled Publicans: They regarded more provisions, and necessaries for their people, then jewels, riches, ease, or delight for themselves. Riches were their servants, not their Maisters. They ruled (as Fathers, not as Tyrantes) their people as children, not as slaves: there was no disaster, could discourage them; and let none

6. "Travail."

thinke they incountered not with all manner of incumbrances. And what have ever beene the workes of the greatest Princes of the earth, but planting of countries, and civilizing barbarous and inhumane Nations, to civilitie and humanitie? whose eternall actions, fill our histories. Lastly, the Portugales, and Spanyards: whose everliving actions, before our eyes will ‖ testifie with them our idlenesse, and **[61]** ingratitude to all posterities, and the neglect of our duties in our pietie and religion we owe our God, our King, and Countrie; and want of charity to those poore salvages, whose Countrie wee challenge, use and possesse; except wee bee but made to use, and marre what our Fore-fathers made, or but onely tell what they did, or esteeme our selves too good to take the like paines. Was it vertue in them, to provide that doth maintaine us? and basenesse for us to doe the like for others? Surely no. Then seeing we are not borne for our selves, but each to helpe other, and our abilities are much alike at the houre of our birth, and the minute of our death: Seeing our good deedes, or our badde, by faith in Christs merits, is all we have to carrie our soules to heaven, or hell: Seeing honour is our lives ambition; and our ambition after death, to have an honourable memorie of our life: and seeing by noe meanes wee would bee abated of the dignities and glories of our Predecessors; let us imitate their vertues to bee worthily their successors.

FINIS.

At London printed the 18. of June, in
the yeere of our Lord 1616.

[62]

To his worthy Captaine,
the Author.

OFt thou hast led, when I brought up the Rere
In bloodie wars, where thousands have bin slaine.
  Then give mee leave, in this some part to beare;
And as thy servant, heere to read my name.
  Tis true, long time thou hast my Captaine beene
In the fierce wars of Transilvania:
  Long ere that thou America hadst seene,
Or led wast captived⁷ in Virginia;
  Thou that to passe the worlds foure parts dost deeme
No more, then t'were to goe to bed, or drinke,
  And all thou yet hast done, thou dost esteeme
As nothing. This doth cause mee thinke
  That thou I'ave seene so oft approv'd¹ in dangers
(And thrice captiv'd, thy valor still hath freed)
  Art yet preserved, to convert those strangers:
By God thy guide, I trust it is decreed.
  For mee: I not commend, but much admire
  Thy England yet unknowne to passers by-her.
  For it will praise it selfe in spight of me;
  Thou it, it thou, to all posteritie.

Your true friend, and souldier,
Ed. Robinson.²

7. Read: "Or was led, taken a captive, in Virginia."
1. Read: "That thou I've seen so oft put to the proof in dangers."
2. For Edward Robinson, see the *True Travels*, 23, and the Biographical Directory.

To my honest Captaine, the Author. [63]

M Alignant Times! What can be said or don,
　But shall be censur'd and traduc't by some!
　　This worthy Work, which thou hast bought so dear,
　　Ne thou, nor it, Detractors neede to fear.
Thy words by deedes so long thou hast approv'd,[3]
Of thousands knowe thee not thou art belov'd.
　　And this great Plot[4] will make thee ten times more
　　Knowne and belov'd, than ere thou wert before.
I never knew a Warryer yet, but thee,
From wine, Tobacco, debts, dice, oaths, so free.[5]
　　I call thee Warrier: and I make the bolder;
　　For, many a Captaine now, was never Souldier
Some such may swell at this: but (to their praise)
When they have don like thee, my Muse shall raise
　　Their due deserts to Worthies yet to come,
　　To live like thine (admir'd) till day of Doome.

Your true friend, somtimes your soldier,
Tho. Carlton.[6]

---

3. "Proved."
4. Map, chart [of New England].
5. These words were all the more remarkable when the private lives of other captains are considered. An example might be Sir Roger Williams, who served under Lord Willoughby in the Low Countries and died of a fever that apparently was brought on by overdrinking and overeating (see Roger Williams, *The Actions of the Low Countries*, ed. D. W. Davies [Ithaca, N.Y., 1964], xl).
6. For Thomas Carlton, see the *True Travels*, 23, and the Biographical Directory.

TEXTUAL ANNOTATION

AND BIBLIOGRAPHICAL NOTE TO

A Description of New England . . .

TEXTUAL ANNOTATION

The page numbers below refer to the boldface numerals in the margins of the present text, which record the pagination of the original edition used as copy text. The word or words before the bracket show the text as emended by the editor; the word or words after the bracket reproduce the copy text. The wavy dash symbol used after the bracket stands for a word that has not itself been changed but that adjoins a changed word or punctuation mark. The inferior caret, also used only after the bracket, signifies the location of missing punctuation in the copy text.

Page.Line

A3ᵛ.5 looke] loooke
4.9 Sagadahock] Sadagahock
4.11 Poppham, Lord] ∼ ˄ ∼
10.3–4 building and the] building the
10.4 and good] and ∼ ∼
10.19 it selfe] if ∼
10.21 however] howevet
10.22 yet who will] ∼ who ∼ ∼
11.22 alledge many] ∼ , ∼ (from *Generall Historie*, 209)
12.24 Puttargo] Puttardo
14.19 State] Sate
22.16 Train oyle] ∼ and ∼ (from *Generall Historie*, 213)
25.8 Plaines, and] ∼ , ∼ and
25.20 trees and gardens] trees gardens (from *Generall Historie*, 214)

Page.Line

29.1 Pennobscot; the] ∼ : ∼
38.23 or if] ∼ ? ∼
41.14 blooming] bloominig
42.3 above its] ∼ it (from *Generall Historie*, 220)
42.20 libertie, profit] ∼ ˄ ∼ (from *Generall Historie*, 220)
47.17 knowne to] ∼ ∼ to
49.14 Sutliffe, Deane] ∼ ˄ ∼
50.18 Stukley, Knight] ∼ ˄ ∼
52.21 nets, and] ∼ , ∼ and
54.6 opportunitie] opportunie
55.7 fish. When] ∼ ˄ when (based on *Generall Historie*, 224)
61.4 want of charity] of want ∼ (from *Generall Historie*, 227)

Hyphenation Record

The following lists have been inserted at the request of the editorial staff of the Institute of Early American History and Culture. The list immediately below records possible compound words that were hyphenated at the end of the line in the copy text. In each case the editor had to decide for the present edition whether to print the word as a single word or as a hyphenated compound. The material before the bracket indicates how the word is printed in the present edition; the material after the bracket indicates how the word was broken in the original. The wavy dash symbol indicates that the form of the word has been unchanged from the copy text. Numerals refer to the page number of the copy text (the boldface numerals in the margin in this edition) and to the line number (counting down from the boldface number) in the present edition.

Page.Line			*Page.Line*		
¶4ᵛ.15	goldesmith]	golde-smith	28.13	Landmarkes]	Land-markes
1.marg.	new-England]	~	28.marg.	landmarkes]	land-markes
1.13	Whale-fishing]	~	29.7	goos-berries]	~
3.5	Northward]	North-ward	50.2	re-accommodated]	~
17.19	New-found]	~	52.marg.	Vice-admirall]	~
25.5	fishpond]	fish-pond	52.marg.	Rere-admiral]	~
27.6	overgrowne]	over-growne	58.22	Newfound-land-man]	~
28.11	Northward]	North-ward			

The list below contains words found as hyphenated compounds in the copy text that unavoidably had to be broken at the end of the line at the hyphen in the present text. In quoting or transcribing from the present text, the hyphen should be retained for these words. Numerals refer to the page number of the copy text (the boldface numerals in the margin in this edition) and line number (counting down from the boldface number).

Page.Line

1.marg.	new-England
29.24–25	Wild-cats
43.1–2	common-weales
52.marg.	Vice-admirall
52.marg.	Rere-admiral

BIBLIOGRAPHICAL NOTE

Entry in the Stationers' Register

3° Junii 1616

Robert Clerke
Entred for his Copie under the handes
of master [John] Sanford and master
[Humphrey] Lownes Warden a booke
called *A Discription of New Englande* by
John Smithe .... vi^d

(Arber, *Registers*, III, 588.)

Editions

Early:

1616. A ‖ DESCRIPTION ‖ of *New England:* ‖ *OR* ‖ THE OBSERVATIONS, AND ‖ discoveries, of Captain *John Smith* (Admirall ‖ of that Country) in the North of *America*, in the year ‖ *of our Lord* 1614: *with the successe of sixe Ships,* ‖ *that went the next yeare* 1615; *and the* ‖ accidents befell him among the ‖ *French men of warre:* ‖ With the proofe of the present benefit this ‖ Countrey affoords: whither this present yeare, ‖ 1616, *eight voluntary Ships are gone* ‖ *to make further tryall.* ‖ [Ornamental rule] ‖ *At LONDON* ‖ Printed by *Humfrey Lownes*, for *Robert Clerke*; and ‖ are to be sould at his house called the Lodge, ‖ in Chancery lane, over against Lin- ‖ colnes Inne. 1616. ‖

Quarto, with one folded map, inserted in some contemporary copies before sig. B1, and one inserted leaf described below; pp. xvi, 64 (62 and 63 unnumbered, 64 blank); ¶ including title page, and A–I in fours. The separate leaf, verso blank, inserted at the front, has an explanatory heading. It is not found in all copies. Two copies of the book have specially printed title pages in place of the usual one with printed presentation inscriptions respectively to Lord Ellesmere, lord chancellor (in the Huntington Library) and Sir Edward Coke, lord chief justice (in the Folger Shakespeare Library). Outside these minor variations, there was but one edition, with one setting of type.

1624. *The Generall Historie of Virginia, New-England, and the Summer Isles* . . . (with some additions and small changes) by John Smith (London), Book VI, 203–227.

Modern:

1837. Massachusetts Historical Society, *Collections*, 3d Ser., VI, 95–140 (Boston).

1837. *A Description of New England* . . . , printed by Peter Force (Washington, D.C.) (repr. 1838).

1865. *A Description of New England* . . . , printed by William Veazie (Boston).

1884, etc. *Captain John Smith . . . Works, 1608–1631*, ed. Edward Arber (Birmingham). See the list of issues of the Arber text in the General Introduction at the beginning of this volume.

1898. *A Description of New England* . . . , in *American Colonial Tracts Monthly*, Vol. II, No. 1 (Rochester, N.Y.).

Letter to Sir Francis Bacon

1618

INTRODUCTION

Background

Prince Henry, heir to the thrones of England and Scotland, received a tenth-birthday gift in 1604 from the lord high admiral in the form of a small, but seaworthy, vessel. Two years later the boy's uncle, King Christian IV of Denmark, gave him the best fighting ship in the Danish royal navy, in token of the prince's nautical bent. Toward the close of that same year Prince Henry's gunner sailed for Virginia with Smith and the other original planters. The sea had already turned Henry's mind in the direction of British expansion overseas.

When Henry died at an early age, and his brother Charles seemed not to have like interests, "suitors" for royal favor such as John Smith turned instead to wealthy noblemen, knights, and merchants for practical help, while continuing to pay token homage to Prince Charles. Thus, after soliciting the latter's grace in the matter of "English names for Indian" in the *Description of New England*, Smith dedicated a personal copy to the lord chancellor, Thomas Egerton, Baron Ellesmere (since 1603), who was created Viscount Brackley on November 7, 1616, some five months after the *Description of New England* was run off. Regrettably for Smith, the viscount, aged seventy-seven, died in March 1617. Sir Francis Bacon immediately took up Egerton's duties.

The Letter to Bacon

Sir Francis had been attorney general, then privy councillor, but he first received the great seal of the lord chancellor with the lesser title of lord keeper (his father had held the same post under Queen Elizabeth). Then, early in 1618, Bacon was raised to the chancellorship, and on July 12 to the peerage as Baron Verulam. Smith resolved to take a bolder step than he had with Egerton. Bacon, a scholar who had written about plantations, now a politician in a position to promote them, was certainly a most promising backer. Smith rapidly set to work to make at least a booklet out of some notes and something he had read.

Obviously, Smith was not the only Englishman to think of approaching the new peer. William Strachey, the ex-secretary of the Jamestown colony,[1]

---

1. See the Introduction to the *Map of Va.*

still hoped in 1618 for employment in Virginia. He, too, turned to Bacon.[2] But neither he nor Smith knew that the great man was plagued by creditors, as well as suitors, and was tarnishing the splendor of his high office by accepting emoluments of a nature not unlike bribes. It is small wonder, then, that Bacon paid no heed to Smith or to Strachey.

Smith's plea-proposal to Bacon holds a watershed position in his career as a writer. From the descriptive, narrative, and explanatory (or justificatory) modes of the *True Relation*, the *Map of Virginia*, and the *Proceedings* (so far as he was involved in this work), Smith seems to have moved in the *Description of New England*[3] to the role of publicist. Although he made a final (and unsuccessful) try at active seafaring life late in 1616, by 1618 he appears to have become at least halfway content with propagandizing for, and pleading the cause of, colonization.

This theory is admittedly at odds with the considered opinions of some modern critics who tend to regard the three New England writings as three versions of a single tract.[4] The editor believes rather that the *Description of New England* should be regarded as a turning point, with the "Letter to Bacon" as the preface to a new presentation of the question of plantations (i.e., the settlement of Englishmen) in New England. Seen in this light, the two versions of *New Englands Trials* are an extended exposition of his proposal to Bacon. It may even be that Smith was already considering rounding out this work with the "history of the Sea," to which he referred years later in his *Advertisements*.[5] If so, the *Generall Historie* came as an interlude, unexpected, yet welcome and surely encouraging; but his thoughts immediately turned again to the sea. He produced the *Accidence* and the *Sea Grammar*, then, under persuasion, the *True Travels*—vainglorious memoirs of all-but-forgotten soldiering a quarter century before, eked out with scraps of recent information from the colonies. This book was still in press when Smith's fiftieth birthday came (possibly with the impact of a modern man's eightieth), and suddenly Smith produced his final warning and encouragement to colonial adventurers and entrepreneurs—the *Advertisements*. Significantly, its stress is on New England, not Virginia.

This long digression has seemed to the editor worth inserting, for without some theory or conjectural commentary the "Letter to Bacon" and the twice-printed *New Englands Trials* seem to form mere collections of fragments tossed off after the 1616 work, while Smith was Micawberishly "waiting for something to turn up."

It should be noted that two addenda were affixed to Smith's "Letter to

2. See fol. 129ᵛ, 129ᵛn, below.
3. See the Introduction to the *Description of N.E.*
4. Cf. Everett H. Emerson, *Captain John Smith* (New York, 1971), 103–118.
5. *Advertisements*, 26.

Bacon," presumably when the State Papers were "redistributed" in the nineteenth century. One of these, a sketch map of Ralegh's Virginia of September 1585 has now been relocated in the Public Record Office.[6] The other is a two-page copy of Smith's list of old and new names in New England, which, on the basis of handwriting, may be assigned to a later date than the "Letter to Bacon"—perhaps even after 1650.[7]

Summary

The "Letter to Bacon" and the two editions of *New Englands Trials* have the same basic content and the same general arrangement, though expanded in each new version. The "Letter to Bacon" opens with a brief explanation of the geographical location of New England, followed by a few words on what Smith has seen and done there. Next, without further ado, comes a compendium of statistical information on fishing and the profits to be made thereby, with seven paragraphs of supporting proofs. The information is presented in a straightforward way and is obviously based on facts or the published testimony of another author. The rest of the "Letter to Bacon" is taken up with side-advantages, particularly the traffic in furs, coupled with an apology of sorts for presenting so unglamorous a proposal to so noble a peer. In short, the "Letter to Bacon" is but a sketch that did not take final form until the second edition of *New Englands Trials* in 1622.

Editorial Method

In transcribing this letter the spelling has been modernized only to the extent that the letter "i" has been changed to "j" and "u" to "v" (or vice versa) where appropriate. In addition, a capital "F" replaces "ff." The editor has not tried to distinguish between a capital "C" and a lowercase "c," however, and in most cases "C" is retained even where the scrivener may have intended "c." The ampersand and other contractions of seventeenth-century handwriting have been expanded. Punctuation added for clarity has been enclosed in brackets.

6. Maps and Plans G. 584 (fig. 3), Public Record Office. The sketch map is fully discussed in David Beers Quinn, ed., *The Roanoke Voyages, 1584–1590* (Hakluyt Society, 2d Ser., CIV–CV [London, 1955]), I, 215–217.

7. This list remains undisturbed in C.O. 1/1, 3886, fol. 134^{r-v}, P.R.O.

To the Right Honorable
SIR FRANCES BACON,
Knight, Baron of Verulam and
Lord high Chauncellor of England.[1]

Right Honorable:

HAVING noe better meanes to acquaint your Lordship with my meaning then this paper, the zeale, love and dutie to God, my Countrie and your Honor, I humbly crave may be my Apologie./.

This 19. yeares[2] I have encountred noe fewe dangers to learne what here I write in these fewe leaves, and though the lynes they containe are more rudely phrased then is meet for the veiwe of so great a judgment, their fruites I am certayne may bring both wealth and honor for a Crowne and a kingdome to his Majesties posterity. The profitts already retourned with so small charge and facillitie according to proportion emboldens me to say it./.

With a stock of 5000.ˡⁱ I durst adventure to effect it[3] though more then 100000.ˡⁱ· hath bene spent in Virginia and the Barmudas to small purpose, about the procuring whereof many good men knowes I have spent noe small tyme, labor nor mony; but all in vaine. Notwithstanding within these fower yeares I have occasioned twice 5000.ˡⁱ· to be imployed that way. But great desyres to ingrosse it, hath bred so many particuler humors, as they have their willes, I the losse, and the generall good, the wrong./.[4]

Should I present it to the Biskayners,[5] French, or Hollanders [129ᵛ] they have made me large offers: But nature doth binde me thus to begg at home, whome strangers have pleased to make a Commaunder abroad.[6] The busines being of such consequence, I hold it

---

1. John Smith to Sir Francis Bacon, C.O. 1/1, 3886, fols. 129–133, Public Record Office. Bacon was made Baron Verulam on July 12, 1618, 28 weeks after his appointment as lord chancellor, and was created Viscount St. Albans in Jan. 1621.

2. I.e., since 1598 or 1599; in 1616 he put it "neere twice nine yeares" (*Description of N.E.*, sig. ¶3ʳ).

3. The meaning is: "with a capital of £5,000, I would dare to undertake to carry out the project outlined here."

4. Read: "But great desires to monopolize the business have bred so many peculiar notions that the investors have had their way, I have had losses, and the general good has suffered."

5. A Spanish document dated Dec. 1616 confirms the existence of contacts, with an eye to whale fishing, between shipowners in the province of Guipúzcoa (capital, San Sebastián) and John Smith (see Philip L. Barbour, *The Three Worlds of Captain John Smith* [Boston, 1964], 475; and Fragments, in Vol. III).

6. A reference to his captaincy, earned in the Balkan "Long War" (*True Travels*, 7).

but my duty to accquaint it to your Honor, knowing you are not only a cheife Patron of your Countrie and state but also the greatest Favourer of all good designes and their Authors. Noe more, but humbly beseeching your goodnes to pardon my rudenes and ponder my plaine meaning in the ballance of good will, I leave the substance to the discretion of your most admired judgment, ever resting

Your Honors ever most truely devoted.
Jo. Smith.[7]

[130ʳ]   Newe England is a part of America[8] betwixt the degrees of 41 and 45. the very meane betweene the North Pole and the line: From 43 to 45. The Coast is mountaynous rockye, barren and broken Isles that make many good Harbours, the water being deepe close to the shore. There is many Rivers and freshe springs[,] a fewe Savages, but an incredible aboundance of fish fowles, wilde fruits and good store of Timber./

From 43 to 41½ an excellent mixed Coast of stone sand and Clay, much Corne, many people, some Isles[,] many good harbors[,] a temperate aire, yron and steele;[9] oare and many other such good blessings, that having but men skilfull to make them simples there growing,[1] I dare ingage myselfe to finde all things belonging to the building and rigging of Shippes of any proportion and good Merchandize for their fraught within a square of 10. or 14. leagues./.

25. Harbors I sounded: 30 severall Lordshipps I sawe, and as nere as I could imagine 3000 men. I was upp one River fortie myles,[2] crossed the mouthes of many whose heads, the Inhabitants report are great Lakes where they kill their beavers inhabited with many people that trade, with them of New England and those of Cannada.[3]

7. This signature seems to be autographic. The tenor of Smith's appeal to Bacon bears comparison with the dedication William Strachey attached to a copy of his "Historie of Travaile," now published as *The Historie of Travaile into Virginia Britannia . . .* , ed. R. H. Major (Hakluyt Society, 1st Ser. [London, 1849]), which he sent to the lord chancellor about the same time.

8. The text of this paper, as Smith calls it, is by and large that of the first edition of *New Englands Trials* (1620). All variations between the two that amount to more than a few words are pointed out in the notes below.

9. The passage "yron and steele . . . myselfe to finde" is omitted in *New Englands Trials* (1620), sig. B1ʳ.

1. The sense seems to be "men to make use of the native (wild) products available there, particularly as medicines." Cf. the *Description of N.E.*, 10.

2. Augusta, Maine, 44 mi. up the Kennebec River, is on the site of Indian Cushnoc, at the head of the tide. Smith seems not to have recorded the name, although he must have stopped not far from there.

3. At the end of this paragraph, *New Englands Trials* (1620), sig. B1ᵛ, has half a page inserted that was based on John Dee's "Brytish Monarchie," followed by a page and a half derived from Tobias Gentleman's *England's way to win wealth . . .* (London, 1614) and (apparently) a MS copy of John Keymor's *Observation made upon the Dutch fishing, about the year 1601 . . .*, which was not printed until 1664 (see *New Englands Trials* [1620], sig. B1ᵛn, B2ʳ, B2ʳnn).

The benefitt of fishing:

The Hollanders raise yearely by fishing (if Records be true) more then	2000000.^{li}

The Hollanders raise yearely by fishing
  (if Records be true) more then   2000000.^{li}
From Newfound land at the least   400000.
From Island and the North Sea   150000
From Hamborough   20000
‖ From Cape Blanke   10000   **[130ᵛ]**

Those five places doe serve all Europe as well the land Townes as Ports and all the Christian shipping with these sorts of Staple fish which is transported from whence it is taken many a thousand myle[:]

Herring	Mullet
Poore John	Purgos
saltfish	Caviare
Sturgeon	Buttargo

Now seing⁴ all these sortes of fish may be had in a land more fertile, temperate and plentifull of all naturall things for the building of Shipps boates howses and the nourishment for man only for a litle labour or the most part of the cheife materialls, the seasons are so propper and the fishing so neare the habitations we may there make./.

That new England hath much advantage of the most of those parts to serve all Europe farr cheaper then they can who have neither wood[,] salt[,] nor foode but at a great rate[,] nothing to helpe them but what they carry in their shipps 2 or 300 leagues from their habitacion? noe Port or harbor but the mayne sea: Wee the fishing at our dores and the helpe of the land for woods, water, fruites, fowle, Corne or what we want to refresh us when we list: And the Terceras Mederas Canaries Spaine Portugall Province Savoy, Cicilia and all Italye as convenient Marketts for our drye fish Greenefish Sturgeon Mullett and Buttargo as Norway Swethland Luttuania Polonia Denmarke or Germany for their Herring, which is here also in aboundance for taking; they retourning but wood, Pitch Tarre Soape ashes, Cordage and such grosse commodityes: we wynes, oyles Sugars Silkes and such marchandize as the Straits afford, whereby our profitt may equallize theirs. ‖ Besides the infinite good by increase of **[131ʳ]** Shipping and Marriners this fishing⁵ would breede. And imployment for the surplusage of many of his Majesties unruely Subjects. And that this may be, these are my proofes. (Vizt)⁶

In the yeare 1614, with two shippes I went from the Downes the third of March and arrived in New England the last of Aprill. I had   1 proofe
          1614

---

4. From here to the top of fol. 131ʳ the MS text is virtually copied in *New Englands Trials* (1620), sig. B2ᵛ–B3ʳ.

5. The phrase "this fishing," omitted by Smith's scrivener, was added in the margin.

6. "Vizt." is an obsolete form of "viz."

but 45. men and boyes[,] we built seven boates[,] 37. did fish[,] my selfe with 8. others raunging the Coast. I made this mappe; gott the acquaintance of the Inhabitants, 1000 Beaver skinns, 100 Martins, and as many Otters. 40000 of drye fish we sent for Spaine with the Saltfish, Traine oyle and furres./. I retourned for England the 18 of July, and arrived safe, with my Company in health in the latter end of August. Thus in six moneths I made my voyage out and home, and by the labour of 45 men gott neere the value of 1500.^li. in lesse then three moneths in those grosse Commodityes./.[7]

2 proofe
1615

In the yeare 1615 the Londoners uppon this sent 4 good Shipps and intertayned[8] the men who retourned with me. They sett saile in Januarye and arrived there in March and found fish inough till halfe June; fraughted a Shipp of 300. Tonnes which they sent for Spaine[.] one went to Virginia to releive that Collonye and two came home with Saltfish, Trayne oyle, furres, and the salt remayned[9] within six moneths.

3 proofe
1615

The same yeare I sett forth from Plymouth with a Shippe of 200 and one of 50 to inhabitt the Countrie according to the Tenor of his Majesties Comission granted to the west parts of England.[1] But ill weather breaking all my Māstes[2] forced me to retourne againe to

[131^v]

Plymouth where reimbarking ‖ myselfe in a small barke but of 60 Tonnes I passed the English Pyrats and the French, but at last I was betrayed by fowre Frenchmen of warr who kept me Prisoner that Sommer and so overthrew my voyage and Plantation. During which tyme my Viceadmirall that sett forth in March arrived there in May. came home fraught with fish[,] Trayne oyle[,] Beavers skinnes[,] and all her men safe in August within 6 moneths and odd dayes./.

4 Proofe
1616

The Londoners ere I retourned sent two shippes more in July to trye the winter:[3] but such courses they tooke by the Canaries, and the Indies, it was 10 moneths ere they arrived, wasting in that tyme their seasons, victuall and healthes: yet within 3 moneths after the one retourned nere fraught with fish Trayne oyle and Beavers./.

5 Proofe
1616

From Plymouth went 4 Shipps only to fish and trade[,] some in February some in March[,] one of 200 Tonnes gott thither in a moneth and went full fraught for Spaine with drye-fish, the rest retourned all well and safe and all full fraught, with Fish furres and oyle in five moneths and odd dayes./.

6 Proofe
1616

From London went two more one of 220 Tonnes gott thither in

7. A sentence is added here in *New Englands Trials* (1620), sig. B3^r.

8. Here, merely "hired."

9. The afterthought regarding the salt is deleted in *New Englands Trials* (1620), sig. B3^r, instead of explained.

1. The passage "to inhabitt . . . parts of England" is omitted at the bottom of sig. B3^r, *ibid.*

2. The significance (if any) of the macron in "Māstes" is not apparent.

3. This was the crux of the question of New England colonial schemes (see the editor's Introduction, above).

6. weekes and within 6 weekes after with 44 men was fraughted with
Fish, furres and oyle[,] and was againe in England within 5 moneths
and a fewe dayes./.[4]

Being at Plymouth provided with 3 good Shippes I was winde   7 Proofe
bound nere 3 monethes as was many a 100 sayle more so that the   *1617*
season being past I sent my Shippes to Newfound land whereby the
adventurers had noe losse./.[5]

There is 4. or 5. saile gone thither this yeare to fish and trade: *1618*
from || London also there is one gone only to fish and trade, each   [132ʳ]
Shippe for her particuler designe and their private endes, but none
for any generall good, where neither to Virginia nor the Bermudas
they make such hast[e]./.

By this your Lordship[6] may perceive the ordinary performance
of this voyage in 6 monethes, the plenty of Fish that is most certainely
approved,[7] and if I be not misinformed from Cannada and Newe
England, within these 4 yeares hath bene gotten by the French and
English nere 36000 Beavers skinnes;[8] That all sortes of Timber for
shipping is most plentifully there; All those which retourned can
testifye, and if ought of this be untrue is easily proved./.

The worst is[9] of these 16. Shippes, 2 or three of them have bene
taken by Pyrates, which hath putt such feare in poore fishermen,
whose powers are but weake. And the desyre of gaine in Marchants
so violent; everyone so regarding his private, that it is worse then
slaverye to follow any publique good, and impossible to bring them
into a bodye, rule, or order, unles it be by some extraordinary power.
But if his Majestie would please to be perswaded to spare us but a
Pinnace, to lodge my men in and defend us and the Coast from such
invasions, the space of eight or tenn monethes only till we were
seated, I would not doubt but ere long to drawe the most part of
Newfound Land men to assist us, if I could be so provided but in due
season: for now ere the Savages grow subtle and the Coast be too
much frequented || with strangers, more may be done with 20.[li] then   [132ᵛ]
hereafter with a 100.[li]

The charge[1] of this is only Salt, Netts, Hookes, Lynes, Knives[,]   The charge.
Course Cloth, beades, glasse, hatchetts and such trash[,] only for
fishing and trade with the Savages, that have desyred me to inhabitt
where I will. And all these Shippes have bene fished within a square

4. What happened to the other is explained in *New Englands Trials* (1620), sig. B3ᵛ.
5. *Sc.*, from Plymouth. *Ibid.*, sig. B4ʳ, clarifies this paragraph somewhat, omitting
the afterthought regarding Virginia, etc., at the end and adding more than two pages
of post-1618 material.
6. Cf. *ibid.*, sig. C1ʳ, where the phrase "your Lordship" is replaced by "all men."
7. Obsolete for "demonstrated, proved."
8. *Ibid.*, sig. C1ʳ, has "neare twenty thousand."
9. Cf. *ibid.*, sig. C1ᵛ, where this paragraph is rewritten.
1. Cf. *ibid.*, where the MS letter, from here to the middle of fol. 133ʳ, is followed
with little change.

of two leagues, the Coast being of the same Condicion the length of two or 3 hundred Leagues, where questionles within one hundred 500 sayle may have their fraught, better then in Iseland Newfounde lande or elswhere, and be at their marketts ere the other can have their fish in their Shippes. From the west part of England the Shippes goe for the third part, that is when the voyage is done the goods are divided into three parts. (vizt) one third for the Shippe: one for the Company, the other for the victualer, whereby with a stock of 5000.[li.] I goe forth with a charge of 15000.[li.] so the transporting this Collonye, will cost litle or nothing, but at the first, because the fishing will goe forward, whether we plant it or noe. for the fishers report it to be the best they knowe in the Sea, and the land in a short tyme may be more profitable.

The facilitye of this Plantation.

Now if a Shippe can gaine 59. or 60.[li.] in the 100. only by fishing, spending as much tyme in going and coming as in staying there, were

[133^r] I there planted seing the Fish || in their seasons serveth the most part of the yeare, and with a litle labour, I could make all the salt I need use, I can conceive noe reason to distrust, but double and triple their gaines, that are at all the former charge and can fish, but two monethes. And if those doe give 20. 30. or 40[s] for an Acre of grounde, or Shipp Carpenters, Forgers of yron or Steele, that buy all thinges at a deare rate grow rich, when they may have as good of all needfull necessaryes for taking, in my opinion should not growe poore, and noe commoditye in Europe doth decay more then wood./.

Thus Right Honorable and most worthy Peere[,][2] I have throwne my Mite into the Treasure of my Countries good beseeching your Lordship well to consider of it, and examine whether Columbus could give the Spaniards any such Certaintyes for his grounds, when he gott 15. sayle[3] from Queene Isabell of Spaine when all the great judgments of Europe refused him: And though I can promise noe mynes of gold, the Hollanders are an example of my projects, whose endevoures by fishing cannot be suppressed by all the kinge of Spaynes golden powers. Truth is more then wealth and industrious Subjects are more availeable to a king then gold. And this is so certaine a course to gett both, as I thinke was never propounded to any

[133^v] State for so small || a charge, seeing I can prove it, both by examples, reason and experience. How I have lived, spent my tyme and bene imployed, I am not ashamed who will examine. Therefore I humbly beseech your Honor, seriously to consider of it; and lett not the povertie of the Author, cause the action to be lesse respected, who desyres noe better fortune then he could finde there./.

---

2. Part of the ensuing peroration has been used in the concluding paragraphs of *New Englands Trials* (1620) (beginning at the bottom of sig. C2^r), but the personal appeal to Bacon is of course missing.

3. Columbus had only 3 ships on his first voyage, but there were 17 in the second fleet in 1493, with a total of 1,500 aboard.

In the interim I humbly desyre your Honor would be pleased to grace me with the title of your Lordshipps servant: Not that I desyre to shutt upp the rest of my dayes in the chamber of ease and idlenes, but that thereby I may be the better countenanced for the prosecution of this my most desyred voyage: for had I but the Patronage of so mature a judgment as your Honors, it would not only induce those to believe, what I know to be true in this matter, who will now hardly vouchsafe the perusal of my relations; but also be a meanes to further it to the uttermost of their powers with their purses. And I shalbe ever ready to spend both life and goods for the honor of my Country, and your Lordships service. With which resolucion I doe in all humility rest,

At your Honors service[4]

4. Smith's scrivener miscopied the word as "serivice." There is occasional other evidence of some haste in preparation.

New Englands Trials

1620

INTRODUCTION

As has been explained in the Introduction to Smith's "Letter to Bacon," the earliest possible date for that appeal would be after July 12, 1618, when Bacon was raised to the peerage. The latest likely date for the first edition of *New Englands Trials* is December 11, 1620, when it was entered for publication in the Stationers' Register. The trivial changes Smith made to convert the "Letter to Bacon" into the first edition of *New Englands Trials* would hardly have kept Smith busy for two years, despite its considerably expanded peroration. Consequently, although the editor has already offered some suggestions elsewhere,[1] a few historical details are added here in an attempt to close the gap.

In the spring of 1618, Sir Walter Ralegh returned from his suicidal Guiana expedition, begun in 1617, and by August 10 he was again in the Tower, accused, as he was in 1603, of high treason. Such was the Spanish ambassador's pressure on the king of England that it was now merely a matter of whether Ralegh would be executed in London or in Spain. On October 29, he was beheaded in London. This has bearing on John Smith in that the separatist group now called the Pilgrims, who had thought of emigrating from Holland to Guiana, then began to look toward North America, but somewhere beyond the direct control of the governor in Jamestown or the Council for Virginia in London. By that time the Virginia Company's administration was under attack, and on April 28, 1619, Sir Edwin Sandys, a staunch Puritan, was chosen to succeed Sir Thomas Smythe as treasurer. Six weeks later, the council granted a patent to the Pilgrims. For one reason or another, it was never used.

Meanwhile, Sir Ferdinando Gorges was organizing still another expedition to New England, but as yet no colony. On December 1, 1619, he appeared in person at a meeting of the Council for Virginia to protest against a fishing expedition off Cape Cod launched from Jamestown, which was an infringement of the dormant, if not defunct, rights of the North Virginia Company. Early in 1620, then, determined to maintain the rights of the West Country entrepreneurs, whom he represented, Gorges petitioned the king for a new patent to replace that of 1606, in the name of the "Council for the Second Colony and Others," or the "Council for New England," as it came to be called. (Parenthetically, it would surely have amused Smith, if he heard it, that the governor in Jamestown authorized a party to fish off

1. Philip L. Barbour, *The Three Worlds of Captain John Smith* (Boston, 1964), 336–349.

"Smith's Island" in New England—not the lord governor's, not Argall's, not Gorges's, but Smith's!) Finally, on November 3, 1620, the charter for New England was properly sealed. By then, *New Englands Trials* was in press. Conceivably Smith had been busy during those two years watching which way the wind was blowing. Perhaps in 1620 the new administration of the Virginia Company would look upon him with more favor; perhaps Gorges's activities would end in a colonial settlement after all. Then, suddenly, Smith apparently decided to get his ideas into print anyway. New England was certainly the watchword late in 1620.

It is time now to explain the meaning of "trials." In Smith's title, "trials" surely meant anything but "tribulations," yet not quite "proofs," as suggested by Emerson.[2] Basically, "trials" meant "things tried," thus "experiments, essays," or, as the *OED* explains, actions adopted in order to ascertain the result of something, investigations by means of experience, the exercise of trial and error.

Smith was always ready to make such trials himself, and at almost any risk; yet he was always willing to, and often did, use the record of other explorers and trailblazers to support his own ideas and plans. His onetime backer Sir Ferdinando Gorges was, oddly, both more skeptical and more patiently persistent in trying than was Smith. Gorges wanted real tests with experimental winter camps before he would seriously consider the establishment of a colony of any size. Smith, with his Jamestown years behind him, was certain that no further testing (or proving) was necessary.[3] But both Gorges and Smith needed financial backing, and so in the long run both of them had to convince merchants or other entrepreneurs that colonization would be profitable, or at least self-sustaining.

In the midst of this, while Gorges was testing, and before Smith's *New Englands Trials* was entered for publication, the Pilgrims from Leiden simply sailed over to Cape Cod Bay and founded the first permanent colony in New England. Religious scruples moved men regardless of Gorges's need for security (a *safe* place in winter) or Smith's need for lucre. Amusingly, when Smith heard about the Pilgrims he did not like the religion that moved them, even though they put into practice precisely what he preached.

Of Smith's book proper, as opposed to the rough, handwritten draft that had been sent to Sir Francis Bacon, there is little to say. The printed work shows that Smith had at least extended his use of data from other sources, such as Robert Hitchcock; John Dee,[4] the inventor of the name "British Empire"; John Keymor,[5] the obscure economist; and Tobias Gentleman,[6]

2. Everett H. Emerson, *Captain John Smith* (New York, 1971), 110.
3. See "Letter to Bacon," fol. 129[r]n.
4. Robert Hitchcock, *A pollitique platt* (London, 1580); John Dee, *General and rare memorials pertayning to the Perfect Arte of navigation . . .* (London, 1577).
5. John Keymor, *Observation made upon the Dutch fishing, about the year 1601 . . .* (London, 1664).
6. Tobias Gentleman, *Englands way to win wealth . . .* (London, 1614).

the even more obscure "fisherman and mariner," as he called himself. Smith had also polished his text with a bit more eloquence. But all in all, he had whipped it into shape so quickly that it amounted to little more than a printed edition of the "Letter to Bacon." It was not until the second edition (1622) that a substantially improved work appeared.

Summary

If a summary be needed for so short a work, it can be pointed out that the first eleven pages, to the bottom of sig. C2^r, are little more than a restatement of the subject matter of Smith's "Letter to Bacon." The remaining four and a half pages include a few additional ideas borrowed from John Dee and a repetition of Smith's by now familiar propaganda for settlement overseas. As has already been mentioned, the second edition (1622) is a trifle better organized and covers the subject more thoroughly. The 1620 work is interesting as a hurried printing of a hurried appeal, with such little polishing as Smith found time to apply.

NEW
ENGLANDS
TRIALS.

Declaring the succeſſe of 26. Ships
employed thither within theſe ſixe yeares:
with the benefit of that Countrey by ſea and
land: and how to build threeſcore ſayle
of good Ships, to make a little
Navie Royall.

Written by Captaine
Iohn Smith.

LONDON,
Printed by *VVilliam Iones.*
1620.

[The editor is grateful to The Newberry Library, Chicago, for permission to reproduce this title page.]

TO THE RIGHT WORSHIPFUL

TO THE RIGHT WORSHIPFUL [A2ʳ]
The Maister, the Wardens, and the Companie
of the Fish-mongers.[1]

To the consideration of your favourable constructions I present these six yeares continued trials from New England: if you please to peruse them, and make use of them, I am richly rewarded. The subject deserveth a farre better habit, but it is as good as the father can give it. Let not therefore a souldiers plainnesse cause you refuse to accept it, how ever you please to dispose of him, that humbly sacreth himselfe and best abilities to his Countries good, and the exquisite judgement of your renowned perfections.

Yours to command,
John Smith.

---

1. In this slim volume the first signature consists of only two leaves. The first leaf contains the title page, the second a dedication. Since but four copies of the book are known to survive and the dedications vary, specific analysis is clearly called for. There are two different dedicatory texts, each of which has two heads. One of the two texts is considered here, the other in n. 2, below. Following the revised *STC*, the "other" will be considered a cancel, or substitute dedication.

The dedication here reprinted is to the Company of Fishmongers (B.L. copy, shelf mark C.33.c.15). A second dedication with identical wording (Bodleian Library copy) is to the just-authorized company of the Adventurers of the Northern Colonie of Virginia (in Smith's words, "the Right honorable and worthy adventers to all discoveries and plantations, espetially to New England"). No reference to Smith's gifts has been found in the records of either of these companies (Terence H. O'Brien, "The London Livery Companies and the Virginia Company," *Virginia Magazine of History and Biography,* LXVIII [1960], 137–155).

TO THE RIGHT HONORABLE,
Sir John Egerton,² Lord Elismere,
Viscount Brackley, Earle of Bridgewater.

Right Honorable,

The great worke contained in this little Booke, requires the patronage of such a one as your Lordship. Though it be but the observations and collections of a plaine Souldier; yet if you please to grace it with your countenance and good acceptance, the Author and it will both thinke themselves happie, and hopes in time to returne you such fruites from those labours, as hereafter may perswade you to pardon their boldnes, and accept them to be your faithful servants.

Your Honours to command,
John Smith.

2. This cancel, or substitute dedication, also survives in two forms: the copy in the Huntington Library is for John Egerton, earl of Bridgwater, son and heir of Sir Thomas Egerton, first Viscount Brackley; the second, in the Ayer Collection, Newberry Library, is for Sir Edward Coke (1552–1634), that personification of English law who lived from the days of Mary I until Charles I began to take the doctrine of divine right of kings too seriously. Bridgwater was wealthy and might have helped Smith; Coke was vaguely interested in the Virginia Company and was a member of the Privy Council. Furthermore, Smith had dedicated his *Description of N.E.* to Bridgwater's father and to the long-lived Coke.

NEW ENGLANDS TRIALS.

EW England[1] is a part of America betwixt
the degrees of 41. and 45. the very meane
betwixt the North Pole and the Line:
From 43. to 45. the coast is mountainous,
rockie, barren and broken Iles that make
many good harbours. The water is deepe
close to the shoare; there are many rivers
and fresh springs: few Salvages, but an incredible aboundance of fish, fowle, wilde
fruites, and good timber. From 43. to 41.
and halfe, an excellent mixed coast of stone, sand, and clay: much
corne, many people, some Iles, many good harbours, a temperate
ayre, and therein all things necessarie; for the building ships of any
proportion, and good merchandize for their fraughts; within a square
of twelve leagues 25. harbours I sounded, thirtie severall Lordships
I sawe, and so neare as I could imagine, three thousand men. I was
up one river fortie miles, crossed the mouths of many, whose heads
are reported to be great Lakes; where they kill their ‖ Bevers; in- **[B1ᵛ]**
habited with many people, who trade with those of New England,
and them of Cannada.

The benefite of Fishing, as that famous Philosopher
Master Dee reporteth in his Brittish Monarchie.[2]

He saith, that more then forty foure yeares agoe, the Herring
Busses out of the Low-countries, under the King of Spaine, were five
hundred, besides one hundred Frenchmen, and three or foure hundred saile of Flemings.

The coasts of Wales and Lankashire was used by three hundred
sayle of strangers.

Ireland at Baltemore[3] fraughted yerely three hundred sayle of

1. This paragraph is almost verbatim from the "Letter to Bacon" (see fol. 130ʳ,
130ʳnn).

2. The reference is to John Dee's *General and rare memorials pertayning to the Perfect
Arte of navigation* . . . (London, 1577), 23–24, the first section of which bears the title
"The Brytish Monarchie." There is material from Dee in both Richard Hakluyt, *The
Principal Navigations, Voyages, Traffiques and Discoveries of the English Nation* (London, 1598–
1600), and Samuel Purchas, *Hakluytus Posthumus, or Purchas His Pilgrimes* . . . (London,
1625). Smith seems to have borrowed directly from the original, probably by courtesy of
Purchas.

3. Baltimore is in Ireland.

Spaniards, where King Edward the sixt intended to have made a strong Castell, because of the straite, to have tribute for fishing.

Blacke Rocke[4] was yearely fished by three or foure hundred sayle of Spaniards, Portugalls, and Biskiners.

Master Gentleman and many Fisher-men and Fishmongers, with whom I have conferred, report:[5]

The Hollanders raise yearely by Herrings, Cod, and Ling, 3000000. pounds.

English, and French by Salt-fish, poore John, Salmons, and Pilchards, 300000. pounds.

Hambrough and the Sound,[6] for Sturgion, Lobsters, and Eeles, 100000. pounds.

Cape Blanke, Tunny and Mullit, by the Biskinners and Spaniards. 30000. pounds.

[B2ʳ]   ### But divers other learned experienced Observers say, though it may seeme incredible:[7]

S.[8]

That the Duke of Medina receiveth yearely tribute, of the Fishers of Tunny, Mullit, and Purgos, more then 10000. pounds.

Lubeck hath seven hundred shippes:[1] Hambrough six hundred: Embden lately a fisher towne, 1400, whose customes by the profit of fishing hath made them so powerfull as they be.

Holland and Zeland, not much greater then Yorkshire,[2] hath thirty walled townes, 400. villages, and 20000. sayle of ships and

4. There are several spots with that name on the Irish coast. This Black Rock is that off Achill Island, County Mayo, and is on the Speed map of Kell.

5. See Tobias Gentleman, *Englands way to win wealth* . . . (London, 1614). While Smith appears to have borrowed little directly from the book, it is evident that Master Gentleman and his fishmonger friends (see *ibid.*, 46) could have supplied Smith with information.

6. "The Sound" refers to the strait between Denmark and Sweden. Below, "Cape Blanke" was the usual English version of Cabo Blanco, on the W coast of Africa in 21° N latitude between Lévrier Bay, Mauritania, and the Atlantic.

7. The identity of Smith's other "Observers" is uncertain, but one of them may have been John Keymor, an economic writer of the period, about whom little is known. Tobias Gentleman writes that Keymor obtained information from him in 1612 or 1613, which he had a "mind to shew . . . unto the right Honourable Counsell" (*Englands way*, 3–4). Keymor, however, wrote his *Observation made upon the Dutch fishing, about the year 1601*, which was not printed until 1664 (in London).

8. Regarding the marginal note "S.," Professor D. B. Quinn has called the editor's attention to John Stoneman's account of Henry Challon's voyage to New England in 1606 and his capture by a Spanish fleet in the Straits of Florida. The duke of Medina Sidonia (1550–1615) attempted to befriend Stoneman and a few others in Challon's party (Purchas, *Pilgrimes*, IV, 1834–1835). Smith may have heard about this from Stoneman personally or through Purchas.

1. This paragraph is certainly based on Keymor's *Observation*, 1. Smith apparently had access to a MS copy.

2. By modern measurements, Holland and Zeeland have a combined area of c. 5,100 sq. mi.; Yorkshire, c. 6,100 sq. mi.

hoyes; 3600. are fishermen, whereof 100. are Dogers, 700. Pinckes
and Welbotes, 700. frand botes, 400. Enaces, 400. gal-botes, Britters
and Todebotes, with 1300. Busses;[3] besides three hundred that
yearely fish about Yarmouth,[4] where they sell their fish for gold; and
15. yeares agoe they had more then 116000. Sea-faring men.

These fishing ships do take yearely 200000. Last of fish,[5] 12.
barrells to a Last; which amounteth to 3000000. pounds by the
Fishermens price that 14. yeres agoe did pay for their tenths 300000.
pound; which venting in Pomerland, Sprusland, Denmarke, Lefland,
Russia, Suethland, Germany, Netherlands, England, or elsewhere,
etc. make their returnes in a yeare about 7000000. pounds; and yet
in Holland they have neither matter to build shippes, nor merchandize to set them foorth, yet they asmuch encrease as other Nations
decay. But leaving these uncertainties as they are, of this I am certaine:

That the coast of England,[6] Scotland, and Ireland, the north   **[B2ᵛ]**
Sea, with Island, and the Sound, New-foundland, and Cape Blancke,
doe serve all Europe, as well the land Townes as Portes, and all the
Christian shipping, with these sorts of Staple fish which is transported; from whence it is taken, many a thousand mile, viz.

Herring.	Tunny.
Salt-fish.	Porgos.
poore John.	Caviare.
Sturgion.	Buttargo.
Mullit.	

Now seeing all these sorts of fish, or the most part of them, may
be had in a land more fertile, temperate, and plentifull of all necessaries for the building of ships, boates and houses; and the nourishment of man: the seasons are so proper, and the fishings so neare the
habitations wee may there make, that New England hath much
advantage of the most of those parts, to serve all Europe farre cheaper
then they can, who at home have neither wood, salt, nor food, but
at great rates; at Sea, nothing but what they carry in their shippes,

3. The paragraph is based on or drawn from Keymor's *Observation*, 2, with some
errors in copying. The correct names as listed by Keymor are: doggers (or dogger-boats),
pinks, well-boats, strand-boats, evers (not in the *OED*), galliots, drivers, and tode-botes.

4. Yarmouth (better known as Great Yarmouth, partly to distinguish it from Yarmouth on the NW coast of the Isle of Wight) was and is a great fishing center in Norfolk
County, 32 km. (20 mi.) E of Norwich (see Gentleman, *Englands way*, 14–17).

5. Here again, Smith seems to have been dependent on Keymor (see *Observation*, 3).
Of the countries mentioned below, Pomerland is now Pomerania, on the Baltic Sea in
East Germany and Poland; Sprusland (or Sprussia), to the E, is part of Poland and the
U.S.S.R., formerly East Prussia; Lefland, also Livonia, is roughly the area now com-
prising Latvia and Estonia; Suethland (for Swethland), is roughly modern Sweden (see
Purchas, *Pilgrimes*, III, for contemporary maps of these areas; and cf. the *Generall Historie*,
228n).

6. Here Smith takes up the text of his "Letter to Bacon" almost verbatim (fol. 130ᵛ).
"Island" was a common spelling of "Iceland."

an hundred or two hundred leagues from their habitation.

But New Englands fishings neare land, where is helpe of wood, water, fruites, fowles, corne, or other refreshings needefull; and the Terceras,[7] Mederas, Canaries, Spaine, Portugall, Provance, Savoy, Sicilia, and all Italy, as convenient markets for our dry Fish, greene Fish, Sturgion, Mullit, Caviare, and Buttargo, as Norway, Sweth-land, Littuania, or Germany, for their Herring, (which is here also in aboundance, for taking;) They returning but wood, pitch, tarre, soape-ashes, cordage, flaxe, waxe, and such like commodities: We **[B3ʳ]** wines, oyles, su- ‖ gars, silkes, and such merchandizes as the Straites affoord, whereby our profites may equalize theirs; besides the increase of Shipping and Mariners. And for proofe hereof:

Proofe 1.[8]
1614.

With two shippes I went from the Downes, the third of March, and arrived in New England, the last of Aprill. I had but fortie five men and boyes, we built seven boates, 37. did fish; my selfe with eight others ranging the coast, I tooke a plot of what I could see, got acquaintance of the inhabitants, eleven hundred bever skinnes, one hundred Martins, and as many Otters: fortie thousand of dry fish we sent for Spaine, with the salt-fish, treine oyle and furres, I returned for England the 18. of July, and arrived safe with my company the latter end of August. Thus in six moneths I made my voyage, out and home, and by the labour of 45. got neare the valew of fifteene hundred pounds in those grosse commodities. This yeare also one went from Plimmouth, spent his victuall, and returned with nothing.[9]

Proofe 2.
1615.

The Londoners, upon this, sent foure good shippes, and because I would not undertake it for them, having ingaged my selfe to them of the West,[1] the Londoners entertained the men that came home with me; They set sayle in January, and arrived there in March: they found fish enough untill halfe June, fraughted a shippe of three hundred Tunnes; went for Spaine with drie fish, which was taken by the Turkes;[2] one went to Virginia, to relieve that Collony; and two came for England, with the greene fish, treine oyle, and furres, within six moneths.

Proofe 3.
1615.

With a labyrinth of trouble[3] I went from Plimmouth with a

---

7. The Azores—from the name of the single island of Terceira.

8. Proofs 1 to 7 as they appear in the "Letter to Bacon" (fol. 131ʳ⁻ᵛ) are repeated with little or no change in both the first and the second editions of *New Englands Trials* (sig. B2ʳ–B3ʳ), except as noted below.

9. The last sentence was added.

1. The clause "and because . . . of the West" has been added.

2. The clause "which was taken by the Turkes" has been added. Cf. M. Oppenheim's apropos remark: "The 'Turks,' the generic name for all Mahommedan pirates, were said to have taken 466 British ships between 1609 and 1616" (M. Oppenheim, ed., *The Naval Tracts of Sir William Monson* . . . [Navy Records Society, *Publications*, XLIII (London, 1913)], 101).

3. Smith's phrase is so unusual for the day that we may suspect that he heard or saw something similar (cf. Shakespeare, *Troilus and Cressida*, II, iii, 2: "What, lost in the labyrinth of thy fury?"). There are a few minor changes in this paragraph.

shippe of two hundred Tunnes, and one of fiftie; || but ill weather **[B3ᵛ]**
breaking all my mastes, I was forced to returne to Plimmouth,
where re-imbarking my selfe in a ship of three score tunnes, how I
escaped the English Pirats, and the French, and was betrayed by
foure Frenchmen of warre, I referre you to the Description of New
England; but my Vice-admirall, notwithstanding the latenesse of
the yeare, setting forth with me in March, the Londoners in January,
she arrived in May, they in March, yet came home well fraught in
August, and all her men well, within five moneths odde dayes.

The Londoners, ere I returned from France, for all their losse   Proofe 4.
by the Turkes, which was valewed about foure thousand pounds,[4]   1616.
sent two more in July: but such courses they tooke by the Canaries to
the west Indies; it was ten months ere they arrived in New England:
wasting in that time, their seasons, victuall, and healths; yet there
they found meanes to refresh themselves, and the one returned, neere
fraught with fish and traine, within two moneths after.

From Plimmouth went foure ships, onely to fish and trade, some   Proofe 5.
in February, some in March; one of two hundred tunnes, got thither 1616.
in a moneth, and went full fraught for Spaine, the rest returned to
Plimouth well fraught, and their men well, within 5 months odde
daies.

From London went two more, one of 220. tunnes, got thither in   Proofe 6.
sixe weekes; and within sixe weekes after, with fortie foure men and 1616.
boyes, was full fraught, and returned againe into England within five
months and a few dayes; the other went to the Canaries with dry fish,
which they solde at a great rate, for royalls of eight, and (as I heard) Proofe 7.
turned Pirates.[5]   1617.

I being at Plimouth, provided with three good ships, || was wind- **[B4ʳ]**
bound three months, as was many a hundred sayle more; so that the
season being past, the shippes went for New-found-land, whereby
my desseigne was frustrate, which was to me and my friends, no small
losse.[6]

There was foure good shippes[7] prepared at Plimouth; but by   Proofe 8.
reason of their disagreement, the season so wasted, as onely two went 1618.
forward, the one being of two hundred tunnes, returned well fraught
to Plimouth, and her men in health, within five moneths; the other
of foure score, went for Bilbow with dry fish, and made a good
returne.

This yeare againe,[8] divers shippes intending to go from Plim- Proofe 9.
mouth, so disagreed, as there went but one of 200. tuns, who stayed 1619.

---

4. The passage "from France, . . . foure thousand pounds" has been added.
5. The passage after the semicolon has been added.
6. The "Letter to Bacon" has "whereby the adventurers had noe loss" (fol. 131ᵛ).
In pointing out here that he himself had a considerable loss, which is explained at greater
length in the 1622 edition (sig. B3ʳ), Smith admits to the full truth. It would have been
highly unwise to admit losses of any kind in his first appeal.
7. This paragraph has been partially rewritten.
8. From here to the second paragraph on sig. C1ʳ, the text is quite new.

in the Countrey about sixe weekes, with thirty eight men and boyes, had her fraght, which she sold at the first penny for 210o. pounds,[9] besides the furres; so that every poore Sayler, that had but a single share, had his charges and sixteene pound ten shillings for his seven moneths worke: but some of the company say, for sixe months in the *Hercules*,[1] they receeved seventeene pound two shillings a share.

Proofe 10.
1620.

For to make triall this yeare there is gone six or seven sayle from the west Country, onely to fish, three of which are returned; and (as I am certainely informed) have made so good a voyage, that every Sayler for a single share had twenty pounds for his seven moneths worke, which is more then in twenty moneths he should have gotten, had he gone for wages any where. Now though all the former ships have not made such good voyages as they expected, by sending opinionated unskilfull men, that had not experienced diligence, to **[B4ᵛ]** save that they tooke, || nor take that there was; which now patience and practise hath brought to a reasonable kinde of perfection in despite of all Detractors, and Calumniations, the Countrey yet hath satisfied all, the defect hath beene in their using or abusing it, not in it selfe, nor me.

For this next
yeare 1621.
it is reported
12. or 20. saile
is a preparing.

Heere I entreate your Honourable leaves to answer some objections. Many do thinke it strange, if this be true, I have made no more use of it, and rest so long without employment. And I thinke it more strange they should tax me before they have tried what I have done, both by Sea and Land, as well in Asia, and Affrica, as Europe and America. These fourteene yeres I have spared neither pains, nor money, according to my abilitie, in the discovery of Norumbega,[2] where with some thirty seaven men and boyes, the remainder of an

---

9. "At the first penny" means at "prime cost," i.e., at what would be normally a wholesale price. Sailors were not paid wages on fishing voyages, but shares, determined by an agreed scale. Prof. D. B. Quinn suggests that the figure "210o pounds" may be an error for £210[.]0[s.], in view of the small "o" and the fact that £2,100 would be an excessive amount for a cargo of fish.

1. This is some otherwise unrecorded voyage. The *Hercules* may have been the same ship that accompanied Lord De La Warr to Virginia in 1610 (see R. H. Major, ed., *The Historie of Travaile into Virginia Britannia . . .*, *by William Strachey* [Hakluyt Society, 1st Ser., VI (London, 1849)], xxiii).

2. Norumbega first appeared on Verrazzano's brother's map of 1529 as Aranbega. Then in 1542, Jean Alfonse (Jean Fontenau of Saintonge) explored the region and stated that "fifteen leagues within this river [the Penobscot, in Maine] is a city called *Norombergue*" (Frank T. Siebert, Jr., book review in the *New England Quarterly*, XVI [1943], 503–504). Quickly, Norumbega became almost as famous as the populous and wealthy Quivira of the Texas-Oklahoma-Kansas region, and just as unreal, though the word itself is definitely of Penobscot Indian origin (*ibid.*). For a discussion of all aspects of Norumbega, see Douglas R. McManis, *European Impressions of the New England Coast, 1497–1620*, University of Chicago Department of Geography Research Paper No. 139 (Chicago, 1972), 49–67, and scattered earlier references. Here Smith most unusually applies the name to "Virginia," as a convenient name for all of the coastal area of North America between Spanish "Florida" and French "Canada." As is usual in Smith, "discovery" means "exploration."

hundred and five, against the fury of the Salvages, I began that
plantation now in Virginia; which beginning (here and there) cost
mee neare five yeares worke, and more then five hundred pound[3]
of my owne estate; beside all the dangers, miseries and incomber-
ances, and losse of other imployments I endured gratìs. From which
blessed Virgin, where I stayed till I left five hundred English, better
provided then ever I was (ere I returned) sprung the fortunate habi-   Burmudos.
tation of Somer Iles.

    This Virgins sister (called New-England, An. 1616 at my
humble suite, by our most gracious Prince Charles) hath bene neare
as chargeable to mee and my friends; from all which, although I
never got shilling, but it cost mee a pound, yet I thinke my ‖ selfe   **[C1ʳ]**
happy to see their prosperities.

    If it yet trouble a multitude to proceede uppon these certainties,
what thinke you I undertooke, when nothing was knowne, but that
there was a vast Land? I never had power and meanes to do any
thing (though more hath beene spent in formall delayes then would
have done the businesse) but in such a penurious and miserable
maner, as if I had gone a begging to builde an University; where,
had men bin as forward to adventure their purses, as to crop the
fruites of my Labours, thousands ere this, had bene bettered by these
designes. Thus betwixt the spurre of Desire, and the bridle of Reason,
I am neare ridden to death in a ring of Despaire;[4] the reines are in
your hands, therefore I entreate you to ease mee: and those blame
mee (beleeve)[5] this little may have taught me, not to be so forward
againe at every motion, unlesse I intended nothing but to carry
newes. For now they dare adventure a shippe, that, when I went
first, would not adventure a groat, so they may be at home againe by
Michaelmasse; but to the purpose.

    By this all men may perceive[6] the ordinary performance of this

    3. According to Purchas, Smith returned to England from soldiering on the Con-
tinent "with one thousand Duckets in his purse" (*Pilgrimes*, II, 1370). Since he had
received 1,500 gold ducats from Zsigmond Báthory, it would appear that he had spent
500 ducats in his travels. The remaining 1,000 would have yielded him upwards of
£450, judging by various travelers' reports, and this would be in line with his statement
that he had spent £500 on Virginia (see the *Generall Historie*, 164, 166, and nn). (Note
that Edward Arber equated £500 with 1,500 ducats, but this would be closer to the rate
of exchange for *silver* ducats [*Captain John Smith . . . Works, 1608–1631*, The English
Scholar's Library Edition, No. 16 (Birmingham, 1884), II, 869].)
    4. The underlying idea of Smith's philosophical reflection is found in Robert
Burton's *The Anatomy of Melancholy* . . . , "A true saying it is, 'Desire hath no rest;' . . . [it
is] a perpetual rack, or a horse-mill, . . . still going round as in a ring" ([London, 1621;
2d ed., "By Democritus Junior," 1624], Pt. 1, Sec. 2, Mem. 3, Subs. XI). Since there
were ties between Smith and Burton (see the Biographical Directory), it is possible that
the passage quoted put Smith's mind to work.
    5. The parentheses are apparently merely for emphasis. At the end of this para-
graph a significant quotation is added in the second edition (see sig. C4ᵛn, below; and
New Englands Trials [1622], sig. D1ᵛ, D1ᵛn).
    6. From here to the bottom of sig. C2ʳ the text is again derived almost verbatim
from the "Letter to Bacon" (fols. 132ʳ–133ʳ), with "all men" being substituted for "your
Lordship."

voyage in five or sixe moneths, the plenty of fish is most certainely approoved; and it is certaine from Cannada and New England hath come neare twenty thousand[7] Bever skinnes, within these five yeares. Now, had each of those shippes transported but sixe, or three pigs, as many goates and hens, fruits, plants and seeds as I projected; by this time there might have beene victuall for a thousand men. But the desire of present || gaine (in many) is so violent, and the indevours of many undertakers so negligent, every one so regarding his private, that it is hard to effect any publique good, and impossible to bring them into a body, rule, or order, unlesse both Authoritie and Mony assist experiences: it is not a worke for every one to plant a Colonie (but when a house is built, it is no hard matter to dwell in it.) This requireth all the best parts of art, judgement, courage, honestie, constancy, diligence and experience to doe but neare well: and there is a great difference betwixt Saying and Doing. But to conclude, the fishing will go forward if you plant it or no; whereby you may transport a colony for no great charge, that in a short time, might provide such fraughts, to buy of us their dwelling, as I would hope no ship could goe or come emptie from New England.

[C1ᵛ]

The charge of this is onely salt, nettes, hookes, lines, knives, Irish rugges,[8] course cloth, beads, hatchets, glasse and such trash, onely for fishing and trade with the Salvages, besides our owne necessarie provisions, whose indevours[9] will quickely defray all this charge; and the Salvages have intreated me to inhabit where I will. Now all those ships have bin fished within a square of two leagues, and not one ship of all these, would yet adventure further, where questionlesse 500. saile may have their fraught, better then in Island, Newfoundland, or elsewhere, and be in their markets before the other can have their fish in their ships. Because New Englands fishing beginneth in mid-February, the other not till mid-Maie, the progression heereof tends || much to the advancement of Virginia, and the Burmudas: and will be a good friend in time of need to the Inhabitants in New-foundland.

[C2ʳ]

The returnes made by the Westerne shippes[1] are commonly divided into 3. parts; one for the owners of the shippe, another for the maister and his company, the third for the victulers; which course being still permitted, will be no hinderance to the plantation, goe

7. The "Letter to Bacon" has 36,000 skins within four years; there is a good deal of rewriting of the "Letter to Bacon" in the next 20 lines or so.
8. This was not included in the "Letter to Bacon." The reference is to coarse woolen coverings, probably the kind called "Irish falinges" by William Strachey (*The Historie of Travell into Virginia Britania*, ed. Louis B. Wright and Virginia Freund [Hakluyt Soc., 2d Ser., CIII (London, 1953)], 71); from the Gaelic *fallaing*, "mantle." See David Beers Quinn, *The Elizabethans and the Irish* (Ithaca, N.Y., 1966), 23–24.
9. I.e., "pains, efforts"; the Indians could supply corn for food, and furs for profit.
1. This paragraph is somewhat clearer than the original in the "Letter to Bacon," fol. 132ᵛ.

there never so many, but a meanes of transporting that yearely for little or nothing, which otherwise will cost many a hundred of pounds.

If a Ship can gaine, twenty, thirty, fifty in the hundred,[2] nay neare three hundred for 100. in seven moneths, as you see they have doone, spending twice so much time in going and coming as in staying there; were I there planted, seeing the varietie of the fishings in their seasons, serveth the most part of the yeare; and with a little labour we might make all the salt we neede use. I can conceive no reason to distrust, but the doubling and trebling their gaines that are at all the former charge, and can fish but two months in a yeare: and if those do give twenty, thirty, or forty shillings for an acre of land, or ship Carpenters, Forgers of yron etc. that buy all things at a deare rate, grow rich, when they may have as good of all needfull necessaries for taking (in my opinion) should not grow poore; and no commoditie in Europe doth more decay then wood.

Maister Dee recordeth[3] in his Brittish Monarchie, that King Edgar had a navie of foure thousand saile, ‖ with which hee yearely **[C2ᵛ]** made his progresse about this famous Monarchy of Great Brittany, largely declaring the benefit thereof: whereupon it seems he projected to our most memorable Queene Elizabeth, the erecting of a Fleete of three score saile, he called a little Navy Royall; immitating the admired Pericles prince of Athens, that could never secure that tormented estate, untill he was Lord and Captaine of the Sea.

At this none neede wonder, for who knowes not, her Royall Majestie during her life, by the incredible adventures of her Royall Navy and valiant Souldiers and Sea-men; notwithstanding all treacheries at home, the protecting and defending France and Holland, and re-conquering Ireland, yet all the world, by Sea or Land, both feared, loved, and admired good Queene Elizabeth.

Both to maintaine and increase that incomparable honour (God be thanked) to her incomparable Successour, our most Royall Lord and Soveraigne King James, etc. this great Philosopher hath left this to his Majesty and his kingdomes considerations.

That if the Tenths of the Earth be proper to God, it is also due by Sea, the Kings highwayes[4] are common to passe, but not to digge for mines or anie thing, so Englands coasts are free to passe, but not to fish, but by his Majesties prerogative.

His Majestie of Spaine, permits none to passe the Popes order for the East and West Indies, but by his permission, or at their perills.

2. The "Letter to Bacon" has "59. or 60.ˡⁱ in the 100. only by fishing," and below, "spending twice so much time" is substituted for "spending as much time."

3. From here to the last two paragraphs (sig. C4ʳ⁻ᵛ) the text was reprinted in the *Generall Historie*, 243–244, with some additions from *New Englands Trials* (1622), sig. D3ᵛ–D4ʳ. The references to John Dee's "Brytish Monarchie" (in Dee, *Perfect Arte of navigation*) are as follows: to King Edgar, p. 56; to the little Navy Royall, p. 3; and to Pericles, pp. 1, 11–12.

4. See Dee, "Brytish Monarchie," in Dee, *Perfect Arte of navigation*, 21–22.

[C3ʳ] If all that world be so justly theirs, it is no injustice for England to make ‖ as much use of her owne, as strangers doe, that pay to their owne Lords the tenth, and not to the owners of those Liberties any thing, whose subjects may neither take nor sell any in their territories; which small tribute, would maintaine his little Navy Royall, and not cost his Majesty a penny; and yet maintaine peace with all forrainers, and allow them more curtesie, then any Nation in the world affords to England.

It were a shame to alledge, that Holland is more worthy to enjoy our fishings as Lords thereof, because they have more skill to handle it then we, as they can our wooll, and undressed cloth, notwithstanding all their wars and troublesome disorders.

To get mony to build this Navy he saith, Who would not spare the hundred penny of his Rents,[5] and the 500. penny of his goods; each servant that taketh 33.s. 4.d. wages, 4. pence, and every forrainer seven yeares of age, 4. pence yearely for 7. yeares; not any of these but yearely they will spend 3. times so much in pride, wantonnesse or some superfluity. And doe any men love the security of their estates that are true subjects, would not of themselves be humble suters to his Majestie, to do this of free will as a voluntary benevolence, so it may be as honestly and truly imployed as it is projected, the poorest mechanicke in this kingdome will gaine by it.

If this be too much, would the honorable Adventurers be pleased to move his Majestie, that but the 200. penny of Rents, and the thousandth peny of Goodes might bee thus collected, to plant **[C3ᵛ]** New England, and but the tenth fish there taken, leaving ‖ strangers as they are. You might build ships of any burden and numbers you please, five times cheaper then you can doe heere, and have good marchandize for their fraught in this unknowne Land, to the advauncement of Gods glorie, his Church and Gospel, and the strengthening and reliefe of a great part of Christendome, without hurt to any: To the terror of Pirates, the amazement of enemies, the assistance of friends, the securing merchants, and so much increase of Navigation, to make Englands Trade and Shipping, as much as any Nation in the world, besides a hundred other benefits, to the generall good of all true subjects, and would cause thousands yet unborne, blesse the time, and all them that first put it in practise.

Now, lest it should be obscured, as it hath bene, to private ends; or so weakely undertaken, by our over-weening incredulitie, that

---

5. See *ibid.*, 13–15. The "hundred penny" would be 4d. on 400d. (400d. = 33s. 4d.); thus a servant earning 33s. 4d. annually would "spare" 4d. annually. As for the "foreigners," there are references to Frenchmen, Dutchmen (Germans), Italians, and Poles sent to Virginia from 1619 to 1621 (Susan Myra Kingsbury, ed., *The Records of the Virginia Company of London* [Washington, D.C., 1906–1935], III, see the Index, under nationalities). Smith himself had had experience with Poles and Germans there in 1608–1609.

strangers may possesse it, whilst we contend for New Englands goods, but not Englands good. I present this unto your Lordship,[6] and to all the Lords in England, hoping (by your honorable good liking and approbation,) to move all the worthy Companies of this noble City, and all the cities and Countries in the whole Land to consider of it, since I can find them wood, and halfe victuall with the aforesaide advantages, with what facility they may build and maintaine this little Navy Royall, both with honour, profite and content, and inhabit as good a countrey as any in the world, within that parallell, which with my life, and what I have, I will indevour to effect, if God please, and you permit.

As for them whom pride or covetousnes lulleth asleepe in a **[C4ʳ]** Cradle of slouthfull carelesnesse; would they but consider, how all the great Monarchies of the Earth have bene brought to confusion: or but remember the late lamentable experience of Constantinople; and how many Cities, Townes, and Provinces, in the faire rich kingdomes of Hungaria, Transilvania, and Wallachia; and how many thousands of Princes, Earles, Barons, Knights, and Merchants, have in one day, lost goods, lives, and honours: or solde for slaves, like beasts in a market place; their wives, children and servants slain, or wandering they knew not whither: dying, or living in all extreamities of extreame miseries and calamities.[7] Surely, they would not onely doe this, but give all they have, to enjoy peace and libertie at home; or but adventure their persons abroad, to prevent the conclusions of a conquering foe, who commonly assaulteth, and best prevaileth, where he findeth wealth and plenty (most armed)[8] with ignorance and securitie.

Much more I could say, but lest I should be too tedious to your more serious affaires, I humbly crave your honorable and favorable constructions and pardons, if any thing be amisse.

If any desire to bee further satisfied, they may reade my Description of Virginia, and New England, and peruse them with their severall Mappes; what defect you finde in them, they shall finde supplied in mee, or in my Authors, that thus freely have throwne my selfe, with my Mite into the Treasury of my Countries good, not doubting but God will ‖ stirre up some noble spirits, to consider and **[C4ᵛ]** examine if worthy Collumbus could give the Spaniards any such cer-

6. Probably the earl of Bridgwater, although there does not seem to be any way of knowing to which "Lordship" Smith was addressing his appeal here. The earl of Bridgwater was not yet a privy councillor and was hardly in a position to "move all the worthy Companies" of London.

7. Smith is obviously recalling his experiences in eastern Europe (see, for example, the *True Travels*, 18).

8. The significance of the parentheses should certainly not be overlooked here. Smith's meaning is that a "conquering foe . . . best prevaileth where he findeth wealth and plenty *most equipped* with ignorance and a false sense of security"—the parentheses indicating emphasis and pointing to the intentional sarcasm.

tainties for his dessigne, when Queene Isabell of Spayne set him forth
with fifteene saile: And though I can promise no mines of golde, yet
the warrelike Hollanders let us immitate, but not hate, whose wealth
and strength are good testimonies of their treasure gotten by fishing.
Therefore (honourable and worthy Countrymen) let not the meannesse of the word Fish distaste you, for it will afford as good golde as
the mines of Guiana, or Tumbatu,[9] with lesse hazard and charge,
and more certaintie and facilitie: and so I humbly rest.

FINIS.

9. "Tumbatu" was in Smith's time a frequent English spelling of "Timbuktu" (today, in the Republic of Mali). The city had been famous in Europe as a market of gold and
salt since the late 14th century. Smith had undoubtedly read about it in John Pory's translation of J. Leo Africanus, *A geographical historie of Africa* (1606), later published in
Purchas, *Pilgrimes*, II, 749–851. Every schoolboy knew about the riches of Guiana from
Sir Walter Ralegh (see *The Discoverie of the large, rich and bewtiful Empyre of Guiana, with a
relation of the great and Golden Citie of Manoa (which the Spanyards call El Dorado)* ... [London,
1596], which Richard Hakluyt reprinted in his *Principal Navigations*, III, 627–662).
Here, we can trace some of Smith's reading habits, as it happens. As a sequel to Ralegh's
Discoverie of Guiana, Hakluyt printed *A Relation of the Second Voyage to Guiana*, by Laurence
Keymis (*Principal Navigations*, III, 666–667). Four pages below there is a quatrain, part
of George Chapman's "De Guiana carmen Epicum." The quatrain caught Smith's
fancy, and when he came to preparing the second edition of *New Englands Trials* he in-
serted it as a bit of prose on sig. D1ᵛ, attributing it to Hakluyt himself (see *New Englands
Trials* [1622]; and cf. sig. C1ʳn, above).

TEXTUAL ANNOTATION

AND BIBLIOGRAPHICAL NOTE TO

New Englands Trials (1620)

TEXTUAL ANNOTATION

The page numbers below refer to the boldface numerals in the margins of the present text, which record the pagination of the original edition used as copy text. The word or words before the bracket show the text as emended by the editor; the word or words after the bracket reproduce the copy text. The wavy dash symbol used after the bracket stands for a word that has not itself been changed but that adjoins a changed word or punctuation mark. The inferior caret, also used only after the bracket, signifies the location of missing punctuation in the copy text.

Page.Line

B2^r.19	elsewhere] e sewhere (in some copies)
B3^r.7	others] Bthers
B3^r.21	Tunnes] Tnnnes (inverted "u")
B3^v.25	dayes] d yes
B4^r.26	voyages] vyages
C1^v.7	parts] pars (from *New Englands Trials* [1622], sig. D1^v)
C2^v.10	and Sea-men] aud ∼ (inverted "n")
C4^r.6	Wallachia] Wallachi (from *New Englands Trials* [1622], sig. D4^r)
C4^v.9	Tumbatu] Tubatu (from *New Englands Trials* [1622], sig. D4^v)

Hyphenation Record

The following lists have been inserted at the request of the editorial staff of the Institute of Early American History and Culture. The list immediately below records possible compound words that were hyphenated at the end of the line in the copy text. In each case the editor had to decide for the present edition whether to print the word as a single word or as a hyphenated compound. The material before the bracket indicates how the word is printed in the present edition; the material after the bracket indicates how the word was broken in the original. The wavy dash symbol indicates that the form of the word has been unchanged from the copy text. Numerals refer to the page number of the copy text (the boldface numerals in the margin in this edition) and to the line number (counting down from the boldface number) in the present edition.

Page.Line

A2^r.10   himselfe]   him-selfe
B2^r.10   fishermen]   fisher-men
B2^r.11   gal-botes]   ~

The list below contains words found as hyphenated compounds in the copy text that unavoidably had to be broken at the end of the line at the hyphen in the present text. In quoting or transcribing from the present text, the hyphen should be retained for these words. Numerals refer to the page number of the copy text (the boldface numerals in the margin in this edition) and line number (counting down from the boldface number).

Page.Line

B4^r.1–2   wind-bound
C1^v.23–24   mid-February
C2^r.2–3   New-found-land

BIBLIOGRAPHICAL NOTE

Entry in the Stationers' Register

11. Decembris [1620]

William Jones
Entred for his Copie under the handes
of Master Doctor [Thomas] Goade and
Master [Humphrey] Lownes warden,
A booke Called *Newe Englands tryall,*
by John Smith.................. vi^d
(Arber, *Registers,* IV, 43.)

Editions

Early:

1620. NEW || ENGLANDS || TRIALS. || Declaring the successe of 26. Ships || employed thither within these six yeares: || *with the benefit of that Countrey by sea and* || land: and how to build threescore sayle || *of good Ships, to make a little* || Navie Royall. || Written by Captaine || *John Smith.* || [Ornament] LONDON, || Printed by *William Jones.* || 1620. ||

Quarto, pp.[20]; [A] including title page in two, B and C in fours. The address (A2) varies. As has been pointed out in Joseph Sabin *et al.*, eds., *A Dictionary of Books Relating to America*, XX (New York, 1927–1928), 248, the book seems to have been "published in a large edition. In the 'Generall Historie,' page 230, Smith says: 'I caused two or three thousand of them to be printed, one thousand with a great many Maps both of Virginia and New-England, I presented to thirty of the chiefe Companies in London at their Halls.' . . . it is now very rare." (Note that this edition was little, or not at all, used in Smith's *Generall Historie* and Purchas's *Pilgrimes*; see *New Englands Trials* [1622].)

Modern:

1873. *New England's Trials Written by Captain John Smith,* with a prefatory note by Charles Deane (Cambridge, Mass.).

1884, etc. *Captain John Smith . . . Works, 1608–1631,* ed. Edward Arber (Birmingham). See the list of issues of the Arber text in the General Introduction at the beginning of this volume.

New Englands Trials

1622

INTRODUCTION

In introducing this small book, it may be well to take what accountants would call a subtotal of Smith's narratives of English expansion overseas, so far. (The grand total will come with his *Advertisements*.) The 1622 edition of *New Englands Trials* was prepared for publication following two noteworthy events in English colonial history: (1) the survival of Jamestown after the Indian massacre of March 1622, and (2) the survival of the Pilgrims in New England through two winters. Thus, two roots of today's United States of America had been planted in different soils with differing objectives, and had proved sturdy and capable of permanence.

Yet Smith's colonial dream was neither realized in full, nor would it be fully realizable for many years. In his *Description of New England* he had written, "I am not so simple, to thinke, that ever any other motive then wealth, will ever erect there a Commonweale; or draw companie from their ease and humours at home, to stay in New England to effect my purposes."[1] Although the presence of the Pilgrims in New England (and the plans of the Puritans to settle there also) shows that Smith was mistaken, yet in a broader sense he was remarkably foresighted, or clairvoyant. The influx of people needed to create the great colony that later became the United States, not just New England, was produced by the opportunities available in America not only to be free, but even more to be rich.

Historians generally, however, have seen early New England as a land settled by people inspired by religious motivation—in the first place by a group that wanted to escape from everybody else, and in the second by a much larger group that wanted to get away from religious bureaucratic oppression in England and that chose to face the presumably tameable "wildmen" of Massachusetts rather than to continue facing the intractability of the likes of Bishop Laud (soon to be elevated to the archbishopric of Canterbury). In other words, the Pilgrims were not colonists in the old Roman sense that surely lurked in the back of Smith's mind, and he had hard things to say about them. But neither were the Puritans who poured out of King Charles's London to seek the shores of the river Charles, more than a thousand leagues away, and they found favor in the eyes of Smith. Years after the publication of the 1622 edition of *New Englands Trials*, Smith thought he saw *his* type of colonist in these resolute and voluntary exiles.

Samuel Eliot Morison, though he claims that Smith was mistaken about

1. *Description of N.E.*, 37.

the importance of wealth as a lure for settlers, has drawn a fine line between those who were driven to New England by religious scruples and the true colonists who went there to better their lot. By way of illustration Morison has quoted J. Franklin Jameson. The story of the Pilgrims, Jameson wrote, is that

of a small and feeble enterprise, . . . always limited by the slender resources of the poor and humble men who originated it [Plymouth]. The founding of the Bay Colony, on the other hand, was less a colonial enterprise than a great puritan emigration. It was organized by men of substance and standing, supported by wealth of a great and prosperous body of the English nation, and consciously directed toward the high end of founding in America a great puritan state.[2]

Smith was "over-glad . . . to see Industry her selfe adventure now to make use of my aged endevours,"[3] as the well-financed Puritan faction dispatched ship after ship across the Atlantic to the shores of Smith's own New England. He was especially happy that a friend of his, John Winthrop of Edwardston (Suffolk), could assure him that "factious Humourists" (like the Pilgrims) would not be suffered to join Winthrop's colonists.

The second edition of *New Englands Trials*, then, completes Smith's story of New England (except for brief supplementary notices in the *Generall Historie* and the *True Travels*) until Smith's final summation of his thoughts on "the Path-way to erect a Plantation" in the *Advertisements*. This edition adds a number of updating details to the first edition, and elaborates on two of his favorite themes: his personal and almost proprietary interest in New England and his experiences with the native inhabitants. Regarding the latter, he finds here his first occasion to refer in print to his rescue by Pocahontas: "God made Pocahontas the Kings daughter the meanes to deliver me."[4] He also seizes an opportunity to mention the prince of Transylvania, Zsigmond Báthory, who not only granted him a kind of coat of arms, but also gave him 1,500 ducats, which he later spent on Virginia.[5]

Summary

New Englands Trials (1622) is easily summarized. From the beginning of the text through sig. B4^r (almost half of the book) the 1620 edition is reprinted, with scattered additions amounting to a total of two and a quarter pages.

2. Samuel Eliot Morison, *Builders of the Bay Colony* (Boston and New York, 1930), 12–13.
3. *Advertisements*, 2.
4. Sig. C2^v, below.
5. See sig. D4^r, below. These and other points are brought out in Everett H. Emerson's *Captain John Smith* (Boston, 1971), 109–112.

None of these is of any great interest. On sig. B4^v begins a long, new passage, which fills almost nine pages. This has to do first with the founding of Plymouth colony, including some correspondence from there that seems not to have been preserved elsewhere. Then comes a bit on the Virginia massacre, which leads Smith to review his own career there (sig. C2^v), including his voyages among the Indians. This is logically followed by examples of some difficulties in New England. Near the bottom of sig. C3^v Smith opens an indirect defense of himself against those who accuse him of being unlucky. Neither the accusation nor the defense seems unusual, granted the superstitious bent of the times and Smith's bias against people who sit at home and risk nothing. Finally, almost all of sig. D (eight pages) is devoted to propaganda for New England, the bulk of it from the first edition.

 Though this volume is not a weighty one, it contains some additional matter of value (particularly, sigs. B4^v–C1^v). It is well worth reading and pondering for its position in the Smith corpus and for the glimpse it gives of Smith's real interest in New England, as well as of the increased breadth of his reading. Possibly the most important part of the book lies in the "documentation" of the New England voyages from his own first voyage in 1614 to about October 16, 1622.[6]

---

6. See sig. C3^v, below.

NEW ENGLANDS TRIALS.

Declaring the succeſſe of 80 Ships employed thither within theſe eight yeares; and the benefit of that Countrey by Sea and Land.

With the preſent eſtate of that happie Plantation, begun but by 60 weake men in the yeare 1620.

And how to build a Fleete of good Shippes to make a little Nauie Royall.

Written by Captaine *Iohn Smith*, ſometimes Gouernour of *Virginia*, and Admirall of *New England*.

The ſecond Edition.

LONDON,
Printed by W I L L I A M I O N E S.
1622.

[The editor is grateful to the British Library for permission to reproduce this title page.]

And Excellent Prince Charles, Prince of Wales;
Duke of Cornewall, Yorke, and Albanie;
Marquis of Ormond, and Rothsey;
and Earle Palatine of Chester;
Heire of Great Britaine, France,
and Ireland, etc.[1]

Sir,

When scarce any would beleeve mee there was any such matter, your Highnesse did not disdaine to accept my description, and calld that New England, whose barbarous names you changed for such English, that none can denie but Prince Charles is the Godfather. Whereby I am bound in all reason and dutie to give you the best account I can how your child ‖ doth prosper: and although as yet it **[A2ᵛ]** is not much unlike the Father in fortune, onely used as an instrument for other mens ends; yet the grace you bestowed on it by your Princely favour, hath drawn so many judgments now to behold it, that I hope shall find, it will give content to your Highnesse, satisfaction to them, and so increase the number of well-willers, New England will be able to reject her maligners, and attend Prince Charles with her dutifull obedience, with a trophie of honour, and a kingdome for a Prince. Therefore the great worke contained in this little booke, humbly desires your Princely patronage. No more but sacring all my best abilities to the exquisite judgement of your renowned vertues, I humbly kisse your gracious hands.

Your Highnesse true and faithfull servant,
Jo. Smith.

---

1. Charles was not yet 22 at the time; see the date supplied on sig. C3ᵛ.

TO THE RIGHT HONORABLE
And Right Worthy Adventurers,
to all Plantations and Discoveries,
their friends and well-willers,
especially of Virginia and New England.

Right Honorable,

I confesse it were more proper for me to be doing what I say, then writing what I know: but that it is not my fault, there is many a hundreth can testifie, if they please to remember what paines I have taken both particularly and generally to make this worke knowne, and procure meanes to put it in practise. What calumniations, doubts, or other mispritions hath opposed my endevours, I had rather forget then remember, but still to expresse my forwardnesse,[2] to the consideration of your favourable constructions I present this short discourse of the proceedings and present estate of New England: if you please to peruse it, and make use of it, I am richly

rewarded, though ‖ they be but the collections and observations of a plaine souldier, yet if you please to grace them with your countenance and good acceptance, I shall therein thinke my selfe happie, and hope that those labours may in time returne you such fruites as hereafter may perswade you to pardon this boldnesse, and accept them to be your honest servants.

Yours to command,
Jo. Smith.

---

2. Eagerness to serve, zeal.

NEW ENGLANDS TRIALS,
and Present Estate.

ONCERNING the description of this Countrey, six yeares ago I writ so largely, as in briefe I hope this may suffice you to remember,[1] that New England is a part of America, betwixt the Degrees of 41. and 45. the very meane betwixt the North Pole and the Line. From 43. to 45. the coast is mountainous, rockie, barren and broken Iles that make many good harbours. The water is deepe, close to the shore; there are many rivers and fresh springs: few Salvages, but an incredible abundance of fish, fowle, wilde fruits, and good timber. From 43. to 41. and a half, an excellent mixed coast of stone, sand and clay, much corne, many people, some Iles, many good harbours, a temperate aire, and therein all things necessary for the building ships of any proportion, and good merchandize for their fraught, within a square of 12 leagues: 25 harbours I sounded; 30 severall Lordships I saw, and so neare as I could imagine, 3000 men. I was up one river fortie miles, crossed the mouths of many, whose heads are reported to be great lakes; where they kill their ‖ Bevers; inhabited with many people, who trade with those of New England, and them of Cannada. [A4ᵛ]

The benefit of fishing, as Master Dee[2] reporteth
in his Brittish Monarchie

He saith that it is more then 44 yeares ago, and it is more then 40 yeares since he writ it, that the Herring Busses out of the Low-countries, under the King of Spaine, were 500. besides 100 French-men, and three or foure hundred saile of Flemmings.

The coasts of Wales and Lancashire was used by 300 saile of strangers.

Ireland at Baltemore fraughted yearely 300 saile of Spaniards,

---

1. After these few introductory lines Smith reprinted the entire 1620 edition of *New Englands Trials*, with some trivial changes, the omission of a few lines, and additional material that amounts to about 44% of the whole. To avoid duplication of the footnotes to the previous work, attention will be called to all material changes in the text, but the annotation will be restricted, with a very few exceptions, to the new material.
2. On John Dee, see *New Englands Trials* (1620), sig. B1ᵛn.

where King Edward the sixt intended to have made a strong Castle, because of the strait, to have tribute for fishing.

Blacke Rocke was yearely fished by three or foure hundred saile of Spaniards, Portugals and Biskiners.

Master Gentleman and many Fisher-men and
Fish-mongers with whom I have conferred, report,

The Hollanders raise yearely by Herring, Cod, and Ling, 3000000 pounds.

English and French by Salt-fish, poore John, Salmons and Pilchards, 300000 pounds.

Hambrough and the Sound, for Sturgion, Lobsters and Eeles, 100000 pounds.

Cape Blanke for Tunny and Mullit, by the Biskiners and Spaniards 30000 pounds.

[B1^r]   But divers other learned experienced Observers
say, though it may seeme incredible,

That the Duke of Medina receiveth yearely tribute of the fishers for Tunny, Mullit and Purgos, more then 10000 pounds.

Lubeck hath 700 ships: Hambrough 600: Embden lately a fisher towne, 1400. whose customes by the profit of fishing hath made them so powerfull as they be.

Holland and Zeland, not much greater then Yorkshire, hath thirtie walled townes, 400 villages, and 20000 saile of shippes and hoyes; 3600 are fishermen, whereof 100 are Doggers, 700 Pinckes and Welbotes, 700 Frand botes, Britters[3] and Tode-botes, with 1300 Busses, besides three hundred that yearely fish about Yarmouth, where they sell their fish for gold; and fifteene yeares ago they had more then 116000 sea-faring men.

These fishing ships do take yearely 200000 Last of fish, twelve barrels to a Last, which amounted to 3000000 pounds by the Fishermens price, that 14 yeares ago did pay for their tenths 300000 pound; which venting in Pumerland, Sprussia, Denmarke, Lefland, Russia, Swethland, Germany, Netherlands, England, or elsewhere, etc. make their returnes in a yeare about 7000000 pounds; and yet in Holland they have neither matter to build ships, nor merchandize to set them foorth; yet by their industrie they as much increase, as other Nations decay. But leaving these uncertainties as they are,

[B1^v] of this I am certaine, ‖ That the coast of England, Scotland, and Ireland, the North Sea, with Ireland[4] and the Sound, New-found land and Cape Blanke, do serve all Europe, as well the land Townes

---

3. For the nomenclature of these vessels, see *ibid.*, sig. B2^rn.
4. Iceland. See the *Generall Historie*, 228n.

as Ports, and all the Christian shipping, with these sorts of Staple fish which is transported, from whence it is taken, many a thousand mile, viz.

Herring.	Tunny.
Salt-fish.	Porgos.
poore John.	Caviare.
Sturgion.	Buttargo.
Mullit.	

Now seeing all these sorts of fish, or the most part of them, may be had in a land more fertile, temperate, and plentifull of all necessaries for the building of ships, boates and houses, and the nourishment of man; the seasons are so proper, and the fishings so neare the habitations we may there make, that New England hath much advantage of the most of those parts, to serve all Europe farre cheaper then they can, who at home have neither wood, salt, nor food, but at great rates; at Sea nothing but what they carry in their ships, an hundred or two hundred leagues from their habitation.

But New Englands fishings is neare land, where is helpe of wood, water, fruites, fowles, corne, or other refreshings needfull; and the Terceras, Mederas, Canaries, Spaine, Portugale, Provance, Savoy, Sicilia, and all Italy, as convenient markets for our dry Fish, greene Fish, Sturgion, Mullit, Caviare, and Buttargo, as Norway, Swethland, Littuania or Germany, for their Herring, which is here also in abundance for taking; they returning but wood, pitch, tarre, soapeashes, cordage, flaxe, waxe, and such like commodities: we, wines, oyles, sugars, silks, ‖ and such merchandize as the Straits affoord, **[B2ʳ]** whereby our profit may equalize theirs; besides the increase of shipping and Mariners. And for proofe hereof:

With two ships sent out at the charge of Captain Marmaduke Proofe 1.
Roydon, Captain George Langam, Master John Buley and W. Skel- 1614.
ton,[5] I went from the Downes the third of March, and arived in New England the last of April, where I was to have stayed[6] but with ten men to keep possession of those large territories, had the Whales proved, as curious information had assured me and my adventurers, (but those things failed.) So having but fortie five men and boyes, we built seven boates, 37 did fish; my selfe with eight others ranging the coast, I tooke a plot of what I could see, got acquaintance of the

---

5. Two lines have been added here in this edition (cf. *New Englands Trials* [1620], sig. B3ʳ), giving the names of Smith's backers. Marmaduke Roydon (also Rawdon, knighted 1643), a merchant who "married money," was one of the first planters (1627) in Barbados (see the Biographical Directory, s.v. "Rawdon"). William Skelton was a London merchant. Capt. George Langham seems to have been from Bury St. Edmunds, Suffolk. Master John Buley is otherwise unknown. See Philip L. Barbour, *The Three Worlds of Captain John Smith* (Boston, 1964), 305–306.
6. The material from here to the end of the sentence has been added to this edition.

inhabitants; 1100 Bever skins, 100 Martins, and as many Otters. 40000 of drie fish we sent for Spaine; with the salt fish, traine oile and Furres, I returned for England the 18 of July, and arived safe with my company the latter end of August. Thus in six moneths I made my voyage out and home; and by the labour of 45, got neare the value of 1500 pounds in those grosse commodities. This yeare also one went from Plimmoth, set out by divers of the Isle of Wight and the West country, by the directions and instructions of Sir Ferdinando Gorge, spent their victuals, and returned with nothing.[1]

Proofe 2.
1615.

The Virginia Company upon this sent 4 good ships; and because I would not undertake it for them, having ingaged my selfe to them of the West, the Londoners entertained the men that came home with me. They set saile in January, and arived there in March; they found fish enough untill halfe June, fraughted a ship of 300 Tuns,

[B2ᵛ] || went for Spaine, which was taken by the Turks; one went to Virginia to relieve that Colonie, and two came for England with the greene fish, traine oile and Furres within six moneths.

Proofe 3.
1615.

In January[2] with 200 pounds in cash for adventure, and six Gentlemen wel furnished, I went from London to the foure ships was promised, prepared for me in the West country, but I found no such matter; notwithstanding at the last with a labyrinth of trouble I went from Plimmoth with a ship of 200 Tuns, and one of fiftie: when the fishing was done onely with 15 I was to stay in the country; but ill weather breaking all my masts, I was forced to returne to Plimmoth, where rather then lose all, reimbarking my selfe in a Bark of 60 Tuns, how I escaped the English pyrates and the French, and was betrayed by foure French men of warre, I referre you to the Description of New England: but my Vice-Admirall, notwithstanding the latenesse of the yeare, setting forth with me in March, the Londoners in January, she arived in May, they in March, yet came home well fraught in August, and all her men well, within 5 months, odde days.

Proofe 4.
1616.

The Londoners ere I returned from France, for all their losse by the Turks, which was valued about 4000 pounds, sent two more in July; but such courses they took by the Canaries to the West Indies, it was ten moneths ere they arived in New England, wasting in that time their seasons, victuall and healths, yet there they found meanes to refresh themselves, and the one returned, neare fraught with fish and traine, within 2 moneths after.

Proofe 5.
1616.

From Plimmoth went 4 ships, onely to fish and trade, some in Februarie, some in March, one of 200 Tuns got thither in a month,

---

1. This last sentence has been added to this edition. The reference is to Capt. Nicholas Hobson's voyage, which began in June 1614 (see James Phinney Baxter, *Sir Ferdinando Gorges and His Province of Maine* . . . [Prince Society (Boston, 1890)], I, 97n).

2. Most of the first half of this paragraph is new to this edition (with the exception of the "labyrinth"), but adds little.

and went full fraught for Spain, ‖ the rest returned to Plimmoth well **[B3ʳ]**
fraught, and their men well, within five moneths, odde dayes.

    From London went two more, one of 200 Tuns, got thither in   Proofe 6.
six weeks, and within six weeks after with 44 men and boyes was full   1616.
fraught, and returned again into England within five moneths and
a few daies; the other went to the Canaries with drie fish, which they
sold at a great rate, for Rials of 8, and as I heard turned pirats.

    I being at Plimmoth provided with 3 good ships, yet but fifteen   Proofe 7.
men[3] to stay with me in the country, was Wind-bound three moneths,   1617.
as was many a hundred saile more, so that the season being past, the
ships went for New-found-land, whereby my designe was frustrate,
which was to me and my friends no small losse, in regard whereof[4]
here the Westerne Commissioners in the behalfe of themselves and
the rest of the Companie, contracted with me by articles indented
under our hands, to be Admirall of that Country during my life, and
in the renewing of their Letters pattents so to be nominated, halfe the
fruits of our endevours theirs, the rest our owne; being thus ingaged,
now the businesse doth prosper, some of them would willingly forget
me; but I am not the first they have deceived.

    There was foure good ships prepared at Plimmoth, but by   Proofe 8.
reason of their disagreement, the season so wasted, as onely 2 went   1618.
forward, the one being of 200 Tuns, returned well fraught for Plimmoth, and her men in health, within five moneths; the other of 80
Tuns, went for Bilbow with drie fish, and made a good returne. In
this voyage[5] Edward Rowcroft, alias Stallings, a valiant souldier,
that had bin with me in Virginia, and seven yeares after went with
me from Plimoth towards ‖ New England with Thomas Dirmer an **[B3ᵛ]**
understanding and an industrious Gentleman to inhabite it; all
whose names with our proceedings you may reade at large in my
description of New England, upon triall before the Judge of the
Admiraltie, how when we had past the worst, for pure cowardize the
Maister and sailers ran away with the ship and all I had, and left me
alone among 8 or 9 French men of Warre in the yeare 1615. This
Stallings went now againe in those ships, and having some wrong
offered him in New England by a French man, he tooke him, and as

---

    3. The detail about the number of men has been added to this edition.
    4. The rest of this paragraph is new to this edition; the most significant new part is
the explanation of how Smith came to have the title of "Admirall of that Country [New
England]." Although there is no record of this in surviving documents, and the editor
is inclined to think that there may have been a misunderstanding, Smith's continued
use of it to the end of his life, with no surviving protest from his "detractors," makes one
hesitant to assume the title was fabricated. See the *Description of N.E.*, caption to the
facsimile title page.
    5. "Bilbow" was a frequent spelling of Bilbao, Spain. The rest of this paragraph has
been added in this edition. Smith and Sir Ferdinando Gorges are the chief sources for
information here (see the excellent account in Richard Arthur Preston, *Gorges of Plymouth
Fort: A Life of Sir Ferdinando Gorges, Captain of Plymouth Fort, Governor of New England, and
Lord of the Province of Maine* [Toronto, 1953], 162–164, and pertinent nn.).

he writ to me, he went with her to Virginia with fish, to trade with them for such commodities as they might spare; he knew both these countries well, yet he promised me the next Spring to meet me in New England; but the ship and he perished in Virginia.

Proofe 9.
1619.

This yeare againe, divers ships intending to go from Plimmoth, so disagreed, as there went but one of 200 Tuns, who stayed in the country about 6 weeks, with 38 men and boyes, had her fraught, which she sold at the first penie, for 2100 pounds, besides the Furres: so that every poore sailer that had but a single share, had his charges, and 16.l. 10.s. for his seven moneths worke.[6] Master Thomas Dirmer having lived about a yeare in New-found-land, returning to Plimmoth, went for New England in this ship, and not only confirmes what I have writ, but so much more approved of it, that he stayed there with five or six men in a little boate; finding 2 or 3 Frenchmen among the savages, who had lost their ship, augmented his companie, with whom he ranged the coast to Virginia, where he was

[B4r] kindly welcomed and well refreshed; thence returned to ‖ New England again, where having bin a yeare, in his back-returne to Virginia, he was so wounded by the savages, he died upon it, them escaped were relieved at Virginia. Let not men attribute their great adventures and untimely deaths to unfortunatenesse, but rather wonder how God did so long preserve them, with so small meanes to do so much, leaving the fruits of their labours to be an encouragement to those our poore undertakings; and this for advantage as they writ unto me, that God had laid this Country open for us, and slaine the most part of the inhabitants by cruell warres and a mortall disease;[7] for where I had seene 100 or 200 people, there is scarce ten to be found. From Pembrocks bay[8] to Harrintons bay there is not 20; from thence to Cape An, some 30; from Taulbuts bay to the River Charles, about 40, and not any of them touched with any sicknes, but one poore Frenchman that died.

Proofe 10.
1620.

For to make triall this yeare there is gone 6 or 7 saile from the West country, onely to fish, three of whom are returned, and as I was certainly informed, made so good a voyage, that every sailer for a single share had 20 pounds for his 7 moneths work, which is more then in 20 moneths he should have gotten had he gone for wages any where. Now though all the former ships have not made such good voyages as they expected, by sending opinionated unskilfull men,

6. A two-line clause of what "some of the company say" has been omitted in this edition. Perhaps it was unfounded. All the rest of the paragraph is new to this edition, and most of it is confirmed in Preston, *Gorges of Plymouth Fort*, 162–164.

7. There is a full note on this in Alexander Young, *Chronicles of the Pilgrim Fathers of the Colony of Plymouth, from 1602–1625* (Boston, 1844), 183–185. The editor would hazard a surmise that the "mortal disease" was smallpox, carried probably by some French sailor.

8. Smith's "Pembrocks bay" is modern Penobscot Bay; "Harrin[g]tons bay" is Casco Bay; "Cape An[ne]" is unchanged; "Taulbuts [Talbots] bay" is Salem harbor; and "River Charles" is unchanged.

that had not experienced diligence to save that they tooke, nor take
that there was; which now patience and practise hath brought to a
reasonable kind of perfection: in despite of all detractors and calumniations, the Country yet hath satisfied all, the defect hath bin in
their using or abusing it, not in it selfe nor me.

A plantation in New England.[9]   [**B4ᵛ**]

Upon these inducements some few well disposed Gentlemen and   Proofe 11.
Merchants of London and other places provided two ships, the one   1620.
of 160 Tunnes, the other of 70; they left the coast of England the 23
of August, with about 120 persons, but the next day the lesser ship
sprung a leake, that forced their returne to Plimmoth, where discharging her and 20 passengers, with the great ship and a hundred
persons besides sailers, they set saile againe the sixt of September, and
the ninth of November fell with Cape James;[1] but being pestred nine
weeks in this leaking unwholsome ship, lying wet in their cabbins,
most of them grew very weake, and weary of the sea, then for want
of experience ranging to and again, six weeks before they found a
place they liked to dwell on, forced to lie on the bare ground without
coverture in the extremitie of Winter, fortie of them died,[2] and 60

9. This is of course the Plymouth colony. From here to the middle of sig. C4ᵛ all the
material is new to this edition. For those who do not want to investigate such thorough
documentation as is to be found in William Bradford's *Plymouth Plantation* or Alexander
Young's *Chronicles of the Pilgrim Fathers*, the editor can suggest the succinct and highly
readable summary of what happened in Samuel Eliot Morison's "The Plymouth Colony
and Virginia," *Virginia Magazine of History and Biography*, LXII (1954), 147–165. In an
even lighter vein (one that Smith would surely have found to his liking), three years
after Morison's article was published, some "Verses on the Puritan Settlement in
America" were accidentally found in the Nottinghamshire Record Office. The date of
these is c. 1631, and the author unknown. The editor offers the first two stanzas as an
example of that lighter view toward the Pilgrims:

> Lett all the paridisean sect
> I meane the Counterfect elect
> All Zealous bankerouts punks devout
> Susspendent preatchers Rable Rout
> Let them sell all out of hand
> Prepare to goe for new England
> To build new bable [Babel] stronge and sure
> Now cald a Churche unspotted pure.

> There milke like springgs from Rivers [flowes?]
> And hony uppon hawthorne growes
> Hempe wooll and flaxe growes there on trees
> The mould is fat and cutts like chees
> All fruits and erbes springe there in feilds
> Tobacco therein plenty yeilds
> And above all thes a Churche the most pure
> Wher you may have salvation sure

(*A Nottinghamshire Miscellany*, Thoroton Society, Record Series, XXI [1962], 37–39).
1. Cape Cod; Smith's flattery never took root.
2. The "exact bill of mortality" was 44 dead, out of a total of 100 (Young, *Chronicles*,
198n).

were left in very weake estate at the ships coming away, about the fift of April following, and arived in England the sixt of May.

Proofe 12.
1620.

Immediatly after her arivall, from London they sent another of 55 Tunnes[3] to supply them, with 37 persons, they set saile in the beginning of July, but being crossed by Westerly winds, it was the end of August ere they could passe Plimmoth, and arived at New Plimmoth in New England the eleventh of November, where they found all the people they left in April, as is said, lustie and in good health, except six that died. Within a moneth they returned here for England, laded with clapboord, wainscot and walnut, with about

[C1ʳ] three hogsheads of Bever skins, ‖ and some Saxefras, the 13 of December,[4] and drawing neare our coast, was taken by a Frenchman, set out by the Marquis of Cera,[5] Govenour of Ile Deu on the coast of Poytou, where they kept the ship, imprisoned the Master and companie, took from them to the value of about 500 pounds; and after 14 days sent them home with a poore supply of victuall, their owne being devoured by the Marquis and his hungry servants; they arived at London the 14 of Februarie, leaving all them they found and caried to New England well and in health, with victuall and corne sufficient till the next harvest.

The copie of Letter sent by this ship.

A Letter from
New Plim-
moth.

Loving cousin,[6] at our arivall at New Plimmoth in New England, we found all our friends and planters in good health, though they were left sicke and weake with very small meanes, the Indians round about us peaceable and friendly, the country very pleasant and temperate, yeelding naturally of it self great store of fruites, as vines of divers sorts in great abundance; there is likewise walnuts, chesnuts, small nuts and plums, with much varietie of flowers, rootes, and herbs, no lesse pleasant then wholsome and profitable: no place hath more goose-berries and straw-berries, nor better, Timber of all sorts you have in England, doth cover the Land, that affoords beasts

---

3. This ship was the *Fortune*.

4. On the *Fortune*'s stay, see William Bradford, *Of Plymouth Plantation, 1620–1647*, ed. Samuel Eliot Morison (New York, 1952), 90–96.

5. The marquis was Jean de Rieux, marquis d'Assérac, sieur de l'Île d'Yeu, Poitou (confirmed in the provincial archives at La Roche-sur-Yon). The full story of what happened is in a document preserved in the P.R.O., which is transcribed in full in Edward Arber, *The Story of the Pilgrim Fathers, 1606–1623 A.D. . . .* (London, 1897), 506–508. The English ship involved was the *Fortune* (see n. above), which was on her way home. Seized by a French man-of-war on Jan. 19, 1622, "some eight leagues off Use," she was escorted to that island. Assérac examined the ship's papers, and despite their proven innocence, the entire ship's company of 13 persons were pillaged, the cargo was rifled, and even private letters from Plymouth to England were confiscated. The commodities alone were worth "£400 at the least." But after 13 days' detention, a young Frenchman who spoke English got them freed on the condition that they sign a paper swearing that Assérac had taken only two hogsheads of skins.

6. This letter has been reprinted in Young, *Chronicles*, 250–251, with a note regarding the author, William Hilton, and his brother Edward, "fishmongers of London."

of divers sorts, and great flocks of Turkies, Quailes Pigeons and Partriges: many great lakes abounding with fish, fowle, Bevers and Otters. The sea affoords us as great plenty of all excellent sorts of sea-fish, as the rivers and Iles doth varietie of wilde fowle of most usefull sorts. Mines we find to our thinking, but neither the goodnesse nor qualitie we know.[7] Better grain cannot be then the Indian corne, if we will plant it upon as good ground as a man need desire. We are all free-holders, the rent day doth not trouble us, and all those good blessings we have, of which and what we list in their seasons for taking. Our companie are for ‖ most part very religious honest **[C1ᵛ]** people; the word of God sincerely taught us every Sabbath: so that I know not any thing a contented mind can here want. I desire your friendly care to send my wife and children to me, where I wish all the friends I have in England, and so I rest

Your loving kinsman
William Hilton.

From the West country went ten or twelve ships to fish, which were all well fraughted; those that came first at Bilbow made 17 pounds a single share, besides Bever, Otters and Martins skins; but some of the rest that came to the same ports that were already furnished, so glutted the market, their price was abated, yet all returned so well contented, they are a preparing to go againe. — *Proofe 13. 1621.*

There is gone from the West of England onely to fish[8] 35 ships, and about the last of April two more from London, the one of 100 Tuns, the other of 30, with some 60 passengers to supply the plantation[9] with all necessary provisions. Now though the Turke and French hath bin somewhat too busie, would all the Christian Princes but be truly at unitie, as his royall Majestie our Soveraigne Lord and King desireth, 70 saile of good ships were sufficient to fire the most of his coasts in the Levant, and make such a guard in the straits of Hellespont, as would make the great Turke himselfe more afraid in Constantinople, then the smallest red crosse that crosses the seas would be, either of any French Piccaroun, or the pirats of Argere.[1] — *For this yeare 1622.*

An abstract of Letters sent from the Collony
in New England, July 16. 1622.

Since the newes of the massacre in Virginia, though the Indians

---

7. I.e., Hilton and his people thought that there were mines in the region, but they did not really know.

8. Smith stresses the point that still no colony was being planned.

9. Arber points out that this was Thomas Weston's plantation at Wessagusset (Edward Arber, ed., *Captain John Smith . . . Works, 1608–1631*, The English Scholar's Library Edition, No. 16 [Birmingham, 1884], 261), about which Governor Bradford wrote lengthily and bitterly (*Plymouth Plantation*, 113–121).

1. "Picarón" was a Spanish name for "corsair," or "privateer." Algiers was a noted haven for pirates (Smith's spelling was in line with the "Argier" of some English merchants and travelers).

[C2ʳ] continue their wonted friendship, yet are we more wary of them then before; for their hands hath bin ‖ embrued in much English blood, onely by too much confidence, but not by force.[2]

Here I must intreate a little your favours to digresse. They did not kill the English because they were Christians, but for their weapons and commodities, that were rare novelties; but now they feare we may beate them out of their dens, which Lions and Tygers would not admit but by force. But must this be an argument for an English man, or discourage any either in Virginia or New England? No: for I have tried them both. For Virginia, I kept that country with 38, and had not to eate but what we had from the savages. When I had ten men able to go abroad, our common wealth was very strong: with such a number I ranged that unknown country 14 weeks; I had but 18 to subdue them all, with which great army I stayed six weekes before their greatest Kings habitations, till they had gathered together all the power they could; and yet the Dutchmen sent at a needlesse excessive charge did helpe Powhatan how to betray me.[3]

Of their numbers we were uncertaine; but them two honorable Gentlemen (Captaine George Percie and Captaine Francis West), two of the Phittiplaces, and some other such noble gentlemen and resolute spirits bore their shares with me, and now living in England, did see me take this murdering Opechankanough now their great King by the long locke on his head, with my pistole at his breast, I led him among his greatest forces, and before we parted made him fill our Bark of twenty Tuns with corne. When their owne wants was **[C2ᵛ]** such, I have given ‖ them part againe in pittie, and others have bought it againe to plant their fields.

For wronging a souldier but the value of a peny, I have caused Powhatan send his owne men to James Towne to receive their punishment at my discretion. It is true in our greatest extremitie they shot me, slue three of my men, and by the folly of them that fled tooke me prisoner; yet God made Pocahontas the Kings daughter the meanes to deliver me: and thereby taught me to know their trecheries to preserve the rest. It was also my chance in single combat to take the King of Paspahegh prisoner, and by keeping him, forced his subjects to worke in chaines, till I made all the country pay contribution, having little else whereon to live.

Twise in this time I was their President,[4] and none can say in all

2. According to Bradford, the first news of the massacre in Virginia was brought to Plymouth by Capt. John Huddleston (May? 1622), and a fort was begun there in June (*Plymouth Plantation*, 110–111). Smith's abstract adds a detail to the general picture.

3. This paragraph is an eloquent expression of Smith's attitude toward the Indians. He continues with two practical examples of how he handled the Indians (Opechancanough and the king of Paspahegh) with little or no bloodshed.

4. This surely should read: "Twice [these things happened, when] I was their President, and none can say. . . ."

that time I had a man slaine: but for keeping them in that feare I was much blamed both there and here: yet I left 500 behind me that through their confidence⁵ in six months came most to confusion, as you may reade at large in the description of Virginia.⁶ When I went first to those desperate designes, it cost me many a forgotten pound to hire men to go; and procrastination caused more run away then went. But after the ice was broken, came many brave voluntaries: notwithstanding since I came from thence, the honorable Company have bin humble suiters to his Majestie to get vagabonds and condemned men⁷ to go thither; nay so much scorned was the name of Virginia, some did chuse to be hanged ere they would go thither, and were: yet for all the worst of spite, detraction and ‖ discouragement, **[C3ʳ]** and this lamentable massacre, there is more honest men now suters⁸ to go, then ever hath bin constrained knaves; and it is not unknown to most men of understanding, how happie many of those Collumners⁹ doe thinke themselves, that they might be admitted, and yet pay for their passage to go now to Virginia: and had I but meanes to transport as many as would go, I might have choise of 10000 that would gladly be in any of those new places, which were so basely contemned by ungratefull base minds.

To range this countrey of New England in like maner I had but eight, as is said, and amongst their bruite¹ conditions I met many of their silly incounters, and without any hurt, God be thanked; when your West country men were many of them wounded and much tormented with the savages that assaulted their ship, as they did say themselves, in the first yeare I was there 1614.² and though Master Hunt then Master with me did most basely in stealing some savages from that coast to sel, when he was directed to have gone for Spaine, yet that place was so remote from Capawuck, where Epenew should have fraughted them with gold ore, his fault could be no cause of their bad success, however it is alledged for an excuse. I speake not this out of vainglory, as it may be some gleaners,³ or some was never there may censure me, but to let all men be assured by those ex-

---

5. Smith apparently used the word here in the same sense as Richard Hooker in the passage, "Their confidence, for the most part, riseth from too much credit given to their own wits" (*Of the Lawes of Ecclesiasticall Politie* [London, (1593)–1597], as quoted in the *OED*).

6. See the *Proceedings*, 105.

7. Although there certainly was talk of sending "criminals" to Virginia, little seems actually to have been done in that direction just then.

8. Variant spelling of "suitors."

9. A misspelling or misprint of a rare variant of "calumniators."

1. Here "rough, rude, 'primitive.'" A few words further, "silly" means "feeble, ineffectual."

2. Although Smith first refers to his own Master Hunt (who kidnapped Indians to sell in Spain), his main reference here is to Gorges's expedition, at the end of which a number of Englishmen and many Indians were hurt or slain (Gorges, "A briefe Relation of the Discovery and Plantation of New England . . . ," in Baxter, *Gorges and His Province*, I, 209–211).

3. Those who glean, or scrape together bits of scandal.

amples, what those savages are that thus strangely doe murder and betray our country men. But to the purpose.

[C3ᵛ]   What is already writ of the healthfulnesse of the aire, ‖ the richnesse of the soile, the goodnes of the woods, the abundance of fruits, fish, and fowle in their season, they stil affirm that have bin there now neare 2 yeares, and at one draught they have taken 1000 basses, and in one night twelve hogsheads of herring. They are building a strong fort, they hope shortly to finish, in the interim they are wel provided: their number is about a hundred persons, all in health, and well neare 60 acres of ground well planted with corne, besides their gardens well replenished with useful fruits; and if their Adventurers would but furnish them with necessaries for fishing, their wants would quickly be supplied. To supply them this 16 of October is going the *Paragon* with 67 persons, and all this is done by privat mens purses. And to conclude in their owne words, should they write of all plenties they have found, they thinke they should not be beleeved.[4]

For the 26 saile of ships, the most I can yet understand is, Master Ambrose Jennens of London, and Master Abraham Jennens of Plimmoth sent (their *Abraham*) a ship of 220 Tuns, and the *Nightingale* of Porchmouth of 100. whose fish at the first penie came to 3150 pounds: in all they were 35 saile: and where in Newfound land they shared six or seven pounds for a common man, in New England they shared 14 pounds; besides six Dutch and French ships made wonderfull returnes in furres.[5]

1622.   Thus you may see plainely the yearely success from New England (by Virginia) which hath bin so costly to this kingdome and so deare to me, which either to see perish or but bleed, pardon me though it passionate me beyond the bounds of modestie, to have bin sufficiently able to foresee it, and had neither power nor meanes how

[C4ʳ] to prevent it. By that ‖ acquaintance I have with them, I may call them my children, for they have bin my wife, my hawks, my hounds, my cards, my dice, and in totall my best content, as indifferent to my heart as my left hand to my right; and notwithstanding all those miracles of disasters[6] have crossed both them and me, yet were there not one English man remaining (as God be thanked there is some thousands) I would yet begin againe with as small meanes as I did at the first; not for that I have any secret encouragement from any I

---

4. Although the precise source of Smith's information is not clear, the standard sources of Plymouth history bear out Smith's statements (e.g., Bradford, *Plymouth Plantation*, and *A Relation or Journall . . . of the English Plantation Setled at Plimoth . . .*, commonly called "*Mourt's Relation*" [London, 1622]).

5. Little seems to be known about this obscure expedition. Abraham Jennings (Jennens), a merchant of Plymouth (Devonshire), was earlier involved in litigation with Gorges in connection with the Sagadahoc colony (Preston, *Gorges of Plymouth Fort*, 398–399, n. 16). The unusual spelling "Porchmouth" is possibly due to confusion with the older village of Porchester at the head of Portsmouth harbor.

6. As is often necessary for understanding Smith's text, the relative "which" or "that" should be inserted for clarity.

protest, more then lamentable experiences: for all their discoveries I can yet heare of, are but pigs of my owne sowe; nor more strange to me then to heare one tell me he hath gone from Billings gate and discovered Greenwich, Gravesend, Tilbery, Quinborow, Lee and Margit,[7] which to those did never heare of them, though they dwell in England, might be made seem some rare secrets and great countries unknowne, except the relations of Master Dirmer.[8]

In England some are held great travelers that have seene Venice and Rome, Madrill and Algere, Prague or Ragousa, Constantinople or Jerusalem, and the Piramides of Egypt; that thinke it nothing to go to the Summer Iles or Virginia,[9] which is as farre as any of them, and I hope in time will prove a more profitable and a more laudable journey. As for the danger, you see our Ladies and Gentlewomen account it nothing now to go thither; and therefore I hope all good men will better apprehend it, and not suffer them to languish in despaire, whom God so wonderfully and so oft hath preserved.

What here I have writ by relation, if it be not ‖ right, I humbly **[C4ᵛ]** intreate your pardons, but I have not spared any diligence to learne the truth of them that have bin actors or sharers in those voyages: in some particulars they might deceive me, but in the substances they could not, for few could tell me any thing, except where they fished: but seeing all those[1] have lived there, do confirme more then I have writ, I doubt not but all those testimonies with these new begun examples of plantation, will move both Citie and Country freely to adventure with me and my partners more then promises, seeing I have from his Majestie Letters Pattents, such honest, free and large conditions assured me from his Commissioners,[2] as I hope wil satisfie any honest understanding.

But because some fortune tellers saith, I am unfortunate; had they spent their time as I have done, they would rather beleeve in God then their calculations, and peradventure have given as bad account of their actions; and therefore I intreat leave to answer those objectors, that think it strange if this be true,[3] I have made no more use of it, and rest so long without emploiment, and hath no more reward nor preferment: to which I say:

7. Billingsgate port or quay (first mentioned in A.D. 979) was half a mi. W of Tower Bridge and was one of the city's two docks with a customhouse for mooring vessels. Greenwich, Gravesend (with Tilbury just opposite), and Leigh were all familiar ports on the Thames; Queenborough on the Medway and Margate on the North Sea were similar ports in Kent.

8. Thomas Dermer, an old associate, was by then far better informed about the coast of New England than Smith was.

9. Something seems to be missing here, but the general drift is understandable.

1. Modern English would require "that" as the next word.

2. This matter of the "Commissioners" (the leaders of the North Virginia group, organized in 1620 as the Council for New England) is intimately entangled with Smith's title of "Admirall" (see sig. B3ʳn, above; and *Description of N.E.*, caption of facsimile title page). It is mentioned again in the *Advertisements*, 16.

3. Here Smith begins to return to the text of the 1620 edition, sig. B4ᵛ.

I thinke it more strange they should taxe me before they have tried as much as I have both by land and sea, as well in Asia and Africa, as Europe and America, where my commanders were actors or spectators, they alwaies so freely rewarded me, I never needed to importunate, or could I ever learne to beg; what there I got, I have thus spent: these sixteen yeares[4] I have spared neither paines nor **[Dɪʳ]** money ac- ‖ cording to my abilitie, first to procure his Majesties Letters pattents, and a Company here to be the means to raise a company to go with me to Virginia, as is said: which beginning here and there cost me neare 5 yeares worke, and more then 500 pounds of my owne estate, besides all the dangers, miseries and incumbrances I endured gratis, where I stayed till I left 500 better provided then ever I was; from which blessed Virgin (ere I returned) sprung the fortunate habitation of Somer Iles.

This Virgins sister, now called New England, an. 1616. at my humble suit by our most gracious Prince Charles hath bin neare as chargeable to me and my friends: for all which although I never got shilling, but it cost me many a pound, yet I thinke my selfe happie to see their prosperities.

If it yet trouble a multitude to proceed upon these certainties, what think you I undertook when nothing was knowne, but that there was a vast land; I never had power and meanes to do any thing, though more hath bin spent in formall delayes then would have done the businesse; but in such a penurious and miserable manner as if I had gone a begging to build an universitie: where had men bin as forward to adventure their purses and performe the conditions they promised me, as to crop the fruites of my labours, thousands ere this had bin bettered by these designes. Thus betwixt the spur of Desire and the bridle of Reason I am neare ridden to death in a ring of despaire; the raines are in your hands, therefore I intreate you to ease me: and those that think I am either idle or unfortunate, may see the cause, and know: unlesse I did see better dealing, I have had warning enough, not to be so forward again at every motion **[Dɪᵛ]** upon their promises, unlesse I intended ‖ nothing but to cary newes. For now they dare adventure a ship, that when I went first, would not adventure a groate, so they may be at home again by Michaelmas: which makes me remember Master Hackluts; oh incredulitie! the wit of fooles, that slovenly do spit at all things faire; a sluggards cradle, a cowards castle, how easie it is to be an infidell:[5] but to the purpose.

4. The number has been changed from "fourteene" in the 1620 *New Englands Trials* to "sixteen" here, and the following passage as far as "till I left 500" has been shortened and made more specific in this edition (cf. *New Englands Trials* [1620], sig. B4ᵛ). Here Smith has obviously oversimplified the process of obtaining the letters patent. It is the editor's conviction that Smith was active in "levying" planters (so to speak) for the original expedition to Virginia, but much work remains to be done in identifying the names on the lists of original planters.

5. The quotation from Richard Hakluyt is in reality a quatrain from George Chap-

By this all men may perceive the ordinary performance of this voyage in five or six moneths, the plenty of fish is most certainly approved: and it is certain, from Cannada and New England within these six yeares hath come neare 20000 Bever skins. Now had each of those ships transported but some small quantitie of the most increasing beasts, fowles, fruit,[6] plants and seeds, as I projected, by this time their increase might have bin sufficient for a thousand men. But the desire of present gain (in many) is so violent, and the endevors of many undertakers so negligent, every one so regarding their private gaine, that it is hard to effect any publick good, and impossible to bring them into a body, rule, or order, unlesse both authoritie and mony assist experiences. It is not a worke for every one to plant a Colonie; but when a house is built, it is no hard matter to dwell in it. This requireth all the best parts of art, judgement, courage, honestie, constancie, diligence and experience to do but neare well: your home bred ingrossing projectors[7] shall finde there a great difference betwixt saying and doing. But to conclude, the fishing wil go forward if you plant it or no; whereby a Colonie may be transported with no great charge, that in a short time might provide such fraughts to buy of us there dwelling, as I would hope no ship should go or come empty from New England.

The charge of this is onely salt, nets, hookes, lines, knives, Irish **[D2ʳ]** rugs, course cloth, beades, glasse, and such trash, onely for fishing and trade with the savages, beside our owne necessary provisions, whose endevours wil quickly defray all this charge; and the savages have intreated me to inhabite where I will. Now all these ships, till this last yeare, have bin fished within a square of two or 3 leagues, and not one of them all would adventure any further, where questionlesse 500 saile may have their fraught better then in Island, Newfoundland, or elsewhere, and be in their markets before the other can have their fish in their ships, because New Englands fishing begins with February, the other not till mid May; the progression hereof

man's "*De Guiana carmen Epicum*" in honor of Laurence Keymis, who in turn dedicated his "Relation of the second Voyage to Guiana" (1596) to Sir Walter Ralegh. The original reads:

> O Incredulitie, the wit of Fooles,
> That slovenly will spit on all things faire,
> The Cowards castle, and the Sluggards cradle
> How easie t'is to be an Infidel?

This was reprinted in Richard Hakluyt's *The Principal Navigations, Voyages, Traffiques and Discoveries of the English Nation* (London, 1598–1600), III, 670, a few pages after the end of Hakluyt's reprint of Ralegh's "Discoverie of . . . Guiana." Here Smith accidentally ran across the bit and not unnaturally attributed it to Hakluyt—only the initials G. C. appear inconspicuously at the end of the whole poem.

6. Arber, *Smith, Works*, 267, omitted "fruit," which appears in all copies the editor has examined. However, for the suggestion that there are some discrepancies among the extant copies of the 1622 edition, see Joseph Sabin *et al.*, eds., *A Dictionary of Books Relating to America*, XX (New York, 1927–1928), 249.

7. Possibly "presumptuous schemers"; there is some sort of play on words here.

tends much to the advancement of Virginia and the Bermudas, whose emptie ships may take in their fraught there, and would be a good friend in time of need to the inhabitants of New foundland.

The returnes made by the Westerne ships, are commonly devided into three parts, one for the owner of the ship, another for the Master and his companie, the third for the victuallers: which course being still permitted, wil be no hindrance to the plantation, go there never so many, but a meanes of transporting that yearly for little or nothing, which otherwise will cost many a hundred of pounds.

If a ship can gaine twentie, thirtie, fiftie in the 100, nay 300 for 100. in 7 moneths, as you see they have done, spending twise so much time in going and coming as in staying there: were I there planted, seeing the varietie of the fishings in their seasons serveth the most part of the yeare, and with a little labour we might make all the salt we **[D2ᵛ]** need use. I can conceive no reason to di- ‖ strust, but the doubling and trebling their gaines that are at all the former charge, and can fish but two moneths in a yeare: and if those do give 20. 30. or 40. shillings for an acre of land, or ship carpenters, forgers of iron, etc. that buy all things at a deare rate, grow rich; when they may have as good of all needful necessaries for taking (in my opinion) should not grow poore; and no commodity in Europe doth more decay then wood.

Master Dee recordeth in his Brittish Monarchie, that King Edgar[8] had a navie of 4000 saile, with which he yearely made his progresse about this famous Monarchie of Great Brittaine, largely declaring the benefit thereof: whereupon it seemes he projected to our most memorable Queene Elizabeth, the erecting of a Fleete of 60 saile, he called a little Navie Royall; imitating the admired Pericles, Prince of Athens, that could never secure that tormented estate, untill he was Lord and Captain of the Sea.

At this none need wonder; for who knowes not, her Royall Majestie during her life, by the incredible adventures of her Royall Navy, and valiant souldiers and sea-men, notwithstanding all trecheries at home, the protecting and defending France and Holland, and reconquering Ireland, yet all the world by sea or land both feared, loved, and admired good Queen Elizabeth.

Both to maintaine and increase that incomparable honour (God be thanked) to her incomparable Successour, our most Royall Lord and Soveraigne King James, etc. this great Philosopher hath left this to his Majestie and his kingdomes consideration: That if the Tenths of the Earth be proper to God, it is also due by Sea: the Kings high wayes are common to passe, but not to dig for Mines or any thing; **[D3ʳ]** so Englands coasts ‖ are free to passe, but not to fish, but by his Majesties prerogative.

8. Edgar reigned from 959 to 975.

His Majesty of Spaine permits none to passe the Popes order for the East and West Indies, but by his permission, or at their perils. If all that world be so justly theirs, it is no injustice for England to make as much use of her own shores as strangers do, that pay to their own Lords the tenth, and not to the owner of those liberties any thing to speake of; whose subjects may neither take nor sell any in their territories: which small tribute would maintain this little Navie Royall, and not cost his Majestie a penny; and yet maintaine peace with all forreiners, and allow them more courtesie, then any nation in the world affoords to England.

It were a shame to alledge, that Holland is more worthy to enjoy our fishings as Lords thereof, because they have more skill to handle it then we, as they can our wooll and undressed cloth, notwithstanding all their wars and troublesome disorders.

To get mony to build this Navy, he saith, who would not spare the 100 peny of his Rents, and the 500 peny of his goods; each servant that taketh 40.s. wages, 4.d; and every forreiner of 7 yeares of age 4.d. for 7 yeares: not any of these but they will spend 3 times so much in pride, wantonnesse, or some superfluitie. And do any men love the securitie of their estates, that of themselves would not be humble suters to his Majestie to do this of free will as a voluntary benevolence, or but the one halfe of this, (or some such other course as I have propounded to divers of the Companies) free from any constraint, taxe, lottery or imposition, so it may be as honestly and truly employed as it is projected, the poorest mechanick in this kingdom would gaine by it.[9] ‖ you might build ships of any proportion and **[D3ᵛ]** numbers you please, five times cheaper then you can do here, and have good merchandize for their fraught in this unknowne land, to the advancement of Gods glorie, his Church and Gospel and the strengthening and reliefe of a great part of Christendome, without hurt to any, to the terror of pyrats, the amazement[10] of enemies, the assistance of friends, the securing[11] of Merchants, and so much increase of navigation to make Englands trade and shipping as much as any nation in the world, besides a hundred other benefits, to the generall good of all good subjects, and would cause thousands yet unborn blesse[1] the time and all them that first put it in practise.

Now lest it should be obscured as it hath bin to private ends, or so weakly undertaken by our overweening incredulitie, that strangers may possesse it, whilest we contend for New Englands goods, but not Englands good; I present this to your Highnes and to all the Lords

---

9. It is obvious that several lines of the 1620 edition were intentionally omitted here, even though sig. D3ᵛ begins without a capital letter or a new paragraph (see *New Englands Trials* [1620], sig. C3ʳ⁻ᵛ).

10. Consternation.

11. Guarding, protecting.

1. Modern English would require "to bless[e]."

in England, hoping by your gracious good liking and approbation to move all the worthy Companies of this noble Citie, and all the Cities and Countries in the whole Land to consider of it, since I can finde them wood and halfe victuall, with the aforesaid advantages, with what facilitie they may build and maintaine this little Navie Royall, both with honour, profit and content, and inhabite as good a country as any in the world, within that parallel, which with my life and what I have I wil endevour to effect, if God please, and you permit. But no man will go from hence,[2] to have lesse freedome there then here; nor adventure all they have, to prepare the way for them that know it not: and it is too well knowne there hath bin so many undertakers of Patents and such sharing of them, as hath bred no lesse discou-

[D4ʳ] || ragement then wonder, to heare such great promises and so little performances. In the interim, you see the Dutch and French already frequent it: and God forbid them in Virginia or any of his Majesties subjects should not have as free libertie as they. To conclude, were it not for Master Pierce[3] and a few private Adventurers with him, what have we there for all these inducements?

This yeare 3 ships went from London, set out by Maister John Farar and his Partners. The *Bona nova* 200 tunns. The *Hopwell* 70 The *Darling* 40.

As for them whom pride or covetousnes lulleth asleep in a cradle of slothfull carelesnes, would they but consider how all the great Monarchies of the earth have bin brought to confusion; or but remember the late lamentable experience of Constantinople; and how many Cities, Townes and Provinces in the faire rich kingdoms of Hungaria, Transilvania, Wallachia and Moldavia; and how many thousands of Princes, Earles, Barons, Knights, Merchants and others, have in one day lost goods, lives and honors; or sold for slaves like beasts in a market place; their wives, children and servants slaine or wandring they knew not whither, dying or living in all extremities of extreame miseries and calamities. Surely they would not onely do this, but give all they have to enjoy peace and libertie at home; or but adventure their persons abroad, to prevent the conclusions of a conquering foe, who commonly assaulteth and best prevaileth where he findeth wealth and plentie (most armed) with ignorance and securitie.

Though the true condition of war[4] is only to suppresse the

2. The material from here to the end of the paragraph has been added.

3. Smith's tribute is worth noting. John Peirce, citizen and clothier of London, obtained a patent from the Virginia Company on Feb. 2, 1620. This patent replaced the Wincop patent, probably because it was more liberal, and became the Pilgrims' basic patent (Bradford, *Plymouth Plantation*, 39n). Because of legal complications and delays, the Pilgrims sailed without any clear rights under either the Wincop or the Peirce patent. It has been suggested that this lack of "patent authority" led the Pilgrims to draw up the Mayflower Compact when the ship reached Cape Cod. In other words, that hallowed document was merely the result of political expediency (Thomas W. Perry, "New Plymouth and Old England: A Suggestion," *William and Mary Quarterly*, 3d Ser., XVIII [1961], 254–256).

4. This paragraph has been added to this edition. It contains the first mention of Zsigmond Báthory, prince of Transylvania, who gave Smith the right to emblazon three Turks' heads in his "shield of Armes" (*True Travels*, 17).

proud, and defend the innocent and humble, as did that most generous Prince Sigismundus Bather, Prince of those countries, against
them, whom under the colour of justice and pietie, to maintaine
their superfluitie of ambitious pride, thought all the world too little
to maintaine their vice, and undoe them, or ‖ keepe them from abilitie   **[D4ᵛ]**
to do any thing that would not admire and adore their honors, fortunes, covetousnes, falshood, bribery, crueltie, extortion, and ingratitude, which is worse then cowardize or ignorance, and all maner of
vildnesse,[5] cleane contrary to all honour, vertue and noblenesse.

Much more could I say, but lest I should be too tedious to your
more serious affaires, I humbly crave your honorable and favourable
constructions and pardons if any thing be amisse.

If any desire to be further satisfied, they may reade my Description of Virginia and New England, and peruse them with their
severall Maps: what defect you finde in them, they shall find supplied in me or my authors, that thus freely hath throwne my selfe
with my mite into the Treasury of my Countries good, not doubting
but God will stir up some noble spirits to consider and examine if
worthy Collumbus could give the Spaniards any such certainties for
his designe, when Queene Isabel of Spaine set him foorth with fifteene
saile. And though I can promise no Mines of gold, yet the warlike
Hollanders let us imitate, but not hate, whose wealth and strength
are good testimonies of their treasure gotten by fishing. Therefore
(honorable and worthy Countrymen) let not the meannesse of the
word Fish distaste you, for it will afford as good gold as the mines of
Guiana or Tumbatu, with lesse hazard and charge, and more certaintie and facilitie; and so I humbly rest.

FINIS.

---

5. "Vileness."

TEXTUAL ANNOTATION

AND BIBLIOGRAPHICAL NOTE TO

New Englands Trials (1622)

TEXTUAL ANNOTATION

The page numbers below refer to the boldface numerals in the margins of the present text, which record the pagination of the original edition used as copy text. The word or words before the bracket show the text as emended by the editor; the word or words after the bracket reproduce the copy text. The wavy dash symbol used after the bracket stands for a word that has not itself been changed but that adjoins a changed word or punctuation mark. The inferior caret, also used only after the bracket, signifies the location of missing punctuation in the copy text.

Page.Line

A2^v.11–12 renowned] renowmed
A4^v.22 Lobsters] Lobste s
B2^r.8 territories, had] ~ . Had
B2^r.9 adventurers] adventures
B2^r.14 Spaine; with] ~ , ~
B2^v.4 cash] cassh
B2^v.27 Februarie] Frebruarie
B3^r.3 From] Fom
B3^r.17–18 ingaged, now] ~ ; ~
B4^r.5 untimely] unimely
C1^r.3 Cera, Govenour] ~ ˄ ~
C1^v.23 crosse that crosses] crosse, crosses (from *Generall Historie*, 236)
C1^v.24 French Piccaroun] ~ , ~
C2^r.16 Powhatan] Powhatam
C2^r.19–20 West), two] ~ , ~

Page.Line

C2^r.21–22 England, did] ~) ~
C2^r.22 Opechankanough] Opechaukanough (inverted "n")
C2^v.4 Powhatan] Powhatam
C2^v.7 Pocahontas] Pocahoutas (inverted "n")
C3^r.19 ore, his] ~ . His
C3^r.25 healthfulnesse] healthfulnsse
C4^v.18 it, and rest] it, rests (from *New Englands Trials* [1620], sig. B4^v)
D2^v.15 Pericles, Prince] ~ ˄ ~
D3^v.14 New Englands goods] ~ ~ good (from *New Englands Trials* [1620], sig. C3^v)
D4^r.25 Bather, Prince] ~ ˄ ~

Hyphenation Record

The following lists have been inserted at the request of the editorial staff of the Institute of Early American History and Culture. The list immediately below records possible compound words that were hyphenated at the end of the line in the copy text. In each case the editor had to decide for the present edition whether to print the word as a single word or as a hyphenated compound. The material before the bracket indicates how the word is printed in the present edition; the material after the bracket indicates how the word was broken in the original. The wavy dash symbol indicates that the form of the word has been unchanged from the copy text. Numerals refer to the page number of the copy text (the boldface numerals in the margin in this edition) and to the line number (counting down from the boldface number) in the present edition.

Page.Line

A4^v.7–8	Frenchmen] French-men
B1^r.10	fishermen] fisher-men
B1^r.11	Tode-botes] ~
B3^r.9	Wind-bound] ~
B3^r.11	New-found-land] ~
C3^r.21	vainglory] vain-glory
D2^v.21	reconquering] re- conquering
D4^v.17	warlike] war-like

The list below contains words found as hyphenated compounds in the copy text that unavoidably had to be broken at the end of the line at the hyphen in the present text. In quoting or transcribing from the present text, the hyphen should be retained for these words. Numerals refer to the page number of the copy text (the boldface numerals in the margin in this edition) and line number (counting down from the boldface number).

Page.Line

A4^v.6–7	Low-countries
B1^v.27–28	soape-ashes
C1^r.24–25	sea-fish
C2^r.15–16	Dutch-men

BIBLIOGRAPHICAL NOTE

["It was not usual to register second and later editions of a Work at Stationers' Hall: therefore this impression does not appear in the *Registers of the Company*" (Arber, *Smith, Works*, I, 250).]

Editions

Early:

1622. NEW ENGLANDS || TRIALS. || Declaring the successe of 80 Ships || employed thither within these eight yeares; || *and the benefit of that Countrey by Sea* || *and Land.* || With the present estate of that happie Plan- || tation, begun but by 60 weake men || *in the yeare* 1620. || And how to build a Fleete of good Shippes || *to make a little Navie Royall.* || Written by Captaine *John Smith*, sometimes Go- || vernour of *Virginia*, and Admirall || of *New England.* || The second Edition. || [Ornament] || *LONDON*, || Printed by WILLIAM JONES. || 1622. ||

   Quarto, pp. [32]; [A]–D in fours. (A revision should be made here of a comment in Joseph Sabin *et al.*, eds., *A Dictionary of Books Relating to America*, XX [New York, 1927–1928], 249: "Mr. [Justin] Winsor, in his 'Earliest Printed Sources of New England History,' 1894, remarks that 'the type of the second edition was probably kept standing for a while, since copies in the British Museum and the Bodleian show changes to be accounted for in that way.' Just what these changes are has not been ascertained." In response to an inquiry by the present editor, a letter of August 22, 1973, from the Bodleian states, "We do not possess a copy of STC. 22793 [the 1622 ed.] and have no record of a copy ever having been in the Library, but we do have a copy of STC. 22792 [the 1620 ed.]." Mr. Winsor's surmise seems to have been derived from some misconception.) In contradistinction to the 1620 edition, that of 1622 was heavily drawn upon in the *Generall Historie*, Bk. VI, as well as in Purchas, *Pilgrimes*, IV, 1837–1842.

Modern:

1837. *New Englands Trials . . . 1622*, ed. P. Force (Washington, D.C.).

1867. *New Englands Trials . . . 1622* (Cambridge, Mass.). (There is a lengthy note on the vicissitudes and variants of this edition in Sabin, *Dictionary*, XX, 250.)

1884, etc. *Captain John Smith . . . Works, 1608–1631*, ed. Edward Arber (Birmingham). See the list of issues of the Arber text in the General Introduction at the beginning of this volume.

1898. *New Englands Trials . . . 1622*, in *American Colonial Tracts Monthly*, Vol. II, No. 2 (Rochester, N.Y.).

1910. *New Englands Trials . . . 1622*, in *Chronicles of the Pilgrim Fathers* (New York).

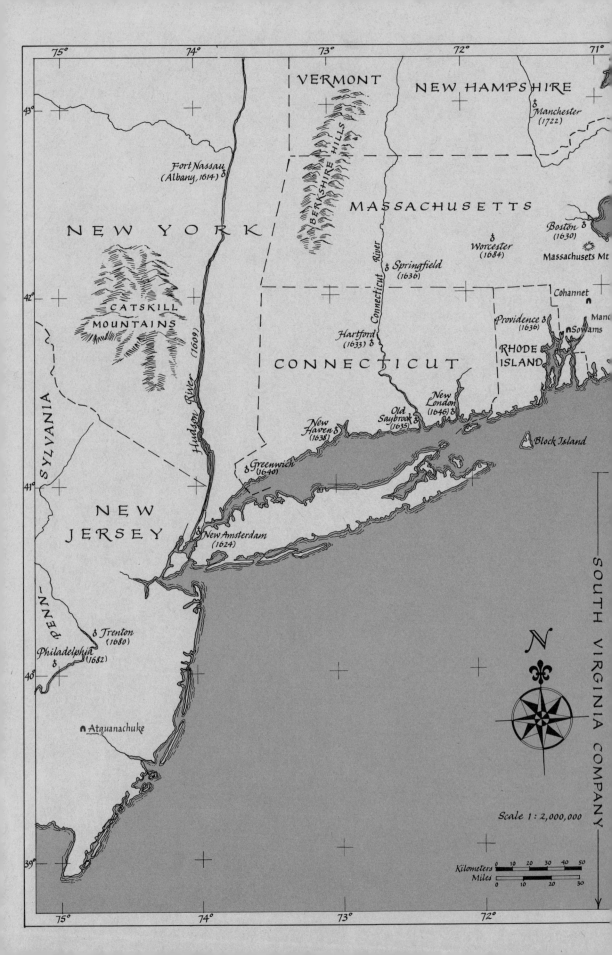